CONTENTS

Chapter 1

"IT'S GOING TO CHANGE YOUR LIFE"

Chapter 2

NURSERY NECESSITIES: CRIBS, DRESSERS & MORE

Chapter 3

BABY BEDDING & DECOR

Chapter 4

THE REALITY LAYETTE: LITTLE CLOTHES FOR LITTLE PRICES

Chapter 5

MATERNITY/NURSING CLOTHES

Chapter 6

FEEDING BABY: BREASTFEEDING, BOTTLES, HIGH CHAIRS

Chapter 7

AROUND THE HOUSE: MONITORS, DIAPER PAILS, SAFETY & MORE

Chapter 8

CAR SEATS

Chapter 9

STROLLERS, DIAPER BAGS, CARRIERS AND OTHER TO GO GEAR

Chapter 10

CONCLUSION: WHAT DOES IT ALL MEAN?

ICONS

Getting Started

Money-Saving Secrets

Sources

Best Buys

Best Online Sources

The Name Game

What Are You Buying?

Do it By Mail

Safe & Sound

Email from the Real World

Smart Shopper

More Money Buys You . . .

Wastes of Money

Bottom Line

CHAPTER 1

"It's Going to Change Your Life!"

Inside this chapter

That had to be the silliest comment we heard while we were pregnant with our first baby. Believe it or not, we even heard this refrain more often than "Are you having a boy or a girl?" and "I'm sorry. Your insurance doesn't cover that." For the friends and relatives of first-time parents out there, we'd like to point out that this is a pretty silly thing to say. Of course, we knew that a baby was going to change our lives. What we didn't realize was how much a baby was going to change our pocketbook.

Oh sure, we knew that we'd have to buy triple our weight in diapers and be subjected to dangerously high levels of the Wiggles. What we didn't expect was the endless pitches for cribs, gear, toys, clothing and other items parents are required to purchase by FEDERAL BABY LAW.

We quickly learned that having a baby is like popping on the Juvenile Amusement Park Ride from Consumer Hell. Once that egg is fertilized, you're whisked off to the Pirates of the Crib ride. Then it's on to marvel at the little elves in StrollerLand, imploring you to buy brands with names you can't pronounce. Finally, you take a trip to Magic Car Seat Mountain, where the confusion is so real, it's scary.

Consider us your tour guides—the Yogi Bear to your Boo Boo Bear, the Fred to your Ethel, the . . . well, you get the idea. Before we enter BabyLand, let's take a look at the Four Truths That No One Tells You About Buying Stuff For Baby.

The Four Truths That No One Tells You About Buying Stuff for Baby

1 **BABIES DON'T CARE IF THEY'RE WEARING DESIGNER CLOTHES OR SLEEPING ON DESIGNER SHEETS.** Let's be realistic. Babies just want to be comfortable. They can't even distinguish between the liberals and conservatives on "Meet the Press," so how would they ever be able to tell the difference between Baby Gucci crib bedding and another less famous brand that's just as comfortable, but 70% less expensive? Our focus is on making your baby happy—at a price that won't break the bank.

2 **YOUR BABY'S SAFETY IS MUCH MORE IMPORTANT THAN YOUR CONVENIENCE.** Here are the scary facts: 63,700 children under age five were injured (requiring emergency room visits) by nursery products. During a recent three-year period (2004-2006), those same baby products caused 80 deaths per year. (Source: 2008 Consumer Product Safety Commission report based on 2006 data).

Each chapter of this book has a section called "Safe & Sound" to arm you with in-depth advice on keeping your baby out of trouble. We'll tell you which products we think are dangerous and how to safely use other potentially hazardous products.

3 **MURPHY'S LAW OF BABY TOYS SAYS YOUR BABY'S HAPPINESS WITH A TOY IS INVERSELY RELATED TO THE TOY'S PRICE.** Buy a $200 shiny new wagon with anti-lock brakes, and odds are baby just wants to play with the box it came in. In recognition of this reality, we've included "wastes of money" in each chapter that will steer you away from frivolous items.

4 **IT'S GOING TO COST MORE THAN YOU THINK.** Whatever amount of money you budget for your baby, get ready to spend more. Here's a breakdown of the average costs of bringing a baby into the world today:

The Average Cost of Having a Baby

(based on industry estimates for a child from birth to age one)

Crib, mattress, dresser, rocker	*$1375*
Bedding / Decor	*$345*
Baby Clothes	*$630*
Disposable Diapers	*$890*
Maternity/Nursing Clothes	*$1210*
Nursery items, high chair, toys	*$520*
Baby Food / Formula	*$960*
Stroller, Car Seats, Carrier	*$675*
Miscellaneous	*$600*
TOTAL	**$7,205**

The above figures are based on a survey of 1000 parents, buying name brand products at regular retail prices.

Bedding/Decor includes not only bedding items but also lamps, wallpaper, and so on for your baby's nursery. Baby Food/Formula assumes mom breastfeeds for the first six months and then feeds baby jarred baby food ($435) and formula ($525) until age one. If you plan to bottle-feed instead of breastfeed, add another $525 on to that figure. (Of course, the goal is to breastfeed your baby as long as possible—one year is a good target.)

Sure, you do get an automatic tax write-off for that bundle of joy, but that only amounts to about $3750 this year (plus you also get up to an additional $3000 child care tax credit, depending on your income). But those tax goodies won't nearly offset the actual cost of raising a child. And as you probably realize, our cost chart is missing some expensive "extras" . . . like medical bills, childcare, saving for college and more. Here's an overview of what can add to the tab.

Scary Number: The Cost of Raising Baby to 18

$204,060. That's what the federal government says it costs to raise a child born in 2010 (the latest year stats are available) to age 18. Those costs include food, transportation, housing, clothes and child care.

But let's talk about child care. Critics point out the federal government grossly underestimates this cost (the feds say parents spend $1220 to $3020 on child care each year for the first two years). But the government averages in parents who pay nothing (grandma watches baby) with those who pay for child care.

So what does child care really cost? According to the National Association of Child Care Resource and Referral Agencies, the average annual bill is $8150. Want to hire a nanny? That can run $30,000 per year in big cities, plus another $6,000 in taxes.

College is another expense the government leaves out of their figures. Four years at a public college now runs $100,000 in many states; private schools are $200,000. Given current rates of return, that means you have to put away $6000 a year every year for 18 years to afford that public school.

The take-home message: raising a baby ain't cheap. It's important to start saving your pennies now, so you can start saving for those important items (college, etc.) down the road.

Reality Check: Does it Really Cost that Much to Have a Baby?

Now that we've thoroughly scared you enough to inquire whether the stork accepts returns, we should point out that children do NOT have to cost that much. Even if we focus just on the first year, you don't have to spend $7205 on baby gear. And that's what this book is all about: how to save money and still buy the best. Follow all the tips in this book, and we estimate the first year will cost you $4196. Yes, that's a savings of $3009!

Now, at this point, you might be saying "That's impossible! I suppose you'll recommend shopping garage sales and dollar stores." On the contrary, we'll show you how to get *quality* name brands and safe products at discount prices. Most importantly, you will learn how not to WASTE your money on dubious gear. And much more. Yes, we've got the maximum number of bargains allowed by federal law.

A word on bargain shopping: when interviewing hundreds of parents for this book, we realized bargain seekers fall into two frugal camps. There's the "do-it-yourself" crowd and the "quality at a discount" group. As the name implies, "do-it-yourselfers" are resourceful folks who like to take second-hand products and refurbish them. Others use creative tricks to make homemade versions of baby care items like baby wipes and diaper rash cream.

While that's all well and good, we fall more into the second camp of bargain hunters, the "quality at a discount" group. We love discovering a hidden factory outlet online that sells goods at 50% off. Or finding a designer stroller on Craigslist at 75% off its original retail. We also realize savvy parents save money by not *wasting* it on inferior goods or useless items.

While we hope that *Baby Bargains* pleases both groups of bargain hunters, the main focus of this book is not on do-it-yourself projects. Books like the *Tightwad Gazette* (check your local library for a copy) do a much better job on this subject. Our main emphasis will be on discount web sites, catalogs, outlet stores, brand reviews and identifying best buys for the dollar.

What? There's No Advertising in This Book?

Yes, it's true. This book contains zero percent advertising. We have never taken any money to recommend a product or company and never will. We make our sole living off the sales of this and other books. Our publisher, Windsor Peak Press, also derives its sole income from the sale of this book and our other publications. **No company recommended in this book paid any consideration or was charged any fee to be mentioned.** (In fact, some companies probably would offer us money to leave them *out* of the book, given our comments about their products or services).

As consumer advocates, we believe this "no ads" policy helps to ensure objectivity. The opinions in the book are just that—ours and those of the parents we interviewed.

We also are parents of two kids. We figure if we actually are recommending these products to you, we should have some real world experience with them. (That said, we should disclose that our sons have filed union grievances with our company over testing of certain jarred baby foods and that litigation is ongoing.)

Of course, given the sheer volume of baby stuff, there's no way we can test everything personally. To solve that dilemma, we rely on reader feedback to help us figure out which are the best products to recommend. We receive over 100 emails a day from parents; this helps us spot overall trends on which brands/products parents love. And which ones they want to destroy with a rocket launcher.

Parents post reviews of products to our web site, message boards and blog. Of course, one bad review from one parent doesn't mean we won't recommend a product—we combine multiple review sources to come up with an overall picture as to which products and brands are best.

What about prices of baby products? Trying to stay on top of this is similar to nailing Jell-O to a wall. Yet, we still try. As much as we can confirm, the prices quoted in this book were accurate as of the date of publication. Of course, prices and product features can change at any time. Inflation and other factors may affect the actual prices you discover in shopping for your baby. While the publisher makes every effort to ensure their accuracy, errors and omissions may exist. That's why we update this book with every new printing—make sure you are using the most recent version (go to BabyBargains.com and click on Book and then Which Version?).

Our door is always open—we want to hear your opinions. Email us at authors@BabyBargains.com or call us at (303) 442-8792 to ask a question, report a mistake, or just give us your thoughts.

So, Who Are You Guys Anyway?

Why do a book on saving money on baby products? Don't new parents throw caution to the wind when buying for their baby, spending whatever it takes to ensure their baby's safety and comfort?

Ha! When our first child was born, we quickly realized how darn expensive this guy was. Sure, as a new parent, you know you've got to buy a car seat, crib, clothes and diapers . . . but have you walked into one of those baby "superstores" lately? It's a blizzard of baby stuff, with a bewildering array of "must have" gear, gadgets and gizmos, all claiming to be the best thing for parents since sliced bread.

Becoming a parent in this day and age is both a blessing and curse. The good news: parents today have many more choices for baby products than past generations. The *bad* news: parents today have many more choices for baby products than past generations.

Our mission: make sense of this stuff, with an eye on cutting costs. As consumer advocates, we've been down this road before.

We researched bargains and uncovered scams in the wedding business when we wrote *Bridal Bargains*. Then we penned an exposé on new homebuilders in *Your New House*.

Yet, we found the baby business to be perilous in different ways—instead of outright fraud or scam artists, we've instead discovered some highly questionable products that don't live up to their hype—and others that are outright dangerous. We were surprised to learn that most juvenile items face little (or no) government scrutiny, leaving parents to sort out true usefulness and safety from sales hype.

So, we've gone on a quest to find the best baby products, at prices that won't send you to the poor house. Sure, we've sampled many of these items first hand. But this book is much more than our experiences—we interviewed over 10,000 new parents to learn their experiences with products. Our message boards have over 20,000 members, buzzing with all sorts of product feedback and advice. We also attend juvenile product trade shows to quiz manufacturers and retailers on what's hot and what's not. The insights from retailers are especially helpful, since these folks are on the front lines, see-

The 7 Commandments of Baby Bargains

Yes, we've come down from the mountain to share with you our SEVEN commandments of *Baby Bargains*—the keys to saving every parent should know. Let's review:

1 **SAFETY IS JOB ONE.** As a parent, your baby's safety is paramount. We never compromise safety for a bargain—that's why hand-me-down cribs or used car seats are not a good idea. Good news: you can subscribe to our free blog to get an email or instant message when a baby product is recalled. Go to BabyBargains.com/ blog and enter your email address in the box at the right.

2 **FOCUS ON THE BASICS.** Big box baby stores are so overwhelming, with a blizzard of baby products. Key on the basics: setting up a safe place for baby to sleep (the nursery) and safe transport (car seats). Many items like high chairs, toys, and so on are not needed immediately.

3 **WEED OUT THE FLUFF.** Our advice: take an experienced mom with you when you register. A mom with one or two kids can help you separate out needed items from the fluff!

ing which items unhappy parents return.

Our focus is on safety and durability: which items stand up to real world conditions and which don't. Interestingly, we found many products for baby are sold strictly on price . . . and sometimes a great "bargain" broke, fell apart or shrunk after a few uses. Hence, you'll note some of our top recommendations aren't always the lowest in price. To be sensitive to those on really tight budgets, we try to identify "good, better and best" bets in different price ranges.

We get questions: Top 5 Questions & Answers

From the home office here in Boulder, CO, here are the top five questions we get asked here at *Baby Bargains*:

1 **HOW DO I KNOW IF I HAVE THE CURRENT EDITION?** We strive to keep *Baby Bargains* as up-to-date as possible. As such, we update it periodically with new editions. But if you just borrowed this book from a friend, how do you know how old it is? First, look

4 **TWO WORDS: FREE MONEY.** As a parent, you NEVER pass up free money! From tax deductions to tax credits, being a parent means freebies. And don't overlook your employer: take advantage of benefits like dependent care accounts—using PRE-TAX dollars to pay for child care will save you HUNDREDS if not THOUSANDS of dollars.

5 **MORE FREEBIES.** Many companies throw swag at new parents, hoping they will become future customers. We keep an updated freebie list on our web site—get free diapers, bottles, and more. Go to BabyBargains.com/freebies for the latest update!

6 **SHOP AT STORES THAT DO NOT HAVE "BABY" IN THEIR NAME.** Costco for diapers? Pet web sites for safety gates? Regular furniture stores for rockers and dressers? IKEA for high chairs? Yes! Yes! Yes! You can save 30% or more by not buying items at baby stores.

7 **ONLINE SHOPPING SAVVY.** Let's face it: as a new mom and dad, you probably won't have much time to hit the mall. The web is a savior—but how do you master the deals? One smart tip: ALWAYS use coupon codes for discounts or FREE shipping before you order. We keep a list (updated daily!) of the best coupon codes on our Bargain Alert Forum on our free message boards (BabyBargains.com).

What you need, when

Yes, buying for baby can seem overwhelming, but there is a silver lining: you don't need ALL this stuff immediately when baby is born. Let's look at what items you need quickly and what you can wait on. This chart indicates usage of certain items for the first 12 months of baby's life:

Item	Months of Use				
	Birth	3	6	9	12+
Nursery Necessities					
Cradle/bassinet	▓▓▓				
Crib/Mattress	▓▓▓▓▓▓▓▓▓▓▓▓				
Dresser	▓▓▓▓▓▓▓▓▓▓▓▓				
Glider Rocker	▓▓▓▓▓▓▓▓▓▓▓▓				
Bedding: Cradle	▓▓▓				
Bedding: Crib	▓▓▓▓▓▓▓▓▓▓▓▓				
Clothing					
Caps/Hats	▓▓▓▓▓▓▓▓▓▓▓▓				
Blanket Sleepers	▓▓▓▓▓▓▓▓▓▓▓▓				
Layette Gowns	▓▓▓				
Booties	▓▓▓▓				
All other layette	▓▓▓▓▓▓▓▓▓▓▓▓				
Around the House					
Baby Monitor	▓▓▓▓▓▓▓▓▓▓▓▓				
Baby Food (solid)	▓▓▓▓▓▓▓▓▓ (from ~4)				
High Chairs	▓▓▓▓▓▓▓ (from ~5)				
Places to Go					
Infant Car Seat	▓▓▓▓▓▓				
Convertible Car Seat*	▓▓▓▓▓▓▓▓▓▓▓▓				
Full-size Stroller/Stroller Frame	▓▓▓▓▓▓▓▓▓▓▓▓				
Umbrella Stroller	▓▓▓ (from ~9)				
Front Carrier	▓▓▓▓▓▓				
Backpack Carrier	▓▓▓▓▓▓ (from ~6)				
Safety items	▓▓▓▓▓▓▓▓▓ (from ~3)				

*You can use a convertible car seat starting immediately with that first ride home from the hospital. However, it is our recommendation that you use an infant car seat for the first six months or so, then, when baby grows out of it, buy the convertible car seat.

at the copyright page. There at the bottom you will see a version number (such as 9.0). The first number (the 9 in this case) means you have the 9th edition. The second number indicates the printing—every time we reprint the book, we make minor corrections, additions and changes. Version 9.0 is the initial printing of the 9th edition, version 9.1 is the first reprint of the 9th edition and so on.

So, how can you tell if your book is current or woefully out-of-date? Go to our web page at BabyBargains.com and click on Book and then "Which version?"—this shows the most current version. (One clue: look at the book's cover. We note the edition number on each cover. And we change the color of the cover with each edition.) We update this book every two years (roughly). About 30% to 40% of the content will change with each edition. Bottom line: if you pick up a copy of this book that is one or two editions old, you will notice a significant number of changes.

2 **WHAT IF I SEE A NEW PRODUCT IN STORES? HOW CAN I FIND INFO ON THAT?** If you can't find that product in our latest book, go to our web page at BabyBargains.com. There you will find a treasure trove of information. First, check out our blog, which tracks the latest news on baby gear. Second, search our message boards section to see if other readers have tried out the product and reported to us on their experiences. Of course, you can email us with a question as well (see the How to Contact Us page at the back of this book). Be sure to sign up for our free e-newsletter to get the latest news on our book, web page, product recalls and more. All this can be done from BabyBargains.com. (A note on our privacy policy: we NEVER sell reader email addresses or other personal info).

You can also read product reviews on our web site, BabyBargains.com. While most of our site is free, the Reviews area requires a subscription—these reviews are the same ones that appear in our book. Updates are posted when available.

3 **I AM LOOKING FOR A SPECIFIC PRODUCT BUT I DON'T KNOW WHERE TO START! HELP!** Yep, this book is 600+ pages long and we realize it can be a bit intimidating. But you have a friend in the index—flip to the back of the book to look up just about anything. You can look up items by category, brand name and more. If that doesn't work, try the table of contents. We sort the book into major topic areas (strollers, car seats, etc).

FYI: some companies have sub-brands—we list these aliases alphabetically and refer you to the main company review (for example, Baby Cache cribs are made by Munire; we discuss Baby Cache in Munire's review.)

4 **WHY DO YOU SOMETIMES RECOMMEND A MORE EXPENSIVE PRODUCT THAN A CHEAPER OPTION?** Yes, this is a book about bargains, but sometimes we will pick a slightly more expensive item in a category if we believe it is superior in quality or safety. In some cases, it makes sense to invest in better-quality products that will last through more than one child. And don't forget about the hassle of replacing a cheap product that breaks in six months.

To be sure, however, we recognize that many folks are on tight budgets. To help, we offer "Good, Better, Best" product suggestions that are typically sorted by price (good is most affordable, best is usually more expensive). Don't torture yourself if you can't afford the "best" in every category; a "good" product will be just as, well, good.

Another note: remember that our brand reviews cover many options in a category, not just the cheapest. Don't be dismayed if we give an expensive brand an "A" rating—such ratings are often based on quality, construction, innovation and more. Yes, we will try to identify the best values in a category as well. But we realize that some folks want to spend more on certain items (car seats, for example)—hence we try to identify the best of the best, not just the cheapest.

Why does our advice sometimes conflict with other publications like *Consumer Reports*? Simple reason: we have different research methods. Most *Consumer Reports* reviews are based on lab tests; we relied on more on parent feedback, culled from hundreds (and sometimes thousands) of reviews and emails. That's our secret sauce.

More often than not, our picks and *Consumer Reports* usually match; when we don't agree, we try to point out the differences, both in our book and blog. Of course, we review and rate many more baby products than *Consumer Reports*, as our focus is just baby gear. We know you want in-depth info to make the best decisions . . . that's why we're here.

5 **WHAT OTHER PARENTING BOOKS DO YOU PUBLISH?** Yes, we do have three other best-selling books: *Expecting 411, Baby 411* and *Toddler 411*. Co-authored by an award-winning pediatrician, these books answer your questions about pregnancy, your baby's sleep, nutrition, growth and more. See the back of this book for details.

What's New in This Edition?

Welcome to the 9th edition—this marks our 17th year of covering the baby biz. Wow, our book will soon get to vote.

As always, we've added dozens of brand reviews for cribs, car seats and strollers. New this year: more eco-friendly baby products. We focus on green cribs and nursery furniture, with an expanded

Get social

Social media sites like Groupon.com are an important new tool in the bargain hunter's toolbox. In case you're new to this world, let's go over a couple of tips on how to use social media to rack up baby bargains.

◆ *Deal of the day sites.* Localized to major cities, sites like Groupon.com post discounted deals every day—restaurants, retail stores, magazine subscriptions and more. When it comes to baby stuff, we've seen 50% off coupons to local baby stores, discounts from local baby proofers and more. Here's how it works: deals change by the day, you buy the certificate the day it appears on Groupon, typically within six hours or before it sells out. Then you take the certificate to the store, restaurant or other location and use it like a prepaid gift card. Share the deal on your Facebook or Twitter page.

◆ *Go deeper.* Of course, there is more than just Groupon! We have a list of deal of the day sites on our web site at BabyBargains/deals. We also recommend checking out DailyDeals.UnRetailMe.com, which aggregates deals from Groupon and several other sites.

◆ *Don't forget:* regular web sites offer deals of the day. Examples include Target, Garnet Hill, Amazon and more. These are typically limited time specials on a small selection of items. Example: TinySoles.com has a Daily Deal. When we last looked at the site, a Pediped shoe for toddlers that retailed for $34 was on sale for $19.95. Many of these sites post their deals on their Facebook and Twitter feeds—"like" or subscribe to keep tabs on sales.

◆ *Cash Back/Rewards sites.* If you are a heavy online shopper, consider signing up with an online cash back or rewards site. Ebates is probably the most well known—you earn cash back when you shop any one of 1200 web sites. Ebates also sends out coupons and promo codes for major sites. Upromise.com is a similar site that helps you pay for a child's college tuition. A great site that compares rebates from various sites is eReward.com.

look at eco-friendly crib mattresses.

What's the best (and most affordable) knock-off of the popular Bugaboo stroller? We've got the scoop in our updated feature, *Bugaboo Smackdown*. This handy comparison chart rates and reviews the best Bugaboo imitators. Also new in strollers: reviews of ten new stroller brands, including the latest European imports like Teutonia.

We've beefed up our car seat reviews with the government's ease of use ratings. And the booster seat reviews now include whether the seat is recommended by the Insurance Institute for Highway Safety.

Look for expanded reviews of carriers in this book, with a model-by-model look at the top brands. We've increased our coverage of video baby monitors, with new reviews of models that are much better than in years' past.

Of course, we've kept the features you love about *Baby Bargains*, including those nifty comparison charts that sum up our picks and our ever-popular baby registry at-a-glance (Appendix B).

Don't forget to check out our extensive online offerings, including an updated blog that covers breaking news and safety recalls. Surf our message boards for news on coupons, sales and deals—updated several times a week. And read reviews of gear posted by our readers.

E-books, web site subscriptions

Baby Bargains is more than just a book. Got a Kindle? Nook? iPad? You can now read our book as an ebook on these devices. Bonus: the Apple iPad ebook version of this book is enhanced with video shopping tip guides.

Subscribe to our web site at BabyBargains.com to get online access to all the reviews in our book, plus online-only exclusive content (example: baby food processors reviews, new products that came out after this book went to press, etc.).

Want to get an updated chapter from this book? You can download a PDF of our latest research direct from our web page. That way if you just want to read about the latest strollers, you can get just that chapter for much less than buying the entire book again.

Check our web page at BabyBargains.com for the latest news on all these new versions of *Baby Bargains*. Or email us at authors@BabyBargains.com if you have a question or suggestion.

Let's Go Shopping!

Now that all the formal introductions are done, let's move on to the good stuff. As your tour guides to BabyLand, we'd like to remind you of one key rule: the Baby Biz is just that—business.

The juvenile products industry is a $8.9 BILLION DOLLAR business. While all those baby stores may want to help you, they are first and foremost in business to make a profit. As a consumer, you should arm yourself with the knowledge necessary to make smart decisions. So let's get rolling!

CHAPTER 2

Nursery Necessities: Cribs, Dressers & More

Inside this chapter

How can you save 20% to 50% off cribs, dressers, and other furniture for your baby's room? In this chapter, you'll learn these secrets, plus discover smart shopper tips that help clarify all those confusing crib options and features. Then, you'll learn which juvenile furniture has safety problems and where to go online to find the latest recall info. Next, we'll rate and review over three dozen top brands of cribs, focusing on quality and value. Finally, you'll learn which crib mattress is best, how to get a deal on a dresser, and several more items to consider for your baby's room.

Getting Started: When Do You Need This Stuff?

So, you want to buy a crib for Junior? And, what the heck, why not some other furniture, like a dresser to store all those baby gifts and a changing table for, well, you know. Just pop down to the store, pick out the colors, and set a delivery date, right?

Not so fast, o' new parental one. Once you get to that baby store, you'll discover that most don't have all those nice cribs and furniture *in stock*. No, that would be too easy, wouldn't it? You will quickly learn that you have to *special order* much of that booty.

To be fair, we should note that in-stock items vary from shop to shop. Some (especially the larger chain stores) may stock a fair number of cribs. Yet Murphy's Law says the last in-stock crib you want was just sold five minutes ago. And while stores may stock a good number of cribs, dressers are another story—these bulky items almost always must be special-ordered.

So, let's cut to chase: when should you order nursery furniture? The answer depends on WHERE you plan to buy furniture. *If you choose an independent baby store, order at your 20th week of pregnancy.* Yes, it really takes 10-14 weeks on average to have specialty-store nursery furniture ordered and delivered (we figured you want it there a few weeks before baby arrives!).

Major caveat: some brands take as long as 16 weeks to order . . . ask your local retailer for advice, as lead times for brands can shift.

What about chain stores like Babies R Us? You need less time than specialty stores, but it isn't lighting quick either. Babies R Us says IF the furniture is in stock at their warehouse, it takes seven to 21 business days to be delivered to a store. If the furniture is NOT in stock, you can cool your heels for four to six weeks. Bottom line: *if you choose a chain store, order at your 25th week of pregnancy.* That way you have left plenty of time, even if the furniture is on a six week delay.

Why does it take so long to get nursery furniture? Most furniture today is made in Asia (primarily China). Manufacturers wait until they receive enough orders of a certain collection before they go into production. Then the furniture is loaded into a shipping container and sent on a four-to-six week ocean journey to the U.S. Assuming all goes well (no hurricanes, port strikes, etc.), the furniture is delivered to a manufacturer's distribution center. From there, it is trucked to the retailer.

Yes, you might get lucky and find your nursery furniture in stock at a manufacturer or retailer's warehouse. But don't bet on it.

We should note that some parents wait until after a baby is born to take delivery of nursery furniture. Why? Certain religious and ethnic customs say it is bad luck to have any baby gear in the house before baby is born. These families will order baby furniture, but not have it delivered until baby is born—needless to say, if you go this route, you have to find a retailer willing to store your furniture until that time.

First-time parent question: so, how long will baby use a crib? Answer: it depends (and you thought we always had the answer). Seriously, most babies can use a crib for two or three years. Yes, some babies are out of the crib by 18 months, while others may be pushing four years. One key factor: when does baby learn they can climb out of the crib? Once that happens, the crib days are numbered, as you can understand. Of course, there may be other factors that push baby out of a crib—if you are planning to have a second child and want the crib for the new baby, it may be time to transition to a "big boy/girl" bed. We discuss more about the transition out of a crib in our other book, *Toddler 411*. See the back of this book for more info.

Cribs: Sources to Find

This year, more than one million households plan to buy infant/nursery furniture, according to a survey by *Kids Today*. That translates into $1.5 billion in sales of infant furniture—yes, this is big business. In their quest for the right nursery, parents have four basic sources for finding a crib, each with its own advantages and drawbacks:

1 **INDEPENDENT BABY SPECIALTY STORES.** Indie baby specialty stores are pretty self-explanatory—shops that specialize in the retailing of baby furniture, strollers, and accessories. Independents come in all sizes: some are small boutiques; others are as large as a chain superstore. A good number of indie retailers have joined together in "buying groups" to get volume discounts on items from suppliers—these groups include Baby Furniture Plus (babyfurniture-plus.com), Baby News (BabyNewsStores.com), NINFRA (ninfra.com) and USA Baby (USAbaby.com). Another good resource to find a specialty store near you is AllBabyAndChildStores.com.

Like other independent stores, many baby specialty shops have been hard hit by the expansion of national chains like Babies R Us. Yet, those that have survived do so by emphasizing service and products you can't find at the chains. Of course, quality of service can vary widely from store to store . . . but just having a breathing human to ask a question of is a nice plus.

The problems with specialty stores? Readers complain the stores only carry expensive brands. One parent told us the only baby specialty store in her town doesn't carry any cribs under $600. We understand the dilemma faced by mom and pop retailers—in order to provide all that service, they have to make a certain profit margin on furniture and other products. And that margin is easier to get on high-end goods. That's all well and good, but failing to carry products in entry-level price points only drives parents to the chains.

Another gripe with some indie stores: some shops can be downright hostile to you if they think you are price-shopping. A reader said she found this out when comparing high-end nursery furniture in her town. "When I asked to price cribs and dressers at two baby stores, I met with resistance and hostility. At one store, I was asked if I was a 'spy' for their competition! The store managers at both baby stores I visited said they didn't want people to comparison shop them on price, yet both advertise they will 'meet or beat' the competition's prices."

The bottom line: despite the hassles, if you have a locally owned baby store in your town, give them a shot. Don't assume chains

The Best Baby Stores in America

Who are the best independent baby stores in America? In researching this book, we have visited hundreds of baby stores from coast to coast during the past 15 years. Along the way, we've met some of the smartest retailers in the U.S.—folks we often turn to to find out what's REALLY happening in the baby gear biz. Which cribs, strollers and car seats are selling and winning raves from parents . . . and what are the bombs.

Readers often tell us they want to support indie stores—but which ones are most reputable? If you are tired of the chains, we offer our list of stores to check out.

A few notes: just in case you are wondering, NO retailers paid us to be on this list. We don't take advertising, commissions or fees to recommend stores in our book or blog. The retailers we think are best earned it the old fashioned way—by focusing on their customers.

We compiled this list from reader feedback and store visits; we also asked baby gear manufacturers to name their top retailers. This list focuses on baby stores in major metro areas (with a few exceptions). Most of these stores sell baby furniture/products in a wide range of prices; these aren't expensive boutiques, but mainstream retailers.

So . . . drum roll . . . here are the Best Baby Stores in America (in alphabetical order):

Baby Furniture Plus (Columbia/Greenville, SC)
~~Baby Super Mart~~ (Broomall, PA)
Baby's 1st (Houston)
Behr's (Metro NY)
Berg's (Cleveland, OH)
Cribs to College Bedrooms (Naperville, IL)
Galt Toys + Galt Baby (Chicago)
Georgia Baby (Atlanta)
Great Beginnings (Washington DC area/Maryland)
Ideal Baby & Kids (Miami); also known as La Ideal.
Juvenile Shop (Sherman Oaks, CA)
Kids Stuff Superstores (South Dakota, Nebraska)
Lazar's (Chicago)
Lone Star Baby (Dallas)
Magic Beans (Boston)
Planet Kids (New York City)
Rockridge Kids (Oakland, CA)
Treasures Room (St Louis)
WONDER! (Chicago)

always have lower prices and better selection. See the box on the last page for our picks of the top indie baby stores in the U.S.

2 **THE CHAINS.** There are two types of chains that sell baby products: specialty chains like Babies R Us who focus on juvenile products and discounters like Walmart, Target, and K-Mart that have small baby departments. We'll discuss each in-depth later in this chapter. The selection at chains can vary widely—some carry more premium brands, but most concentrate on mass-market names to appeal to price-conscious shoppers. Service? Fuggedaboutit—often, you'll be lucky to find someone to help you check out, much less answer questions.

In recent years, we've seen a third type of chain enter the baby market: specialty chains such as Pottery Barn Kids (PBK) and Restoration Hardware. The former has stores that sell some baby furniture; the latter (Restoration Hardware) has an online-only baby boutique.

3 **ONLINE.** Long before the web, companies tried to sell furniture via mail order, albeit with mixed results. Perhaps the best example is JCPenney (jcpenney.com), whose mail-order catalog (and now web site) specializes in affordable cribs and dressers. Despite the challenge of shipping bulky items like dressers, web sites and specialty retailers are still piling into the online nursery niche. We'll discuss the pros and cons if this approach later in the chapter.

Some web sites try a hybrid approach: online and retail. The RightStart.com has nine stores including a Denver flagship that has nursery furniture displays. You can see it in the store and then have it drop-shipped to your home.

Even if you decide to order your entire nursery online, there are several roadblocks. Given the weight and bulk of cribs and dressers, only a few (mostly lower-end) brands are typically sold online. Shipping charges can be exorbitant—and that assumes you can get items shipped at all (most sites don't ship furniture to Hawaii, Alaska, Canada or military addresses). With shipping, you then have the issue of damage, delays and worse. Given the limitations of drop-shipped furniture delivery, it is more realistic to use online sites to buy accessories (lamps, rockers, décor) for your nursery rather than an entire furniture suite.

4 **REGULAR FURNITURE STORES.** You don't have to go to a "baby store" to buy juvenile furniture. Many regular furniture stores sell name-brand cribs, dressers and other nursery items. Since these stores have frequent sales, you may be able to get a better price than at a juvenile specialty store. On the other hand, the salespeople may not be as knowledgeable about brand and safety issues.

NURSERY NECESSITIES

What Are You Buying?

Ok, let's break this down. Outfitting a nursery usually means buying three basic furniture items: a crib, dresser (which doubles as a place to change baby's diaper) and rocker. Here's a quick discussion of each.

◆ **Crib.** Crib prices start at $150 for an inexpensive crib at a discounter like Kmart. The mid-range for cribs is probably best typified by what you see at chains stores such as Babies R Us and Baby Depot—most of their cribs are in the $200 to $600 range (the stores seem to be a bit more pricey while their online sites offer more lower price options). Specialty stores and catalogs tend to carry upper-end cribs that run $400 to $800. And what about the top end? We'd be remiss not to mention the modern-design cribs, which run $1000 to $2000.

Surprise! The vast majority of cribs don't come with mattresses; those are sold separately ($60 to $300). Bedding is also extra ($100 to $500). We'll discuss mattresses later in this chapter; bedding gets its own entire chapter (Chapter 3).

◆ **Dresser.** Most nurseries need a place to store clothes, diapers, supplies and so on. Known in the baby biz as case pieces (because they are, uh, a case), dressers range from simple, ready-to-assemble four-drawer chests to elaborate armoires (and their smaller cousins, chiffarobes).

Now, there is no federal law that says you MUST buy a dresser or armoire that exactly matches the finish of your crib. Some folks simply re-purpose a dresser from another room to baby's nursery— or pick up a dresser second-hand or at a discount from a regular furniture store. That's fine, of course.

But . . . we realize the allure of matching nursery furniture convinces many new parents to pony up the bucks. So here are some general price guidelines: a ready-to-assemble dresser from IKEA or a discount store runs $150 to $200.

Now, if you'd like to have something fancier (and already assembled), prices for dressers range from $200 to $800 in chain stores. Step into a specialty store and you'll find plenty of fancy dressers, armoires and chiffarobes . . . for $500 to $1000 and higher.

Most dressers also double as a place to change baby—some have tops specifically designed for that purpose. These changer tops remove after baby is done with diapers (usually right before college). So most parents today do not need to buy a separate changing table.

◆ **Rocker.** A place to sit and nurse baby is an important part of any nursery's function—so the next question is . . . where to sit? Again, you can re-purpose a rocker from grandma's house or pick up one secondhand. If you have the room, a small loveseat or over-sized chair is a workable solution for nursing baby.

Brand new "glider-rockers" run the gamut from wooden chairs with thin pads to fully upholstered models. And the price range reflects this: you can spend as little as $100 to $200 for a rocker from Target or Walmart . . . as much as $1300 for a tricked out leather model from a specialty store. Most folks probably buy a basic model from chain stores like Babies R Us for about $300. Yes, ottomans are a nice extra—but cost $100 to $300 more.

Glider rockers get their own section later in this chapter.

The Grand Total. As you can see, the bare-bones budget for a nursery would be $600 (simple crib, mattress, basic dresser and rocker). The mid-range would run about $1100 . . . and on the designer end, you could easily spend $2000 to $3000 on nursery furniture.

And these figures are BEFORE you get to any of the other décor items: bedding, lamps, paint, artwork, curtains, etc.

More Money Buys You . . .

Here's a little secret expensive crib makers don't want you to hear: ALL new cribs (no matter what price) sold in the U.S. or Canada must meet federal safety standards. Yes, the governments of both the U.S. and Canada strictly regulate crib safety and features—that's one reason why most cribs have the same basic design, no matter the brand or price. So, whether you buy a $150 crib special at K-Mart or a $1500 wrought iron crib at a posh specialty boutique, either way you get a crib that meets federal safety requirements.

Now, that said, when you spend more money, there are some perks. The higher the price-tag of the crib (generally), the fancier the design (thicker corner posts, designer colors, etc.). That's all nice, but is it really necessary? No—a basic, safe crib in a simple finish is all a baby needs.

The biggest sales pitch for cribs is convertibility: more expensive cribs are convertible. They morph into beds for older kids: toddler bed (basically, a crib with one side removed and a short rail), day bed (no rail) and (finally) full-sized bed. That latter uses the sides of the crib to become a headboard and footboard—some cribs even transform into queen-size adult beds.

Convertible cribs are pitched to parents as "lifetime cribs" (your child will take the bed to college with them, we suppose) and smart investments, because it "grows with your child." Here's what the pitch leaves out: to convert the crib, you often have to buy a conversion kit (sold separately, naturally). And think about the SIZE of the average kids' bedroom these days: most can barely squeeze in

Three Golden Rules of Buying Nursery Furniture

◆ **Don't over buy**—think about your needs first. Here's a common first time parent mistake: rushing out to a local baby store and falling in love with that fancy cognac finish on a chiffarobe. Instead, think about what you really NEED. Start with the size of your baby's nursery—most secondary bedrooms in a typical suburban home are small (10' x12' is common). That barely leaves room for a crib, dresser and rocker. Don't let a baby store sell you on a double dresser PLUS an armoire when you don't have room. For urban apartment dwellers, space is at a premium. Closets need to be tricked out to provide maximum storage. Expect furniture to do double duty.

◆ **Three words: set a budget.** Don't waste your time with designer furniture if you haven't done the math. As you saw from the discussion on the last few pages, a three-piece nursery set (crib, dresser, rocker) runs anywhere from $600 . . . up to $3000. Pick a budget and stick with it. Then read the brand reviews later in this chapter—you'll quickly realize which ones are in your budget and which aren't! Again, it pays to think outside the box: can you re-purpose a dresser from another room? Get a hand-me-down rocker from a friend or off Craigslist?

◆ **Decide on nursery style.** There are two theories of nursery design: either a baby's room should look, well, babyish . . . or it should be more adult-looking, able to adapt as the child grows. There is no right or wrong answer. If you subscribe to the baby-theme, then go with a simple (non-convertible) crib and dresser that you will later swapped out for a twin bed and computer desk/hutch. If you prefer the other path, then buy a convertible crib (which converts to a full size bed) and dresser that can do double duty. Some brands have dressers that are first a changing area for diapers . . . and then convert to a computer area complete with pull out keyboard drawer.

a TWIN bed and dresser . . . a full or queen size bed is often impossible. We'll discuss this issue more, later in the chapter.

Some crib extras also have dubious value—take the under-crib storage drawer. Often seen on cribs that run $500 or more, this feature appeals to parents who have a storage crunch in their home (you can put blankets, extra clothes in the drawer). The problem? The drawer usually doesn't have a top. So, anything inside will be a dust magnet.

Ok, so now you know the typical prices of nursery furniture . . . and what more money really buys you. How do you decide what is best for your baby's nursery? See the previous box for our Three Golden Rules of Buying Nursery Furniture.

Safe & Sound

Here's a fact to keep you up at night: cribs are the third-biggest cause of injuries and deaths among all nursery products. In the latest year for which statistics are available, 11,300 injuries and 32 deaths were blamed on cribs and mattresses.

And you couldn't click on a news web site in the past year without seeing another crib recall: since 2007, over four MILLION cribs were recalled. The recalls involved both cribs sold in pricey specialty stores and lower-end models sold in Babies R Us and Walmart. The problems? Defective slats that could break, poor side rail design, lead paint and more.

New crib safety standards went into effect in June 2011, effectively banning the sale of drop-side cribs and mandating strength requirements for side rails. Yet even with the new rules, there are safety guidelines and considerations for nursery shopping. Here's an overview:

◆ **Don't buy a used or old crib.** Let's put that into bold caps: **DON'T BUY A USED OR OLD CRIB.** And don't take a hand-me-down from a well-meaning friend or relative. Why? Because old cribs account for most of the injuries and deaths when it comes to cribs. Surprisingly, these old cribs may not be as old as you think—cribs made before 2011 don't meet current standards.

Most folks realize that cribs made in the 70's and 80's aren't safe . . . but that never seems to stop a well-meaning relative to bring down a "family heirloom" crib from the attic. These are death traps: spindles that are too far apart, cutouts in the headboard, and other hazards that could entrap your baby. Decorative trim (like turned posts) that looks great on adult beds are a major no-no for cribs—

they present a strangulation hazard. (Note: cribs with TALL posts are fine; it is the shorter posts that are prohibited—see the graphic on the next page).

Some old cribs have lead paint, a dangerous peril for a teething baby. Another hazard to hand-me-down cribs (regardless of age): missing parts and directions. It only takes one missing screw or bolt to make an otherwise safe crib into a danger. Without directions, you can incorrectly assemble the crib and create additional safety hazards. So, even if your friend wants to give/sell you a recent model crib, you could still have problems if parts or directions are missing.

It may seem somewhat ironic that a book on baby bargains would advise you to go out and spend your hard-earned money on a new crib. True, we find great bargains on Craigslist and second-hand stores. However, you have to draw the line at your baby's safety. Certain second-hand items are great deals—toys and clothes come to mind. However, cribs (and, as you'll read later, car seats) are no-no's, no matter how tempting the bargains.

And second hand stores have a spotty record when it comes to selling safe products. A recent report from the CPSC said that a whopping two-thirds of all U.S. thrift/second-hand stores sell baby products that have been recalled, banned or do not meet current safety standards (specifically 12% of stores stocked old cribs). Amazingly, federal law does not prohibit the sale of cribs (or other dangerous products like jackets with drawstring hoods, recalled playpens or car seats) at second-hand stores.

Readers often ask us why we don't give tips for evaluating old or hand-me-down cribs. The reason is simple: it's hard to tell whether

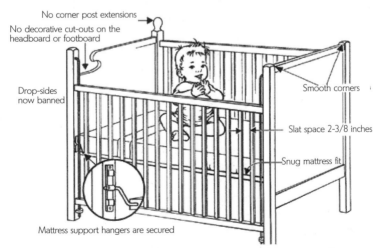

No corner post extensions

No decorative cut-outs on the headboard or footboard

Drop-sides now banned

Smooth corners

Slat space 2-3/8 inches

Snug mattress fit

Mattress support hangers are secured

Older cribs typically have many hazards. Here's a graphic of what is dangerous. Note: all new cribs sold today are required by law to NOT have any of these features.

an old crib is dangerous just by looking at it. Cribs don't always have "freshness dates"—some manufacturers don't stamp the date of manufacture on their cribs. Was the crib made before or after the current safety standards went into effect in 2011? Often, you can't tell.

Today's safety regulations are so specific (like the allowable width for spindles) that you just can't judge a crib's safety with a cursory examination. Cribs made before the 1970's might contain lead paint, which is difficult to detect unless you get the crib tested. Another problem: if the brand name is rubbed off, it will be hard to tell if the crib has been involved in a recall. Obtaining replacement parts is also difficult for a no-name crib.

What about floor model cribs? Is it safe to buy a crib that has been used as a floor sample in a baby store? Yes—as long as it is in good working condition, has no missing/broken parts, etc. Floor model cribs CAN take a tremendous amount of abuse from parents, who shake them to check stability and so on. As a result, the bolts that hold the crib together can loosen. Obviously, that can be fixed (just have the store tighten the bolts) . . . and as a result, we think floor model cribs are fine. That isn't what we mean by avoiding a "used" crib!

What if a relative insists you should use that "family heirloom" crib we mentioned earlier? We've spoken to dozens of parents who felt pressured into using an old crib by a well-meaning relative. There's a simple answer: don't do it. As a parent, you sometimes have to make unpopular decisions that are best for your child's safety. This is just the beginning.

Don't

◆ **Cribs with fold-down rails.** A handful of cribs have fold-down rails—the upper one-third of the railing is hinged and folds down. These are also called swing gate cribs (see picture).

One major crib maker uses these rails for some of their models: Baby's Dream. While we like the quality of Baby's Dream's furniture overall, we do not recommend any crib with a fold-down rail. Why? Older babies who can stand (which happens around a year of age) can get a foothold on the hinged rail to climb out of the crib, injuring themselves as they fall to the floor.

A reader in Seattle, WA recently emailed us with exactly that story: her 13 month old son fractured his fibula (calf bone) after falling out of his Baby's Dream drop-gate crib. "We liked how the drop gate was easy to operate and worked better for a shorter person," she said. "However, we didn't foresee that the drop gate would provide a ledge for him to prop his foot on and fall out."

◆ *Inspect and tighten bolts monthly.* Many cribs that were recalled in the past year had defective hardware or spindles that broke. While drop-side cribs (which had more hardware failures than static side cribs) are no longer on the market, all cribs should be inspected monthly. Make sure all bolts are tightened, no slats are loose, etc.

The new 2011 crib safety standards require hardware that doesn't need to be retightened—however, wood furniture is wood furniture. Changes in humidity or temperatures in a nursery may still require hardware or bolts to be tightened from time to time.

If something has broken on your crib, immediately stop using it. Don't attempt to repair it yourself—and never use a crib with missing, broken or loose parts.

◆ *Lead paint.* The lead paint scare of 2007 is still fresh in the minds of many consumers—and that concern has translated into fears of cribs made in China. So, here's the scoop:

While there have been numerous toys and other children's products recalled for lead paint, there was only one nursery furniture recall for this reason (Munire recalled 3000 cribs and 5000 matching dressers for lead paint in 2008). Most nursery furniture companies have their paint and stains independently tested to verify they are lead-free—one (Sorelle) even posts its test results online. Yet, as the Munire recall shows, even a diligent company can have lapses.

Still, we realize some folks still don't trust China and want to avoid Chinese-made furniture. To help, we have a box on page 49 that lists all the nursery furniture makers who make their furniture in countries other than China.

◆ *Formaldehyde.* Most of us are familiar with this chemical from those middle school biology classes. A gas at room temperature, formaldehyde is an organic compound that was classified as a probable human carcinogen back in 1987. It is linked to increased risk of childhood asthma and allergies.

Of course, you probably don't plan to be dissecting frogs in your child's nursery, so there's no need to worry about formaldehyde, right? Wrong—formaldehyde sneaks into your house in other ways. It is found in furniture, specifically the glue in engineered wood products like particle board, chip board and some types of medium density fiberboard (MDF).

The Environmental Protection Agency regulates the amount of formaldehyde that can off-gas from furniture and other wood products. And some states (California) have even stricter limits. In fact, the state of California sued five baby furniture makers in 2008 for unsafe levels of formaldehyde. The suit was prompted by a report from Environment California, which found certain furniture items from Child Craft, Delta, Stork Craft, South Shore and Jardine had unsafe levels of the chemical.

So how can you avoid this hazard in your nursery? One alternative is to stick with solid wood furniture, but this can be pricey (that's why furniture makers use engineered wood like MDF and particle board: it's cheaper). A second recommendation is to consider furniture that is GREENGUARD certified (greenguard.org). In order to pass this certification process, furniture must meet strict chemical emission limits.

Yes, it is an environmental paradox: engineered wood products like MDF are better for the environment, since you don't have to cut down a tree to make a dresser. But the resin that holds MDF together can contain formaldehyde, which contributes to bad indoor air quality. To get around this conundrum, some eco-friendly nursery companies claim they use MDF that has low-emission glue. While this is hard to verify this (unless you had a testing lab), this might be something to consider if you have a history of allergies and/or asthma in your family.

◆ **Stripped screws.** Cheap cribs often have screws that attach directly to the wood of the headboard. The problem? The screws can strip over time (especially if the crib is assembled several times) and that can weaken the crib's support . . . which is very dangerous. If you ever discover you are not able to tighten the screws or bolts used to hold your crib together, immediately stop using it. When you are crib shopping, look at how the mattress support is attached to the headboards—look for metal screwed into metal.

◆ *Be aware of the hazards of putting a baby in an adult bed.* Co-sleeping is where a baby shares a bed with adults. While common in other parts of the world, co-sleeping is controversial here in the U.S.—on one side are attachment parenting advocates, who insist it is safe, a big convenience for nursing moms and an important part of parent/child emotional bonds.

On the other side are safety advocates, including the Consumer Product Safety Commission and the American Academy of Pediatrics. A CPSC report released in 2002 blamed 122 infant deaths in a previous three-year period on co-sleeping. Of those deaths, many were caused when a child's head became entrapped between the adult bed and another object (a headboard, footboard, wall, etc). Other deaths were caused by falls or suffocation in bedding. The American Academy of Pediatrics agreed with the CPSC's concerns, issuing a recommendation against co-sleeping in 2005 and again in 2011.

We have an expanded discussion of this debate in our other book, *Baby 411.* Our basic advice: the safest place for a baby to sleep is a separate sleep space (a crib or bassinet that meets current safety standards).

◆ **When assembling a crib, make sure ALL the bolts and screws are tightened**. A recent report on *Good Morning America* pointed out how dangerous it can be to put your baby in a miss-assembled crib—a child died in a Child Craft crib when he became trapped in a side rail that wasn't properly attached to the crib. How did that happen? The parent didn't tighten the screws that held the side rail to the crib. Cribs (including the Child Craft one here in question) are safe when assembled correctly; just be sure to tighten those bolts!

◆ **Recalls: where to find information.** The U.S. Consumer Product Safety Commission has a toll-free hotline at (800) 638-2772 and web site (cpsc.gov) for the latest recall information on cribs and other juvenile items. Both are easy to use—you can also report any potential hazard you've discovered or an injury to your child caused by a product. Write to the U.S. Consumer Products Safety Commission, Washington, D.C. 20207 or file a complaint online at cpsc.gov. FYI: The CPSC takes care of all juvenile product recalls, except for car seats—that's the purview of the National Highway Traffic Safety Administration (nhtsa.gov).

A great "all-in-one" site for recalls is Recalls.gov. Also: subscribe to our blog—we will send you an email or text message when a product is recalled. Go to BabyBargains.com/blog and enter your email at the box at the right and hit subscribe. It's free!

◆ **Safety is more than a crib.** Be sure to have a smoke and carbon monoxide detector for your baby's nursery. And if you haven't had your home tested for radon yet, this would be a good time. (We discuss radon and other environmental hazards in our book, *Toddler 411*. See the back of this book for details).

Smart Shopper Tips

Smart Shopper Tip #1
The Art and Science of Selecting the Right Crib.

"How do you evaluate a crib? They all look the same to me. What really makes one different from another?"

Selecting a good crib is more than just picking out the style and finish. You should look under the hood, so to speak. Here are our nine key points to look for when shopping for a crib:

◆ ***Brand reputation.*** Later in this chapter, we will rate and review the biggest crib brands. Our advice: stick with a brand that gets a B or better rating. We formulate these ratings from parent feedback (some of which is posted on our web site, where readers rate and review various crib brands) as well as our analysis of a brand's track record. We look at recall history, customer service, delivery reliability and overall quality to assign a rating.

◆ ***Mattress support.*** Look underneath that mattress and see what is holding it up. The best cribs use a metal spring platform or a grid of wooden slats. Other cribs use cheap vinyl straps or a piece of particle board. We think the last two are inferior—vinyl straps aren't as secure as metal springs or wood slats; and concerns have been raised over formaldehyde emissions with particle board (see earlier discussion).

◆ ***Static side rails.*** All cribs sold in the U.S. and Canada are now stationary or static side cribs. In years past, cribs with drop sides (where one side lowers to give assess to the baby) were linked to numerous safety recalls. Although you won't see drop-side cribs sold in stores, there are still many listed for sale on Craigslist and in second-hand stores—we say avoid them.

One exception to the no-drop side rule: one crib maker, Baby's Dream, still offers some cribs with a fold-down rail). Instead of lowering, the rail has a hinge that allows the top portion to fold down. The CPSC deems these rails to be safe; we aren't big fans of fold-down rails for reasons we outlined earlier in this chapter.

◆ ***Hardware/bolts: hidden or exposed?*** Some cribs have visible bolts that attach the crib rails to the headboard; others are hidden. Is there a difference in safety or durability? No, it's just aesthetics. The more money you spend, the more likely the hardware/bolts will be hidden.

◆ ***How stable is the crib?*** Because all cribs sold today have stationary sides, this is less of an issue than in years past. Stationary cribs by virtue of have no moving parts, tend to be more stable then the drop-side cribs of years past. And yes, more expensive cribs are typically heavier with thicker posts and slats than low-priced options—and that makes them more stable.

◆ ***How do you move the crib?*** Few cribs sold today have wheels. When you move a crib, it is a two-person job. And some cribs weigh in excess of 100 pounds. Never drag a crib across the carpet, as you can damage the headboard. One idea: if your crib has legs or bun feet, use Magic Sliders (magicsliders.com, $7) to make it easier to move a crib to clean or vacuum behind it.

◆ **How easy is it to assemble?** Ask to see those instructions—most stores should have a copy lying around. Make sure they are not indecipherable. Yes, some stores offer set-up and delivery, but with chain superstores, you are typically on your own. Sadly, some crib makers don't put a high priority on easy-to-understand assembly instructions—check first before you buy! The good news: some crib makers now have instructions you can download from their web sites.

◆ **Compare the overall safety features of the crib.** In a section earlier in this book, we discuss crib safety in more detail.

◆ **Which wood is best?** Most cribs are made of hardwoods: birch, beech, oak, etc. In recent years, crib makers have also made some models in pine. The problem? Pine is a softwood that isn't as durable as hardwood—it tends to nick, scratch and damage. Of course, not all pine is the same. North American pine is the softest, but pine grown in really cold climates (Northern Europe, for example) is harder.

Another recent trend: modern furniture made of medium-density fiberboard (MDF) with a glossy lacquer finish. Made of wood fibers and resin, MDF has a smooth, grain-free surface, which enables manufacturers to add that high-gloss finish.

So, which wood is best? We recommend you go with a hardwood crib—it doesn't matter whether it is birch, beech, mahogany or even ramin (also called rubber wood). The latter is an Asian hardwood that is often seen in low-price cribs.

We caution against pine furniture—even "hardwood pine" can be more susceptible to nicks, scratches and damage than other woods like birch or beech. If you decide to buy pine baby furniture, just prepare yourself for the inevitable ding here or there.

What about MDF? We aren't fans of composite wood—MDF simply isn't as durable as hardwood. Yes, we realize fans of modern furniture are more sold on the aesthetic here . . . MDF with a glossy lacquer makes for a sleek look. But you'll be paying through the nose for this (some modern cribs run $1000+) for a crib that isn't made from solid wood.

Another quick point: don't confuse finish with wood. Some stores and web sites tout "cherry" cribs when they are actually referring to the finish, not the actual wood. It may be a "cherry" stain, but the wood is probably not.

Smart Shopper Tip #2
Cyber-Nursery: Ordering furniture online

"We don't have any good baby stores nearby, so I want to order furniture online. How do you buy items sight unseen and make sure they arrive in one piece?"

Sure, you can buy just about everything today online, but when it comes to nursery furniture, we have one word of advice: don't.

Despite the fact that most stores selling nursery items have online sites offering furniture, our readers report that the actual experience of buying a crib or dresser online leaves them frustrated.

You probably guessed the reason: bulk. Cribs and dressers are heavy and bulky—this makes them expensive to ship and susceptible to damage. If there is a problem, you have to deal with a customer service agent half way across the country.

Our advice: order from a local store and have the items delivered/set-up. If the store doesn't have items in stock, see if they have a "site to store" shipping option—you order online, but the item is delivered to a local store where you pick it up. This helps eliminate shipping damage.

Wastes of Money

1 **LOW QUALITY "BABY" FURNITURE THAT WON'T LAST.** Baby furniture stores (both chains and independents) are sometimes guilty of selling very poor quality furniture. Take a dresser, for example. Many dressers made by juvenile furniture companies have stapled drawers, veneer construction (instead of solid wood), cheap drawer glides and worse. Now, that wouldn't be so bad if such dressers were low in price. But often you see these dressers going for $500 and up in baby stores—it's as if you are paying a premium to merely match the color of your crib. While we don't see a problem buying low-end "disposable" furniture at a good price (IKEA is a prime example), paying a fortune for a poorly made dresser is ridiculous. In this chapter, we will point out brand names that provide more quality for the dollar. Look for solid wood construction, dovetail drawers, and smooth drawer glides if you want that dresser to last.

2 **UNDER-CRIB DRAWERS.** It sounds like a great way to squeeze out a bit more storage in a nursery—the drawer that slides out from under a crib. Getting a crib with such a feature usually costs an extra $100 or $150. The problem? Most of these drawers do NOT have tops . . . therefore anything kept in there will get dusty in a hurry. So that nixes storing extra blankets or clothes. We say skip the extra expense of an under-crib drawer.

3 **THE TODDLER BED.** Some crib makers tout cribs that convert to toddler beds. Smaller than a twin bed, a toddler bed uses the crib mattress and is pitched as a transition between the crib and a big boy/girl bed. But, guess what? Most kids can go straight from a crib to a regular twin bed with no problem whatsoever. The toddler bed is a waste of money, in our opinion.

4 **CRADLE.** Most pediatricians recommend "rooming in" with your newborn to help with breastfeeding. But where will the baby sleep? Cradles and bassinets are one option, but can be pricey. Cradles (basically a mini crib that rocks) run up to $400, while separate bassinets (a basket on a stand) can cost $200. A more affordable solution: just set up the crib in your room. After you establish that breastfeeding rhythm, the baby and crib can move to the nursery. If you don't have room in your master bedroom to set up the crib, consider a playpen with bassinet feature like the Graco Pack N Play. We'll discuss the best buys on bassinets on page 102; playpens like the Pack N Play are reviewed in Chapter 7, Around the House.

5 **CRIBS WITH "SPECIAL FEATURES."** Some stores carry unique styles of cribs and that might be tempting for parents looking to make a statement for their nursery. An example: elliptical cribs. The only problem: special cribs like this may require additional expenses, such as custom-designed mattresses or bedding. And since few companies make bedding for these cribs, your choices are limited. The best advice: make sure you price out the total investment (crib, mattress, bedding) before falling in love with an unusual style.

6 **CHANGING TABLES.** Separate changing tables are a big waste of money. Don't spend $90 to $200 on a piece of furniture you won't use again after your baby gives up diapers. A better bet: buy a dresser that can do double duty as a changing table. Many dressers you'll see in baby stores are designed with this extra feature—just make sure the height is comfortable for both you and your spouse. Other parents we interviewed did away with the changing area altogether—they used a crib, couch or countertop to do diaper changes.

E-Mail from The Real World
Spending $385 for a $50 dresser

A reader in Ohio shared this bad experience with shopping for a dresser online:

"I ordered a three drawer combo dresser from a well-known baby gear web site. It had all of the things suggested in your book and was $385. The manufacturer is Angel Line. The item arrived with split wood on the corner, a knob missing, a missing wall strap and one of the drawers didn't shut completely and was crooked. I called the site and they said I had to contact the manufacturer directly to get the problem resolved. It took four calls and the best I could get was another knob and drawer sent to me with corners that did not fit together. So, I essentially paid $400 for something that looks like a dresser that's $50 at a garage sale."

Top 8 Things Baby Stores Won't Tell You About Buying Nursery Furniture

◆ *Our store may disappear before your nursery furniture arrives.* It's a sad fact: baby stores come and go. Most retailers that close do so reputably—they don't take special orders for merchandise they can't fill. A handful are not so honest . . . they take deposits up until the day the landlord padlocks their doors. Our advice: always charge your purchase to a credit card. If the store disappears, you can dispute the charge with your credit card company and (most likely) get your money back. Another red flag: stores that ask for payment up front on a special order. The typical deal is half down with the balance due upon delivery. Stores that are desperate for cash might demand the entire purchase price upfront. Be suspicious. Another piece of advice: keep a close eye on what's going on with your furniture maker. How? Read our blog or surf our message boards at BabyBargains.com. Over the years, we've seen it all—strikes, floods, fires, port shutdowns and more. You name it, it can happen to the factory that makes your furniture. When we get a whiff of a problem, we send out the news to our readers via our e-newsletter, blog or on our message boards. That way you can switch to another brand if you've haven't placed an order yet . . . or formulate a plan B if your furniture is caught by a delivery delay.

◆ *Never assume something in a sealed box is undamaged.*

Always OPEN boxes and inspect furniture before taking it out of a store. Yes, that is a hassle, but we've had numerous complains about boxed furniture that someone has driven 50 miles home, only to discover a major gash or other damage. Or the wrong color is in the right box. Or a major piece is missing. A word to the wise: inspect it BEFORE going home.

◆ *If it is in stock, BUY IT.* Let's say you see a crib that is in stock, but the matching dresser is on back order. Do you get the crib now and wait on the dresser? Or special order both? Our advice: if an item is sitting there in a store (even if it is a floor sample), it is ALWAYS better to take the in-stock item now.

◆ *Your special order merchandise will be backordered until 2014, despite our promise to get it to you before your baby is born.* Almost all furniture today is imported . . . we are not talking from close-by countries like Canada or Mexico. Nope, odds are your furniture will be made in China, Vietnam, Eastern Europe or South America. And a myriad of problems (labor strikes, port shut-downs, Latvian Independence Day) can delay the shipment of your nursery furniture. Our advice: ORDER EARLY. If the furniture store says it will take six weeks, plan on 12. Or 15.

◆ *Just because the crib maker has an Italian name doesn't mean your furniture is made in, say, Italy.* Not long ago, you had domestic makers of cribs (Child Craft, Simmons) and the imports, most of which were from Italy. Those days are long gone—today almost all nursery furniture is imported from Asia (specifically, China).

Here's where it gets confusing: sometimes the very same brand will import furniture from different countries. Sorelle, for example, started out as an Italian importer. Today, Sorelle imports most of its cribs and furniture from China, Brazil and Latvia in Eastern Europe. Ditto for Bonavita, which despite the Italian sounding name, imports most of its furniture from China and other factories in Asia.

Bottom line: key on the brand's reputation for quality and cus-tomer service, not so much the country the crib is made in. Yes, we realize some folks are nervous about Chinese-made products. To address those concerns, we have a box on page 49 that points out the brands not made in China. However, we don't think a crib or dresser made in China is inherently dangerous—again, it is the com-pany's reputation for quality and customer service that is key, not the country of origin.

◆ *That special mattress we insist you buy isn't necessary.* Some baby stores are trying a new tactic to sell their pricey in-house brand of crib mattress: scaring the pants off new parents. We've heard all the stories—only OUR mattress fits OUR crib, a less expensive foam mattress is DANGEROUS for your baby and so on. Please! Government standards require both cribs and mattresses to be within standard measurements. Yes, fancy boutiques might make their mattress a bit larger to give a tighter fit . . . but that doesn't mean a regular mattress won't work just as well (and is just as safe). It's no wonder stores push the in-house mattress—it can cost $300 or more. Our advice: save your money and get a plain crib mattress for half the price at another store.

♦ *Just because we say this item is discontinued does NOT mean you can't find it anywhere else.* This is especially true for chain stores—just because Babies R Us says the crib you've fallen in love with is now discontinued does NOT mean you can't find it from another store. That's because chains discontinue items all the time . . . and not just because the manufacturer is discontinuing it. Chains replace slow moving merchandise or just make way for something new. Meanwhile, the very same furniture (or for that matter, any baby gear) is sold down the street at another store.

♦ *The finish on that expensive special-order dresser may match your crib . . . or not.* Here's something baby stores don't advertise: the finishes on that expensive nursery furniture you special ordered may not match. Why? Many furniture companies use different wood for different pieces—say birch for a crib, but pine for a dresser. The problem: each takes stain differently. As a result, a birch crib in cherry may not match a pine dresser in the same cherry stain. While the difference may be small, it bugs some folks more than others. The take home message: if matching stain is important to you, confirm all the pieces of your furniture are made of the same wood—and try to see a sample of the stain on a real piece of furniture to confirm colors (don't rely on online photos).

 Money Saving Secrets

1 **CHECK OUT REGULAR FURNITURE STORES FOR ROCKERS, DRESSERS, ETC.** Think about it—most juvenile furniture looks very similar to regular adult furniture. Rockers, dressers, and bookcases are, well, just rockers, dressers, and bookcases. And don't you wonder if companies slap the word "baby" on an item just to raise the price 20%? To test this theory, we visited a local discount furniture store. The prices were incredibly low. A basic four-drawer pine dresser was $200. Even maple or oak four-drawer dressers were just $350.

The same quality dresser at a baby store by a "juvenile furniture" manufacturer would set you back at least $500, if not twice that. We even saw cribs by such mainstream names as Bassett at decent prices in regular furniture stores. What's the disadvantage to shopping there? Well, if you have to buy the crib and dresser at different places, the colors might not match exactly. But, considering the savings, it might be worth it.

2 GET SOCIAL. Social media is more than just status updates and tweets—sign up for "deal of the day sites" like Groupon or Zulily.com. As the name implies, deal of the day sites have one great deal (up to 70% off) available for a limited time. For Groupon, that might be a 50% discount on a local maternity store. Zullily, founded by the folks who started Blue Nile, offers cribs, designer kids clothes and baby gear at deep discounts. Of course, part of the fun with these sites is sharing the deals with your friends on Facebook.

3 THINK TWICE ABOUT MOD. Modern furniture is the rage in high-end boutiques, but what do you get for that ultra-mod look? Many "modern" cribs and furniture are made of MDF, particle board and laminates . . . and for this you're supposed to shell out $800 for a crib and $1600 for a dresser? Can someone explain to us why modern furniture costs TWICE as much as "regular" cribs and dressers that are made of all wood? Sure that mod furniture has a few extra coats of lacquer and looks all shiny. But we still don't get it—especially since nearly all nursery furniture (yes, even the mod stuff) is imported from Asia. Our advice: If you decide to go mod, stick with the more affordable options like IKEA (even Walmart now sports a modern furniture collection at reasonable prices).

4 COMPARE ONLINE PRICES. Do you wonder if that local baby store has jacked up the price of nursery furniture? We know some of you live in towns or communities with little or no local competition for nursery items. One obvious solution: hit the web. Now, we realize we listed all sorts of caveats for online orders earlier in the book (high shipping fees, problems with damage, etc)—but let's face it. In some parts of the country, this is really your best option. As always, don't ASSUME local stores will be higher in price than the web. Do your homework first. And always ask local retailers if they will price match what you see online. Many quietly do! One good source to compare crib prices: BabyCribCentral.com doesn't sell cribs, but provides a handy price comparison engine.

A caveat to online shopping: if you live in Alaska or Hawaii (or are overseas military with an APO address), you may be out of luck. While Walmart and Target will ship some items to Alaska and

Hawaii, other sites refuse.

5 **ONE WORD: IKEA.** Sure, it's basic and no frills . . . but it's hard to beat the price! IKEA's ultra affordable cribs and dressers make even Walmart look expensive. Example: the HENSVIK crib for $139 and matching wardrobe for $149. Yes, you will have to assemble it yourself. And no, it won't last through three kids. But hey—it's hard to beat the price. (See the brand reviews later for more on IKEA, including some key things to know before you buy).

6 **GO NAKED.** Naked furniture, that is. An increasing number of stores sell unfinished (or naked) furniture at great prices. Such places even sell the finishing supplies and give you directions (make sure to use a non-toxic finish). The prices are hard to beat. At a local unfinished furniture store, we found a three-drawer pine dresser (23" wide) for $100, while a four-drawer dresser (38" wide) was $175. Compare that to baby store prices, which can top $400 to $700 for a similar size dresser. A reader in California e-mailed us with a great example of this trend in the Bay Area: "Hoot Judkins" has two locations (Redwood City and Millbrae; hootjudkins.com) that sell unfinished furniture. She found a five-drawer dresser in solid birch for just $229 and other good deals on nursery acces-sories. Another idea: Million Dollar Baby/Da Vinci (see review later in this chapter) is one of the few crib makers to offer unfinished crib models (Jenny Lind, M0391). While unfinished cribs are somewhat rare, naked furniture stores at least offer affordable alternatives for dressers, bookcases, and more.

7 **SKIP THE SLEIGH CRIB.** Lots of folks fall in love with the look of a sleigh-style crib, which looks like (you guessed it) a sleigh. The only problem? Most sleigh cribs have solid foot and head-boards. All that extra wood means higher prices, as much as TWICE that of non-sleigh styles. If you have your heart set on a sleigh style, look for one with slats on the headboard instead of solid wood.

8 **CONSIDER AN AFFORDABLE CONVERTIBLE CRIB.** Before you jump on the bandwagon and consider a convertible crib, there is key question to ask: do you have room in the nursery for the crib to convert to a full-size bed? If the answer is yes, then con-sider an affordable convertible. At chains stores like Babies R Us convertible cribs run $300 to $500. At specialty stores, brands like Munire and Westwood offer convertibles in the $400 to $600 range. Don't forget to factor in the price of the kit to convert the crib to a twin or full-size bed—this is another $60 to $200. At press time, Costco was selling a convertible crib by CaféKids convertible crib (including the conversion kit) for a mere $364 (see review of CaféKids below). One tip: make sure the design has a true headboard and shorter footboard (many low-end convertible cribs cheat on this point by having the same size head and foot boards). This looks much better when converted to a double bed.

9 **TRY CRAIGSLIST.ORG.** As you probably know, Craigslist's popular online classified site has versions for dozens of cities, with a special "for sale" section for baby/kids stuff. Use Craigslist to find a local family that is unloading unneeded nursery furniture, gear and other items (but do NOT buy a used crib, as we've discussed earlier).

10 **DON'T WAIT ON THE CONVERSION KIT OR NIGHTSTAND.** Many parents like the concept of a convertible crib that can grow with your child from crib to twin or full-size bed. But to make that transition, you often need to buy a separate conversion kit (bedrails and other hardware). We recommend buying the conversion kit (and other matching items like a nightstand) when you first order your nursery furniture, instead of waiting until your child needs the crib converted. Why? Styles and colors can be discontinued at the drop of a hat; some manufacturers disappear altogether. If you wait and the conversion kit is no longer available, you've just spent a fortune on a convertible crib that can't be converted!

Baby Superstore Reviews: The Good, Bad & Ugly

There's good news and bad news when it comes to shopping for baby. Good news: there are an amazing number of stores to shop for baby gear. Bad news: there are an amazing number of stores to shop for baby gear.

And as a first-time parent, you probably have never been in these stores (except for that time you bought a gift for a pregnant co-worker). Walking into a baby superstore for the first time can give even the most levelheaded mom or dad-to-be a case of the willies. It is a blizzard of pacifiers, strollers, cribs and more in a mind-numbing assortment of colors, features and options. So, as a public service, here's our overview of the major players in the baby store biz.

Babies R Us 888-BABYRUS; babiesrus.com. The 800-pound gorilla of baby stores, Babies R Us has 260+ stores nationwide and is the country's leading baby gear retailer. Love 'em or hate 'em, you'll probably find yourself in a BRU at some point—in some communities, BRU is the only game in town.

FYI: Babies R Us comes in several flavors: there are the 260 stand-alone stores. Then there are 109 side-by-side stories (where a Toys R Us and Babies R Us are side-by-side). There are also 26 "R" super-stores that combine a Toys R Us with a Babies R Us. Finally, the chain has a flagship store in Union Square that is a Babies R Us on steroids.

For the uninitiated, Babies R Us is your typical chain store—big on selection, decent prices . . . but service? That's not the point. Sure, our readers occasionally report they found a knowledgeable sales clerk. But other times, you are lucky to find a person to check you out, much less give advice on a car seat.

To its credit, Babies R Us is trying to fix this by adding registry concierges—specially trained associates whose mission in life is to guide parents-to-be through the registry process. So far, the chain has rolled out this program at 36 stores and may add it chainwide by the time of this writing.

In the furniture section, Babies R Us carries brands that are exclusive to the chain: Baby Cache (Munire), and Carter's (Butterfly Living). BRU's strategy is to price its cribs higher than discounters like Target but less than specialty stores. And since you can't find Jardine in any other stores, you can't price shop that specific model.

Unfortunately, this strategy came back to bite BRU in the butt in

How to snag the best deals on Craigslist

Sure there are great deals on Craigslist, but how do you use this online wonder to save the most? Here are a few tips:

◆ **Be patient.** When you first go on Craigslist, you will be amazed at the prices and think you have to snap up deals quickly. But take some time to see what really are the *best* prices. A reader says she thought she got a good deal when she hastily bought a Baby Bjorn carrier off Craigslist for 50% retail—until she noticed the going rate is more like 75% off.

◆ **Use Craigslist list to find garage sales.** On Friday night or Saturday morning, just do a quick search in the garage sale listings for "baby."

◆ **Deals are even better than they look.** That's because there is no shipping or sales tax. Examples from our readers: a Dutailier rocker and ottoman for $260 (retail $600+), Boppy pillow for $5 (retail $35), cradle swing for $60 (retail: $140).

2008 after a massive recall of a 375,000 Jardine cribs. The way BRU handled this recall sparked a large number of complaints (we covered this story on our blog), tarnishing the chain's image among parents.

While we aren't wild about most of BRU's furniture offerings, the rest of the store is better: you'll see Britax in the car seat section and Maclaren in strollers, both better brands. And BRU wins kudos for their web site, which has been upgraded to include a gift-finding tool, store inventory levels and wish lists. The web site features additional brands not sold in BRU's stores (Bugaboo strollers, for example).

Babies R Us' ace in the hole is their gift registry, which now has a quick start option and other online tools. While no gift registry is perfect (and BRU's registry has seen its fair share of complaints on our message boards), we have noted that readers lately seem happier with BRU's registry after the company divorced itself from a disastrous partnership with Amazon a few years ago.

FYI: Watch for high dollar coupon books that Babies R Us distributes in January—ask your local store for details.

So, how to grade Babies R Us? For selection, make it an A-, service gets a C, pricing a B+ and the registry, an A. Overall, let's call it a B. ***Rating: B***

Baby Depot *800-444-COAT; burlingtoncoatfactory.com.* Baby Depot is a store-within-a-store concept. Tucked inside the cavernous Burlington Coat Factory, Baby Depot is a nook stuffed with nursery furniture, strollers and a smattering of other gear.

Even though there as many Baby Depots as Babies R Us stores (370+ at last count), Baby Depot has always played second-fiddle to BRU. Part of the problem has been marketing strategy: Baby Depot could use one. Burlington/Baby Depot operates in a wide range of locations, some in shiny new suburban power centers and others in dingy warehouses.

The selection of brands at Baby Depot is decent, but merchandising isn't exactly Baby Depot's strong suite. The aisles of the stores are often disorganized and cluttered.

The service at Baby Depot makes Babies R Us look like Nordstroms. We get frequent letters from Baby Depot furniture customers, complaining about late orders, botched orders and worse.

On the plus side, Baby Depot has changed their draconian return policy—now you can return items within 30 days and get cash back (as long as you have a receipt and the tags are still attached).

So, here's our advice: if you see something here that is in stock and the price is right, go for it. But forget about special ordering anything such as furniture. ***Rating: C-***

Buy Buy Baby *BuyBuyBaby.com*. Owned by the Bed, Bath & Beyond chain, Buy Buy Baby is our top pick in this category. Yes, they only 50+ locations, but the chain is expanding and may be worth a trip if one is nearby.

Service is the strong point here—folks at Buy Buy Baby know their stuff. Now, we realize that this might not be a fair fight—can Babies R Us with its zillion stores ever compete on service with a much smaller rival? It will be interesting to see if Buy Buy Baby can maintain that advantage as it expands into new stores.

Given the urban slant to its locations, the brands and selection skew toward the expensive. Yes, there are Graco travel systems here . . . but also Bugaboo's $900 models. Ditto for the furniture, with Million Dollar Baby sharing floor space with more pricey options from Young America (by Stanley), Baby Appleseed and Westwood.

The stores are merchandised a bit like Bed Bath and Beyond— that is crowded, with stacks of merchandise rising to the ceiling. While Babies R Us is a bit easier to navigate, Buy Buy Baby has more selection in several categories.

If we had to pick one point on which Buy Buy could improve, it would have to be their lackluster web site. Poor organization and little in the way of buying advice—Buy Buy Baby's web site might have done the trick five years ago, but now it is among the weakest online entries. Yes, the web site has just added user reviews (what took so long?); overall, Amazon and Babies R Us are light years ahead.

Despite their web site, we still give Buy Buy Baby our top rating among chain stores—if you happen to be near one, this store is a keeper. ***Rating: A***

The Discounters: Target, Walmart, K-Mart

Any discussion of national stores that sell baby items wouldn't be complete without a mention of the discounters: Target, Walmart, K-Mart and their ilk. In recent years, the discounters have realized one sure-fire way to drive store traffic—discount baby supplies! As a result, you'll often see formula, diapers and other baby essentials at rock-bottom prices. And there are even better deals on "in-house" brands. The goal is to have you drop by to pick up some diapers . . . and then walk out with a big-screen TV.

Of all the discounters, we think Target is best (with one big caveat—their ruthless return policy, see below for a discussion). Target's baby department is a notch above Walmart and K-Mart when it comes to brand names and selection. Yes, sometimes Walmart has lower prices—but usually that's on lower-quality brands. Target, by contrast, carries Perego high chairs and a wider selection of products like baby monitors. The best bet: Super Targets, which have expanded baby products sections.

One important trend: discounters have bulked up their web sites with brands, products and models that are NOT carried in their stores. Sometimes you'll even find an upscale brand online at discount prices. We'll discuss the discounter web sites specifically below.

Of course, there are some downsides to the discounters. If you're looking for premium brand names, forget it. Most discounters only stock the so-called mass-market brands: Graco strollers, Cosco car seats, Gerber sheets, etc. And the baby departments always seem to be in chaos when we visit, with items strewn about hither and yon. K-Mart is probably the worst when it comes to organization, Walmart the best. We like Target's selection (especially of feeding items and baby monitors), but their prices are somewhat higher than Walmart. What about service? Forget it—no matter which store you're in, you're on your own.

While we do recommend Target, we should warn readers about their return policy. Once among the most generous, Target now requires a receipt for just about any return. A raft of new rules and restrictions greet customers (sample: exchanges now must be made for items within the same department). This has understandably ticked off a fair number of our readers, especially those who have unfortunately chosen to register at Target for their baby gifts. Among the biggest roadblocks: Target won't let you exchange duplicate baby gifts if you don't have a gift receipt (and there are numerous other rules/restrictions as well). Of course, your friends may forget to ask for a gift receipt or throw it away. And watch out: gift receipts have expiration dates; be sure to return any item before that date. Target also limits the number of returns you can do in one year.

After receiving a fair amount of consumer complaints about this, Target now allows returns of registry gifts without a gift receipt IF the item is listed on your registry. The rub: you will get the lowest sales price in the last 90 days, not necessarily what your guest paid for it. That's a special gotcha for new parents—many baby products and clothes go on sale frequently, rendering your gift almost worthless on an exchange. This and other concerns with Target have spawned many complaints about their registry and even blogs dedicated to dissing the chain.

Our advice: think twice about registering at Target. While we get complaints about all baby registries (even industry leader Babies R Us), be sure to read the fine print for ANY baby registry before signing up. Ask about returns and exchange policies, including specifically what happens if you have to return/exchange a duplicate item without a gift receipt. And check for limits on the number of returns you can do within a certain time period. Finally, ask about HOW the store integrates your registry with the web site—if someone buys an item online instead of at a store, will this be reflected on your registry? Check our blog and message boards for the latest buzz on baby registries.

Each of the major discounters sells baby products online. Here's an overview of each site:

◆ **WalMart.com** Hit the baby tab and you'll find yourself in Walmart's extensive online baby gear department. We like how the chain has expanded online offerings in recent years—there's much more on the web site than in the stores (particularly strollers). Walmart has steadily improved the site over the last year or so—now you can search by brand, read product reviews and get a product delivered to a nearby store at no charge. And, of course, the prices are excellent.

◆ **Kmart.com** K-Mart's online outpost is a winner—we liked the graphics and easy navigation. You can search by brand, price and more. We also liked the Deals tab for the latest specials. The only bummer: unlike Target, K-Mart's online selection brand-wise is much the same as the store—heavy on low-end brands like Baby Trend. And the site is confusing in some areas—in car seats, Kmart mixes infant, convertible and booster seats. That's not very helpful.

◆ **Target.com** is our pick as the best discounter web site—their online offerings go way beyond what's in the stores. We also like the user reviews, as well as the ability to sort any category by brand, price or best-sellers. Perhaps the biggest drawback with Target.com (as with other sites) is the sometimes skimpy product descriptions. You can often find more about a product by reading the user reviews than Target's own descriptions.

◆ **Diapers.com** New kid on the block, Diapers.com started off selling diapers online (naturally) and evolved into a baby gear behemoth in recent years. The reason: big discounts and quick shipping. As of this writing, the site was offering free two-day shipping on orders of $49. This has sparked a war with Amazon, which recently rolled out a similar free two-day shipping program dubbed Amazon Mom. Then Amazon just up and bought Diapers.com. No word on any changes to the web site and it's great shipping program. At press time, Diapers.com's site featured excellent organization and the occasional upscale brand (Q Collection in cribs; Mutsy in strollers). A Green Baby tab highlights eco-friendly diapers, gear and clothing. For bargain hunters, zero in on the Sale tab for the latest discounts and clearance items.

Specialty Chains That Sell Baby Furniture

Inspired by the success of Pottery Barn Kids, several chains have ventured into the nursery business. An example: Room & Board (RoomandBoard.com), an 11 store chain (plus an outlet) with locations in California, Colorado, Illinois, Minnesota, Georgia and the New York City area. Their well-designed web site has a nursery section with a couple of cribs ($700 to $1000), dressers and accessories. Quality is good, say our readers who've ordered from them.

And that's just the beginning: Land of Nod, a subsidiary of Crate & Barrel, has an extensive website (landofnod.com) with nursery offerings (ten cribs) as well as five stores in Chicago and Seattle. FYI: Even though Land of Nod is owned by Crate & Barrel, you can't use gift cards from one chain at the other.

What's driving this is a boom in babies, especially to older moms and dads. Tired of the cutesy baby stuff in chain stores, many parents are looking for something more sophisticated and hip. Of course, it remains to be seen what this means for bargain shoppers. On one hand, more competition is always good—having a wide diversity of places to buy nursery furniture and accessories is always a plus. On the downside, most of these chains are chasing that "upscale" customer with outrageously priced cribs and bedding. "As much as parents love the furniture at Pottery Barn Kids, some wince at the prices," said the *Wall Street Journal* in a recent article on this trend. And we agree—while we love the PBK look, our goal in life is to try to find that same look . . . at half the price!

Outlets

There are dozens of outlets that sell kids' clothing, but when it comes to furniture the pickings are slim. In fact, we found just a handful of nursery furniture outlets out there. Here's a round up:

Pottery Barn Kids has eight outlets for their kids catalog, scattered around the country (there's a list on their web site). Readers report some good deals there, including a changing table for $100 (regularly $200) and a rocker for $200 (down from $700). The outlet also carries the PBK bedding line at good discounts. A reader in Georgia said the PBK outlet there features 75% off deals on furniture and you can get a coupon book at the food court for an additional 10% discount. "The best time to shop is during the week—they run more specials then," she said. "And bring a truck—they don't deliver." One final tip: call AHEAD before you go. The selection of nursery furniture can vary widely from outlet to outlet . . . some may have no stock during certain months.

Live in the Northeast? Check out **Baby Boudoir Outlet**, an offshoot of a baby store in New Bedford, MA (babyboudoiroutlet.com, 800-272-2293, 508-998-2166). The store is an authorized dealer for Pali, Baby's Dream, Bonavita, Romina and Munire. The Baby Boudoir Outlet has 1000 cribs in stock at any one time at prices from $250 to $450. The store also carries glider rockers, bedding and other baby products at 30% to 70% off retail. FYI: There is both a Baby Boudoir store and a warehouse outlet—you want to visit the outlet for the best deals. The outlet is around the corner from the main store.

Readers have been mixed on their opinions of the Baby Boudoir outlet. One described it as a "bare bones warehouse in a bad neighborhood." However, another reader described the outlet as "in an urban area, but safe"; she found the warehouse itself "clean and well-organized."

Don't forget that **JCPenney** has 21 outlet stores nationwide. The stores carry a wide variety of items, including children's and baby products (always call before you go to confirm selection). Check out the web site Outlet Bound (outletbound.com) for a current listing of locations.

The Name Game: Reviews of Selected Manufacturers

Here's a look at crib brands sold in the U.S. and Canada. Our focus is on the most common nursery furniture brands you see in chains stores, independents and other furniture outlets. If you've discovered a brand that we didn't review, feel free to share your discovery by calling or emailing us (see our contact info at the end of the book).

How did we evaluate the brands? First, we inspected samples of cribs at stores and industry trade shows. With the help of veteran juvenile furniture retailers, we checked construction, release mechanisms, mattress supports, and overall fit and finish. Yes, we did compare styling among the brands but this was only a minor factor in our ratings (we figure you can decide what looks best for your nursery).

Readers of previous editions have asked us how we assign ratings to these manufacturers—what makes one an "A" vs. "B"? The bottom line is quality *and* value. Sure, anyone can make a high-quality crib for $800. The trick is getting that price down to $400 or less while maintaining high-quality standards. Hence, we give more bonus points to brands that give more value for the dollar.

What about the crib makers who got the lowest ratings? Are their cribs unsafe? No, of course not. ALL new cribs sold in the U.S.

and Canada must meet minimum federal safety standards. As we mentioned earlier in this chapter, a $150 crib sold at Walmart is just as safe as a $1500 designer brand sold at a posh boutique. The only difference is styling, features and durability—more expensive cribs have thick wood posts, fancy finishes and durability to last through two or more kids. The best companies have the best customer service, taking care of both their retailers and consumers.

Brands that got our lowest rating have poor quality control and abysmal customer service. Serious safety recalls also impacts a brand's rating.

The Ratings

A **EXCELLENT**—*our top pick!*
B **GOOD**— *above average quality, prices, and creativity.*
C **FAIR**—*could stand some improvement.*
D **POOR**—*yuck! could stand some major improvement.*

ABC. *See Million Dollar Baby. Sold exclusively at JCPenney.*

AFG Furniture. *This crib brand is reviewed in the bonus section on our web site, BabyBargains.com/cribs*

Alexander Designs. *See Dorel. Sold exclusively at JCPenney.*

Aldi *See Natart.*

Amy Coe. *See Butterfly Living. Sold exclusively at Babies R Us.*

Angel Line *This crib brand is reviewed in the bonus section on our web site, BabyBargains.com/cribs*

A.P. Industries *apindustries.com.* Quebec-based crib maker A.P. Industries (also known as Generations) offers stylish cribs and case pieces, which are available in 25 different collections. A.P. has survived the recent shake-out of Canadian crib makers, but not without some serious changes: most of A.P.'s cribs ($500 to $700) are imported from China (although the company does offer a made-in-Canada option for cribs as well—these cost a third more than the Chinese cribs).

All of AP's dressers are made in Canada; this is a change from years past. Prices top $1000 for a typical dresser.

At this point, you might be saying, whoa! $700 for a Chinese-made crib? Yes, we had the same reaction—but A.P.'s key feature is a choice of 35 different finishes and knob styles. You can even mix and match two tone finishes. It's that level of customization that makes this brand unique. And A.P.'s take on modern (the Element; Lollipop) has been a good seller.

As for dresser quality, the company uses different draw glide systems depending on the collection (the Blue Note has self-closing drawers). A.P.'s customer service has been up and down in recent years. Overall, we'll give this brand a B—somewhere in the middle of the pack for quality and value.

FYI: A.P. is typically sold in specialty stores, but we noticed Amazon is carrying a smattering of cribs now for $735 to $839. **Rating: B**

Argington. *argington.com* Argington puts a green spin on their modern furniture: New York-based designers Andrew Thornton and Jenny Argie strive to use only solid wood ("virtually no MDF, particle board other similar engineered wood products.") All Argington's wood is FSC certified as part of its "sustainable manufacturing" (glues are low-emission, etc). The brand's main crib offering is the two-toned Sahara for $685 with matching dresser for $500.

New in the past year, the Bam Collection is Argington's value offering—it starts as a bassinet that converts to a crib for $585 (conversion kit included). You can buy just the bassinet ($359) and buy the conversion kit later for $329. A toddler bed conversion kit is also available for $100 and a matching changing table for $400.

Argington also offers a limited selection of organic cotton crib bedding ($185 for a set). Reader feedback on Argington's quality is positive and the pricing is slightly more reasonable when compared to the $1000+ modern cribs Argington competes against.

Argington is sold in specialty stores and some Buy Buy Baby's, as well as on quite a few online stores. **Rating: B+**

Babee Tenda *See box on page 52-53.*

Baby America *See Young America by Stanley.*

Baby Appleseed *babyappleseed.com. See Nursery Smart.*

Baby Cache *See Munire.*

babyletto. *See Million Dollar Baby.*

Baby Mod. *See Million Dollar Baby.*

Baby Relax. *See Dorel.*

Baby's Dream *BabysDream.com.* Georgia-based Baby's Dream's claim to fame is convertible cribs. The company was among the first to launch the trend in 1990—they were convertible before convertible was cool.

In the past, the company divided its offerings into two brands: Baby's Dream and Cocoon. In 2011, Baby's Dream folded Cocoon into the Baby's Dream line. Which is all well and good, because there wasn't much difference style-wise between the two. One big difference, however, is country of origin: Baby's Dream is made in Chile; Cocoon was imported from China. The company told us the majority of the line will be made Chile going forward, but a hand-

Baby Gift Registries: Disappointing

We have a plea for tomorrow's computer science college graduates: fix the gift registries at chain stores—please!

Sure, computers can pilot a spaceship to Pluto or solve the most complex microbiology problem . . . but for some reason, such computer smarts elude the baby gift registry programmers at chain stores.

No matter how sweet the promises are about computerized registries ("Look Ma! I'm changing an item on the registry at 2 am!") the reality falls WAY short of utopia. Judging from our reader mail and message boards, folks are steamed when they must deal with registry snafus . . . and who can blame them.

While the process of registering at any chain is relatively straightforward (you can scan items in the store or pick them off a web site), USING the registry is where things start to fall apart. You name it, we've heard it: duplicate gifts, out of stock items (with no notice to the parent), endless backorders and other goofs.

Here are the frustrations:

◆ *Online versus offline.* Many stores carry items online that aren't in stores. And in some cases, items can only be found in stores, not online. So if you register online at a major retailer, your friends who visit the retailer's stores may find a large chunk of your registry can't be purchased in the store. Another frustration: at Babies R Us, online-only items can't be returned to BRU stores—they can only be returned via the mail. And then the gift-giver receives the credit, not you.

◆ *Returns.* Stores have Byzantine return policies that can frustrate the seemingly simple task of returning a duplicate gift (which shouldn't happen with registries, right?). Many stores require a gift receipt for returns—but whoops! Your gift-giver for-

ful of styles will still come from China.

Baby's Dream offers both static and fold-down rails on their cribs and a raft of accessories (armoires, mirrors, toy chests, etc). Cribs start at $350, but the average Baby's Dream crib sells for $500. A double dresser runs $500 to $600.

New in the past year, Baby's Dream debuted the "Cube," their first modern collection with a $500 crib and $700 changer that morphs into a desk. The Cube is imported from China.

Pine is the most common wood in this line, although a few styles are made from birch.

If there is an award for the most snakebit crib maker in America,

got to include that. No problem, just print out a copy of your registry from the web site? Whoops! The store deleted your registry 14 days after your baby was born. And so on.

◆ **Discontinued items.** You try to be smart and register early for that baby shower—but now several items are discontinued. Does the registry email you with notice? Are you kidding? Registries expect you to monitor your registry and replace items as needed. And product may disappear from an online registry, but still be available in stores.

Some of the problems with a gift registry only become apparent AFTER you've received a gift. Example: Pottery Barn's policy on gift certificates. If you want to use a gift certificate for an online or telephone purchase at Pottery Barn Kids, you must MAIL the certificate in and cool your heels for a two to three week processing period. How convenient.

Babies R Us runs the country's biggest gift registry—and comes in for a regular barbequing from our readers. To its credit, BRU has fixed many of the glitches that were apparent in recent years . . . but we still hear from readers who have problems with returns, discontinued items and more. FYI: Babies R Us changed their return policy for gift registry purchases in the past year—now you have 90 say from your *due date* (not when the items where purchased) to return items.

Bottom line: take a second and read the gift registry feedback from recent parents on our web site (hang out in the "Lounge" forum or do a search on the site). Always READ the return policies of any gift registry BEFORE you sign up—is there a time limit for returns? Must you have a gift receipt? Are you limited to X number of returns or exchanges? Know ALL the fine print before you plunge in!

it would have to go to Baby's Dream. The company suffered through not one but two factory fires in Chile back in 2007. And then came the 2010 Chilean earthquake. As a result, Baby's Dream suffered numerous delays and other set-backs in shipments. That said, during those occasional moments when a disaster hasn't befallen the company, Baby's Dream does get decent marks on deliveries and customer service.

One gripe: if your crib has a defective part, there may be a long wait for replacement parts. That's because Baby's Dream doesn't stock replacement rails or headboards—you have to wait until the next boat arrives from Chile (which could be weeks or months of waiting). While this is a problem that plagues many imported furniture lines, Baby's Dream could do a better job at quality control and not ship out defective furniture to begin with.

While we recommend Baby's Dream, there is one caveat: we do NOT recommend Baby's Dream's cribs with fold-down rails. As we discussed earlier, we aren't fans of this design. Fortunately, Baby's Dream also offers models with static rails—go for that option if you like this brand.

Finally, readers have asked us about this contradiction: how can we recommend Baby's Dream but warn against buying nursery furniture that is made of pine (and most Baby's Dream furniture is pine)? That's because Baby's Dream furniture imported from Chile is made from South American pine, which is harder (and more durable) than North American pine.

Of course, not all Baby's Dream furniture is made in Chile—the Chinese-imports Cube and Cocoon are made of Asian pine. We'd suggest sticking with the Chilean furniture if you choose this brand. **Rating (Chilean furniture only): A**

Babi Italia *See LaJobi.*

Babies Love by Delta *See Delta.*

Bassettbaby *bassettbaby.com.* Sold in mostly big box stores, Bassett divides its line into three brands: First Choice, Bassettbaby and private label offerings for Babies R Us and Restoration Hardware.

First Choice is Bassett's most affordable line and features simple cribs and smaller-size, ready-to-assemble dressers. The brand offers four crib styles in Walmart and Target, with prices running $200 to $400 (cribs) and $225 to $300 (dressers).

Bassettbaby offers an upgrade in both styling and features: fancier finishes and fully assembled dressers with French dovetail drawer construction. Example: a pine 4-in-1 crib is $300 at Target; a matching three-drawer dresser is $350.

Not made in China

From lead paint in toys to tainted baby formula, China has had its share of, uh, quality control issues lately. And some of our readers have asked us, not surprisingly, how to furnish a nursery with products NOT made in China. While that sounds simple, it isn't: 90% or more of baby furniture sold in the U.S. is made in China—so avoiding Chinese-made items takes some effort.

But there is good news: there ARE a handful of companies that make their furniture somewhere other than China. And yes, there are still firms that make furniture in the U.S.: Newport Cottages and ducduc are examples, as is El Greco (which sells cribs via the Land of Nod chain) and Muu, Q Collection and Stanley. Oak Designs (oakdesigns.com) makes dressers and twin beds domestically.

Other furniture makers import goods from countries *other* than China: Romina makes furniture in Romania; Munire imports from Indonesia. Creations, Westwood and Bratt Décor have factories in Vietnam. Oeuf imports its furniture from Latvia. Natart is made in Canada and Denmark.

Some companies make PART of their furniture line in China—and the rest in other factories. Example: Sorelle makes some items in Brazil and Latvia while the rest is made in China.

A few caveats to this advice: first, production often shifts, so before you order, reconfirm with the manufacturer or retailer where the furniture is being made. Second, manufacturers that split production between China and other countries often don't publicize which furniture is made where. You have to ask which furniture is made where.

Generally, Bassett's strategy is to add a bit more bling to the BRU and Restoration Hardware versions of its furniture to justify prices that are $100 or more than competing imports. (See Restoration Hardware's review later in this section for a discussion of Bassett's cribs made for that chain.)

All Bassett furniture is imported from China. How's the quality? We like Bassett's cribs, which we think are a good value. Yes, Bassett had two recalls in 2008 for its Wendy B cribs (one for defective bolts; another for spindles that were too far apart), but overall, Basset has a good quality record.

While we like Bassett's cribs, the case pieces are another story. Take a look at IKEA—they offer better quality ready-to-assemble furniture at a lower price. And Bassett's assembled dressers didn't impress us with their overall fit and finish.

Bottom line: Bassett's cribs in chain stores (not counting Babies R Us) are a good value, but skip the dressers. **Rating: B+**

Bedford Baby *See Westwood.*

Bella D'Este *See Dorel.*

Bellini *bellini.com.* Bellini pitches itself as the antidote to giant baby superstores. Instead of a cavernous building stacked to the ceiling with baby gear and clueless salespeople, Bellini boutiques are about 4,000 square feet and carry their own in-house line of furniture and accessories. The goal is personal service and a narrow focus on better merchandise. Example: some stores stock nursery accessories made by local artists.

This franchised chain had its heyday in the 80's and 90's—during those decades, its business model was selling imported Italian nursery furniture with $700 price tags. Of course, that was long before Buy Buy Baby and Pottery Barn Kids, not to mention the slew of luxury baby web sites.

In the last decade, like many independent retailers, Bellini found itself struggling to compete against chains selling better quality goods and the online world of baby gear discounters. After closing some locations, the chain now has 28 stores, including international outposts in Panama and Dubai.

Facing a strong euro, Bellini abandoned its Italian import strategy and now imports its furniture from China. Cribs run $500 to

Who Is Jenny Lind?

You can't shop for cribs and not hear the name "Jenny Lind." Here's an important point to remember: Jenny Lind isn't a brand name; it refers to a particular *style* of crib. But how did it get this name? Jenny Lind was a popular Swedish soprano living in the 19th century. During her triumphal U.S. tour, it was said that Lind slept in a "spool bed." Hence, cribs that featured turned spindles (which look like stacked spools of thread) became known as Jenny Lind cribs. All this begs the question—what if today we still named juvenile furniture after famous singers? Would we have Lady Gaga cribs and Beyonce dressers? Nah.

$950, with an average price of $700. A three-drawer dresser is $750; a double dresser is $1000. Delivery takes about ten to 12 weeks on average, although some orders can be filled in just two to three weeks.

Quality of the furniture is good (the company has never had a safety recall) . . . but the real question here is: does Bellini's customer service justify the price premium? After all, you can buy similar furniture at a Buy Buy Baby for 20% to 30% less.

Reviews of Bellini from our readers and posted on sites like Yelp and Lilaguide are decidedly mixed. The Bellini in Boca Raton, FL gets good marks on customer service, while the locations in/near New York City? Not so much.

Of course, some of this can be chalked up to the nature of a franchised chain, where each store is independently owned. But if Bellini wants to compete against high-end specialty stores and chains like Buy Buy Baby, it can't be inconsistent. It shouldn't matter whether you walk in a Bellini in New Jersey or California.

So, it is a mixed review for this chain. We can certainly see a niche in the market for a small boutique aimed at parents underwhelmed by baby superstores. But the jury is still out on whether the customer service here justifies the high price tags. ***Rating: B-***

Bergamo. *See Dorel.*

Bethany James Collection *See Dorel.*

Bloom *BloomBaby.com* Known for its modern high chairs and accessories, Bloom's offering in the crib category is a mini-crib called the Alma. With two mattress heights, the Alma folds for storage and is designed for babies under one year of age.

In spite of its $400 price tag, the Alma earns generally good reviews from parents. Dissenters say the mini-crib is too small for even six month olds—some folks were unhappy they couldn't use it for much longer than a bassinet. Of course, Bloom doesn't pitch the Alma as a crib replacement. Overall, we can see this as a bassinet alternative for urban parents who are starved for space. For others, a playpen with a bassinet feature (that you'd leave set up in your bedroom) would be a more practical alternative.

New for 2012, Bloom is debuting a full-size version of the Alma, dubbed the Alma Papa. Like the mini, the full-size Papa fold ups and features casters for mobility. Although it isn't set to debut until January, we noticed Giggle has it now for $700. A conversion rail ($140) turns the Papa into a toddler bed. ***Rating: B-***

Bonavita *See La Jobi.*

Boori *Boori.com* One can safely say that Australia's influence on the American nursery market has been somewhere between zero and none. Boori aims to change that when it debuts its first collection here in 2011. The company dominates the Aussie crib market (cribs are designed in Australia, but made in China), but is largely unknown outside of its home country. Typical of their offerings is the $970 Royale crib, a sleigh-style model with wide slats. Dressers run $1070 for a four-drawer model. At those prices, you'd expect the furniture should knock your socks off . . . but we were under-

Babee Tenda's "safety" seminar: Anatomy of a Hard Sell

We got an interesting invitation in the mail during our second pregnancy—a company called "Babee Tenda" invited us to a free "Getting Ready For Baby" safety seminar at a local hotel. The seminar was described as "brief, light and enjoyable while handing out information on preventing baby injuries." Our curiosity piqued, we joined a couple dozen other expectant parents on a Saturday afternoon to learn their expert safety tips.

What followed was a good lesson for all parents—beware of companies that want to exploit parents' fears of their children being injured in order to sell their expensive safety "solutions." Sure enough, there was safety information dispensed at the seminar. The speaker started his talk with horrific tales of how many children are injured and killed each year. The culprit? Cheap juvenile equipment products like high chairs and cribs, he claimed. It was quite a performance—the speaker entranced the crowd with endless statistics on kids getting hurt and then demonstrated hazards with sample products from major manufacturers.

The seminar then segued into a thinly veiled pitch for their products: the Babee Tenda high chair/feeding table and crib. The speaker (really a salesperson) spent what seemed like an eternity trying to establish the company's credibility, claiming Babee Tenda has been in business for 60 years and only sells its products to hospitals and other institutions. We can see why—these products are far too ugly and expensive to sell in retail stores.

How expensive? The crib sells for $600+ and the feeding table for about $400.

We found Babee Tenda's sales pitch to be disgusting. They used misleading statistics and outright lies to scare parents into thinking they were putting their children in imminent danger if they used store-bought high chairs or cribs. Many of the statistics and "props" used to demonstrate hazards were as much as 20 years old and

whelmed when we viewed the collection recently. The Aussies just haven't done their homework on the American market. Example: most of the furniture is made of pine in various natural and light wood finishes. However, what's most popular here is "espresso"— that is, dark finishes. While we liked the dressers with their solid wood drawers and dove-tail joints, the use of metal glides and a lack of corner blocks simply won't cut it at this price level. And, oddly, Boori plans to offer several ready-to-assemble pieces, including an armoire. Style-wise, Boori also misses the mark with its plain

long since removed from the market! Even more reprehensible were claims that certain popular juvenile products were about to be recalled. Specifically, Babee Tenda's salesperson claimed the Evenflo Exersaucer was "unsafe and will be off the market in six months," an accusation that clearly wasn't true.

The fact that Babee Tenda had to use such bogus assertions raised our suspicions about whether they were telling the truth about their own products. Sadly, the high-pressure sales tactics did win over some parents at the seminar we attended—some forked over nearly $800 for Babee Tenda's items. Since then, we've heard from other parents who've attended Babee Tenda's "safety seminars," purchased the products and then suffered a case of "buyer's remorse." Did they spend too much, they ask?

Yes, in our opinion. While we see nothing wrong per se with Babee Tenda's "feeding table" (besides the fact it's god-awful ugly), you should note it costs nearly four times as much as our top recommended high chair, the very well made Fisher Price Healthy Care. There's nothing wrong with the crib either—and yes, Babee Tenda, throws in a mattress and two sheets. But you can find all this for much less than the $600 or so Babee Tenda asks.

A new twist to the Babee Tenda pitch: invitations sent by a Babee Tenda distributor in Virginia in 2004 carried a line that their seminar is sponsored "in conjunction with the Consumer Product Safety Commission and the National Highway Traffic Safety Administration." Whoa, sounds official! Except it isn't true—neither the CPSC nor NHTSA have anything to do with Babee Tenda's seminars . . . in fact, the federal government successfully sued Babee Tenda to stop the practice. In 2007, a federal judge ruled Babee Tenda committed mail fraud, calling their sales tactics "deceitful and reprehensible."

So, we say watch out for Babee Tenda (and other similar companies like Babyhood, who pitches their "Baby Sitter" in hotel safety seminars). We found their "safety seminar" to be bogus, their high-pressure sales tactics reprehensible and their products grossly overpriced.

vanilla dressers and cribs. Again, if you want to charge these prices, you better wow the market. Boori is more of a head-scratcher. Since it is so new, we don't have any reader feedback yet and will wait to assign a rating. FYI: Buy Buy Baby has an exclusive version of this line, called Boori Regency. **Rating: Not Yet.**

Bratt Décor brattdecor.com. At least you have to give this company bonus points for creativity—Bratt Decor made their name with offerings like the "Casablanca Plume" crib that was topped with (and we're not making this up) ostrich feathers. That (and the $1050 price tag) enabled Bratt Décor to earn a distinguished place on our list of the most ridiculous baby products in a previous edition of this book.

In the past year, Bratt has expanded their line to include a series of wood cribs in various "vintage" and whimsical looks. The Chelsea Sleigh crib comes in several finishes, including "antique silver." Price: $1320. Overall, prices for Bratt Décor's cribs range form $715 to $1400.

Bratt Décor's wood cribs are made in Vietnam; the metal models are imported from China. New for 2012, Bratt Decor has an oval iron crib that coverts from a cradle to full-size crib ($1250).

What parents seem to like here is the style and colors of the cribs (Bratt Décor is one of the few crib makers out there today that does a navy blue or bright red finish). They also have matching accessories such as nightstands, mirrors, bookcases and other decorative options. FYI: Bratt Décor is one of the few crib brands that sells direct via their web site. Bratt also has a company store in Baltimore, in addition to regular retail dealers. The store gets good marks for customer service.

How's the quality? Readers say it is very good—one reader said after two years, her Bratt Décor crib "has held up beautifully."

On the down side, this company can be incredibly slow at shipping—one source told us Bratt Décor orders require a wait of 25+ weeks on some items. Yes, that is half a YEAR. The company also discontinues product frequently—at one point last year, they dropped half their line. And the company generally seems disorganized, with reports of unreturned phone calls, etc.

Hence it is a mixed review for Bratt Décor: kudos for the clever design and overall quality. But concerns over shipping delays and discontinued product temper our rating. **Rating: C+**

Bright Future See JCPenney.

Bright Steps. See BSF Baby.

BSF Baby BSF Baby is new e-commerce company that started in

Certifications: Do they really matter?

As you shop for cribs and other products for your baby, you'll no doubt run into "JPMA-Certified" products sporting a special seal. But who is the JPMA and what does its certification mean?

The Juvenile Products Manufacturers Association (JPMA) is a group of over 300 companies that make juvenile products, both in the United States and Canada. Over twenty-five years ago, the group started a volunteer testing program to head off government regulation of baby products. The JPMA enlisted the support of the Consumer Products Safety Commission and the American Society of Testing and Materials (ASTM) to develop standards for products in several categories, including cribs, high chairs and more.

Manufacturers must have their product tested in an independent testing lab and, if it passes, they can use the JPMA seal. The JPMA touts its seal as "added assurance the product was built with safety in mind."

So is a product like a crib safer if it has the JPMA seal? No, not in our opinion. In fact, the biggest crib recall in history (one million Simplicity cribs in 2007 after three deaths) involved cribs that were JPMA certified. How did that happen?

Well, the JPMA certification is a MINIMUM set of standards that mostly address adequate warning labels. While detailed warning labels for products are helpful, it doesn't stop defective design or faulty instructions (the problem in the Simplicity recall).

The Simplicity recall tarnished the JPMA's certification program—and the JPMA's actions in the past year (accusations of misleading the public on the safety of crib bumpers and lobbying against baby bottle regulations) have undermined the association's safety message. See our blog at BabyBargains.com (click on news/updates) for details about these stories on bedding and bottles.

The take-home message: the JPMA seal is no guarantee of safety.

What about other certification programs? GREENGUARD (greenguard.org) certifies nursery furniture and mattress makers who comply with its strict standard on chemical emissions. Since this is done by an independent third party, we think GREEN-GUARD certification has merit—as of this writing, furniture by Young America by Stanley and Q Collection are GREENGUARD certified. Mattresses by Colgate, Naturepedic and Simmons are certified.

2008 as Bright Steps Furniture. It is sold online at BabiesRUs.com, Amazon and Target among other sites (as well as a few retailers). The emphasis here is on low price cribs ($150 to $300) and ready-to-assemble dressers ($200 to $250).

New for 2012, BSF is launching a new line, Heritage Baby, which features a bit more fancy styling and some already-assembled dressers. Prices for cribs and dressers will run $200 to $500.

All BSF cribs and dressers are made in China of New Zealand pine—as we've discussed, we are not big fans of this wood for nursery furniture (pine tends to scratch and ding easily).

We've had little reader feedback on this line, given its still relatively low profile. It's hard to believe that even though its been in business for nearly four years, BSF Baby still lacks a functioning web site. As a result, we'll take a wait and see approach here. ***Rating: Not Yet.***

Build a Bear *pulaskifurniture.com* Sold at Buy Buy Baby and online, these mid-price dressers win kudos for quality and customization options. Made by Pulaski, the parent of Creations (reviewed later in this section), Build a Bear also sells twin beds, loft beds and other items. Parent feedback has been positive—the dressers feature English dovetail joints, dust-proofing, safety drawer stops and interchangeable drawer knobs and front panels. Prices run $650 to $800 for a double dresser, placing this brand in the middle of the pack price-wise. No, this furniture isn't solid wood (instead, you get veneers over hardwood), but the other quality touches and customizable design make it a decent buy. We've had little parent feedback on this brand, so no rating yet. ***Rating: Not Yet.***

Butterfly Living *summerinfant.com* Better known for its video monitors, Summer Infant jumped into the nursery furniture market when it acquired Butterfly Living in 2009. Started by a group of former Graco alums, Butterfly Living imports most of its furniture from Asia (Indonesia, China and Vietnam).

Summer Infant has largely phased out the Butterfly Living brand and now markets these cribs under a license from Carter's. Just to make it more confusing, these cribs are marketed several ways: Carters, Carters Child of Mine, My Nursery by Child of Mine. FYI: Summer also markets these cribs under the name Disney Princess and its own name.

Prices range from $150 for a Child of Mine by Carter's crib at Walmart to a $350 Carter's convertible crib at Bed Bath & Beyond. Dressers are $230 to $280; most are ready-to-assemble.

In a nutshell, most of these cribs are simple in styling with few bells and whistles. The styling echos Pottery Barn and the dressers have a touch of Shaker design.

Parent feedback on the brand has been mostly positive: fans like the sturdy construction, easy assembly and included conversion kit. Detractors point out the mattress support is an MDF board and the ready-to-assemble dressers are nothing special, quality-wise. **Rating: B**

C&T International *See Sorelle.*

CaféKid *Cafekid.com.* Better known for its older kid furniture (bunk beds, etc.), CafeKid also sells a crib and dresser at Costco, both online and in the warehouses. The Sydney ($390 in store, $650 online—includes shipping and handling) is your standard convertible crib and features rather conservative styling.

We saw the Sydney crib in a Costco warehouse and were impressed—made in Thailand, it features a wood slat mattress platform and converts to a full-size bed. The price includes the conversion rails to a full-size bed . . . and that's a great deal.

As for the dresser, it featured dovetail drawers, corner blocks and laminate drawer boxes. The metal glides, however, were cheap. Still, not a bad value at $390, but not as good of a deal as the crib.

Of course, the problem with any deal at Costco is availability. These items will probably only be at the warehouse for a limited time. Meanwhile, you can sometimes order the Sydney online from Costco for $650 crib, $1250 for the crib plus dresser or $1600 for a three piece set that includes crib, dresser and bookcase. While those prices include shipping and handling, you can buy a crib and dresser from most of our top-rated brands for less than $1250.

So it is a split opinion on CafeKid—if you can find it in a Costco warehouse, go for it. Otherwise, unless you live in Montana and the nearest baby store is miles away, these offerings are too pricey. **Rating: B (store only)**

Capretti Home *caprettihome.com.* Launched in 2007, Capretti Home is the brainchild of Mitchell Schwartz, one of the key players who worked at the old Ragazzi label. After Ragazzi was sold to Stork Craft, Schwartz launched Capretti Home as his own label. It's perhaps no big surprise that the furniture takes design cues from the old Ragazzi—but Capretti tries to up the quality quotient with solid poplar construction, high-quality finishes and dresser drawers that are smooth and sanded on the inside. Among the most popular features: self-closing drawer glides that prevent pinching.

Prices are high—$900 for a convertible crib; a double dresser can run $1000. PoshTots.com sells the Roma crib for $1200. One major negative: finish/color options are limited and the accessories selection (mirrors, other accents) is thin compared to other lines.

On the plus side, Capretti's crib price includes the conversion kit and toddler rail—other furniture makers charge you $200 to $300 for these items. When you back that out of the price for a Capretti crib, the company compares favorably to Munire and Creations, although still about 10% to 20% more in price.

Quality wise, Capretti started out strong back in 2007 (we gave them an A) when their initial shipments met our quality standards. Yet Capretti soon struggled with one big problem: freight damage. Capretti furniture often arrived damaged, thanks to poor packing at their Asian plants. When you are paying $1000+ for a crib, you expect it to be perfect.

To put this in perspective, we should point out that many furniture makers suffer from this problem—improperly packed furniture and other problems often result in freight damage. But Capretti's problem was severe, indicating a lack of quality control at the factory.

To the company's credit, Capretti worked on fixing this problem in 2009 and now their freight damage levels are in the normal range. Unfortunately, all these troubles drove away retail dealers. Capretti lost several major retailers over this issue and now is sold in just a handful of independent stores. To supplement its rather sparse retail coverage, Capretti also sells direct from its web site.

In the past year, Capretti has focused more on quality control than new designs, although the company does plan to launch two new collections in mid 2012. *Rating: B+*

Caramia *This crib brand is reviewed in the bonus section on our web site, BabyBargains.com/cribs*

Carter's/Child of Mine *See Butterfly Living.*

Chanderic *This crib brand is reviewed in the bonus section on our web site, BabyBargains.com/cribs.*

Child Craft *childcraftindustries.com.* Here's a sad case study of American business. Child Craft, the Indiana-based crib maker that traces its roots back to 1911, was once among the top brands of nursery furniture. In recent years, however, the company has had a slow, painful slide into obscurity. Some of this has been bad luck (a 2004 flood knocked the company offline for several months) . . . while most of the blame can be laid at the company's leadership, which never fully adapted to the influx of Asian-produced nursery furniture, both on the high and low end of the market.

Adding insult to injury, the company has gone through several changes in ownership. The latest: commercial crib maker Foundations acquired the assets of Child Craft in 2009.

Organic baby furniture

What makes nursery furniture green? As with many products marketed as organic or natural, there isn't a consensus as to what that means—and that's true with baby furniture as well.

Furniture, by its very nature, isn't the most green product on earth. A toxic brew of chemicals is used to manufacture and finish most items. Example: most furniture isn't made of solid wood but veneers (a thin strip of wood over particle board). Glue is often used to adhere the veneer onto particle board for dresser tops and sides. Some glues contain formaldehyde—as we discussed earlier on page 24, some baby furniture makers have been sued by the state of California for unsafe levels of this chemical.

For many folks, green means sustainable. So green baby furniture should be made from sustainable wood. But which wood is more eco-friendly? Some say bamboo is the most green (Natart's new Tulip line of furniture is made from bamboo, but is very pricey). Others say rubber wood (ramin) is green since the tree it comes from (Para rubber tree) is usually cut down anyway after it is used to produce latex.

Given all the confusion, here is our advice for green nursery furniture shoppers:

◆ *Look for solid wood furniture that is certified.* There are a handful of non-profit environmental organizations that certify wood as sustainable: the Forest Stewardship Council (FSC) is among the best known. FSC-certified crib makers include Arglington, and Oeuf (both are reviewed in this chapter).

◆ *Consider a water-based paint or stain.* Romina offers a "Bees wax" finish that is about as organic as it gets. Pacific Rim also has a similar option: 100% pure tung oil with a beeswax sealant. Stokke's Sleepi crib features a formaldehyde-free varnish.

◆ *Avoid dressers made entirely of MDF or particle board.* The more solid wood, the better.

◆ *Consider an organic mattress.* We review mattresses later in this chapter.

Foundations relaunch of the Child Craft brand has been bumpy. The company has abandoned Child Craft's high-end label (Legacy) and now just sells entry-price point cribs under the Child Craft (blue) label. Example: the low-profile London crib is $180 to $220 and available on sites like Amazon to Target.

That crib gets good reviews from parents who like its low height and over all quality. Less enthusiastic are the reviews of Child Craft's dressers, which are made by ready-to-assemble king Sauder. We heard more than one parent complain about freight damage to the dressers; assembly is rather difficult.

Style-wise, we were a bit underwhelmed with Child Craft's relaunch. We can't quite put our finger on what was wrong, but the company's plain vanilla styling seemed about ten years behind current trends.

So it is a mixed review for Child Craft: a thumbs up for the affordable cribs (especially the London). But skip the dressers. *Rating: B*

Child of Mine by Carter's See Butterfly Living.

Chris Madden See Bassett.

Cocoon See Baby's Dream.

E-MAIL FROM THE REAL WORLD
Leg got stuck in crib slats

"Yesterday, my nine month old somehow wedged his leg between two slats of the crib. I heard him scream shortly after I put him to bed for his afternoon nap and found his leg entrapped up to the thigh. I couldn't pull the slats apart and get his leg out myself, so I called 911. A police officer was able to pull the slats apart just enough so I could gently guide by son's leg back through. I took him to the doctor and he's fine, other than a bruise on his leg. Any tips on how we can avoid this in the future?"

Crib slats are required by federal law to be a certain maximum distance apart (2 3/8"). This is done to prevent babies from getting their heads trapped by the crib spindles or slats, a common problem with cribs made before 1973 when the rule was enacted. Of course, just because baby can't get a head stuck in there doesn't mean an arm or leg can't be wedged between the slats. A solution: Breathable Baby (breathablebaby.com) makes a "Crib Shield System" ($30) and "Breathable Crib Bumper" ($37) that uses Velcro to attach to a crib (it is compatible with most, but not all cribs). It is made of breathable mesh and is sold online at BabiesRUs.com and OneStepAhead.com. It is rather uncommon for a baby to get their arms or legs wedged in the slats. But if you do discover this is a problem, that's one solution.

College Woodwork *collegewoodwork.org* Started by a Seventh-day Adventist high school in a suburb of Toronto, College Woodwork began as a wood working class in 1921. The goal was to provide students of the bible school experience at furniture building. Still owned by the school (now called Kingsway College), College Woodwork employs students who turn out bedroom furniture, both adult and nursery. FYI: College Woodwork does all the manufacturing for the Kidz Decoeur line, reviewed later in this section.

The non-profit's four nursery collections feature traditionally styled furniture—cribs are made of solid beech, imported from Europe but assembled and finished in Canada. All the cribs convert into toddler and then double beds. Dressers are made of solid wood (no MDF or particle board)—each collection features a choice of four-drawer, five-drawer or armoire. Quality touches include dovetail joints, customizable hardware and metal drawer glides.

Of course, all this solid wood goodness comes at a price: cribs are $1000 to $1200 and dressers top $1000—yes that is similar to lines like Romina. But the quality is excellent (with one exception: dresser backs are stapled on; they should be screwed in at this price point) and the customization options (15 finishes are available) may make it worth the expense. We also like the wide variety of accessories (about two dozen options such as night stands, toy chests, etc.) in each collection.

One caveat: College Woodwork's distribution is rather limited with few dealers in the U.S.

Bottom line: great quality but the high prices drag down this brand's overall rating. At this price, we'd expect more styling pizzazz and no staples on the dresser backs. ***Rating: B***

Concord *This crib brand is reviewed in the bonus section on our web site, BabyBargains.com/cribs*

Corsican Kids *corsican.com.* Looking for a wrought iron crib? California-based Corsican Kids specializes in iron cribs that have a vintage feel, with detailed headboard and footboard decoration. Before you fall in love with the look, however, be sure to turn over the price tag. Most Corsican Kids iron cribs sell for a whopping $1300 to $3000! And that pumpkin crib will set you back a cool $4300.

Yes, you can choose from a variety of cool finishes like pewter and antique bronze. So if you just won the lottery and have to have a crib no one else on the block has, here's your brand. ***Rating: C+***

Cosco *See Dorel.*

Creations *CreationsBaby.com.* If you owned an adult furniture company, launching a nursery collection should be a slam dunk, right? After all, furniture is furniture—dressers and cribs aren't too far removed from adult beds and dressers?

So thought the folks at furniture giant Home Meridian International (home of such furniture brands as Pulaski and Samuel Lawrence Furniture, SLF), which launched Creations back in 2007 with a former executive of Baby's Dream. The goal was to make nursery furniture that was more like adult furniture—Creation's dressers are 21″ deep (as are most adult dressers) versus the 18″ seen in most juvenile furniture. Creations dressers have full-extension drawers, dust proofing under each drawer and wood-on-wood glides—again, mimicking adult furniture.

Unfortunately, Home Meridian quickly learned some hard lessons about the nursery furniture business. First, most nursery furniture is sold as special orders (parents who want this model in that finish). Second, the retailers in the high-end nursery business are still dominated by small mom-and-pop retailers, not large chains (Creations is sold in Buy Buy Baby under the name Lullabye CoCo Bear, but not Babies R Us). In order to succeed in this market, you must run a tight ship at your factories.

In a nutshell, Creations bombed. The brand's launch was a disaster, with quality problems, delivery delays and worse. So, the company hit the reset button and for a while, things were improving. Then came 2010, and again, the company had a melt-down in production—shipments were late, finishes didn't match and worse. Many retailers gave up on the brand.

So, now it is time for Creations 3.0. The company replaced its management, hiring industry veteran Kevin Walker (formerly with Pali, and Young America by Stanley) to right the ship. Walker shifted production to factories that specialize in juvenile furniture (Creations at first tried to do production in Pulaski's adult furniture plants, which was a disaster). Cribs are now in stock and the company's three Vietnam factories are churning out good quality with finishes that match.

The company has also hired a new designer, who clearly brings a new traditional/conservative spin to the brand. And for 2012, Creations will lower prices, with entry-price point cribs that start at $300 (most Creations cribs are in the $500 to $600 range). Dressers are $600 to $800. Finishes are limited—most groupings only have one or two options.

Bottom line: so far, Creations 3.0 has been a success. Of course, we've been there before and have been burned by this brand's inconsistency. Yes, other high-end furniture makers have struggled with shipments and quality as well (see Ragazzi, screw-ups by). So we'll give Creations a qualified recommendation—we'd like to see a sustained effort here before giving them a higher rating. **Rating: B+**

Cub *See NettoCollection.*

DaVinci *See Million Dollar Baby.*

Delta *DeltaEnterprise.com.* Imported from China and Indonesia, Delta (also known as Delta Luv and Babies Love by Delta) is perhaps best known for their low-price cribs sold in big box stores.

Unfortunately, the company became known for something else in 2008: one the biggest crib recalls in history. Nearly 1.6 million Delta cribs were recalled by the CPSC for defective hardware—two babies suffocated in their Delta cribs after the cribs' side rails detached. The 2008 recall comes on the heels of two smaller recalls in 2004 (Delta cribs had high levels of lead paint) and 2005 (defective slats).

Obviously, this was a big black eye for Delta, which responded by redoubling their safety testing. The company built an extensive testing laboratory in their New Jersey warehouse, which the New York Times described:

"Eight hours a day, five days a week, cribs are beaten and battered by machines, subjected to the kind of malevolence a demonic toddler could only dream of doling out." Of course, Delta had little choice in setting up this lab—tougher new safety standards for

Rug Burn:
How to save on nursery rug prices

Yes, it's always exciting to get that new Pottery Barn Kids catalog in the mail here at the home office in Boulder, CO. Among our favorites are those oh-so-cute rugs Pottery Barn finds to match their collections. But the prices? Whoa! $300 for a puny 5' by 8' rug! $600 for an 8' by 10' design! Time to take out a second mortgage on the house. We figured there had to be a much less expensive alternative out there to the PBK options. To the rescue, we found **Fun Rugs** by General Industries (funrugs.com; 800-4FUNRUGS). This giant kids' rug maker has literally hundreds of options to choose from in a variety of sizes. Fun Rugs makes matching rugs for such well-known bedding lines as California Kids and Olive Kids. Now, their web site lets you see their entire collection, but you can't order direct from Fun Rugs. Instead, go to one of their dealers like **American Blind & Wallpaper** (American Blinds.com), **RugsUSA** (RugsUSA.com) and **NetKidsWear** (netkidswear.com search for rugs). All of those web sites sell Fun Rugs at prices that are significantly below similar rugs at PBK. In fact, we found most of those web sites sell rugs for 40% less than PBK or posh specialty stores.

cribs went into effect in 2011 and that forced low-price king Delta to face an unsettling reality: it's low-end cribs wouldn't be allowed to be sold without improving their quality and durability.

So far, Delta has been recall free since the meltdown of the last decade. Prices range from $130 to $500, although most Delta cribs sold in chains like Babies R Us are $200 to $300. Among Delta's big selling point: the cribs don't require any tools to assemble.

In our last review, we gave Delta an F—Delta earned that grade after their disastrous run of recalls in the past few years. However, the company has turned over a new leaf. Quality of Delta cribs is now good and we'll give them a recommendation.

FYI: Delta also owns the Simmons brand, reviewed separately. **Rating: B-**

Disney Princess See Butterfly Living.

Domusindo domusindo.com. See JCPenney.

Dorel djgusa.com Canadian conglomerate Dorel is best known for their Eddie Bauer car seats and Safety 1st gadgets—but the company is also a big player in the nursery furniture biz. Just don't look for Dorel nursery furniture under the name Dorel.

Dorel's furniture subsidiary Dorel Asia employs a blizzard of aliases in the furniture market: Jardine (Babies R Us), Bella D'Este (Babies R Us), Vintage Estate (Sears), Heritage Collection (K-Mart), Bethany James/Secure Reach and Baby Relax (Walmart) and so on. Baby Gap at one point launched its own Dorel-made crib line (under the moniker Dorel Fine Furnishings).

Why more aliases than a Jason Bourne movie? Perhaps it has to do with the numerous recalls that Dorel endured during the 1990's under their main Cosco label. In fact, Dorel/Cosco was fined nearly $2 million for failure to report product defects to the government at the start of this decade.

So, if you were the marketing whiz at Dorel, what would you do? Start calling your furniture anything but Dorel or Cosco.

Unfortunately, the company's safety woes didn't end with the name change. Jardine suffered one of the biggest crib recalls in history in 2008 when 320,000 cribs were yanked from Babies R Us for defective slats. Readers flooded our blog with complaints about how the recall was handled (Jardine and Babies R Us set up a Byzantine process to replace the defective cribs, with multiple steps and long waits).

Given Dorel's longstanding troubles with safety in this segment, we don't recommend their nursery furniture, no matter what name they use. **Rating: F**

Co-sleepers

If you can't borrow a bassinet or cradle from a friend, there is an alternative: the ***Arm's Reach Bedside Co-Sleeper*** (armsreach.com). This innovative product is essentially a bassinet that attaches to your bed under the mattress and is secured in place. The three-sided co-sleeper is open on the bed side. The result: you can easily reach the baby for feedings without ever leaving your bed, a boon for all mothers but especially those recuperating from Caesarean births. Best of all, the unit converts to a regular playpen when baby gets older (and goes into a regular crib). You can also use the co-sleeper as a diaper changing station. The cost for the basic model? $210 to $245, which is a bit pricey, considering a plain playpen with bassinet feature is about $130. But the unique design and safety aspect of the Arm's Reach product may make it worth the extra cash layout.

In recent years, Arm's Reach has rolled out several variations on its co-sleeper. The "Universal" model ($240 to $250) is redesigned to fit futons, platform and European beds. The removable sidebar and new liner can also be positioned at the top level of the play yard to create a four-sided freestanding bassinet.

One of Arm's Reach most popular models is the "Mini Co-Sleeper," which does not convert to a playpen ($160). Arm's Reach has expanded the Mini line to include a Curved Mini ($165), a Euro Mini ($150), and a Mini Convertible, which converts into a mini play yard among other designs.

Of course, Arm's Reach isn't the only co-sleeper on the market. ***The Baby Bunk*** (BabyBunk.com) is a wood co-sleeper that is either purchased for $240 to $300 or rented by the month. That's right, you can rent one for just $40 a month (with a refundable deposit) in case you want to see if this is for you. That might be the best bargain of all when it comes to co-sleepers. Baby Bunk also sells a series of accessories for their co-sleepers, including sheets, mattresses, bumpers and more.

While we like the co-sleeper, let us point out that we are not endorsing the concept of co-sleeping in general. Co-sleeping (where baby sleeps with you *in your bed*) is a controversial topic that's beyond the scope of this book. We discuss co-sleeping (along with other hot parenting issues) in our other book, *Baby 411* (see back of this book for details).

Dream on Me *DreamOnMe.com*. The portable/folding crib market has been rife with problems in recent years, with major players like Evenflo and Delta recalling their models for safety reasons. Yet small player Dream on Me has a winner with their "2 in 1 Portable mini crib." Sold online for about $150-$200, this crib is a good bet for Grandma's house—it converts from a crib to a playpen and changing table.

Dream on Me also makes full-size cribs that fold for $270.

Overall, quality is good. Negatives include vague directions that make first-time assembly difficult, say some parents. Dream on Me's iffy customer service (unreturned emails, phone calls) is another drag on this brand. ***Rating: B-***

ducduc *ducducnyc.com*. New York-based ducduc was among the first entrants into the modern nursery category with an eco twist: all furniture is made in the U.S. (their plant is in Connecticut), contains no MDF or particleboard and features finishes that are air pollutant-free. Of course, all this eco-fabulousness is going to cost you: a ducduc crib runs $1300 to $2400; matching dressers are $1600. No wonder this company's distribution is limited to pricey boutiques on the coasts (new this year, you can buy ducduc direct from their web site). In the past year, ducduc debuted a new canopy crib ($1445) as well as a crib with customizable fabric panels (you provide the fabric or choose one of theirs; $1425).

Quality is good, but we have blogged about one customer's disappointment with the ducduc's "white glove delivery." Given that experience, perhaps one would be better off buying this brand from a boutique instead of direct from the manufacturer. ***Rating: B***

Dutailier *dutailier.com*. Canadian rocker-glider maker Dutailier launched its nursery furniture line in 2004 after acquiring fellow Canadian crib maker EG. The line features nine collections—most are traditionally-styled.

Until recently, Dutailier imported much of its furniture from China. Given China's recent woes, however, the company decided to switch most production back to Canada.

The big news at Dutailier for 2012 is a new modern collection of nursery furniture, featuring zebra wood and colored accents. Example: the Papaya.

This a marked contrast to Dutailier's past efforts in this category, which mostly featured traditionally styled furniture. The traditional cribs are $400 to $700 and dressers are $600 to $1000; the modern styles are $1000 for both a crib and dresser.

You can choose from 32 finish choices and Dutailier offers many accessories (computer desks, night stands, etc).

How's the quality? All in all, we like Dutailier—the company's

cribs

Two guys, a container and a prayer

Back in ancient times (say, the 1970's), if you wanted to make and sell cribs, you needed a factory. This required a significant amount of capital, as well as the know-how to engineer cribs to comply with safety standards, finish cribs to match dressers and market the resulting furniture nationwide.

Fast forward to today: most start-up nursery furniture companies today are two guys, a shipping container from China . . . and a prayer.

We realize the days of domestic manufacturing are long gone for many basic items like furniture . . . yet the stark new reality of imported goods creates challenges for new parents—which brands can a parent trust to make safe furniture for their baby's nursery? Will their special ordered furniture arrive sometime before the child goes to college? Will the company be around in a few years to fill a parts or service request?

But the biggest question remains: will the furniture ever ship? Since nearly all furniture is imported from China or other Asian countries, it can take 12 weeks or more from the time the furniture is ordered until it lands in a container at a West Coast port. Then it must be trucked to a distribution center and finally, out to stores (and consumers). And that doesn't count any disruptions (Chinese New Year, port strikes, bad weather, etc). It's no surprise that delayed shipments are a common complaint in our reader email and message boards.

Quality control is a problem that dogs many of today's new furniture brands. Why? The smaller companies often do NOT have a person there at the factory in Vietnam or China, watching out for quality problems. Hence problems are only discovered once items are shipped to retailers or consumers.

Customer service is another issue for today's furniture importers. Let's be honest: customer service in the baby business ranges from grossly inadequate to merely abysmal. And that's being charitable. When you are talking about a small furniture importer, customer service often means one lone person sitting at a phone or answering emails. You are lucky to get a reply to an email (beyond a canned response) or a returned phone call.

The take home message for new parents: go into this process with your eyes open. Don't wait until the last minute to place an order—leave PLENTY of lead time. Stick to the better brands reviewed in this chapter. And once your furniture arrives, carefully inspect items for damage or incorrect assembly.

attention to detail in its dressers and accessories is evident.

Examples: the drawer casings are made of solid wood and drawers use French dovetail assembly. Dutailier has recently added dust proofing to the bottom of its drawers. One disappointment: the new modern collection lacks corner blocks in the dresser drawers.

A couple of caveats: waits can be long for some items (up to 18 weeks, reported one reader who ordered a Dutailier crib). And Dutailier makes it somewhat difficult to find its nursery furniture on its web site, burying it in the section with its gliders. Each collection page has an embedded PDF with dimensions and options, which is a clunky way of displaying the info.

Despite their web shortcomings, we recommend Dutailier. It will be interesting to see if the new modern collection will be a hit, given the price point. ***Rating: B+***

Dwell Studio *DwellStudio.com* Fashionable home designer Dwell Studio made a splash with their licensed bedding line in Target a few years ago. Now, the company is debuting a nursery furniture collection—but don't look for it in discount stores.

The first effort is the Century Crib, available in three finishes (French White, Natural and Espresso). It is sold on Amazon and Giggle for $980. As we said, this one won't be in Target!

The basic crib features an unusual "x-base structure" and tapered cone-shaped legs. The effect is a minimalist aesthetic (Dwell dubs it "vintage classic")—but we wonder if it will be darn difficult to vacuum under the thing. Made in Canada, the crib has exposed bolts, which is odd for this price range.

To compliment the crib, Dwell sells a matching three-drawer dresser for $1080, which has ball-bearing drawer glides, dove-tail joints and a "soft-close" drawer mechanism. The dresser is also made in Canada and features both solid birch and birch veneer, as well as something Dwell dubs "recovered wood." So for those keeping score at home, a Dwell crib and dresser will run $2060. And, oh, the toddler rail for the crib is another $195. And, no the crib doesn't convert to a full-size bed.

Dwell Studio's nursery furniture joins a crowded modern nursery furniture market, where a sagging economy has seen competitors such as Oeuf roll out less expensive versions of their $1000+ cribs. On the other hand, Dwell has a well-known brand name and good reputation . . . so perhaps it will find success at a price point that is hard to sell in today's economy.

Since this crib just started shipping recently, we haven't received any real world feedback yet. And we haven't had a chance to see it in person, as it appears only Giggle is carrying it at retail. So we'll wait to assign a review until we get more feedback. ***Rating: Not Yet.***

cribs

Bait and Switch with Floor Samples

Readers of our first book, *Bridal Bargains,* may remember all the amazing scams and rip-offs when it came to buying a wedding gown. As you read this book, you'll notice many of the shenanigans that happen in the wedding biz are thankfully absent in the world of baby products.

Of course, that doesn't mean there aren't ANY scams or rip-offs to be concerned about. One problem that does crop up from time to time is the old "bait and switch scheme," this time as it applies to floor samples of baby furniture. A reader in New York sent us this story about a bait and switch they encountered at a local store:

"We ordered our baby furniture in August for November delivery. When it all arrived, the crib was damaged and both the side rails were missing paint. We were suspicious they were trying to pass off floor samples on us—when we opened the drawer on a dresser, we found a price tag from the store. The armoire's top was damaged and loose and the entire piece was dirty. There was even a sticky substance on the door front where a price tag once was placed. Another sign: both the changing table and ottoman were not in their original boxes when they were delivered."

The store's manager was adamant that the items were new, not floor samples. Then the consumer noticed the specific pieces they ordered were no longer on the sales floor. After some more haggling, the store agreed to re-order the furniture from their supplier.

Why would a store do this? In a tough economy, a store's inventory may balloon as sales stall. The temptation among some baby storeowners may be to try to pass off used floor samples as new goods, in order to clear out a backlog at the warehouse. Of course, you'd expect them to be smarter about this than the above story—the least they could have done was clean/repair items and make sure the price tags were removed! But some merchants' dishonesty is only matched by their stupidity.

Obviously, when you buy brand new, special-order furniture that is exactly what you deserve to get. While this is not an everyday occurrence in the baby biz, you should take steps to protect yourself. First, pay for any deposits on furniture with a credit card—if the merchant fails to deliver what they promise, you can dispute the charge. Second, carefully inspect any order when it arrives. Items should arrive in their original boxes and be free of dirt/damage or other telltale signs of wear. If you suspect a special-order item is really a used sample, don't accept delivery and immediately contact the store.

Echelon *See Munire.*

Eden *EdenBaby.com.* This LA-based crib importer sells a small collection of traditional and convertible cribs to a handful of independent stores nationwide. Eden offers five collections with matching dressers, armoires, hutches and combo dressers. The styling is very plain vanilla, with prices running $300 to $450 for a regular crib, $500 or more for convertible models. A three-drawer dresser is about $400. This brand is imported from China and is sold online by Sears and Amazon, among other sites.

In the past year, Eden has expanded their modern and contemporary-styled offerings. Example: the Madison crib is $430 and a matching dresser is the same price.

As for Eden's quality, we are not impressed (some dressers featured stapled drawers that lacked a smooth glide). Given the competition on the market, Eden needs to step up the quality in order to better compete. **Rating: C+**

El Greco *ElGrecoFurniture.com.* Here's a rare bird in the nursery furniture business: a company that still makes its furniture in the U.S. Based in Jamestown, New York, El Greco has been making furniture since 1975 but largely flies under the radar of the industry. Why? Because most of El Greco's cribs and dressers are sold as private label offerings by Land of Nod, Room & Board and Relics. Yes, the brand is also sold in a handful of furniture stores, but most are regular furniture stores, not baby retailers. Quality is excellent—cribs are made of poplar and maple, although some of the dressers are made of MDF. Dressers have corner blocks, dovetail joints, metal glides and solid wood drawer faces.

FYI: Readers in upstate NY have told us they have been able to buy furniture direct from El Greco's Jamestown factory—one snagged a crib for $200 under the price she saw in a North Carolina store. As for El Greco's regular prices, be prepared to spend a pretty penny for a U.S.-made crib: most are $650 to $800 at Land of Nod. A six drawer double dresser is $800. Despite the high prices, we will give El Greco our highest rating—for parents who want to avoid Chinese-made furniture and can afford the price tags, this is an excellent choice. **Rating: A**

Europa Baby *See LaJobi.*

First Choice *See Bassettbaby.*

Fisher Price *See Stork Craft.*

Generations *See A.P. Industries.*

Giggle *giggle.com.* Specialty chain Giggle sells cribs from Oeuf, Netto, Boon and Stokke, but the company also imports a few exclusive models. An example is the new "Better Basics" Harper crib for $500-$550. This crib is actually made by Latvian manufacturer Troll Nursery (troll.lv), which has been in business since 1994 and mostly sells cribs in Europe and Russia. The Harper crib features birch rails and plywood end panels and uses low VOC paint. A matching changing table is $325 and a conversion kit (to a toddler bed) is $100. The Harper is available in two finishes: natural and walnut. Giggle claims the glue used in the plywood end panels is nontoxic, but the crib is not GREENGUARD certified, so it is hard to verify any emission claims. The Harper is brand new as of this writing, so no reader feedback yet. **Rating: Not Yet.**

Golden Baby *See Sorelle.*

Graco *See LaJobi.*

Hart *See Westwood.*

Heritage Collection *See Dorel.*

IKEA *ikea.com.* IKEA is an incredibly affordable option for cribs and other nursery furniture items. For example, their simple Sniglar is just $70. IKEA has four other crib options: Gulliver ($100-$130), Hensvik ($120), Sundvik ($120) and Leksvik ($130).

New to the line up is the Mammut, IKEA's most expensive offering at $220 in blue or pink.

IKEA carries much more than just cribs: you can buy dressers ($80 to $300), twin beds ($100), lamps, bedding and more.

So what's the catch? Well, most items require assembly that can drive just about any sane person off a cliff. And the quality of IKEA's dressers and other furniture items can best be described as no-frills (we weren't impressed with their thin crib mattress, for example).

Yet most of our readers are happy with their IKEA purchases. If you can survive the assembly process (especially for the dressers), then this is a good choice. **Rating: A**

Icon *See Westwood.*

Issi *See LaJobi.*

Jardine *See Dorel.*

JCPenney *jcpenney.com*. JCPenney is a big player in the online crib business—their site has nearly three-dozen crib styles to choose from, along with a raft of other nursery furniture and accessories.

Penney's takes a different approach to the nursery furniture biz than other chains: it uses aliases of big crib makers to make the furniture look exclusive to the company. Hence, most furniture sold here is made by major manufacturers under assumed names. Example: Bedford Baby is really Westwood, ABC/DaVinci is Million Dollar Baby. Alexander Designs is Dorel and Sweet Pea is Delta. Only the Rockland and Savanna furniture are Penney's private label. These are made by Yu Wei, a Taiwan-based furniture company, exclusively for JCPenney

Despite having some brand names listed online, the company doesn't reveal the manufacturer for about 20% of its furniture and that is frustrating. As for Rockland and Savannah, most readers tell us they are happy with the quality. Prices for cribs range from $250 to $500; most of the dressers are $250 to $400.

In the past year, we've noticed Penney's has added several three-piece nursery collections to their web site, with prices in the $700 to $1300 range for a crib plus changer and four-drawer chest.

On the upside, Penney's has a good reputation for safety. Yes, the company has had recalls for some defective side rails and drop-side cribs in the past two years, but overall Penney's has had a good safety track record.

Penney's customer service has been up and down in recent years. Although complaints are generally down compared to five years ago, we still see stories like this posted to our message board: a reader ordered a nursery set and it arrived three weeks early. So far so good, right? Yes, but when the reader opened the box with the dresser, she found it damaged (dropped on the corner and the top had buckled). Interestingly, the box was flawless, so someone had dropped the dresser before it had been packed.

So the customer takes the dresser back to Penney's, which promise to ship a replacement. The replacement arrives a week later . . . but is the wrong color. When the customer calls back Penney's to get this fixed, she finds the entire set has now been discontinued. Bottom line: our reader has to return the entire nursery set and start again.

The moral of this story is that, yes, freight damage can happen with any furniture order. But Penney's compounds the error by shipping the wrong color as a replacement—there's no excuse for that.

Bottom line: we only recommend Penney's if you live in a place with few other retail baby store alternatives. **Rating: C+**

Jenny Lind *This is a generic crib style, not a brand name. We*

explain what a Jenny Lind crib is in the box on page 50.

Jesse *See Natart.*

Jessica McClintock *See Simmons.*

Kathy Ireland *See La Jobi.*

Kidz Décoeur *kidzdecoeur.com.* A former executive from Ragazzi has teamed up with College Woodwork to create an eco-friendly, made-in-Canada furniture line sold in specialty stores. As a division of College Woodwork, Kidz Decoeur features the same quality finish as the main line (dovetail drawer construction, full-extension slides, solid birch construction, etc). The difference is mostly styling: while College Woodwork is traditional, Kidz Decoeur has a more modern/clean aesthetic. The Greenwich collection features two-tone finishes, while the Augusta features curved legs on both the crib and dresser. Six finishes are available, including Toasted Cranberry (we didn't realize you could toast a cranberry, but we digress). Prices are similar to College Woodwork ($1000 for a crib or dresser). At that level, you are competing with the likes of Romina, whose construction and drawer glides are arguably superior to College Woodwork. Initial quality reports on this line are encouraging. Since this line is so new, however, we'll have to wait to assign a rating. **Rating: Not Yet.**

LA Baby *lababyco.com.* Importer LA Baby's main business is commercial-grade, portable cribs sold to hotels and day care centers. In addition, LA Baby also has a line of full-size convertible cribs made in China for $240 to $280, with matching dressers (about $350). The company also has a line of organic crib mattresses.

We saw LA Baby's furniture at a recent trade show and weren't impressed. Drawers on the dressers are stapled, not dovetailed. The full-size cribs are ok, but there are better choices at this price level. **Rating: C**

LaJobi *lajobi.com.* LaJobi started as an importer of Italian cribs in the '80's, sold to both chain stores and indie retailers. To avoid raising the ire of specialty stores, LaJobi has marketed its wares under many aliases—it currently uses Babi Italia in Babies R Us, Europa Baby in Buy Buy Baby and Bonavita in specialty channels. (Each brand has its own web site—go to LaJobi.com to access these sites).

When the Euro rose sharply against the dollar a few years ago (making Italian furniture costly to import), LaJobi switched to Asian imports from Vietnam, Thailand and China. This transition was bumpy—quality glitches and delivery problems dogged this line for several years in the mid 2000's. The company pulled through and was acquired in 2008 by Russ Berrie (now called Kid Brands). FYI: Kid Brands also owns bedding brands Kids Line and Cocalo as well as Sassy feeding products.

LaJobi's main market niche is value—and unlike their competitors, they've always been aggressive about marketing their goods in chain stores. While the brand typically is the most expensive price point for chains, the company gives you more style and features for the buck. Look at the $400 Babi Italia convertible crib sold at Babies R Us. Similar cribs from Munire and other brands would probably run 20% to 30% more. (FYI: Walmart sells a non-convertible version of this crib for $150).

Compared to other brands sold in chain stores, LaJobi not only outdoes these other competitors style-wise, but also with quality touches like fit and finish. A typical Babi Italia crib at BRU is $300 to $400—a good buy for parents who want something better than a $200 Delta crib, but can't afford the $500 cribs sold in specialty stores.

LaJobi divides its brands into three price ranges: entry-level (Graco, Nursery 101), mid-price (Babi Italia, Europa Baby) and high-end (Bonavita). Just to confuse you, sometimes the company blurs the lines a bit: Babi Italia is sold in Babies R Us as a mid-price brand, but also in Walmart at the entry-price level.

At the entry-price level, LaJobi's Graco brand is sold in chains like Target and Walmart. A simple Graco crib at Walmart is $120 to

Hotel cribs: hazardous at $250 a night?

Sure, your nursery at home is a monument to safety, but what happens when you take that act on the road? Sadly, many hotels are still in the dark ages when it comes to crib safety. A recent survey by the CPSC found unsafe cribs in a whopping 80% of hotels and motels checked by inspectors. Even worse: when the CPSC invited hotel chains to join a new safety effort to fix the problem, only the Bass Hotel chain (Inter-Continental, Holiday Inn, Crowne Plaza) agreed to join. That chain pledged to have their staff inspect all cribs, making sure they meet current safety standards. We urge other hotels to join this effort, as research shows children under age two spend more than seven MILLION nights per year in hotels and motels. And if you find yourself in a hotel with your baby, don't assume the crib you request is safe—check carefully for loose hardware, inadequate size sheets and other problems. Another tip: consider bringing your own sheets to ensure safety.

$200. How's the quality? Excellent, in our opinion. These are probably the best low-price cribs on the market today, especially compared to similarly priced competitors like Delta and Cosco.

That said, LaJobi isn't perfect here: the company had to recall 200,000 Graco cribs in 2010 for defective drop-sides (hardware that broke, causing the side rail to detach). Of course, all drop-side cribs by most crib makers have been recalled in the past two years, so LaJobi isn't alone here. While the massive recall was not LaJobi's best moment, we should note that the new static side cribs get good reviews from readers.

In the past year, LaJobi has rolled out a new entry level brand: Nursery 101. Sold in chain stores like Walmart, Nursery 101 offers affordable packages of furniture: a basic crib plus changing table is $200; a crib plus changing table and dresser is $250. A Nursery 101 crib only at Target is $130.

Europa Baby is a mid-price brand where a crib runs $280-$400; a double dresser is $500. Babi Italia in Babies R Us is similarly priced.

On the upper end, Bonavita cribs run $400 to $700. Dressers from this line can be pricey, with prices ranging from $500 for a simple chest to $900 for an armoire. New at Bonavita: eco-nursery furniture. The company is debuting its first "eco-friendly" collection (Madre) which has water-based finishes and is made with wood from certified "sustainable" forests.

So is it worth it to shell out the extra bucks on the Bonavita line? No—the difference is just aesthetics. These cribs have more details like scalloped edges on the side rail or fancier finishes (the distressed finish on the Francaise Collection, for example). We'd just save the money and buy a basic Babi Italia or Graco crib.

Dressers are another story, however. When you spend more money on a Bonavita dresser, you get more than fancy styling. Bonavita's dressers are fully assembled, for example, while the lower-end Graco dressers are do-it-yourself. Graco dressers are made of "veneered composites," while Bonavita uses more solid wood.

New in the past year, LaJobi rolled out a new high-end license: the Kathy Ireland Collection. This line features dresser with all wood drawer glides, corner blocks and dovetail construction. We liked the little touches such as a hutch that comes with feet so it can convert to a bookcase. Prices are $650 to $700 for a crib, $730 for a five-drawer dresser.

We previewed the new Kathy Ireland furniture and thought it was well-designed. Yet compared to similarly priced Munire or Young America, the quality isn't quite up to the same level (Munire), nor does it have the same green pedigree (Young America).

In 2012, LaJobi is debuting the "Historic Collection," which as the name implies, has both vintage and antique design elements.

Examples include a rope bed replica crib, a dresser that resembles a pie safe and distressed finishes. Yes, party like its 1799!

Bottom line: overall, LaJobi offers good quality and decent value, especially the Graco and Babi Italia brands. **Rating: A**

Land of Nod *landofnod.com.* An off shoot of the Crate and Barrel chain, the Land of Nod (LON) catalog and web site offers nine cribs and a selection of matching accessories (including bedding, bassinets, and other gear.) It ain't cheap: cribs range from $700 to $800 (although occasional sales see prices drop to $600).

The company has shifted its furniture strategy over the years. For a while, they sold Million Dollar Baby cribs with custom finishes. After a China safety scare (LON recalled 2000+ cribs in 2006 for lead paint), the catalog now offers cribs from El Greco, a U.S.-based manufacturer we reviewed earlier.

As for Land of Nod's customer service and quality, readers give the company high marks. But one reader was upset that her furniture order arrived damaged—twice. Land of Nod was accommodating in shipping out replacement pieces, but getting it right in the first place would be nice for a brand that sells such pricey items.

All in all, we like Land of Nod—the El Greco-made cribs are safe and sturdy. And while the prices aren't a bargain, many readers say the custom finishes and other coordinating accessories make it worth the investment. Style and quality-wise, these cribs aren't much different than what you see on Target.com for a $200 Graco crib. The difference is the made-in-the-U.S. label. If that's important to you and you're willing to pay the premium, the Land of Nod is a good alternative. **Rating: A**

Lea *See Simmons.*

Leander *See Natart.*

Legacy *See Child Craft.*

Legacy Classic Kids *legacyclassickids.com.* No, this brand isn't related to Child Craft, which used the Legacy brand on some of its nursery furniture. Legacy Classic Kids is a North Carolina-based importer of bunk beds and teen furniture that launched in 1999 and then branched into nursery in 2008. Made in China, cribs run $500 to $800, while dressers are $500 to $600. Legacy Classic Kids dressers feature corner blocks, but no dove-tail drawer joints. Some designs feature wood-on-wood drawer glides, while newer models feature metal glides. We liked the fact that the cribs feature metal spring mattress supports, but most models also come with under-crib storage drawers. As we've discussed, these drawers are less practical then they seem—since they lack tops, they are dust collectors. FYI: Legacy Classic Kids' distribution is a bit limited: instead of chains like Babies R Us, you're more likely to find it in large furniture stores. Bottom line: this brand offers neither innovative styling, nor amazing value. ***Rating: Not Yet.***

Li'l Angels *This crib brand is reviewed in the bonus section on our web site, BabyBargains.com/cribs*

Little Miss Liberty *This crib brand is reviewed in the bonus section on our web site, BabyBargains.com/cribs*

Little Miss Matched littlemissmatched.com Little Miss Matched started off selling socks and recently branched out into girls clothes, bath accessories, (and you guessed it) nursery furniture. We saw their latest effort at Babies R Us, which was selling a crib for $429 and four drawer dresser and shelf for $600. The key feature was color accent panels that can be swapped out for different looks. The crib was made of rubber-wood with a metal spring mattress platform, but the dresser was less impressive: wood-on-wood drawer glides, MDF with birch veneers. We suppose the appeal here is the multi-function nature of the furniture: a combo dresser ($500) morphs into a desk with a $150 conversion kit.

Early reviews on this line are positive—most parents find the crib easy to assemble and quality is good. One negative: the crib does have visible bolts, something you don't normally see in the $400+ price range. ***Rating: B+***

Lullabye Coco Bear *See Creations.*

Luna *This crib brand is reviewed in the bonus section on our web site, BabyBargains.com/cribs.*

Lusso *See Sorelle.*

Million Dollar Baby milliondollarbaby.com. Million Dollar Baby (MDB) is one of the industry's best survival stories—among the first to jump on the import bandwagon (the company launched in 1989), MDB has thrived by selling its wares in a large variety of stores under a series of aliases. It also didn't hurt that the company was the first to see the potential of the Internet to sell furniture.

Even though this company got its start selling low-price Jenny Lind cribs to discount stores, you'll now find it everywhere from specialty stores to Walmart. The company's cribs are sold under the aliases ABC in JCPenney and Baby Mod at Walmart.

The company divides its line into four brands: Million Dollar Baby (MDB), DaVinci, Babyletto and Nurseryworks. MDB is an entry-level price point, sold in retail stores, DaVinci is basically the same price as MDB but is an online-only brand. Meanwhile, Babyletto and Nurseryworks are modern, high-end brands sold in specialty stores.

Style-wise, MDB and DaVinci are similar. The difference: DaVinci's dressers are ready-to-assemble (and hence easier to ship), while MDB are pre-assembled.

Cribs in the Million Dollar Baby/DaVinci lines are $150 to $550 (most are $200 to $300); dressers are $260 to $500, with MDB's offerings being slightly more expensive.

Babyletto's modern cribs are $350 to $400, although Walmart sells a version called Baby Mod with less fancy detailing for $200 to $300. A bundle (crib plus matching dresser) runs $500 to $600.

Nurseryworks, however, is priced at the premium end of the market: their modern Aerial crib is $900; the two-toned Loom crib is $600 to $750.

New for 2012, Million Dollar Baby is rolling out an entire new brand: Franklin & Ben. Described as "new traditionalist," this furniture takes its cues from Federalist styling and features American poplar accents and birch veneers over MDF. The result is sort of an updated vintage feel, complete with antique walnut and weathered grey finishes. Cribs will run $600; and a four-drawer dresser will be $600. Franklin & Ben will be in specialty stores only in January.

So, how's the quality overall for Million Dollar Baby? The cribs are good; the dressers are average. Our biggest beef with MDB: their heavy use of Asian pine, which is softer than other pine on the market and more susceptible to damage. We wish MDB had more hardwood groupings in their line and less pine.

Readers like the Baby Mod and Babyletto modern cribs, but the dressers are made of low-quality materials that scratch easily.

Even MDB's upper-end furniture cuts corners on quality: dressers lack corner blocks and the basic metal glides don't stack up well to the competition. Franklin & Ben will be interesting to watch: MDB will add in quality touches to this line, including ball-bearing drawer glides and freebies like free toddler rails with each crib. Of course, this line wasn't shipping as of press time, so we'll have to wait to see the final product. The $600 price level for cribs is a crowded field with the likes of Munire—whether MDB can compete here on quality is an open question.

How is MDB's customer service? We've heard mixed reports. Retailers seem happy with MDB's customer service and deliveries. Consumers are less enthusiastic, telling us about unreturned emails, poor assembly instructions and overall lackluster customer service.

Bottom line: this is a good brand if you just have to have that modern look on a budget—Baby Mod and Babyletto are standouts. We recommend the cribs from this line, but skip the dressers. *Rating: B*

Morigeau/Lepine *This company closed in 2008.*

Mother Hubbard's Cupboard *This crib brand is reviewed in the bonus section on our web site, BabyBargains.com/cribs*

Munire *munirefurniture.com.* The big news at Munire is the recent launch of their new made-in-America sub-line, Echelon. More on that in just a minute.

Munire is a successful importer of furniture that got its start back in 2002—their niche is adult-looking nursery furniture (with an emphasis on style and quality) at prices that are a few notches below the other players on the market.

A typical offering: the Urban with its clean lines ($500 to $600 crib, $750 for a double dresser). While a couple of Munire collections are less expensive (the Essex crib is $400 to $450), most Munire cribs are in the upper $500's; all are imported from Indonesia.

Overall, a three-piece Munire furniture collection (crib, dresser, armoire) runs about $2000. Yes, that's more than some lower-end competitors, but you do get quality touches like dove-tail drawers and architectural details such as bun feet on the dressers. In fact, it is the quality that most impressed us about Munire: drawers feature a double-track, ball-bearing system for smooth glides, center supports, corner blocks and more. Most of Munire's collections are made of solid wood, although a few have painted MDF veneers.

Finish options are a bit limited—most collections come in four or five choices, although a few just have two. Munire's furniture is conservatively styled (lots of dark espresso finishes), although the company took a shot at modern recently with the Cirque grouping.

In the past year, Munire debuted a handful of simple, non-convertible cribs dubbed Safe-side for $350. With a lower-to-the-ground profile, Safeside addresses a complaint some parents voiced about the height of Munire's regular cribs that makes it tough to lay down a baby when the mattress is in its lowest position. While the Safeside cribs convert into a toddler/day bed with an optional toddler rail, they don't covert into a full-size bed.

If you like the Munire look but can't spend $600 for a crib, check out the brand's sister line at Babies R Us under the name Baby Cache. Basically, this is Munire Lite—similar design, but less fancy detailing. Baby Cache's five collections at BRU run $330 to $530 for cribs, $420 to $600 for a dresser. Hence, a three-piece Baby Cache nursery is about $1500. The downside? Baby Cache doesn't have the accessories Munire offers (such as night stands) and finishes are limited.

Munire is also sold under the name Suite Bebe at Baby Depot, where a simple crib (the Hampshire) is $360 and a six-drawer dressers is $440. Suite Bebe has its own web site at suite-bebe.com—the brand is just like Baby Cache: a scaled back, less fancy version of Munire.

New in the past year, Munire debuted Echelon, a made-in-America brand (Munire and Baby Cache are imported from Indonesia). Munire built a $5 million factory in Indiana to make Echelon, which features all wood construction (no MDF or particle board), self-closing/full extension drawers and other upper-end touches. Prices: $900 for a crib, $1000 for a dresser. In the coming year, Munire will expand the Echelon line with two new collections.

How's the quality for Munire overall? Munire is like the Toyota Camry of nursery furniture brands: well-made, solid value but not top-of-the-line. Yes, other brands might have better quality, but you're going to pay more. Ragazzi's drawer glides are nicer . . . but a comparable dresser is $100 to $200 more than Munire. And Romina uses 100% solid beech wood . . . but its cribs and dressers are 30% to 40% more than Munire. The new Echelon furniture aims for a higher quality mark, but of course, you'll pay for it.

Munire is making improvements to its quality. New for 2012, Munire dressers will now have new side-mounted drawer glides, which the company says will give its drawers a smoother glide. Also new: a "Cherry Espresso" finish which has more of a reddish look that enables you to see the wood grain underneath.

So, what's not to like about Munire? Well, detractors say some Munire cribs styles need to be completely disassembled to adjust the mattress height. One reader pointed out the dimensions of Munire's dresser drawers are smaller than competitors (hence, less storage). And Munire suffered a black eye with an embarrassing recall in late 2008 for lead paint in one finish of one collection: 3000 Newport cribs in "rubbed black" had a red paint undercoat that contained lead. While the company vows to toughen its testing of paint, this was still a major lapse.

We've also received a scattered number of complaints about the finish on some Munire collections; readers say it scratches way too easily. One reader who ordered the Essex in cherry said it has been a "headache from the beginning. After a few months of use, the finish is scratched up." We're not sure if this was a quality control issue on a particular batch of cribs since other readers report no problems—but we expect more consistency at this price level.

Despite these issues, we still think Munire is a good brand and we recommend it. Whenever our readers have sent us a complaint about the company, Munire has been quick to correct the problem. So while the brand isn't perfect, the customer service and overall value of the brand earns them a top rating in our book. **Rating: A-**

Muu *muukids.com* Los Angeles-based Muu joins the crowded modern furniture market with an eco-spin: it's furniture is made in the U.S. (by El Greco) and features locally-sourced hardwood and "MDF from certified environmentally friendly recycled wood fibers." Style-wise, Muu's cribs add a bit of design whimsy with interchangeable fabric panels that give their furniture a bit of Zen-like bling. Prices range from $800 for a basic crib to $1175 for the aforementioned panel crib, available in a series of designs and colors. Feedback on Muu has been rather sparse, as it is sold in just a handful of boutiques (as well as their own web site). But we will give them bonus points for creative design. And with prices about 20% to 30% below that of other modern crib makers, Muu is a good alternative for those parents seeking to combine both modern aesthetics and a made-in-the-U.S. label. **Rating: B**

Natart *natartfurniture.com.* Quebec-based Natart has had to face the market challenges that beset their fellow Canadians in recent years, including a strong Canadian dollar and a surge of low-cost imports from Asia. But, while those market forces drove a half

True Colors: Swatches and Samples

What's the difference between oak and pecan? When you order baby furniture, those terms don't refer to a species of wood, but the color of the stain. And many parents have been frustrated when their expensive nursery furniture arrives and it looks nothing like the "cherry" furniture they expected. Here's our advice: when ordering furniture, be sure to see ACTUAL wood samples stained with the hue you want. Don't rely on a web site picture or even a printed catalog. And remember that different types of wood take stain, well, differently. If you order your furniture in a pecan finish, but the crib is made of beech wood and the dresser is pine, they may NOT match. That's because beech and pine would look slightly different even when stained with the exact same finish.

Ordering online makes this more of a challenge. Most sites don't offer wood samples—you have to rely on an online picture (and how that is displayed on your monitor). Bottom line: you'll have to be flexible when it comes to what the final stain looks like. But if you have your heart set on a particular hue for your nursery furniture, it might be best to order off-line . . . and see a stained wood sample first.

dozen of Natart's Canadian compatriots from the market, Natart itself is still here today.

It's been a bumpy ride. Natart has shifted strategies several times in recent years—when we first reviewed them Natart was a made-only-in-Canada brand. Then it switched to importing goods from China, which was a disaster. Next, the company tried to do a hybrid, with some items made in Canada and others imported from China. That only served to muddy the brand's image.

So Natart is back to Canada-only production. And frankly, that's probably for the best—Natart is a pricey, boutique brand with unique designs and (when it's made in Canada), good quality. In recent years, the brand has added an eco focus: all their cribs are GREENGUARD certified.

Natart's Tulip sub-line takes the eco-angle one step further: all its cribs and dressers feature "all engineered recycled wood (MDF) and bamboo components." Tulip cribs run about $1000; by contrast, Natart features all solid-wood construction and runs about $800 for a crib. Dressers are similarly priced. (For 2012, Natart is introducing a new lower-price crib, the Barcelona for about $500).

New to the Natart family is the Leander line, which is made in Denmark and features an oval crib that converts to a twin bed (like the Stokke Sleepi). Price: $1300, which includes the conversion rails.

Quality-wise, we liked Natart's dressers, which features self-closing glides, center stabilizer bars and other quality touches.

In a nutshell, Natart is a good brand if you want to avoid Chinese-made furniture and are wiling to pay extra for the eco-focus. Yes, the prices are higher than in year's past (gone is the low-end Aldi crib imported from China), but we think Natart is probably better off focusing on what they do well: made in Canada, high quality furniture. ***Rating: B+***

NettoCollection *maclarenbaby.com* New York designer David Netto helped launch the modern/minimalist design wave with his NettoCollection in 2002. An interior designer by trade, Netto's furniture comes in two collections: Netto (which is more expensive) and an entry-level line, Cub.

On the upper end, the "Modern Crib" ($1600) is typical of the Netto aesthetic with solid white lacquer panels and natural ash side rails. A shelf under the crib can hold optional $115 linen boxes. A matching dresser is $1750. Yes, a two-piece Netto nursery will set you back close to $3500.

If that's too rich, Netto's Cub Kids line is designed as a slightly less-expensive alternative. The Cub 2.0 crib is $890, as is the matching three-drawer dresser. You get the same two-toned, minimalist aesthetic, but Cub is made in Vietnam (Netto is imported from

Poland). And Cub is clearly a scaled down version of Netto (the end panels aren't as thick, etc).

So, how's the quality? With all the MDF in this line, it's hard to justify these prices. Yes, Netto is a style leader (the new curvy Louis crib has a whimsical touch . . . for $900), but you can find many of these looks for much less elsewhere. Another caveat: Cub dressers are ready-to-assemble (Netto is fully assembled).

In 2009, NettoCollection was sold to stroller maker Maclaren, which has since added the furniture to its web site. It is unclear what plans Maclaren has for Netto—in the past year, the company has rolled out a new model (the Louis), but otherwise hasn't change the line much. As Maclaren tries to transition from being just a stroller company to a baby gear conglomerate, we'll have to wait and see what role Netto will play. ***Rating: C+***

NE Kids *ne-kids.com* New Energy (NE) Kids is a Virginia-based importer of bunk beds as well as loft beds and captain's beds. They recently added nursery furniture to their line. At present, they offer two crib styles (Richmond and Charleston), which are available in four finishes. Prices range from $450 for a crib and $500 for a dresser. NE Kids has average quality; perhaps the biggest issue with this line is back orders. Some pieces go on back order for a long time—and then are discontinued. ***Rating: C+***

Newport Cottages *newportcottages.com.* When it comes to over-the-top nursery furniture, Newport Cottages turns the knob to 11. With their trademark look of two-toned case pieces with distressed finishes, Newport Cottages is a mix of both vintage and contemporary aesthetics. But it will cost you: a simple, colorful crib is $1200 to $1400. A dresser will set you back $1500. Yep, that is pricey . . . but at least the furniture is manufactured in the U.S. (which makes Newport Cottages one of the few remaining domestic makers of nursery furniture). Quality is a mixed bag—the samples we previewed looked fine, but this company has struggled with consistency when it comes to quality and shipping. And at that these prices, we'd expect perfection. On a side note, as we went to press, Newport Cottages still had a smattering of drop-side cribs on their web site. We assume they will turn these designs into static rail cribs in 2011 to comply with new federal safety regulations, but just an FYI in case you notice these for sale online. ***Rating: C***

Nursery 101 See LaJobi.

Nursery Smart *nurserysmart.com; babyappleseed.com.* Nursery Smart injects a bit of eco-activism into their Baby Appleseed furniture collection: when you buy one of their cribs, the company will plant ten trees in your baby's name, thanks to a partnership with the non-profit American Forests.

Nursery Smart is probably best known for its Baby Appleseed cribs sold in Buy Buy Baby: the Davenport ($700), Millbury ($650) and Beaumont ($900). There are four styles of dressers available; a five-drawer, armoire, nightstand and dresser with hutch. Each style comes in four finishes, except the Beaumont which is available in one finish.

Baby Appleseed's cribs are made of poplar wood; the dresses are poplar with birch veneers.

On a recent visit to Buy Buy Baby, we asked the clerk in the crib department to give us her top recommendation—she pointed to the Baby Appleseed Davenport and praised its durable finish, which prevents scratches and nicks. It's clear Buy Buy Baby is this brand's biggest account, which hasn't gained much traction outside that chain.

That's probably because Baby Appleseed/Nursery Smart had teething problems during its launch five years ago—production delays, quality issues and other woes. To their credit, the company has worked hard to fix production and quality issues in the past year. Hence, there haven't been many new designs or other news here.

Besides Baby Appleseed, Nursery Smart also sells cribs under its own name. Their main offering, the Chelsea, is sold in stores and online on sites like Amazon. Nursery Smart's prices are lower than that of Baby Appleseed—the Chelsea retails for $430. A four-drawer dresser (ready to assemble) is $400.

Readers have mixed reviews on Baby Appleseed and Nursery Smart. While the brand gets generally good marks, more than one reader complained about difficult assembly. The finish on the lower end Nursery Smart crib also came in for criticism: it scratches too easily. While that isn't a problem with the pricey Baby Appleseed cribs, we found it odd the brand offers two starkly different levels of quality.

We'll tick up this brand's rating a bit for this edition, reflecting their successful efforts to address quality issues. However, the assembly issues and lackluster customer service hold Nursery Smart/Baby Appleseed back from receiving a top rating. **Rating: B-**

Nurseryworks *See Million Dollar Baby.*

Oeuf *Oeufnyc.com.* Oeuf (French for egg and pronounced like the "uff" in stuff) traces its roots to 2003, when French-American designers Sophie Demenge and Michael Ryan launched the company (and a family) in Brooklyn, New York. Their goal: pair eco-consciousness with modernist design elements. The result: the Oeuf crib (now called the Classic), which takes its cues from minimalist Euro styling.

The Oeuf crib's fixed side rails, headboard and footboard remove, converting the whole unit to a toddler bed. Like many modern cribs, the Oeuf Classic has a wood base (in this case, birch) and MDF panels covered in a white lacquer finish. Price: $940. A matching four-drawer dresser is $1150. Oeuf also sells a variety of other baby items, including mattresses, clothes and toys.

In recent years, Oeuf debuted a slightly less expensive line of furniture (Sparrow), with cribs at $730 and dressers for $820. Sparrow features natural birch wood accents—there is no MDF in this crib (although the dresser is made of MDF with Baltic birch plywood drawer fronts).

Along the same more affordable lines, the Robin features solid pine end panels and birch slats— $590 for a crib, $600 for a dresser. While this is the most affordable Oeuf collection yet, we weren't impressed with the water-based finish on the Robin dresser—we realize this makes it eco-friendly, but we are concerned about durability.

New for 2012, Oeuf is debuting a six-drawer dresser that will work with any of their cribs. Price: $1400. It features self-closing drawer glides and a changing tray option.

So where does Oeuf fit in the modern furniture universe? Price-wise, Oeuf is on the more affordable end of the modern crib biz— especially the Sparrow and Robin. With modern crib prices often topping $1000, it's nice to have an option that doesn't break the bank. What's disappointing is the quality of the dressers—we noticed the drawers lack corner blocks and had low-end metal glides. When you are paying $800+ for a Sparrow three drawer dresser, you are in the same price range as Munire and other better brands. Compared to the competition, Oeuf loses, in our opinion.

We understand the point here of all the eco-goodness, made-in-Europe pedigree and minimalist design aesthetic. And to its credit, Oeuf has good customer service, according to retailers we've interviewed. Whether the brand is worth the price tag compared to competitors that use more solid wood and better dresser construction is an open question. *Rating: B+*

Pacific Rim Woodworking This crib brand is reviewed in the bonus section on our web site, BabyBargains.com/cribs

Paintbox See El Greco.

Pali pali-design.com. Italian furniture maker Pali traces its roots to 1919, when the Pali family started out making chairs in Northern Italy. The company switched gears and focused on juvenile furniture in 1962 and then rode a wave of popularity in the 90's, when its Italian-made cribs and dressers won fans for their craftsmanship and stylish looks.

Unfortunately, the last decade hasn't been kind to Pali. The company blundered by keeping prices too high, a result of a stubborn insistence on keeping production in Europe when every other competitor switched to Asia. By shunning most big box stores and Internet sales, the company placed its bets on selling furniture through a dwindling base of specialty stores. At the same time, competitors like Munire undercut Pali's prices and gained market share at their expense.

Pali realized its mistakes and has tried to shift course. In recent years, the company switched production to Vietnam (made with wood from Europe). Pali is now selling some of its furniture online at ToysRUs.com

In the past year, Pali has lowered their prices—cribs now run $400 to $550, down from $600 to $800 in years past. A double dresser in the mod-looking Trieste collection is $870; other dressers are in the $600 to $700 range.

Pali recently introduced two new collections that use solid beech wood (except for drawer bottoms, which are made of MDF). The Onda features a $900 crib and $1200 double dresser with self-closing drawer glides. The other collection, the Aria, features similar prices and a bead board design.

New for 2012, Pali is debuting furniture sets (crib plus dresser) for $900 to $1000, a good value. Also new: cribs can either be ordered with a high or flat headboard.

How's the quality? Better—Pali has worked out the early snafus we complained about with their first imports. Yes, Pali uses birch veneers in some collections instead of solid wood like Romina. Of course, you'll pay much more for a Romina dresser than Pali. FYI: Pali is now using three woods in its collections: poplar, New Zealand pine and rubber wood.

Since Pali has lowered prices in the past year, its quality level is in the ballpark with what other brands offer. Bottom line: Pali is a good, mid-price brand that offers a dash of European design flash and decent quality. ***Rating: B+***

Pamela Scurry *See Bassettbaby.*

Pottery Barn Kids *potterybarnkids.com.* It's rare that one retailer/catalog can change an entire industry. Pottery Barn Kids (PBK) scored that coup earlier this decade when their contemporary nursery décor (accented by vintage motifs and a bright color palette) literally changed the rules. Out went cutesy baby-ish décor; in came a more modern yet still whimsical look, thanks to PBK.

Pottery Barn Kids sells a mixture of name brand and private label furniture from their site. Prices range from the $400 simple crib to the massive $1000 sleigh-style design. The company also sells a Bratt Décor iron crib (see earlier review).

Matching dressers from PBK run $400 for a three-drawer to

$1000 for a double dresser. Of course, PBK has all manner of accessories: nightstands, armoires, bookcases, and more.

Watch out for shipping surcharges—PBK charges a "delivery surcharge" of $100 to $150 on items dressers (but not on some cribs). That charge is in addition to shipping fees, making the final price much higher than what you see online. Example: an $800 dresser actually costs $980 after all these fees.

While most parents are happy with PBK's customer service and delivery, we've had more than one parent tell us about quality woes with PBK furniture: peeling paint on a crib, splintering wood on a dresser, etc. To PBK's credit, the web site or store usually takes care of the problem and replaces the defective item. But as one reader, who told us PBK's home delivery service miss-assembled her crib, described it, "it's always a canned apology with a pipe dream solution—we'll send someone out, but they never show up."

Quality-wise, you are paying a premium for the PBK look (many items have custom finishes only available at PBK). But take a look under the hood: that $600 crib is cute, but why so much cash for a crib with exposed bolts and hardware? You could spend a $100 less on a similar Baby Cache crib from Babies R Us and get a more finished look. And competitors have long since caught up with PBK on style and design, so we're not sure the price premium is justified anymore.

Bottom line: use this catalog for décor items like bedding or lamps and order the furniture elsewhere. ***Rating (furniture): C***

Ragazzi *ragazzi.com.* Ragazzi is a nursery furniture brand with nine lives. The company started in the 70's as a Quebec-based manufacturer of upper-end baby furniture and had its heyday in the '90's. Ragazzi's long rein at the top of the luxury nursery market ended in 2006, when the company suddenly declared bankruptcy and shuttered its Canadian factory. In the end, Ragazzi fell victim to the same forces that doomed other Canadian furniture makers: high costs, competition from Asian imports and a strong Canadian dollar.

Enter Stork Craft, the Vancouver, Canada-based furniture importer best known for its low-end cribs sold in Walmart. For an undisclosed figure, Stork Craft bought the rights to the Ragazzi name and re-launched the brand as an upper-end line in 2008.

We were skeptical this was going to ever work—and at times, we still have our doubts. The relaunch took a year longer than planned . . . and then a switch of factories in 2010 meant Ragazzi was out stock for much of last year. That's right—Ragazzi was missing in action for most of 2010.

To say this frustrated both retailers and consumers is an understatement—we heard from more than one reader whose special order Ragazzi furniture was caught in special-order hell.

As we went to press, Ragazzi was back in production and promising this time things will be different. We'll have to see.

For 2012, Ragazzi plans to debut six new collections and will add "media centers" to their dresser options.

FYI: Prices for Ragazzi cribs range from $300 to $900 (most are in the $600 range). As for dresser options, Ragazzi offers the gamut, from three/five drawer chests to armoires, night tables and combo dressers. Most dressers are $850. (Side note: we see Amazon is selling a handful of less-expensive Ragazzi styles for $300 to $400).

Quality is impressive: top drawers feature felt-lining, dove-tail joints, self-closing drawers, corner blocks and more. How does that stack up against its other competitors in the premium segment? Compared to Munire, Ragazzi has nicer drawer hardware. But Ragazzi pales a bit next to Romina, which uses 100% solid beech wood (Ragazzi has some veneers). Of course, Romina charges $1200 for a double dresser . . . almost 50% more than Ragazzi.

Bottom line: if you choose this brand, make sure your dealer gives you an honest accounting of their current shipping status, back-orders and so on. Last time out, we gave Ragazzi an A; this time, we've knocked down their rating a letter grade to reflect their recent delivery snafus. ***Rating: B***

Relics Furniture *This crib brand is reviewed in the bonus section on our web site, BabyBargains.com/cribs*

Restoration Hardware. *RHBabyandChild.com* Restoration Hardware in the past year joined other chains like Pottery Barn in rolling out a luxe kids line, complete with furniture, linens, lighting, apparel, gifts and more. Sold online only, Restoration Hardware's neo-classical nursery furniture is arranged in ten collections, each with crib, dresser, bookcase and armoire. Finish options are limited: white or espresso in most cases.

All of Restoration Hardware cribs are made by Bassettbaby, reviewed separately. Obviously, these are upgraded models compared with what Bassett sells to other chain stores—hidden hardware, distressed finishes, etc. Dressers include English dovetail joints, cedar-lined drawers and tip guards.

While the web site calls out the maker on its cribs, Restoration Hardware is mum on who makes the matching dressers. We assume it is Bassett, but we couldn't confirm this as of press time.

So, what's not to like? Well, the prices are in the stratosphere: $800 to $1300 for a crib. And that doesn't include "unlimited delivery" fees ($95-$295, depending on your distance to a PBK store) and hotel mini-bar prices for accessories (a $500 bookcase, anyone?).

And here's the kicker: cribs only convert to toddler beds (and goofy looking ones at that), not twin or full size beds as most convertible cribs. Hard to imagine, but Restoration Hardware has managed to make even the most expensive nursery brands sold in specialty stores look like a bargain. At least if you are spending $1000 for a crib in such stores, most likely you are getting a convertible model that turns into a full-size bed. We suppose the point is you are supposed to go back to Restoration Hardware and spend another $800 on a big kid bed.

Reader feedback has been mixed on RH—one reader complained that much of her nursery furniture order was on backorder . . . for months! And the quality? "Many of the things I ordered (the mobile in particular) were sub par in terms of quality or arrived broken, however highly priced."

So it is a mixed review for RH: we liked the coordinated collections and the upgraded Bassett furniture . . . but at these prices, we are hard pressed to give RH anything higher than an average rating. The value just isn't there—you can spend HALF the price of these cribs and dressers and get BETTER quality and durability. **_Rating: C_**

Restore & Restyle _Target's in-house brand of baby furniture is reviewed on our web site, BabyBargains.com/cribs_

Rockland _See JCPenney._

Romina _RominaKidsFurniture.com._ The collapse of Canadian premium furniture maker Ragazzi back in 2006 produced two surprising results: first, Stork Craft re-launched the brand as an Asian import (see review earlier). And second, Ragazzi's former crib supplier, Romina, decided to enter the U.S. market on their own.

Yes, Romina used to supply Ragazzi with unfinished cribs . . . but could Romania-based Romina successfully launch their own line in the U.S.? As it turns out, the answer is yes.

Romina's success here could be attributed to two factors: first, good timing. Romina launched in the midst of the Chinese recall crisis—with furniture made in Romania, Romina is one of the few non-China options out there.

Second, Romina doesn't cut corners when it comes to quality— the line features 100% solid beech wood construction. No MDF, no rubberwood, no veneers over particle board, etc. Romina dressers feature dove-tail joints, corner blocks and self-closing drawer glides that are smooth "like butter," as one retailer described them.

Of course, this isn't cheap—and if you want Romina, you're going to pay for it. Cribs run $850 to $1300; a double dresser is $1200 to $1400. Yes, that's $400 to $500 more than Munire or

Ragazzi charges for a similar dresser—you'll have to decide if avoiding an Asian import is worth that premium.

Romina's other major emphasis is their eco-friendly "Bees Wax" finish, which as the name implies, is all-natural. Romina touts it as the ultimate organic finish. If you prefer a darker stain or painted look, Romina also offers eight other finishes, including a navy, white and brown metallic.

Design-wise, Romina furniture is traditionally styled; the Ventianni

8 tips to lower the risk of SIDS

Sudden Infant Death Syndrome (SIDS) is the sudden death of an infant under one of year of age due to unexplained causes. Sadly, SIDS is still the number one killer of infants under age one—over 2500 babies die each year.

So, what causes SIDS? Scientists don't know, despite studying the problem for two decades. We do know that SIDS is a threat during the first year of life, with a peak occurrence between one and six months. SIDS also affects more boys than girls; and the SIDS rate in African American babies is twice that of Caucasians. Despite the mystery surrounding SIDS, researchers have discovered several factors that dramatically lower the risk of SIDS. Here is what you can do:

Put your baby to sleep on her back. Infants should be placed on their back (not side or tummy) each time they go to sleep. Since the campaign to get parents to put baby to sleep on their backs began in 1992, the SIDS rate has fallen by 50%. That's the good news. The bad news: while parents are heeding this message, other care givers (that is, grandma or day care centers) are less vigilant. Be sure to tell all your baby's caregivers that baby is to sleep on his back, never his tummy.

Encourage tummy time. When awake, baby should spend some time on their tummy. This helps prevent flat heads caused by lying on their backs (positional plagiocephaly). Vary your child's head position while sleeping (such as, turning his head to the right during one nap and then the left during the next nap). Minimize time spent in car seats (unless baby is in a car, of course!), swings, bouncer seats or carriers—any place baby is kept in a semi-upright position. A good goal: no more than an hour or two a day. To learn more about plagiocephaly, go online to plagiocephaly.org.

Forget gadgets. Special mattresses, sleep positioners, breathing monitors—none have been able to reduce the risk of SIDS, says the American Academy of Pediatrics. Just put baby to sleep on her back.

Use a pacifier. Consider giving baby a pacifier, which has been shown in studies to reduce the rate of SIDS. Why? Scientists don't know exactly, but some speculate pacifiers help keep the airway open.

group is the company's only bow to the modern, two-tone finish look. We liked all the available accessories: each collection features nightstands, armoires, book cases and the like. New in the past year: an over-the-top crib (Cleopatra) that looks like a handlebar mustache, complete with a footboard that can be carved with your baby's name.

All in all, this is one of the best nursery furniture lines on the market . . . there are many expensive nursery furniture brands on the

Okay, we should acknowledge that pacifiers are controversial—key concerns include breastfeeding interference, tooth development and ear infections. But if you introduce the pacifier after breast-feeding is well-established (around one month), there are few problems. Stop using the pacifier after one year (when the SIDS risk declines) to prevent any dental problems. While pacifiers do increase the risk of ear infections, ear infections are rare in babies when the risk of SIDS is highest (under six months old). Bottom line: Use pacifiers at the time of sleep starting at one month of life for breastfed babies. If the pacifier falls out once the baby is asleep, don't re-insert it. Stop using pacifiers once the risk of SIDS is over (about a year of life).

Don't smoke or overheat the baby's room. Smoking during pregnancy or after the baby is born has been shown to increase the risk of SIDS. Keep baby's room at a comfortable temperature, but don't overheat (do not exceed 70 degrees in the winter; 78 in the summer). Use a werable blacket or swaddle baby with a blanket.

Bed sharing: bad. Room sharing: good. Why does bed sharing increase the risk of SIDS? Scientists say the risk of suffocation in adult linens (pillows, etc) or entrapment between bed frame and mattress, or by family members is a major contributor to SIDS. That said, *room sharing* (having baby in the same room as the parents, either in a bassinet or a product like the Arm's Reach Bedside co-sleeper) is shown to reduce the rate of SIDS. Again, researchers don't know exactly why, but it's possible parents are more attuned to their baby's breathing when baby is nearby.

No soft bedding. Baby's crib or bassinet should have a firm mattress and no soft bedding (quilts, pillows, stuffed animals, bumpers, etc). We will discuss soft bedding more in depth in the next chapter. Also: consider using a swaddling blanket, footed sleeper or SleepSack instead of a blanket. More on these items in Chapter 3.

Make sure all other caregivers follow these instructions. Again, you might be vigilant about back-sleeping . . . but if another caregiver doesn't follow the rules, your baby could be at risk. Make sure your day care provider, grandma or other caregiver is on board.

market that aren't worth the asking price when it comes to quality. Romina is the real deal. ***Rating: A***

Room & Board *This nine-store chain with locations in Chicago, San Francisco and New York is reviewed in the bonus section on our web site, BabyBargains.com/cribs*

Room Magic *This crib brand is reviewed in the bonus section on our web site, BabyBargains.com/cribs*

Sauder *This crib brand is reviewed in the bonus section on our web site, BabyBargains.com/cribs*

Savanna *See JCPenney.*

SB2 *See Sorelle.*

Secure Reach by Bethany James *See Dorel.*

Simmons *simmonskidsfurniture.com.* Here's a sad story about the rise and fall of an American company. Simmons Juvenile was once one of the country's biggest nursery furniture makers, selling cribs and dressers to many generations of parents. Started in 1917 by Thomas Alva Edison to provide wooden cabinets for one of his recent inventions (the phonograph), Simmons morphed into a furniture company that also made mattresses. The company spun off its juvenile division in the 1980's (just to confuse you, there is still a Simmons company that makes mattresses).

Then the company began its slow decline. Simmons made a couple major mistakes, chief among them a decision in the 90's to concentrate on selling its furniture in chain stores (forsaking the independent stores that built its business over the decades). The biggest goof: Simmons never adapted to the changing nursery furniture market, which soon became flooded with low-price imports from Asia. Simmons stuck to making its cribs and dressers in plants in Wisconsin and Canada.

By 2004, Simmons' deteriorating fortunes prompted the management to sell their crib mattress biz and then shutter the Wisconsin plant. Simmons sold the rights to their name to Delta, which then relaunched Simmons as a separate, upscale division aimed at specialty stores. Ironic, no?

However, the re-launch of Simmons has been bumpy for Delta. Their first collection (imported from China and Vietnam) was a bust— $800 cribs, $700 dressers were met with little enthusiasm from shoppers.

Delta/Simmons went back to the drawing board and decided to change strategies: instead of competing in the upper end of the market, they'd aim for the entry-level price point among specialty stores. Hence, Simmon's recent Slumber Time collection features cribs that start at just $300 and has five mix-and-match finish options.

Simmons other offerings run $400 to $600 for cribs, $500 to $600 for dressers. At the top end, Simmons' Jessica McClintock line of cribs features three collections running $600 to $1000 for a crib, $700 to $1000 for a dresser.

The industry reaction to Simmons' new collection has been a collective yawn. While the new lower prices are a step in the right direction, the bland styling of the line has resulted in lackluster sales. And quality-wise, the company is all over the board: the upper-end McClintock features self-closing drawers and other quality touches. But the lower end Simmons features drawer glides more at home on a Delta dresser at Walmart than a specialty store.

So it is a mixed review for Simmons: kudos for the new lower prices . . . but the plain vanilla styling and scattershot quality drag down their overall marks. It seems Simmons is still a brand in search of an identity. **Rating: C+**

Sorelle *sorellefurniture.com.* Sorelle is one of the baby gear industry survival stories. In business since 1977, the company has constantly changed and morphed over time.

The company first imported Italian cribs. It switched gears in the last ten years to importing furniture from Canada, Brazil, Latvia, Vietnam and China (today most items are imported from Vietnam). Few companies have diversified production like Sorelle while this strategy could have ended up clouding its brand identify, Sorelle has succeeded by pursuing a value niche: its furniture is generally regarded as giving consumers more bang for the buck.

Sorelle has also survived by selling its furniture in a zillion venues: specialty stores (under the Sorelle brand), chains stores (under Golden Baby and C &T) and online.

In recent years, Sorelle has decided to divide its brand into three parts: Lusso, Sorelle and SB2.

Lusso is sold just in specialty, brick-and-mortar stores—prices range from $500 to $700 for cribs, which includes the toddler conversion rail. Quality touches here include dove-tail drawer construction and poplar wood.

Sorelle is the brand you'll see in chain stores—it is similar to Lusso in quality, but scaled down a bit. Cribs run $280 to $500.

SB2 is Sorelle's new entry-price point brand sold online. Cribs run $200 to $350; dressers are ready-to-assemble. Under the SB2 brand, Sorelle offers entire five-piece nursery sets for $400 to $500—crib, four-drawer dresser, hamper, changing table, toddler conversion rail.

Style-wise, Sorelle is middle-of-the-road traditional furniture; yes there are one or two modern groupings with two-tone finishes, but that is the exception to the rule.

So, how's the quality? If you take a look at the two-dozen reviews of Sorelle posted to our web site, you'll note the opinions are all over the board. For every parent who tells us they are pleased with the quality and finish of their Sorelle furniture, another will write to blast a series of problems—defective side rails, "nonexistent and rude" customer service, poor assembly instructions, missing parts and more.

It's the lack of customer service that bothers us most here: the attitude at Sorelle seems to be "you're getting a good price on this furniture, so don't complain if we don't return your call for parts." Sorry, but that doesn't cut it.

Bottom line on this brand: great prices but a mixed quality picture and weak customer service drag down their rating **Rating: C+**

Spot on Square *spontonsquare.com*. California-based Spot on Square launched its modern nursery furniture in 2007. The company offers three crib styles, all with an eco-angle: low VOC paints and formaldehyde-free glue. Like most modern furniture companies, Spot on Square uses MDF (which it pitches as a recycled material) along with birch, bamboo and walnut. Prices are moderate, at least for modern: the Eicho crib is $595, while a matching changing table is $675. The hiya crib comes in three color variations, ranging in price from $750 (all white MDF) to $900 for a version with bamboo end panels. New in the past year is the high-end Roh crib made of walnut for $1800 to $2250.

Overall, we were a bit disappointed in the lack of accessories: only the hiya collection has a matching nightstand and dresser (the others just have a dresser or changing table). Spot on Square's cribs do not convert to full size beds. It might be hard seeing this furniture in person, as distribution is limited to a handful of small boutiques (although you can buy pieces direct through their company web site). With little reader feedback and the lack of a hands-on inspection, we'll have to wait to give this brand a rating. **Rating: Not yet**

Stanley *See Young America.*

Status. *storkcraft.com.* Stork Craft's mid-price line is positioned as a step up from Stork Craft's furniture sold in chain stores, yet less expensive than their premium Ragazzi brand. Sold in specialty stores and made in China, Status offers 12 collections. Each features a static convertible crib and two dresser options (combo or double dresser). Five finishes are available. Cribs run $350 to $600 (most are in the $400 range); a combo dresser is $680; armoires are around $700.

Unlike Stork Craft's ready-to-assemble dressers, Status comes fully assembled and features all hardwood construction (pine). The downside? The drawers lack dovetail construction and feature basic wood-on-wood glides (most upper-end nursery furniture has metal glides). We also noticed visible bolts on the cribs, which is something you'd see on a $250 crib at discount store . . . but not usually at this price.

All in all, this line is a head scratcher. What is the point? At these prices, Status competes directly with Munire and Westwood—but the quality and design isn't up to par. **Rating: C**

Stokke/Sleepi *stokke.com.* Color us skeptical when we first heard about this Norwegian company's ultra-expensive crib "system:" The Sleepi morphs from a bassinet to a crib, then a toddler bed and finally two chairs . . . for a cool $1000. You can buy just the crib for $800 (without the toddler bed conversion kit).

A separate changing table (the Care) converts to a play table and desk for $500. As with all these funky European products, you'll have to buy specially made bedding with limited choices ($40 for a sheet; $320 for a set). Yes, you read that right: $40 for a single sheet.

Yet the parent feedback on the Sleepi has been very positive—fans love its clever oval shape (fits through narrow doorways) and overall ease of use. The Sleepi is perhaps best suited to urban apartment dwellers with little space for a standard-size crib. Given positive reader reviews, we will up the rating of the Stokke Sleepi—yes, it is outrageously expensive and a niche product, but for those who are space-deprived, this is a good solution. **Rating: A-**

Stork Craft *storkcraft.com.* Stork Craft is probably best known as an entry-level brand that's sold in chain stores from Walmart to Babies R Us.

Stork Craft's cribs start at $120 online at Walmart, although most are in the $150 to $200 range. At the top end, s $350 crib model features sleigh styling and the ability to convert to a full-size bed.

All Stork Craft furniture is imported from China.

Stork Craft also makes a wide array of matching accessories, including dressers, rocker gliders and other items—the dressers are an affordable $180 to $300. All of the furniture is ready-to-assemble; readers report assembly ranges from difficult to frustrating, thanks to minimal directions and a lack of labeling for screws and parts. A significant amount of patience is necessary, say most readers.

New in the past year, Stork Craft began selling fully assembled dressers for $500.

So, let's talk quality. Parents generally give Stork Craft low marks, based on reviews posted to our web site. Fans like the affordable pricing and the fact you can order most of this furniture online. But detractors say items often arrive damaged, with missing parts and worse. One parent who paid $450 for a Stork Craft crib said she was extremely disappointed in the poor finish which looked very cheap—and the under-crib drawer's bottom constantly fell off its track when moved. Another parent who bought a $300 Stork Craft dresser said it arrived severely damaged and "looks as if it were purchased at a garage sale." Customer service also came in for criticism, with delays in fixing defective merchandise and parts among the top gripes.

Finally, Stork Craft has downgraded the quality of its cribs in recent years, in our opinion. Example: gone are the spring mattress supports. Now Stork Craft uses a MDF board to support the mattress, which is not our preferred choice.

Our suspicions about this brand were sadly confirmed in 2009 when over two million Stork Craft drop-side cribs were recalled for defective hardware.

Stork Craft competes against Million Dollar Baby (Baby Mod), Graco (made by LaJobi) and Carter's (Summer) in this price range. We'd recommend any of those companies over Stork Craft.

Bottom line: if you have your heart set on this brand, stick with the low-price items (the $150 cribs at Walmart are a good bet). Skip the dressers, glider rockers and anything expensive (those $250+ cribs). And be sure to set your expectations accordingly. ***Rating: C-***

Suite Bebe *See Munire.*

Summer *See Butterfly Living.*

Sweet Pea *See Delta.*

Today's Baby *This crib brand is reviewed in the bonus section on our web site, BabyBargains.com/cribs*

Tulip *See Natart.*

Vintage Estate *See Dorel.*

Westwood Design *westwoodbaby.com.* Westwood Design was launched in 2005 by several veteran nursery furniture executives who partnered with an adult furniture company for distribution expertise. The company has found success in a crowded market by offering a high-quality product at affordable prices.

Westwood is sold in a variety of outlets, from specialty stores to chains like Buy Buy Baby and online on Amazon. You'll find the brand under the aliases Bedford Baby at JCPenney and Hart at Baby Depot. At the chains, a Westwood crib runs $350 to $450; dressers are similar in price.

In specialty stores, Westwood tends to be a bit fancier in style and higher in price. Example: a new modern two-tone grouping features a $600 crib; dressers are in the $500 to $700 range. New in the past year, Westwood added a $350 crib (the Copa), as well as several scaled-down furniture pieces (the company calls them "euro-sized") for folks trying to fit furniture in a small nursery.

In the coming year, Westwood is introducing a new alias: Icon, a brand it plans to use in specialty stores. Same furniture, just a different name for indie baby stores. Westwood's entry-level crib for specialty stores (the Jonesport) is about $500; most other styles are in the upper $500's.

For 2012, there have been a few changes to Westwood. First, the company no longer is making pine furniture. Also, certain Westwood cribs now come with "always there hardware"—pre-installed hardware that doesn't detach from the crib. That makes it safer when you disassemble and reassemble a crib. Finally, Westwood is introducing a line of "no tools assembly" case goods. The company is touting these as easy-to-assemble chests, combos and bookcases.

FYI: All Westwood furniture is made in Vietnam.

Quality-wise, Westwood is a good value. Most of the cribs and dressers are made from solid hardwood, although the company does use some cherry veneers and painted MDF (in their modern grouping). You'll see some adult furniture touches here and there (hutches with built-in lights; dressers with height-adjustable feet), which is unusual in the nursery market.

We also like how transparent the company is—Westwood even posts pictures of their Vietnam factory to their company blog. That's unusual: most companies don't like talking about their factories, treating their locations like a national security secret.

The downsides? Well, the company only offers a limited number of finishes. And Westwood probably uses more veneers and MDF than its competitors in this price range. That said, parent feedback on Westwood has been very positive—readers love the sturdy construction, ease of assembly on the cribs and overall finished look. Another plus: customer service at Westwood is excellent. ***Rating: A***

NURSERY NECESSITIES

Young America by Stanley youngamerica.com. Adult furniture maker Stanley entered the juvenile market in 2003 with "Young America," a collection of nursery furniture with a wide range of accessories.

This brand has gone through several changes over the years. It started out as a high-end brand that was made in the U.S. Then Stanley switched to imports from Asia to lower prices. In 2010, Stanley made the decision to bring production back to the U.S. and added an eco-focus (it is one of the few brands on the market to earn GREENGUARD certification).

Stanley's mojo is their "built to grow" theme—cribs that can turn into full-size beds, added accessories like desks/study areas for older kids, trundle storage options and more. It's the plethora of accessories that sets Stanley's Young America apart from its competitors, where offering a matching nightstand is about as "built to grow" as they get.

Price-wise, Stanley is on the premium end of the market: a crib runs $700 to $900. A double dresser runs $1000 to $1500. Armoires are $1250 to $1700. Heck, a Young America nightstand can set you back $600. FYI: this brand is sold in specialty stores and chains like Buy Buy Baby, where it is known as Baby America.

So, is it worth it? Well, if you want made-in-the-U.S. nursery furniture that is GREENGUARD certified, then Stanley is your brand. Fans love the numerous finishes and accessory items—most crib styles can be purchased in over 30 color finishes. That's right, when other brands limit you to three versions of brown, Stanley lets you customize to your heart's content here.

Critics of this brand point out the plain vanilla styling makes it hard to justify the prices. Compare the styling here to Munire and Romina and you'll see what we are referring to—Young America by Stanley needs a bit more zing to justify their $800 price tags.

Quality-wise, Young America doesn't stack up well against competitors like Romina, which offers solid wood construction (Stanley's dressers are more often veneers) and better drawer glides. Yes, Stanley offers felt-lined top drawers and dove-tail construction. That alone doesn't justify these prices. If you want to charge folks a $1000 for dresser, we'd like to see self-closing glides and more solid wood construction. We are happy to see that in the past year, Stanley has tried to address the quality gap by adding touches like corner blocks and dust proofing to dresser drawers.

Quality control is another problem that dogs Young America by Stanley; retailers complain that too many shipments arrive damaged. Some of this is probably due to poor packaging, but other issues are just poor quality control on Stanley's part (damaged furniture that shouldn't have shipped from the plant in the first place).

So if you order this brand for your nursery, it would help to have plenty of time for your retailer to fix any glitches.

Bottom line: it's clear what you are paying for here is the made-in-the-U.S. label and numerous finish colors and accessories. If you care more about solid wood dresser construction or fancier styling, this isn't your brand. Nonetheless, we recommend Young America by Stanley for filling an important niche in the market. **Rating: B+**

See the chart on pages 100 to 101 for a summary of the major crib brands.

Brand Recommendations: Our Picks

Good. The best budget crib is made by LaJobi under their Graco license. Specifically, we like the *Graco Sarah* ($150-$170) or *Lauren* ($145-$165; pictured). Both are simple, all-wood, static-side cribs. Another option: *IKEA's Sniglar*
crib is $70. Funky name, good value. The same goes for *IKEA's Gulliver* crib ($100 in white; $130 in natural).

Quick FYI on the Graco cribs: yes, they are made of pine. Yes, we usually don't recommend pine as a wood for cribs as it easily scratches. However, the prices on these cribs are so low, we think it is a worthwhile exception to the rule.

Better. Step up to the $300 to $500 range and you'll find more convertible models that turn from a crib to full-size bed. Our favorites here include *Baby Cache's Heritage* crib (made by Munire, $480, Babies R Us exclusive; pictured) and *Bedford Baby's Tribeca* crib (made by Westwood, $400, JCPenney.com).

Best. Who's got the very best quality when it comes to cribs and dressers? In the $500 to $700 range, we like *Munire* and *Westwood*. Each makes excellent cribs and very good dressers.

Is someone buying you nursery furniture as a gift? Do you want to avoid Chinese-made nursery furniture? If so, we suggest *Romina* or *El Greco*. Romina offers sold-wood cribs ($850 to $1100) and dressers imported from Romania. El Greco makes its cribs and dressers in the U.S.; they are sold online at sites like Land of Nod. Prices: $600 to $750 for a crib.

Continued on page 102

CRIB RATINGS

NAME	RATING	COST	WHERE MADE?
A.P. INDUSTRIES	B	$$$	CANADA/CHINA
ARGINGTON	B+	$$$	CHINA
BABYS DREAM	A	$$ TO $$$	CHILE/CHINA
BASSETTBABY	B+	$ TO $$	CHINA
BELLINI	B-	$$$	CHINA
BLOOM	B-	$$ TO $$$	CHINA
BOORI	N/A	$$$	CHINA
BRATT DECOR	C+	$$$	VIETNAM/CHINA
BSF BABY	N/A	$ TO $$	CHINA
BUTTERFLY LIVING	B	$ TO $$	VIETNAM/CHINA
CAPRETTI HOME	B+	$$$	CHINA
CHILD CRAFT	B	$	ASIA
COLLEGE WOODWORK	B	$$$	CANADA
CORSICAN KIDS	C+	$$$	USA
CREATIONS	B+	$$ TO $$$	VIETNAM
DELTA	B-	$ TO $$	ASIA
DUCDUC	B	$$$	USA
DUTAILIER	B+	$$ TO $$$	CANADA/CHINA
EDEN BABY	C+	$$ TO $$$	CHINA
EL GRECO	A	$$$	USA
IKEA	A	$	ASIA
JCPENNEY	C+	$$	ASIA
KIDZ DECOEUR	N/A	$$$	CANADA
LA JOBI	A	$ TO $$$	VIETNAM/CHINA
LAND OF NOD	A	$$$	USA
MILLION $ BABY/DA VINCI	B	$ TO $$$	ASIA
MUNIRE	A-	$$ TO $$$	INDONESIA
NATART	B+	$$$	CANADA
NETTOCOLLECTION	C+	$$$	POLAND/VIETNAM (CUB)
NEWPORT COTTAGE	C	$$$	USA
NURSERY SMART	B-	$$$	VIETNAM
OEUF	B+	$$$	LATVIA
PALI	B+	$$ TO $$$	VIETNAM
POTTERY BARN KIDS	C	$$$	ASIA
RAGAZZI	B	$$ TO $$$	CHINA
RESTORATION HARDWARE	C	$$$	ASIA
ROMINA	A	$$$	ROMANIA
SIMMONS	C+	$$ TO $$$	CHINA/VIETNAM
SORELLE	C+	$ TO $$$	BRAZIL/VIETNAM
STOKKE/SLEEPI	A-	$$$	SLOVENIA
STORK CRAFT	C-	$ TO $$	CHINA
WESTWOOD	A	$$$	VIETNAM
YOUNG AMERICA	B+	$$$	USA

Key: **RATING:** Our opinion of the manufacturer's quality and value.
COST: $=under $250, $$=$250-500, $$$=over $500.
JPMA: Are these cribs JPMA-certified? See page 55 for details.

JPMA	COMMENTS
	Good quality; 35 color choices. Dressers made in Canada
	Green spin on modern furniture.
◆	Still have some folding rails; Chile-made cribs best bet.
◆	Cribs good; case pieces bad. Sold at Restoration Hardware
◆	Sold only in namesake pricey boutiques.
	Alma mini crib good bassinet alternative for urbanites.
	Designed in Australia, plain styling.
	Vintage looks, bright colors. Sells direct via own site.
	Sold mostly online. Made of New Zealand pine.
	Sells under Carter's/Disney brands. Owned by Summer.
	Pricey, but cribs include conversion kit and toddler rail.
◆	Affordable, but quality/service has slipped.
	Great quality, but very high prices.
	Very pricey wrought-iron cribs; vintage feel.
◆	Conservative styling; shipping problems in past year
◆	Low prices but low quality; major safety recalls in past years
◆	Retro, modernist furniture; high gloss finish. Expensive.
	Quality has improved; expensive, 32 finishes.
	Unimpressive quality, especially for dressers.
	Excellent quality, sold at Land of Nod
	Do-it-yourself assembly; low prices; very simple styling.
◆	Good quality; offers several private label brands.
	Made by College Woodwork; eco-focus. Pricey.
◆	Graco line sold in chain stores; Bonavita in specialty stores.
	Stylish but pricey; good service, Made by El Greco.
◆	Da Vinci brand sold online; modern cribs under Baby Letto
◆	Excellent quality; adult looks. Sold as Baby Cache in BRU.
	Innovative storage; whimsical touches but very pricey.
◆	Modern/minimalist; Cub line: do-it-yourself assembly.
	Two-tone, distressed finishes; quality/service inconsistent.
◆	Adult looks; struggles with customer service issues.
	Eco-style meets modernism; lowest price of modern group.
	Lowered prices in the past year; good quality.
	Design leader but overpriced; high shipping charges.
	Many accessories. Adult looks. Recent delivery snafus.
◆	Upgraded line made by Bassett; very pricey.
	Pricey, but very well-made furniture.
◆	Owned by Delta; average quality, new lower prices.
◆	Decent prices; mixed customer service reputation.
	Pricey crib "system" best for those with little space.
◆	Low price (sold on Walmart.com), but low quality.
◆	Traditional looks; high quality. Pricey but worth it.
◆	40 color finishes; many accessories. Greenguard certified.

If space is tight (yes, we are talking to you, New Yorkers), we'd suggest the **Stokke Sleepi**. Ok, it isn't cheap ($1000), but when your urban lifestyle requires a compact crib/bassinet, the Sleepi is the answer.

Short. If you are under 5'5", you may find reaching into a standard-size stationary crib challenging. Since drop-side cribs were phased out in the past year, shorter parents may find it difficult putting baby in a stationary crib when the mattress in its lowest position. For those parents, a lower profile crib may just the ticket. A good bet: **babyletto's Modo 3-in-1** crib is made from New Zealand pine and is relatively affordable at $380.

Green. **Romina** wins the crown in the green nursery race—their uber-natural "Bees Wax" finish is offered on any of their five furniture collections. Romina also earns green points for their 100% solid bueech wood and formaldehyde-free construction (no particle board or MDF). Another plus: all furniture is made in Romania.

A runner-up in the green category is **Young America by Stanley**—with GREENGUARD certification and a made-in-the-U.S. pedigree, Young America is eco-conscious but also about 20% less expensive than Romina. Also worth a look: **Natart's Tulip**, made in Canada from recycled wood (MDF) and bamboo.

Grandma's house. If you need a secondary crib for Grandma's house, consider a portable mini crib from Dream on Me for $160, which folds for easy storage or transport.

Bassinets, Cradles & Mini Cribs

A newborn infant can immediately sleep in a full size crib, but some parents like the convenience of bassinets or cradles to use for the first few weeks or months. Why? These smaller baby beds can be kept in the parents' bedroom, making for convenient midnight feedings.

What's the difference between a bassinet and a cradle? Although most stores use the terms interchangeably, we think of bassinets as small baskets that are typically put onto a stationery stand (pictured at top right). Cradles, on the other hand, are usually made of wood and rock back and forth.

A third option in this category is "Moses baskets," basically woven baskets (right) with handles that you can use to carry a newborn from room to room. (Moses-Baskets.com has a good selection; but you can even find Moses baskets on sites like Target.com). Moses baskets can only be used for a few weeks, while you can typically use a bassinet or cradle for a couple of months.

Mini cribs are yet another alternative: most are similar in size to a bassinet (40″ long by 28″ wide). By comparison, a full-size crib is about 52″ long and 28″ wide. We recommend a specific mini crib on page 102 (see Grandma's house). FYI: mini cribs, like bassinets, are NOT a substitute for a full-size crib, which is the safest place for a baby to sleep after the first few weeks or months. Mini cribs are fine for newborns or at grandma's house for the occasional overnight visit.

As for bassinets, we noticed a Badger Basket bassinet (a rather common brand, badgerbasket.com) starts at $80 at chain stores including the "bedding" (sheets, liners, skirts and hoods). Fancier bassinets with pleated skirts and height adjustable drape canopies go for as much as $200. Cradles, on the other hand, run about $120 to $400 but only need a mattress and a sheet. Moses baskets run $50 to $200 and include all the bedding.

So, which should you buy? We say none of the above. As we mentioned at the beginning of this section, a newborn will do just fine in a full-size crib. If you need the convenience of a bassinet, we'd suggest skipping the ones you see in chain stores. Why? Most are very poorly made (stapled together cardboard, etc) and won't last for more than one child. The bedding is also low-quality. One reader said the sheets with her chain store-bought bassinet "were falling apart at the seams even before it went into the wash" for the first time. And the function of these products is somewhat questionable. For example, the functionality of a Moses basket, while pretty to look at, can be easily duplicated by an infant car seat carrier, which most folks buy any way.

Instead, we suggest you borrow a bassinet or cradle from a friend. . . or buy a portable playpen with a bassinet feature. We'll review specific models of playpens in Chapter 7, but basic choices like the Graco Pack 'N Play run $60 to $300 in most stores. The bassinet feature in most playpens (basically, an insert that creates a small bed area at the top of the playpen) can be used up to 15 pounds, which is about all most folks would need. Then, you simply remove the bassinet attachment and voila! You have a standard size playpen. Since many parents get a playpen anyway, going for a model that has a bassinet attachment doesn't add much to the cost and eliminates the separate $80 to $200 expense of a bassinet.

Another way to save: consider a stroller with a bassinet option. Yes, you can typically add this as an accessory to full-size strollers for $100 to $200—and some companies even sell a bassinet stand for use in your bedroom. See the stroller chapter for prices and options.

Mattresses

Now that you've just spent several hundred dollars on a crib, you're done, right? Wrong. Despite their hefty price tags, most cribs don't come with mattresses. So, here's our guide to buying the best quality mattress for the lowest price.

Safe & Sound

The key issue in mattress safety is Sudden Infant Death Syndrome (SIDS), the leading cause of death among infants under one year of age, claiming over 2000 lives per year. We have a detailed discussion of SIDS in our book, *Baby 411* (see back of this book for info), but here is the take-home message when it comes to SIDS and mattresses: buy a FIRM mattress that correctly fits your crib, bassinet or cradle. See the box on page 90 for more tips on preventing SIDS.

Another point to remember: while mattresses come in a standard size for a full-size crib, the depth can vary from maker to maker. Some mattresses are just four inches deep; others are six. Some crib sheets won't fit the six-inch thick mattresses; it's unsafe to use a sheet that doesn't snugly fit OVER the corner of a mattress and tuck beneath it.

Mattresses should fit your crib snugly with no more than two finger's width between the mattress and all sides of the crib when *centered* on the mattress platform. Since most cribs and mattresses are made to a standard size, this is usually not a major problem. Occasionally, we hear from a parent who has purchased a crib in Europe only to find that they can't find a mattress here that fits (Europe has a different standard for crib sizes).

Smart Shopper Tips

Smart Shopper Tip #1
Foam or Coil?
"It seems the choice for a crib mattress comes down to foam or coil? Which is better? Does it matter?"

Yes, it does matter. After researching this issue, we've come down on the foam side of the debate. Why? Foam mattresses are lighter than those with coils, making it easier to change the sheets in the middle of the night when Junior reenacts the Great Flood in his crib. Foam mattresses typically weigh less than eight pounds, while coil mattresses can top 20 or 30 pounds! Another plus: foam mattresses are less expensive, usually $100 to $160. Coil mattresses can be pricey, with some models running $200+.

Sounds easy, right? Just buy a foam mattress? Well, as always, life can be complicated—many baby stores (and even chains like Babies R Us) only sell coil mattresses, claiming that coil is superior to foam. One salesperson even told a parent that foam mattresses aren't safe for babies older than six months! Another salesperson actually told a parent they should expect to replace a foam mattress two to three times during the two years a baby uses a crib. Neither of these claims are true.

We've consulted with pediatricians and industry experts on this issue and have come to the conclusion that the best course is to choose a *firm* mattress for baby—it doesn't matter whether it's a firm coil mattress or a firm foam one. What about the claim that foam mattresses need to be replaced constantly? In the 15 years we've been researching this topic, we've never heard from even one parent whose foam mattress had to be replaced!

What's going on here? Many baby stores try to make up for the thin profit margins they make on furniture by pitching parents to buy an ultra-expensive mattress. The latest rage are so-called "2 in 1" mattresses that combine foam *and* coil (foam on one side; coil on the other). These can run $200 or more! While these mattresses are nice, they are totally unnecessary. A $100 foam mattress will do just as well.

So why all the pressure to get the fancy-shmancy double dip mattress? Such mattresses cost stores just $40 at wholesale, yet they sell for $200 or more!

Bottom line: foam mattresses are the best deal, but can be hard to find (they are sold online). As a result, we'll recommend mattresses in both the coil and foam categories just in case the baby stores near you only stock coil.

Smart Shopper Tip #2
Coil Overkill and Cheap Foam Mattresses
"How do you tell a cheap-quality coil mattress from a better one? How about foam mattresses—what makes one better than the next?"

Evaluating different crib mattresses isn't easy. Even the cheap ones claim they are "firm" and comparing apples to apples is difficult. When it comes to coil mattresses, the number of coils seems like a good way to compare them, but even that can be deceiving. For example, is a 150-coil mattress better than an 80-coil mattress?

Well, yes and no. While an 80-coil mattress probably won't be as firm as one with 150 coils, it's important to remember that a large number of coils do not necessarily mean the mattress is superior. Factors such as the wire gauge, number of turns per coil and the temper of the wire contribute to the firmness, durability and strength of the mattress. Unfortunately, most mattresses only note the coil count (and no other details). Hence, the best bet would be to buy a good brand that has a solid quality reputation (we'll recommend specific choices after this section).

What about foam mattresses? The cheapest foam mattresses are made of low-density foam (about .9 pounds per cubic foot). The better foam mattresses are high-density with 1.5 pounds per cubic foot. Easy for us to say, right? Once again, foam mattresses don't list density on their packaging, leaving consumers to wonder whether they're getting high or low density. As with coil mattresses, you have to rely on a reputable brand name to get a good foam mattress (see the next section for more details).

Smart Shopper Tip #3
New crib mattress = dangerous fumes?

"I read on the 'net that some crib mattresses give off dangerous fumes that can cause SIDS."

This internet myth has its roots in New Zealand. In the mid 90's, a New Zealand chemist launched a web site that claimed Sudden Infant Death Syndrome was caused by toxic gasses given off by crib mattresses. His solution: wrap the mattress in a gas-impenetrable cover, which naturally, was sold on his web site.

This theory has been discredited by SIDS researchers and scientists, who have studied SIDS causes for years and have found no link between mattress chemicals and infant deaths. Yet, there is still much online buzz about this theory, amid general concern over exposure of infants to household chemicals.

It is true that conventional crib mattresses (whether foam or coil) are made from scary-sounding chemicals. Most mattresses have these chemicals to meet fire retardant standards, which are mandated by both federal and state rules. *Bottom line: to date, there is no research that links sleeping on traditional crib mattresses to any disease or illness.*

That said, we can understand why new parents want to limit their newborns exposure to environmental hazards—you can't control all chemical exposure, but one place you do have some say is your child's nursery. In recent years, an entire industry of organic crib mattresses have sprung up to meet this concern.

Here's the take-home message: we think conventional crib mattresses (foam or coil) are safe. If you decide you want to go the organic route, however, we will provide some recommendations in that category later in this section.

Here are a few more shopping tips/myths about crib mattresses:

◆ **What's the best way to test the firmness of a crib mattress?** Test the center of the mattress (not the sides or corners)—place the palm of one hand flat on one side of the mattress and then put your other hand on the opposite side. The greater the pressure needed to press your hands together, the more firm the mattress.

◆ **Are all crib mattresses the same size?** No, they can vary a small amount—both in length/width and thickness. Most coil mattresses are 4" to 6" in depth. What's the best thickness? It doesn't matter, but 5" should be fine. FYI: 5" mattresses are often less expensive then 6" mattresses.

Remember the safest crib mattress is the one that snugly fits your crib—you shouldn't be able to fit more than two fingers between the headboard/side rails and the mattress. A tip: the mattress should be CENTERED on the crib mattress platform, not jammed up to one side or the other!

FYI: For the curious, full-size cribs sold in the U.S. and Canada must be between 27 5/8" and 28 5/8" wide (and 51 3/4" to 53" in length). Hence most crib *mattresses* are about 27 1/4" to 28 5/8" in width.

◆ **All foam mattresses look alike—what separates the better ones from the cheaper options?** Test for firmness (see above). The more firm, the better. Another clue: weight. A slightly heavier foam mattress usually means they used a better-quality foam to make the product. Finally, look at the cover: three layers of laminated/reinforced vinyl are better than a single or double layer. What about quilted covers? They are a waste of money, in our opinion.

Smart Shopper Tip #4
Mattresses & bacteria
"I saw a study that linked crib mattresses with a lack of waterproofing to SIDS. What should I do to protect my baby?"

In a study published in 2008 in the Journal of Applied Microbiology, scientists from the United Kingdom discovered foam crib mattresses that lacked waterproofing near an infant's head could cause bacteria growth. Some researchers believe this can be linked to Sudden Infant Death Syndrome.

Of course, most mattresses sold in U.S. have water-resistant covers (typically a layer of vinyl). However, a new crop of "organic" mattresses without such waterproofing have come on the market, appealing to parents who don't want any petrochemical-based products in their baby's nursery.

Here's our recommendations:

◆ *Get a mattress with a vinyl cover that is triple-laminated* (this provides better waterproofing).

◆ *Use a waterproof pad* over the mattress. Some "sheet savers" (Ultimate Crib Sheet) have waterproof backing that would provide extra protection to keep liquid out of the mattress. Many organic mattress companies sell mattress protectors as an accessory.

◆ *Don't use a hand-me-down mattress*, since it might not have been water-protected.

◆ *Consider changing out the mattress with each child* (new baby, new mattress) since no matter how hard you try, some leakage might happen.

The Name Game: Reviews of Selected Manufacturers

Colgate colgatekids.com Colgate has long been one of our favorite brands for affordable foam crib mattresses. The company offers three types of mattress: foam, innerspring and natural/organic. All of Colgate's foam mattresses (regular or organic) are GREEN-GUARD certified to be low in chemical emissions, which is unique in this segment. Perhaps the best selling Colgate mattress is their simple Classica 1 ($150) foam mattress with a triple layer nylon reinforced cover. Colgate also sells an "eco" version of this mattress (cleverly called the Eco Classica, $190) that replaces most of the petrochemical foam with plant-based foam. Of course, Colgate sells more than just two models—they sell several versions of the Classica mattress, some of which have dual firmness zones, memory foam and other upgrades. That's nice, but unnecessary.

Colgate is releasing a couple new mattresses for 2012. The first, called EcoFoam Supreme, is made of a unique foam. Instead of soy foam, like many of their competitors, this foam is derived from non-food plants which grow in rocky soil. It has square corners and a damask cover that is coated on the underside to be waterproof. The other new mattress is the Postura mattress, a dual firmness option with one inch thick memory foam and a medical grade water proof cover of PVC3. Again, it has square corners plus inverted seams. Prices are reasonable: $130 for the EcoFoam Supreme and the Postura is $260. Overall, we're impressed with Colgate's wide range of offerings. **Rating: A-**

Greenbuds Baby *GreenBudsBaby.com This brand is reviewed on the free side of our web site, BabyBargains.com.*

Kolcraft *kolcraft.com* Baby gear maker Kolcraft is also a big player in crib mattresses and one key reason is price: these are some of the most affordable mattresses on the market. An example is their Pediatric 2000 coil mattress with 150 coils for $65 online—a good deal if you want to go for coil. The company also sells eco-mattresses under their Contours brand, including the Soybean-Latex Foam 2-Stage crib mattress ($319). This features a rayon (bamboo) cover treated with Crypton technology for resistance to bacteria as well as a soybean foam core. Ok, that's not so affordable at $319, but Kolcraft also makes the Sealy brand, which has several affordable options in both coil and foam that are $125 or less (example: the Sealy Soybean Foam-Core mattress for $122 on Amazon). Good news, Kolcraft is expanding the Sealy eco line with even more options in 2012.

In the past year, Kolcraft added a new brand for eco mattresses called Stearns & Foster, which is a kids' version of the luxury adult mattress line. They're offering two options: the Baby Dynasty Eco Foam 2-Stage Infant-Toddler mattress (foam only, $300), and the Baby Dynasty Eco-Luxe 2-Stage Infant-Toddler mattress (foam and coil, $250). Both use high density soy foam and include Crypton Green covers. **Rating: A**

LA Baby *lababyco.com* This company is probably better known for its mini-crib, but they also sell a line of mattresses that include foam, inner spring and natural. An example is the Organic Cotton mattress for $200, which the company claims is made from certified organic cotton. Unfortunately, LA Baby's web site is woefully lacking on info (there are just pictures of the mattresses, with little or no additional details). We've seen these mattresses in person and think they are ok, quality-wise. However, Colgate and Naturepedic are superior when it comes to materials, covers, etc. **Rating: C**

Lullaby Earth *lullabyearth.com* Lullaby Earth is a new division of Naturepedic (reviewed separately) that is aiming for affordable eco crib mattresses priced under $200. Yes, you read that right—an eco crib mattress priced as a conventional mattress.

Set to debut in 2012, Lullaby Earth's Super Lightweight mattress is made of polyethylene foam (a non-toxic, food-grade foam that requires no fire retardant chemicals) and weighs just 6.5 lbs. (Most other foam mattresses on the market are made of polyurethane). It will feature seamless edges and Greenguard-certification. Price: $150. A two-stage firmness model will be available for $200.

Since this wasn't out on the market as of this writing, we don't a have a rating yet. But if Lullaby Earth is able to pull this off, it will open up the eco-crib mattress market to many more parents at this price point. **Rating: Not Yet.**

Moonlight Slumber *moonlightslumber.com.* Moonlight Slumber was one of the entrants into the "premium" crib mattress market when they debuted a few years ago. The mojo: "medical grade" and natural crib mattresses. Moonlight Slumber defines medical grade as PVC/vinyl free, non-toxic, antimicrobial and hypoallergenic. Of course, to claim something is medical grade is fuzzy, as there is no formal definition. But Moonlight Slumber points to their welded seams and a "medical grade" stretch knit fabric cover. The company's Starlight Support mattress ($245) comes in both foam and innerspring versions, as well as in various sizes (crib, bassinet, cradle, etc). Readers tell us they love the dual-zone firmness, with a less-firm side for toddlers. They also have a Starlight Support Supreme all foam for $270. FYI: Moonlight Slumber makes a standard and supreme version of its mattress—the latter ($270) has a layer of memory foam. And the company makes a more affordable version of their foam mattress (the Little Dreamer, $150 for one firmness to $185 for dual firmness), which is five inches thick (the Starlight is 6"). **Rating: A**

Natura *naturaworld.com. This brand is reviewed on the free side of our web site, BabyBargains.com.*

Naturalmat *naturalmatusa.com* UK-based Naturalmat offers three organic mattresses made of coir (the husk of a coconut), latex or mohair. Priced at $400 each, none of these are water-proof; for that, you need a $70 mattress protector that Naturalmat sells as an add-on. Amazon occasionally has them for as little as $325 while we saw the mohair version for $454 on Amazon. As for quality, readers generally praise Naturalmat, especially for the coconut mattress (Coco Mat). While the prices are high, you at least are getting a high-quality, natural mattress. **Rating: B+**

Naturepedic *naturepedic.com* Naturepedic's "No-Compromise" Classic coil mattress ($260) features 150 coils, organic cotton fabric and filling and a food-grade polyethylene cover that is waterproof. The company also makes this mattress in a seamless version (like Moonlight Slumber's design) for $280 to $300 and a 252-coil version for $300.

The Organic Cotton Lightweight mattress swaps out the coils for closed-cell air pockets made from food-grade polyethylene. As a result, this mattress is half the weight of a traditional coil mattress. This seamless mattress is $260; a dual-firmness model is $300 and an "organic cotton ultra" with Wavesupport Plus is $330.

The Ultra series is new and comes with a stronger, more durable cover and support for $360 to $400. Quality is good—Naturepedic is GREENGUARD certified. We also liked the company's detailed web site, with extensive FAQ's, articles and a blog about shopping for a natural mattress. ***Rating: A***

Nook *nooksleep.com* And now for a crib mattress that costs more than most cribs: the $550 Nook Pebble Organic features a natural latex and wool core, eucalyptus fiber and cotton cover (make sure there are no koala bears around your home) and a unique pebble wrap that is machine washable/dryable. The company claims the pebbled cover design "creates valleys for airflow on the mattress surface."

Made in the U.S., Nook also sells a lighter weight version of the mattress (Pebble Lite, 16 lbs.) that features a non-toxic eco-foam core for $295. While these mattresses are certainly unique (they come in six bright colors), neither has a water-proof cover (they claim it is "water resistent").

New for 2012, Nook is adding the Pebble Pure mattress ($395). This mattress has a coconut and latex foam core.

We've received little feedback on Nook, which is still relatively new and is sold in a handful of baby specialty stores. ***Rating: Not Yet.***

Sealy. *See Kolcraft.*

Serta by La Jobi. *lajobi.com* Crib maker La Jobi licenses the well-known Serta name for its crib mattresses. An example is the best-seller Serta Nightstar Extra Firm crib mattress ($80), a coil mattress with a 25-year warranty. Most readers say this is a good, basic crib mattress, but a few dissenters say it isn't as firm as the competition. Of course, La Jobi/Serta hasn't ignored the eco trend—their Nightstar Eco-friendly mattress runs $133. We're not sure what makes this coil mattress eco-friendly, save for the layer of organic cotton on the top of the mattress. We noticed this mattress appears to be unavailable at this time. Stay tuned for more.

Overall, readers are happy with this brand, which provides decent value for basic crib mattresses. ***Rating: B***

Simmons *simmonskids.com* Tracing its roots back to 1870, Simmons has long been a player in crib mattresses and for a while, even made cribs and nursery furniture (that part of the business was sold to Delta a few years ago). Simmons makes mattresses under the names Slumber Time, Beautyrest Beginnings, and Soja Dream Haven, their eco-friendly line. A typical example is Simmons Kids Pampering Sleep Supreme with 234 coils for $117. It features a firmer foam side for babies, a coil side for toddlers. Readers are somewhat mixed on the feedback for this brand. The lower-priced Slumber Time Evening Star mattress (under $100) is knocked for poor quality (it sags in the middle, among other problems). Simmons more expensive mattresses do somewhat better, but over-all we think there are better bets out there. *Rating: C+*

Sopora SoporaSleep.com Sopora is the new mattress division of fur-niture maker Munire. Munire has partnered with mattress industry veteran Terri Paul (formally of Moonlight Slumber) to launch the com-pany, which aims to do a new generation of healthy crib mattresses.

Sopora has four made-in-the-US models that feature Baby Safe "sealed seams" to keep out fluid, bed bugs and dust mites. The mat-tress covers are medical-grade, with no vinyl or phthalates and the corners are square.

So what's unique here? Sopora uses CertifPUR, a lightweight foam made of soy and caster oil. The company claims this is health-ier and lighter than foam made by competing manufacturers.

Sopora offers four models: The Classic is a 5" foam model with coated nylon for $152. The Premium is also 5" with a dual firmness zone for $164. The Deluxe ($230) and the Ultimate ($260) are 6" thick and have stretch knit covers with a waterproof urethane coat-ing. The Ultimate has dual firmness zones for babies and toddlers.

We found these prices to be quite affordable compared to sim-ilar mattresses by Moonlight Slumber. Quality is very good, but since this company is brand new, we don't have any real world feedback yet. *Rating: Not Yet.*

Brand Recommendations: Our Picks

Good. The *Sealy Soybean Foam-Core* crib mattress is a good deal at $120. Yes, the core is foam made from soybeans. At just 8.3 pounds, this lightweight but firm mattress makes changing sheets easy.

Better. *Moonlight Slumber's Little Dreamer* foam crib mattress is $170-$185 and features stitched seams and a PVC-free, "hospital-grade" vinyl cover. Bonus: it has two firmness zones (one for baby, another for toddler).

Best. *Naturepedic's Organic Cotton Lightweight* mattress, which swaps out coils for closed-cell air pocket made from food-grade polyethylene. As a result, this mattress is half the weight of a traditional coil mattress. It runs $260; a dual-firmness model is $300. If you want a coil mattress, Naturepedic's Organic Cotton Classic 150 coil mattress is a good bet at $260. In a nutshell, Naturepedic balances the best of both worlds: organic cotton filling, a firm foam or coil innerspring AND a waterproof cover. All of Naturepedic's mattresses contain no PVC's, polyurethane foam or chemical fire retardants.

Green. *Naturepedic* would be our top pick here—see above for model info. A runner-up best pick in the green category goes to *Naturalmat's Coco Mat* ($400), made from coconut fiber. The only bummer: the cover isn't waterproof (you have to add a $70 mattress protector to get that feature).

Dressers & Changing Tables

Now that you've got a place for the baby to sleep (and a mattress for her to sleep on), where are you going to put all those cute outfits that you'll get as gifts from Aunt Bertha? The juvenile trade refers to dressers, armoires, and the like as "case pieces" since they are essentially furniture made out of a large case (pretty inventive, huh?).

Of course, a dresser is more than just a place to store clothes and supplies. Let's not forget that all-too-important activity that will occupy so many of your hours after the baby is born: changing diapers. The other day we calculated that by our baby's first birthday, we had changed over 2300 diapers! Wow! To first-time parents, that may seem like an unreal number, but we're not exaggerating. On average, that is about SEVEN diaper changes a day during the first year . . . but for a newborn, expect up to 15 diaper changes a day. So, where are you going to change all those diapers? Most parents use the dresser top, but we'll also discuss changing tables in this section.

What are You Buying

1 **DRESSERS.** As you shop for baby furniture, you'll note a wide variety of dressers—three drawer, four drawer, armoires, combination dresser/changing tables, and more. No matter which type you choose, we do have three general tips for getting the most for your money.

First, choose a model whose drawers glide easily. Test this in the store—drawers with an easy glide typically have tracks on BOTH sides of the drawer. Cheaper dressers have drawers that simply sit on a track at the bottom center of the drawer. As a result, they don't roll out as smoothly and are prone to coming off the track.

Our second piece of advice: look at the drawer sides—the best furniture makers use "dove-tailed" drawer joints. There are two types of dove-tail drawers: English and French (see pictures at right). Either is OK; the cheapest dressers do not have dove-tailed drawers. Instead, the drawer and drawer front are merely stapled together.

A third quality indicator: drawers with corner blocks (pictured below). Pull the drawer out and turn it over to look at the corners— if there is a small block that braces the corner, that's good. Cheaper dressers omit this feature, which adds to the stability of the drawer. Also check the sides of the drawers: are they solid wood? Or particle board?

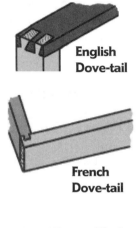

English Dove-tail

French Dove-tail

Corner Block

Drawer glides are another key point: some dressers have simple metal glides, while others use more elaborate mechanisms including self-closing glides (you push the drawer nearly closed and it automatically/slowly closes the rest of the way). A few dresser makers use wood-on-wood glides, more commonly seen in adult furniture.

When it comes to drawers, consider how far they extend: fully extending drawers are better than partial.

Step back a moment and look at the entire dresser—do the drawers fit? Are the hinges for an armoire adjustable (like what you'd see in good kitchen cabinets)? Is the back of the dresser a flimsy piece of chipboard that is stapled? We've been amazed to see the quality (or lack thereof) when it comes to dressers in chain stores.

Let's talk about wood for a second. Unlike cribs (most of which are made of solid wood), dressers are usually a compromise—solid wood on the parts you see (drawer fronts, front panels) and wood substitutes for the parts you don't see (basically, everything else).

Most dresser makers use fiberboard (sometimes referred to as MDF, medium density fiberboard) and particleboard as well as veneers (thin strips of wood glued over particleboard).

The key shopping tip: how much solid wood is there in the dresser? The better quality the dresser, the more solid wood. While one furniture maker (Romina) uses all solid wood that is the exception. The better quality furniture makers use solid wood drawer boxes, drawer fronts, tops and sometimes even sides. Or if veneers are used, they are over less expensive solid hardwood instead of MDF (Pali uses birch veneers over rubber wood, for example).

In recent years, we've seen more MDF used in baby furniture. Why? It's cheap, easy to sculpt and smooth (there is no wood grain or knots). Many modern/minimalist furniture designers are using MDF (usually coated with a high-gloss lacquer) as a design statement. While we don't see anything wrong with that, we do object to the sky-high prices for this—paying $1500 for a dresser made of MDF is like spending four-figures for a fake-leather jacket.

What are the concerns with MDF and other wood substitutes? In general, fake wood isn't as durable as solid wood, which means more possible warping in very humid or dry climates. Why? MDF is made by compressing/gluing together wood waste fibers. That compression/gluing can be affected by the moisture content in the air—and hence your expensive MDF dresser can warp.

Another concern with MDF: formaldehyde. This chemical can be found in high concentrations in MDF and particle board, thanks to that glue that binds the fibers together. The more MDF or particle board, the more possible formaldehyde, which can lead to unhealthy indoor air. In high concentrations, formaldehyde can cause a burning sensation and nausea . . . as well as a possible link to cancer.

But there is good news on this front: a new California law that went into effect in 2009 limits the amount of formaldehyde emissions from furniture. Since California is a big furniture market, manufacturers will have to adjust their entire production to limit use of these glues (and substitute them for soy-based glue).

The take-home message: when evaluating a dresser, look beyond the pretty finish. Evaluate drawer construction, glides, corner blocks and the amount of solid wood.

2 CHANGING AREA. Basically, you have two options here. You can buy a separate changing table or use your dresser as a changing area. As mentioned earlier, we think a separate changing table is a waste of money (as well as a waste of space).

So most folks look for dressers to do double duty: not only a place to store clothes, but also change diapers. Basically, you need a changing area of the right height to do this—evaluate your and your spouse's heights to see what you'd need.

FYI: We aren't big fans of those combination cribs, where a changing table or dresseer is attached to the crib. The reason is safety: attached dressers give older babies a place to climb out of the crib and potentially fall from a higher distance.

In fact, a 2011 study from the Nationwide Children's Hospital found 9,600 babies and toddlers are injured a year in cribs, most from falls.

While the study didn't have specific statistics on falls from cribs with attached dressers, we think these items are an obvious hazard.

Where do you keep the diaper changing supplies? Well, you can use a drawer in the dresser. Or, a rolling storage cart is another solution (cost: about $25 in many catalogs and stores such as Container Store (containerstore.com).

Safe & Sound

Safety doesn't stop at the crib—consider these items:

◆ **Anchor dressers to the wall.** Why? When baby starts exploring her nursery, she can tip over dressers, bookcases or shelves—no matter how heavy they are. Some furniture brands include anchor straps; in other cases, you'll need to visit a local hardware store. One solution: the Anti-Tip Kit ($10) from HangmanProducts.com.

◆ **Baby proof the diaper station.** If your diaper changing area has open shelves, you may have to baby proof the bottom shelves. As your baby begins to climb, you must remove any dangerous medicines or supplies from easily accessible shelves.

◆ **Air out all that new nursery paint, furniture and decor.** A University of Maryland study suggests new parents should air out freshly painted or wallpapered rooms before baby arrives. New furniture and mattresses also "out-gas" fumes for a brief time, so consider ventilating the nursery when they arrive as well. How much ventilation? The study suggested four to eight weeks of open window ventilation. Another idea: look for environmentally friendly paints that have lower out-gas emissions. If you install new carpet in the house, leave during the installation and open the windows (and turn on fans) for two days.

Our Picks: Brand Recommendations

Our picks for dressers mirror what we picked for cribs. For contact information on these brands, refer to the reviews earlier in this chapter. Here's a round up:

Good. IKEA's affordable dressers (about $130 to $250) are our top pick if money (or space) is tight. Let's be honest: IKEA's dressers aren't for the long haul and are nothing to fancy to look at. Plus you have to assemble everything yourself, which can be challenging. But if you need something on a temporary basis (and plan to swap out all the nursery furniture as your child grows older), IKEA is the answer.

Better. The dressers from brands like *Babi Italia (La Jobi)* and *Baby Cache (Munire)* are better quality than what you'd see in discount stores like Walmart. A simple four-drawer dresser from Baby Italia is $300 to $500; Baby Cache runs in the $500 to $600 range.

Best. Our top picks for dressers are *Munire* and *Westwood.* Each sells dressers in the $500 to $700 range, although Munire and Westwood sell less-expensive options in the chains under names Baby Cache and Bedford Baby/Hart, respectively.

If you've got more cash to burn, the very best quality in dressers can be found in *Ragazzi* and *Romina*. A double dresser from Ragazzi is $850 and features felt-lined top drawers and top notch construction. Romina is even better, with all solid-wood construction—but a double dresser from this brand runs a whopping $1200.

Changing Table Pads. The best bets here are the Simmons' Two Sided Contour Changing Table Pad with Non-Skid Bottom ($30 to $40) we like as well as Summer Infant's Contoured Changing Pad ($16 to $25). If you're looking for a natural version, consider Naturepedic's Organic Cotton Changing Table Pad. It's expensive at $100 but avoids synthetic fabrics.

Glider Rockers

More than a mere rocking chair, glider rockers feature a ball-bearing system so they glide with little or no effort.

Is a glider-rocker a waste of money? Some parents have written to us with that question, assuming you'd just use the item for the baby's first couple of years. Actually, a glider-rocker can have a much longer life. You can swap the cushions after a couple of years (most makers let you order these items separately) and move the glider-rocker to a family room. Making this transition even easier is the trend toward all upholstered gliders (earlier models had exposed wood; the newer ones are all fabric). Yep, they are more expensive, but they can go from the nursery to the family room in a single bound.

Here are some shopping tips when looking at rocker gliders:

a) Go for padded armrests. You'll be cradling a newborn and spending many hours here. All in all, the more padding in the chair, the better.
b) Consider a chair with a locking mechanism. Some brands

(notably Shermag) have an auto-locking feature; when you stand up, the chair can no longer rock. Very helpful if you have a curious toddler who might end up with pinched fingers.

c) Extra width is always smart. Some of the cheapest glider rockers are quite narrow, which might not seem bad if you are a small person. But remember you will most likely be using a nursing pillow with your newborn . . . and having the extra width to accommodate this pillow is most helpful!

The Name Game: Reviews of Selected Manufacturers

Best Chair besthf.com. This Indiana-based rocking chair maker entered the baby biz in 2002, although they trace their roots to the 1960's. We were very impressed with their quality and offerings. Basically, Best specializes in upholstered chairs with over 100+ fabric choices. They claim their gliders have the longest glide in the industry. They also offer an optional 10-position glide lock that makes it easier to get in and out of the chair. Delivery is four weeks and prices are decent for an all-upholstered look: most are $500 to $700. A matching ottoman is $200 to $300. Best is sold only in specialty stores as well as JCPenney. **Rating: A**

Brooks brooksfurnitureonline.com. *This brand is reviewed on the free side of our web site, BabyBargains.com.*

Dutailier dutailier.com. Quebec-based Dutailier is to glider-rockers what Google is to online searches—basically, they own the market. Thanks to superior quality and quick delivery, Dutailier probably sells one out of every two glider rockers purchased in the U.S. and Canada each year.

Dutailier has an incredible selection of 45 models, seven finishes, and 80 different fabrics. The result: over 37,000 possible combinations. All wood is solid maple or oak and features non-toxic finishes. You have to try real hard to avoid seeing Dutailier—the company has 3500 retail dealers, from small specialty stores to major retail chains. New for 2012, Dutailier's new Montreal designer has added a cool modern-style chair ($800 and up) to match its Papaya crib, dresser and night stand (see cribs for more info).

Prices for Dutailier start at about $350 for their "Ultramotion" line sold at discount stores like Target.com. The Ultramotion gliders are entry-level: you get basic fabric cushions and exposed wood accents. Their Value line ($550 to $600) ships in one box.

Dutailier's mid-price line (about $450 to $530) is sold at chains like Babies R Us and features upgraded fabric and more fabric choices. Of course, the price can soar quickly from there—Dutailier's specialty store line lets you customize a glider-rocker to your heart's content . . . add a swivel base, plush cushions or leather fabric and you can spend $600. Or $1000. The latest rage: all upholstered glider rockers (Prestige) run $1000 to $1200.

If you like the upholstered look but don't have that much coin, Dutailier offers an option: the Grand Modern chairs, with fully upholstered arms (but open bases) for $600 to $650 with ottoman in six fabrics and five finishes. Basically, much the same look, half the price.

Dutailier's Matrix line of ergonomic gliders echoes the look of those high-end office chairs with mesh backs ($800 to $1000). The Matrix gliders have memory-foam seats and are aimed at the modern nursery market. Matrix Too gliders are a lower-price version of the Matrix for $600 to $700 (ottoman $250); it omits the mesh seat and height adjustments.

Dutailier offers an "auto lock" feature on some chairs—it's always locked when no one is sitting in it and then automatically unlocks when you sit down. Also new: a "nursery chair" for $430 with drop-down nursing pillows.

If we had to criticize Dutailier on something, it would have to be their cushions. Most are not machine washable (the covers can't be zipped off and put into the washing machine). As a result, you'll have to take them to a dry cleaner and pay big bucks to get them looking like new. A few of our readers have solved this problem by sewing slipcovers for their glider-rockers (most fabric stores carry pattern books for such items). Of course, if the cushions are shot, you can always order different ones when you move the glider-rocker into the family room—but that can be expensive, as replacement cushions are $150 to $300.

It can take ten to 12 weeks to order a custom Dutailier rocker (more for leather options), but the company does offer a "Quick Ship" program—a selection of 17 chair styles in two or three different fabric choices that are in stock for shipment in two weeks. We have received occasional complaints about how long it takes to order a Dutailier—one reader special-ordered a Dutailier from Babies R Us, only to find out some weeks later that the fabric was discontinued (Dutailier "forgot" to tell Babies R Us, who, to their credit, tried to fix the problem immediately). Other readers complain about fabric backorders, which cause more delays in delivery. Our advice: make sure the store double checks the order with Dutailier.

An optional accessory for glider rockers is the ottoman that glides too. Prices range from $130 to $300. We suggest forgetting the ottoman and ordering an inexpensive "nursing" footstool ($32 from sites like Motherwear.com). Why? Some moms claim the ottoman's height puts additional strain on their backs while breast-feeding. While the nursing footstool doesn't rock, it's lower height puts less strain on your back. (That said, we should note that some ottoman fans point out that once their mom/baby get the hang of nursing, that gliding ottoman is a nice luxury).

One safety note: don't leave an older child sitting in a glider-rocker. Many can be tipped over by a toddler when they climb out of it. (Safety tip: some glider rockers have a lever that locks it in position when not in use). *Rating: A*

Jardine Made by Dorel Asia, Jardine's rocker gliders are sold in discount stores for $250 chair, $100 ottoman. The quality is disappointing—these chairs don't rock as easily as a Dutailier or Shermag. We say pass on this one. *Rating: D*

Little Castle littlecastleinc.com. Expensive, but good quality is how we'd describe Little Castle's glider rockers. Little Castle specializes in all-upholstered, swivel gliders made in California. An example is their popular Cottage Chase, a soft, over-stuffed chair for $825. Other styles start at $300 and go over $1000. As you'd expect for that price level, you get a wide choice of fabrics (all of which are online at Little Castle's web site) and other perks like a hidden release button to recline the chair. While Little Castle has two chair styles in five colors available for quick shipping, most custom chair orders take six to eight weeks (and sometimes, up to 12 weeks). So plan in advance.

New for 2012, Little Castle has a leatherette chair ($700 to $800 in white, brown or black) that can be customized with cushions using fabric from their entire line or your own fabric. These extra cushions run $130 for a set.

Readers generally like this company, but we heard from more than one that had quality issues with their expensive Little Castle gliders. One had a spring that popped out of the bottom of the chair; another said her Cottage Chase glider developed a hole in the arm after just eight months of use. Worse, Little Castle told the reader there was nothing they could to do help her since the fabric was discontinued (even though the chair comes with a one year warranty). As a result of these complaints, we have ticked down their rating this year. *Rating: B*

Newco Sold online at Walmart and Costco, Newco makes upholstered gliders at discount prices. Walmart currently has a $388 Newco glider that features chenille fabric and matching ottoman for $155. Feedback on the chair has been limited, but most folks are happy. One reader told us she was a bit surprised at how short the back of the chair was (and she wasn't a tall person). Otherwise, folks seem happy to be able to score an upholsterered glider for much less than what you'd typically see in stores. **Rating: B+**

Shermag/Chanderic *shermag.com.* Canada-based Shermag's strategy is to under-price Dutailier. Their $220 gliders (which include an ottoman) are sold online at Walmart, Amazon and in Target stores. Shermag's focus is the entry glider market, similar to Dutailier's Ultramotion rockers.

So what's the catch with Shermag's affordable line? First, these styles are a bit smaller in size than other glider-rockers—they fit most moms fine, but those six-foot dads may be uncomfortable. The color choices are also limited (just one or two, in most cases). And you should try to sit in these first to make sure you like the cushions (no, they aren't as super comfy as more expensive options but most parents think they're just fine).

Shermag's pricier options are found at stores like Babies R Us, where $350 (including ottoman) is the average price. For that extra money, you'll get a bigger chair, more fabric and frame color options.

How's the quality of Shermag gliders? While the low-end glider rockers get good marks from our readers, we did hear more complaints about Shermag's mid and upper price models. Perhaps the expectations are much higher here, but we were disappointed to note that readers thought the quality and durability of these $300 to $500 was not as good as Dutailier. As a result, we've dropped Shermag's rating in this edition. **Rating: B**

Stork Craft Like their cribs and dressers, Stork Craft's glider rockers are priced for the entry-level part of the market: about $140 to $260. And the company also makes upper-end gliders under its Ragazzi label. The quality here is only average. Bottom line: there are better options than Stork Craft when it comes to gliders. **Rating: C**

Nursery gift ideas

Need a small light to see baby during 2am diaper changes? We like the BabeeBrite, a hands-free mobile light source with an automatic on/off timer. $15; web: MommyBeeHappy.com.

If you have a preemie and your doctor wants you to track feedings and diaper changes, the Itzbeen Baby Care Timer is a good solution. The handheld timer tracks when baby last napped, ate or had a diaper change. Optional alarms will remind you if a time limit has been reached. Cost: $25; Itzbeen.com.

The Bottom Line:
A Wrap-Up of Our Best Buy Picks

For cribs, you've got two basic choices: a simple model that is, well, just a crib or a convertible model that eventually morphs into a twin or full size bed.

For a basic crib, the Graco Lauren ($145-$165) or Sarah ($150-$170) are good choices.

When it comes to convertible cribs, look at Munire (Baby Cache) or Westwood. These models run $400 to $600. Yep, it costs more money up-front but you get a crib that converts to a full-size bed.

Whatever crib style you pick, check under the hood to look at the mattress support. We like metal springs or wood slats; avoid cheap boards made of MDF. Choose a crib made of hard wood that will resist scratches and nicks.

The best mattress? We like **Sealy Soybean Foam-Core** crib mattress for $120. If you want a coil mattress, Naturepedic's Organic Cotton Classic 150 coil mattress is a good bet at $260. For organic mattresses, **Naturepedic's Organic Cotton Lightweight** mattress is our top pick at for $260.

The best dressers for your baby's nursery should have dove-tail drawers and smooth glides; the more solid wood, the better. Avoid pine and other soft woods, since these show scratches and other damage. The best dressers are the same as our crib picks: Munire, Westwood or Romina.

For glider rockers, Dutailier earns our top mark. A simple glider rocker runs $350, but fancy all-upholstered styles can push $1000.

So, here's a sample budget for an affordable nursery

Graco Sarah crib	$150
Sealy Soybean Form mattress	$120
Baby Cache (Munire) dresser	$500
Dutailier Ultramotion glider-rocker	$350
Miscellaneous	$200

TOTAL   **$1320**

By contrast, if you bought a designer modern crib ($1500) and paired it with a high-end dresser (plus mattress, glider rocker, etc.), you'd be out $3500 by this point. So by following our budget, you will have a safe yet affordable nursery . . . and saved $2225.

Of course, you don't have any sheets for your baby's crib yet. Nor any clothes for Junior to wear. So, next we'll explore those topics and save more of your money.

CHAPTER 3

BABY BEDDING

Baby Bedding & Decor

Inside this chapter

Where can you find brand new, designer-label bedding for as much as 50% off the retail price? We've got the answer in this chapter, plus you'll find eight smart shopper tips to help get the most for your money. We'll share the best web sites for baby linens. Learn the ten important tips that will keep your baby safe and sound. Finally, we've got reviews of the best bedding designers and a must-read list of seven top money-wasters.

Getting Started: When Do You Need This Stuff?

Begin shopping for your baby's linen pattern in the sixth month of your pregnancy, if not earlier. Why? If you're purchasing these items from a baby specialty store, they usually must be special-ordered—allow at least four to eight weeks for delivery. If you leave a few weeks for shopping, you can order the bedding in your seventh month to be assured it arrives before the baby does.

If you're buying bedding from a store or web site that has the desired pattern in stock, you can wait until your eighth month. It still takes time to comparison shop, and some stores may only have certain pieces you need in stock, while other accessories (like wall hangings, etc.) may need to be special ordered.

No matter where you buy your baby's bedding, make sure you take the time to wash it (perhaps more than once) to make sure it doesn't shrink, pill or fall apart. You'll want to return it as soon as possible if there is a problem with the quality.

Sources

There are five basic sources for baby bedding:

1 BABY SPECIALTY STORES. These stores tend to have a limited selection of bedding in stock. Typically, you're expected to choose the bedding by seeing what you like on sample cribs or by looking through manufacturers' catalogs. Then you have to special-order your choices and wait four to eight weeks for arrival. And that's the main disadvantage to buying linens at a specialty store: THE WAIT. On the upside, most specialty stores do carry high-quality brand names you can't find at discounters or baby superstores. But you'll pay for it—most specialty stores mark such items at full retail.

2 DISCOUNTERS. The sheer variety of discount stores that carry baby bedding is amazing—you can find it everywhere from Walmart to Target, Marshall's to TJ Maxx. As you'd expect, everything is cash and carry at these stores—most carry a decent selection of items in stock. You pick out what you like and that's it; there are no special orders. The downside? Prices are cheap, but so is the quality. Most discounters only carry low-end brands whose synthetic fabrics and cheap construction may not withstand repeated washings. There are exceptions to this rule, which we'll review later in this chapter.

3 DEPARTMENT STORES. The selection of baby bedding at department stores is all over the board. Some chains have great baby departments and others need help. For example, JCPenney carries linen sets by nearly ten such manufacturers like CoCaLo and Carter's (see the reviews of these brands later in this chapter), while Sears carries lines like Lambs & Ivy and Baby Boom. Prices at department stores vary as widely as selection; however, you can guarantee that department stores will hold occasional sales, making them a better deal.

4 BABY SUPERSTORES. The superstores reviewed in the last chapter (Babies R Us, Baby Depot, Buy Buy Baby etc.) combine the best of both worlds: decent prices AND quality brands. Best of all, most items are in stock. Unlike in Walmart or K-Mart stores, you're more likely to see 100% cotton bedding and better construction. Yet, the superstores aren't perfect: they are often beaten on price by online sources (reviewed later in this chapter). And superstores are more likely to sell bedding in sets (rather than a la carte), forcing you to buy frivolous items.

5 **ONLINE.** Most of our readers shop for their bedding online. And if there were a perfect baby product to be sold on-line, crib bedding is it. The web's full-color graphics let you see exactly what you'll get. And bedding is lightweight, which minimizes shipping costs. The only bummer: you can't feel the fabric or inspect the stitching. As a result, we recommend sticking to well-known brand names when ordering online. See the next section on best online sources for baby bedding and don't forget to check out online-only bedding on Walmart and Target's web sites.

Best Online Bargains

Baby Catalog of America

babycatalog.com. Baby Catalog is one of the best online baby gear web sites out there. They not only sell strollers and car seats, but they have pretty good selection of bedding. You'll find lines like Kids Line, Skip Hop, and Lambs & Ivy. They also sell bedding basics like solid sheets, blankets, port-a-crib sheets, sheet savers and bassinet/cradle sheets. If you're looking for bassinet or cradle mattresses, this site has quite a few options. All these items are priced 20% to 50% off retail. And you can get another 10% off with the purchase of an annual membership ($25 per year or $50 for three years). If you're active duty military, you qualify for free membership for one year. Our only complaint: the site could use some reader reviews of different products. ***Rating: A-***

Baby Supermall

babysupermall.com. As you'd expect from a site with "mall" in its name, BabySupermall tries to be all things to moms and dads. From safety gear to furniture to toys, this site carries quite a wide selection. In the baby bedding department, they had 351 different bedding options available. Manufacturers include Sumersault, Genna Jean, Bananafish and MiGi. Prices are usually affordable, although frequent sales (up to 50% off) make this site a real bargain. You can even click on a link for a bedding set and BabySupermall will send you an email when that bedding goes on sale in the future.

Perhaps the best part of the site is its baby bedding finder. You can choose categories like gender, price range, color, brand and up to four themes. These themes include flora, bugs and butterflies, frogs and 17 other options. Another plus: free shipping if you spend over $69 and fabric samples are available for a small charge. The site claims to have the fastest delivery because they warehouse "nearly 10,000 nursery bedding sets" at their shipping facility.

Our only complaint: the site is very cluttered. It can be as over-whelming visually as your first visit to a Babies R Us store. ***Rating: A***

Baby Supermarket

babysupermarket.com. This online outlet for a Jackson, MS baby store is a good option to consider for bargain bedding. They carry about ten bedding lines, including some of our top picks (Cotton Tale, Sumersault and Lambs & Ivy) and prices are good. For example they sell a six-piece set from CoCaLo for $147 (regular price $200). Baby Supermarket also has a decent selection of separates including the Ultimate Crib Sheet and bedding for cradles and small cribs. Baby Supermarket has improved the site since our last review with easier drop down menus to get you where you're going. ***Rating: B***

Baby Universe

babyuniverse.com. We're impressed with the calm, uncluttered look of Baby Universe's web site. For a change, we aren't bom-barded with tons of ads and superfluous information. You do have to drill down a bit to get to bedding sets or separates, however. The selection is impressive with over 170 crib bedding sets and over 30 bassinet and cradle sets. Manufacturers include Cocalo, KidsLine, Picci, Trend Lab and more with search options for price range, brand, theme and gender. Free shipping offers and other rotating discounts are available plus the site has an online outlet store with deals up to 30% off. ***Rating: B+***

Diapers.com

diapers.com. Diapers.com is really the land of discounts. Everywhere you look when you visit there are coupon codes, cash back offers, free shipping over $49, and free returns. The site is a bit busy with all the free/discount offers, but you can easily narrow your search by gender, theme, brand and price. We were impressed that they offered so many mini crib sets and sheets (87 total on our visit). These can be tough to find, so here's a great resource.

Manufacturers include the usual crowd as well as some different names like Clouds & Stars zip off sheets (see box later in this chap-ter), Egg by Susan Lazar and Natures Purest organic sets. The site calls out sale prices and any out of stock items clearly, a nice plus. Overall, Diapers.com is one of our favorites for great selection and price. ***Rating: A***

Overstock

overstock.com. Overstock.com is a master at finding closeout deals in all kinds of categories. We always buy our regular bed sheets from these guys in amazing Egyptian cotton with incredibly high thread counts. So we figured they'd have some great deals on baby bedding too. And we weren't disappointed. On a recent visit we saw over 160 baby bedding sets from companies like Trend Lab, Sumersault, Cotton Tale and more. Prices are 25% to 50% off. For example, we noticed a N. Selby Designs 4 piece set for a mere $198, half off retail.

But remember, if you see something you want on Overstock.com, don't wait too long. They sell out quick! And some designs do not offer a la carte sheets so you're stuck with what comes in the package. Be sure you check customer reviews before you buy to verify you're really getting a deal. ***Rating: A***

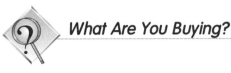

What Are You Buying?

Walk into any baby store, announce you're having a baby, and stand back: the eager salespeople will probably pitch you on all types of bedding items that you MUST buy. We call this the "Diaper Stacker Syndrome," named in honor of that useless (but expensive) linen item that allegedly provides a convenient place to store diapers. But what do you really need? Here's our list of the absolute necessities for your baby's linen layette:

◆ ***Fitted sheets***—at least three to four. This is the workhorse of your baby's linens. When it comes to crib sheets, you have three choices: woven, knit and flannel. Woven (also called percale) sheets are available in all cotton or cotton blend fabrics, while knit and flannel sheets are almost always all cotton. As to which is best, it's up to you. Some folks like flannel sheets, especially in colder climates. Others find woven or knit sheets work fine. One tip: look for sheets that have elastic all-around the edges (cheaper ones just have elastic on the corners). See the "Safe & Sound" section for more info on crib sheet safety issues.

If you plan to use a bassinet/cradle, you'll need a few of these special-size sheets as well . . . but your choices here are pretty limited. You'll usually find solid color pastels or white. Some specialty linen manufacturers do sell bassinet sheets, but they can get rather pricey. And you may find complete bassinet sets that come with all the linens for your baby. Just be sure to check the fabric content (all cotton is best) and washing instructions. By the way, one mom improvised bassinet sheets by putting the bassinet mattress inside a king size pillowcase. You may want to secure the excess fabric under the mattress so it doesn't un-tuck.

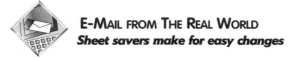

E-MAIL FROM THE REAL WORLD
Sheet savers make for easy changes

Baby bedding sure looks cute, but the real work is changing all those sheets. Karen Naide found a solution:

"One of our best buys was 'The Ultimate Crib Sheet.' I bought one regular crib sheet that matched the bedding set, and two Ultimate Crib Sheets. This product is waterproof (vinyl on the bottom, and soft white poly/cotton on the top) and lies on top of your regular crib sheet. It has six elastic straps that snap around the bars of your crib. When it gets dirty or the baby soils it, all you have to do is unsnap the straps, lift it off, put a clean one on, and that's it! No taking the entire crib sheet off (which usually entails wrestling with the mattress). It's really quick and easy! While the white sheet may not exactly match your pattern, it can only be seen from inside the crib, and as you have so often stated, it's not like the baby cares about what it looks like. From the outside of the crib, you can still see the crib sheet that matches your bedding. Anyway, I think it's a wonderful product, and really a must."

*Summer Infant makes the **Ultimate Crib Sheet** (summerinfant.com). It sells for $20 and is available at Babies R Us, Target and other baby web sites..*

Of course, there are several other companies that sell similar sheets; we've seen them on general websites like One Step Ahead (Breath-Easy Crib Sheet Saver, two for $20) and Baby Catalog of America (American Baby Sheet Savers, $7 to $11).

*One of the coolest new products we found was the **Quick Zip** crib sheet from Clouds and Stars (cloudsandstars.com). Here's how it works: the sheet base covers the bottom of the mattress and stays in place. The top of the sheet is secured via a plastic zipper. Baby's diaper leaks at two in the morning, you zip off the top of the sheet and zip on a spare. No lifting of the mattress (except when you first set it up). The white or ecru sheet sets are $35 to $60 for the starter set (a zipper base plus top sheet) and additional top sheets are $19 to $38.*

◆ *Mattress Pads/Sheet Protector.* While most baby mattresses have waterproof vinyl covers, many parents use either a mattress pad or sheet protector to protect the mattress or sheet from leaky diapers. A mattress pad is the traditional way of dealing with this problem and is placed between the mattress and the crib sheet. A more recent invention, the sheet protector, goes on top of the crib sheet.

A sheet protector has a waterproof vinyl backing to protect against leaking. And here's the cool part: it Velcro's to the crib's posts, making for easy removal. If the baby's diaper leaks, simply pop off the sheet protector and throw it in the wash (instead of the fitted crib sheets). You can buy sheet protectors in most baby stores or online. See "Email from the Real World" on the previous page for information on sheet savers.

◆ *Blanket?* Baby stores love to pitch expensive quilts to parents and many bedding sets include them as part of the package. But remember this: *all babies need is a simple, thin cotton blanket.* Not only are thick quilts overkill for most climates, they can also be dangerous. The latest report from the Consumer Product Safety Commission on Sudden Infant Death Syndrome (SIDS) concluded that putting babies face down on such soft bedding may contribute to as many as 30% of SIDS deaths each year in the U.S. (As a side note, there is no explanation for the other 70% of SIDS cases, although environmental factors like smoking near the baby and a too-hot room are suspected). Some baby bedding companies have responded to these concerns by rolling out decorative flannel-backed blankets (instead of quilts) in their collections.

But what if you live in a cold climate and think a cotton blanket won't cut it? Consider crib blankets made from fleece (a lightweight 100% polyester fabric brushed to a soft finish) available in most stores and online. For example, *Lands End* sells a micro fleece crib blanket for $20. Of course, polar fleece blankets are also available from mainstream bedding companies like *California Kids* (reviewed later in this chapter). Or how about a "coverlet," which is lighter than a quilt but more substantial than a blanket? Lightweight quilts (instead of the traditional thick and fluffy version) are another option for as little as $30 online.

We found a great product to keep baby warm and avoid a blanket altogether. *Halo Innovations'* (halosleep.com) SleepSack is a "wearable blanket" that helps baby avoid creeping under a blanket and suffocating. Available in three sizes and fabrics, the SleepSack is $24 to $33. A portion of the sale price goes to First Candle/SIDS Alliance.

Swaddling blankets are now the rage (although most folks can figure out how to swaddle a baby with a regular blanket without much effort). Examples include the *Miracle Blanket* ($30; miracleblanket.com) and the *Kiddopotamus Swaddle Me* ($10). See the box on the next page for more swaddling blanket picks.

Swaddling & Wearable Blankets

Ever since the Consumer Product Safety Commission first began their "Back to Sleep" campaign in 1994, parents have struggled with how to keep baby both warm at night and safe. With strict orders to stay away from soft bedding and only cover baby up to her chest with a blanket, some parents were stumped. Along came some bright entrepreneurs who invented an easy way to keep baby safe and warm with wearable blankets. The original *SleepSack* (made by Halo) started the trend and is still available in a variety of fabrics for $25 to $40. They are a bit like a sleeping bag with arms (or sleeveless).

Halo has expanded their line to include swaddling blankets. Swaddling has become a huge trend among parents. So the Halo SleepSack morphed into a swaddling blanket (SleepSack Swaddle $27 to $29) with the addition of flaps that fold over and Velcro to hold baby's arms close to their body.

Of course, there's more than just the SleepSack out there. Here are some of our reader favorites for swaddling blankets.

Aden & Anais (AdenandAnais.com) make one of the most popular lines of swaddling blankets. Available from their web site as well as in stores like Target and Buy Buy Baby, these cotton muslin blankets are a simple option. They don't have Velcro or any special secret fold, but they are just the right shape and size for easy swaddling. The site offers online graphic and video demonstrations for novice parents. Prices range from $30 for a four pack on Target.com to $45 per four pack on Aden & Anais web site. Double layer blankets, organic and bamboo collections are available for a bit more.

Another option: *Swaddle Designs* (swaddledesigns.com) swaddlers and wearable blankets are also excellent, say readers. This site offers both a wearable blanket option called the zzZipMe Sack ($32 to $45) with a cool two-way zipper for easy diaper changes plus their Ultimate Receiving blanket ($25) and Marquisette Swaddling blanket ($14 to $27). Both blankets have easy directions, shown on a sewn-on tag.

Finally, a small company out of Connecticut makes a wearable blanket/swaddler called the *Woombie* (thewoombie.com). This option is similar to a wearable blanket without the arm holes. You just zip it up and it hugs your baby's arms to his chest. Cost: $28 to $30. Winter weight, summer weight and organic fabrics are available.

More Money Buys You . . .

Baby bedding sets vary from as little as $40 in discount stores up to nearly $1000 in specialty stores. The basic difference: fabric quality and construction. The cheapest bedding is typically made of 50/50 cotton-poly blends with low thread counts (120 threads per inch). To mask the low quality, many bedding companies splash cutesy licensed cartoon characters on their offerings. So what does more money buy you? First, better fabric. Usually, you'll find 100% cotton with 200 thread counts or more. Cheap quality crib sheets often lack elastic all the way around and some shrink dangerously when washed (see Safe and Sound next for details), while more money buys you preshrunk or oversized (to allow for shrinkage) sheets with elastic all around the edge.

Beyond the $300 price point, you're most likely paying for a designer name and frilly accessories (coordinating lamp shade, anyone?). At the upper end of the crib bedding market, you find luxury fabrics—silks, brocades, matte lasse, etc.

Safe & Sound

When it comes to baby safety, most folks think of outlet covers and coffee table bumpers—but your baby's crib bedding should be a key priority. Why? Your baby will be spending more time in the crib than any other place in the house. Here are several safety points to remember:

◆ *Make sure the crib sheets snugly fit the mattress.* Let's talk about crib sheets. As you might guess, it is the elastic on a sheet that helps it fit snugly to a mattress. But not all sheets have the same amount of elastic.

One quality sign: check to make sure the sheet's elastic extends around the ENTIRE sheet (cheaper quality crib sheets only have elastic on the ends, making a good fit more difficult to achieve).

Another issue to consider with crib sheets: shrinkage. *Never use a sheet that has shrunk so much it can no longer be completely pulled over the bottom corners of the mattress.*

Unfortunately, some sheets shrink more than others. Generally, the cheapest sheets sold in discount stores shrink the most. We will review and rate bedding brands later in this chapter—those brands we recommend typically have sheets that are pre-shrunk. Others make their sheets larger to allow for shrinkage.

Our advice: for any crib sheet you buy, be sure to wash it several times *according to the directions* and see if it correctly fits your crib. If not, return it to the store.

In response to concerns about ill-fitting cribs sheets, a few new crib sheet alternatives have come on the market. Example: The *Stay Put* safety sheet (babysheets.com; $20 each) works like a pillowcase on your

mattress. The only downside: the fabric is 50% poly, 50% cotton. Another option to consider: "pocket" sheets wrap around the crib mattress and close easily with Velcro. These sheets are manufactured by *Halo* (halosleep.com), the makers of the SleepSack mentioned earlier. Also consider the Ultimate Crib Sheet and the QuickZip sheet discussed on page 128 as other safe sheet options.

Finally, if you want a safety sheet that is customized to your nursery décor, take a look at *Sweet Pea's Heirlooms* (sweetpeasheirlooms.com). These sheets completely encase the mattress (like a pillowcase) then snap on the end. And, best of all, you can get the sheet made-to-order (with a print on one side and a solid on the other, or any combination of fabric). A 200-thread count cotton sheet from Sweet Pea starts at $25, with flannel and fleece options as well.

◆ *No soft bedding in the crib.* Yes, we've said it before and here it is again: studies on Sudden Infant Death Syndrome (SIDS, also known as crib death) have linked SIDS to infants sleeping on fluffy bedding, lambskins, or pillows. A pocket can form around the baby's face if she is placed face down in fluffy bedding, and she can slowly suffocate while breathing in her own carbon dioxide. The best advice: put your infant on her back when she sleeps. And don't put pillows, comforters or other soft bedding or toys inside a crib.

Sheets with All Around Elastic

Here is a partial list of manufacturers who make their crib sheets with elastic all around the sheet:

BB Basics	Kids Line	Restoration
Baby Basics	Lands End	Hardware
Baby Gap	Luv Stuff	Sweet Kyla
Carousel	Maddie Boo	Wamsutta
Circo (Target)	Bobble Roos	
Fleece Baby	Nava's Designs	
Garnet Hill	Nurseryworks	
Hoohobbers	Pitter Patter	

The Consumer Product Safety Commission now recommends that parents not use ANY soft bedding around, on top of, or under baby. If you want to use a blanket, tuck a very thin blanket under the mattress at one end of the crib to keep it from moving around. The blanket should then only come up to baby's chest. Safest of all: avoid using any blankets in a crib and put baby in a blanket sleeper (basically, a thick set of pajamas) and t-shirt for warmth. (More on blanket sleepers in the next chapter). See the picture at right for an example of the correct way to use a blanket.

One mom wrote to tell us about a scary incident in her nursery. She had left a blanket hanging over the side of the crib when she put her son down for a nap. He managed to pull the blanket down and get wrapped up in it, nearly suffocating. Stories like that convince us that putting any soft bedding in or near a crib is risky.

How much bedding is too much? A new father emailed us this question: "With all the waterproof liners, fitted sheets and ultimate crib sheets we're worried that our firm mattress is now becoming soft and squishy. How many layers are safe?"

Good point. We know that some parents figure it is easier to change crib sheets at 2 am if they simply pile on several layers of sheets on the crib mattress. (This way, you simply remove the top wet layer when changing the sheets). While we admire the creative thinking, we suggest NOT doing this. One sheet over a waterproof liner is enough. Or use an Ultimate Crib Sheet over your sheet—you won't need an additional liner since the Ultimate Crib Sheet is waterproof. The take-home message: any more than TWO layers on top of a mattress is dangerous.

◆ **Beware of ribbons and long fringe.** These are possible choking hazards if they are not attached properly. Remove any questionable decoration.

◆ **We DO NOT recommend crib bumpers.** Do not use bumpers in your baby's crib, cradle or bassinet. They are a risk factor for suffocation.

Yes, in past editions of this book, we tried to discourage people from using bumpers, but did not outright reject them. Why did we change our mind? New evidence shows that bumpers can and do cause suffocation deaths in infants. A recent investigation by the *Chicago Tribune* detailed a link between crib bumpers and two dozen infant deaths in the past decade. The article ("Hidden Hazard of Crib Bumpers," December 12, 2010) prompted the CPSC to open a review of the safety of crib bumpers.

An earlier study by a Washington University pediatrician, Dr. Bradley Thach "concluded that 27 babies' deaths were attributed to bumper pads from 1985 to 2005." This study, however, has been largely ignored by both the industry and the CPSC, although the American Academy of Pediatrics discourages parents from using bumpers.

As a side note, Canada has discouraged bumper use for many years. One Canadian reader noted: "We are not supposed to use bumper pads due to the increased risk of SIDS. No one I know uses them. When the health nurse comes to visit you in the home, she checks to make sure you don't have bumper pads." It's time parents in the U.S. followed similar guidelines.

Now we know what you're thinking: "What if my baby hits his head on the hard wood slats?" or "What if she gets her arm or leg stuck between the slats?" First, realize these issues are rare—few kids are injured by knocking their heads against the slats and even fewer get limbs stuck. However, there are a couple of bumper alternatives that can help; we'll review these products (the CozyWedge, Wonder Bumper, Breath Easy Bumper and Crib Shield) later in the Name Game in this chapter. Most of these items are either breathable mesh or firm, shock absorbing foam that don't pose a suffocation risk. Again, most folks will not needs these bumper alternatives.

◆ **Never use sleep positioners.** A recent recall of sleep positioners lead us to urge parents not to use them. These $10 to $20 blocks of foam are supposed to hold baby in place on their back when sleeping. However, the Consumer Product Safety Commission (CPSC.org) issued a "warning to parents and caregivers to stop using sleep positioners." They have received reports of 12 infants who suffocated when positioners were used. In past editions, we discouraged sleep positioners because they were a waste of money, but now we know they are also a serious hazard. Simply put your baby to sleep on his back—no pillows, no rolled up towels.

◆ **Never use an electric blanket/heating pad.** Babies can dangerously overheat, plus any moisture, such as urine, can cause electric shock.

◆ **Avoid blankets that use nylon thread.** Nylon thread melts in the dryer and then breaks. These loose threads can wrap around your baby's neck, fingers or toes or break off and become a choking hazard. Cotton thread is best.

◆ ***Watch out for chenille.*** Its popularity has waned in recent years, but we still see some chenille accents on baby bedding and in luxe items like blankets. The problem? With some chenille, you can actually pull out fibers from the fabric backing with little effort. And that might be a choking hazard for baby.

◆ ***Travel.*** Now that you've created a safe nursery at home, what about when you travel? Parents who frequently travel are often frustrated by hotels, which not only have unsafe cribs (see previous chapter) but also questionable sheets. At one hotel, we were given queen size bed sheets to use in a crib! A solution: one reader recommended bringing a crib sheet from home. That way you know your baby will be safe and sound. (When you reserve a crib at a hotel, find out if it is a portable crib or a standard crib so you know what size sheet to bring.) Check with some of our recommended safety sheet manufacturers listed earlier in this chapter and consider buying their port-a-crib versions for travel.

◆ ***All linens should have a tag*** indicating the manufacturer's name and address. That's the only way you would know if the linens were recalled. You can also contact the manufacturer if you have a problem or question. While this is the law, some stores may sell discounted or imported linens that do not have tags. Our advice: DON'T buy them.

Smart Shopper Tips

Smart Shopper Tip
Pillow Talk: Looking for Mr. Good Bedding

"Cartoons or more cartoons—that seems to be the basic choice in crib bedding at our local baby store. Since it all looks alike, is the pattern the only difference?"

There's more to it than that. And buying baby bedding isn't the same as purchasing linens for your own bed—you'll be washing these pieces much more frequently, so they must be made to withstand the extra abuse. Since baby bedding is more than just another set of sheets, here are nine quality points to look for:

1 RUFFLES SHOULD BE FOLDED OVER FOR DOUBLE THICKNESS— INSTEAD OF A SINGLE THICKNESS RUFFLE WITH HEMMED EDGE. Double ruffles hold up better in the wash.

2 **COLORED DESIGNS ON THE BEDDING SHOULD BE PRINTED OR WOVEN INTO THE FABRIC, NOT STAMPED** (like you'd see on a screen-printed t-shirt). Stamped designs on sheets can fade with only a few washings. The problem: the pieces you wash less frequently (like dust ruffles and bumpers) will fade at different rates, spoiling the coordinated look you paid big money for. In case you're wondering how to determine whether the design is printed rather than stamped, printed fabrics have color that goes through the fabric to the other side. Stamped patterns are merely applied onto the top of the fabric.

3 **MAKE SURE THE PIECES ARE SEWN WITH COTTON/POLY THREAD, NOT NYLON.** While nylon threads can be a safety problem (see earlier discussion), they also are a quality issue. When nylon threads break in a dryer, the filling can bunch up.

4 **CHECK FOR TIGHT, SMOOTH STITCHING ON APPLIQUÉS.** If you can see the edge of the fabric through the appliqué thread, the work is too skimpy. Poor quality appliqués will probably unravel after only a few washings. We've seen some appliqués that were actually fraying in the store—check before you buy.

5 **HIGH THREAD-COUNT SHEETS.** Unlike adult linens, many packages of baby bedding do not list the thread count. But, if you can count the individual threads when you hold a sheet up to the light, you know the thread count is too low. High thread-count sheets (200 threads per inch or more) are preferred since they are softer and smoother against baby's skin, last longer and wear better. Unfortunately, most affordable baby bedding has low thread counts (80 to 120 thread counts are common)—traditionally, it's the design (not the quality) that sells bedding in the baby biz. But there is good news on this front: several upstart brands (reviewed later) actually tout high thread counts for their sheets.

6 **THE DUST RUFFLE PLATFORM SHOULD BE OF GOOD QUALITY FABRIC**—or else it will tear. Longer, full ruffles are more preferable to shorter ones. As a side note, the dust ruffle is sometimes referred to as a crib skirt.

7 **REMEMBER THAT CRIB SHEETS COME IN DIFFERENT SIZES—** bassinet/cradle, portable crib, and full-size crib. Always use the correct size sheet.

Wastes of Money/Worthless Items

"I have a very limited budget for bedding, and I want to avoid spending money on stuff that I won't need. What are some items I should stay away from?"

It may be tempting to buy every matching bedding accessory. And you'll get a lot of sales pressure at some stores to go for the entire "coordinated" look. Yet many baby-bedding items are a complete waste of money—here's our list of the worst offenders:

1 **DIAPER STACKER.** This is basically a bag (in coordinating fabric, of course) used to store diapers—you hang it on the side of a changing table. Apparently, bedding makers must think stacking diapers on the shelf of your changing table or storing them in a drawer is a major etiquette breach. Take my word for it: babies are not worried if their diapers are out in plain sight. Save the $30 to $50 that bedding makers charge for diaper stackers and stack your own. By the way, we've even seen $100 diaper stackers—these typically coordinate with equally expensive bedding sets.

2 **PILLOWS.** Some bedding sets still include pillows or pillowcases. Are the bedding designers nuts, or what? Haven't they heard that it's dangerous to put your baby to sleep on a pillow? What a terrible safety hazard, not to mention a waste of your money. We don't even think a decorative pillow is a good idea—what if another caretaker puts your baby to sleep in her crib and forgets to remove the decorative pillow? Forget the pillow and save $30 to $50.

3 **SETS OF LINENS.** Sets may include useless or under-used items like those listed above as well as dust ruffles and window valances. Another problem: sets are often a mixed bag when it comes to quality. Some items are good, while others are lacking. Here's an example from Overstock.com: a 13-piece set on sale for $104 included a quilt, two valances, skirt, crib sheet, bumper, diaper stacker, toy bag, two pillows and three wall hangings. No surprise, this set was made of a poly/cotton blend fabric. A better bet: many baby stores or even chains now sell bedding items a la carte. That way you can pick and choose just the items you need—at a substantial savings over the all-inclusive sets.

4 **CANOPIES.** Parents-to-be of girls are often pressured to buy frilly accessories like canopies. The pitch is a feminine look for her nursery. Don't buy into it. The whole set-up for a canopy is going to be more expensive (you'll need a special crib, etc.)—it'll set you back $60 to $175 for the linens alone. And enclosing your baby's crib in a canopy won't do much for her visual stimulation or health (canopies are dust collectors).

5 **ALL-WHITE LINENS.** If you think of babies as pristine and unspoiled, you've never had to change a poopy diaper or clean spit-up from the front of an outfit. We're amazed that anyone would consider all-white bedding, since keeping it clean will probably be a full-time job. Stick with colors, preferably bright ones. If you buy all-white linens and then have to go back to buy colored ones, you'll be out another $100 to $200. (Yes, some folks argue that white linens are easier to bleach clean, but extensive bleaching over time can yellow fabric.)

Money Saving Secrets

1 **IF YOU'RE ON A TIGHT BUDGET, GO FOR A GOOD BLANKET AND A NICE SET OF HIGH THREAD-COUNT SHEETS.** What does that cost? A good cotton or fleece blanket runs $10 to $20, while a decent quality fitted sheet is another $10 to $20. Forget all the fancy items like embroidered comforters, duvet covers, window valances, diaper stackers and dust ruffles. After all, your baby won't care if she doesn't have perfectly coordinated accessories.

2 **DON'T BUY A QUILT.** Sure, they look pretty, but do you really need one? Go for a nice cotton blanket, instead—and save the $50 to $200. Better yet, hint to your friends that you'd like receiving blankets as shower gifts.

3 **SKIP EXPENSIVE WALL HANGINGS—DO DECOR ON THE CHEAP.** One of the best new products we've discovered for this is Wall Nutz (wallnutz.com). These innovative iron-on transfers let you create paint-by-number masterpieces in your baby's room. Paint a six-by-eight foot mural or just add some decorative borders. Cost: $40 (plus the cost of paints).

A new idea: wall decals. These creative graphic "stickers" can be positioned and repositioned, removed and replaced. Choose from animals, flowers, abstract designs and more. Two companies offer these cool décor options: *Blik Re-Stik* (whatisblik.com; eight pieces for $30) and *WallPops!* (wall-pops.com; kits starting at $20). While these are reusable, take care when removing them as they may fray along the edges. *Wallies* (wallies.com) are similar to decals except that they are pre-pasted shapes. You wet the backing and stick them wherever you like. FYI: Some Wallies aren't reusable—you have to strip them off like wallpaper. A pack of 25 small flowers runs about $10. They now offer bigger, mural size Wallies starting at $45.

Of course, crafts stores are another great source for do-it-yourself inspiration. Michaels Arts & Crafts (michaels.com) sells stencils and supplies for nursery decor.

4 **MAKE YOUR OWN SHEETS, DUST RUFFLES AND OTHER LINEN ITEMS.** Think that's too complicated? A mom in Georgia called in this great tip on curtain valances—she bought an extra dust ruffle, sewed a curtain valance from the material and saved $70. All you need to do is remove the ruffle from the fabric platform and sew a pocket along one edge. I managed to do this simple procedure on my sewing machine without killing myself, so it's quite possible you could do it too. A good place for inspiration is your local fabric store—most carry pattern books like Butterick, Simplicity and McCalls, all of which have baby bedding patterns that are under $10. There are other pattern books you can purchase that specialize in baby quilts—some of these books also have patterns for other linen items like valances, crib skirts or wall hangings. Even if you buy good quality fabric at $10 per yard, your total savings will be 75% or more compared to "pre-made" items.

5 **SHOP AT OUTLETS.** Scattered across the country, we found a few outlets that discount linens. Among the better ones Garnet Hill and Carousel (also known as babybeddingonline.com)— see their reviews in this chapter. Another reader praised the Pottery Barn Outlet. They have ten locations at the time of this writing. The discounts start at 50% on bedding and furniture from their web sites and retail stores. Other outlets: Carter's, Baby Gap, and Nautica. Check Outlet Bound (www.outletbound.com) for locations.

6 **DON'T PICK AN OBSCURE BEDDING THEME.** Sure, that "Exploding Kiwi Fruit" bedding is cute, but where will you find any matching accessories to decorate your baby's room? Chances are they'll only be available "exclusively" from the bedding's manufacturer—at exclusively high prices. A better bet is to choose a more common theme with lots of accessories (wall decor, lamps, rugs, etc.). The more plentiful the options, the lower the prices. Winnie the Pooh is a good example, although you'll find quite a few accessories for other common themes like Noah's Ark, teddy bears, rocking horses, etc.

7 **Go for solid color sheets and use themed accessories.**
Just because you want to have a Disney-themed nursery does-
n't mean you have to buy Disney *bedding*. A great money-saving
strategy: use low-cost solid color sheets, blankets and other linen
items in the crib. Get these in colors that match/compliment theme
accessories like a lamp, clock, poster, wallpaper, rugs, etc. (Hint: register for these items, which make nice shower gifts). You still have the
Disney look, but without the hefty tag for Disney bedding. Many of
the online sites we reviewed earlier in this chapter are excellent
sources for affordable, solid-color bedding. Another bonus: solid
color sheets/linens from these web sites we recommend are often
much higher quality (yet at a lower price) than theme bedding.

8 **Surf the web.** Earlier in this chapter, we discussed the best
web sites for baby bedding deals. The savings can be as
much as 50% off retail prices. Even simple items like crib sheets can
be affordably mail ordered.

The Name Game:
Reviews of Selected Manufacturers

Here are reviews of some of the brand names you'll encounter
on your shopping adventures for baby bedding. Note: we include
the phone numbers, web sites and addresses of each manufacturer—this is so you can find a local dealer near you (most do not sell
directly to the public, nor send catalogs to consumers). We rated
the companies on overall quality, price, and creativity, based on an
evaluation of sample items we viewed at retail stores. We'd love to
hear from you—tell us what you think about different brands and
how they held up in the real world by emailing authors@
BabyBargains.com.

SAFETY NOTE: We do not recommend parents use bumpers in
their babies' cribs. See the Safe and Sound section earlier for an in
depth explanation. Note that many brands reviewed below sell
bedding sets that include bumpers.

The Ratings

A **Excellent**—*our top pick!*
B **Good**— *above average quality, prices, and creativity.*
C **Fair**—*could stand some improvement.*
D **Poor**—*yuck! could stand some major improvement.*

Annette Tatum *annettetatum.com.* Also known as Little House, this bedding collection also goes by its designer's name. The look here is part of the shabby chic trend, sold exclusively in baby boutiques and the designer own store in Santa Monica, CA. At $300 to $400 for a three-piece set (bumper, sheet and skirt), Annette Tatum is not cheap. Extra sheets run a whopping $66! You'd think they were embroidered in gold thread at that price. And who's going to buy only one sheet? The fabric is 100% cotton poplin in a wide array of pastel mix and match patterns. Quality is good, as you'd expect at these prices. FYI: If you like the look here but not the price, look online for past seasons' sets. We saw a few under the Little House brand label for $300 for a five-piece set, 25% less than Tatum's current retail. ***Rating: B***

Baby Bedding Online *See Carousel.*

Baby Basics *See Carter's.*

BananaFish *bananafishinc.com.* "Sophisticated" and "tailored" is how we'd describe this California-based bedding maker. BananaFish's emphasis is on all-cotton fabric with adult-like finishes (such as pique) and muted color palettes (see picture for example). They also offer a sub line called MiGi. The colors are a little more subdued and the style is very whimsical. They also hold the license for Skip Hop bedding, an über modern grouping with a polka dot design.

How's the quality? Overall, excellent, say readers. FYI: Part of BananaFish's line is made in China; the balance is still produced in the U.S. Fair warning: it's not cheap—prices range from $220 to $600 at retail for a four-piece set. The exception: the MiGi line starts at $145. ***Rating: B***

BB Basics Online *buybuybaby.com.* Private-label brands of bedding are commonplace among the chains. Target has it's Circo brand while Babies R Us has Koala Baby...so it's no surprise that Buy Buy Baby now has its own line, BB Basics (or BB Couture). This label offer three types of sheets: 200 and 400-thread count cotton percale and 180-thread count cotton jersey knit. Sheets are available in three sizes: crib, play yard and bassinet. All sheets have all around elastic and prices are rather affordable. A percale crib sheet is $10 each for 200-thread count and $18 for 400-thread count. Knit crib sheets are $10. So how's the quality? Feedback is mixed. One mom complained that the fit was too loose and the stitching came undone after the first washing. But another reader praised the knit sheets: "they're pretty good quality for the dollar." ***Rating: B-***

Bedtime Originals *See Lambs & Ivy.*

Bobble Roos *BobbleRoos.com.* Mr. Bobbles Blankets is now Bobble Roos! As you know, we love the Graco Pak N Play and other playpens for their convenience . . . with one exception: those darn cheap playpen sheets! Active babies easily pull off the sheets that come with most playpens and the thin, low-thread count cotton makes them a cold place for baby during winter months. To the rescue comes Bobble Roos, which besides its namesake blankets, also makes a No-Slip Play Yard Sheet for $20. We had a reader give this product a test-run and the verdict was positive. Made of 100% cotton flannel, the "very soft" sheets come in "cute fabrics" and "held up well after several washings," said our reviewer. And true to its claims, the sheet does not slip off the mattress—it is designed like a pillow sham so it doesn't easily pull off the corners. **Rating: A**

Brandee Danielle *brandeedanielle.com. An archived review of this manufacturer is available on our website BabyBargains.com under Bonus Material.*

Breathe Easy by Summer *See Summer.*

Caden Lane *cadenlane.com.* Caden Lane designer Katy Mimari got her start in the baby biz when she designed unique diaper bags. From there, she was inspired by her own pregnancy to design a line of baby bedding. Today, she has a total of 18 bedding sets as well as diaper bags and matching accessories.

Bedding sets are divided into the Classic Collection (stripes, dots and circles), Modern Vintage (Moroccan inspired prints), Luxe Collection (stripes, swirls and damask patterns), and the new Boutique Collection. Most of the line is made up of four piece sets including a 100% cotton, 230-thread count sheet, skirt, bumper and blanket. Price: a hefty $400. If that's too rich, the new Boutique collection has only three pieces (no blanket) and runs $389. Extra sheets are $38 and blankets run $44 to $48. Extra fabric is available by the yard and you can order swatches for only $5. A new "Limited Edition" collection is affordably priced at under $200 with no bumpers (hurray for Caden Lane!).

Overall, the fabrics and patterns are lovely and Caden Lane's style is certainly different. Prices are rather high compared to other brands. The jury is still out on the quality of this relatively new brand—we've received little reader feedback on Caden Lane, so no rating yet. **Rating: Not Yet**

California Kids calkids.com. One of our favorite bedding lines, California Kids specializes in bright and upbeat looks. In recent years, they've added more girl-oriented themes as well as a line of coordinating lamps. The quality is excellent; everything is 100% cotton.

California Kids used to make all their bedding in (you guessed it) California. Today, about 5% of the total line (or six collections out of 80) are made in India. Prices run $250 to $350 for a four-piece set (the average is about $300). Most of California Kids past sets included four-pieces, but some are only a three-piece set with the sheet, quilt and bumper. It's a clever way to raise prices since they don't include that fourth piece, but charge the same price. With an amazing array of options (60+ patterns at last count), California Kids is sold in specialty stores and upper-end department stores. Available accessories include wall hangings, lampshades and fabric by the yard. Their web site has improved quite a bit with more information on accessories and options. But we'd like to see a bit more info about fabrics. *Rating: A*

Carousel/Baby Bedding Online babybedding.com. Carousel/Baby Bedding Online used to sell its line of bedding exclusively through retail stores at about $250 to $450 per set. Several years ago, however, they decided to change to an Internet-only sales model online at BabyBedding.com. Selling directly to consumers resulted in lower prices—today their sets run $175 to $388. Can't beat those prices for an all cotton bedding line (with elastic all around). And best of all, Carousel doesn't do this half way. The web site offers eight fabric swatches for $4 and other goodies.

FYI: many of the solid sheets on this website are 200 thread count and the sateens are 260. However, some of the printed patterns are less than 200 thread count (160). Their customer service is

---

Affordable Artwork

Framed artwork for baby's room has to be very expensive, right? Nope, not if you buy a framed print from **Creative Images** (www.crimages.com). This Florida-based company sells prints, growth charts, wall hangings and more at very affordable prices—just $30 to $100. Each print is mounted on wood and laminated (no glass frame) so baby can enjoy it at eye-level (just sponge it off if it gets dirty). Best of all, there are hundreds of images in any theme to choose from: Pooh, bunnies, Noah's Ark, plus other collections of animals, sports and pastels. Check out their web site for samples.

great about answering questions regarding sheet thread count, we just wish they put this information online to save time.

Looking for quality portable crib sheets or matching cradle sheets? How about rocking chair pads and high chair pads? They've got them. They will even custom design your baby bedding set for as low as $79 for the skirt, comforter and bumper set. Lastly, Baby Bedding has an online outlet store with the same great deals (up to 75% off) at their old physical outlet in Atlanta, but you don't have to live near Atlanta to get them. FYI: many of the solid sheets on this website are 200 thread count and the sateens are 260. However, some of the printed patterns are less than 200 thread count (160).

What if you want to custom design your baby's bedding? This is where Carousel really shines. The site's Nursery Designer tool allows parents to mix and match any of the patterns and colors available, using drop and drag swatches. For example, let's say you plan to get a comforter (not for use in a crib, but for play on a floor). You can pick a fabric for the front then a different fabric for the back. Or another color/pattern for the sheets. Or you might like your sheets to come in two or three different patterns. The crib skirt can also be customized. Then you'll be able to see the final nursery on line with all the different patterns and colors. When you pick your first pattern, the site will recommend some solids and patterns that go together—but you can pick anything you like. A three-piece custom set runs $240—that's a great deal for a custom look.

What do parents think about Carousel? Universally parents praise Carousel's great prices and quality. One mom noted that not only were the prices great, but even after repeated washing the crib set "still looks new!" Overall, we recommend Carousel—good designs, great quality and affordable prices. *Rating: A*

Carter's carters.kidslineinc.com. Kids Line is now producing the Carter's line of bedding (with a separate web site at carters.kidsline.com). Kids Line has given the Carter's bedding a much needed style upgrade—there are 12 complete collections (double the number compared to our last edition) as well as a baby basics mix and match line. Look for a couple new, cute patterns called Laguna and Wonder. A four-piece set is priced at $180 although we've seen significant discounts online. Sheets ($11-17 each) are 200 thread-count, 100% cotton and quite a step up from the old Carter's sheets we reviewed in the past. Jersey knit sheets for cribs, mini-cribs and bassinets are available as are velour sheets for extra warmth. Kids Line has definitely improved both the quality and design. *Rating: B*

Circo See Target

License Translator
Who makes what brand of bedding

One of the hottest trends in crib bedding is licensed characters—just about every cartoon character imaginable has been licensed to one of the big bedding makers for use in juvenile bedding. But how can tell you tell who makes what? Here is a list of popular licensed characters and their bedding makers:

LICENSE	SEE BEDDING MAKER
Baby Looney Tunes	Crown Crafts
Care Bears	Baby Boom
D.C. Super Friends	Crown Crafts
Disney Baby	Pem America
Disney Baby	Kids Line
Dr. Seuss	Trend Lab
Dora the Explorer	Baby Boom
Eddie Bauer	Crown Crafts
Fisher-Price	Crown Crafts
Hello Kitty & Friends	Lambs & Ivy
Kathy Ireland	Thank You Baby
Laura Ashley	Pem America
Maisy	Sleeping Partners
NauticaKids	Crown Crafts
Nojo	Crown Crafts
Organically Grown	Crown Crafts
Precious Moments	Baby Boom
Sesame Street	Crown Crafts
Snoopy	Lambs & Ivy
Thomas and Friends	Baby Boom
Too Good by Jenny	Pem America
Wamsutta	Spring
Winnie The Pooh	Crown Crafts
Zutano	Kids Line

Classic Pooh *See Crown Craft*

CoCaLo *cocalo.com.* CoCaLo has certainly gone through a lot of changes over the years. In May 2008, the original owners were bought out by Russ Berrie, who also own KidsLine (see review later).

Cocalo has been around for years, first as an independent brand, and more recently as part of Russ Berrie, which also owns Kids Line (see review later). They started out with their own line plus a few licensed lines, but have given up the licenses to concentrate on expanding their sub lines.

Those five lines include Cocalo Baby, Cocalo Couture, Petit Tresor, Natures Purest and CoCo & Company. Cocalo Baby is their flag-ship line available in six or eight piece sets. Sets are running from $180 to $210 although it appears the company is changing from 6-pice to 8-piece sets without bumpers, so prices may change.

Cocalo Couture and Petit Tresor are Cocalo's high end bedding sets. Cocalo Couture runs $225 to $350 with more tailored designs and sophisticated color pallets. Petit Tresor is designed by Nina Takesh and Samantha Winch, who have a boutique called Petit Tresor in Beverly Hills. Both have worked for European fashion houses in the past and bring a European flair to their embroidered designs. Price: $230 for a four-piece set (which unfortunately includes bumpers).

On the other end of the spectrum in CoCo & Company, an affordable all-cotton line featuring simple yet charming graphical treatments of animals, flowers, sports or airplanes for under $100 for four pieces. Finally, Cocalo makes Natures Purest, which is made of 100% natural color cotton and bamboo that is organically grown. They offer two 4-piece bedding sets (sheet blanket, diaper stacker and bed skirt) for about $160.

Cocalo's biggest news this year is with bumpers. They are no longer including them in most of their sets, but are continuing to sell them separately (we don't recommend bumpers).

Overall, CoCaLo is a good value, with decent quality for the price and many options that are bumper free—or you can use their matching mesh bumpers. ***Rating: B+***

Company Kids companykids.com. A subsidiary of the Company Store, Company Kids offers a selection of sheets, blankets and quilts plus a crib comforter cover in a variety of patterns and solids. Everything is priced a la carte. Sheets (200-thread count cotton) run $14 each while comforters are $60 to $70 each. You have a choice of either down comforters or down free. Not a bad deal at all for 100% cotton percale fabrics.

While the prices are decent, we've received complaints about Company Kids' poor customer service and quality. Backordered items are a common gripe. Another reader was frustrated when her sheets ripped after several washings while another complained that the sheet shrunk after washing. Overall, quality reviews were mixed—some fans say the brand is good, comparable to Pottery Barn Kids. Others are less generous.

Given the mixed reviews, we'll tick down the Company Kids rating this time out. While the web site is easy to navigate and the prices are decent, quality and customer woes drag down this brand. ***Rating: B-***

Cotton Tale cottontaledesigns.com. Cotton Tale has been one of our favorite bedding lines for a long time and for good reasons: originality and quality. There are no licensed cartoon characters or trendy fabrics like chenille here. Instead, you'll see beautiful soft pastels, whimsical animal prints and adorable appliqués. Best of all, Cotton Tale's prices are affordable—most range from $150 to $300 for a four-piece set. We'd love to see Cotton Tale make sets available without bumpers, however. Most of the fabrics are 100% cotton, although some trim may be a blend.

Cotton Tale's sub-line N. Selby Designs kicks up the sophistication a notch with more luxurious looks. You'll find bold colors as well as fun accents like tiers of ruffles and lots of polka dots. A four-piece set of N. Selby Designs sells for $250 to $320.

New this year, most of the collections are now made in the U.S. (except those with embroidery or heavy appliqués): the fabric is printed in Mississippi and the items are sewn in California.

Our only beef with the company is that their sheets only have elastic at the ends, not all the way around. That's disappointing. But all in all, we'll give Cotton Tale a big thumbs up for the innovative designs and beautiful patterns. ***Rating: A-***

CozyWedge cozywedge.com. As we've discussed earlier in this chapter, traditional crib bumpers are not recommended. But if you've got an active baby who keeps bonking his head against the crib, is there a safe solution? The CozyWedge is an option: this bumper is made from very firm foam with a removable, washable cotton slipcover. Unlike other bumpers that are soft and pose a suffocation risk if baby gets trapped up against or below the bumper, the CozyWedge is hard foam . . . sort of like a swimming noodle. And it's only a few inches tall, so babies can't use it to boost themselves out of the crib once they start standing. The CozyWedge provides protection for babies without the concerns of traditional crib bumpers. The price is $60 (about the same as a regular bumper) and the organic cotton cover comes in eight solid colors. Bottom line: you don't need to rush out and get this product—but it is a potential solution if you have a little head banger in the house. ***Rating: A***

CribShield & Breathable Bumper *Made by Trend-Lab.* breathablebaby.com. Here's a mom-invented product that is a simple solution for babies who get their arms or legs caught in the crib spindles: a "breathable" bumper made of mesh that Velcros on to the crib. Unlike other traditional bumpers, this one allows for airflow and baby can't get trapped between it and the mattress. And it's affordable: $32 to $40 ($25 for port-a-cribs and cradles) and available in stores or online (Walmart.com carries it). The company makes two versions of the product: the Breathable Bumper (one style for beds with slats all around and one for cribs with solid ends) and the CribShield. The latter covers the entire crib from bottom rail to top rail, while the bumper is just 11" deep. New this year are "fashion trim bumpers" with contrasting polka dot trim as well as six new versions where the mesh is printed with stripes, animals, flowers, and a sports theme.

Detractors of these products say they don't fit all cribs (given the wide variety of models out there, that isn't a big surprise) and older babies can rip them off the crib. The web site addresses the fit problem with a Crib Fit Guide. And the manufacturer recommends using these products only until your baby reaches nine months of age. Bottom line: we think this a good solution if you have a baby who keeps getting stuck. Like the CozyWedge (reviewed elsewhere on the site), there's no need to get this product before baby is born. Only a small percentage of babies will get their arms or legs caught in a crib's spindles. But if that is you, this might be a solution. This is one of the few options for bumpers we recommend. **Rating: A**

Crown Crafts www.ccipinc.com or www.nojo.com. Baby bedding behemoth Crown Crafts used to hold the license on just about every cartoon character you could think of. Today, however, they've paired it down to a more manageable group of eight: Disney Baby (and Toddler), Fisher-Price, Nautica Kids, Eddie Bauer, Sesame Street, and Baby Looney Tunes. They also have an organic cotton line called Organically Grown. These are all very basic sets, many made of cotton/poly blends at prices as low as $70 (some are better quality and cost up to $300) and sold in chains like Walmart and Babies R Us.

But the flagship of the Crown Craft's baby bedding lines is NoJo. Each year they release a dozen or more designs made of 100% cotton in sets of four or six (four-piece sets now include the comforter, sheet, dust ruffle and blanket—no bumpers). Prices are reasonable, in the range of $150 to $200. The designs are definitely very babyish with lots of cotton candy pink and baby blue. Appliqué is okay and designs are heavy on cute bugs, flowers and jungle animals. NoJo also has a few sub lines like Little Bedding by NoJo (priced around $100), Naturally for Baby by Nojo and Kimberly Grant (reviewed separately later in this section).

New for 2012, NoJo is offering a Crib Safety Liner—essentially a mesh bumper with coordinating fabric binding. These new mesh bumpers address the issue of fluffy bedding in the crib. It's great that they now offer this option and sell their sets without bumpers of any kind.

Overall quality with Crown Crafts is basically that you get what you pay for. Higher end items have better appliqué and stitching while low end sets won't wash and wear as well. Bottom line: stick with the better quality sets (Nojo, Eddie Bauer) and avoid the cheap-o character-theme sets (Disney Baby). **Rating: C+**

Disney *See Kids Line.*

Dwell *dwellshop.com.* When modern style cribs first emerged as a new style aesthetic, there weren't many bedding options that matched the look. Dwell Studio aimed to fill that niche, albeit at a rather high price.

Made of 210 to 320-thread count and 100% cotton, Dwell offers a simple, yet sophisticated look. Example: Gio Aqua is a stylized

Tips on green bedding

Like many organic products today, there is no standard for organic baby bedding. This leaves it up to bedding manufacturers to determine for themselves what's organic. So, let's review some terms you'll see.

Organic cotton simply means cotton that's been grown with a minimum amount of toxic pesticides or fertilizers. That's right, there is no guarantee that organic cotton is completely pesticide- and fertilizer- free. But it is as close as you can get!

So, you want to go for organic cotton sheets—but what about the sheet's color? Since conventional sheets are dyed with synthetic chemicals, can an organic sheet be colored anything than the natural shade of cotton (that is, an off-white)?

Turns out, the answer is yes. Organic cotton can be grown in a few colors. Yes, that's right, just like you can buy naturally orange or purple cauliflower, you can buy colored cotton. Three colors are available: pink, light brown and green. Nature's Purest by Summer Infant Products is one bedding option that uses grown-in colors (SummerInfant.com, click on Organic; a four-piece set is $230).

Another solution: vegetable dyes. Kids Line (Kidsline.com; $160 for six-piece set) and Gap Baby (GapBaby.com; $19 for an organic crib sheet) sell baby bedding made of low-impact vegetable dyed cotton.

William Morris animal print in aqua, blue and brown hues. The price: $360 (we saw it for $300 online) for a set that includes a fitted sheet, padded bumper, crib skirt and blanket (items are also available a la carte). Dwell even makes several designs of oval bedding to fit the Stokke crib. We should note that the prices on Dwell's web site are significantly higher than you can find from other online resellers.

Parent reviews have been positive on this brand—readers laud the softness and fit. One summed it up as "expensive, but worth it."

What about Dwell Studio for Target bedding? It features 100% cotton, 200-thread count sheets and is priced at $80 for a three-piece set. That's the same look at a fraction of the regular Dwell price. The sheets were surprisingly soft with all around elastic. Parent feedback has been positive. ***Rating: B+ (for both lines)***

Eddie Bauer. *See Crown Craft*

Fleece Baby So, you live in a part of the country where winter is colder than (fill in your own punch line here)? Given all the warnings about soft bedding and heavy quilts, how do you keep baby warm during those cold winter months? One solution is fleece baby sheets. Fleece Baby makes a wide variety of crib sheets, blankets, play yard sheets and more . . . all made of 100% polar fleece. Crib sheets run $28 and are sold online at BabyCenter.com and various other sites. And the best part: their extra fabric around the ends keep sheets on the mattress better than regular sheets. We had a reader road test the play yard version of the Fleece Baby sheet ($20) and she gave it two thumbs up. The only concern: after washing, the sheet lost a bit of its softness, but still overall it was a winner. One tip: use unscented dryer sheets on this bedding to retain softness. As we went to press, we noticed Fleece Baby's web site is no longer active—however, the sheets are still sold on Amazon and Diapers.com ***Rating: A***

Garnet Hill *garnethill.com*. Garnet Hill sells a small selection of all-cotton percale and flannel crib bedding. In addition a few themed sets, the company sells basics like the Dot-To-Dot sheets in flannel ($15) and percale ($18). Quality is high: all sheets are 200-thread count with elastic all around. ***Rating: B***

Gerber *gerber.com*. While Gerber offers some cute patterns in their bedding line and they're available almost everywhere, the bedding's quality leaves much to be desired. One reader emailed us this typical story: "I bought several of the Gerber Everyday Basics knit sheets. They fit my 5" thick Sealy mattress well when I bought them, they were super soft, and had elastic all the way around for safety. But then . . . I washed them on the delicate cycle in cold water and dried on low/delicate as instructed in the package. They shrunk so much I couldn't even get them on the mattress anymore!." We can't recommend this brand. *Rating: D*

Glenna Jean *glennajean.com*. Glenna Jean has notched over 30 years in the bedding biz by adapting to the times—their current line features bold patterns and bright color palettes.

Overall, Glenna Jean sets (either four or six pieces) start at $225 and go up to $700. The average price is between $300 and $385. Most of the designs are made in the US of 100% cotton with the exception of some of the trim. Higher priced sets include luxury fabrics like taffeta, velvet and moiré.

Glenna Jean also sells a lower priced line called Sweet Potato, which starts at $200. Designs for this line have a more mod look. Yes, this departs a bit from Glenna Jean's traditional look, but we liked the geometric designs and brighter colors—and the prices are certainly more reasonable than other mod bedding brands.

FYI: Glenna Jean is one of the few bedding manufacturers who makes nearly all its bedding in the US. *Rating: B+*

Graham Kracker *grahamkracker.com*. This e-commerce company specializes in custom bedding. You can mix and match your own selections from nearly 100 different fabrics or you can provide your own fabric. The price? A whopping $595 for a five-piece set which includes sheet, skirt, comforter, bumper and baby pillow (don't use these last two items in the crib, please!). Everything is 100% cotton and there are all sorts of matching accessories. Most of the fabrics are bright, cheerful designs, but not too cutesy. Swatches are available for $10 and shipping time is two to three weeks. *Rating: B*

Green Collection *See Kids Line.*

Holly Hobby *See Crown Craft.*

Hoohobbers *hoohobbers.com*. Hoohobbers has over 40 crib bedding designs; their style aesthetic tends toward interesting color combinations in both bright jewel tones and pastels. Prices for all their four-piece collections are $390; that's expensive, but everything is 100% cotton and well constructed (the sheets feature all-around elastic, for example). You can see and purchase any of their patterns on their web site. All bedding is made at Hoohobbers' Chicago factory (they have a factory outlet store in Chicago too). FYI: Hoohobbers' bassinets and Moses baskets come in coordinating fabrics as well. In fact, the company makes a wide range of accessories including furniture, bouncer seat covers and more. *Rating: B+*

Jessica McClintock *PacificCoastHomeFurnishings.com* Remember those lacy Jessica McClintock homecoming and prom dresses? Or her old-fashioned wedding gowns? We do (maybe we're showing our age), so it's not surprising that Jessica McClintock is bringing that lacy, Victorian look to crib bedding. Made by Pacific Coast Home Furnishings (which licensed the name), the designs are mostly 100% cotton with satin, silk, plush and even hand painted accents. Good news: even with the fancy fabrics and lace, the whole line is machine-washable. Prices range from $300 to $400 for a five-piece set (each set has both a blanket and a quilt/wall hanging). ***Rating: B-***

JoJo Designs *jojodesigns.com.* JoJo Designs offers a rather amazing bedding deal: a nine-piece bedding set for only $110 to $250. What does that include? You get a comforter, bumper, sheet, skirt, two valances, diaper stacker, toy bag and throw pillow (never use this or bumpers in your crib!). Sets include 100% cotton sheets and come in all the popular themes plus some new modern styles this year. Some sets do include fabric touches like microsuede. JoJo is available in a few specialty stores but we've mostly seen it online on quite a few websites like Amazon.com and BeyondBedding.com as well as their own site. Extra crib sheets and other accessories are available a la carte. Overall, there are about 100 design choices.

But how's the quality? Well, you're not getting top of the line fabric and designs here, but readers tell us the sets hold up well in the wash; they don't fade or fall apart. For a low price line, the quality here beats Gerber or Crown Craft's low price line. ***Rating: B***

Katie Little *See Kids Line.*

Kids Line *kidslineinc.com.* Kids Line has been on a roll in recent years, designing sets with luxury touches while keeping prices affordable ($100 to $200 for a six-piece set). New in the past year they've added organic cotton sets that use eco-friendly vegetable dyes. Check out Bunny Meadow, for example, with a mod brown and green motif including a cute green bunny silhouette. The 100% cotton set is $145 for a six-piece set. Other sub lines include Disney Baby and Mod Pod.

Kids Line has expanded their accessories line to include bath coordinates as well as blankets, wall hangings, lamps and more. And that seems to have resonated with our readers: parents tell us they love all the accessory options with Kids Line's patterns. How's the quality? Well, reviews are mixed. Some items are cotton-poly blends and parents have reported that shrinkage is sometimes a problem. On the plus side, colors hold up well in the wash and their sheets have elastic all around.

FYI: Kids Line also makes the Tiddliwinks line of bedding available mostly at Target. This lower-end line runs $70 to $90 for a four-piece set. While it has 100% cotton sheets with all around elastic, we found the overall quality of Tiddliwinks to be disappointing. And we suspect these sheets will shrink, since the washing instructions are cold-water only. Our advice: avoid Tiddliwinks.

Kids Line also makes the Carter's line (see review earlier) and in 2011, they are introducing Zutano bedding as well as a "hotel collection" similar to Restoration Hardware's look. We weren't able to view these two lines at press time.

Overall it is a mixed review for Kids Line—nice designs and great accessories . . . but a bit iffy on the quality (especially Tiddliwinks, the Target-exclusive). The Carter's separates are a better bet, quality wise. ***Rating: B***

Kimberly Grant kimberlygrant.com. If you're looking for bedding designs that are a bit lower key and not too cutesy, Kimberly Grant is a great option. Now produced by Crown Crafts (see review earlier in section), Grant has moved away from the adult looks to a more cartoony style. Prices run $150 to $400 for a four-piece set. Overall, we like the quality. ***Rating: A-***

Koala Baby Available exclusively at Babies R Us. Koala Baby is Babies R Us' attempt at establishing an in-house brand of bedding (Koala Baby is actually made by Crown Craft). The line is sold a la carte: blankets are $18 to $25, a two pack of sheets range from $10 to $18. That's affordable. So what's the downside? Quality, for one. As one reader put it, "This brand is TERRIBLE! I washed the fitted sheet before putting it on my crib mattress and it shrunk about 6" in length! I wouldn't recommend these sheets to anyone." The good news: BRU apparently listened to the complaints. Feedback is more positive now with compliments on the deep corner pockets and softness of these sheets. So we'll raise their rating a bit. ***Rating: C+***

Lambs & Ivy lambsivy.com. Barbara Lainken and Cathy Ravdin founded this LA-based bedding company in 1979. Their specialty: cutesy baby bedding that is sold in discount and mass market stores (you'll also see them sold on JCPenney's web site and on many others). This year they've added some whimsical looks along with vintage prints and licensed characters including Snoopy and Hello Kitty. Quality of the Snoopy line is actually good—instead of using stamp printing, Lambs & Ivy uses photo-quality heat transfer technology.

This is a clever way of achieving a nicer look without big cost (you have to see the bedding in person to note the difference). Prices are still reasonable at $150 to $285 for a six-piece set. One cool side note: quilts have a sewn on rod pocket so you can use it as decoration. Bedtime Originals, a sub-line of Lambs & Ivy, is lower in price (around $60 to $85 for a three piece set) and quality. We'd rank the overall quality of Lambs & Ivy a bit ahead of other mass-market bedding brands. Yes, some of the fabrics are blends (50-50 cotton/poly), but the stitching and construction is a cut above. *Rating: B+*

Land of Nod *landofnod.com.* This stunning site (owned by Crate & Barrel) features attractive layouts of baby's and kid's rooms, replete with cute linens and accessories. Even if you don't buy anything, the Land of Nod is a great place to get decorating ideas.

Land of Nod's in-house bedding is sold a la carte as well as in sets. Some designs only have a quilt, sheet and bumpers available. The fabric is 100% cotton, 200-thread count with quite a few available in organic cotton. The Natural Born Organic Crib Set is an affordable $159 for three pieces. A three-piece set runs $160 to $220, while a single sheet can cost $24. Yes, bumpers are available (we don't recommend them). What bugs us a bit is that the different designs are most obvious on the bumpers. So that means you have to buy a bumper to get the feel of the collection. Check out the featured design to see what we mean.

Overall, we loved the color palettes, which ranged from patchwork denim to bright pastels. Check out the whimsical lamps and other accessories. *Rating: B*

Laura Ashley *See Pem America.*

Little Bedding *See Crown Crafts.*

Living Textiles *livingtextiles.com.* Australian bedding manufacturer Living Textiles has made a big splash in the US market with their affordable four and five piece, all cotton bedding sets. A neat option: all their quilts can be beefed up with an optional duvet ($31, inserted in the quilt cover) so you can use in them colder climates— of course, never use a quilt in a crib with a baby under one year of age. Until then, you could use the quilt as a play mat.

Accents on Living Textiles' sets include faux suede, velour, and dimensional appliqués. Prices run $190 for five-piece sets including wall decals. Accessories abound and include valances, mobiles, lamps and decals. Additional sheets range from $20 to $30 each. Living Textiles baby bedding is available online at Amazon and Babies R Us, but the brand is so new, we've had little reader feedback. One mom told us her Living Textiles set washed well, so that's a good sign. We'll wait for more feedback before assigning a rating. ***Rating: Not Yet.***

Luv Stuff *Luvstuffbaby.com* Texas-based Luv Stuff's claim to fame is their unique, hand-trimmed wall hangings, which match their custom bedding. You can mix and match to your heart's content (all items are sold a la carte). The quality is high: the company's exclusive fabrics are mostly 100% cotton with high-thread count, plus all their collections are made in-house in Texas and they have ties both top and bottom and elastic around the whole sheet. As you might expect, however, all this quality isn't free—a four-piece ensemble (sheet, comforter, bumper, dust ruffle) runs $550 to $750. And Luv Stuff's bumpers aren't very consumer friendly—they are surface clean (with a mild detergent) or dry-clean only. Despite this, we liked the brand's unique and bold styles. This bedding is a tour de force of color and contrast. ***Rating: B***

Maddie Boo *maddieboobedding.com.* You can just imagine seeing Maddie Boo baby bedding in an Architectural Digest spread. And we will give this line bonus points for sophistication—some of their designs would look great on adult beds! Of course, you'll be paying Architectural Digest prices. Four-piece sets run $400 to $600.

Made in Houston, Texas, the sets are 100% cotton with high thread counts, and the accent fabrics include silk and linen. Sheets have all around elastic.

Surprisingly, Maddie Boo bedding can be found on sites like Amazon as well as in specialty stores. That doesn't mean you'll be able to find it at a discount, however, but the wide distribution is impressive. Occasional sales on their web site are worth checking out. Quality of the samples we viewed was high; but the prices drag down their overall rating. ***Rating: B***

Mod Pod *See Kids Line.*

My Baby Sam *mybabysam.com.* This bedding line is an off-shoot of a baby gift dot-com (NewArrivalsInc.com) and is widely avail able, both in specialty stores and online at sites like Target.com, BabiesRUs.com and JCPenney. Four-piece sets start at $160 with most costing around $190, a decent value for an all-cotton set. But…we noticed the set is cold-water wash only, which is not a good sign when it comes to shrinkage. Quality is good—readers praise the soft fabrics and overall construction. ***Rating: B+***

NauticaKids *See Crown Craft*

Nava's Designs *navasdesigns.com.* So, Warren Buffet is your uncle...and he wants to give you a gift of baby bedding. Who you gonna call? Try Nava's, the most over-the-top bedding on the market today. The fabrics in this line are simply amazing—damask, silk dupioni, matte lasse and so on. Owner Nava Shoham has been designing nurseries since 1986 and her credits include numerous celebrities such as (and we are not making this up) Slash's nursery. Yes, that Slash. Fill in your own joke here. So, how much does this cost? Are you sitting down? Nava's bedding runs $980 to $1780 for a three-piece set. And, yes, some of the fabrics have to be dry-cleaned. But seriously, we dare you to find more sumptuous bedding on the market. We're impressed with Nava...making it over 20 years in this biz by selling these linens at these prices, well, that's an achievement in its own right. New this year: Nava is selling direct through her own online store. **Rating: B**

NoJo *See Crown Craft.*

N. Selby Designs *See Cotton Tale.*

Pem America *See Too Good By Jenny.*

Picci *Imported by Mutsy. picci.com.* Picci is a high-end bedding line imported from Italy. Here's an oddity of the baby market here: many European-made products are a big hit in the U.S. (Baby Bjorn, Perego strollers), but bedding is not among them. Why? Part of the blame is that what sells well in Europe for nurseries (garish colors, frilly treatments like canopies) just doesn't translate well across the Atlantic. To solve that dilemma, Picci researched American design sensibilities and went with a more toned down look. The result is impressive. In a market stuffed with cheaply made imports from Asia, Picci actually pulls off a tasteful line with a high-end feel made from Italian and Spanish fabrics. The only caveat is the prices: $329 to $489 for a set. Expensive, but we give Picci bonus points for creativity and quality. **Rating: B+**

Pine Creek Bedding/Over the Moon *pinecreekbedding.com.* Pine Creek Bedding has long been a favorite for their warm and fuzzy flannel crib sets. But that's not all they make. They have two options for parents: a custom made bedding set or their Over the Moon "pre-designed" options. Over the Moon offers 23 bedding sets. Styles run the gamut from (literally) plain Vanilla to toile offerings, strips and floral prints. Prices range from $300 to $550 for a four-piece set.

If you're interested in a custom bedding option, Pine Creek Bedding offer an easy, yet pricey way to design your own look.

Choose your fabric, mix and match for different pieces and so on. Prices for these custom options range from about $300 to $500 for a comforter, $200 to $278 for a bumper, $100 to $200 for a dust ruffle, and $48 to $66 for sheets depending on the chosen fabric. Hence, a custom four-piece set can top $1000.

Overall, we liked Pine Creek—their "pre-designed" sets feature excellent quality. ***Rating: A-***

Pooh *Classic Pooh/Disney Pooh bedding are made by Crown Craft.*

Pottery Barn Kids *potterybarnkids.com.* No web site has shaken up the baby bedding and décor business in recent years like Pottery Barn Kids (PBK). Their cheerful baby bedding, whimsical accessories and furniture blew past competitors. PBK isn't cutesy-babyish or overly adult. It's playful, fun and bright.

PBK's bedding is 100% cotton, 200-thread count. The sheets have 10" corner pockets . . . and they used to have elastic that went all the way around the edge. We're disappointed to say that they now only make their crib sheets with elastic on the ends. And that elastic is the source of frustration among some parents we talked to—one PBK customer said she had to exchange several sheets after the elastic popped off or simply wore out after only one washing. By the way, PBK's spin on why they don't have elastic all the way around is that it is "for safety purposes." We disagree—we prefer sheets with all around elastic.

On the plus side, recent parent feedback has consistently praised the softness of PBK sheets. Their "chamois" sheets ($29; polyester fleece) have also come in for great praise. Readers say PBK's fleece sheets stay softer than fleece sheet brands.

PBK has added several new sets to its organic line of baby bedding and they are touting their Oeko-Tex certified organic cotton (for more information: oeko-tex.com). Two of their organic sets are licensed products: Curious George and Dr. Seuss. Prices for sheets range from $16 to $19 PBK also sells Peter Rabbit and the Very Hungary Caterpillar licensed sets.

Prices for quilts range from $90 to $135 and sheets are $14 to $30. While the prices are generally affordable, the nagging quality issues give us pause in recommending PBK's crib bedding. On the plus side, frequent sales make more expensive items like lamps and rugs even more affordable. The best deal: PBK's outlet stores. One reader saw sheets on sale for $8, duvet covers for $15 and even a crib for $175 at the outlet (see earlier in the chapter for locations). What really seems to be PBK's strong suit is accessories. The site is stuffed with so many rugs, lamps, storage options and toys, you can shop one place for a complete look.

New this year: Pottery Barn kids has taken a page from Pine Creek and Carousel with their new "Design the Perfect Crib" option. You select a crib color, then a fitted sheet, bumper, quilt and bed skirt. Then Pottery Barn adds it all up for you and lets you buy your choices together with one button. You can even choose a wall paint color. Of course, it's not as custom as Pine Creek or Carousel, but it is a nice way to look at different pieces and how they work together. And no, there is no discount when you purchase a "set" this way.

Bottom line: it is a mixed bag for PBK: readers love the chamois sheets, but unless you're buying at outlet prices, forego the bedding sets. ***Rating: C+***

Precious Moments *See Crown Craft.*

Restoration Hardware *rhbabyandchild.com.* Six hundred thread count. That's right, Restoration Hardware sells crib sheets that are 600 thread count. We're not sure many adults sleep on 600 thread count sheets! And will your baby really know the difference between regular 200 thread count and 600? We don't think so.

Pardon the rant—back to our review of Restoration Hardware. As it turns out, not all RH's cribs sheets are 600 thread count. Some have a mere 210 thread count. All sheets feature all-around elastic and finishes include linen, matelasse, jersey knit, voile and sateen. Three-piece sets run $200 to $300. Individual sheets are around $60 each. The site also offers a variety of accessory pieces.

So how's the quality? Pretty good. But. . .(you knew there had to be a but), RH's customer service leaves a lot to be desired. Readers have reported long back orders, accessories that arrive broken, no fabric swatches and frustrating returns.

So while we like the style and quality of RH baby bedding, we'll be dropping the rating this time around for the service snafus. ***Rating: B-***

Serena & Lily *serenaandlily.com.* Serena & Lily's web site is such a pleasure to visit. Calm not cluttered, sweet but not too babyish. The bedding sets have a clean, light, unfussy style. Unfortunately, the prices are in the stratosphere.

Good news! Serena & Lily has dropped the price of some of their sets down to $325 from $395. Don't see that too often in the high end bedding lines. The sets include one sheet, bumper and skirt. Fabrics are 100% cotton 300-count sateen for most collections. The collections are usually very striking graphic prints with uniquely designed bed skirts. Colors are mostly understated pastels with a few exceptions like the Rye collection's eye-popping teal.

Come into some Lottery cash? Serena & Lily's got you covered—the company has a couple of intricately embroidered crib bedding sets for $1000.

Other accessories are available including quilts, pillows (as you know, never in a crib), even an organic crib mattress ($460). Swatch cards area available for $6 and if you'd like to re-create the entire room pictured on their web site, they offer the glider rocker, rug, lamp, and furniture. They even sell the paint colors. It's a one stop shopping experience.

Serena & Lily also offer custom crib bedding and what they call their Nursery Basics. Nursery Basics skirts run $68 and sheets are $36 each or three for $99. These simple white pieces have a choice of three color accents (blue, pink, green). You can coordinate with plain white sheets or choose from several complimentary patterned sheets for each color option. Quality is excellent.

Bottom line: Serena & Lily's Nursery Basics line is a good choice if you want a simple, clean look for your nursery. ***Rating: B+***

Sesame Street *See Crown Craft*

Skip Hop *See Bananafish*

Sleeping Partners *sleepingpartners.com or tadpolesbedding.com.* Sleeping Partners' mojo is embroidered and appliquéd bedding sets. This year, they've lowered prices and added an organic line.

Tadpoles is Sleeping Partners flagship line. We noticed a simple four or five-piece set ranges from $90 to $200 online (Sleeping Partners is sold on sites like BabyUniverse.com and in some stores like Buy Buy Baby). Tadpole Organics sets are made of organic cotton in brown, sage and pink. It's affordable too: only $180 for a four-piece set. All sheets are 100% cotton with elastic all around.

The Tadpole Basics line available at Target, comes in mostly solid colors and ginghams as an a la carte option. Coverlets are $30 and sheets are two for $30. Again, this line is all cotton, 200 thread count.

New this year, Sleeping Partners has a line called Seed Sprout sold exclusively at Walmart. Priced at a mere $80 for a four piece set, the 100% cotton line has a few simple designs available online.

Overall, Sleeping Partners' bedding sets wash well. Another plus: we spied a 15% coupon on their web site. ***Rating: B***

Sumersault *sumersault.com.* Veteran bedding designer Patti Sumergrade has an eye for beautiful fabrics—the results are Sumersault's whimsical bedding collection. We loved the plaids and patchwork, all done with a sophisticated spin. Compared to other lines, Sumersault leaves most of the cutesy touches to optional wall hangings. A four-piece set retails for $110 to $300. Sumersault is now making sets to rival JoJo Designs with ten pieces for as little as $100 on Target and other sites. The feedback on these jumbo sets has been positive for the most part. Overall, the quality of Sumersault is excellent. **Rating: A**

Summer *summerinfant.com*. We've talked about a few of Summer's bedding products earlier in the chapter including the Ultimate Crib Sheet and their organic bedding line. But wait, there's more!

One of Summer's more interesting bedding items is the BreatheEasy Baby Bumper System and EZ Change Sheet ($41). This "system" Is a one-piece design that incorporates mesh bumpers with the sheet so there are no gaps between them. The idea is to keep babies from getting arms and legs caught in the slats or scooting under the bumpers. Plus, it's lightly padded to avoid bumps and bruises if your baby is really active. While we don't recommend bumpers, this would be an acceptable alternative if your little one keeps getting a leg stuck in his crib slats.

Summer also offers a line of bedding basics including porta crib, play yard and bassinet sizes in 100% cotton. A few regular, non-organic bedding sets are also available in four and six piece sets. A four-piece set runs $65 to $100. That's very affordable, but unfortunately some pieces are 55% cotton, 45% polyester—we wouldn't recommend a blend for crib sheets. Rating: A for the Ultimate Crib Sheet, B-for the rest of the bedding line. **Rating: A for the Ultimate Crib Sheet, B- for the rest of the bedding line.**

Sweet Kyla *sweetkyla.com*. Canadian bedding maker Sweet Kyla has popped up stateside in USA Baby Stores among other outlets. We liked their take on crib bedding, which often uses mixed textures (a touch of faux suede, for example) and patchwork motifs. Most fabrics are all-cotton and customer service and delivery is excellent. Readers who have purchased this line have been impressed with the quality (all cotton sheet with elastic all around). One caveat: all items must be washed in cold water on delicate settings. Only the sheets can be dried in the dryer. Sets are around $240 to $330 or you can order pieces a la carte. Sets are also available without bumpers for about $200—hurray! Fabric is available by the yard. One parent who bought this brand for her son's nursery raved about their excellent fabric, saying the sheets in particular were "very soft and cozy." Sweet Kyla also offers organic bedding called Wee Organics. Made of 100% cotton knit, this bedding uses low impact dies or you can purchase a set in natural colored fabric. Prices for a three-piece bumperless set are $200. **Rating: A**

Tadpole *See Sleeping Partners.*

Target *target.com.* Target not only sells bedding lines like Dwell Studio for Target (see more in the Dwell review), Tadpole (by Sleeping Partners) and Tiddliwinks (by Kids Line), they even have their own in-house line of basics called Circo. Quality is so-so; Circo gets mixed reviews from our readers. Folks love the prices— $60 for a three-piece set—and the cute prints. Yes, it is all-cotton and the sheets feature elastic all around, but many readers complain of shrinkage and low thread counts. Our advice: buy a sheet or two to test before investing much in this brand. **Rating: C**

Tiddliwinks *See Kids Line.*

Too Good by Jenny *toogoodbyjenny.com.* Playboy model and actress Jenny McCarthy launched her own bedding line in 2010, dubbed Too Good by Jenny. The pitch: "affordable, non-toxic juvenile products (for) mainstream consumers with the highest regard for safety, health and enjoyment."

Oy vey. Where to begin?

McCarthy's emphasis on "non-toxic" bedding raises the obvious question: what baby bedding is toxic? The answer is, of course, none. But who are we to get in the way of a feel-good eco pitch when there are parents to scare and bedding to sell.

Too Good By Jenny is actually made by Pem America, which is better known for its older kids and teen twin bedding. There's nothing wrong with the bedding itself: sets feature 100% cotton, 200-thread fabrics and run about $119 to $200 for a five-piece set. One clever element: the bumpers and quilt are reversible for a different look. Of course, you aren't supposed to user bumpers or a quilt in a crib, but we digress.

Our beef with this brand isn't with the bedding, but Jenny McCarthy herself. In addition to being an actress and book author, McCarthy has been an outspoken autism advocate after her son was diagnosed in 2005. McCarthy blames vaccines for her son's autism and has allied herself with anti-vaccine advocates that include disgraced researcher Andrew Wakefield.

According to the British Medical Journal, Wakefield engaged in an "elaborate hoax" to tie the MMR vaccine with autism. Despite being exposed for fraud and faked research, McCarthy still defended Wakefield despite the damage this scare is dong to public health and the health of children. That is reprehensible.

So we can't divorce McCarthy from her controversial stands on children's heath—while she's entitled to her opinion, we can't recommend our readers buy anything with her name on it. **Rating: F**

Trend Lab Baby *trend-lab.com.* Trend Lab may sound more like a chemical beaker maker than a bedding designer, but this brand is a hit in the under-$150 crib bedding market. Sold on Target.com and other discounters, Trend Lab offered (mostly) 100% cotton bedding in the $50 to $150 range for a four-piece set. In the past year, however prices have started to creep closer to $200. Now they're attempting to compete with JoJo Designs by offering 12 to 14 piece sets from $225 to $325.

So what does Trend-Lab offer? You'll see design elements like textured fabric (waffle weave and knit jersey, for example) as well as attractive embroidery and appliqué. And parents love their sheets. As one parent noted on our web site: "the crib sheets from Trend Lab are big enough to fit the mattress perfectly . . . and the quality is high." The downside: some items may shrink (note the cold-water washing instructions) and a few items are poly/cotton blends. But for the price, parents tell us Trend Lab is still a decent value.

As we went to press, Trend Lab announced that it has acquired the license for Nickelodeon—yep, that means they'll soon be making SpongeBob, Blue and Dora the Explorer bedding for infants and toddlers. ***Rating: B-***

Wamsutta *See Crown Crafts.*

Waverly *See Crown Crafts.*

Whistle & Wink *whistleandwink.com.* One of your lovely authors' (Denise's, actually) mothers, Helen, is a big fan of needlework. From childhood, Denise has been leafing through needlecraft books and magazines. So when she opened the Whistle & Wink catalog (a new designer that debuted in 2007), her first thought was how the embroidery reminded her of those old patterns from childhood. Truly, the look of many of W & W's designs are vintage motifs you might have seen in the mid-20th century. Beyond embroidery, the line also showcases toile fabrics and fun accents like rick rack, tassels and more. The cost for this 100% cotton, 240 count bedding is $400 for a three-piece set (bumper, sheet and bed skirt). That's definitely pretty expensive. Reader feedback on this line has been limited, but what we've heard so far is positive. ***Rating: B+***

Wonder Bumpers *gomamagodesigns.com.* Go Mama Go Designs' Wonder Bumpers are an alternative to traditional crib bumpers—essentially, they are fabric-covered soft tubes that zip around each individual crib slat. As a result, you get the same protection of a bumper without the risk of suffocation or a child using them to climb out of a crib. Sets come in either 24 or 38 count—the site estimates that most cribs have 30 to 60 rails so you'll need either one set of 38 or two sets of 24. Extras are available from their web site in two count packages. And they fit on any type of side slat: flat or round. Two can be zipped together for larger rails over 2.5″ wide. Packs of two bumpers run $13; a pack of 24 is $100 and 38 bumpers are $160. Those prices are for the basic colors—they also sell several fancier designs that can top $200. And the site also sells complete bedding sets (sheet, dust ruffle, bumpers) for $240 to $500. Reader feedback on this has been positive—most folks love this alternative to bumpers, which don't have to be removed when the sheets are changed. Pricey, yes, but a worthwhile investment if your little one likes to bang his head against the crib slats. ***Rating: A***

Zutano See Kids Line.

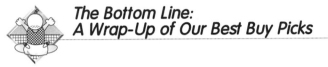

The Bottom Line: A Wrap-Up of Our Best Buy Picks

For bedding, we think California Kids, Carousel, Cotton Tale, Sumersault and Sweet Kyla are your best bets. And if money is no object, try Nava's.

Of course, there's no law that says you have to buy an entire bedding set for your nursery—we found that all baby really needs is a set of sheets and a good cotton blanket. Web sites like BabyBeddingOnline.com sell affordable (yet high-quality) sheets for about $20. Crib blankets at LandsEnd.com are $20 to $25. Instead of spending $300 to $500 on bedding sets with uneeded items like bumpers and quilts, use creative solutions (like wall decals) to decorate the nursery affordably and leave the crib simple.

The take-home message: decorate your baby's room, not the crib.

If you fall in love with a licensed cartoon character like Pooh, don't shell out $300 on a fancy bedding set. Instead, we recommend buying solid color sheets and accessorizing with affordable Pooh items like lamps, posters, rugs, etc.

Who's got the best deals on bedding? Web sites like BabyCatalog.com, BabySuperMall.com, Diapers.com and Overstock. com have the best bargains. If you're lucky to be near a manufacturer's outlet, search these stores for discontinued patterns.

Let's take a look at the savings:

Continued on page 166

BEDDING RATINGS

Name	Rating	Cost	Organic?
Annette Tatum	B	$$ to $$$	◆
BB Basics Online	B-	$	
Banana Fish	B	$ to $$$	
Caden Lane	N/A	$$ to $$$	
California Kids	A	$$ to $$$	
Carousel	A	$ to $$	
Carter's	B	$	
CoCaLo	B+	$ to $$	◆
Company Kids	B-	$ to $$$	
Cotton Tale	A-	$$ to $$$	
Crown Crafts	C+	$ to $$	◆
Dwell	B+	$ to $$	
Gerber	D	$	
Glenna Jean	B+	$$ to $$$	
Hoohobbers	B+	$$	
Jessica McClintock	B-	$$ to $$$	
JoJo Designs	B	$ to $$	
Kids Line	B	$	◆
Kimberly Grant	A-	$ to $$	
Koala Baby	C+	$	
Lambs & Ivy	B+	$ to $$	
Land of Nod	B	$$	◆
Living Textiles	N/A	$	
Maddie Boo	B	$$ to $$$	
My Baby Sam	B+	$	
Nava's Designs	B	$$$	
Picci	B+	$$ to $$$	◆
Pine Creek	A-	$$ to $$$	
Pottery Barn	C+	$$	◆
Restoration Hardware	B-	$$	◆
Serena & Lily	B+	$$ to $$$	
Sleeping partners	B	$ to $$	◆
Sumersault	A	$ to $$	
Summer	A/B-	$	◆
Sweet Kyla	A	$$	◆
Target (Circo)	C	$	
Too Good By Jenny	F	$	
Trend Lab	B-	$ to $$	
Whistle & Wink	B+	$$$	

Key *See next page*

A quick look at some top crib bedding brands

Fiber Content	Notes
100% COTTON	Used to be known as Little House.
100% COTTON	Buy Buy Baby's private label; quality is mixed.
100% COTTON	MiGi line starts at $145 per set. Also does Skip Hop.
100% COTTON	Modern vintage collections; Moroccan designs.
100% COTTON	60+ patterns, most made in California.
100% COTTON	Nursery designer tool online for custom looks
100% COTTON	Baby Basics is mix-and-match separates line.
MIX	Good quality; decent value for the dollar.
100% COTTON	Mixed reviews on customer service/quality.
100% COTTON	All made in the USA. Innovative designs.
MIX	Baby-ish designs; sold in major chain stores.
100% COTTON	Dwell Studio line at Target earns kudos.
POLY/COTTON	Cute patterns, but poor quality.
MIX	Made in the USA; higher-end fabrics.
100% COTTON	Made in the USA; 40 patterns. Many accessories.
100% COTTON	Lacey, Victorian looks. Mid-price.
100% COTTON	9-piece beddings sets offer value; sold online.
MIX	Expanded accessory line; make Tiddliwinks brand.
100% COTTON	Luxe fabrics, made by Crown Craft.
100% COTTON	BRU store brand, sold as separates.
POLY/COTTON	Quilts have sewn-on rod pocket for hanging.
100% COTTON	Nice selection of accessories like lamps.
MIX	Affordable 5-pc sets, designed in Australia.
100% COTTON	Sophisticated looks, accented by silk and linen.
100% COTTON	Affordable, readers love quality and soft fabrics.
100% COTTON	Over the top luxe looks; prices start at $680.
100% COTTON	New organic line features corn-based fill
100% COTTON	Custom-made or off-the-shelf designs, pricey.
100% COTTON	Curious George and Dr. Seuss themed sheets.
100% COTTON	600 thread count sheets; customer service issues.
100% COTTON	Embroidery, bold designs. Many accessories.
100% COTTON	Lowered prices recently; new organic line.
100% COTTON	10 pc sets sold on Target.com and other sites.
100% COTTON	Maker of Ultimate Crib Sheet; separates line.
100% COTTON	Quality is good; sets can be ordered w/o bumpers
100% COTTON	Low price, low thread counts. Shrinkage issues.
100% COTTON	Reversible bumpers.
MIX	12 to 14 pc sets; readers like sheets.
100% COTTON	Vintage looks with embroidery accents.

Our suggested bedding budget

Pottery Barn cotton fitted sheets (two)	$38
Wearable blanket (instead of a blanket)	$20
Miscellaneous (lamp, other decor)	$100
TOTAL	**$158**

By contrast, if you go for a designer brand and buy all those silly extras like diaper stackers, you could be out as much as $800 on bedding alone—add in wall paper, accessories like wall hangings, matching lamps and you'll be out $1100 or more. So, the total savings from following the tips in this chapter could be nearly $1000. Now that your baby's room is outfitted, what about the baby? Flip to the next chapter to get the lowdown on those little clothes.

CHAPTER 4

REALITY
LAYETTE

The Reality Layette:
Little Clothes for Little Prices

Inside this chapter

What the heck is a "Onesie"? How many clothes does your baby need? How come such little clothes have such big price tags? These and other mysteries are unraveled in this chapter as we take you on a guided tour of baby clothes land. We'll reveal our secret sources for finding name brand clothes at half off retail prices. Which brands are best? Check out our picks and our nine tips from smart shoppers on getting the best deals. Next, read about the many outlets for children's apparel that have been popping up all over the country. At the end of this chapter, we'll even show you how to save big bucks on diapers.

When Do You Need This Stuff?

◆ **Baby Clothing.** You'll need basic baby clothing like t-shirts and sleepers as soon as you're ready to leave the hospital. Depending on the weather, you may need a bunting (a snug-fitting, hooded sleeping bag of heavy material) at that time as well.

You'll probably want to start stocking up on baby clothing around the seventh month of your pregnancy—if you deliver early, you will need some basics. However, you may want to wait to do major shopping until after any baby showers to see what clothing your friends and family give as gifts.

Be sure to keep a running list of your acquisitions so you won't buy too much of one item. Thanks to gifts and our own buying, we had about two thousand teeny, side-snap shirts by the time our baby was born. In the end, our son didn't wear the shirts much (he grew out of the newborn sizes quickly and wasn't really wild about them anyway), and we ended up wasting money.

◆ **Diapers.** How many diapers do you need for starters? Are you sitting down? If you're going with disposables, we recommend 600 diapers for the first six weeks (about 14 diapers a day). Yes, that's six packages of 100 diapers each (purchase them in your eighth month of pregnancy, just in case Junior arrives early). You may think this is a lot, but believe us, we bought that much and we still had to do another diaper run by the time our son was a month old. Newborns go through many more diapers than older infants because they feed more frequently. Also, remember that as a new parent, you'll find yourself taking off diapers that turn out to be dry. Or worse, you may change a diaper three times in a row because baby wasn't really finished.

Now that you know how many diapers you need for the first six weeks, what sizes should you buy? We recommend 100 newborn-size diapers and 500 "size one" (or Step 1) diapers. This assumes an average-size baby (about seven pounds at birth). But remember to keep the receipts—if your baby is larger, you might have to exchange the newborns for size one's (and some of the one's for two's). Note for parents-to-be of multiples: your babies tend to be smaller at birth, so buy all newborn diapers to start. And double or triple our recommended quantity!

If you plan to use a diaper service to supply cloth diapers, sign up in your eighth month. Some diaper services will give you an initial batch of diapers (so you're ready when baby arrives) and then await your call to start up regular service. If you plan to wash your own cloth diapers, buy two to five dozen diapers about two months before your due date. You'll also probably want to buy diaper covers (six to ten) at that time. We'll discuss cloth diapers in depth later in this chapter.

Even if you plan to use disposable diapers, you should pick up one package of high-quality, flat-fold cloth diapers. Why? You'll need them as spit-up rags, spot cleaners and other assorted uses you'd never imagined before becoming a parent.

Sources

There are nine basic sources for baby clothing and diapers:

1 BABY SPECIALTY STORES. Specialty stores typically carry 100% cotton, high-quality clothes, but you won't usually find them affordably priced. While you may find attractive dressy clothes, play clothes are typically a better deal elsewhere. Because the stores themselves are frequently small, selection is limited. On the upside, you can still find old-fashioned service at specialty stores—and that's helpful when buying items like shoes. In that case, the extra help with sizing may be worth the higher price.

As for diapers, you can forget about it—most specialty baby stores long ago ceded the diaper market to discounters and grocery stores (who sell disposables), as well as mail-order/online companies (who dominate the cloth diaper and supply business). Occasionally, we see specialty stores carry an offbeat product like Tushies, an eco-friendly disposable diaper. And some may have diaper covers, but the selection is typically limited.

2 DEPARTMENT STORES. Clothing is a department store's bread and butter, so it's not surprising to see many of these stores excel at merchandising baby clothes. Everyone from Sears to Nordstrom sells baby clothes and frequent sales often make the selection more affordable.

3 SPECIALTY CHAINS. Our readers love Old Navy (see money-saving tips section) and Gap Kids. Both sell 100% cotton, high-quality clothes that are stylish and durable. Not to mention their price adjustment policies—if you buy an item at Gap/Old Navy and it goes on sale within seven days, you get the new price. Old Navy's selection of baby clothes is somewhat limited compared to Gap Kids. Other chains to check out include Gymboree, and Children's Place. All are reviewed later in this chapter.

4 DISCOUNTERS. Walmart, Target and K-Mart have moved aggressively into baby clothes in the last decade. Instead of cheap, polyester outfits that were once common at these stores, most discounters now emphasize 100% cotton clothing in fashionable styles.

Target has vastly expanded their baby clothes with their in-store brand, Cherokee. Not only have they expanded, but the quality is terrific in most cases. We shop Target for all cotton play clothes and day care clothes. Durability is good.

Diapers are another discounter strong suit—you'll find both name brand and generic disposables at most stores; some even carry a selection of cloth diaper supplies like diaper covers (although they are the cheaper brands; see the diaper section later in this book for more details). Discounters seem to be locked into an endless price battle with warehouse clubs on baby items, so you can usually find deals.

5 BABY SUPERSTORES. Babies R Us, Baby Depot and Buy Buy Baby carry a decent selection of name-brand clothing at low prices.

Most of the selection focuses on basics, however. You'll see more Carter's and Little Me than the fancy brands common at department stores. Over the years, Babies R Us has tried to upgrade their clothing options with a bit of embroidery here or an embellishment there. They've added sporty lines too like Nike track suits and more.

Diapers are a mixed bag at superstores. Babies R Us carries them, but Baby Depot doesn't. When you find them, though, the prices are comparable to discounters. We've seen diapers priced 20% to 30% lower at Babies R Us than grocery stores.

6 **WAREHOUSE CLUBS.** Members-only warehouse clubs like Sam's, Costco and BJ's sell diapers at rock-bottom prices. The selection is often hit-or-miss—sometimes you'll see brand names like Huggies and Pampers; other times it is an in-house brand. While you won't find the range of sizes that you'd see in grocery stores, the prices will be hard to beat. The downside? You have to buy them in "bulk," huge cases of multiple diaper packs that might require a forklift to get home.

Check out clubs' infant and toddler clothing as well. We'll talk later about some of the bargains we've found.

7 **WEB SITES.** There are a zillion catalogs and web sites that offer clothing for infants. The choices can be quite over-whelming, and the prices can range from reasonable to ridiculous (don't worry, we'll give you the best bets). It's undeniably a great way to shop when you have a newborn and just don't want to drag your baby out to the mall. Another strength of the web: cloth diapers and related supplies. Chains and specialty stores have abandoned these items, so mail order suppliers have picked up the slack. Check out Best Online Sources on page 171 for the complete low-down on web sites that sell clothing. Cloth diaper web sites are discussed on page 200.

8 **CONSIGNMENT OR THRIFT STORES.** You might think of these stores as dingy shops with musty smells—purveyors of old, used clothes that aren't in great shape. Think again—many consignment stores today are bright and attractive, with name brand clothes at a fraction of the retail price. Yes, the clothes have been worn before, but most stores only stock high-quality brands that are in excellent condition. And stores that specialize in children's apparel are popping up everywhere, from coast to coast. Later in this chapter, we'll tell you how to find a consignment store near you.

9 **GARAGE/YARD SALES.** Check out the box on page 172 for tips on how to shop garage sales like the pros.

Baby Clothing

So you thought all the big-ticket items were taken care of when you bought the crib and other furniture? Ha! It's time to prepare for your baby's "layette," a French word that translated literally means "spending large sums of cash on baby clothes and other such items, as required by Federal Baby Law." But, of course, there are some creative (dare we say, sneaky?) ways of keeping your layette bills down.

At this point, you may be wondering just what does your baby need? Sure you've seen those cute ruffled dresses and sailor suits in department stores—but what does your baby *really* wear everyday?

Meet the layette, a collection of clothes and accessories that your baby will use daily. While your baby's birthday suit was free, outfitting him in something more "traditional" will cost some bucks. In fact, a recent study estimated that parents spend $13,000 on clothes for a child by the time he or she hits 18 years of age—and that sounds like a conservative estimate to us. Baby clothes translate into a $20 *billion* business for children's clothing retailers. Follow our tips, and we estimate that you'll save 20% or more on your baby's wardrobe.

Best Online Sources

Bargain Childrens Clothing

bargainchildrensclothing.com. This site carries lots of "workhorse" brands like Hanes, Gold Toe and OshKosh, as well as character items from Sesame Street, Barbie and Dora the Explorer. The site also carries higher-quality brands such Wes and Willy, Izod or Flapdoodles,

CPSC Issues Thrift Shop Warning

Do second-hand stores sell dangerous goods? To answer that question, the Consumer Product Safety Commission randomly surveyed 301 thrift stores a few years ago, looking for recalled or banned products like clothing with drawstrings (an entanglement and strangulation hazard). The results: 51% of stores were selling clothing (mostly outerwear) with drawstrings at the waist or neck. This is particularly disturbing since 22 deaths and 48 non-fatal accidents since 1985 have been attributed to drawstrings. If you buy clothing at a consignment or thrift store or from a garage sale, be sure to avoid clothes with drawstrings. Another disturbing finding: about two-thirds of the stores surveyed had at least one recalled or banned product on the shelves.

at discounts of up to 85%. For example, we found an infant three-piece velour pant set by MulberrieBush regularly priced at $56 for only $29.90, a 47% savings. The site is a bit of a mishmash making it difficult to find the good stuff, but take your time and you'll see some really great money saving bargains. **Rating: A-**

Forget Me Not Kids

foregetmenotkids.com. Selection at Forget Me Not Kids is amazing. You'll see brand names like Miniman, Pepper Toes, Baby Lulu,

---

Garage & Yard Sales
Eight Tips to Get The Best Bargains

It's an American bargain institution—the garage sale.

Sure you can save money on baby clothes online or get a deal at a department store sale. But there's no comparing to the steals you can get at your neighbor's garage sale.

We love getting email from readers who've found great deals at garage sales. How about 25¢ onesies, a snowsuit for $1, barely used high chairs for $5? But getting the most out of garage sales requires some pre-planning. Here are the insider tips from our readers:

1 **CHECK THE NEWSPAPER/CRAIGSLIST FIRST.** Many folks advertise their garage sales a few days before the event—zero in on the ads/posts that mention kids/baby items to keep from wasting time on sales that won't be fruitful.

2 **GET A GOOD MAP OF THE AREA.** Find those obscure streets and cul de sacs. Print out a Google Map of the area or use your smart phone to pinpoint sales before you jump in the car.

3 **START EARLY.** The professional bargain hunters get going at the crack of dawn. If you wait until mid-day, all the good stuff will be gone. An even better bet: if you know the family, ask if you can drop by the day before the sale. That way you have a first shot before the competition arrives. One trick: if it's a neighbor, offer to help set-up for the sale. That's a great way to get those "early bird" deals.

4 **DO THE "BOX DIVE."** Many garage sale hosts will just dump kids clothes into a big box, all jumbled together in different sizes, styles, etc. Figuring out how to get the best picks while three other moms are digging through the same box is a challenge. The best advice: familiarize yourself with the better name brands in this chapter and pluck out the best bets as fast as possible. Then evalu-

---

Hartstrings and Klim Baby. We also saw shoes, baby blankets, hair bows, dress-up clothes and accessories, even diaper bags, slings and carriers for parents. While regular prices can be quite stiff, selection is great and they were offering nine pages of sale items when we visited. ***Rating: B***

Hanna Andersson

hannaandersson.com Hanna Andersson claim to fame is "Swedish quality" 100% cotton clothes. Unfortunately, Swedish quality is

ate the clothes away from the melee.

5 CONCENTRATE ON "FAMILY AREAS." A mom here in Colorado told us she found garage sales in Boulder (a college town) were mostly students getting rid of stereos, clothes and other junk. A better bet was nearby Louisville, a suburban bedroom community with lots of growing families.

6 HAGGLE. Prices on big-ticket items (that is, anything over $5) are usually negotiable. Another great tip we read in the newsletter *Cheapskate Monthly*: to test out products, carry a few "C" and "D" batteries with you to garage sales. Why? Most swings, bouncers and other gear use such batteries. Pop in your test batteries to make sure items are in good working order!

7 SMALL BILLS. Take small bills with you to sales—lots of $1's and a few $5's. Why? When negotiating over price, slowly counting out small bills makes the seller feel like they are getting more money. A wad of 20 $1's for a high chair feels like a more substantial offer than a $20 bill.

8 DON'T BUY A USED CRIB OR CAR SEAT. Old cribs may not meet current safety standards. It's also difficult to get replacement parts for obscure brands. Car seats are also a second-hand no-no— you can't be sure it wasn't in an accident, weakening its safety and effectiveness. And watch out for clothing with drawstrings, loose buttons or other safety hazards.

9 BE CREATIVE. See a great stroller but the fabric is dirty? And non-removable so you can't throw it in the washing machine? Take a cue from one dad we interviewed. He takes dirty second-hand strollers or high chairs to a car wash and blasts them with a high-pressure hose! Voila! Clean and useable items are the result. For a small investment, you can rehabilitate a dingy stroller into a showpiece.

going to set you back some big American bucks. For example, a simple romper styled like a rugby shirt was a whopping $40. At that price, it's hard to imagine buying a complete wardrobe here, no matter how cute their clothes are.

These aren't clothes you'd have your baby trash at daycare—Hanna Andersson's outfits are more suitable for weekend wear or going to Grandma's house. One note of caution: while the quality is very high, some items have difficult diaper access (or none at all). Another negative: Hanna Andersson uses "European sizing," which can be confusing. Thankfully, they are now including the age range for each size. On the plus side, we liked their web site especially the sale section—makes them a bit more reasonable. *Rating: B-*

LL Bean

llbean.com Rugged basics are what LL Bean is known for, and that's reflected in their baby collection. Lots of fleece, flannel and fashion are what you'll find on their site. We love the bold floral prints for girls and the lumberjack plain for boys. While the collection isn't huge, the quality is terrific. No shrink cottons top our list of great buys at $10.95 for short sleeve t-shirts. Sales prices are about 25% off making and they sell lots of cold weather items plus some gear like BOB strollers. *Rating: B*

MiniBoden

bodenusa.com Designed in London, MiniBoden is a children's off-shoot of Boden, a terrific women's and men's clothing line. Chock full of fun patterns and great colors, we were thrilled when they added a kids line. Ok, it's not cheap, but Boden offers many year-round sales and the children's line is sold at Nordstrom.com, where sales are common as well. The Brits have great fashion sense and style—these aren't the same old t-shirts and jeans. Quality is excellent as well. *Rating: B+*

Naartjie

naartjiekids.com Naartjie is a western US chain that originally started in South Africa. In fact, "naartjie" (pronounced nar chee) is an Afrikaans word for small, sweet citrus fruit. Sounds delish! Anyway, we first heard about this chain from one of our readers and were excited to have a store near us we could visit. We agree with our reader: the quality is comparable to Gymboree and Hanna Andersson. And yes, this line is full of cute stuff. We saw embroidered tunics for $17, corduroy pants for $15 and even some great dress up clothes. We loved the outfit ideas section on their web site with those adorable baby models. Very inspiring if you're just too tired to make decisions. *Rating: A*

Patsy Aiken

patsyaiken.com or chezami.com. Once upon a time, independent baby stores carried a much wider selection of adorable outfits for babies. And the brand they all carried was Patsy Aiken. You can't get it from a store anymore, but thankfully they have a web site you can visit. And the clothes are still as wonderful as we remember. These U.S.-made clothes are all cotton with amazing embroidery and appliqué. You'll find beautiful, bright colors with fun accents. They've cut out a lot of the super dressy designs and seem to be concentrating on fun casual clothes. Prices average around $30 to $50 for the typical dress or overall. Not cheap but the quality is terrific. This is a great site for grandmas looking for a cute shower gift.

Since Patsy Aiken has decided to discontinue selling the line in stores, they've added a new method of buying their designs. Called Chez Ami, it's a take off on the old Tupperware parties. You get a group of your friends together and have a Patsy Aiken clothing party. Check out the web site for more details. ***Rating: A***

Preemie.com

preemie.com Preemie.com is a wonderful oasis for parents of preemies. Sizes start as small as one to three pounds! If you need clothes for the NICU like IV shirts, open sided shirts, NICU wraps and more, this is the place. But that's not all. Basic gowns and onesies as well as designer baby clothes for preemies are available at super low prices on this site. Organic options are called out as are christening gowns and even preemie pacifiers! The site is run by the mom of a former preemie and she really knows what parents need. We highly recommend this site for parents of preemies. ***Rating: A***

TrendiTikes

trenditikes.com Looking for something really specific for your child? Here's a site that allows you to shop by designer, price, style and size. Organization seems to be their forte. We're impressed with the brands as well: Sara's Prints, Junk Food (love their t-shirts), Monkey Bar Buddies, Mim Pi and more. Prices are regular retail, but sales are frequent as are free shipping deals. ***Rating: A-***

Wooden Soldier

woodensoldier.com If you really need a formal outfit for your child for a wedding or special occasion, Wooden Soldier has the most expansive selection of children's formalwear we've ever seen. Unfortunately, the prices are quite expensive—a girls' silk plaid dress with velvet collar is $148; a boy's vest and pant set with shirt is $118. And those are for infant and toddler sized clothes (6 to 24 months)!

On the plus side, the quality is certainly impressive. And you won't find a bigger selection of dressy clothes around. They even offer some matching adult outfits. Wooden Soldier also continues to expand their casual offerings, which now include overalls, jump-suits and cotton sweaters. If you've got the cash and the occasion for these clothes, they're pretty cool. But for most people, these items, even the casual clothes, are way out of range. ***Rating: B-***

What Are You Buying?

Figuring out what your baby should wear is hardly intuitive to first-time parents. We had no earthly idea what types of (and how many) clothes a newborn needed, so we did what we normally do—we went to the bookstore to do research. We found three-dozen books on "childcare and parenting"—with three-dozen different lists of items that you *must* have for your baby and without which you're a very bad parent. Speaking of guilt, we also heard from relatives, who had their own opinions as to what was best for baby.

All of this begs the question: what do you *really* need? And how much? We learned that the answer to that last, age-old question was the age-old answer, "It depends." That's right, nobody really knows. In fact, we surveyed several department stores, interviewed dozens of parents, and consulted several "experts," only to find no consensus whatsoever. So, in order to better serve humanity, we have developed THE OFFICIAL FIELDS' LIST OF ALMOST EVERY ITEM YOU NEED FOR YOUR BABY IF YOU LIVE ON PLANET EARTH. We hope this clears up the confusion. (For those living on another planet, please consult our *Baby Bargains* edition for Mars and beyond).

Feel free to now ignore those lists of "suggested layette items" provided by retail stores. Many of the "suggestions" are self-serving, to say the least.

Of course, even when you decide what and how much to buy for your baby, you still need to know what *sizes* to buy. Fortunately, we have this covered, too. First, recognize that most baby clothes come in a range of sizes rather than one specific size ("newborn to 3 months" or "3-6 months"). For first time parents buying for a new-born, *we recommend you buy "3-6 month" sizes (instead of new-born sizes).* Why? Because the average size newborn will grow out of "newborn" sizes way too fast. The exception to this rule: pre-emies and multiples, which tend to be on the small side. (See previous section for a great preemie website).

No matter how big or small your newborn, a smart piece of advice: keep all receipts and tags so you can exchange clothes for larger sizes—you may find you're into six-month sizes by the time your baby hits one month old! (Along the same lines, don't wash *all* those new baby clothes immediately. Wash just a few items for the initial few weeks. Keep all the other items in their original packaging to make returns easier).

Ever wonder how fast your baby will grow? *Babies double their birth weight by five months . . . and triple it by one year!* On average, babies grow ten inches in their first year of life. (Just an FYI: your child will average four inches of growth in her second year, then three inches a year from ages 3 to 5 and two inches a year until puberty.) Given those stats, you can understand why we don't recommend stocking up on "newborn" size clothes.

Also: remember, you can always buy more later if you need them. In fact, this is a good way to make use of those close friends and relatives who stop by and offer to "help" right after you've suffered through 36 hours of hard labor—send them to the store!

We should point out that this layette list is just to get you started. This supply should last for the first month or two of your baby's life. Also along these lines, we received a question from a mom-to-be who wondered, given these quantities, how often do we assume you'll do laundry. The answer is in the next box.

The "Baby Bargains" Layette

Let's talk quality when it comes to baby clothes.
First, you want clothing that doesn't shrink. Look at the washing

---

E-MAIL FROM THE REAL WORLD
How Much Laundry Will I Do?

Anna B. of Brooklyn, NY had a good question about baby's layette and laundry:

"You have a list of clothes a new baby needs, but you don't say how often I would need to do laundry if I go with the list. I work full time and would like to have enough for a week. Is the list too short for me?"

Our answer: there is no answer. Factors such as whether you use cloth or disposable diapers (cloth can leak more; hence more laundry) and how much your baby spits up will greatly determine the laundry load. Another factor: breast versus bottle-feeding. Bottle-fed babies have fewer poops (and hence, less laundry from possible leaks). An "average" laundry cycle with our layette list would be every two to three days, assuming breast feeding, disposable diapers and an average amount of spit-up.

instructions. "Cold water wash/low dryer setting" is your clue that this item has NOT been pre-shrunk. Also, do the instructions tell you to wash with "like colors?" This may be a clue that the color will run. Next check the detailing. Are the seams sewn straight? Are they reinforced, particularly on the diaper area?

Go online and check message boards for posts on different brands. On our boards (Babybargains.com), parents comment frequently on whether a brand shrinks, has plenty of diaper room, falls apart after a few washings, etc. Spend a little time online to get some intel on the best brands—and which ones to avoid.

Now, let's get to the list:

◆ **T-Shirts.** Oh sure, a t-shirt is a t-shirt, right? Not when it comes to baby t-shirts. These t-shirts could have side snaps, snaps at the crotch (also known as onesies or creepers) or over-the-head openings. If you have a child who is allergic to metal snaps (they leave a red ring on their skin), you might want to consider over-the-head t-shirts. (FYI: While some folks refer to onesies as a generic item, the term onesie is a trademarked clothing item from Gerber.)

By the way, is a onesie t-shirt an outfit or an undergarment? Answer: it's both. In the summer, you'll find onesies with printed patterns that are intended as outfits. In the winter, most stores just sell white or pastel onesies, intended as undergarments.

HOW MANY? T-shirts usually come in packs of three. Our recommendation is to buy two packages of three (or a total of six shirts) of the side-snap variety. We also suggest buying two packs of over-the-head t-shirts. This way, if your baby does have an allergy to the snaps, you have a backup. Later you'll find the snap-at-the-crouch t-shirts to be most convenient since they don't ride up under clothes.

◆ **Gowns.** These are one-piece gowns with elastic at the bottom. They are used as sleeping garments in most cases. (We'll discuss more pros/cons of gowns later in this chapter.)

HOW MANY? This is a toss-up. If you want to experiment, go for one or two of these items. If they work well, you can always go back and get more later.

◆ **Sleepers.** This is the real workhorse of your infant's wardrobe, since babies usually sleep most of the day in the first months. Also known as stretchies, sleepers are most commonly used as pajamas for infants. They have feet, are often made of flame-retardant polyester, and snap up the front. As a side note, we've seen an increase in the numbers of cotton sleepers in recent years. Another related item: cotton long johns for baby. These are similar to sleepers, but don't have feet (and hence, may necessitate the use of socks in winter months).

One parent emailed us asking if she was supposed to dress her baby in pants, shirts, etc. or if it was OK to keep her daughter in sleepers all day long. She noted the baby was quite comfortable and happy. Of course, you can use sleepers exclusively for the first few months. We certainly did. As we've said all along, a comfortable baby is a happy parent!

How MANY? Because of their heavy use, we recommend parents buy at least four to eight sleepers.

◆ *Blanket Sleepers/wearable blankets.* These are heavyweight, footed one-piece garments made of polyester. Used often in winter, blanket sleepers usually have a zipper down the front. In recent years, we've also seen quite a few fleece blanket sleepers, their key advantage being a softer fabric and a resistance to pilling.

How MANY? If you live in a cold climate or your baby is born in the winter, you may want to purchase two to four of these items. As an alternative to buying blanket sleepers, you could put a t-shirt on underneath a sleeper or stretchie for extra warmth.

Another option is a wearable blanket or swaddling blanket. See page 130 for a box on "Swaddling and Wearable Blankets." We have a few recommendations for parents who want to try one of these items. You may want to put a t-shirt on baby and then wrap her up in a swaddling blanket or wearable blanket.

 ◆ *Coveralls.* One-piece play outfits, coveralls (also known as rompers) are usually cotton or cotton/poly blends. Small sizes (under 6 months) may have feet, while larger sizes don't.

How MANY? Since these are really play clothes and small infants don't do a lot of playing, we recommend you only buy two to four coveralls for babies less than four months of age. However, if your child will be going into daycare at an early age, you may need to start with four to six coveralls.

 ◆ *Booties/socks.* These are necessary for outfits that don't have feet (like gowns and coveralls). As your child gets older (at about six months), look for the kind of socks that have rubber skids on the bottom (they keep baby from slipping when learning to walk).

How MANY? Three to four pairs are all you'll need at first, since baby will probably be dressed in footed sleepers most of the time.

◆ **Sweaters.** HOW MANY? Most parents will find one sweater is plenty (they're nice for holiday picture sessions). Avoid all-white sweaters for obvious reasons!

◆ **Hats.** Believe it or not, you'll still want a light cap for your baby in the early months of life, even if you live in a hot climate. Babies lose a large amount of heat from their heads, so protecting them with a cap or bonnet is a good idea. And don't expect to go out for a walk in the park without the baby's sun hat either.

HOW MANY? A couple of hats would be a good idea—sun hats in summer, warmer caps for winter. We like the safari-style hats best (they have flaps to protect the ears and neck).

◆ **Snowsuit/bunting.** Similar to the type of fabric used for blanket sleepers, buntings also have hoods and covers for the hands. Most buntings are like a sack and don't have leg openings, while snowsuits do. Both versions usually have zippered fronts.

FYI: Snowsuits and buntings should NOT be worn by infants when they ride in a car seat. Why? Thick fabric on these items can compress in an accident, compromising the infant's safety in the seat. So how can you keep your baby warm in an infant car seat? Check out page 389 for a discussion of several car seat cover-ups/warmers that keep baby toasty without compromising the safety of the seat.

HOW MANY? Only buy one of these if you live in a climate where you need it. Even with a Colorado winter, we got away with layering clothes on our baby, then wrapping him in a blanket for the walk out to a warmed-up car. If you live in a city without a car, you might need two or three snowsuits for those stroller rides to the market.

◆ **Kimonos.** Just like the adult version. Some are zippered sacks with a hood and terry-cloth lining. You use them after a bath.

HOW MANY? Are you kidding? What a joke! These items are one of our "wastes of money." We recommend you pass on the kimonos and instead invest in good quality towels.

◆ **Saque Sets.** Two-piece outfits with a shirt and diaper cover.

HOW MANY? Forget buying these as well.

◆ **Bibs.** These come in two versions, believe it or not. The little, tiny bibs are for the baby that occasionally drools. The larger versions are used when you begin feeding her solid foods (at about six months). Don't expect to be able to use the drool bibs later for feedings, unless you plan to change her carrot-stained outfit frequently.

HOW MANY? Skip the drool bibs (we'll discuss why later in this chapter under Wastes of Money). The exception: if your baby really can't keep dry because he's drooling the equivalent of a bathtub full every day, consider buying a few of these. When baby starts eating solid foods, you'll need at least three or four large bibs. One option: plastic bibs for feeding so you can just sponge them off after a meal.

◆ **Washcloths and Hooded Towels.** OK, so these aren't actually clothes, but baby washcloths and hooded towels are a necessity. Why? Because they are small and easier to use . . . plus they're softer than adult towels and washcloths.

Clothing: What you need, when

If you're new to this baby thing, you may be wondering how to pair the right clothing with your baby's developmental stage (if you're back for another round, think of this as a refresher). Here's a little primer on ages and stages.

◆ **0-3 months:** Newborns aren't even lifting their heads and they aren't able to do much besides eat, sleep and poop. Stick with sleepers, wearable blankets, and nightgowns for these guys. They don't need overalls or shirts and pants. Look for items sized by weight if possible since 0-3 month sizes can be all over the board.

◆ **3-6 months:** By the end of this stage your little one will be rolling over, sitting up and sleeping somewhat less. Still need those sleepers, but you're probably going to expand the wardrobe to include a few more play clothes. Two new items you will need now: bibs and socks. Depending on your baby's growth, you may find that you're buying nine and 12-month sizes.

◆ **6-12 months:** Finally, your baby is crawling, standing, maybe even cruising. At the end of a year she's likely tried those first tentative steps! Play clothes are a layette mainstay during these months. You'll also need good, no-skid socks that stay on (or very flexible shoes). You may find you're buying into the 18-month sizes.

HOW MANY? At first, you'll probably need only three sets of towels and washcloths (you get one of each per set). But as baby gets older and dirtier, invest in a few more washcloths to spot clean during the day.

◆ **Receiving Blankets.** You'll need these small, cotton blankets for all kinds of uses: to swaddle the baby, as a play quilt, or even for an extra layer of warmth on a cold day.

HOW MANY? We believe you can never have too many of these blankets, but since you'll probably get a few as gifts, you'll only need to buy two or three yourself. A total of seven to eight is probably optimal.

What about the future? While our layette list only addresses clothes to buy for a newborn, you will want to plan for your child's future wardrobe as well. For today's baby, clothes come in two categories: play clothes (to be used in daycare situations) and dress-up clothes. Later in this chapter, we'll discuss more money-saving tips and list several recommended brands of play and dress-up clothes.

More Money Buys You . . .

Even the biggest discounters now offer good quality clothing. But with more money you tend to get heavier weight cottons, nicer fasteners, better quality embellishments and more generous sizing. At some point, however, considering how fast your little one is growing, it's a waste to spend top dollar on baby clothes!

Safe & Sound

Should your baby's sleepwear (that is, the items he'll wear almost non-stop for the first several months of life) be flame retardant? What the heck does "flame retardant" mean anyway?

According to the Consumer Product Safety Commission (CPSC), items made of flame retardant fabric will not burn under a direct flame. Huh? Doesn't "flame retardant" mean it won't burn at all? No—that's a common myth among parents who think such clothes are a Superman-style second skin that will protect baby against any and all fire hazards.

Prior to 1996, the CPSC mandated that an item labeled as sleepwear be made of "flame retardant fabric." More often than not, that meant polyester because the alternative (untreated cotton fabric)

DOES burn under direct flame. While there are a few companies that make cotton sleepwear that is chemically treated to be fire retardant, the prices of such items were so high that the de facto standard for children's sleepwear for many years was polyester.

Then the government changed its mind. The CPSC noticed that many parents were rebelling against the rules and putting their babies in all-cotton items at bedtime. After an investigation, the CPSC revised the rules to more closely fit reality.

First, pajamas for babies nine months and under were totally exempt from the flame-retardant rules. Why? Since these babies aren't mobile, the odds they'll come in contact with a fire hazard that would catch their clothes on fire is slim. What if the whole house catches fire? Well, the smoke is much more dangerous than the flames—hence, a good smoke detector in the nursery and every other major room of your house is a much better investment than fire-retardant clothes.

What about sleepwear for older babies? Well, the government admits that "close-fitting" all-cotton items don't pose a risk either. Only flowing nightgowns or pajamas that are loose fitting must meet the flame retardant rules today.

If you still want to go with "flame retardant" baby items, there are a couple of options beyond plain polyester. Look for fleece PJ's—Old Navy cells fleece sleepers for $16.50. There use to be a few treated cotton pajama options on the market, but now that the rules have changed to allow close fitting, untreated cotton pajamas, we don't see the treated ones anymore.

Finally, one last myth to dispel on this topic: does washing flame-retardant clothing reduce its ability to retard flames? Nope—fabrics like polyester are *naturally* flame retardant (that is, there is no magic chemical they've been doused with that can wash out in the laundry).

There is one exception to the laundry rule: if you do choose to buy flame-retardant clothing, be sure to avoid washing such clothing in soap flakes. Soap flakes actually add a flammable chemical residue to clothes. And so do dryer sheets and liquid softeners. For more advice on washing baby clothes, see the discussion on page 185.

What about other safety hazards with children's clothing? Here are a few more to consider:

◆ *Check for loose threads.* These could become a choking hazard, or the threads could wrap around fingers or toes, cutting off circulation.

◆ *Be careful about appliqués.* "Heat-welded" plastic appliqués on clothes can come off and cause choking. Poorly sewn appliqués can also be a hazard as the thread can unravel. Look for appliqués

REALITY
LAYETTE

One Size Does Not Fit All

A six month-size t-shirt is a six-month-size t-shirt, right? Wrong. For some reason, baby clothing companies have yet to synchronize their watches when it comes to sizes. Hence, a clothing item that says "six-month size" from one manufacturer can be just the same dimensions as a "twelve-month size" from another. All this begs the question: how can you avoid widespread confusion? First, open packages to check out actual dimensions. Take your baby along and hold items up to her to gauge whether they'd fit. Second, note whether items are pre-shrunk—you'll probably have to ask (if not, allow for shrinkage). Third, don't key on length from head to foot. Instead, focus on the length from neck to crotch—a common problem is items that seem roomy but are too tight in the crotch. Finally, forget age ranges and pay more attention to labels that specify an infant's size in weight and height, which are much more accurate. To show how widely sizing can vary, check out the following chart. We compared "six-month" t-shirts from six major clothing makers (sold at Babies R Us and Amazon.com) plus two popular web sites, Hanna Andersson, and Baby Gap. Here's what these six-month t-shirts really translated to in terms of a baby's weight and height:

What a six month t-shirt really means

MAKER	WEIGHT	HEIGHT
Baby Gap	17-22 lbs.	27-29"
Carter's/OshKosh	12.5-16.5 lbs.	24-26.5"
Gymboree	17-22 lbs.	25-29"
Hanna Andersson	14-21 lbs.	26-30"
Gerber	16-22 lbs.	25-28"
Little Me	12-16 lbs.	24-27"
Luvable Friends	16.5-20.5 lbs.	26.5-28.5"
SpaSilk	12-18 lbs.	24-26.5"

Here's another secret from the baby clothing trade: the more expensive the brand, the more roomy the clothes. Conversely, cheap items usually have the skimpiest sizing. What about the old wives' tale that you should just double your baby's age to find the right size (that is, buying twelve-month clothes for a six-month old?). That's bogus—as you can see, sizing is so all over the board that this rule just doesn't work.

that have thick layers of thread attaching them to the clothing.

◆ *Avoid outfits with easy-to-detach, decorative buttons or bows—these may also be a choking hazard.* If you have any doubts, cut the decorations off.

◆ *Watch out for drawstrings.* In recent years, most manufacturers have voluntarily eliminated such drawstrings. But if you get hand-me-downs or buy second-hand clothes, be sure to remove any strings. We're amazed, however, at the continued use of draw-strings by some manufacturers of new children's clothing. We get frequent alerts from the Consumer Product Safety Commission (CPSC) about recalls of new items with drawstrings.

◆ *Lead in jewelry.* Cheap jewelry from China has consistently turned up on the CPSC's recall list. These items are sold in mall stores and from vending machines. Best bet: never purchase jewel-ry for infants and toddlers. Items like necklaces are likely to end up in their mouths and can be a potential lead and choking hazard. If you choose to pierce your child's ears, stick with high-quality hypoallergenic metals like gold.

Laundry Conundrum: What's Best for Baby's Clothes?

Ever since Dr. Spock's best-selling tome on taking care of baby came out in 1946, most parenting authors have advised washing baby's clothes and linens in mild soap or detergents. The implication is that baby's skin is delicate and could be irritated by harsh chemicals.

So should baby's clothes be washed only in expensive deter-gents like Dreft? The answer is a definite no. But we do recommend you choose a dye-free, fragrance-free detergent like *All Free & Clear*, which, by the way, is HALF the cost of Dreft.

More advice: do not use fabric softeners on any sleepwear. Most sleepwear is polyester, which is a flame retardant material. However, fabric softeners will leave a residue on polyester and that residue is flammable.

What if your child develops eczema or a reaction to your deter-gent? Consider cleaning your baby's clothes with a natural pure soap product. We have used *Cal-Ben's Seafoam Liquid* laundry soap (CalBenPureSoap.com) and would recommend it to parents of kids with severe skin issues. Unfortunately, soap does NOT clean as well as detergent, especially in the laundry, so be prepared. And it's expensive: $29 for one gallon of liquid laundry detergent, about 20% more expensive than Dreft.

Soap flakes are another laundry option. Ivory Snow and Dreft no longer make soap flakes so you have to buy them online. One brand, **Dri-Pak,** is available at Soap-Flakes.com. Soap flakes can also leave a residue on flame retardant clothing—don't use it for sleepwear.

Pure soap products are hard to find and expensive, although some natural food stores carry these brands as well. What about "natural" detergents found in health food stores? Read the labels carefully before you buy since some items contain detergents and others may have allergenic fruit or vegetable ingredients.

Smart Shopper Tips

Smart Shopper Tip
Tips and Tricks to Get the Best Quality
"I've received several outfits from friends for my daughter, but I'm not sure she'll like all the scratchy lace and the poly/cotton blends. What should she wear, and what can I buy that will last through dozens of washings?"

Generally, we recommend dressing your child for comfort. At the same time, you need clothes that can withstand frequent washings. With this in mind, here are our suggestions for baby clothing:

1 SEE WHAT YOUR BABY LIKES BEFORE INVESTING IN MANY GAR-MENTS. Don't spend $90 on fancy sweaters, only to find baby prefers cotton Onesies.

2 WE GENERALLY RECOMMEND **100%** COTTON CLOTHING. Babies are most comfortable in clothing that breathes.

3 IF YOUR CHILD DEVELOPS A RED, ITCHY RASH, IT COULD BE AN ALLERGY. Culprits could include metal snaps on a t-shirt, zippers or even the ink on tagless labels. One idea: consider alternatives such as shirts that have ties or that pull over the head. Stick with clothes that have plastic snaps and zippers.

4 IN GENERAL, BETTER-MADE CLOTHES WILL HAVE THEIR SNAPS ON A REINFORCED FABRIC BAND. Snaps attached directly to the body of the fabric may tear the garment or rip off.

5 IF YOU'RE BUYING **100%** COTTON CLOTHES, MAKE SURE THEY'RE PRE-SHRUNK. Some stores, like Gymboree (see review later in this chapter), pre-wash their clothes to prevent shrinkage. With other brands, it's hard to tell. Our advice: read the label. If it says, "wash in cold water" or " tumble dry low," assume the garment will shrink (and hence buy a larger size). On the other hand, care instructions that advise "wash in warm water and tumble dry" usually indicate that the garment is already preshrunk.

6 **GO FOR OUTFITS WITH SNAPS AND ZIPPERS ON BOTH LEGS, NOT JUST ONE.** Dual-leg snaps or zippers make it much easier to change a diaper. Always check a garment for diaper accessibility—some brands actually have no snaps or zippers, meaning you would have to completely undress your baby for a diaper change! Another pet peeve: garments that have snaps up the back also make diaper changes a big hassle.

7 **BE AWARE THAT EACH COMPANY HAS ITS OWN WARPED IDEA ABOUT HOW TO SIZE BABY CLOTHES.** See the box "One Size Does Not Fit All" earlier in this chapter for more details.

8 **BEWARE OF APPLIQUES.** Some appliqué work can be quite scratchy on the inside of the outfit (it rubs against baby's skin). Feel the inside of the outfit before you buy to make sure it's soft. Some manufacturers will use additional fabric between the appliqué and baby's skin.

9 **KEEP THE TAGS AND RECEIPTS.** A reader emailed us her strategy for dealing with baby clothes that shrink: until she has a chance to wash the item, she keeps all packaging, tags and receipts. If it shrinks, she returns it Immediately.

Wastes of Money

Waste of Money #1
Clothing that Leads to Diaper Changing Gymnastics
"My aunt sent me an adorable outfit for my little girl. The only problem: it snaps up the back making diaper changes a real pain. In fact, I don't dress her in it often because it's so inconvenient. Shouldn't clothing like this be outlawed?"

It's pretty obvious that some designers of baby clothing have never had children of their own. What else could explain outfits that snap up the back, have super tiny head, leg and arm openings, and snaps in inconvenient places (or worse, no snaps at all)?

One mother we spoke with was furious about outfits that have snaps only down one leg, requiring her baby to be a contortionist to get into and out of the outfit.

Our advice: stay away from outfits that don't have easy access to the diaper. Look instead for snaps or zippers down the front of the outfit or on the crotch. If your baby doesn't like having things pulled over his head, look for shirts with wide, stretchie necklines.

Waste of Money #2
The Fuzz Factor

"My friend's daughter has several outfits that aren't very old but are already pilling and fuzzing. They look awful and my friend is thinking of throwing them out. What causes this?"

Your friend has managed to have a close encounter with that miracle fabric known as polyester. Synthetics such as polyester will often pill or fuzz after washing, making your baby look a little rag-tag. Of course, this is less of a concern with sleepwear—the flame retardancy of polyester fabric outweighs the garment's appearance.

However, when you're talking about a play outfit, we recommend sticking to all-cotton clothes. They wash better, usually last longer, and generally look nicer—not to mention they feel better to your baby. Cotton allergies are rare, unlike sensitivities to the chemicals used to make synthetic fabrics. You will pay more for all-cotton clothing, but in this case, the extra expense is worth it. Remember, just because you find the cheapest price on a polyester outfit doesn't mean you're getting a bargain. The best deal is not wasting money on outfits that you have to throw away after two washings.

If you get polyester outfits as gifts, here's a laundry tip: wash the items inside out. That helps lessen pilling/fuzzing. And some polyester items are better than others—polar fleece sweatshirts and pajamas are still made of polyester, but are softer and more durable.

Waste of Money #3
Do I Really Need These?

"My mother bought me a zillion gowns before my baby was born, and I haven't used a single one. What the heck are they for?"

"The list of layette items recommended by my local department store includes something called a saque set. I've never seen one, and no one seems to know what it is. Do I really need one?"

"A bath robe with matching towel and washcloth seems like a neat baby gift for my pregnant friend. But another friend told me it probably wouldn't get used. What do you think?"

All of these items come under the heading "Do I Really Need

These?" Heck, we didn't even know what some of these were when we were shopping for our baby's layette. For example, what in the world is a saque set? Well, it turns out it's just a two-piece outfit with a shirt and diaper cover. Although they sound rather benign, saque sets are a waste of money. Whenever you pick up a baby under the arms, it's a sure bet her clothes will ride up. In order to avoid having to constantly pull down the baby's shirt, most parents find they use one-piece garments much more often than two-piece ones.

As for gowns, the jury is still out on whether these items are useful. We thought they were a waste of money, but a parent we interviewed did mention that she used the gowns when her baby had colic (that persistent crying condition; see our other book *Baby 411* for a discussion). She believed that the extra room in the gown made her baby more comfortable. Still others praise gowns for their easy access to diapers, making changes easy, especially in the middle of the night. Finally, parents in hot climates say gowns keep their infants more comfortable. So, you can see there's a wide range of opinions on this item.

There is no question in our minds about the usefulness of a baby bathrobe, however. Don't buy it. For a baby who will only wear it for a few minutes after a bath, it seems like the quintessential waste of your money (we saw monogrammed options for a whopping $90!). Instead, invest in some good quality towels and washcloths and forget those cute (but useless) kimonos.

Waste of Money #4
Covering Up Those Little Piggies
"I was looking at baby shoes the other day and I saw a $40 pair of Nike Jordan Retro sneakers! This is highway robbery! I can't believe babies' shoes are so expensive. Are they worth it?"

Developmentally, babies don't need shoes until after they become quite proficient at walking. In fact, it's better for their muscle development to go barefoot or wear socks. While those expensive Merrells might look cute, they're really a waste of time and money. Of course, at some point, your baby will need some shoes. See the box on the next page for our tips on how to buy babies' first shoes.

Waste of Money #5
To Drool or Not to Drool
"I received a few bibs from my mother-in-law as gifts. I know my baby won't need them until she's at least four to six months old when I start feeding her solids. Plus, they seem so small!"

What you actually received was a supply of *drool* bibs. Drool bibs are tiny bibs intended for small infants who drool all over everything. Or infants who spit-up frequently. Our opinion: they're pretty useless—they're too small to catch much drool or spit-up.

When you do buy bibs, stay away from the ones that tie. Bibs that snap or have Velcro are much easier to get on and off. Another good bet: bibs that go on over the head (and have no snaps or Velcro). Why? Older babies can't pull them off by themselves.

Stay away from the super-size vinyl bibs that cover the arms, since babies who wear them can get too hot and sweaty. However, we do recommend you buy a few regular-style vinyl bibs for trav-

Baby Needs a New Pair of Shoes

As your baby gets older, you may find she's kicking off her socks every five minutes. And at some point she's going to start standing, crawling and even walking. While we suggest waiting to buy shoes until walking is firmly established, there will come a day when you will need to buy that first set of shoes. Here are some suggestions:

First, look for shoes that have the most flexible soles. You'll also want fabrics that breath and stretch, like canvas and leather—stay away from vinyl shoes. The best brands we found were recommended by readers. Reader Teri D. wrote us about Canada's **Robeez** (robeez.com, now a division of Stride Rite). "They are the most AWESOME shoes—I highly recommend them," she said in an email. And Teri wasn't the only one who loves them. Our email has been blitzed by fans. Robeez are made of leather, have soft, skid-resistant soles and are machine washable. They start at $28 for a basic pair (see above). Another reader recommended New Zealand-made **Bobux** shoes ($26.50, bobuxusa.com). These cute leather soft soles "do the trick by staying on extremely well," according to a reader. Finally, we also like **PediPeds** (pedipeds.com). The soft-soled shoes are hand stitched and made of leather. They are sized from 0 to five years and sell for around $32 to $40.

What about shoes for one or two year olds? We've found great deals at Target, where a wide selection of sizes and offerings was impressive. Another good source: Gap Kids/Baby Gap. Their affordable line of sneakers are very good quality. Parents have also told us they've had success with Babies R Us' in-house brand; others like Stride Rite shoes, which are often on sale at department stores. Many of the sites we list in the Best Online Sources earlier in this chapter sell shoes as well.

el. You can wash them off much more easily than the standard terry-cloth bibs. As for sources of bibs, many of the catalogs we review in this book carry such items. Readers have also recommended the long sleeve bib from **A Better Bib** (abetterbib.com). Made of soft, breathable fabrics, these bibs run $17.

Reader Sharon F. from Chicago wrote in to praise **Pelican Bibs** (pelican-bib.com): "I want to strongly recommend Pelican bibs! They really protect clothing and catch dropped food" better than other bibs. Pelican bibs have a wide lip for catching spills. Cost: $15.

Money Saving Secrets

1 REMEMBER THESE TWO STORES: OLD NAVY AND THE CHILDREN'S PLACE. Old Navy (oldnavy.com) is the hip, discount offshoot of the Gap (gap.com) with 1000+ stores in the U.S. and Canada. Readers rave about the buys they find at Old Navy (sample: "adorable" 100% cotton Onesies for just $12.50 per 3-pack; gripper socks, $6), although most admit the selection is limited. The options change rapidly and Old Navy's sales and clearance racks are "bargain heaven," say our spies. An insider tip to Old Navy and Gap Kids: the stores change out their merchandise every six weeks, moving the "old" stuff to the clearance racks rather quickly. Ask your local Old Navy or Gap Kids which day they do their markdowns (typically it is Tuesday night, effective Wednesday).

Here's another tip for folks who shop Old Navy or the Gap regularly: check to see if your recent purchases have been marked down. You may be able to get a refund if items you've bought are marked down even more. One reader emailed us her great deal: "Last month I found a hooded sweatshirt for baby on clearance. It was originally $15 marked down to $10.50. The next week, I went back and the same sweatshirt had been marked down from $10.50 to $1.99. So they refunded me $8.60!" Both Old Navy and the Gap allow you a price adjustment within 14 days of purchase. You don't have to bring the clothes back, just your receipt.

A Gap employee emailed us the inside scoop on their markdowns. She told us that prices ending in $.97 are the lowest price you'll see on the markdown rack. After 14 days at the $.97 price, the stores have the authority to cut the price in half to "kill" the item. Finally, if you have a Gap credit card, you can get an additional 10% off everything on the first Tuesday of every month. And our source says don't forget to take the register surveys—they'll save you 10% as well.

The Children's Place (childrensplace.com) has over 900 stores in the US and Canada. They're about as ubiquitous as Old Navy, and the prices are just as good. They offer their clothing in sizes newborn to 4T. One reader wrote: "I found that this chain has really great looking and durable clothes for extremely reasonable prices." She did note that sizes run a bit small, so buy up a size. An example of their offerings: we saw a white, ruffled girl's cardigan for a mere $16.95. If you order online, the site offers a flat $5 shipping fee plus you can make returns at their stores.

2 **WAIT UNTIL AFTER SHOWERS AND PARTIES TO PURCHASE CLOTHES.** Clothing is a popular gift item—you may not need to buy much yourself.

3 **STICK WITH BASICS—T-SHIRTS, SLEEPERS, CAPS, SOCKS AND BLANKETS.** For the first month or more, that's all you need since you won't be taking Junior to the opera.

4 **SALES!** The baby area in most department stores is definitely SALE LAND. At one chain we researched, the baby section has at least some items that are on sale every week! Big baby sales occur throughout the year, but especially in January. You can often snag bargains at up to 50% off the retail price. Another tip: consider buying for the future during end-of-season sales. If you're pregnant during the fall, for example, shop the end-of-summer sales for next summer's baby clothes. Hint: our research shows the sale prices at department stores are often better deals than the "discounted" prices you see at outlets.

5 **CHOOSE QUALITY OVER LOW PRICE FOR PLAYCLOTHES AND BASICS.** Sure that polyester outfit is 20% cheaper than the cotton alternative. HOWEVER, beware of the revenge of the washing machine! You don't realize how many times you'll be doing laundry—that play outfit may get washed every couple of days. Cheap polyester clothes pill or fuzz up after just a few washings—making you more likely to chuck them. Quality clothes have longer lives, making them less expensive over time.

6 **FOR SLEEPWEAR, TRY THE AFFORDABLE BRANDS.** Let's get real here: babies pee and poop in their sleepers. Hence, fancy designer brands are a money-waster. A friend of ours who lives in Texas uses affordable all-cotton Onesies as sleepwear in the hot summer months. For the winter here in Colorado, we use thermal underwear, which we've found for as little as $15 in Target.

7 **CAN'T RETURN IT?** Did you get gifts of clothing you don't want but can't return? Consign it at a local thrift store. We took a basketful of clothes that we couldn't use or didn't like and placed them on consignment. We turned these duplicates into $40 cash.

8 **SPEAKING OF CONSIGNMENT STORES, HERE IS A WONDERFUL WAY TO SAVE MONEY:** Buy barely used, consigned clothing for your baby. We found outfits ranging from $5 to $7 from high quality designers like Alexis. How can you find a consignment or thrift shop in your area specializing in high-quality children's clothes? Besides looking in the phone book, check out web sites like the National Association of Resale & Thrift Shops (narts.com, click on the shopping guide icon). Here are two tips for getting the best bargains at second-hand stores: First, shop the resale stores in the richest part of town. Why? They are most likely to stock the best brands with steep discounts off retail prices. Such stores also have clothes with the least wear (we guess rich kids have so many clothes they don't have time to wear them all out)! Second: ask the consignment store which day is best to shop. Some stores accept new consignments on certain days; others tell us that days like Tuesday and Wednesday offer the best selection of newly consigned items.

9 **CHECK OUT DISCOUNTERS.** In the past, discount stores like Target and Walmart typically carried cheap baby clothes that were mostly polyester. Well, there's good news for bargain shoppers: in recent years, these chains have upgraded their offerings, adding more all-cotton clothes and even some brand names.

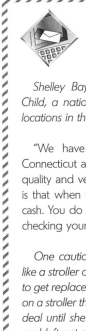

E-MAIL FROM THE REAL WORLD
Second-hand bargains easy to find

Shelley Bayer of Connecticut raved about Once Upon A Child, a nationwide chain of resale stores with well over 200 locations in the US and Canada (OUAC.com).

"We have seven locations of Once Upon A Child in Connecticut and I love them! The clothes and toys are of great quality and very affordable. The good thing about these stores is that when you take something in to be sold, they pay you cash. You do not have wait for something to be sold and keep checking your account like a traditional consignment shop."

One caution about second-hand stores—if you buy an item like a stroller or high chair at a resale shop, you may not be able to get replacement parts. One mom told us she got a great deal on a stroller that was missing a front bar . . . that is, it was a great deal until she discovered the model was discontinued and she couldn't get a replacement part from the manufacturer.

For basic items like t-shirts and play clothes that will be trashed at day care, these stores are good bets. Walmart sure impressed one of our readers: "I spent $25 for a baby bathing suit in a specialty store, and for a little over twice that (about $60) I bought my daughter's entire summer wardrobe at Walmart—shorts, t-shirts, leggings, Capri pants, overalls and matching socks. Some of the pieces were as low as $2.88." And don't forget other discounters like Marshalls, TJ Maxx and Ross. Bargain tip: ask the manager when they get in new shipments—that's when selection is best.

By the way, Carter's makes Child of Mine brand clothing sold at Walmart, Little Layette at Buy Buy Baby and Just One Year at Target.

10 WAREHOUSE CLUBS. Warehouse clubs like Sam's, BJ's and Costco carry baby clothes at prices far below retail. On a recent visit to Costco we saw Carter's fleece sleepers for only $7.29. All-cotton play clothes were a mere $13 while all-cotton pajamas (2T-10) were $12. Even baby Halloween costumes and kids outerwear (raincoats, fleece jackets) are terrific seasonal deals.

11 DON'T FORGET ABOUT CHARITY SALES. Readers tell us they've found great deals on baby clothes and equipment at church-sponsored charity sales. Essentially, these sales are like large garage/yard sales where multiple families donate kids' items as a fund-raiser for a church or other charity.

Outlets

Here's a round up of our favorite outlet stores for baby and kids clothes. Remember: outlet locations open and close frequently—check their web sites or OutletBound.com for up-to-date information on locations.

CARTER'S
Locations: Over 150 outlets.

It shows you how widespread the outlet craze is when you realize that Carter's has over 150 outlets in the U.S. That's right, 150. If you don't have one near you, you probably live in Bolivia.

We visited a Carter's outlet and found a huge selection of infant clothes, bedding, and accessories. Prices were generally marked 50% off retail although sharp-eyed readers noted that department store sale prices are often just as good.

The best deals, however, are at the outlet's yearly clearance sale in January when they knock an additional 25% to 30% off their already discounted prices. A store manager at the Carter's outlet we visited said that they also have two other sales: back-to-school and a "pajama sale." In the past, we noted that all the goods in their outlet stores were first quality. However, they have added a couple "seconds" racks (called "Oops" racks) in most of their stores with flawed merchandise. Our readers report that most seconds have only minor problems and the savings are worth it.

GAP
Locations: Over 170 outlets.

Gap sells such great play clothes, you probably find yourself buying them at full retail sometimes. But now you don't have to. With so many outlet stores, you can buy your baby those cute little mini skinny jeans, Fair Isle sweaters and itty bitty swim trunks at drastically reduced prices. And check out the $1.99 rack. Readers tell us these are amazing deals. Some parents complain that the outlet stores are a bit trashed, but pants for $4 and shirts for a dollar make it worth the mess.

HANNA ANDERSSON
Outlets Stores: Lake Oswego, OR; Michigan City, IN; Kittery, ME; Woodinville, WA; Williamsburg, VA

If you like Hanna Anderson's catalog, you'll love their outlet stores, which feature overstocks, returned items and factory seconds. For more information on Hanna Anderson, see Best Online Sources earlier in this chapter.

HARTSTRINGS
Locations: 28 outlets

Hartstrings' 27 outlet stores specialize in first-quality apparel for infants, boys, and girls and even have some mother/child outfits. Infant sizes range from three months to 24 months; savings up to 50%.

JCPENNEY
Locations: 22 outlets

A reader in Columbus, Ohio emailed her high praise for the Penney's outlet there. She snagged one-piece rompers for $5 (regularly $25) and hand-loomed coveralls for $2.99 (compared to $28 in stores). She also found satin christening outfits for both boys and girls for just $5 that regularly sell for as much as $70! The outlet carries everything from layette to play clothes, at discounts of 50% or more. (Hint: the outlet stores also have maternity clothes).

OshKosh

Locations: 147 outlets.

OshKosh, the maker of all those cute little overalls worn by just about every kid, sells their clothes direct at over 154 outlet stores. With prices that are 30% to 70% off retail, buying these play clothes staples is even easier on the pocketbook. For example, footed sleepers were $7.70 (regularly $11), and receiving blankets were $18.20 (regularly $24).

We visited our local OshKosh store and found outfits from infant sizes up to size 16. They split the store up by gender, as well as by size. Infant and toddler clothes are usually in the back of the store.

The outlet also carries OshKosh shoes, socks, hats, and even stuffed bears dressed in overalls and engineer hats. Seasonal ensembles are available, including shorts outfits in the summer and snowsuits ($42) in the winter. Some clothes are irregulars, so inspect the garments carefully before you buy.

One complaint: a parent wrote telling us she was disappointed that OshKosh had cheap elastic around the legs and didn't wash well. In her opinion, the quality of Carter's was much better in comparison.

FYI: OshKosh was purchased by Carter's in 2005.

The Name Game: Our Picks for the Best Brands

Walk into any department store and you'll see a blizzard of brand names for baby clothes. Which ones stand up to frequent washings? Which ones have snaps that stay snapped? Which are a good value for the dollar? We asked our readers to divide their favorite clothing brands/stores into three categories: best bets, good but not great and skip it.

The Best Bets tend to be clothes that were not only stylish but also held up in the wash. The fabric was usually softer and pilled less. Customer service also comes into play with the best brands. Hanna Andersson is a great example of a company that bends over backwards for their customers. Gymboree, on the other hand, seems to be less satisfactory for many parents, souring them on the brand. Keep in mind, some brands are pricey, so look for sales and second hand deals. Or just point Grandma to these sites!

Good but not Great clothes were pretty good, just not as soft or as stylish as Best Bets. The Skip-It brands were most likely the poorest quality: they shrunk in the wash, pilled up or fell apart. Inconsistent sizing was also a problem with brands like Babies R Us' Koala Kids.

Some of these brands sell direct; others just through retailers.

Best Bets

BABY GAP	(800) GAP-STYLE	BABYGAP.COM
BABY LULU		BABYLULU.COM
CARTER'S	(770) 961-8722	CARTERS.COM
COZY TOES		COZYTOES.COM
FIRST IMPRESSIONS		MACYS.COM
FLAP HAPPY	(800) 234-3527	FLAPHAPPY.COM
FLAPDOODLES	(302) 731-9793	FLAPDOODLES.COM
FUNTASIA! TOO	(214) 634-7770	FUNTASIATOO.COM
H & M		HM.COM
HANNA ANDERSSON		HANNAANDERSSON.COM
HARTSTRINGS/KITESTRINGS	(212) 868-0950	HARTSTRINGS.COM
HEDGEHOG		HEDGEHOGUSA.COM
JAKE AND ME	(970) 352-8802	JAKEANDME.COM
JANIE AND JACK		JANIEANDJACK.COM
KISSY KISSY		KISSYKISSYONLINE.COM
LITTLE LUBBALOO		LITTLELUBBALOO.COM
LITTLE ME	(800) 533-5497	LITTLEME.COM
LL BEAN		LLBEAN.COM
MINIBODEN		MINIBODEN.COM
MULBERRIBUSH (TUMBLEWEED TOO)		MULBERRIBUSH.COM
NAARTJIE		NAARTJIE.COM
OLD NAVY		OLDNAVY.COM
OSHKOSH B'GOSH	(800) 692-4674	OSHKOSHBGOSH.COM
PATSY AIKEN	(919) 872-8789	PATSYAIKEN.COM
PUMPKIN PATCH		PUMPKINPATCHUSA.COM
SARAH'S PRINTS	(888) 477-4687	SARASPRINTS.COM
SWEET POTATOES/SPUDZ	(800) 634-2584	SWEETPOTATOESINC.COM
TEA COLLECTION		TEACOLLECTION.COM
WES & WILLY		WESANDWILLY.COM
ZUTANO		ZUTANO.COM

Good But Not Great

CHILDREN'S PLACE		CHILDRENSPLACE.COM
GOOD LAD OF PHILA.	(215) 739-0200	GOODLAD.COM
GYMBOREE	(877) 449-6932	GYMBOREE.COM
LANDS END		LANDSEND.COM
LE TOP	(800) 333-2257	LETOP-USA.COM
TARGET (LITTLE ME, CLASSIC POOH, HALO, TYKES, CIRCO)		TARGET.COM
WALMART (FADED GLORY)		WALMART.COM

Skip It: GERBER, HANES, KOALA KIDS (BABIES R US), DISNEY, CARTER'S JUST ONE YEAR AT TARGET, GEORGE BY WALMART

Our Picks: Brand Recommendations

What clothing brands/catalogs are best? Well, there is no one correct answer. An outfit that's perfect for day care (that is, to be trashed in Junior's first painting experiment) is different from an out-fit for a weekend outing with friends. And dress-up occasions may require an entirely different set of clothing criteria. Hence, we've divided our clothing brand recommendations into three areas: good (day care), better (weekend wear) and best (special occasions). While some brands make items in two or even three categories, here's how we see it:

Good. For everyday comfort (and day-care situations), basic brands like Carter's, Little Me, and OshKosh are your best bets. We also like the basics (when on sale) at Baby Gap (Gap Kids) for day-care wardrobes. For great price to value, take a look at Old Navy and Target.

Better. What if you have a miniature golf outing planned with friends? Or a visit to Grandma's house? The brands of better-made casual wear we like best include Baby Gap, Flapdoodles, and Gymboree. Also recommended: Jake and Me, MulberriBush, and Wes and Willy. For online sites, we like the clothes in Hanna Andersson and MiniBoden as good brands.

Best. Holidays and other special occasions call for special outfits. We like Patsy Aiken, and the dressier items at Baby Gap. Of course, department stores are great sources for these outfits, as are consignment shops. As for catalogs, check out Wooden Soldier.

Diapers

The great diaper debate still rages on: should you use cloth or disposable? On one side are environmentalists, who argue cloth is better for the planet. On the other hand, those disposable diapers are darn convenient.

Considering the average baby will go through 2300 diaper changes in the first year of life, this isn't a moot issue—you'll be dealing with diapers until your baby is three or four years old (the average girl potty trains at 35 months; boys at 39 months). Yes, you read that last sentence right . . . you will be diapering for the next 35 to 39 MONTHS.

Now, in this section, we've decided NOT to rehash all the environmental arguments pro or con for cloth versus disposable. Fire up your web browser and you'll find plenty of diaper debate on parenting sites like BabyCenter.com or ParentsPlace.com. Instead, we'll focus here on the FINANCIAL and PRACTICAL impacts of your decision.

Let's look at each option:

Cloth. Prior to the 1960's, this was the only diaper option available to parents. Fans of cloth diapering point to babies that had less diaper rash and toilet trained faster. From a practical point of view, cloth diapers have improved in design over the years, offering more absorbency and fewer leaks. They aren't perfect, but the advent of diaper covers (no more plastic pants) has helped as well.

Another practical point: laundry. You've got to decide if you will use a cloth diaper service or launder at home. Obviously, the latter requires more effort on your part. We'll have laundry tips for cloth diapers later in this chapter. Meanwhile, we'll discuss the financial costs of cloth in general at the end of this section.

Final practical point about cloth: most day care centers don't allow them. This may be a sanitation requirement governed by state day care regulators and not a negotiating point. Check with local day care centers or your state board.

Disposables. Disposable diapers were first introduced in 1961 and now hold an overwhelming lead over cloth—about 95% of all households that have kids in diapers use disposables. Today's diapers have super-absorbent gels that lower the number of needed diaper changes, especially at night (which helps baby sleep through the night sooner). Even many parents who swear cloth diapers are best often use disposables at night. The downside? All that super-absorbency means babies are in no rush to potty train—they simply don't feel as wet or uncomfortable as babies in cloth diapers.

The jury on diaper rash is still out—disposable diaper users generally don't experience any more diaper rash than cloth diaper users.

Besides the eco-arguments about disposables, there is one other disadvantage—higher trash costs. In many communities, the more trash you put out, the higher the bill.

The financial bottom line: Surprisingly, there is no clear winner when you factor financial costs into the diaper equation.

Cloth diapers may seem cheap at first, but consider the hidden costs. Besides the diapers themselves ($100 for the basic varieties; $200 to $300 for the fancy ones), you also have to buy diaper covers. Like everything you buy with baby, there is a wide cost variation. The cheap stuff (like Dappi covers) will set you back $3 to $6 each. And you've got to buy several in different sizes as your child grows, so the total investment could be nearly $100. If you're lucky, you can find diaper covers second-hand for $1 to $3. Of course, some parents find low-cost covers leak and quickly wear out. As a result, they turn to the more expensive covers—a single Mother-Ease (see later for more info on this brand) is $12.25. Invest in a half dozen of those covers (in various sizes, of course) and you've spent another $240 to $480 (if you buy them new).

What about laundry? Well, washing your own cloth diapers at home may be the most economical way to go, but often folks don't have the time or energy. Instead, some parents use a cloth diaper service. In a recent cost survey of such services across the U.S., we found that the average is about $750 a year. While each service does supply you with diapers (relieving you of that expense), you're still on the hook for the diaper covers. Some services also don't provide enough diapers each month. You'll make an average of eight changes a day (more when a baby is newborn, less as they grow older), so be sure you're getting about 60 diapers a week from your service.

Proponents of cloth diapers argue that if you plan to have more than one child, you can reuse those covers, spreading out the cost. You may also not need as many sizes depending on the brands you use and the way your child grows.

So, what's the bottom line cost for cloth diapers? We estimate the total financial damage for cloth diapers (using a cloth diaper service and buying diaper covers) for just the first year is $850 to $1200.

By contrast, let's take a look at disposables. If you buy disposable diapers from the most expensive source in town (typically, a grocery store), you'd spend about $650 to $750 for the first year. Yet, we've found the best deals are buying in bulk from the discount sources we'll discuss shortly. By shopping at these sources, we figure you'd spend $400 to $500 per year (the lowest figure is for private label diapers, the highest is for brand names).

The bottom line: the cheapest way to go is cloth diapers laundered at home. The next best bet is disposables. Finally, cloth diapers from a diaper service are the most expensive.

Best Online Sources: Cloth Diapers

Families that use disposable diapers really have it easy. After all, there are only three main manufacturers and a few in-store brands to choose from. Yes, each manufacturer may have a few sub lines with different features, but a disposable is still basically a disposable.

Life's not that easy for cloth diaper aficionados—the choices seem endless. After researching this topic for fifteen years, we realize cloth diaper parents are like snowflakes—no two are exactly alike. Some like pockets, some love prefolds. Others think wool is great while still others like microfiber. And some use one product during the day and another at night. A few of our readers have confessed to being cloth diaper obsessed: they've collected a wide variety of different brands and types. So if you don't find all the answers here, we recommend you check out cloth diapering message boards, both on our site and others.

Here are a few web sites our readers have recommended for both cloth and disposable diapers (in that order).

ClothDiaper.com

clothdiaper.com. Home of the OsoCozy line of cloth diapers, ClothDiaper.com offers just about everything parents need for cloth diapering: covers, inserts, swim diapers, training pants and more. Package deals are available as well. When we first reviewed these guys, we were impressed by their All-in-One diapers. The system has soft cotton inside against baby's skin (gauze in the bleached version, birdseye weave in the unbleached), a polyurethane waterproof liner, adjustable Velcro-style closures and elastic leg openings. The cost: $15 each with quantity discounts available. The advantage of the all-in-one is pretty obvious, but if you'd rather buy prefolds or flat diapers, they are also available on this site as are organic fabric options. Package options are available on both fitted and prefolds

Break glass for emergency diaper

In our never-ending quest to discover cool baby products and share them with our readers, we scour trade shows each year, meeting with hundreds of entrepreneurs who are convinced they've invented the next Diaper Genie. While the hype doesn't often match reality, we occasionally unearth a something really amazing.

Exhibit one: Diaper Buds.

Diaper Buds are vacuum-sealed, disposable diapers that you can fit in your jeans pocket. The idea? Diaper Buds are an emergency diaper—when you're fresh out of diapers and something bad happens. And since they are vacuum-packed, they take up little space. Diaper Buds are individually wrapped and when opened expand into a full size diaper. They come in sizes 2 to 5 and sell for $6 to $18, depending on size and quantity. You can purchase a sample from their web site (DiaperBuds.com) for just $1 per bud.

at up to 35% off. Cloth Diaper.com does sell FuzziBunz and GroVia diapers as well as Bummi, Imse Vimse, Whisper Pant and Gerber diaper covers. Finally, we love this sites "all the diapers your baby will need" options. Let's say you want to buy all the fitted diapers your baby will need up to 18 lbs and you don't want to wash too often. That package sells for $465.95. If the items were purchased separately, the cost would be $735. What a deal! **Rating: B**

Diapers.com

diapers.com. So you think Walmart and Amazon are aggressive discounters? You ain't seen nothin' till you've shopped at Diapers.com. Deals abound here: on a recent visit they were offering 30% cash back on diapers for three months and 10% off everything else. Impressive.

Diapers.com's regular price on Huggies Snug & Dry sizes 1&2: $37.99 for 192 pack. Cost per diaper runs 20¢ each. But. . . you can use a coupon and save $3 per package (now 18¢ each) or that promotion we mention earlier of 30% cash back for three months (this works out to 14¢ per diaper). At that price, Diapers.com is among the cheapest sources for diapers in the U.S.

So why are diapers such a deal here? Because Diapers.com sells diapers as a loss leader, hoping that when you come to their site for diapers, you'll stay to buy a few of their over 25,000 additional products. But the real mojo of the site is their free two-day delivery if you buy at least $49 worth of stuff.

Thanks to those prices and super-fast shipping, Diapers.com has quickly become one of the top sites selling baby gear. The site became such a threat to Amazon that the company acquired them in late 2010. We're not sure how Amazon will change this site, but for now Diapers.com is a winner and worth a visit. **Rating: A**

Green Mountain Diapers

greenmountaindiapers.com. Looking for some help figuring out the cloth diapering options out there? Check out Green Mountain Diapers. This site may not look as sophisticated as others, but the info and photos make it a useful resource. Most helpful: photos of real babies wearing the products they sell, which helps new cloth diaper parents get a better idea of what each product is like. Green Mountain Diapers sells a wide variety of products, include preemie cloth diapers. Wool and cotton is the specialty here, with flat-rate shipping. **Rating: A**

Mother-Ease

mother-ease.com. Mother-Ease has been around for over 20 years, manufacturing their own line of cloth diapers. They offer all-in-one diapers, one size diapers (in two levels of absorbency), and two types of diaper covers. Prices start at $12 for the original One Size diaper and range up to $14.75 depending on the type of fabric (choose from unbleached cotton, bleached cotton, bamboo/cotton and organic cotton). Sandy's diapers come in two sizes for a more custom size and are priced the same as the One Size option. All in One diapers run $16 to $18 each. While parents like Mother-Ease diapers, options are limited to their three styles—if one of these doesn't work, you'll have to look elsewhere. **Rating: B+**

Nicki's Diapers

nickisdiapers.com. Nicki's Diapers is a popular site mentioned often on our message boards here at *Baby Bargains.* And with good reason. They carry a wide range of cloth diapering supplies including their Best Bottom diapers. Best Bottoms are a water-proof, adjustable shell with a snap-in insert inside. Inserts are available in three different sizes and different materials (microfiber or hemp/organic cotton) as well. Shells sell for $17 while inserts range from $4 to $7 each. Nicki's recommends buying eight to ten shells and 18 to 24 inserts per size. But that's not all. Nicki's sells a huge number of brands including FuzziBunz, GroVia, Happy Heiny's, Bumkins, bumGenius and many more. Readers praise their customer service and give this web site a cloth diapering thumbs up. **Rating: A**

Zoolikins.com

zoolikins.com. A reader recommended Zoolikins (formerly Wild Flower Diapers) for their amazing inventory of cloth diapering products as well as their great articles. They carry products from Babykicks, Thirsties, Bummis, Little Beetle, FuzziBunz, bumGenius, and our favorite: Knickernapies. Prices are regular retail, but if you live in Phoenix, you can pick up amazing bargains at their retail location, including used diapers for as little as $1. Zoolikins has a sale section online. **Rating: B**

Our Picks: Brand Recommendations

Disposables. The evolution of disposable diapers is rather amazing. They started out in the 1960's as bulky and ineffective at stopping leaks. In the last 60 years, disposables morphed into ultra-thin, super-absorbent miracle workers that command 95% of the market.

And writing about disposable diaper brands is like trying to nail Jell-O to a wall—every five minutes, the diaper makers come out with new features and new gimmicks as they jostle for a piece of the nearly $27 billion worldwide diaper market. In the 16 years since the first edition of this book came out, the constant innovation in this category is amazing. We used to talk about three types of diapers:

basic (thick, tape tabs), ultrathin (with the gel and tape tabs) and supreme (fabric-like outer layer, Velcro tabs). But in recent years, almost all diapers have added Velcro tabs, nicer outer layers and the ubiquitous super absorbent gels. So what separates the good from the bad diapers? *The key is good fit, no leaks and comfort for baby.*

No matter what brand you try, remember that sizing of diapers is all over the board. The "size two" diaper in one brand may be cut totally different from the "medium" of another, even though the weight guidelines on the package are similar. Finding a diaper that fits is critical to you and your baby's happiness.

Now, let's answer some common questions about disposables:

Q. What makes one brand different from another?

A. Surprisingly, the absorbency of diapers varies little from brand to brand. A *Consumer Reports* test of 14 families with infants and toddlers is a case in point. They tested seven types of disposable diapers. Five of them tested "very good" or "excellent" for leak protection. No matter what brand you choose, you'll probably have a diaper that fits well and doesn't leak. Yes, the premium/supreme diapers scored highest in CR's tests, but the difference between them and the cheaper options was minimal (except for the price, of course).

In 2010, Houston, Texas TV station KPRC did a blind test of diapers with local viewers—and the results were similar to what *Consumer Reports* found. KPRC reporter Amy Davis gave two unmarked packages of diapers to viewers, asking them to score them on quality and fit. The station compared both national brands and private label options from Walmart, Target and Babies R Us.

The winner? Parents named the Babies R Us' Supreme Diaper brand (a private label) as their favorite. BRU's diapers are priced below national brands, but a bit more than store brands at Walmart and other discounters.

Q. What about store brands like Babies R Us and others? Is there much difference?

A. Although store diapers used to be less impressive than name brands, as we noted above, they've caught up in terms of cloth like covers, Velcro fasteners and ultra absorbency. And they cost as much as 30% less too.

Q. Do certain brands work better for boys or girls?

A. We used to hear anecdotal evidence from our readers that Huggies were better for boys and Pampers better for girls. In recent years, however, parents tell us there doesn't seem to be a gender difference at all.

Q. How many diapers of each size is a good starting point?

A. Most babies go through 12 to 14 diapers *per day* for the first few months. That translates into about 500 to 600 diapers for the first six weeks. As you read at the beginning of the chapter we recommend buying 100 "newborn" size diapers and 400 to 500 "size one" diapers before baby is born. Caveat: some families have large babies, so keep the receipts just in case you have to exchange some of those newborns for size 1.

So how many do you need of the larger sizes? Starting with a case of each size as you transition to larger diapers is a good idea. There are typically 100 diapers or more in a case. As you near a transition to a larger size, scale back the amount of smaller size diapers you buy so you don't have any half opened packs lying around.

Finally, remember that as your baby grows, she will require fewer diaper changes. Once you add solid foods to her feeding schedule you may only be doing eight to ten changes a day (we know—eight to ten a day still seems like a ton of changes; but it will feel much less than baby's first few weeks). Plus you'll be much more experienced about when a diaper really is wet.

Check out our comments on different diaper brands. They are arranged alphabetically. By the way, all their web sites offer coupons of some sort—check them out and sign up for the deals.

◆ *Babies R Us Supreme diapers.* As we mentioned above, BRU's Supreme diapers won a blind test run by a Houston TV station in 2010. Fans of these diapers like their overall quality—the liner is hypoallergenic and contains vitamin E, aloe and zinc. They also have a waterproof cover and stretchy waistband. And the price is right: size 1's are just 13¢ each. But the verdict on these diapers isn't unanimous. Critics say leaks are a problem—and the stretchable grip tabs don't stretch enough.

◆ *Huggies (huggies.com).* Huggies has been a strong brand for years. They now offer five diaper options: Pure & Natural, Little Snugglers, Little Movers, Snug & Dry and Overnight. One of the best features of the line are the pocketed waistbands designed to avoid blowouts. This feature is available on the Pure & Natural and Little Snugglers/Movers lines.

Huggies Pure & Natural have an organic cotton exterior and are hypoallergenic with aloe and vitamin E. The liner is also recyclable and they use less ink on the graphics on these diapers. Obviously, this is an attempt to convince parents that these diapers are more eco-friendly. You'll pay for it—on Walmart.com we priced size 1 Pure & Natural at 25¢ per diaper while the size 1 Little Snugglers was 23¢ per diaper. Hence using the more eco-friendly Huggies will run you about $50 a year.

Little Snugglers (formally Huggies Supreme) feature a cloth-like outer cover, wetness indicator and pocketed waistband. Huggies Snug & Dry are their less expensive option with leak lock (layers to "lock wetness away") and the SnugFit elastic waistband. The Snug & Dry Diapers are about 20% cheaper than Little Snugglers.

Overnights are made to be even more absorbent so babies can actually sleep through the night (and parents too!). And they still have their "Little Swimmers" swim diapers—great for the pool or beach.

As for wipes, Huggies offers five varieties from Sensitive to Natural Care to Soft Skin. Feedback from parents was a thumbs up on the wipes, no matter the type.

Reader feedback on Huggies is positive. Parents note that the pocket waistband (they call it the "poop pocket") really does help avoid up-the-back blowouts.

◆ *Luvs (luvsdiapers.com).* Made by Procter & Gamble (who also makes Pampers), Luvs are marketed as a lower-price brand. They are often less expensive than even store brand diapers.

Thankfully, Luvs doesn't try to be all things to all people with multiple diaper options. They just have one diaper with basic features. Luvs stresses their Ultra Leakguard guarantee that claims Luvs will have fewer leaks that your current brand—or your money back.

So, do they work? Readers were mixed in their appraisal of Luvs. Some said they leaked, but others praised the low price and thought they worked fine. In the blind test in Houston mentioned earlier, parents ranked Luvs in the middle of the pack (in a tie with Huggies). Walmart.com's price for size 1 Luvs was an amazing 13¢ per diaper. Compared to Huggies Little Snugglers at 23¢ per diaper, we'd say try Luvs first!

◆ *Pampers (pampers.com).* Pampers continues to offer an extensive line of diapers including Swaddlers Sensitive, Swaddlers with Dry Max, Cruisers (also with Dry Max) and Baby Dry diapers. Their new Dry Max technology has been a bit controversial. Pampers was stung by parent criticism that claimed their babies got a rash from the super absorbing technology, a claim Pampers denies. In fact, Pampers has aggressively countered the bad press with a money-back guarantee and online FAQ's addressing the controversy. An inquiry from the Consumer Product Safety Commission found no evidence the diapers caused rashes.

So what makes the Dry Max technology so special? The company claims their Dry Max diapers are two times drier than standard diapers and 20% thinner. The company has added five times more absorbent gel and eliminated much of the filler that made diapers bulky.

Baby Dry diapers are Pampers' lower-priced line. They don't use the Dry Max technology and offer pretty basic features like contoured fit and absorbent core.

Swaddlers Sensitive are Pampers' hypoallergenic option with an absorbent liner like the Baby Dry diapers.

Walmart.com sells the Baby Dry diapers and Swaddlers with Dry Max (size 1) for 18¢ per diaper; Swaddlers Sensitive (size 1) sell for 22¢ each. Overall, reader feedback on the Pampers line has been positive.

◆ *Parent's Choice by Walmart.* Walmart's private label brand, Parent's Choice, has features similar to name-brand diapers: a cloth-like cover, absorbent core, elastic leg openings and flexible fit waistband. But the price is what's impressive. On their web site, we found a 200 pack of size 1 diapers for only $27.50. The per diaper price: 14¢, among the lowest prices out there. So what do readers think of Parent's Choice? Fans note that Walmart has re-engineered

Who's got the cheapest diapers?

What's the best place to buy disposable diapers? We did a price comparison among several major sources, listed here from least to most expensive:

STORE OR WEB SITE	DIAPER TYPE	COUNT	PRICE	PER DIAPER
BABIESRUS.COM**	HUGGIES #1	264	$36.89	14¢
SAM'S CLUB	HUGGIES #1-2	264	$38.88	15¢
COSTCO	HUGGIES #2	258	$39.99	15¢
AMAZON.COM**	HUGGIES #1-2	192	$30.65	16¢
WALMART.COM**	HUGGIES #1	192	$35.00	18¢
TARGET.COM**	HUGGIES #1	84	$16.99	20¢
DIAPERS.COM***	HUGGIES #1-2	192	$37.99	20¢
GROCERY STORE*	HUGGIES #2	42	$9.77	23¢

Per Diaper: The cost per diaper.

* Checked at Kroger (King Soopers).
** Free shipping; minimum dollar amount may be required.
*** Diapers.com offers coupons and cash back offers that lower the price down to 14¢ per diaper.

Note: Prices checked as of 2011.

their diapers, changing the tabs and sizing to compare more with Pampers' diapers. Reviews have been generally positive, although in the blind test we mentioned above, Parent's Choice ranked dead last. This is a great brand to consider taking to daycare if you have to provide the diapers.

◆ *Up & Up by Target.* Target's in store brand, Up & Up sells for an amazing 13¢ per diaper for a pack of size 1's. That's even less than Walmart's Parents' Choice. These diapers feature leak guards, and the usual contoured shape. They are hypoallergenic, chlorine free and latex free. Parents apparently liked an earlier version of the diapers better—recent reviews complain they now leak and are smaller and thinner. They also scored near the bottom in the Houston test. As a result, we wouldn't recommend this brand.

Eco-friendly Disposables. Are there diapers that combine the convenience of disposables with the ecological benefits of cloth diapers? Yes—here's an overview of so-called eco-friendly disposables:

Tushies, first invented by a Denver pediatrician in the late 1980's, bills its diapers as a gel-free, latex-free, perfume-free alternative to name brand disposables. Made with non-chlorine bleached wood pulp surrounding an absorbent cotton core, Tushies also has a "cloth-like" cover. Tushies mentions that without the gel, their diapers won't "explode" in the swimming pool.

The disadvantages to Tushies? They are considerably thicker than regular diapers. And like most "all-natural" versions of consumer goods, Tushies ain't cheap. Amazon.com sells a case of 160 size small diapers for $43.63. That's a whopping 27¢ per diaper. Yes, that's twice the price of discounted regular diapers.

Seventh Generation (seventhgeneration.com) is another brand of chlorine-free disposable diapers with a thinner design than Tushies. The diapers have a cloth like outer layer, reusable tabs, and are latex and fragrance free. Made of wood pulp, a polyolefin backing and a polyolefin outer cover, Seventh Generation also includes an absorbent polymer gel. They are careful to explain that the gel they use is non-toxic, non-carcinogenic and non-irritating. In fact, you can view material safety data sheets on all the diaper's components on their web site. A reader also recommends the company's wipes saying they are "free of chemicals and full of good stuff for my baby's skin."

You can find these diapers online at Amazon or in stores such as Whole Foods and Vitamin Cottage. On Amazon.com, a pack of 176 stage 1 Seventh Generation diapers was $39.99 (a pricey 23¢ per diaper). Coupons are available on Seventh Generation's web site.

Another newcomer to the eco-friendly disposable is *Nature Babycare* diapers by Naty (naty.com). These diapers are chlorine free and use no plastics (corn-based materials). They were designed by a Swedish mom and are compostable. They are slightly less expensive Tushies (26¢ per diaper) for the small size, but still considerably more than standard disposables. You'll find them on web sites like Diapers.com and Target.com.

Here's a popular new diaper that isn't quite a disposable, nor a cloth diaper—**gDiapers** are flushable cloth diapers. Yep, you read it right. Flushable. To be precise, part of a gDiaper is flushable.

A gDiapers starter kit comes with six reusable "little g" pants (like cloth diaper covers) and 640 diaper refills for $130 on Diapers.com. Once you are ready to dispose of the diaper refills, you have a choice: flush them, compost the wet diapers or throw them in the garbage. GDiapers notes you never compost a poopy diaper, only flush it. But what about throwing them out? Isn't that the same as disposables? Not necessarily since there is no plastic in gDiapers, so they degrade fast (supposedly 50 to 150 days) . . . if you don't put them in a plastic trash bag, of course.

GDiapers' web site has several videos showing their product at work. And we've heard from several moms who love this idea. It is a nice compromise in the cloth versus disposable debate. One caveat: you'll find gDiapers aren't as absorbent as disposables, simply because they use only wood pulp (fluffed for extra absorbency) rather than that super absorbent gel in most diapers. Price is probably the biggest stumbling block with gDiapers. Additional washable "little g" pants range from $14 to $18. Refills start at 33¢ each for a 160 of the small size. Ouch! That's more than twice the price of disposables when bought at discount stores! You can also buy reusable snap-in liners, $20 for six.

Ultimately, while these products are promising options for parents looking for a natural alternative to mainstream disposables, the price of all these options severely limits their popularity. And there is still an issue of where these diapers will go. Until recycling centers with composting options become more widely available, there's a question as to whether these diapers won't still end up buried under tons of earth and trash waiting to decompose.

Cloth Diapers. As we noted earlier, if you ask 100 parents for their recommendations on cloth diapers you're likely to get 100 different opinions—it seems everyone has their special system or favorite brand! So what's an aspiring CD'er (cloth diaperer) to do? First let's take you through the basics with Karen F., our CD guru from our message boards:

A cloth diaper has three basic functions. Working from the inside out:

1. Wick it away. This layer is intended to keep baby from sitting in her pee. This layer lets moisture through in one direction but not back towards the skin. In cloth diapers, this layer is fleece or suede-cloth, but only certain kinds of fleece will do this. Some people just cut rectangles of fleece and lay them inside the diaper. Some diapers are lined with fleece, sewn in place while others are pocket diapers with the fleece next to the skin. And there are some people who skip this layer and change the diaper as soon as baby pees.

2. Soak it up. Typically, the absorbent layer in cloth diapers is made of cotton or hemp and is sewn in layers. There are also some diapers with a micro fiber towel for the absorbent layer. Some people add an extra layer called a "doubler" which is just layers of cloth sewn together. This allows parents to increase absorption when needed (overnight, for example). See page 212 for a discussion of

---

E-MAIL FROM THE REAL WORLD
Cloth diaper laundry tips

Once you make the decision to use cloth diapers, you'll want to research the "art" of cleaning them. Too many harsh chemicals can damage and fade cloth diapers and covers, not enough will leave diapers looking less than pristine. So what's a parent to do? Here's some advice from readers who've experienced lots of diaper cleaning.

Rowan Cerrelli writes:

"I do not like to use chlorine bleach to wash out diapers since they are expensive and the chlorine ruins them. There are some products out there that use natural enzymes to predigest 'stuff' out of the diapers, therefore eliminating the need for bleach. Companies that have these products include Seventh Generation and Ecover. They are also available in natural food grocery stores."

Catherine Advocate-Ross recommends:

"I use BioKleen laundry powder on the diapers. Works great and you need very little."

BioKleen's web site biokleenhome.com explains their products and directs consumers to stores or web sites that carry them. They have an extensive line including liquid as well as powder detergent and stain and odor eliminator. The main ingredient in the line is grapefruit seed and pulp extract.

Kelly Small, from Wallingford, CT emailed us to say:

"I highly recommend OxyClean— it is great on the poop stains!!!"

---

the different options for this layer.

3. Keep the rest of the world dry. Remember those awful plastic/rubber pants of yesteryear? Uncomfortable for baby and noisy too! Today's options are much more comfortable to wear and touch. Cloth diaper covers can be polyurethane laminate (PUL) over cotton or polyester, nylon, wool or fleece. Wool is naturally water repellent when it has natural lanolin in it. (Otherwise sheep would bulk up like a sponge in a rainstorm!). The type of fleece that is used as diaper covers is water repellent."

Okay, now that you know the mechanics of cloth diapering, what should you use for your little guy or gal? First, here's the lingo you'll need to master:

Finally, Rebecca Parish has some practical advice on cloth diapers:
"We (my friends and I) have run across a shortcut that I had not heard about before we attempted cloth diapering. Mainly, we have found it entirely unnecessary to rinse diapers out at all before laundering them. We own a four-day supply of pre-fold diapers and wraps. When our baby poops, we take an extra diaper wipe with us to the toilet, and use it to scrape what easily comes off into the toilet. Then we throw the dirty diaper into our diaper pail, right along with all the other dirty diapers. There's no liquid in the pail for soaking—they just sit in there dry. About every three or four days we throw the entire contents of the diaper pail into the laundry machine, add regular detergent (we use Cheer) and two capfuls of bleach (about 4 teaspoons), and run the machine. The diapers and wraps all come out clean. Just two extra loads of laundry a week (which is nothing compared to the extra loads of clothes we now wash), and no dipping our hands into toilet water. I generally use about five diaper wipes every time I change a messy diaper as it is, so using one extra one for scraping poop into the toilet seems like no big deal.

I think washer technology has improved significantly enough in recent years to allow for this much easier diaper cleaning. We own a fairly new front-loader washer. I don't think the brand name is important; we have a friend who owns a different brand of front-loader, and gets equally good results. However, one of our friends with an older top-loader uses our same system but ends up with stains; she doesn't care but I would. "

Bottom line: new technologies (detergents, additives and washers) have led to great improvements in the cleaning of cloth diapers.

1 PREFOLDS (CPF for Chinese prefolds or DSQ for diaper-service quality). These are what most parents think of when they envision cloth diapers. They are heavyweight 100% cotton cloths that have been prefolded (so that there is extra padding in the middle) and sewn down. This process leads to a diaper with six to eight layers in the middle and two to four layers on the sides. They can then be pinned onto your baby (not our favorite idea) or folded into a diaper cover. Avoid flat fold diapers—these are really just burp pads and great dust cloths!

2 FITTED DIAPER: Sometimes called pre-fitteds, these are prefolded diapers that have elastic sewn in for the leg openings. They don't have snaps or Velcro so they have to be secured with pins or in a cover. You'll get a more snug fit around the leg openings with these.

3 DOUBLER (ALSO CALLED LINER). Available in paper, cotton, microfiber or even silk, doublers are used when you need extra absorbency. They are inserted between the diaper and baby's bottom. These would be a great option at night or on a long car trip.

4 DIAPER COVER/WRAP. This item is placed over the diaper to stop leaks. One style of diaper cover is called a wrap—think of it as baby origami. You'll wrap your baby up and secure the Velcro tabs to the front strip. Some covers snap in place and there are other pants that can be pulled on (elastic waist).

5 ALL-IN-ONE. Just what you'd think, an all-in-one (AIO) is a diaper and cover sewn together. There are pluses and minuses to this design. Yes, the convenience of grabbing one item and snapping or Velcro-ing it on your baby is great, but if your baby makes a mess, you have to wash the whole thing. With a traditional diaper/cover combination, you won't have to wash the cover every time unless baby gets poop on it. So you'll end up buying more all-in-ones to keep yourself from doing laundry constantly.

6 POCKET DIAPER. Made famous by Fuzzi Bunz, the pocket diaper is an all-in-one with a pocket sewn into the lining. You can then customize the diaper for more absorbency by adding an insert or a prefolded diaper.

7 SNAPPI FASTENERS. Made in South Africa, these cutting-edge diaper fasteners replace the traditional (and potentially painful) diaper pin. Check out their website at snappibaby.com for a look at how they work.

Whew! That's a lot to remember. So anyway, what's the bottom line? What should you buy? Great question. Here's what our cloth diaper guru recommends if you're just starting out and have a newborn: Buy two to three dozen prefold diapers and four to six diaper covers. You may also want to get a few pocket diapers or all-in-ones and a couple Snappis.

Now you probably want to know which brands to buy. So we polled our readers to find out their favorites. Right off the bat, they told us "it depends." Depends on your baby's body type, whether you're looking for nighttime leak protection and many other factors. A couple of the brands readers *could* agree on were Fuzzi Bunz (fuzzibunz.com) and Snap-EZ Fleece Pocket diapers (snap-ez.com). Here is a list of the other brands readers recommend:

◆ **Fitted Diapers:**
Happy Heiney (happyheiny.com)
Kissaluvs (kissaluvs.com)
Monkey Toe Diapers (monkeytoediapers.com/sugarplumbaby)
Nicki's (nikisdiapers.com)

◆ **Diaper Covers:**
Aristocrat (wool) (aristocratsbabyproducts.com)
FLIP (flipdiapers.com)
gDiapers (gdiapers.com)
Imse Vimse Bumpy (imsevimse.us)
Swaddlebees ABC Snap Wraps (swaddlebees.com)

◆ **All-In–Ones:**
Bum Genius (bumgenius.com)
Daisy Doodles (daisy-doodles.com)
DryBees (drybees.com)
Gro Via (gro-via.com)
Lullaby Diapers (lullabydiapers.com)
Swaddlebees Simplex (swaddlebees.com)

◆ **Pockets:**
bumGenius (bumgenius.com)
Fuzzi Bunz (fuzzibunz.com)
Happy Heiny's (happyheinys.com)
Nicki's (nickisdiapers.com)
Olive Branch Baby Marathon (obbdiapers.com)
Thirsties (thirstiesbaby.com)

◆ **Inserts/Doubler:**
Babykicks Hemparoo Joey Bunz (babykicks.com)
bumGenius Stay Dry Doubler (bmgenius.com)
FLIP (flipdiapers.com)

FuzziBunz Hemp Inserts (fuzzibunz.com)
gDiaper—disposable and reusable (gdiaper.com)
Gro Via Stay Dry Booster (gro-via.com)
Happy Heiney's Stuffins (happyheineys.com)
Imse Vimse Stay Dry Liners (imsevimse.us/)

Need more information? A good book on using cloth diapers is
Diaper Changes by Theresa Rodriquez (M. Evans and Co., publisher; $15, Amazon.com). Also, check out our online message boards on
our web site at babybargains.com. They have extensive commentary
from cloth diaper parents with tips and recommendations.

Wipes. Like diapers, you have a basic choice with wipes: name
brand or generic. Our advice: stick to the name brands. We polled
our readers and their top pick was: **Huggies Natural Care**. The
reviews were more mixed with Pampers wipes: some parents
thought they were too wet and too expensive.

We found most cheap generic wipes to be inferior. With less
water and thinner construction, store brand wipes we sampled
were losers. There are a couple exceptions to this rule, however:
Costco's Kirkland brand wipes, and Walgreens Comfort-Smooth
Sensitive baby wipes. One mom emailed: "Kirkland are not as rigid
as Huggies or Pampers, have a lighter scent and are stronger than
any other wipe we tried." And it's hard to beat the price: $19 for
900 (that's 2.1¢ per wipe). As for Walgreens' brand, a mom emailed
saying they "are as good at Huggies in thickness and durability."
And they cost about 3¢ a wipe. Another mom really loves BJ's
Berkely & Jensen brand of wipes. She thought they were softer
than Costco, more like Huggies for less than 2¢ a wipe.

Money Saving Secrets

Here are some tips for saving on disposable diapers (cloth diaper bargain advice is at the end of this section):

1 **THINK PRICE PER DIAPER.** Stores sell diapers in all sorts of package sizes—always compare diaper prices per diaper, not per
box.

2 **BUY IN BULK.** Don't buy those little packs of 20 diapers—look
for the 80 or 100 count packs instead. You'll find the price per
diaper goes down when you buy larger packs. That's why grocery
stores are usually the most expensive place to buy diapers—they sell

diapers in small packages, with the highest per diaper price.

3 **GO FOR WAREHOUSE CLUBS.** Both Sam's (samsclub.com) and Costco (costco.com) wholesale clubs sell diapers at incredibly low prices. For example, Costco sells a 258-count package of Huggies stage 2 for just $39.99 or about 15¢ per diaper. We also found great deals on wipes at the wholesale clubs. Another warehouse club is BJ's (bjs.com), which has nearly 200 locations in 15 states, most in the Eastern U.S. The downside? You buy a membership to shop at clubs, which runs about $50 a year. And clubs don't stock the usual sizes of diapers—Costco carries "size 1-2" Kirkland diapers, instead of just size 1 or 2. Readers are frustrated with this combined sizing, according to our message boards.

4 **BUY STORE BRANDS.** As mentioned earlier, many parents find store brand diapers to be equal to the name brands. And the prices can't be beat—many are 20% to 30% cheaper. Chains like Target, Walmart and Toys R Us/Babies R Us carry in-house diaper brands, as do many grocery stores. See the reviews earlier on these store brands. Warehouse clubs also carry in store brands: Costco's Kirkland, BJ's Little Bundles and Sam's Club's Member's Mark. Sample price: Costco's Kirkland diapers are just 14¢ each.

5 **FORGET BRAND LOYALTY.** Buy whatever diaper is on sale this week at your favorite store. Ok, some diapers are losers (Target's Up & Up are an example), but if Huggies are on sale this week, go for the Huggies. When Pampers go on sale next week, buy those. Since the name brands and most private label diapers are equivalent in quality, it doesn't pay to be brand loyal.

6 **CONSIDER TOYS R US.** You may not have a wholesale club nearby, but you're bound to be close to a Toys R Us (or their sister division, Babies R Us). And we found them to be a great source for affordable name-brand diapers. The best bet: buy in bulk. You can often buy diapers (both name brand and generic) by the case at Toys R Us, saving you about 20% or more over grocery store prices. A recent price check by Houston TV station KPRC found Babies R Us had the lowest prices on diapers in that city—beating out grocery stores, Target and even warehouse clubs (once you factor in the annual membership cost). A year's worth of diapers ran $365.70 at BRU versus $370 at Costco or Sam's, the station reported. Bonus: TRU and BRU often offer in-store coupons for diapers—combine these with manufacturer's coupons for double savings.

7 **ONLINE DEALS MAY BEAT IN-STORE PRICES.** Hard to believe, but sometimes buying diapers online and having them shipped to your house is cheaper than buying at a store. Why? Online sites often sell bigger packages of diapers than stores—and the bigger the package, the lower the cost per diaper. Walmart.com is an example—it sells Pampers for 17% less online (with free shipping) than in the store . And sites like Diapers.com sell diapers at or below cost to lure in customers. With many sties offering free or low-cost shipping, online dealers may be better than shopping in store.

8 **WHEN BABY IS NEARING A TRANSITION POINT, DON'T STOCK UP.** Quick growing babies may move into another size faster than you think, leaving you with an excess supply of too-small diapers.

9 **DON'T BUY DIAPERS IN GROCERY STORES.** We compared prices at grocery stores and usually found them to be sky-high. Most were selling diapers in packages that worked out to 20¢ per diaper. We should note there are exceptions to this rule, however: some grocery chains (especially in the South) use diapers as a "loss-leader." They'll sell diapers at attractive prices in order to entice shoppers into the store. Also, store brands can be more attractively priced, even at grocery stores. Use coupons (see below) to save even more.

10 **USE COUPONS.** You'll be amazed at how many coupons you receive in the mail, usually for 75¢ off diapers and 50¢ off wipes. One tip: to keep those "introductory" packages of coupons coming, continue signing up to be on the mailing lists of the maternity chain stores (apparently, these chains sell your name to diaper manufacturers, formula companies, etc.) or online at diaper manufacturers' web sites.

11 **IF HAVE TO BUY YOUR DIAPERS FROM A GROCERY STORE OR PHARMACY, SIGN UP FOR A LOYALTY CARD**. Yes, we just said don't buy diapers at the grocery store. But we know—sometimes the grocery store is the most convenient choice for a 2 am diaper run. Our advice: sign up for the store's loyalty card, which often offers discounts on items like diapers and wipes. Combine this with in-store sales and manufacturer's coupons and you might find the price per diaper approaching what you'd pay at a discount store. If you have multiple coupons, buying multiple packages sometimes achieves the maximum savings.

12 **ASK FOR GIFT CERTIFICATES.** When friends ask you what you'd like as a shower gift, you can drop hints for gift certificates/cards from stores that sell a wide variety of baby items—including diapers and wipes. That way you can get what you really need, instead of cute accessories of marginal value. You'd be surprised at how many stores offer gift certificate programs.

13 **FOR CLOTH DIAPER USERS, GO FOR "INTRODUCTORY PACKAGES."** Many suppliers have special introductory deals (Mother-Ease offers their One-Size diaper, a liner and cover for $22 to $25 including shipping). Before you invest hundreds of dollars in one brand, give it a test drive first.

14 **BUY USED CLOTH DIAPERS.** Many of the best brands of cloth diapers last and last and last. So you may see them on eBay or cloth-diaper message boards. Buy them—you can get some brands for as little a buck or two. As long as you know the quality and age of the diapers you're buying, this tip can really be a money saver.

15 **REUSE THEM.** Okay, we know this may be obvious, but hang onto your cloth diapers and use them for your next child. Every child is different, so even if you buy a brand and it doesn't fit your baby well, it may work on your next child. And of course, you can always sell them on eBay or Craigslist when you're all finished.

16 **MANUFACTURERS' SECONDS.** Diaper site Kissaluvs.com emailed us this tip: every six to eight weeks, the site offers diaper seconds at a huge discount. The diapers are still perfectly fine, they just have minor flaws that don't affect their quality like a slightly too large waistline, a button a millimeter out of place or stitching in the wrong color. If you have a favorite cloth diaper brand, consider checking directly with the manufacturer to see if they offer any seconds deals as well.

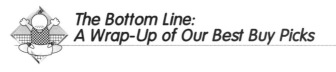

The Bottom Line: A Wrap-Up of Our Best Buy Picks

In summary, we recommend you buy the following layette items for your baby (see chart on next page).

QUANTITY	ITEM	COST
6	T-shirts/onesies (over the head)	$18
6	T-shirts (side snap)	$20
4-6	Sleepers	$64-$96
1	Blanket Sleeper	$12.50
2-4	Coveralls	$50-$100
3-4	Booties/socks	$10-$12
1	Sweater	$16.50
2	Hats (safari and caps)	$20
1	Snowsuit/bunting	$20
4	Large bibs (for feeding)	$24
3 sets	Wash cloths and towels	$36
7-8	Receiving blankets	$20

TOTAL   **$311 to $395**

These prices are from discounters, outlet stores, or sale prices at department stores. What would all these clothes cost at full retail? $500 to $600, at least. The bottom line: follow our tips and you'll save $100 to $300 on your baby's layette alone. (Of course, you may receive some of these items as gifts, so your actual outlay may be less.)

Which brands are best? See "Our Picks: Brand Recommendations" earlier in this chapter. In general, we found that 100% cotton clothes are best. Yes, you'll pay a little more for cotton, but it lasts longer and looks better than clothes made of polyester blends (the exception: fleece outerwear and sleepwear). Other wastes of money for infants include kimonos, saque sets, and shoes.

What about diapers? We found little financial difference between cloth and disposable, especially when you use a cloth diaper service. Cloth does have several hidden costs, however—diaper covers can add hundreds of dollars to the expense of this option although the cost can be spread out among additional children.

For disposables, we found that brand choice was more of a personal preference—all the majors did a good job at stopping leaks. The best way to save money on disposable diapers is to skip the grocery store and buy in bulk (100+ diaper packages) from a warehouse club. Diapers from discount sources run about $300 to $375. The same diapers from grocery stores could be $600 or more. Another great money-saver: generic, store-brand diapers from Babies R Us, Walmart, Target and the like. These diapers performed just as well as the name brands at a 20% to 30% discount.

Whew! Now that you have an advanced degree in baby clothing and diaper deals, let's talk about maternity clothes, up next!

CHAPTER 5

Maternity & Nursing

Inside this chapter

Love 'em or hate 'em, every mother-to-be needs maternity clothes at some point in her pregnancy. Still, you don't have to break the bank to get comfortable, and, yes, fashionable maternity items. In this chapter, we tell you which sources sell all-cotton, casual clothes at unbelievably low prices. Then, we'll review the biggest maternity chains and reveal our list of top wastes of money. Finally, you'll learn which nursing clothes moms prefer most.

Maternity & Nursing Clothes

Getting Started: When Do You Need This Stuff?

It may seem obvious that you'll need to buy maternity clothes when you get pregnant, but the truth is you don't actually need all of them immediately. The first thing you'll notice is the need for a new bra. At least, that was my first clue that my body was changing. Breast changes occur as early as the first month and you may find yourself going through several different bra sizes along the way.

Next, it's time for the bump. Yes, the baby is making its presence known by making you feel a bit bigger around the middle. Skirts and pants feel tight as early as your third month. Maternity clothes at this point may seem like overkill, but some women do begin to "show" enough that they find it necessary to head out to the maternity shop.

If you have decided to breastfeed, you'll need to consider what type of nursing bras you'll want. Buy two or three in your eighth month so you'll be prepared. You may find it necessary to buy more nursing bras after the baby is born, but this will get you started. As for other nursing clothes, you may or may not find these worth the money. Don't go out and buy a whole new wardrobe right off the bat. Some women find nursing shirts and tops to be helpful while others manage quite well with regular clothes. More on this topic later in the book.

Sources

1 **MATERNITY WEAR CHAINS.** Pea in the Pod, Destination Maternity and Motherhood are probably the best known maternity stores—all owned by the same company. More on these chains later in the chapter.

2 **MOM AND POP MATERNITY SHOPS.** These small, independent stores sell a wide variety of maternity clothes, from affordable weekend wear to high-priced career wear. Some baby specialty stores carry maternity clothes as well. The chief advantage to the smaller stores is personalized service—we usually found salespeople who were knowledgeable about the different brands. In addition, these stores may offer other services. For example, some rent formal wear for special occasions, saving you big bucks. Of course, you may pay for the extra service with higher prices. While you're shopping at the independents look for better quality lines from manufacturers like Meet Me in Miami (meetmeinmiami.com), Juicy Couture Maternity and Olian (olianmaternity.com).

3 **CONSIGNMENT STORES.** Many consignment or thrift stores that specialize in children's clothing may also have a rack of maternity clothes. In visits to several such stores, we found some incredible bargains (at least 50% off retail) on maternity clothes that were in good to excellent condition. Of course, the selection varies widely, but we strongly advise you to check out any second-hand stores for deals.

4 **DISCOUNTERS.** When we talk about discounters, we're referring to chains like Target, Walmart and K-Mart. Now, let's be honest here—these discounters probably aren't the first place you'd think of to outfit your maternity wardrobe. Yet, each has a surprisingly nice selection of maternity clothes, especially casual wear. Later, we'll tell you about the incredible prices on these all-cotton clothes.

5 **DEPARTMENT STORES.** As you might guess, most department stores carry some maternity fashions. The big disadvantage:

maternity

the selection is usually rather small. Selection is much greater, however, on store websites. And department stores like Penney's and Sears often have end-of-the-season sales with decent maternity bargains. Look for maternity sections at Kohl's, JCPenney, Sears, Macy's, Nordstrom, Neiman Marcus and Saks Fifth Avenue.

6 **WEBSITES.** Shopping online has a hidden benefit for maternity clothes—many sites offer more generous return policies than retail stores. While maternity chains limit returns to a short period and only for store credit, online sites from the very same chains give you cash back and a longer return window. Another bonus to online shopping: it's easier to find sale items. And sites show what the clothes look like on real people, instead of a hanger.

7 **NON-MATERNITY STORES.** Maternity stores don't have a monopoly on pregnancy clothes—and you can save big bucks by shopping at stores that don't have the word "maternity" in their name. Some of our favorites: Old Navy, the Gap, Ann Taylor Loft. Their maternity clothes are both stylish and affordable.

8 **YOUR HUSBAND'S CLOSET.** Where's a good place for comfy weekend wear? Look no further than the other side of your closet, where your husband's clothes can often double as maternity wear.

9 **OUTLETS.** Yes, there are several outlets that sell maternity clothes and the prices can be a steal. Many of the chain maternity stores we discuss later in this chapter have outlets.

10 **YOUR FRIENDS.** It's a time-honored tradition—handing down "old" maternity clothes to the newly pregnant. Of course, maternity styles don't change that much from year to year and since outfits aren't worn for a long time, they are usually in great shape. Just be sure to pass on the favor when you are through with your pregnancy.

Best Online Bargains and Sources

2 Chix

Check out the sassy maternity t-shirts on 2 Chix. Potato sacks these are not. Form fitting tank tops as well as short and long sleeved T's are the rule here, many with cutesy sayings like "Does this BABY make my BUTT look big?" These 100 % cotton, preshrunk tops are $38 and work great for weekends. The site also sells maternity dresses, pants and even skirts that fit throughout your pregnancy and after with lots of stretch and cute detailing plus a drawstring at the waist. We also chuckled at the dad shirts with sayings like "he shoots, he scores." Not that you'd want him to wear this around your dad, but his friends would be amused. ***Rating: A-***

Ann Taylor LOFT

loft.com Ann Taylor's fashion esthetic seems to be more focused on designs for work than weekend lounging. They offer in house brands, designs by Olian and Cotton Glam. We like their trousers, top-of-the-knee length skirts and corduroys. They work well with cute cardigans, comfy jersey tops and tailored shirts. Our favorite designs are the dresses: a couple sweater dresses and jersey knit dresses in great shapes and colors were affordably priced between $75 and $115. The site's fit guide is helpful with pictures of their three belly panel options. ***Rating: A***

Due Maternity

duematernity.com Due Maternity is a combo web site: they sell their in house brand as well as a plethora of designer maternity brands like Nuka, Maternal America, Olian and Egg. They have one of the nicest collections of formal wear for pregnant moms, with a wider variety of styles than we've seen on most sites. Prices are up there, but most run less than $200—not bad for formal wear. We like the section of under-garments too: belly bands, slips and camis, Spanx hose and more. They even carry jeggings. Nursing clothes are available from Japanese Weekend, Bravado, Majamas and Boob (we're not making that up). Styles are attractive, selection is great but prices are regular retail— check out sale items for better deals. ***Rating: B+***

Expressiva

expressiva.com Wow! That's all we could say when we took a look at Expressiva's designs. You really never would know these are nurs-ing clothes. And they don't make you look like a sack of potatoes. Tops, dresses, casual clothes, bras, swimsuits and sleepwear are avail-able here. Sizes range from extra small to 3X and the site includes hints about sizing for specific outfits. We love the special collection for plus sizes. Eight styles of nursing openings are available and the site shows you exactly how each type works (click on the "why nursing wear" link). Prices are reasonable for the quality. ***Rating: A***

Gap

gap.com You probably already shop the Gap for basics like jeans or t-shirts, but you can also find maternity here. There are some stores with maternity sections, but the best selection is online. You'll find classics like cardigans and jeans as well as stretch shirts, swim suits and more. Check out the Fit & Style Guide with style secrets, size charts and tips. We also like their Starter Styles (lots of basics like classic shirts, tanks and pants) and their Work Essentials section. If you've never been pregnant before, this is a great resource. Sizes range from 00 to 16-18 plus inseams go up to 34". Check frequently for sale items—they seem to offer more sales than most maternity retailers. Readers have been impressed with the quality of Gap maternity, according to our email. Note: the Gap only accepts mailed in returns of maternity clothes bought online—you can't take them back to the store. You also have to pay the return shipping. A few readers report they were able to return online maternity purchases to Gap maternity stores, but not regular Gap outlets. **Rating: A**

Isabella Oliver

isabellaoliver.com This stylish site offers the usual categories like work and casual, but also includes fourth trimester clothes and resort wear. While the designs are very hip, they are expensive. Sale items however, are a great deal. And we like the attitude on this site. The designers have a blog—they offer good fashion advice and interesting "style notes." **Rating: B+**

JCPenney

jcpenney.com JCPenney may not be the source you turn to for everything in your maternity wardrobe, but you might want to take a look at some of their basics. T-shirts, jeans, bras, maternity belts and pajamas are priced reasonably. We found a lot of sale items as well: twill cargo pants marked down from $36 to $13 and more. Yes, the fashion could use a little updating, but the basics are a good value. **Rating: B-**

Motherwear

motherwear.com "This site makes the best clothes for nursing!" gushed one mom in an email to us and we have to agree—this is a great catalog and web site. The quality is excellent with prices in the reasonable range (a special occasion dress for $69, anyone?). They have a clearance section as well, and don't forget to check their weekly specials. Motherwear also has a factory outlet on eBay. The web site has detailed info on how their 12 different nursing openings work, with photos. Motherwear has a satisfaction guarantee and easy return policy. **Rating: A**

Mine For Nine

MineForNine.com If the thought of buying thousands of dollars worth of pregnancy clothes to wear for a mere four or five months makes your head spin, consider renting. Mine for Nine is a new web site that offers designer maternity clothes for rent at up to 75% off the retail price. Dresses, suits, pants, skirts and more from designers like Ripe Maternity, Olian and Maternite can be rented for amazing prices. Example: a beautiful silk floor length gown that sells for $293 can be rented for just $73 for one month. For weddings, New Years and other special events, this is a great deal.

How does it work? You can rent by the month or longer if you want work or casual clothes . . . and more than one item can be rented at a time. Evening clothes can be rented for as little as 14 days. Amazingly, there are no late fees if you keep the clothes longer (you pay for the extra days on a pro-rated basis). Clothes are either new or "like new" which means they have been professionally dry cleaned and inspected. The site has plenty of information on how to get the right fit, plus any order over $75 qualifies for free shipping. To ship your items back, use the return shipping label that comes in the box. Mine for Nine is sort of like Netflix for maternity clothes. You can even buy the clothes if something really impresses you. ***Rating: A***

Old Navy

oldnavy.com Like their parent company the Gap, Old Navy also sells maternity. Yes, the quality is less impressive here, but the prices are a steal. The category selection is similar to Gap—they carry jeans and pants, dresses and skirts, even pajamas and nursing clothes. A short sleeve nursing top in cotton jersey goes for a mere $19.50. At this price, you can try one without investing a huge amount. We like their Favorites categories like "shop by semester" and "wear to work."
Rating: B

One Hot Mama

onehotmama.com Nursing clothes are where One Hot Mama got their start, but they have expanded into maternity clothes as well. Their niche: hip styles from manufacturers like Glamourmom and Prego. Fun fabrics and colors are highlighted in the selection on this site. Prices are regular retail and sizing ranges from 2 to 18. ***Rating: B***

What Are You Buying?

What will you need when you get pregnant? There is no shortage of advice on this topic, especially from the folks trying to sell you stuff. But here's what real moms advise you to buy (divided into two topic areas, maternity clothes and then nursing clothes):

Maternity Clothes

◆ ***Maternity Bras.*** Maternity bras are designed to grow with you as your pregnancy progresses; these bras also offer extra support (you'll need it). Maternity bras are available just about everywhere, from specialty maternity shops to department stores, mail order catalogs and discount chains. More on this topic later in this chapter; look for our recommendations for maternity underwear.

HOW MANY? Two in each size as your bust line expands. I found that I went through three different sizes during my pregnancy, and buying two in each size allowed me to wear one while the other was washed.

◆ ***Sleep Bras.*** Why a sleep bra, you ask? Well, some women find it more comfortable to have a little extra support at night as their breasts change. Toward the end of pregnancy, some women also start to leak breast milk (to be technical, this is actually colostrum). Sleep bras hold breast pads in place to soak up any leaks. And once the baby arrives, a sleeping bra (about $10-$20) also keeps you from leaking when you inadvertently roll onto your stomach—yes, there will come a day when you can do that again. Some women just need light support, while others find a full-featured bra a necessity.

HOW MANY? Two sleep bras—one to wear while one is in the wash.

◆ ***Underpants.*** In the past, our recommendation for maternity underpants extolled the virtues of traditional maternity underwear. But time rolls on—and fashion has changed. Most women today are wearing bikini-style underpants as standard gear. And, readers note, you can continue to wear those same styles when you're pregnant. So, save yourself some money and forget the maternity underpants. If you're already wearing bikini styles, stick with them. But now is a good time to consider upgrading your underpants wardrobe in case you've let your skivvies wear out a bit. After all, you'll be going to lots of check ups and eventually the hospital—your mom would be embarrassed if your unmentionables were full of holes!

HOW MANY? If you need new underpants or plan to ignore our advice and buy maternity underpants, we recommend at least eight pairs.

◆ ***Maternity belts.*** Pregnancy support belts can be critical for some moms. For example, Pam A., one of our readers sent the following email when she was 7 1/2 months along:

"Last week I got the worst pain/cramp that I have ever had in my life. It kept coming and going while I was walking, but it was so bad that I doubled over in pain when it hit. I went to my doc-

Plus-size Maternity Clothing

What's the number one frustration with maternity wear? Finding the right size, particularly if you're looking for plus-size maternity clothes, say our readers. Some maternity clothing manufacturers think only women with supermodel bodies get pregnant. But what to do if you want to look attractive and your dress size starts at 16 or above? Our readers have recommended the following sites:

Baby Becoming	babybecoming.com
JCPenney	jcpenney.com
MomShop	momshop.com
Motherhood	maternitymall.com
Expressiva	expressiva.com
Plus Maternity	plusmaternity.com

tor and she said that the baby was pushing on a ligament that goes between the abdomen and the leg. She recommended that I get a "Prenatal Cradle" (prenatalcradle.com). I'll tell you what—it is the most wonderful purchase I have ever made in my life. It was about $70, but it works wonders. It does not totally eliminate the pain, but it gives enough support that it drastically reduces the pain and even gives me time to change positions so that it does not get worse. I have even found that wearing it at night helps to alleviate the pain at night rolling over in bed."

In our pregnancy book, *Expecting 411*, obstetrician Michele Hakakha explains the need for maternity belts for some women:

"(During pregnancy) the curvature of your spine changes and so does your center of gravity. The bigger your belly gets, the more you will feel the aching. This usually happens earlier and earlier with each subsequent pregnancy. (Maternity belts) really help lift the belly up and relieve the pressure and discomfort. But you have to wear them correctly to get relief. You need to try on many different styles and decide what fits best before you purchase."

HOW MANY? Kind of obvious, but one or two should be enough.

◆ **Career Clothing.** Our best advice about career clothing for the pregnant mom is to stick with basics. Buy yourself a coordinating outfit with a skirt, jacket, and pair of pants and then accessorize.

Now, we know what you're saying. You'd love to follow this advice, but you don't want to wear the same old thing several times a week—even if it is beautifully accessorized. I don't blame you. So, go for a couple dresses and sweaters too. The good news is you don't have to pay full price. And chances are you know someone who is finished with her pregnancy and will lend you some clothes.

Thanks to casual office wear trends, pregnant woman can spend hundreds of dollars LESS than they might have had to ten or twenty years ago. Today, you can pair a pencil skirt with a sweater set for most office situations.

◆ **Casual Clothes.** Your best bet here is to stick with simple basics, like jeans and cords. You don't necessarily have to buy these from maternity stores. In fact, later in this chapter, we'll talk about less-expensive alternatives. If you're pregnant in the summer, dresses can be a cooler alternative to pants and shorts.

◆ **Dress or Formal Clothes.** Forget them unless you have a full social calendar or have many social engagements associated with your job. Sometimes, you can find a local store that rents maternity formalwear for the one or two occasions when you might need it. Look at sale items on some of our recommended web sites. You may be able to find a nice outfit at a great price, especially right after holidays.

◆ **Spanx.** Spanx has become famous for their "slimming intimates" and their Mama Spanx support hose expand that philosophy to maternity. Made especially for pregnant bellies, these hose will smooth you out, front and back (the part you seldom see and forget about sometimes!). Available in footless and full lengths for $28, they are worth the money. And if you're not interested in hose but still want some reshaping, Power Mama ($32) is a thigh length shaper made to accommodate your pregnant belly, support your back and smooth out the bulges—and It will eliminate panty lines.

Nursing Clothes

◆ **Nursing Bras.** The one piece of advice every nursing mom gives is: buy a well-made, high quality, nursing bra *that fits you.* Easier said than done you say? Maybe. But we can offer some tips we gleaned from a reader poll we took.

Nursing bras have special flaps that fold down to give baby easy access to the breast. Access is usually with a hook or snaps either in the middle or on top of the bra near the straps. So first, our readers insist new moms should look for the easiest access they can find with a nursing bra. You'll need to be able to open your nursing bra quickly and with only one hand in most cases.

Next, avoid under wire bras at all cost. They can cause plugged ducts, a very painful condition. If you sport a large cup size, you'll need a bra that is ultra supportive. Also, in most cases, nursing moms require a sleep bra too—some for support, some just to hold nursing pads.

Mothers living near a locally owned maternity shop or specialized lingerie store recommended going in and having a nursing bra fitted to you. One reader reported that "I was wearing a bra at least three cup sizes too small. The consultant fitted me properly and I couldn't believe how comfortable I was!" In fact this should probably be our first tip: make sure your bra is comfortable! Straps shouldn't dig into your shoulders or chest, cups shouldn't look as if they are "overflowing" (we're talking to you, Kardashian sisters!) If you don't have the luxury of a shop full of specialists, Motherwear (motherwear.com) has good online tips and information (click the link for "how does it work") and Bravado (bravadodesigns.com) offers extensive sizing tips for different bras models.

If you plan to nurse, you should probably buy at least two bras during your eighth month (they cost about $30 to $45 each). Why then? Theoretically, your breast size won't change much once your baby is born and your milk comes in. I'd suggest buying one with a little larger cup size (than your eighth month size) so you can compensate for the engorgement phase. You can always buy more later and, if your size changes once the baby is born, you won't have invested too much in the wrong size. If you want more advice on nursing bras, you can check out Playtex's cool web site at playtex.com. Click on the link to "Expectant Moments," their maternity brand.

How many? Buy one to two bras in your eighth month. After the baby is born, you may want to buy a couple more.

◆ **Nursing Pads.** There are two options with nursing pads: disposable and reusable. Common sense tells you that reusable breast pads make the most economical sense, particularly if you plan to have more children. Still, if you aren't a big leaker, don't plan to breast feed for long or just need something quick and easy when you're on the go, disposables are handy.

When we polled our readers, we were surprised to learn that the majority preferred disposables. Those by Lansinoh (lansinoh.com; $7.50 for 60 at drugstore.com) were by far the favorite followed by Johnson and Johnson ($5.80 per 60), Gerber (60 for $5.69) and Curity (12 for $1.44). What's the secret to these disposables? The same type of super absorbent polymer that makes your baby's diapers so absorbent. That makes them super thin too so you aren't embarrassed by telltale "bulls-eyes" in your bra. Moms also love the individually wrapped pads because they can just grab a couple and throw them in the diaper bag on the way out of the house. Interestingly, moms were divided on whether they like contoured or flat pads or those with adhesive strips or without. New options on the market include

NUK ($7 for 60), First Years ($5 for 30), and Evenflo ($7.50 for 48). We don't have feedback yet on the performance of these pads.

While there wasn't one discount source mentioned for disposable breast pads, moms tell us when they see their favorite brands on sale at Walmart, Target or Babies R Us, they snapped up multiple boxes.

For the minority who preferred reusable, washable pads, Medela ($6 per pair), Avent ($6.50 for three pair) and Gerber ($7 for three pair) made the top of the list. Some moms recommend Bravado's (bravadodesigns.com) Cool Max pads ($16 for three pair) for superior absorption. A few parents have raved about Danish Wool pads (danishwool.com). These soft, felted pads contain natural lanolin, a godsend for moms with sore, cracked nipples. They aren't cheap ($21 to $31 per pair) but we thought them worth the mention. Another pad recommended by a reader is LilyPadz by Lilypadz.com. She told us they are streamlined and reusable, can be worn with or without a bra and cost about $23 per pair.

If you have nipple soreness (you have our sympathies!), Jeri from Stoneham, MA recommended a product called Soothies made by Lansinoh. These reusable gel pads can be slipped into your bra to cool and soothe painful nipples. You can find them online or in drugstores for $10 to $12.

HOW MANY? With disposable pads, buy the smaller package—don't buy the Costco-sized box. You may not need that many or may not like the brand. As for reusable pads, we recommend starting with three pair. That give you one to wear, one to wash and an extra just in case.

◆ **Nursing Clothes.** You may not think so (especially at 8 1/2 months), but there will come a day when you won't need to wear those maternity clothes. But what if you want to nurse in public after baby is born? Some women swear by nursing clothes as the best way to be discreet, but others do just fine with loose knit tops and button front shirts as well as discrete blanket placement. Bottom line: one obvious way to save money with nursing clothes is not to buy any. If you want to experiment, buy one or two nursing tops and see how they work for you. By the way, parents of twins found it difficult if not impossible to use a nursing top when nursing both babies at the same time. See the box on the next page for more reader feedback on nursing clothes.

Reader Tracy G. suggested that working moms who are nursing or expressing milk might want to check into getting a nursing camisole or tank top. "I wear them under a regular shirt and don't feel so exposed when I pump at work or nurse in public." Her favorite: a Walmart brand camisole. She thought it was softer than Motherhood Maternity options.

Another tip: a reader, Sandra F., came up with an ingenious way to use her breast pumps hands free. While Sandra's sister bought a special hands free bra, Sandra bought a zip-up-the-front sports bra and cut holes in it. She emailed us to say it worked better at holding the pumps phalanges to her breasts than her sister's, which was a tube top style that kept slipping. And Sandra saved some big bucks: her sports bra was a $6 sale item while her sister bought a $40 special pumping bra.

◆ **Nursing Pajamas.** Looking for something comfortable to sleep in that allows you to nurse easily? Nursing PJ's are one

Reader Poll: Nursing clothes brands

When we polled our readers about nursing clothes we were immediately chastised by at least half the respondents for even considering recommending them. "A waste of money," "ugly!" and "useless" were a few of the more charitable comments from these readers. As many as one third had never even used a single nursing top. They preferred to wear button up shirts or t-shirts and loose tops that they just pulled up. One mom told us "I got pretty good at being discreet in public with my regular clothes and no one was the wiser."

But other moms loved nursing clothes. And their favorites were those from **Motherwear** (motherwear.com). In our poll over 100 respondents mentioned Motherwear as the best source for well-made, comfortable nursing clothes. The biggest complaint about Motherwear was that their clothes are expensive. Readers suggested buying them used from ebay.com. The next closest company was **One Hot Mama** (onehotmama.com) with 17 votes.

Other sites recommended by parents included **Expressiva** (expressiva.com), and **Birth and Baby** (birthandbaby.com).

Regardless of where nursing clothes were purchased, moms were universal in thinking that the best tops have two vertical openings over the breasts. Forget the single center opening! And no buttons either. Too hard, our moms said, to open with one hand while baby is screaming in your ear. Twin sets and cardigan sweaters were the preferred styles. Readers thought they looked least like nursing clothes. And lots of moms thought just having a few nursing camisoles and t-shirts to wear under a regular shirt was the way to go. Finally, several parents recommended the Super Secret Nursing Shirt from One Hot Mama ($68).

Want to make your own nursing clothes? Creative sewers will find great patterns on **Elizabeth Lee's** web site (elizabethlee.com).

answer, although only a few moms we interviewed use them. Most hated nursing gowns and found it much simpler to sleep in pajamas with tops they could pull up or unbutton quickly

If you are interested in a specific nursing pajama, check out **Majamas** (majamas.com). One of our product testers tried out their nightgown ($60 online) with her newborn and thought it was great, worthy of a recommendation. It allowed her to sleep without wearing a nursing bra since it had pockets for holding breast pads and had easy nursing access. They have several pajama pant and gown designs and have expanded the line to include maternity clothes.

More Money Buys You . . .

Like any clothing, the more you spend, the better quality fabric and construction you get. Of course, do you really need a cashmere maternity sweater you'll wear for only a few months? Besides fabric, you'll note more designer names as prices go up. For example, Lilly Pulitzer and Juicy Couture are making maternity clothes now.

Smart Shopper Tips

Smart Shopper Tip #1
Battling your wacky thermostat

"It's early in my pregnancy, and I'm finding that the lycra-blend blouses that I wear to work have become very uncomfortable. I'm starting to shop for maternity clothes—what should I look for that will be more comfortable?"

It's a fact of life for us pregnant folks—your body's thermostat has gone berserk. Thanks to those pregnancy hormones, it may be hard to regulate your body's temperature. And those lycra-blend clothes may not be so comfortable anymore.

Our advice: stick with natural fabrics as much as possible, especially cotton, silk, light wools and some high tech fabrics. You need fabrics that breathe. Unfortunately, a lot of lower-priced maternity clothing is made of polyester/cotton blend fabrics.

Smart Shopper Tip #2
Seasons change

"Help! My baby is due in October, but I still need maternity clothes for the hot summer months! How can I buy my maternity wardrobe without investing a fortune?"

Unless you live in a place with endless summer, most women have to buy maternity clothes that will span both warm and cold seasons. The best bets are items that work in BOTH winter or summer—for example, lightweight long-sleeve shirts can be rolled up in the summer. Cropped pants can work in both spring and fall. Another tip: layer clothes to ward off cold. Of course, there's another obvious way to save: borrow items from friends. If you just need a few items to bridge the seasons (a coat, heavy sweater, etc), try to borrow before buying.

Smart Shopper Tip #3
Petites aren't always petite

"I'm only 5 feet 2 inches tall and obviously wear petite sizes. I ordered a pair of pants in a petite size from an online discounter, but they weren't really shorter in the leg. In fact, I'd have to have the pants reconstructed to get the right fit. What gives?"

Many maternity web sites advertise that they carry a wide range of sizes but in truth you may find the choices very limited. And in some cases, "petite" is really just sizes 2 to 4. Translation: these pants aren't really shorter in the leg. How can you tell without ordering and then having to return items? Your best bet is to try on items before you buy. That's not always easy, of course, especially when ordering online. In that case, check the size charts on each site to be sure they offer *real* petites. And if a manufacturer (like the Gap, for example) makes petites that fit you in their regular clothing, chances are their maternity line will be comparable.

Here are our readers recommendations for petite maternity: Kohl's, JCPenney, Old Navy, Gap, Japanese Weekend, Juicy Couture, Rebel jeans and Lands End.

Smart Shopper Tip #4
Tall isn't easy either

"At nearly six feet, I can't find any maternity pants that don't look dorky. Help!"

Just as with petites, we see lots of sites promising a wide range of sizes . . . only to find they have one style that comes in a 31" inseam. And you need a 34." I feel your pain. At 5'9" myself, I recall finding almost nothing in the right length for me. There are more choices today for tall women, but you may find yourself forced to wear more skirts and dresses than pants during your pregnancy.

Here's a partial list of sites that carry tall maternity: Mommy Long Legs (mommylonglegs.com), JC Penney, Isabella Oliver (isabellaoliver.com), Gap, and Old Navy, Long Tall Sally (longtallsally.com), and

RG Maternity (rgmaternity.com). If you discover any new sites or stores with tall sizing, email us and we'll add them.

Our Picks: Brand Recommendations for Maternity Undergarments

Here are our readers top picks for maternity undergarments.

God bless Canada—those Maple Leaf-heads make one of the best maternity bras in the world. Toronto-based *Bravado Designs'* (bravadodesigns.com) maternity/nursing bra of the same name is just incredible. "A godsend!" raved one reader. "It's built like a sports bra with no under wire and supports better than any other bra I've tried . . . and this is my third pregnancy!" raved another.

Bravado makes five different styles and one nursing bra tank top. Prices start at $35 for the basic Original Nursing Bra. Other styles include the Body Silk Seamless bra ($49), the Bliss ($54), the Sublime ($49) and the Allure ($54). Sizes range from a B cup to J/K (a few go to H/I). The nursing tank top option includes a built in full bra (not a shelf bra) and goes up to a G cup for $49.

Another plus: the Bravado reps are knowledgeable and helpful with sizing questions. In the past, some of our readers criticized the Bravado for not providing enough support, but the Supreme should answer those concerns. Our readers have noticed great prices on Bravado Bras at WearstheBaby.com ($32 including shipping).

Playtex Expectant Moments brand was mentioned by our readers as a good choice as well. They offer two nursing bra choices, an underwire and an underwire alternative. Sizes range from B to DDD cups and 34" to 44." A nice touch, they offer sizing advice specifically for maternity and nursing customers on their web site at playtex.com. You'll find these bras at stores like JCPenney. *Medela*, as you'd imagine, also has a big following for their bras. Five options are available: Comfort, Seamless Underwire, Seamless Soft Cup, Sleep Bra and a new Nursing Camisole. Some are also available in extended sizes from 36F to 46H. Prices average around $40 for the nursing bras.

Finally, many readers have recommended Leading Lady maternity and nursing bras (leadinglady.com). They are available widely in many department stores and maternity outlets. Leading Lady has quite a wide assortment of bras in a huge range of sizes.

Looking for maternity shorts/tights for working out? One of the best is *Fit Maternity* (fitmaternity.com; 800-961-9100). They offer an unbelievable assortment of workout clothes including unitards, tights, swimsuits, tennis clothes and more. On the same subject, *Due Maternity* (duematernity.com) offers several yoga and workout pants as well as swimsuits.

Our Picks: Brand Recommendations for Nursing Bras, Pads and Clothes

Nursing pads are a passionate topic for many of our readers with disposables beating out reusables as moms' favorites. They loved both **Lansinoh** and **Johnson & Johnson** disposable by an overwhelming number. **Medela**, **Advent** and **Bravado** make great reusable nursing pads.

Bravado is also quite popular as a nursing bra for all but the largest of cup sizes as are **Playtex** and **Medela**. If you need a size larger than DD, consider **Motherhood Maternity's** brand as well as **Leading Lady**. The web is the best place to find bras on deal including **Decent Exposures** (decentexposures.com) and **Birth and Baby** (birthandbaby.com).

Most moms found that specialized nursing clothes weren't a necessity, but for those who want to try them, nearly everyone recommended **Motherwear** (motherwear.com). **One Hot Mama** (onehotmama.com) and **Expressiva** (expressiva.com) are other stylish sites to consider. Look for discounts on clearance pages or eBay.

Fetal Monitors: Good or Bad Idea?

Can you buy your own Doppler ultrasound monitor to listen to your baby's heartbeat? Sure . . . but is it a good idea? To answer that question, we turned to our favorite obstetrician, Dr. Michele Hakakha. Michele is the co-author of our new book on pregnancy, *Expecting 411.* Here's why she says pass on these gizmos:

"First of all, home Dopplers are very expensive (around $500 to purchase; $25 to $50 a month to rent). Secondly, using the Doppler requires the experienced hands of someone who has used one about a thousand times. And even in those experienced hands, it can be hard to find the baby's heartbeat, especially early in the pregnancy.

What ends up happening is that the pregnant couple can't detect the baby's heartbeat at home and they frantically rush into their practitioner's office. Other times, couples listen cheerfully to mom's pulse instead of baby's heartbeat!

You can do a much better job of tracking the health of your unborn baby by following your baby's *movements* in the womb. So, skip the panic (you'll have your share of that as new parents), save your money (you'll need it for the college fund), and leave the Fun-With-The-Doppler game up to your practitioner."

Wastes of Money

Waste of Money #1
Maternity Bra Blues

"My old bras are getting very tight. While visiting a store to get a larger size, a salesperson suggested I purchase a maternity bra for more comfort and support. Should I buy a regular bra in a larger size or plunk down the extra money for a maternity bra?"

We've heard from quite a few readers who've complained that expensive maternity bras were very uncomfortable and/or fell apart after just a few washings. Our best advice: try on the bra before purchase and stick to the better brands. Compared to regular bras, the best maternity bras typically have thicker straps, more give on the sides and more hook and eye closures in back (so the bra can grow with you). Most of all, the bra should be comfortable and have no scratchy lace or detailing. Readers tell us that a good sports bra can also be a fine (and affordable) alternative.

As a side note, FDA says that fetal heart monitors are a medical device and, as such, require a prescription from a doctor to use at home. While some sites will not rent or sell a monitor to a parent without a prescription, others assume you have your doctor's okay.

Why do you need a prescription? After all, isn't a heart monitor just a Doppler ultrasound that checks the heartbeat? What's the big deal?

Doppler ultrasound devices use acoustical energy that is emitted continuously from the unit. It's the "continuous" part that has doctors and the FDA concerned. In your doctor's office, he or she will use a fetal heart monitor for a few minutes. But unsupervised parents at home may decide to use it every day for longer periods of time. The risk: the unit could heat up, causing damage to the fetus.

Our advice: don't bother with a fetal heart monitor.

As for the "entertainment value" of hearing your baby's heartbeat and sharing it with others we'd recommend a simple option—consider buying a good stethoscope. Then have your doctor teach you how to use it to hear your baby's heartbeat. By about 18 weeks you can usually hear a heartbeat with a stethoscope. And you can buy one for as little as $100.

Waste of Money #2
Overexposed Nursing Gowns/Tops

"I refuse to buy those awful nursing tops! Not only are they ugly, but those weird looking panels are like wearing a neon sign that says BREASTFEEDING MOM AHEAD!"

"I plan to nurse my baby and all my friends say I should buy nursing gowns for night feedings. Problem is, I've tried on a few and even though the slits are hidden, I still feel exposed. Not to mention they're the ugliest things I've ever seen. Can't I just wear a regular gown that buttons down the front?"

Of course you can. And considering how expensive some nursing gowns can be ($35 to $50 each), buying a regular button-up nightshirt or gown will certainly save you a few bucks. Every mother we interviewed about nursing gowns had the same complaint. There isn't a delicate way to put this: it's not easy to get a breast out of one of those teenie-weenie slits. Did the person who designed these ever breastfeed a baby? I always felt uncovered whenever I wore a nursing gown, like one gust of wind would have turned me into a centerfold for a nudist magazine.

And can we talk about nursing shirts with those "convenient button flaps for discreet breastfeeding"? Convenient, my fanny. There's so much work involved in lifting the flap up, unbuttoning it, and getting your baby positioned that you might as well forget it. My advice: stick with shirts you can pull up or unbutton down the front. These are just as discreet, easier to work with, and (best of all) you don't have to add some expensive nursing shirts (at $30 to $75 each) to your wardrobe.

Another tip: if possible, try on any nursing clothing BEFORE you buy. See how easy they are to use. You might be surprised how easy (or difficult) an item can be. Imagine as you are doing this that you have an infant that is screaming his head off wanting to eat NOW, not five seconds from now. You can see why buying any nursing clothes sight unseen is a risk.

Waste of Money #3
New shoes

"Help! My feet have swollen and none of my shoes fit!"

Here's a little fact of pregnancy that no one tells you: your feet are going to swell. And, sadly, after the baby is born, those tootsies won't necessarily shrink back to your pre-pregnancy size. A word to the wise: don't buy lots of new shoes at the start of your pregnancy. But no need to despair. After your baby is born, you'll likely have a built-in excuse to go shoe shopping!

Another suggestion from reader Gretchen C. of Rochester, WA: "It is never too early to buy shoes that don't tie! I go to the gym every morning, and it was getting to be a huge ordeal just to get my shoes tied. I bought some slip on shoes at 20 weeks and I still think it's one of the smartest things I've done."

Money-Saving Secrets

1 CONSIDER BUYING "PLUS" SIZES FROM A REGULAR STORE. Thankfully, fashion continues to be heavy on casual looks . . . even for the office. This makes pregnancy a lot easier since you can buy the same styles in larger ladies' sizes to cover your belly without compromising your fashion sense or investing in expensive and often shoddy maternity clothes. We found the same fashions in plus-size stores for 20% to 35% less than maternity shops (and even more during sales).

One drawback to this strategy: by the end of your pregnancy, your hemlines may start to look a little "high-low"—your expanding belly will raise the hemline in front. This may be especially pronounced with dresses. Of course, that's the advantage of buying maternity clothes: the designers compensate with more fabric in front to balance the hemline. Nonetheless, we found that many moms we interviewed were able to get away with plus-size fashions for much (if not all) of their pregnancy. How much can you save? In many cases, from 25% to 50% off those high prices in maternity chains like Pea in the Pod.

2 DON'T OVER-BUY BRAS. As your pregnancy progresses, your bra size is going to change at least a couple times. Running out to buy five new bras when you hit a new cup size is probably foolish—in another month, all those bras may not fit. The best advice: buy the bare minimum (two or three).

3 TRY BRA EXTENDERS, BELLA BAND. You may be able to avoid buying lots of maternity bras by purchasing a few bra extenders. Available from fabric stores, OneHanesPlace.com and even Amazon.com among other sites, these little miracles cost as little as $1.50. You simply hook the extender onto the back of your bra and you can add up to two inches around the bust. You may still need to purchase new bras at some point, but with extenders, you can continue to use your pre-pregnancy bra for quite a while.

By the way, Candy from San Diego wrote to us about a similar product for pants called the Bella Band (bellaband.com).: "I bought the Bella Band early on in my pregnancy and love it so much that I recently bought another one. It was perfect for keeping my "normal" clothes on when I couldn't button them anymore. Then it helped me keep maternity pants on when they were still a little too big but I couldn't fit in my regular clothes anymore." Keep in mind the Bella Band is really for use in early pregnancy before you're big enough to buy true maternity pants and skirts. It will allow you to wear your regular pants during that stage where you're just not ready for maternity. Another, similar product called the Baby Be Mine Belly Band (Amazon.com) was only $16 for one while a three pack of BellaBands was $74.

4 **BUT DON'T SKIMP ON QUALITY WHEN IT COMES TO MATERNITY BRAS.** Take some of the money you save from other parts of this book and invest in good maternity underwear. Yes, you can find cheap bras for $20 at discount stores, but don't be penny-wise and pound-foolish. We found the cheap stuff is very uncomfortable and falls apart, forcing you to go back and buy more. Invest in better-quality bras if you plan to have more than one child—you can actually wear it again for subsequent pregnancies. No need to purchase special maternity underpants—use your own and save money.

5 **CONSIDER DISCOUNTERS FOR CASUAL CLOTHES.** Okay, I admit that I don't normally shop at K-Mart or Target for my clothes. But I was surprised to discover these chains (and even department stores like Sears) carry casual maternity clothes in 100% cotton at very affordable prices. Let's repeat that—they have 100% cotton t-shirts, shorts, pants, and more at prices you won't believe. Most of these clothes are in basic solid colors—sorry, no fancy prints. At Target, for example, I found a cotton/spandex maternity shirt (long sleeves) for $15. Jeans were only $30. Even a rayon jersey dress was a mere $30. The best part: Liz Lange designs a big part of the Target line. Our readers say the quality is a bit less than Liz's regular, specialty store version, but the style is good and the prices can't be beat. Don't forget to check Target's sale rack too. One reader found items for as little as $4 on sale.

While the discounters don't carry much in the way of career wear, you'll save so much on casual/weekend clothes that you'll be ecstatic anyway. Witness this example: at A Pea in the Pod, we found a striped cotton-knit, short-sleeved top and ponte knit pants. The price for the two pieces: a heart-stopping $245. A similar all-cotton tank top/pants outfit from Target was $50. Whip out a calculator, and you'll note the savings is an amazing 80%. Need we say more?

By the way, don't forget to check out stores like Kohl's, Marshall's,

Ross and TJ MAXX. One reader told us she found maternity clothes at 60% off at TJ MAXX. Of course, as we've mentioned, readers like Old Navy and the Gap as well. Corrie, a reader from Chicago, did all her maternity shopping on line at Old Navy. She spent a total of $365 for eight pairs of pants, one pair of jeans, eleven sweaters, eight long sleeve tops, three button-down shirts, five sleeveless tops and two cardigans. This works out to less than $10 per piece!

For fans of the hip discounter H&M, there's great news: the chain has a maternity section in 20 of their stores! Granted most of them (11) are in New York, but if you live in a major metropolitan area and have an H & M, check to see if yours has a maternity section. Dubbed "Mama," our readers report these departments are selling tops for $12 to $16, camisoles for $8 and more. They carry pretty much everything except underwear. Prices are fantastic.

6 **RENT EVENING WEAR—DON'T BUY.** We found that some indie maternity stores rent eveningwear. For example, a local shop we visited had an entire rack of rental formalwear. An off-white lace dress (perfect for attending a wedding) rented for just $50. Compare that with the purchase price of $200+. Sadly, places that rent maternity wear are few and far between, but it might be worth a look-see in your local community. Another idea: try RentMaternityWear.com as an online source for rentals! Pregnant moms can rent the company's dresses for $39 to $79. Rent Maternity Wear also allows moms to rent two sizes of an item to make sure it really fits well. Shipping is a flat $8 and you can specify the exact date you want a dress. Such a deal!

7 **CHECK OUT CONSIGNMENT STORES.** You can find "gently worn" career and casual maternity clothes for 40% to 70% off the original retail! Many consignment or second-hand stores carry only designer-label clothing in good to excellent condition. If you don't want to buy used garments, consider recouping some of your investment in maternity clothes by consigning them after the baby is born. You can usually find listings for these stores in the phone book or online. (Don't forget to look under children's clothes as well. Some consignment stores that carry baby furniture and clothes also have a significant stock of maternity wear.) One web source to find consignment shops is narts.org.

 FIND AN OUTLET. Go to OutletBound.com to find a maternity outlet near you.

 BE CREATIVE. Raid your husband's closet for over-sized shirts and pants.

10 **SEW IT YOURSELF.** A reader in California emailed in this recommendation: she loved the patterns for nursing clothes by Elizabeth Lee Designs (elizabethlee.com). "I would think anyone with a bit of sewing experience could handle any of the patterns, which don't LOOK like nursing dresses or tops." In addition to patterns, Elizabeth Lee also sells ready-made dresses and tops. Another bonus: the company has one of the largest selections of nursing bras we've seen, including Bravado Bras.

Pattern companies like Simplicity (simplicity.com) and McCall (mccall.com includes Butterick and Vogue as well) sell their patterns online and in fabric stores. You'll find a limited selection of designs, but if you're a sewing maven, here's a way to avoid the high prices and frustrating return policies of retail maternity stores.

11 **BEG AND BORROW.** Unless you're the first of your friends to get pregnant you know someone who's already been through this. Check around to see if you can borrow old maternity clothes from other moms. In fact, we loaned out a big box after our second baby was born and it has made the rounds of the whole neighborhood. And don't forget to be generous after your baby making days are over too.

12 **CHECK OUT CLEARANCE AREAS IN CATALOGS AND ONLINE.** Many of our most devoted discount shopping readers have scored big deals on their favorite web sites' clearance pages.

13 **WHEN ORDERING MATERNITY CLOTHES FROM WEB SITES, POOL YOUR ORDERS!** Most web sites offer a free shipping option on orders of $75 to $100 or more (especially after holidays and during end of season sales). Check to see what deals they're offering when you visit. Also, some chain stores will let you return items to your local store, saving you the return-shipping fee.

The Name Game: Reviews of Selected Maternity Stores

Usually this section is intended to acquaint you with the clothing name brands you'll see in local stores. But now there is only one giant chain of maternity wear in North America—Destination Maternity Corp., which operates stores under three brand names. This company is the 800 pound gorilla of maternity clothes with over 1700 locations, many of which are leased departments in chains like Babies R Us, Macy's, Sears, Kohl's and other stores.

Destination Maternity has over a 40% share of the $1.2 billion maternity clothing market in the US. There are also 36 Motherhood stores in Canada.

FYI: keep in mind that these chains often offer a larger selection of maternity clothing online than what you see in the stores. This is, of course, frustrating since you can't try them on. On the upside, the draconian return policies of the bricks and mortar stores don't apply to online purchases. So you'll be able to return online purchases more easily.

So let's take a look at these three divisions, a new concept they've added, and their web site.

◆ **Motherhood.** Motherhood is the biggest sister in the chain with 567 locations. While most stores are located in malls and power centers, 232 are also leased departments within Kohl's (called Oh! Baby by Motherhood). Motherhood carries maternity clothes in the lowest price points. As an example, dresses at Motherhood range from $20 to $50.

◆ *A Pea in the Pod.* A Pea in the Pod (APIP) is Destination Maternity's most expensive division. With dress prices ranging from $59 to $325, A Pea in the Pod's 56 stores are positioned as designer boutiques. They even have a line designed by Heidi Klum called "lavish."

Watch out for return policies!

Have you bought a maternity dress you don't like or that doesn't fit? Too bad—most maternity stores have draconian return policies that essentially say "tough!"

Motherhood Maternity stores (including their sister chain A Pea in the Pod) only allow returns to their stores if you have the receipt, the item is unworn, unopened and with all the tags. The item also must have been purchased within 10 days. These returns are only for store credit or exchange—no money back. Independent maternity stores may have a similar returns policy.

Online return policies are a bit more generous from Motherhood.com: you can get cash back, given you returned the item within 30 days and have all the tags attached. Unfortunately, returning an online purchase to a Motherhood or Pea in the Pod store only gets you store credit, no cash.

The take-home message: if you are unsure about an item, consider buying it online and then return it by mail.

◆ **Destination Maternity Superstore.** These stores combine
A Pea in the Pod and Motherhood Maternity under one roof. More
than just a clothing store, some of these locations also boast a spa
and classes in yoga, financial planning and scrapbooking. As of this
writing, there are 75 Destination Maternity Superstores.

All these stores carry merchandise designed in house, exclusively
for the different divisions, as well as well known brands like Spanx,
C&C California, Lucky Brand and Lilly Pulitzer.

Now that you know the basics, what do real moms think of
Destination Maternity's stores? First and foremost, moms dislike, no,
hate their return policy. The policy is pretty basic: once you've
bought an item, you have ten days to return it for store credit or
exchange only (you must have the tags and receipt too). No
refunds. What if it falls apart in the wash on day 11? Too bad for
you. By the way, if you order an item online from Mother Works
web site, you'll find a more generous return policy: *Items can be
returned for refund or exchange and you have 30 days to return
the clothing.* You cannot return items bought online to the store or
vice versa, but at least you get extra time and even the money back
with an online return. Our advice, if you see it in the store, try it on.
If you like it, go home and order it online.

And don't forget that Motherhood has in-store "boutiques" in
Kohl's department stores as well as other department stores. In
these cases, the leased stores have to comply with the same generous return policy of the department store where they lease
space.

As for individual chains, most moms agreed that the quality at
Motherhood is poor. Although some readers have praised their
maternity and nursing bras, in general, most agree with this reader's sum-up: "I have found the quality to be inconsistent. I've
bought shirts that have unraveled within a few months. . . trashy!"
The consensus seems to be that if you buy at Motherhood, you
should stick to the sale rack and don't expect high quality except
for their bras. However, a recent reader took issue with our review
of Motherhood's quality. She told us: "Motherhood clothes are just
as well made, if not better made, than Old Navy maternity."

A Pea in the Pod is just way too expensive. That's the general
feeling among our readers about this store. Most moms don't think
the style of clothing at this chain is anything special. Certainly not to
spend $60 for a cotton t-shirt. Considering how short a time a
pregnancy is it's a huge waste of money to spend over $245 on a
Pea in the Pod pants outfit. And what about their "legendary" service, as Pea in the Pod likes to tout? It's a joke, say our readers. One
mom summed it up best by saying: "For the price that one is pay-

ing, one expects a certain degree of customer service and satisfaction, both of which are lacking in this over-priced store. What a complete and utter disappointment!"

Consumer alert: one new mom warned us about giving personal info to a maternity chain when you make a purchase (clerks may ask you if you want to receive sales notices). The problem: you often end up on junk mailing lists. In the case of our reader, even though she specifically requested the chain not sell her information to third parties, they did so. Once on those lists, it's tough to stop the junk from arriving in your mailbox.

E-MAIL FROM THE REAL WORLD
Stay fit with pregnancy workout videos

Sure, there are plenty of workout DVDs targeted at the preggo crowd. But which are the best? Readers give their top picks, starting with Margaret Griffin:

"As a former certified aerobics instructor, I have been trying out the DVD workouts for pregnancy. I have only found three DVDs available in my local stores, but I wanted to rate them for your readers.

"*Buns of Steel: Pregnancy & Post-Pregnancy Workouts* with Madeleine Lewis ($13) gets my top rating. Madeleine Lewis has excellent cueing, so the workout is easy to follow. Your heart rate and perceived exertion are both used to monitor your exertion. There is an informative introduction. And I really like the fact that the toning segment utilizes a chair to help you keep your balance, which can be off a little during pregnancy. Most of the toning segment is done standing. This is a safe, effective workout led by a very capable instructor and I highly recommend it."

"A middle rating goes to *Denise Austin's: Fit & Firm Pregnancy* ($15). Denise has a good information segment during which she actually interviews a physician. She also provides heart rate checks during the workout. However, there are a couple of things about this workout that I don't particularly like. First, during the workout, there are times when safety information is provided regarding a particular move. This is fine and good, but instead of telling you to continue the movement and/or providing a picture-in-a-picture format, they actually change the screen to show the safety information and then cut back into the workout in progress. Surprise! You were supposed to keep doing the movement. Second, Denise Austin is a popular instructor, but I personally find that her cueing is not as sharp as I prefer and sometimes she seems to be a little offbeat with the music. My suggestion is get this DVD to use in addition to other DVDs if you are the type who gets easily bored with one workout."

Reader Laura McDowell recommended a few different workout DVDs. **Leisa Hart's FitMama** ($4) workout DVD was a favorite. "I loved it! Leisa has great energy and her peppy attitude made me smile through the whole workout. It has about 20 minutes of salsa dancing and then modified yoga." Laura also enjoyed **Kathy Smith's Pregnancy Workout** (discontinued by manufacturer, but still available used on Amazon). It was "a total 80's throwback; fun and energizing. She moves through the steps fast at times, but is always clear about offering ways to slow down if you need to. The hair, outfits and music are highly entertaining so the workout goes fast and feels great."

Another reader recommended **The Perfect Pregnancy Workout** DVD ($25). "It's by a former Cirque du Soleil acrobat, who leads the exercises with a French accent. It also offers beginner, intermediate and advanced options for each exercise."

Yoga is a terrific low impact exercise that does a wonderful job of stretching muscles you'll use while carrying and delivering your child. It's a terrific option for pregnant moms. And it's definitely become one of the most popular exercise options in North America. So it was only a matter of time before our readers began reviewing yoga DVDs. Here are some of their comments:

Reader Sheri Gomez recommended Yoga Zone's DVD **Postures for Pregnancy** ($15), calling it "wonderful for stretching and preventing back problems. It's beginner friendly and not too out there with the yoga thing." Her only complaint: there is no accompanying music, so she played her own DVDs along with the tape.

Reader Eufemia Campagna recommended Yoga Journal's **Prenatal Yoga** with Shiva Rea ($20). She noted that each segment of the tape is done using three women at different stages of pregnancy. "The segments are all accompanied by lovely, relaxing music and the instructor's directions are so clear that you don't even have to look at the TV to know what you need to do!" Another reader, Carolyn Oliner, also complimented this DVD: "It's not so much of a traditional yoga workout but a great series of poses and stretches that work for pregnant women and leave you feeling warm and stretched and (more gently) exercised." Finally, another reader noted that this workout is "really gentle (pretty easy for experienced yogini)."

Finally, we should note that Pilates has also been adapted for pregnancy exercise. You'll find several options on DVD including **Pilates During Pregnancy, Jennifer Gianni's Fusion Pilates for Pregnancy**, and **Prenatal Pilates** as well as many others.

Note: Amazon.com is a great source to find these DVDs. If you have any favorite DVDs, email us your review of them and we'll add them to our collection. One of our readers noted that NetFlix (netflix.com) has a huge assortment of pregnancy DVDs for rent, so you can try before you buy.

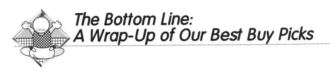

The Bottom Line: A Wrap-Up of Our Best Buy Picks

For career and casual maternity clothes, we thought the best deals were from the Old Navy, the Gap and H&M stores. Compared to retail maternity chains (where one outfit can run $200), you can buy your entire wardrobe from these places for a song.

If your place of work allows more casual dress, check out the prices at plus-size stores or alternatives like Old Navy. A simple pair of jeans that could cost $140 at a maternity shop are only $36 or less at Old Navy. And if you prefer the style at maternity shops, only hit them during sales, where you can find decent bargains. Another good idea: borrow from your husband's closet—many items can do double-duty as maternity clothes.

For weekend wear, we couldn't find a better deal than the 100% cotton shirts and shorts at discounters like Target, Walmart and K-Mart. Prices are as little as $10 per shirt—compare that to the $34 price tag at maternity chain stores for a simple cotton shirt.

Invited to a wedding? Rent that dress from a maternity store and save $100 or more. Don't forget to borrow all you can from friends who've already had babies. In fact, if you follow all our tips on maternity wear, bras, and underwear, you'll save $700 or more. Here's the breakdown:

1. **Career Wear:** $300.

2. **Casual Clothes:** $100.

3. **Underwear:** $150 to $200.

Total damage: $550 to $650. If you think that's too much money for clothes you'll only wear for a few months, consider the cost if you outfit yourself at full-price maternity shops. The same selection of outfits would run $1300 to $1700.

Notes

CHAPTER 6

FEEDING

Feeding Baby

Inside this chapter

How much money can you save by breastfeeding? What are the best options for pumps? Which bottles are best? We'll discuss these topics as well as ways to get discount formula, including details on which places have the best deals. And of course, we'll have tips and reviews on the next step in feeding: solid food. Finally, let's talk about high chairs—who's got the best value? Durability? Looks?

Breastfeeding

As readers of past editions of this book know, we are big proponents of breastfeeding. The medical benefits of breast milk are well documented, but obviously the decision to breast or bottle-feed is a personal call for each new mom. In the past, we spent time in this chapter encouraging breast-feeding . . . but we realize now we are preaching to the choir. Our time is better spent discussing how to save on feeding your baby, no matter which way you go. So, we'll leave the discussion of breast versus bottle to our other book *Baby 411* (as well your doctor and family). Let's talk about the monetary impact of the decision, however.

Breastfeed Your Baby and Save $500

Since this is a book on bargains, we'd be remiss in not mentioning the tremendous amount of money you can save if you breast-feed. Just think about it: no bottles, no expensive formula to prepare, no special insulated carriers to keep bottles warm/cold, etc.

So, how much money would you save? Obviously, NOT buying formula would be the biggest money-saver. Even if you were to use the less-expensive powdered formula, you would still have to spend nearly $25 per 25.7-ounce can of powdered formula. Since each can makes about 188 ounces of formula, the cost per ounce of formula is about 13¢. And, by the way, the American Academy of Pediatrics and the American Dental Association now say that parents who use powdered formula should use bottled water when they make up a bottle for baby. What kind of bottled water? Purified, demineralize, deionized, distilled or reverse osmosis filtered water. So that's going to cost you too—about a penny per ounce.

That doesn't sound too bad, does it? Unless you factor in that a baby will down 32 ounces of formula per day by 12 weeks of age. Your cost per day would be $4.48. Assuming you breastfeed for at least the first six months, you would save a grand total of $806 just *on formula alone*. The American Academy of Pediatrics recommends breastfeeding for 12 months (with solid foods added to the mix at six months), so in that case your savings could be as much as $1600! That doesn't include the expense of bottles, nipples and accessories! By the way, statistically speaking, nearly 74% of American moms breastfeed their babies at birth. By six months, however, the number of breastfeeding moms drops to nearly 43% (although this is an improvement up from 33% in 2007).

To be fair, there are some additional expenses that might go along with breastfeeding too. The biggest dollar item: you might decide to buy a breast pump. Costs for this item range from $50 for a manual pump to $380 for a professional-grade breast pump. Or you can rent a pump for $45 a month (plus a kit—one time cost of about $50 to $60). And of course, you'll also need some bottles—but arguably fewer than if you formula-feed.

If $806 doesn't sound like a lot of money, consider the savings if you had to buy formula in the concentrated liquid form instead of the cheaper powder. A 32-ounce can of Enfamil ready-to-eat liquid costs about $6.69 at a grocery store and makes up only eight 4-ounce bottles. The bottom line: you could spend over $1000 on formula for your baby in the first six months alone!

Of course, we realize that some moms will decide to use formula because of a personal, medical or work situation—to help out, we have a section later in this chapter on how to save on formula, bottle systems and other necessary accessories.

Sources: Where to Find Breast Feeding Help

The basis of breastfeeding is attachment. Getting your new little one to latch onto your breast properly is not a matter of instinct. Some babies have no trouble figuring it out, while many others need your help and guidance. In fact, problems with attachment can lead to sore nipples and painful engorgement. Of course, you should be able to turn to your pediatrician or the nurses at the hospital for breastfeeding advice. However, if you find that they do not offer you the support you need, consider the following sources for breastfeeding help:

1 **LA LECHE LEAGUE** (llli.org). Started in 1956 by a group of moms in Chicago, La Leche League has traditionally been the most vocal supporter of breastfeeding in this country. You've got to imagine the amount of chutzpah these women had to have to buck the bottle trend and promote breastfeeding at a time when it wasn't fashionable (to say the least).

In recent years, La Leche has established branches in many communities around the world, providing support groups for nursing moms. Their web site also offers reviews and recommendations of books and videotapes on nursing, as well as other child care topics.

2 **NURSING MOTHERS' COUNCIL** (nursingmothers.org). Similar in mission to La Leche League, the Nursing Mothers' Council differs on one point: the group emphasizes working moms and their unique needs and problems.

3 **LACTATION CONSULTANTS**. Lactation consultants are usually nurses who specialize in breastfeeding education and problem solving. You can find them through your pediatrician, hospital, or the International Lactation Consultants Association (iblce.org). New eligibility requirements for members of this group in 2012 will include "90 contact hours of re-exam education in human lactation and breastfeeding and either be a registered/licensed/recognize health professional in their country or have completed high education in 14 subjects" before they can take the licensing exam.

At some hospitals, resident lactation consultants are available to answer questions by phone at no charge. If a problem persists, you can set up an in-person consultation for a minimal fee (about $65 to $90 per hour, although your health insurance provider may pick up the tab).

Unfortunately, the availability and cost of lactation consultants seems to vary from region to region. Our advice: call area hospitals before you give birth to determine the availability of breastfeeding support. Another good source for a referral to a lactation consultant is your pediatrician.

4 **HOSPITALS.** Look for a hospital in your area that has breastfeeding-friendly policies. These include 24-hour rooming in (where your baby can stay with you instead of in a nursery) and breastfeeding on demand. Pro-nursing hospitals do not supplement babies with a bottle and don't push free formula samples.

5 BOOKS. Although they aren't a substitute for support from your doctor, hospital, and family, many books provide plenty of info and encouragement. Check the La Leche League web site for titles.

6 THE WEB. The web site *Bosom Buddies* (bosombuddies.com) has a good selection of breastfeeding articles, product information and links to other breastfeeding sites on the web.

Of course, our message boards (BabyBargains.com, click on community) are also a good place to find help—we have a special board on feeding where you can ask other moms for advice, tips and support.

7 HEALTH INSURANCE PROVIDERS. Some health insurance plans offer extensive breastfeeding resources; check your benefits.

Best Online Sources

Medela

medela.com Medela's web site offers useful info, tips and advice on breastfeeding. "Tips and Solutions" is an excellent FAQ for nursing moms. You can even submit questions to online lactation consultants. **Rating: A**

Nursing Mother Supplies

nursingmothersupplies.com Not only does this site carry breast pumps and supplies from Medela and Ameda Egnell, they also offer support to customers after they buy. We liked the extensive FAQ and breast pump comparison charts. Nursing pillows, storage options, Medela bottles and pads are also available. This site isn't too preachy—we like their low-key approach to encouraging breastfeeding. **Rating: A**

Breast Pumps Direct

breastpumpsdirect.com Breast Pumps Direct is an online discounter of breast pumps. They carry the major brands (Medela, Avent), as well as accessories and other items. Overall, we found their prices about 5% to 10% below other discounters. The advice section includes pump reviews, comparison charts and more. **Rating: A**

◆ *Other web sites:* Here is a site with a name that speaks for itself: *Affordable-medela-pumps.com*. Readers have mentioned it as a great site for pumps from Medela, Ameda, and Avent to name a few. *Mommy's Own* (mommysown.com) carries nearly every brand of recommended pump, bottle, breast pad and more. You'll find Boppy pillows, Majamas nursing clothes and LilyPadz breast pads at decent prices plus advice and forums you can join. Finally, a reader, Cherie Kannarr, thought that ***BreastFeeding.com*** "is a wonderful site, filled with facts, stories, humor, and support for nursing mothers."

What Are You Buying?

Even if you exclusively breastfeed, you probably will find yourself needing to pump a bottle from time to time. After all, you might want to go out to dinner without the baby. Maybe you'll have an overnight trip for your job or just need to get back to work full or part time. Your spouse might even be interested in relieving you of a night feeding. The solution? Pumping milk. Whether you want to pump occasionally or every day, you have a wide range of options. Here's an overview:

◆ ***Manual Expression:*** OK, technically, this isn't a breast pump in the sense we're talking about. But it is an option. There are several good breastfeeding books that describe how to express milk manually. Most women find that the amount of milk expressed, compared to the time and trouble involved, hardly makes it worth using this method. A few women (we think they are modern miracle workers) can manage to express enough for an occasional bottle; for the majority of women, however, using a breast pump is a more practical alternative. Manual expression is typically used only to relieve engorgement.

◆ ***Manual Pumps:*** Non-electric, hand-held pumps are operated by squeezing on a handle. While the most affordable option, manual pumps are generally also the least efficient—you simply can't duplicate your baby's sucking action by hand. Therefore, these pumps are best for moms who only need an occasional bottle or who need to relieve engorgement.

◆ ***Mini-Electrics:*** These battery-operated breast pumps are designed to express an occasional bottle. Unfortunately, the sucking action is so weak that it often takes twenty minutes per side to express a significant amount of milk. And doing so is not very comfortable. Why is it so slow? Most models only cycle nine to fifteen times per minute—compare that to a baby who sucks the equivalent of 50 cycles per minute!

◆ **High-End Double Pumps:** The Mercedes of breast pumps—
we can't sing the praises of these work horses enough. In just ten to
twenty minutes, you can pump both breasts. And high-end double
pumps are much more comfortable than mini-electrics. In fact, at first
I didn't think a high-end pump I rented was working well because
it was so comfortable. The bottom line: there is no better option for
a working woman who wants to provide her baby with breast milk.

Today, you have two options when it comes to these pumps: rent
a hospital-grade pump (which often is called a piston-electric) or
buy a high-end consumer grade double-pump.

Rental Pumps. These are what the industry refers to as hospital-grade or piston electric pumps. They are built to withstand continuous use of up to eight to ten times a day for many years. Often
they are much heavier than personal use pumps like the Medela
Pump-In-Style. And all the interior parts are sealed to prevent contamination from one renter to the next. *In fact, the Food and Drug
Administration (FDA) certifies rental pumps for multiple use.* The only
item each renter must buy is a new collection kit.

Where to find: Pediatricians, lactation consultants, doulas, mid-
wives, hospitals, maternity stores and home medical care companies
are sources to find rental pumps. You can also call La Leche League
(800-LALECHE; web: lalecheleague.org) or other lactation support
groups for a referral to a rental company in your area.

How much: Prices generally average about $45 to $65 per month
to rent a breast pump. Common brands of hospital-grade pumps
include Hygeia and White River Concepts, although consumer
brands Medela and Ameda also have hospital versions. Collection kits
cost about $45 to $60 for the bottles, shields and tubes.

Professional-Grade Electric Pumps. These electric pumps
are available for sale to consumers and are intended to be used no
more than three or four times a day. Unlike rental pumps, they are
lighter weight and easier to carry around (to work or elsewhere).
Examples of these pumps include the Medela Pump-In-Style and
the Ameda Purely Yours.

These pumps have an open system without sealed parts and are
therefore only recommended as a single-use item. *The FDA, lactation consultants, pediatricians and manufacturers DO NOT recommend using a second-hand personal pump.* Even if you change the
tubes and shields, there is a possibility of cross contamination. (The
exception is the Bailey Nurture III breast pump, which is one of the
very few pumps certified by the FDA for multiple users).

Where to find: Online is a primary source. Also most independent baby stores and Babies R Us carry a selection of electric breast

FEEDING

	Manual	Mini-Elec.	Professional	Rental*
BREAST PUMPS — Which pump works best in which situation?				
Do you need a pump for:				
A missed feeding?	■	◆		
Evening out from baby?	■	◆		
Working part-time.	■	◆		
Occasional use, a few times a week.	■	◆		
Daily use; full-time work			●	●
Premature or hospitalized baby?			●	●
Low milk supply?			●	●
Sore nipples/engorgement?	■		●	●
Latch-on problems or breast infection?			■	●
Drawing out flat or inverted nipples?	■	◆	●	●

Key: ■ = Good ◆ = Better ● = Best
*Rental refers to renting a hospital-grade pump. These can usually be rented on a monthly basis.
Source: Medela.

pumps. See earlier in the chapter for some of our favorite sources.

How much: Prices range from about $150 to $350 depending on the brand and accessories included. We will review pumps on page 258 and include prices.

Safe and Sound

As we mentioned in the last section, we don't recommend buying a used breast pump. Models like Medela's Pump In Style can actually collect milk in the pump mechanism. So, let's state it clearly: DO NOT PURCHASE A USED BREAST PUMP. The risk of exposing your baby to any pathogens isn't worth the savings.

Of course, it is fine to re-use your own breast pump for another child down the road. Just replace the tubing and collection bottles to make sure there are no bacteria left over from previous uses.

One more safety tip: if it hurts stop. No kidding! Pumping to express milk for your baby should not be a painful experience.

Smart Shopper Tip

Smart Shopper Tip #1
When to buy that pump.

"I don't know how long I want to breastfeed. And I'll be going back to work soon after my baby is born. When should I get a pump?"

We'd suggest waiting a bit before you invest in a breast pump or even nursing clothes. Many moms start with breast-feeding, but can't or don't want to continue it after a few weeks. For them investing in a pump would be a waste of money. If you aren't sure how long you want to breast feed, but you'd like to pump some extra bottles of milk anyway, consider renting a hospital grade pump first and trying it out before you invest a couple hundred dollars. You can often rent for as little as one month, which will be much cheaper than buying a pump that can run $200 to $350.

The best milk storage options

Once you've decided to express breast milk for your child, you'll need to consider how to store it. Freezer bags are the most common method and most major pump manufactures and bottle makers sell bags. So, who's got the best storage bags? *Lansinoh* (sold in Target; 50 pack for $10)) is the hands-down winner. "They are sturdy, stand on their own and have an excellent double lock seal closure," said one mom. Others echoed that recommendation. Lansinoh also sells BPA-free storage bottles that fit most breast pumps ($10 for four at Target.com).

Another good choice is *Medela*, the king of breast pumps. Their bags attach to any Medela pump and feature a zipper-top. Amazon.com sells a box of 50 for $17. Medela also sells 80 ml. breast milk containers and lids (12-pack is $13) and plastic collection bottles ($3.25 each). Both options are compatible with Medela breast pumps and are BPA free.

A completely different alternative is *Mothers Milk Mate* (mothersmilkmate.com). For $29, you get a ten-bottle storage system with rack. The 5 oz. bottles are BPA free and the set comes with freshness dating labels.

Speaking of labels, it's pretty important to know when milk has been expressed so you don't your feed baby milk that is past its freshness date. One solution: *BabaBaby's* storage bottles, with a calendar cap you twist to date. Invented by mom

Waste of Money

Even Cows Opt for the Electric Kind

"I'm going back to work a couple of months after my baby is born. My co-worker who breastfeeds her baby thinks manual and mini-electrics pumps are a waste of money. Your thoughts?

While they may be useful to relieve engorgement, manual pumps aren't very practical for long-term pumping when you're at work. They are very slow, which makes it hard to get much milk. Mini-electric breast pumps are better but are really best only for occasional use—for example, expressing a small amount of milk to mix with cereal for a baby who's learning to eat solids. The problem with mini-electrics: some are painful and most are too slow.

Your best bet if you plan to do some serious pumping is to rent a hospital-grade pump. These monsters maintain a high rate of extraction with amazing comfort. A lactation consultant we inter-

and actress Tara Strong (best known as the voice of cartoon characters on such shows as the *Powerpuff Girls* and *Ben 10*), BabaBaby bottles (babababy.com) are BPA-free and run $17.50 for two.

Medela offers a new storage system that includes a storage tray, two labeling lids and two 5 oz. bottles. The tray holds up to six bottles or storage bags upright in your freezer making them easy to see. Arrows mark which bottle is supposed to be used next so you don't grab the wrong one. The included lids (which can also be ordered separately) track the day and time the milk was pumped. The system sells for $16 and a six-pack of lids sells for $9.50

Yet another great option for freezer storage: **Milk Trays** by Sensible Lines (SensibleLines.com). It's hard to believe no one has thought of this before—Milk Trays are like old-fashioned ice cube trays but with a twist. The tray's 16 one-ounce capacity cubes are shaped like skinny cylinders, small enough to fit into any baby bottle. They come with lids to block freezer burn and are made from BPA-free, phthalate-free plastic. The trays sell for $22 for two.

Don't forget there are numerous apps for your smart phone that can help you keep track of your frozen or refrigerated expressed milk, baby feedings, diapers changes and more. Baby logs range in price from free up to $5.

viewed said these pumps can empty both breasts in about ten to 15 minutes—contrast that with 20 to 30 minutes for mini-electrics and 45 minutes to an hour for manual pumps.

We note later in our reviews of pumps that the manual pump that received top rating from our readers is the Avent Isis—and even though it is a vast improvement over previous options, it still is a MANUAL pump. It may not work well for moms who plan to work part or full-time and still nurse their baby. That said, one solution is to use two pumps—a mom we interviewed uses a Medela Pump In Style when she's tired (during the evening or night-time) and an Avent Isis at work (it's much quieter; doesn't need electricity, etc).

Money Saving Tips

1 **GET A FREE PUMP—COURTESY OF YOUR HEALTH INSURANCE.** One reader noted that her insurance provider would pay $50 toward the purchase of a breast pump; yet another reader found her medical insurance covered the entire cost of a $280 pump! Other insurance providers will only pay for a pump if there is a medical reason (premature birth, etc). You may have to get a "note from your doctor" to qualify. FYI: Medela has downloadable forms for insurance reimbursement online (medelabreastfeedingus.com, click on For Professionals, then LC Information). Good news: in 2011, the Internal Revenue Service ruled you can use pre-tax money in flexible spending accounts to purchase breastpumps and other supplies.

2 **CONSIDER EBAY.** Many readers have noted that breast pumps, including Medela's Pump In Style Advanced, are available for sale on eBay.com at huge discounts. We saw one, new in the box, for only $200. Some of them are older models or even used, so you'll need to educate yourself on what you're buying. Again, our advice: don't buy a used pump—only a new one.

3 **DON'T FEEL LIKE YOU HAVE TO BUY THE "TOP BRAND."** There are several manufacturers of breast pumps besides Medela. And our readers say their products work just as great for a lot less money (we discussed these alternative brands next in this chapter). For example, the Ameda Purely Yours pump averages only $200, while the Medela Pump in Style Advanced is a whopping $300+ retail and the Avent ISIS iQ is $350. However, we recommend sticking with manufacturers who specialize in breastfeeding. The First Years, for example, makes a ton of other products from spoons to bath tubs as well as breast pumps. We aren't as impressed with the quality of their pumps compared to other brands, however.

Breast Pumps (model by model reviews)

Manual Pumps

AVENT ISIS MANUAL (SCF310/20)
Web: AventAmerica.com
Price: $40.
Type: Manual.
Comments: Our readers love this pump, which
Avent claims is as efficient as a mini-electric (it takes
about eight to ten minutes to empty a breast). You can buy the Isis
by itself, or as part of a kit that includes extra bottles, cooler packs
and more. Good news: they've dropped the price this time around
making it more competitive with the Harmony. **Rating: A**

EVENFLO SIMPLYGO MANUAL
Web: Evenflo.com
Price: $23.
Type: Manual.
Comments: Evenflo's SimplyGo manual pump is
touted for its lightweight design. Another plus: a
new "Advance MemoryFlex" fastener to improve milk expression
plus silicone inserts for different size nipples. The unit comes with one
5 oz. collection bottle and a carry case. So what do parents think?
The biggest complaints were a lack of suction. While some readers
were able to express enough for an occasional bottle, many thought
the pump wasn't worth it. **Rating: C**

LANSINOH MANUAL
Web: Lansinoh.com
Price: $30-$35.
Type: Manual.
Comments: Readers think this pump is a good
runner up to Medela or Avent—Lansinoh's manual pump is easy to use and has few parts to clean.
A few dissenters say it doesn't quite have the suction of the Medela,
however. That was confirmed by our lactation consultant, who said
her measurements showed the Lansinoh pump had about 20% less
suction compared to the Avent or Medela. FYI: Lansinoh plans a
revision of this pump for 2011 with new ComfortFit breast flanges
(purple rings). Our concern: after you sterilize the pump, we worry
these flanges would stiffen over time, making the pump less comfortable. **Rating: B**

MEDELA HARMONY
Web: Medela.com
Price: $35.
Type: Manual.
Comments: The Harmony is a winner. Similar to the Avent Isis, it has fewer parts to wash than the Avent and is easier to assemble. One mom with larger breasts found this pump worked better for her than the Isis. The Harmony is more affordable than the Isis. **Rating: A**

SIMPLISSE MANUAL BREASTFEEDING COMPANION
Web: Simplisse.com
Price: $40.
Type: Manual.
Comments: New kid on the block Simplisse says their manual pump mimics Mother Nature better than other manual pumps, which have a suck-and-release action. Fans love the soft breast cup; dissenters say it isn't as good as the Medela or Avent models. One online reviewer chimed in, saying "the name 'Simplisse' must be French for many ridiculous steps for assembly and disassembly and miserable to clean." **Rating: C+**

Mini Electric Pumps

EVENFLO SIMPLYGO DUAL ELECTRIC
Web: Evenflo.com
Price: $40 single, $60 dual.
Type: Mini-electric.
Comments: Evenflo has completely revamped its line of breast pumps under the moniker SimplyGo. The SimplyGo Dual Electric breast pump is a double pump mini electric which sells for an affordable $60 (a single version is available for $40). The pump features an adjustable vacuum which Evenflo claims allows moms to customize the comfort level. It also has a silicone insert to "accommodate different nipple sizes" and comes with an AC adapter, cooler pack with two ice packs, two 5 oz. collection bottle, and a sample of their SimplyAbsorbant breast pads. Evenflo only recommends this pump for occasional use. In fact, they note on their web site that moms should not use it more than two times per day.

So far, feedback is very sparse but not very positive. Evenflo's track record in this category is poor, but this pump is too new to assign a rating yet. **Rating: Not Yet.**

FIRST YEARS MIPUMP
Web: learningcurve.com
Price: $46 single; $62 double.
Type: Mini-electric.

Comments: With both a single and double mini-electric version (pictured), the First Years MiPump is affordable and quiet—but the suction is inadequate. And more than one reader criticized the overall quality of the MiPump. Several reports of the pump breaking within one month of purchase make this one a loser. **Rating: F**

MEDELA SINGLE DELUXE BREAST PUMP
Web: Medela.com
Price: $53 to $65.
Type: Mini electric.
Comments: While Medela is among the top brands for breast pumps, the brand's entry in the mini-electric category receives decidedly mixed reviews from readers. For every mom who loved this pump, another complained about motors that burned out right after the warranty period was up and other woes. Yes, the Medela Swing (see below) costs more than twice this pump, but it is a much better choice. **Rating: D**

MEDELA SWING BREAST PUMP
Web: Medela.com
Price: $130-$160.
Type: Mini electric.
Comments: This single electric pump offers Medela's 2 Phase Expression (the same system as Medela's more expensive pumps), which is supposed to copy baby's natural sucking rhythm. The pump has two different modes: first to stimulate letdown and then to simulate baby's normal sucking pattern. Moms applaud this pump's ease of use and comfort. The only negative: it's a single pump and hence is best for occasional use. In fact, some moms wished it came as a double version. Despite that, we will give it our highest rating. **Rating: A**

PLAYTEX PETITE DOUBLE ELECTRIC PUMP
Web: playtex.com
Price: $80
Type: Mini electric.

Comments: Playtex has discontinued its Embrace Deluxe breast pump, but it's new entry, the Petite, still has soft silicone breast shields, a closed system design and air cushioned opening of the earlier model. It's smaller (as the name implies) which might make it a lot easier to carry and use. Another plus: it works directly with Playtex wide bottle system. The downsides? Parents complained that suction didn't work well at emptying both breasts compared to Medela pumps and Purely Yours. The motor even burned out on several readers! The weak suction and poor quality is a deal-killer—we don't recommend this pump. **Rating: F**

More mini-electrics: You'll see several other brands of mini-electric breast pumps on the market today. With the exception of the Medela Swing, most of these pumps fair poorly according to our reader feedback. For occasional use, you are better off getting a simple manual pump. Or if you need a serious pump for daily pumping, the professional-grade options (reviewed below) are the best bets.

Professional-Grade Pumps

AMEDA PURELY YOURS

Web: Ameda.com
Price: $160 for the pump only; $210 for the Carry All version; $230 for the Backpack; $300 Ultra.
Type: Professional.
Comments: It's smaller! It's lighter! And its less expensive—the Ameda Purely Yours has won a legion of fans for its Purely Yours Pump, which comes in four versions: pump only (use your own bag), Carry All and Backpack. A new "Ultra" version throws in an extra tote bag, cooler bag and six bottles. The pump weighs about five pounds and has eight suction settings and nine speeds. The backpack includes a car adapter. The Ameda has a built-in AA battery pack, versus the Medela, which has a separate battery pack. Best of all, the Ameda is easy to maintain (milk can't get into the tubes, which means less cleaning than the Medela). The downside? Medela is sold in many more retail outlets than Ameda meaning you can get spare parts and supplies easier (although to its credit, Ameda has great customer service). The Lansinoh is a branded version of the same pump for $150. FYI: Ameda is now a division of Evenflo. **Rating: A**

AVENT SINGLE/TWIN ELECTRIC

Web: AventAmerica.com
Price: $130-$170 single; $160-$300 double.
Type: Professional.
Comments: Perhaps the coolest thing about Avent's electric breast pumps is the

customization feature. Moms can adjust the suction strength, the length of suction time and the rest period—that's fantastic.

So how does it work? You start by pumping manually, then the pump "copies" your preferences. You can continue to tweak the settings with "infinite variable controls" and it remembers your latest settings.

So what's the downside to the Avent electric pumps? Well, there are a lot of parts to assemble, but most moms noted that with practice it's pretty easy. We did hear from one mom who complained that when set up on a desk, the Isis iQ can be rather tippy to use. She also noted that milk gets stuck in the diaphragm and has to be emptied at the end.

And finally, the price is a big stumbling block. Although you can find it discounted online to $160 for the double version, the price in some stores is closer to $300 . . . that is nearly twice the Ameda Purely Yours. At least Avent doesn't skimp on what comes with the pump: besides the pump itself, you get two Avent 4 oz. bottles, four bottles stand/funnel covers, and an electric adapter in a microfiber bag. But compared to the old Isis IQ, that's a bit skimpy. The Isis came with an insulated carry bag and eight gel packs for cold storage. So the price is about the same, but the amenities are less spectacular. It's comparable to the top-of-the-line Medela Pump In Style Advanced without the nice bag.

Our readers are generally split into two camps when it comes to pumps: Medela vs. Avent. Medela fans like the wide availability of parts and Medela's excellent customer service. Avent fans love the pump's overall quality and compatibility with Avent's very popular bottles—the pump connects directly to the bottles, etc.

Aside from the price, moms thought it was quiet, comfortable and easy to clean. And it does the job. **Rating: A-**

Pumps: Have a Plan B

If you plan to return to work and will rely on pumping to feed your baby, make sure you have a Plan B in case your breast pump breaks. Yes, pumps are just machines and sometimes they break down—that means tracking down replacement parts at a store across town. Or waiting for parts to arrive by mail. The best advice: have a Plan B, like a back-up manual or mini-electric pump on hand. This is especially important if you choose a brand (like Ameda) that is mostly sold online—the only way to get replacement parts for such pumps is through the mail!

Nursing Pillows

Many nursing moms find a nursing pillow makes breastfeeding easier and more comfortable. Our readers have emailed us positive comments for *My Brest Friend* by Zenoff Products (zenoffprod-ucts.com). Okay, it probably qualifies as the Most Stupid Name for a Baby Product Ever award, but it really works—it wraps around your waist and is secured with Velcro. It comes in original, deluxe, professional, travel and twins models. The Original retails for about $40.

An old favorite is the *Boppy* pillow. Sold for $25 to $35 online, this perennial favorite doesn't have a waist strap, but many moms swear by it as a simple, affordable nursing pillow.

Got twins? Check out *EZ-2-NURSE's* pillow (we found it on Amazon.com) A mom told us this was the "absolute best" for her twins, adding, "I could not successfully nurse my girls together without this pillow. It was wonderful." Cost: $55.

If you're not sold in the idea of a big, bulky nursing pillow, we did find an alternative. *Utterly Yours* (utterlyyours.com) makes a small, hand-sized pillow that you position directly under the breast. Cost: $24 (including pillow cover).

BAILEY MEDICAL NURTURE III
Web: BaileyMed.com
Price: $120 basic, $160 deluxe.
Type: Professional
Comments: This pump comes in two versions—basic ($120) and deluxe ($160). It's claim to fame: the Nurture III is the only small pump approved for multiple users by the FDA. Hence you can buy this pump and hand it down to a friend or sell it online. The Nurture III features adjustable suction and manual cycling, where mom can control the cycling pattern. This feature takes some practice, say our readers—and isn't a plus for sleep-deprived moms. Fans say it does a great job at expressing milk, but others have a problem letting-down with the Nurture III. The deluxe version includes an insulated carry bag with ice pack and four extra bottles (pictured). Bottom line: this is a good pump, but hard to find in stores. It is mostly sold online. **Rating: B+**

HYGEIA ENJOYE
Web: Hygeiababy.com
Price: $305
Type: Professional
Comments: A reader recommended this

brand to us—she loved her EnJoye pump, which is comparable in suction to hospital-grade pumps. It comes in three versions: a rechargeable battery version (LBI; $305, pictured), one with an external power supply (EPS, $220) or an external battery pack (EXT, $260). The only bummer: Hygeia doesn't make smaller size flanges. Hygeia isn't as well known as Medela or Avent, but a worthy alternative to consider. **Rating: A**

LANSINOH AFFINITY
Web: Lansinoh.com
Price: $130-$150.
Type: Professional.
Comments: Lansinoh's last effort in this category was to merely repackage an Ameda pump (see review). This time, however, the company has their own design: the Affinity is an affordable pump that is lightweight and has the same stimulation model (one-touch let-down) that Medela offers. We liked the improved white membrane, which should make it less likely to tear and need replacement. The filter in the model is much like Medela's Freestyle. Also good: multiple suction and cycle settings let you customize pumping plus the company guarantees milk will not back up into the tubing or motor.

On the downside, the suction isn't as strong as Medela's pumps (about 10% less, based on our measurements). And readers say the Affinity is rather loud and not as comfortable as other pumps. Also: there is just one size flange (24 mm), so it won't be as accommodating for smaller or larger breasts. Finally, we aren't wild about that purple lip around the flange—like the manual pump, we worry it would stiffen over time after you sterilize the pump (making it uncomfortable). So it's a mixed review for the Lansinoh Affinity— good price and decent features make it a better bet than other low price models like Evenflo and First Years. But it still can't hold a candle to our top rated picks in this category (Ameda and Medela). **Rating: B**

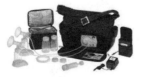

MEDELA PUMP IN STYLE ADVANCED
Web: Medela.com
Price: $260 to $370.
Type: Professional
Comments: It's the 800-pound gorilla of the breast pump category: the Medela Pump In Style (PIS).

So what's all the fuss about? If you are serious about pumping every day, the Pump In Style allows you to carry a high quality pump with you to work. You can empty both breasts in a short amount of time with great comfort. As a nursing mom, I remember

using the Original version and found it pretty comparable to a hospital-grade pump.

The PIS has evolved over the years—gone is the basic "Original" version and now we have the Advanced, which comes in three flavors: backpack ($280), shoulder bag ($280) and metro bag ($310).

In general, the Advanced features Medela's new "2-Phase Expression" technology that mimics the way infants nurse at the breast. At first, infants apparently nurse quickly to simulate let down. Then they settle into a deeper, slower sucking action—the Pump In Style Advance simulates this pattern.

The Advanced three versions are similar: they all have the same pump, just a different bag. The Metro is slightly different (and $30 more expensive): it has a removable pump motor and storage bags.

So what's the disadvantage of the Pump In Styles? Cost is a biggie: the PIS is $100 or so more than the Ameda Purely Yours, which is smaller, lighter and has several other attractive features. Medela's higher price is no doubt attributable to their "minimum advertised price" policy, which prevents Internet discounters from selling their pumps below a certain price. Hence, you'll see Medela priced about the same on most sites.

Fans of Medela love the availability of parts (sold in many retail stores) and Medela's excellent customer service. So, all in all, we will recommend the Pump in Style—it is an excellent pump. **Rating: A**

MEDELA FREESTYLE BREAST PUMP
Web: Medela.com
Price: $380
Type: Professional
Comments: The Freestyle is Medela's latest pump and they pulled out all the stops: hands-free option, LED display, pumping session timer, memory function and more.

How does it differ from the Pump in Style (PIS)? Well, the Freestyle can be removed from its bag (unlike the PIS backpack or shoulder bag) and it features a rechargeable battery for three hours of pumping (the PIS can use AA batteries or a wall outlet). Most moms only have to charge it once a week.

Yet it is the hands-free option that is the killer app here: fans call it "life changing," especially for moms with another toddler at home (and hence the need to multi-task). Of course, at $380, this pump better be darn impressive. And it's amazing that all this comes from a pump that basically fits in the palm of your hand (ok, if you have big hands).

So why buy the Freestyle instead of the Pump In Style? Fans of the Freestyle say it is easier to use and clean than the PIS. Even the breast shields are softer and more comfortable. The downside? The Freestyle isn't exactly quiet, although no louder than the Pump In Style. And if you don't keep the bottles at the right angle, milk can spill out. Also the Freestyle can be a bit fussy to assemble—if you don't assemble the parts just so, you can get less suction. Those cons aside, we still think this is an excellent pump. The Freestyle is highly recommended. **Rating: A**

SIMPLISSE DOUBLE ELECTRIC BREASTFEEDING COMPANION
Web: Simplisse.com
Price: $285.
Type: Professional.

Comments: New kid on the block Simplisse's Double Electric Companion pump features "gentle compression technology to gently elicit milk expression." The pump also has flexible breast cups for better fit and adjustable pump pressure settings, as well as a purse-like tote bag that includes a cooler pack and four milk collection bottles. This pump is still rather new, so there's not as much feedback on it as we have on other models. However, the first adopters in general weren't that impressed—it is too loud, says one reader who also knocked the suction as sub-par. Fans, however, say the pump is very comfortable, although even they say the lack of accessories (no vehicle adapter car, for example) hampers its usefulness. **Rating: C+**

Our Picks: Brand Recommendations

◆ *Manual Pump:* The best manual pumps are the *Avent Isis* (SCF310/20; $40) and *Medela Harmony* ($35). Between the two, the Medela Harmony has the edge, given its lower price and easier-to-clean design.

◆ *Mini Electric Pump:* The *Medela Swing* mini-electric is pricey ($130-$160) but very good quality. Yes, you may be tempted by other mini-electric pumps in discount stores for $40 and $50, but we have one word of advice: don't.

◆ *Professional Grade Pump:* You can't go wrong with either, so we'll make it a tie: the *Medela Pump In Style* ($265 to $370) and *Ameda Purely Yours* ($160 to $300) are the co-champs. For daily pumping, they are the standard. If hands-free operation is important, then consider the excellent Medela Freestyle ($380).

Before you buy a pump, we suggest RENTING a hospital-grade pump first for a week or two (or a month). After you decide you're committed to pumping and you're comfortable with how double pumps work, then consider buying one of your own. Given the hefty retail prices, it makes sense to buy only if you plan to pump for several months or have a second child.

Formula

Is there any nutritional difference between brands of formula? No, the federal government mandates that all formula have the same nutritional value (the amount of protein, etc). That's right—the "generic" formula sold at a discounter is nutritionally no different than pricey name brands. How pricey? A 25-ounce can of name brand powdered formula runs $25.83 today. Yep, 25 bucks a tub. At these prices, you can see how buying formula can take a bite out of your baby budget in a hurry. As we mentioned earlier, the American Academy of Pediatrics and the American Dental Association now say that parents who use powdered or concentrated formula should use bottled water when they make up a bottle for baby. What kind of bottled water? Purified, demineralize, deionized, distilled or reverse osmosis filtered water. So that's going to cost you too—add about a penny per ounce to the cost of powdered formula. Let's talk formula!

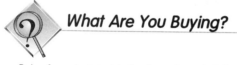

What Are You Buying?

Baby formula is just baby formula, right? Nope, it is more complicated that—formula comes in several versions (powdered, liquid concentrate, ready-to-drink) as well as types (cow's milk, soy, etc). Not to mention organic, specialty formulas and more. Here's a quick overview:

◆ **Versions.** Formula comes in three different versions: powder, liquid concentrate and ready-to-drink. Powder is least expensive, followed by liquid concentrate—you add water to both these. Ready-to-drink is the priciest. A recent online price survey revealed the lowest cost per ounce of powdered formula is 11¢ (we include the cost of bottled water per oz of 1¢). Compare that to liquid concentrate at 21¢ (also includes 1¢ per oz. bottled water expense), and ready to drink at 28¢ per ounce.

◆ **Infant stages.** Manufacturers are now making different formulas for different ages and stages of infancy. For example, Enfamil makes a formula for newborns to three month olds with additional vitamin D.

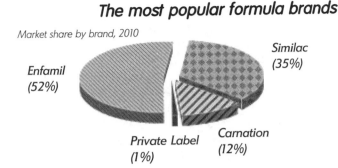

The most popular formula brands

Market share by brand, 2010

Enfamil
(52%)

Similac
(35%)

Private Label
(1%)

Carnation
(12%)

formula

Meanwhile, Enfamil's regular formula (for newborns up to 12 months) has added prebiotics to aid in the growth of good bacteria in the gut. Similac has a "Go & Grow" formula for older babies (nine-24 months).

◆ *Toddler formula.* First created by Carnation ("Follow Up" formula, now marketed under the Nestle name), then copied by other formula manufacturers, "toddler" formulas are intended to be used for older children (typically nine months old and up) instead of regular cows milk or soymilk. Typically, parents move to whole milk or soymilk when their child reaches one year of age. In order to hang on to consumers longer, formula manufacturers have developed these toddler formulas. So what's the big difference between baby formula and toddler formula? All these toddler formulas add calcium and iron as well as a variety of vitamins (E, C, D) depending on the brand.

◆ *Types.* Beside cow's milk-based formula, there is also soy-based formula. Which is best? Cow's milk formula with iron—this formula is tolerated best by the most babies and recommended first by most doctors. Of course, there are many specialty formulas for babies with special problems—we call these the "gourmet" formulas, described in more detail below. Our advice in a nutshell: buy the cheapest cow's milk based formula you can find to start with.

◆ *Organic.* These formulas are certified "antibiotic, pesticide and growth hormone free." Organic formula is almost always more expensive than regular formulas, just like organic foods typically cost more. Whole Foods and other natural grocery stores carry organic formula as well as many regular grocery chains. Other options are available online. These are the brands we've found in our research:

Baby's Only Organic Baby Formula—for toddlers only, not for infants (naturesone.com)
Earth's Best Infant Formula (earthsbest.com)
Kroger Private Selection Organic Formula

O Organic Formula (safeway.com)
Parents Choice (parentschoiceformula.com)
Similac Advance Organic (similac.com)

◆ *Gourmet formula.* Formula makers have been busy rolling out additional formula to accommodate a range of baby needs. For example, there is a lactose-intolerant formula (Enfamil LactoFree), Isomil DF for babies with a stomach virus and Enfamil AR for babies with gastro esophageal reflux. We discuss these formulas in greater detail in our other book, *Baby 411* (see our web site for more information). Just for fun, here is the entire list of Enfamil gourmet formulas: they have formulas for fussiness & gas (cow and soy versions), frequent spit-up, colic due to cows' milk protein allergy, for feeling full longer, premature growth, trouble absorbing fat, severe cows' milk allergy, and metabolic formulas.

◆ *Packaging.* Concerns about Bisphenol-A (BPA; see the bottle discussion later in this chapter for more on BPA) has prompted formula makers to change their packaging in recent years. Newer plastic tubs and bottles are BPA-free. Other manufacturers like Nature's One have never lined their cans with BPA.

That's just a brief overview of formula—we have an in-depth discussion of formula in our *Baby 411* book. Co-written with a pediatrician, Dr. Ari Brown, the book extensively discusses breastfeeding, formula and feeding challenges for all infants. It's all in a fun-filled chapter called "Liquids." Check our web site (Baby411.com) for Dr. Brown's blog, which covers breaking news items on infant feeding.

 *Safe and Sound*

Formula is one of the most closely regulated food items in the US. The Food and Drug Administration has strict guidelines about what can and cannot go into baby formula. The FDA requires expiration dates, warning labels and so on. So what are the safety hazards you might run up against? Here are a few:

1 **ASK YOUR DOC FIRST.** Never switch formula types or brands without discussing it with your pediatrician first. While our recommendation is to buy the cheapest cow's milk you can find, some babies have health problems that require special formula.

2 **CONFUSING CANS CONFRONT SOY FORMULA USERS.** Soy formula now accounts for 17% of the infant formula market. Yet, a case of mistaken identity has caused problems. Some parents mistakenly thought they were feeding their babies soy formula, when in fact they were using soymilk. The problem: soymilk is missing important nutrients and vitamins found in soy formula. As a result, babies fed soymilk were malnourished and some required hospitalization. Adding to the confusion, soymilk is often sold in cans that look very similar to soy formula. The government has asked soymilk makers to put warning labels on their products, so most should be labeled. If you use soy formula, be careful to choose the right can.

3 **IRON.** Another concern: low-iron formula. A myth among some parents is that the iron in standard formula causes constipation—it does not, says pediatrician Dr. Ari Brown, co-author of *Baby 411*. Yes, constipation can be a problem with ALL formulas. But babies should NEVER be on low-iron formula unless instructed by a pediatrician.

4 **EXPIRED FORMULA.** While formula comes in sealed cans and tubs that look like they have an infinite shelf life, they do have expiration dates. And many of our readers have written to tell us that stores don't always remove expired formula from the shelves in a timely manner. That includes grocery stores, discounters and even warehouse clubs. So read the label carefully and check your own supply of formula before you open a tub or bottle. Also, watch out for formula sold on auction sites. Be sure to ask about expiration dates.

5 **DON'T BUY OFF BRAND FORMULA IN ETHNIC GROCERY STORES.** While the 2008 melamine scare mainly affected families in China, a few cans did make it into the U.S. through ethnic grocery stores. Federal law bans such black market imports, but that doesn't mean they don't happen. Stick to name brand formula bought in mainstream stores.

6 **DON'T FORGET THE BOTTLED WATER.** As we mentioned several times already, you'll need to mix your powdered or concentrated formula with special water. What kind? Purified, demineralize, deionized, distilled or reverse osmosis filtered water. The American Academy of Pediatrics and the American Dental Association recommend this to help avoid consuming too much fluoride which causes tooth discoloration. You can use tap water if it contains less than .3 ppm of fluoride or if you have a reverse osmosis filter. For everyone else, there will be an extra expense. Be sure to buy your water in bulk—gallon jugs are the most economical. A reasonable price per ounce will be about 1¢. For more details on fluoride and your baby, check out our *Baby 411* book (see the end of this book for more information).

Money Saving Tips

1 **STAY AWAY FROM PRE-MIXED FORMULA.** Liquid concentrate formula and ready-to-drink formula are 50% to 200% more expensive than powdered formula. Yes, it is more convenient but you pay big time for that. We priced name brand, ready to drink formula at a whopping 28¢ per ounce.

Guess what type of formula is given out as freebies in doctors' offices and hospitals? Yes, it's often the ready-to-drink liquid formula. These companies know babies get hooked on the particular texture of the expensive stuff, making it hard (if not impossible) to switch to the powdered formula later. Sneaky, eh?

What's the most popular type of formula in the US? Powder. Over 60% of the formula sold in the US is powdered while liquid concentrate accounts for only 27% of formula sales.

2 **CONSIDER GENERIC FORMULA.** Most grocery stores and discounters sell "private" label formula at considerable savings, at least 30% to 40%. At one grocery store chain, their generic powdered formula worked out to just 5¢ per fluid ounce, a 50% savings.

The largest maker of generic formula is PBM Products (PBMProducts.com). This company makes generic formula under several different brand names including Bright Beginnings (BrightBeginnings.com), Member's Mark (sold at Sam's Club) and Parent's Choice (sold at Walmart). Generic formula has come a long way in recent years—now you can buy generic organic formula as well as several other special varieties.

We should note that some pediatricians are concerned about recommending generic formula—doctors fret that such low-cost formula might discourage breastfeeding.

3 **BUY IT ONLINE.** Yep, you can buy formula online from eBay. You can save big but watch out—some unscrupulous sellers try to pawn off expired formula on unsuspecting buyers. Be sure to confirm the expiration date before buying formula online. And watch out for shipping charges—formula is heavy and shipping can outweigh any deal, depending on the price you pay.

4 **BUY IN BULK.** We found wholesale clubs had the best prices on name brand formula. For example, Costco (Costco.com) sells a 34 oz. can of Similac Advance for $25.89 (10¢ per oz. of mixed formula). That is 27% less than grocery stores. And generic formula at wholesale clubs is an even bigger bargain. Costco's Kirkland brand formula was $16.49 for a 36 oz can (6¢ per oz. of mixed formula). Don't forget to pick up bottled water to mix with formula at the wholesale club as well.

5 **ASK YOUR PEDIATRICIAN FOR FREE SAMPLES.** Just make sure you get the powdered formula (not the liquid concentrate or ready to pour). One reader in Arizona said she got several free cases from her doctor, who simply requested more from the formula makers.

6 **SHOP AROUND.** Yes, powdered formula at a grocery store can run $20 to $25 for a 28-ounce can (approximately)—but there's no federal law that says you must buy it at full retail. Readers of our book have noticed that formula prices vary widely, sometimes even at different locations of the same chain. In Chicago, a reader said they found one Toys R Us charged over a dollar less per can for the same ready-to-feed formula than another TRU across town. "They actually have a price check book at the registers with the codes for each store in the Chicagoland area," the reader said. "At our last visit, we saved $13.20 for two cases (about 30% of the cost), just by mentioning we wanted to pay the lower price."

Another reader noticed a similar price discrepancy at Walmart stores in Florida. When she priced Carnation Good Start powdered formula, she found one Walmart that marked it at $6.61 per can. Another Walmart (about 20 miles from the first location) sells the same can for $3.68! When the reader inquired about the price discrepancy, a customer service clerk admitted that each store independently sets the price for such items, based on nearby competition. That's a good lesson—many chains in more rural or poorer locations (with no nearby competition) often mark prices higher than suburban stores.

7 **FORGET TODDLER FORMULA.** When your child is ready for whole milk (usually at one year of age, according to most pediatricians), you can switch from formula (about 11¢ per ounce) to milk (about 3¢ per ounce). Yep, that is a savings of nearly 70%! No, you don't need toddler formula.

What about the claim that toddler formulas have extra calcium, iron and vitamins? Nutritionists point out that toddlers should be getting most of their nutrition from solid foods, not formula. Toddlers should only be drinking about two cups a day of whole milk. Additional calcium can be found in foods as diverse as yogurt and broccoli; iron in red meat and spinach; vitamins in a wide variety of foods.

But what if you don't think your child is getting enough of those nutrients? Adding a vitamin and mineral supplement to your child's diet would still be less expensive than blowing your money on toddler formulas.

You may be wondering, in the day of increasing concern about obesity, why whole milk is recommended. Pediatricians tell us toddlers between 12 and 24 months of age need the fat in whole milk to foster brain development. At age two, you should switch to skim milk or 1%. For more on toddler development and nutrition, check out our *Toddler 411* book. See the back of this book for more information.

8 **CHECK OUT AMAZON.** Yep, Amazon sells formula (and even diapers) in their health and personal care store. Prices for formula were about 10% to 15% cheaper than full retail and if you order more than $25 (which is pretty easy), you may qualify for free shipping. Sign up for Amazon Mom—a free membership program that gives you free two-day shipping with Amazon Prime and 30% off items like diapers and wipes. You get additional months of free two-day shipping the more you buy from Amazon's baby store.

9 **JOIN A FORMULA CLUB.** Several formula makers have frequent buyer clubs. Example: Enfamil's Family Beginnings offers checks for purchasing formula, a free diaper bag, and more. It's free (sign up at Enfamil.com) but be prepared to fill out lots of forms asking for information on where you live, when your baby is due and your attitudes toward breast and formula feeding.

Bonus savings idea: Sam's Club accepts Enfamil's checks, which lets you stretch those freebies even farther! And you can find lots of checks for sale on eBay.com at great prices.

Bottles/Nipples

What are you buying?

What's the best bottle for baby? Actually, it's more than just the bottle. The nipple (how the milk is delivered to baby) is just as important as the container.

When it comes to nipples, there are a myriad of choices. Your first decision will be the shape of the nipple. They come in orthodontic (bulb shaped), flat-topped or original (bell shaped). See graphics at right. Experts tell us that the bell shaped nipple seems to work best for breast fed babies who are either taking an occasional bottle or permanently transitioning from breast to bottle.

Most nipples are made of latex or silicone. We recommend silicone. They last longer, don't have any flavor, are heat resistant and may resist bacteria better than latex. Latex can be allergenic as well.

Orthodontic

Finally, nipples have different flow levels. If you are starting immediately with bottle feeding, begin with a low flow nipple so your baby doesn't become overwhelmed with formula and gag. This is also a good idea for parents who are giving an occasional bottle to a breast fed baby—it forces your baby to work harder, more like when breastfeeding. As baby grows, you may *Flat-topped* need to buy a faster flow nipple.

What about the bottle itself? After the government issued a report in 2008 that questioned the safety of a chemical (Bisphenol-A or BPA) used in polycarbonate bottles, manufacturers began making BPA-free *Bell shaped* bottles. So, pretty much all the new bottles on the shelves today are BPA-free. (We've posted a Q&A about BPA on our web site BabyBargains.com, click on Bonus Material). Some parents prefer glass bottles since they have always been a safe, chemical free option.

Of course, there may be older baby bottles still on the back of some store shelves—a word to the wise: make sure the package says BPA-free before buying any bottle, breast pump or sippy cup. And if a friend offers you her old baby bottles, we say politely decline. You likely wouldn't be able to tell if they had BPA or not.

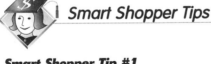

Smart Shopper Tips

Smart Shopper Tip #1
Bottle confusion?

"How many bottles will I need if I formula feed? What nipple sizes do I need? Do I need a bottle sterilizer?"

Yes, the questions about bottles and feeding baby can be rather endless! To help, on our web site, we've posted a great email from a mom who's been there, done that. This email actually appeared first as a thread on our message boards, but we thought it was the most comprehensive discussion of bottle-feeding we've ever seen. Since it is eight pages long, however, we didn't have room to reprint it here. Go to Babybargains.com/Bonus to read it.

Smart Shopper Tip #2
Getting started
"I think I'm going to bottle feed for at least some of the time, but I don't want to spend a fortune on bottles. What should I buy?"

Consider getting a starter kit from one or two of our top recommended bottle makers (see Our Picks below). Starter kits usually include a selection of bottle sizes, slow flow nipples and bottle caps. They may also have accessories like a bottle brush included. Prices range from $15 to $60 depending on brand and number of items included.

Our Picks: Brand Recommendations

Good. First Years offers an interesting option to parents looking for a good bottle to help with the transition between bottle and breast. Their **Breastflow** bottles have a unique double nipple that forces baby to use both suction and compression—just like at mother's breast. Priced at about $5 per 5 oz. bottle. While feedback from parents is mostly positive, some thought the double nipple design was hard to clean and using them required practice.

Better. *Tommee Tippee's Closer to Nature* bottles are new, debuting in the past year. The feedback from parents is mostly positive, especially if your baby is transitioning from breast to bottle and back. The extra wide nipple (made of silicone) stretches and flexes like a human breast. They also include an "easi-vent" valve that helps avoid gas and colic. A newborn starter kit sells for $40 and includes four 9 oz. bottles, two 5 oz. bottles, three formula dispensers and a bottle/nipple cleaner. A two pack of 9 oz. bottles sells for $17. Perhaps the biggest criticism of this bottle is collapsing nipples (where the nipple doesn't fill up with liquid)—the company has advice on how to avoid this on their web site (TommeeTippee.us).

Best. Tied for first place in the bottle battle are *Avent* and *Dr. Brown's*. It's a real toss up as to which is best. Our readers seem to be split evenly. Avent gets a nod for its well-designed nipple, which is clinically proven to reduce colic (uncontrollable, extended crying that starts in some babies around one month of age). Ditto for Dr. Brown's Natural Flow bottle (handi-craft.com), which has a patented vent system that eliminates bubbles and nipple collapse. Avent and Dr. Brown's are pricey, however—they cost about $5 to $8 a bottle. That compares to $2 to $4 for other bottles from makers like Evenflo and Playtex.

Best Glass Bottle. Nobody beats *Evenflo's* glass bottles. They are very affordable, available in several sizes and quantities and the best choice for folks who don't want plastic. Prices range from $2 to $3.50 per bottle. The more expensive versions have elasticized plastic sleeve to help avoid breakage if dropped.

One quick note: in most cases, bottles and nipples aren't interchangeable. You can't use an Avent nipple on a Gerber bottle and so on. The exception: Dr. Brown's nipples DO fit on Evenflo's glass bottles (see above), report our readers—a bit of trimming on the vent tube is required.

Bottle Warmers & Sterilizers

Do you need to sterilize bottles every time you use them? Or boil water for formula? Or use bottled water?

The answers are no, no and yes.

There's no need to sterilize baby bottles every time you use them—yes, run them through the dishwasher when you first open the package. But you can clean bottles with warm, soapy water thereafter (or use the dishwasher again).

There's also no need to boil water for formula. That's because most tap water in the U.S. is treated and is safe to drink. However, the standard recommendation today is to use bottled water to mix with formula—we have a full discussion of this in our other book, *Baby 411*.

As for the temperature of a bottle of formula, room temperature is fine—bottles neither need to be heated nor cooled.

The take-home message: bottle warmers and sterilizers are purely optional. Since we realize some readers still want to purchase these items, here are our recommendations:

Avent seems to win the sterilizer war with their "Microwave Steam Sterilizer." This model holds up to six Avent bottles or two Avent Breast Pumps and two bottles for $32. If you prefer a plug in sterilizer, the Digital Steam Sterilizer sterilizes six bottles in six minutes and keeps bottles sterile for up to 24 hours. Like the microwave version, it can also sterilize up to two breast pumps. Cost: about $75.

While Avent makes a good sterilizer, we would suggest getting the matching sterilizer for your bottle brand. For example, if you decide to use Born Free bottles, then the ***Born Free sterilizer*** ($45) is a good bet. Why? Sterilizers for one brand can sometimes damage other brand's bottles—for example, we did receive a report that ***Medela's Quick Clean Micro-Steam bags*** can melt Born Free bottles.

What about bottle warmers? Avent makes a couple, including the iQ Electronic Bottle and Baby Food Warmer ($60). The digital readout lets parents know how soon the bottle or food will be ready and warms them automatically. The Electric Bottle and Baby Food Warmer ($60) warms a room temperature bottle in about four minutes. Both

Pacifiers: Good or Bad?

Should your baby use a pacifier? Surprisingly, this is a controversial topic.

Some experts argue that early use of pacifiers may interfere with breastfeeding. But new studies show that pacifier use in children actually reduces the risk of Sudden Infant Death Syndrome (SIDS). It's unclear why pacifiers work, but studies clearly show a lowered risk of SIDS.

So, here are our recommendations for pacifier use: wait to give your child a pacifier until breastfeeding is well established (about a month of age). Discontinue pacifier use by six months of age. Why? Ninety percent of SIDS deaths occur between one month and six months of age. For more on the health benefits of pacifiers, see our other book, *Baby 411*.

So, now that you know what's good about a pacifier, which type of pacifier is best? There are two types—regular pacifiers have round nipples, while "orthodontic" pacifiers have flat nipples. Either is fine—but consult with your pediatrician if you have concerns on this topic. Our resident pediatrician, Dr. Ari Brown recommends "Soothies" (soothie-pacifiers.com) brand to her patients.

models fit baby food jars and all types of baby bottles (not just Avent).

New to the bottle warmer market is the **Kiinde Kozii** ($70). This new universal bottle warmer accepts frozen breast milk storage bags, liner bottles, plastic bottles, glass bottles and even food containers—any type, any brand. Kiinde's SAFEHeat technology consists of a "circulating bath of warm water" to heat a bottle. Since the water is about room temperature, Kiinde claims to prevents hot spots and allays concerns that boiling water can cause chemicals like BPA to leach out of older bottles. A timer and automatic shutoff means it won't overheat and the water reservoir does not require parents to add water each time it's used.

The Kiinde Kozii is too new for a rating yet, but the initial feedback on it has been positive.

Baby Food

At the tender age of four to six months, you and your baby will depart on a magical journey to a new place filled with exciting adventures and never-before-seen wonders. Yes, you've entered the SOLID FOOD ZONE.

Best Online Sources

Looking for a schedule of what foods to introduce when? Earth's Best's web site has a comprehensive chart with suggestions (earthsbest.com, click on Health & Nutrition, then Doctor's Corner, then Infant Feeding Schedule). Gerber's slick web site (gerber.com) also has lots of information. Unfortunately, you'll have to sign up on the site to get to information like recommended feeding schedules. Watch out for lots of spam from this site.

We also liked Beechnut's site (beechnut.com), which includes suggested menus and feeding tips. Although it is designed for Canadian parents, Heinz's baby food web site, heinzbaby.com contains extensive nutritional advice and menu planners among other information. Canadians can take advantage of rebate offers and other deals on this site (hopefully, they'll add the rest of North America to the coupon deals soon).

Safe & Sound

1 **FEED FROM A BOWL, NOT FROM THE JAR.** Why? If you feed from a jar, bacteria from baby's mouth can find its way back to the jar, spoiling the food much more quickly. Also, saliva enzymes begin to break down the food's nutrients. The best strategy: pour the amount of baby food you need into a bowl and feed from there (unless it's the last serving from the jar). And be sure to refrigerate any unused portions.

2 **DON'T STORE FOOD IN PLASTIC BAGS.** If you leave plastic bags on the baby's high chair, they can be a suffocation hazard. A better solution: store leftover food in small, Tupperware-type containers.

3 **DO A TASTE TEST.** Make sure it isn't too hot, too cold, or spoiled. We know you aren't dying to taste the Creamed Ham Surprise from Gerber, but it is a necessary task.

Another tip: a dental hygienist wrote to remind us that parents should taste baby's food with a different spoon than the one baby will be using. Why? "The bacteria from your mouth can be transferred to the baby's mouth when you use the same spoon."

4 **CHECK FOR EXPIRATION DATES.** Gerber's jarred food looks like it would last through the next Ice Age, but check that expiration date. Most unopened baby food is only good for a year or two. Use opened jars within one to two days.

5 **AVOID UNPASTEURIZED MILK, MILK PRODUCTS AND JUICES.** Babies don't have the ability to fight off serious bacterium like e. coli. Avoid these hazards by feeding your child only pasteurized dairy and juice products.

Also steer clear of feeding honey to children less than one year of age. Botulism spores can be found in honey—while not harmful to adults and older kids, these spores can be fatal to infants.

6 **WHAT ABOUT INTRODUCING HIGH ALLERGENIC FOODS?** When can you introduce nuts like peanuts and tree nuts to your baby? The advice on this has changed over the years. Until 2008, the American Academy of Pediatrics (AAP) recommended waiting on introducing peanuts and other highly allergenic foods (like shellfish) until age 3 to prevent lifelong allergies. However, the latest studies indicate there is no benefit to waiting—and even the AAP now says there is no need to wait. Our advice: consult with your pediatrician on this one, especially if you have a family history of food allergies.

Smart Shopper Tips

Smart Shopper Tip #1
Tracking Down UFFOs (Unidentifiable Flying Food Objects)
"We fed our baby rice cereal for the first time. It was really cute, except when baby knocked the bowl to the floor . . . multiple times! Should we have bought some special stuff for this occasion?"

Well, unless you want your kitchen to be redecorated in Early Baby Food, we do have a few suggestions. First, a bowl with a bottom that suctions to the table is a great way to avoid flying saucers. Plastic spoons that have a round handle are nice, so baby can't stick the spoon handle in her eye (yes, that does happen—babies do try to feed themselves even at a young age). Spoons with rubber coatings are also recommended; they don't transfer the heat or cold of the food to the baby's mouth and are easier on the gums. One clever spoon is Munchkin's "White Hot Infant Spoon" (web: munchkininc.com, four for $5). This spoon uses a special coating that changes color when baby's food is too hot (over 110°).

Smart Shopper Tip #2
Avoiding Mealtime Baths

"Our baby loves to drink from a cup, except for one small problem. Most of the liquid ends up on her, instead of in her. Any tips?"

Congratulations! You have a child who is ready to join the rest of the world and give up the bottle or breast. You may have mixed feelings about this, especially when you have to wash all those additional bibs, the floor and yourself more frequently. But this is a cool milestone. Babies are developmentally able to use a cup between ten and 16 months.

So what's the solution to the inevitable mess your baby will make when learning to drink from a cup? Most parents turn to sippy cups. But we don't recommend them. Why? Sippy cups aren't exactly beloved by doctors and dentists. Turns out babies use the same sucking action to get milk from a sippy cup as they do when sucking from a baby bottle. Hence they are not learning how to drink from a cup. Plus, sippy cups direct the flow of liquid straight at the back of baby's top front teeth—this promotes tooth decay.

Is there an answer to this dilemma? When being clean and pristine aren't that important (say when eating at home in the kitchen with lots of clean up gear handy) let your baby practice with a regular plastic cup. But also try to teach her to use a straw. That way, when you're out at a restaurant, she won't be taking a bath in public.

 ## *Money-Saving Tips*

1 MAKE YOUR OWN. Let's be honest: baby foods like mashed bananas are really just . . . mashed bananas. You can easily whip up this stuff with that common kitchen helper, the food processor. Many parents skip baby food altogether and make their own. One tip: make up  a big batch at one time and freeze the leftovers in ice cube trays. Check the library for cookbooks that provide tips on making baby food at home. A reader suggestion: "Top 100 Baby Purees" by Annabel Karmel ($16, Atria). This 128-page book is a best-selling guide to making your own baby food.

2 FYI: TOYS R US AND BABIES R US SELL BABY FOOD. If you think your grocery store is gouging you on the price of baby food, you might want to check out the prices at Babies R Us. We found Gerber 1st Foods in a two-pack of 2.5-ounce jars for $1.27—that works out to about 25¢ per ounce or about 15% less than grocery store prices. Toys R Us also sells four-packs of assorted dinners from Gerber's 2nd and 3rd Food collections.

3 **COUPONS! COUPONS! COUPONS!** Yes, we've seen quite a few cents-off and buy-one-get-one-free coupons on baby food and formula—not just in the Sunday paper but also through the mail. Our advice: don't toss that junk mail until you've made sure you're not trashing valuable baby food coupons. Another coupon trick: look for "bounce-back" coupons. Those are the coupons put in packages of baby food to encourage you to bounce back to the store and buy more.

4 **GO FOR A LESSER-KNOWN BRAND.** Example: Bay Valley Foods' Nature's Goodness (formerly owned by Del Monte) makes good quality baby food, but is not as well known as Gerber or Earth's Best. It is priced about 20% less than the competition. The only drawback: it isn't available everywhere.

5 **SUBSTITUTE COMPARABLE ADULT FOODS.** What's the difference between adult applesauce and baby applesauce? Not much, except for the fact that applesauce in a jar with a cute baby on it costs several times more than the adult version. (One caveat: make sure the regular applesauce is NOT loaded with extra sugar). Another rip-off: "next step" foods for older babies. Gerber loves to tout its special toddler meals in its "Graduates" line. What's the point? When baby is ready to eat pasta, just serve him small bites of the adult stuff. Bottom line: babies should learn to eat the same (hopefully healthy) foods you are eating, with the same spices and flavors. Toddler or graduate foods are a waste of time and money.

6 **GO FOR THE BETTER QUALITY.** That's a strange money-saving tip, isn't it? Doesn't better quality baby food cost more? Yes, but look at it this way—the average baby eats 600 jars of baby food until they "graduate" to adult foods. Sounds like a lot of money, eh? Well, that only works out to $150 or so in total expenditures (using an average price of 25¢ per jar). Hence, if you go for the better-quality food and spend, say, 15% to 20% more, you're only out another $30. And feeding baby food that tastes more like the real thing makes transitions to adult foods easier.

How about organic baby food? Well, there is no scientific data that shows any health benefit for organic baby food. But, we think the key issue here is exposure to pesticides. Organic foods are certified pesticide-free; since pesticide residues affect the small bodies of infants and children more than adults, avoiding such exposure with organic food for infants makes sense.

The Name Game: Reviews of Selected Manufacturers

Here's a round up of some of the best-known names in baby food. We should note that while we actually tried out each of the foods on our baby, you may reach different conclusions than we did. Unlike our brand name ratings for clothing or other baby products, food is a much trickier rating proposition. We rated the following brand names based on how healthy they are and how much they approximate real food (aroma, appearance, and, yes, taste). Our subjective opinions reflect our experience—always consult with your pediatrician or family doctor if you have any questions about feeding your baby. (Special thanks to Ben and Jack for their help in researching this topic.)

The Ratings

A **EXCELLENT**—*our top pick!*
B **GOOD**— *above average quality, prices, and creativity.*
C **FAIR**—*could stand some improvement.*
D **POOR**—*yuck! could stand some major improvement.*

Beech-Nut beechnut.com. Beech-Nut was one of the first baby food companies to eliminate fillers (starches, sugar, salt) or artificial colors/flavors in its 120 flavors. While Beech-Nut is not organic, the company claims to be made of "all-natural ingredients." Our readers gen-erally give Beech-Nut good marks (some like it better than Gerber). Beechnut is affordable: we've seen it on sale for as little as 17¢ per oz.

The only bummer about Beech-Nut baby food: it can be hard to find (not every state has stores that carry it). You can use their "where to buy" function to find a store that carries it. And check out their "Beech-Nut Rewards" for info on money saving programs. **Rating: B+**

Del Monte See Nature's Goodness.

Earth's Best earthsbest.com. Earth's Best's emphasis is organic baby food. Started in (where else?) Vermont, Earth's Best has gone through several owners before landing in the lap of natural foods conglomerate Hain Celestial (parent of Celestial Seasonings Tea). Despite all the changes in ownership, Earth's Best has maintained its focus, with the largest line of "natural" baby foods on the market—all vegetables and grains are certified organically grown (no pesticides are used), and meats are raised without antibiotics or steroids. Another advantage: Earth's Best never adds any salt, sugar or modified starches to its food. And the foods are only made from whole grains, fruits and vegetables (instead of concentrates). Yes, Earth's Best is more expensive (30¢ per oz.; or 15% more than conventional baby food) but as we pointed out earlier, that's works out to only about $90 more per year and ready to print coupons are easy to find on their web site.

Reader feedback on Earth's Best has been positive—fans like the extensive choice and commitment to organic principals. All in all, Earth's Best is a much-needed natural alternative to the standard fare that babies have been fed for far too many years. **Rating: A**

Gerber gerber.com. Dominating the baby food business with a whopping 79% market share (that's right, three out of every four baby food jars sold sport that familiar label), Gerber sure has come a long way from its humble beginnings. Back in 1907, Joseph Gerber (whose trade was canning) mashed up peas for his daughter, following the suggestion of a family doctor. Today Gerber sells $2 billion in baby food a year.

Over the years, Gerber has tried to expand beyond jarred baby food. It launched microwavable toddler meals in 2002 and has licensed its name out for a variety of baby products, including cups, infant toys and even baby skincare items. Yet controversy has constantly dogged Gerber—in the 90's, consumer pressure forced the company to stop adding sugar and starch to its baby foods. The Federal Trade Commission has accused the company of deceptive advertising when it claimed a survey showed that four out of five pediatricians recommended the brand (the actual number was 16%).

E-MAIL FROM THE REAL WORLD
Making your own baby food isn't time consuming

A mom in New Mexico told us she found making her own baby food isn't as difficult as it sounds:

"My husband and I watch what we eat, so we definitely watch what our baby eats. One of the things I do is buy organic carrots, quick boil them, throw them in a blender and then freeze them in an ice cube tray. Once they are frozen, I separate the cubes into freezer baggies (they would get freezer burn if left in the ice tray). When mealtime arrives, I just throw them in the microwave. Organic carrots taste great! This whole process might sound complicated, but it only takes me about 20 minutes to do, and then another five to ten minutes to put the cubes in baggies."

On the upside, Gerber offers parents two key advantages: choice and availability. The line boasts an amazing 200 different flavors. And Gerber is sold in just about every grocery store on Earth at around 25¢ per oz. We have to give Gerber credit: bowing to consumer interest in all things organic, they rolled out "Gerber Organic" to compete with Earth's Best. The new line is made with "whole grains and certified organic fruits and vegetables" and costs around 35¢ per oz. (note that Gerber's regular line still uses fruit and vegetable concentrates). Finally, we noticed that Gerber is now packing its first foods in plastic rather than glass. While we like the changes Gerber has made, we still have problems with the brand: we think their "Graduates" line of "toddler" foods is a waste of money. And their juice line is overpriced compared to others on the market. Quality-wise, we will give Gerber an average rating. **Rating: C**

Frozen, gourmet baby food: worth it?

Frozen and organic aren't two words that normally go together, but a collection of entrepreneurs is trying to shake up the baby food market with new offerings that do just that. Sold online on Amazon and in stores like Whole Foods, *Jack's Harvest* (jacksharvest.com) features an all-organic food line. It is frozen into 1 oz. and 3 oz. heart-shaped portions. Interesting flavors like carrots with a pinch of ginger or mango with lime make these a more adventurous baby food choice. Price: $1.20 to $1.32 per oz.

Bella Baby (bellababy.com) also freezes its organic (and Kosher) foods. You can order directly from their site with a minimum of six packages for a flat price of $7.33 per item (includes shipping). Each package includes ten 1.5 oz. packets. That works out to 77¢ per ounce; Amazon also sells this brand.

Other organic baby food makers take a different approach: sealing baby food in vacuum-packed pouches. *Plum Organics* (plumorganics.com), *Happy Baby* (happybaby.com), and *Sprout* (sproutbabyfood.com) take this route. To serve, you submerge the packages in warm water or serve at room temperature (no microwaving). Prices range from 33¢ per oz. to 81¢ per oz.

Most of these sites offer coupons and some even have "starter sets" at discounted prices.

So is this pricey baby food worth it? No. We can't help but think you can basically replicate these gourmet baby foods with a simple food processer and an ice cube tray—at a much lower price.

Healthy Times *healthytimes.com*. Healthy Times got its start selling one of the first health-food baby products back in 1980: a teething biscuit. Since then, the company has expanded their baby food offerings to include 22 jarred baby foods, baby cereal, snacks and toiletry items. The baby food line is certified organic and contains no soy, flour or other fillers. You'll find single fruits and vegetables (stage 1), fruit and veggie blends (stage 2) and dinners (combos of several veggies, and meat and veggies). You can buy Healthy Times online on the company's web site for 33¢ per oz. jar for stage one foods. We also saw Healthy Times foods on Amazon.com. **Rating: A-**

Nature's Goodness *naturesgoodness.com*. Formerly owned by Heinz and then Del Monte, Nature's Goodness was sold to Bay Valley Foods in 2006. We like the fact that the company's website posts its nutritional labels online—and we noted the lack of added sugars or starches in most of the line. Cost: a 4-ounce jar of apple-sauce goes for 25¢ per oz. The feedback from parents on this line is positive; the only drawback is availability—Nature's Goodness isn't in as many stores as Gerber. **Rating: A**

"Toddler" foods: a waste of money?

When the number of births leveled off in recent years, baby food companies began looking around for ways to grow their sales. One idea: make foods for older babies and toddlers who have abandoned the jarred mushy stuff! To boost sales in the $1 billion baby food market, Gerber rolled out "Gerber Graduates" while Heinz debuted "Toddler Cuisine," microwaveable meals for kids as old as 36 months. What do nutritionists and doctors think of these foods? Most say they are completely unnecessary. Yes, they are a convenience for parents but, besides that, so-called "toddler foods" offer no additional nutritional benefit. In their defense, the baby food companies argue that their toddler meals are meant to replace the junk food and unhealthy snacks parents give their babies. We guess we can see that point, but overall we think that toddler foods are a complete waste of money. Once your baby finishes with baby food, they can go straight to "adult food" without any problem—of course, that should be HEALTHY adult food. What's best: a mix of dairy products, fruits, vegetables, meat and eggs. And, no, McDonald's French fries don't count as a vegetable!

High Chairs

As soon as Junior starts to eat solid food, you'll need this quin-tessential piece of baby furniture—the high chair. Surprisingly, this seemingly innocuous product generates over 11,700 injuries each year. So, what are the safest high chairs? And how do you use them properly? We'll share these insights, as well as some money-saving tips and brand reviews in this section.

Safe and Sound

1 STRAP ME IN. *Most high chair injuries occur when babies are not strapped into their chairs.* Sadly, one to two deaths occur each year when babies "submarine" under the tray. To address these types of accidents, new high chairs now feature a "passive restraint" (a plastic post) under the tray to prevent this. Note: some high chair makers attach this submarine protection to the tray; others have it on the seat. We prefer the seat. Why? If it is on the tray and the tray is removed, there is a risk a child might be able to squirm out of the safety belts (which is all that would hold them in the chair). As a side note, some wooden high chairs only seem to have a crotch strap—no plastic post. Again, not much is keeping baby safely in the chair.

FYI: Even if the high chair has a passive restraint, you STILL must strap in baby with the safety harness with EACH use. This prevents them from climbing out or otherwise hurting themselves.

2 THE SAFETY STANDARDS FOR HIGH CHAIRS ARE VOLUNTARY. Unlike the mandatory safety rules for cribs or car seats, high chair makers only have a series of voluntary standards. This will change shortly, when the government issues mandatory safety standards for high chairs as part of the 2008 Consumer Product Safety Improvement Act. But . . . as of press time, high chair safety standards are purely voluntary.

3 INSPECT THE SEAT PAD. Make sure it won't tear or puncture easily.

4 LOOK FOR STABILITY. It's basic physics: the wider the base, the more stable the chair. Another tip: never put the high chair near a wall—babies have been injured in the past when they pushed off a wall or object, tipping over the chair. This problem is rare with the newest high chairs (as they have wide, stable bases), but you still can tip over older, hand-me-down models.

high chairs

5 **CAREFULLY INSPECT THE RESTRAINING SYSTEM.** We prefer a five-point harness (straps that go over the baby's shoulders and around the waist); some high chairs only have three-point harnesses (just a waist belt).

6 **DOES THE SEAT RECLINE?** Many high chairs have a reclining seat function that makes it easier to feed a young infant. The problem? Feeding a baby solid foods in a reclining position is a choking hazard. If you want to use the reclining feature, it should be exclusively for bottle-feeding. We do think the recline feature is a plus for another reason, however: it is easier to move baby in and out of the high chair when it is reclined. And when babies start out with solid foods, they may go back and forth between the bottle and solid food during meals. Hence, the recline feature is helpful when they need to take a bottle break.

More Money Buys You

Whether you spend $30 or $500, most high chairs do one simple thing—provide you with a place to safely ensconce your baby while he eats. The more money you spend, however, the more comforts there are for both you and baby. As you go up in price, you find chairs with various height positions, reclining seats, larger trays, more padding, casters for mobility and more. From a safety point of view, some of the more expensive high chairs feature five-point restraint harnesses (instead of just a waist belt). As for usability, some high chairs are easier to clean than others, but that doesn't necessary correspond to price. Look for removable vinyl seat covers that are machine-washable (cloth covers are harder to clean). And watch out for crevices in seats, pads and trays—these are food magnets. Models with seamless trays, seats and pads may cost more but will be easier to keep clean.

Smart Shopper Tips for High Chairs

Smart Shopper Tip #1
High Chair Basics 101
    "What's the difference between a $50 high chair and one that's $400? And does it matter what color you get? I like white best."
    The high chair market is basically divided into four camps:

◆ *Low-end chairs* sold in discount stores aimed at Grandma. These cost around $50 and are bare bones, without many features.

◆ *Multi-function chairs.* These range from $100 to $250 and feature seat recline, adjustable height positions, footrests and upgraded pads. The more expensive models have toys, designer fabrics and other upgrades.

◆ *Modern high chairs.* Pricey at $300 to $450, these chairs are sold mostly on aesthetics—their ultra-modern looks appeal to parents who want to make a style statement.

◆ *Wood high chairs.* Either all wood or a hybrid of wood and plastic (wood base, plastic tray), these high chairs run $150 to $200. Wood high chairs appeal to traditionalists who are turned off by the plastic-y look of most high chairs. The trade-off is a lack of features or adjustments.

As you can see, high chairs are often sold more on aesthetics than function—and that's a classic first-time parent mistake. A pretty high chair that is impossible to clean is a big headache. And while we understand that a high chair that sits in middle of your kitchen shouldn't be an eyesore, consider these practical features before falling in love with a high chair:

◆ *Tray release.* The best high chairs have a one-hand tray release that enables you to easily remove the tray with a quick motion. Of course, some are easier to use than others. Our advice: take a second in the store and remove the tray a few times from sample models. You'll note some trays are sticky; other "one-hand" tray releases really require two hands.

◆ *Dishwasher-safe trays—NOT!* Most high chairs today come with a dishwasher-safe tray insert. This cover snaps off the main tray and pops in the dishwasher for clean-up . . . or does it? In the reviews in this section, we'll note some models whose dishwasher-safe trays are too big to fit in an actual dishwasher. A word of advice: measure the bottom rack of your dishwasher and take that dimension with you when high chair shopping.

◆ *Tray height.* Some parents complain the tray height of certain high chairs is too high—making it hard for smaller babies to use. A smart tip: take your baby with you when you go high chair shopping and actually sit them in the different options. You can evaluate the tray heights in person to make sure the chair will work for both you and baby. We'll note which chairs have the best/worst tray heights later in our reviews. Generally, a chair with a tray height of less than 8″ should work for most babies. A few models have tray heights over 8″—those can be a major problem since a child

high chairs

can't reach the food on the tray. Why is this important? Some day (we know it seems light years away), your baby will feed himself . . . and being able to see and reach the food is important!

◆ *Seat depth.* Most chairs have multiple tray positions and reclining seats. But what is the distance between the seat back when it is upright and the tray in its closest position? A distance of 5″ to 7″ is acceptable. Over 7″ and you run the risk that there will be a large gap between your baby and the tray—and all their food will end up in their lap. Again, take your baby with you when shopping for a chair, as smaller babies may be harder to fit.

◆ *Cleanability.* Here's an obvious tip some first-time parents seem to miss: make sure the high chair you buy has a removable, washable seat cover OR a seat that easily sponges clean. In the latter category, chairs with VINYL trump those made of cloth—vinyl can be wiped clean, while cloth typically has to be washed. This might be one of those first-time parent traps—seats with cloth covers sure look nicer than those made of vinyl. But the extra effort to machine wash a cloth cover is a pain . . and some cloth covers can't be thrown in the dryer! That means waiting a day or more for a cover to line dry.

Watch out for seat pads that have ruffles or numerous crevices—these are food magnets and a bear to keep clean.

What color cover should you get? Answer: anything but white. Sure, that fancy white "leatherette" high chair looks all shiny and new at the baby store, but it will forever be a cleaning nightmare once you start using it. Darker colors and patterns are better.

Of course, keeping a chair clean involves more than just the pad—look at the seat and tray itself. Avoid models with numerous crevices and cracks. Seamless seats and trays are best.

FYI: Many high chair trays claim they are dishwasher safe. But some have cracks that let water collect inside the tray—this can be a mold hazard, as it is hard to get the tray to dry properly. We will note these models in our reviews later in this section.

Smart Shopper Tip #2
Tray Chic and Other Restaurant Tips

"We have a great high chair at home, but we're always appalled at the lack of safe high chairs at restaurants. Our favorite cafe has a high chair that must date back to 1952—no straps, a metal tray with sharp edges, and a hard seat with no cushion. Have restaurateurs lost their minds?

Some folks who run restaurants must search obscure foreign countries to find the world's most hazardous high chairs. The biggest problem? No straps, enabling babies to slide out of the chair, submarine-style. The solution? When the baby is young, keep her in her infant car seat; the safe harness keeps baby secure. When your baby is older (and if you eat out a lot), you may want to invest in a portable booster seat. We'll discuss and recommend hook on chairs and booster seats later in this chapter.

If you decide to use the restaurant high chair, you may want to do a quick clean with baby wipes just to make sure. Nothing grosser than a dirty restaurant high chair. In fact, there are some grocery cart covers (reviewed on page 488) can also be used in restaurant high chairs.

high chairs

The Name Game: Reviews of High Chair Makers

Here's a round up of the best high chairs on the market today:

The Ratings

A   EXCELLENT—*our top pick!*
B   GOOD— *above average quality, prices, and creativity.*
C   FAIR—*could stand some improvement.*
D   POOR—*yuck! could stand some major improvement.*

Baby Bjorn babybjorn.com Best known for its iconic baby carrier, Baby Bjorn has been slowly expanding into other categories in recent years. First there was the Bjorn potty, then a bouncer, and a playpen last year. And given their recent debut of kitchen ware (bowls, spoons, bibs), it's not too surprising to see Bjorn introduce its first high chair, cleverly dubbed the Baby Bjorn High Chair.

The Bjorn high chair has all the Swedish minimalist design you'd expect from a Bjorn—the white/black color motif, seamless seat design and so on. Of course, Bjorn hasn't forgotten about safety: the high chair features a "Smart Safety Lock," which is a two-stage lock that Bjorn says "ensures that children cannot open or close the safety table on their own." This is probably the Bjorn's most unique feature: the tray pivots down to enable a parent to put a child in or out of the chair. That differs from other high chairs, where the entire tray is removable—or the tray slides forward to let you move a child in or out.

So what's not to love? Well, first of all, the price: at $300, the chair is seriously overpriced. At this lofty price point, the Bjorn high chair is competing against modern high chairs such as the Bloom Fresco and Boon Flair (both beat the Bjorn on style) and multi-function models like the Perego Tatamia, which transforms into a baby swing and recliner. The Bjorn doesn't transform into anything. And considering Bjorn's emphasis on safety, we were disappointed to see the chair lacks a five-point harness (instead it has a three-point harness).

Real world feedback on the Bjorn high chair has been thin, as it just started shipping (as of this writing). Initial reports are mixed—parents like the seamless design (easy to clean up) and easy assembly. The compact fold (a mere 10″ wide when folded) also is a plus. But the small size of the seat had more than one parent grumbling that, despite Bjorn's claim the chair will work up to three years of age, it is too small for bigger toddlers.

Other negatives: while the tray has a three-position adjustment (to allow more room for growing babies), there is no height adjustment for the chair. While we understand that Bjorn's intention is to have the high chair fit most kitchen tables, this seems like a major oversight. Ditto for the lack of casters to make the chair more mobile. Finally, we should note the seat doesn't recline—as a result, you won't be able to use this chair with newborns who don't have any head control. Add in the lack of a five-point harness and we are left scratching our heads at how this chair ever got out of Bjorn's R & D lab.

For 2012, we hear Bjorn may add a second color choice beyond the white model now in stores.

All in all, this feels like a 1.0 version product. Nice first try, but Bjorn needs to rethink some of this chair's features to make it worthy of the $300 price tag. ***Rating: Not Yet.***

Baby Trend *babytrend.com.* Baby Trend's high chair was one of our top picks in a previous edition of this book, but our rating of this chair continues to drift down as complaints from readers stack up. Yes, it is a credible knock-off of the Perego and Chicco chairs, yet sells for 40% less ($80 to $100 in most stores). You get all the standard features you'd expect: five-point harness,  four-position reclining seat, three-position tray with one hand release, six height positions, compact fold and casters. Some models have a separate dishwasher-safe tray. And, yes, the Baby Trend high chair is generally easier to use than competitors (it requires little assembly and the seat recline is easy to adjust, for example).

Baby Trend sells a $60 version (Trend 86) of their high chair at Walmart and an $70 to $100 version (Trend 88) elsewhere. The more expensive model has a fully reclining seat and is fully assembled (the cheaper one has a partial seat recline and requires assembly). All in all, Baby Trend churns out 24 different versions of the Trend, most of which are just variations in fashion.

New in the past year, Baby Trend has debuted a new version of the high chair: the Deluxe Feeding Center. This is basically the same as the Trend high chair, but adds the ability to attach a Baby Trend infant car seat. We are scratching our head at that last feature, as we don't see the point of using a car seat in a high chair frame.

Given Baby Trend high chairs' features, why all the complaints? The pad is this chair's Achilles' heel. We've received several reports that the cloth pad (which has a reversible vinyl side) fell apart or bunched up after machine washing. Even Baby Trend, in an email to us, admitted the pad "responds best to hand washing." Gee, that's nice—too bad the instructions for the chair say to machine wash the pad on the gentle cycle . . . with no mention of hand washing. Add that to the fact the pad has to be line dried and you have a deal-breaker here. Another major complaint centers on the tray height, which is way too high for average-size babies. Of course, not all the reviews are negative: some parents have had success with this high chair. And we give Baby Trend bonus points for improving the chair over the years. But Baby Trend's customer service stumbles and the pad washing issue have convinced us that this chair isn't worthy of a recommendation. ***Rating: C+***

Bloom *bloombaby.com* Bloom's Fresco high chair is the latest entrant in the space-age, Jetsons-style high chair category. It's egg-shaped, seamless seat and circular base echo the Boon Flair with one big exception: the Bloom Fresco can recline, making it suitable for infants. And we liked the micro-suede seat upholstery (in nine colors) and pneumatic-assist height adjustment. But the price? $400 is way too high, in our opinion.

In the past year, Bloom debuted an all-black version of the chair dubbed the Fresco Loft, which extends an extra six inches in height for $500. They have since added 12 colors to the Bloom Loft line including a silver leatherette ($520). New for 2012, Bloom plans to add even more colors to the line, including a denim version.

Feedback on the Bloom Fresco has been mixed. For every fan who loves the chair's Jetsons' look and function, others say it just isn't worth the money (instructions can be confusing; the color fades after a year or two, etc). Quality is a major complaint area: one reader said the chair's lift feature worked well for a week . . . and then broke. The Bloom Fresco is also hard to clean.

Bloom has a second high chair model: the Nano, which is tagged as an "iconic minimalist" model with a flat fold and "micro leather" seat in six colors. Price: $180—that's about three times the price of other simple high chairs that don't recline, lack wheels and fold up flat. In the past year, Bloom modified the Nano so it has a smaller footprint.

Feedback on the Nano is similar to the Fresco: for every parent who likes the Nano, we found another who knocked its difficulty to clean and fold.

As a result of the mixed feedback on this brand, we've decided to lower Bloom's rating this time. Prices are too high and the quality is too low. Yes, these chairs are cool to look at, but that's about it. ***Rating: C***

Boon *booninc.com.* Boon's Flair high chair debuted in 2007, part of the modernist wave sweeping the baby products biz at the time. At least this chair features something unique: a pneumatic lift, which gives the chair "effortless height adjustment." Basically, a button on the base will automatically lower the chair. We do like the seamless seat, which is easier to clean than other high chairs (where food finds its way into  every last crack and crevice). The pad and harness remove for cleaning and a dishwasher-safe tray within a tray is easy to use. The Flair retails for $280, but we've seen it on Amazon for $229. (We can't help but wonder if the folks at Boon were watching a DVD of *Office Space* when they named this chair).

There haven't been many changes to the Flair in the past year, except for a few new colors.

The only negative for the Flair: the seat doesn't recline, making this chair inappropriate for smaller infants who are bottle-feeding. A reclining seat is a standard feature on almost all high chairs, so we wonder why Boon left this out. Reader feedback on the Flair is positive: fans love how easy it is to clean and the small footprint. Their only complaint: the straps should tighten a bit more for smaller babies. And the lack of a chest buckle means the harness can slide off the shoulders of some kids. Yet, most folks love this chair, whose sleek look is the big draw. ***Rating: A***

Carter's *See Summer.*

Chicco *chiccousa.com.* Chicco's Polly high chair is the successor to the Mamma, a high chair we only gave a C in a previous edition of this book. So is the Polly an improvement? Yes.

Retailing for $120 to $155, the Polly features an adjustable footrest, compact fold, three-position seat recline, seven height positions and removable dishwasher-safe tray. You also get two pads—one can be on the chair while the other is being cleaned. (FYI: an older model Polly with a single pad can still be found online for $80 or so).

Fans of the Chicco Polly like the tray, which can be removed with one-hand and hung off pegs on the back of the frame. The compact fold is nice, but the chair doesn't stand well by itself. Readers who like the Polly love the stylish look—it comes in one of 12 snazzy color combinations.

As for negatives, the Polly's pad is not machine-washable, which is a bummer. You can only spot clean it. Cleanability is a major negative to the Polly: the chair and tray have numerous seams, cracks and crevices that are food magnets. Also: the submarine protection is attached to the tray and not the seat, as we prefer for safety reasons. To top it off, the harness can be difficult to adjust.

FYI: a few older Polly's still have cloth pads—we'd avoid these and stick with the newer, vinyl seat versions (much easier to clean).

In the past year, Chicco teased U.S. parents with ads for a new version of the Polly, dubbed the Polly Magic. It is similar to the regular Polly, but adds an upgraded leatherette pad, toys and a storage basket. Where's the magic? That's the price, which magically rises to $180. As of this writing, the Polly Magic is a Toys R Us exclusive and is going for $160. Since the chair is still quite new to the market, we've had little parent feedback on it yet.

So it's a mixed review for the Chicco Polly: fans like the stylish design and easy fold—and when the chair is discounted like it is on Walmart for $116, it is a good deal. But the negative reviews outweigh the positives in our research, so the Chicco Polly only earns an average rating. There are better options out there than this.
Rating: C+

Cosco djgusa.com. Like most things Cosco makes, their high chairs define the entry-level price point in this market. The Cosco Flat Fold high chair (pictured) is a bare bones model for $29 at Walmart. This would do the trick for grandma's house—this simple chair has a three-position seat recline plus, as the name implies, a flat fold for storage. Nothing too fancy to look at, but how many bells and whistles does Grandma need?

While these high chairs are fine for occasional use at Grandma's house, we aren't keen on these offerings as a primary high chair. Why? A lack of safety features (example: three-point harnesses instead of a five-point) make these chairs better for occasional use. And the pad doesn't remove from the chair, making it harder to clean after repeated use. Oddly, the seat in this chair doesn't sit up right, so the baby is always reclined—hence this may not be a good choice until your baby can sit up unassisted.

FYI: Cosco has an older version of this chair, called the Convenience that is still for sale for $35 at Walmart. It is basically the same as the Flat Fold, but doesn't fold as compactly. ***Rating: C+***

Dwell Studio *Sold at Target, this chair is made by Fisher Price. As of press time, it was discontinued.*

Eddie Bauer *djgusa.com.* Cosco/Eddie Bauer offers a mash-up here: a hybrid wood chair with plastic tray. Yep, in the category of "everything old is new again," the Eddie Bauer Classic high chair ($125-$145; this chair is also called the Newport) combines the look of wood with the convenience of plastic.

So, what are the trade-offs? Well, you can forget about many of the features you'll find in plastic chairs—Eddie Bauer's chair lacks wheels, height adjustments, seat recline and more.

Reader feedback on this chair has turned sharply negative over the past year. When it first debuted, the Eddie Bauer wood high chair had a full pad that covered the entire seat; in the past year, the pad design changed to a smaller size, showing more wood. We speculated last year this would make it harder to clean (more food would get on the wood) and we were right—the negative reviews shot up after the design change.

"It's pretty out of the box, but impossible to keep that way," said one reader, who summed up the frustrations of many parents. Food sticks to the dark wood finish, the slats on the side of the seat, just about anywhere—and it is impossible to clean. The finish also comes off, say others, indicating Cosco cut some corners here.

In a past edition of this book, we gave this seat our recommendation and a high rating. That's changed now, as we drop the rating to reflect poor consumer reviews after the design change. ***Rating: D***

Evenflo *evenflo.com.* Evenflo has long been an also-ran in the high chair market, thanks to quality woes and designs that lack pizzazz.

Exhibit A: Evenflo's Right Height high chair. This $80 chair features a dishwasher-safe tray insert, three-position seat recline, six height adjustments and compact fold. While we liked the fact the removable pad can be machine-washed, it is disappointing to only see a three-point safety harness . . . a five-point harness is more common at this price.

Evenflo's other high chair offering is a Walmart exclusive: the

Snap. This simple $45 model is meant to compete against ⌐ low-end chairs. The Snap features a compact fold, dishwasher-s⌐ tray insert and three-point harness. At this price, you only get a tray with a three-position adjustment (no reclining seat, no seat height adjustment). Between the Evenflo or the Cosco, we'd suggest the Cosco model—it has the same features but is $15 cheaper at Walmart.

New for 2012, Evenflo will release the Convertible high chair, which, as the name suggests, will convert to a table and chair ($50). Also new: a hip offering, the Modern Kitchen ($90-$120) with a neoprene chair pad and foam seat.

Our biggest beef with Evenflo is their quality control—we've heard many stories of parts that break, screws that come out of the seat and so on. That suspicion was verified in 2008 when Evenflo recalled nearly 100,000 Majestic high chairs because "plastic caps and metal screws can loosen and fall out, posing both a fall and choking hazards to children," reported the CPSC.

Bottom line: Evenflo isn't much of a player here. *Rating: C-*

Fisher-Price *fisher-price.com.* Folks, we have a winner! Fisher-Price has hit a home run with its well-designed line-up of high chairs, including the best-sellers, Healthy Care and Space Saver.

The Healthy Care high chair features a three-position seat recline, five-point restraint, one-hand tray removal, dishwasher-safe tray liner, and various height adjustments. FYI: The Healthy Care comes in three versions: a basic model (Healthy Care) that starts at $70 in Walmart and then fancier versions (dubbed Ocean Wonders, Adorable Animals or Precious Planet Sky Blue) for $80 to $125. Basically, these are the same high chair, but the more expensive versions include a fancier pad and more toys.

Parents universally praise the Healthy Care for its ease of use and cleanability (yep, those harness straps and toys can be thrown into the dishwasher). The major negative to this chair is the fashion—those cutesy color schemes fall flat with some folks.

Some complain the chair tends to collect food in crevices of the seat pad. And the Healthy Care requires quite a bit of assembly. Despite that, this is a best bet in the high chair market and we give the Healthy Care our highest rating.

Fisher Price has tried to address the complaints about the cutesy designs with two new designs that are similar to the Healthy Care: the Dreamsicle 3-in-1 ($140, yes it is orange) and the Brentwood Baby high chair (discussed below). The Dreamsicle converts to a booster that can be attached to a kitchen chair.

other high chairs: Space lection wood hybrid. The 0) is the first high chair that sort of a souped-up boost-er; see pic___ model features a full-size tray and three-position recline—plus it converts to a toddler booster. If you are short of space (think New York City apartment), this is a great choice. Detractors point out that once you strap this thing to a chair, you can't push the chair under the table—hence defeating the space saving concept. We see that point, but still think this is a great solution for urban condos with little space to store a bulky high chair. Reader feedback on the Space Saver is very positive—we recommend it.

Fisher Price's first wood hybrid chair, the Zen, debuted in the past year. This $105 to $150 high-chair features a plastic seat with three-position recline, a tray with dishwasher-safe insert and three-position height adjustment. The Zen is actually a combination of plastic, wood and metal—the chair is plastic (with a vinyl cover), the legs are metal and the footrest and support bars are wood.

The Zen is quite a departure for Fisher Price—this company is not exactly known for its design aesthetic. Most folks have to hide their Fisher Price chairs when guests come over; this one you can leave out and it will fit most contemporary kitchens.

Reader feedback on the Zen is mixed, especially considering the glowing reviews for the Healthy Care or Space Saver. Critics of the Zen say the lack of a compact fold is a negative, as is the dishwasher safe tray, which is too easy for baby to remove. Although the main tray is dishwasher safe, water can get into it and that can create a mold problem if not properly drained. Bottom line: save the $50 and get a regular Healthy Care instead.

FYI: Even though the Zen has an official retail of $150, we see it discounted online to $105 on many sites. And Fisher Price sells a version of Zen called the Brentwood at Amazon for $113; same design, less fancy seat.

In the past year, Fisher Price has debuted a new model called the EZ Clean. If you hadn't guessed by the name, this $90 chair's main focus is cleanability: it features a seamless pad (no crevices for food to stick), coated straps and a seamless dishwasher-safe tray. Of course, you also get the standard high chair features like four position seat recline, one-hand tray release and more. Reader feedback on this new model has been quite positive (folks love the seamless pad), but a few dissenters knock the lack of wheels on the back of the chair (there are only wheels upfront). This makes it difficult to move around the kitchen. A few parents with bigger toddlers also found the seat too snug. Overall, however, we would recommend the EZ Clean.

Also new: the Home & Away 3-in-1 high chair ($130) converts from a high chair to a booster pitched for use at restaurants as an alternative to grimy high chairs. As of this writing, it is a Babies R Us Exclusive and is brand new, so no parent feedback yet.

Bottom line: Fisher Price is our top pick for high chairs. We like the Healthy Care and Space Saver best; skip the Zen. **Rating: A**

Graco *gracobaby.com.* Graco has had mixed results in the high chair category. For every inno- vation (the Graco Contempo high chair featured the most compact fold on the market), the com- pany seems to also take a step backward. Graco had to recall 1.2 million Harmony high chairs (now discontinued) in 2010 after screws holding the front legs loosened and the high chair tipped over

unexpectedly. This defect injured 24 babies. This recall came on the heals of a similar problem in 2006. Graco offers seven high chair models, divided into three categories: all-in-one models (Blossom, pictured, Duo Diner, SimpleSwitch), "classic" high chairs (Meal Time, Contempo, Cozy Dinette) and wood models (Classic Wood).

Graco's flagship "all-in-one" high chair is the Blossom, which strikes a much more modern pose than most Graco models. It has all the standard features you expect from today's chairs (three-position recline, six-position height adjustment, dishwasher-safe tray insert) plus a few surprises: an adjustable footrest and a parent tray under the chair. The Blossom's key feature: it converts to a toddler booster with a seat back insert that adjusts in size. Price: $145 to $180. Feedback for this chair has been positive, with fans citing its clean- ability and ease of use. One negative: the t-bar is attached to the tray, not the seat (as we prefer for safety reasons). And the Blossom lacks a fold feature, which means you can't store it away.

Graco's Duo Diner is similar to the Blossom—it also converts to a booster seat for use with older children. But it is much more afford- able ($120) and can be folded for storage. Readers are generally happy with the Duo Diner.

If you need a compact fold, consider The Graco Contempo ($92 to $130). Feedback on this model has been much more positive, with folks loving the ultra compact fold and extra seat pad. You also get six-position height adjustment, three-position recline and a dishwasher-safe tray insert. On the more affordable price spectrum, the Graco Meal Time high chair ($70 to $80) features a one-hand, three-position recline, dishwasher-safe tray, four height adjustments, casters and one-hand tray release. Readers like the Meal Time, but the praise isn't as positive compared to the Contempo. Fans like the vinyl seat cover and smaller seat dimensions, but critics say this chair is rather bulky and the tray insert can easily be removed by baby (which of course, is not good!).

After watching their competition roll out wood high chairs to great success, Graco joined the market in the past year with their Classic Wood offering ($125 to $150). Graco's spin: their chair is all wood, except for the seat pad and clear plastic tray cover, which is dishwasher safe. Fans like the Classic Wood chair's easy assembly and machine washable pad—this chair is much easier to clean than the comparable Eddie Bauer model. But . . . this is a wood high chair, so you don't get a seat that reclines or adjusts in height, nor a tray that removes with one hand. And some parents told us the under-tray wood bar that prevents a child from sliding out is not adjustable and hence too tight for older babies/toddlers. Bottom line: we say skip this model. (FYI: As of this writing, it looks like Graco is phasing out the Classic Wood high chair, as it has disappeared from most sites).

The Graco Cozy Dinette is a $100 high chair with a flip-open third tray and seat recline indicator. Feedback on this chair has been mostly positive, but not the glowing reviews we see for the Contempo (it lacks that model's ease of use).

New in the past year, Graco debuted the SimpleSwitch, which converts from a high chair to booster seat (similar to the Fisher Price Dreamsicle). At $80, the SimpleSwitch features a three position recline, five position height adjustment and washable pad. Reader feedback on the SimpleSwitch has been positive.

So to sum up, Graco high chairs generally earn positive reviews from readers, especially the Contempo. However, the company's safety record in this category tempers our enthusiasm. ***Rating: B+***

IKEA ikea.com. IKEA has four simple high chairs offerings. The Antilop ($20; pictured) is a plastic chair with metal legs . . . but doesn't include a tray (that's $5 extra) and doesn't fold up. The Blames ($60) is a wood high chair with plastic tray. The Gulliver is a wood high chair without a tray for $60.

The Spoling is a $40 high chair without tray (but with a safety belt) that folds for storage. These chairs are clearly designed for older kids, but the lack of five-point harness (the "safety belt" doesn't quite cut it) or other adjustments make these a hard sell. That said, readers have generally given good reviews to the Antilop—one mom said it was incredibly easy to clean and just the ticket for her twins. ***Rating: C+***

Inglesina inglesina.com. Italian stroller company Inglesina has jumped into the high chair market with the pricey Zuma, which attempts to be both high style and practical. The rounded seat echoes modern seats by Bloom and Boon, but the more traditional base echoes a bit of Pali.

The Zuma has eight height positions, three-position seat recline and a hefty price tag: $250 (although Amazon has it for as little as $200). As a newcomer to the high chair market, Inglesina has made a few mistakes: the tray requires two hands to remove and the dishwasher-safe tray insert doesn't cover the entire main tray. The gap between baby and the tray is too far, in our opinion (as a result, food ends up in baby's lap).

Reader feedback on the Zuma is mixed—some laud the design, while others find its negatives (food sticks to the Velcro that holds the seat, making it hard to clean) too much for the price. FYI: In the past year, the company has redesigned the tray to sit closer to baby.

Inglesina also has a second, simpler high chair: the Club ($120). This chair doesn't really do anything but look pretty. The Club is probably best for toddlers who aren't ready for a booster seat yet. The feedback on the Club is more positive than the Zuma. ***Rating: C***

Joovy *joovy.com.* Joovy is best known for its strollers, but its Nook high chair ($110 to $140) is worth a look. It features a swing-open tray, plush seat cushion, dishwasher-safe insert and compact fold. We liked the five-point harness and most reader feedback on the chair has been positive.

Critics note the large gap between the tray and seat means too much food ends up in baby's lap. The sleek look has its fans, but the chair lacks wheels. This chair is relatively easy to clean and that super-compact fold makes this one a winner. We liked the $130 price, which is below that of similar simple high chair offerings from Inglesina, Bloom and Valco. ***Rating: A-***

Mamas & Papas *mamasandpapas.com.* British manufacturer Mamas & Papas is like the Graco of the UK. Now the company has landed on this side of the Atlantic with a collection of strollers, bouncers and two high chair models. The Go Eat high chair ($180, pictured) features a compact fold and five-point harness. We liked

the fact the seat pad can be removed for cleaning, but the tray doesn't have a dishwasher-safe insert. The lack of adjustments (the tray doesn't adjust, nor does the seat back or the height) is disappointing. Basically, what we have here is a $180 chair that . . . folds.

The Loop ($360) has many more features than the Go Eat—it features a seat that rotates 360 degrees, height adjustment, seat recline, five point harness and machine washable pad. But the lack of wheels is a curious omission at this price. No reader feedback on this chair yet, as it was too new as of press time.

New for 2012, Mamas & Papas plans to introduce the Juice ($150), which has a 2-in-1 pitch: the high chair's seat pops off and it becomes a little chair for toddlers. Also new: the Pixie high chair ($110) features a compact fold. **Rating: Not Yet.**

Minui *minuihandysitt.com.* Minui's Handy Sitt bills itself as the only high chair with a portable seat. That's not quite true (both Graco and Fisher Price make similar models), but Handy Sitt does feature a portable high chair that can strap to a chair at grandma's house. The chair morphs from a high chair for baby to a chair for older toddlers and later a kids' floor chair. It's rather spendy—the chair is $170; the baby seat is $130, a baby kit (five-point harness and cushion) runs $65. Hence, the total investment here would be $365, making it one of the most expensive chairs on the market. While we like the modern wood and steel design and overall flexibility, we've received little reader feedback on this new option. So no rating for now. **Rating: Not Yet.**

OXO Tot *oxotot.com.* Kitchen gadget maker OXO's first high chair trikes an über modern pose, with its wooden legs and plastic seat. We liked the overall design, with its two height positions, adjustable footrest and more. But at $250, we'd expect to see a dishwasher-safe insert stray (it lacks this) and a compact fold (it doesn't fold). The  Sprout comes in two base colors, a light birch and dark walnut. The birch comes with either an orange or taupe pad; the dark walnut just has green.

The OXO Tot was released in May 2011 and since it is still rather new, we've seen limited real world feedback. However, the initial reviews we've seen are quite positive, with folks liking the chair's small footprint and easy assembly. It also gets good marks on cleanability, but more than one parent notes the lack of a dishwasher-safe tray (which we noted above) is a strange omission for a $250 chair. OXO doesn't plan any major changes to this chair for 2012; there may be some new colors, however.

Overall, we would recommend the OXO Tot. FYI: OXO will debut shortly its first booster seat: the Seedling Youth Booster will be $40 and will fold up for easy transport. **Rating: B+**

Peg Perego *perego.com.* Yes, the Prima Pappa has been a best seller but its day has come and gone. Sure, it looks stylish and features a four-position reclining seat, seven height adjustments, a dishwasher-safe dinner tray, five-point restraint and compact fold. And the fabrics! Tre chic!

But let's look at the chair's key flaw: the tray. It sits a whopping 8.5" above the seat, making it too tall except perhaps for Shaq's kids. Another problem: the tray sits 7" from the back of the seat, creating a gap the size of the Grand Canyon between your baby and her food. (There is some good news on this front: for 2012, Peg is adding a new-born cushion to one model of the Pappa, the Best, to address this issue).

Then let's talk about this chair's cleanability—it's notorious for collecting food in every little nook and cranny. And the dishwasher-safe tray insert is too big to fit in most dishwashers. All this for $200+! Wow, what a deal.

Perego makes three versions of the Prima Papa: the Best, Diner and Newborn. The Best ($230, pictured) features an upgraded, tailored seat cushion. The Diner ($200) has a seat pad made of microfiber. The Newborn ($180 retail, $136 Amazon) has a fully reclining seat for newborns. The seat removes completely so you can fold the frame flat. Otherwise, the chairs are basically the same. (FYI: It appears Perego may be soon discontinuing the Newborn, as it doesn't appear in their current line-up on their web site).

We should note that you can occasionally find Peg high chairs (especially last year's models) for as little as $140 online.

Perhaps the best thing about the Perego high chair is how it looks—the fabrics are gorgeous. And this chair is made in Italy. But when you actually use the chair, the design flaws (it lacks a compact fold, the tray is sticky and tough to remove with one hand, lack of cleanability, etc.) quickly outweigh how pretty it looks. As one mom summed it up in an online review: "this chair should only be sold together with a 2000 psi power washer!"

Perego's other high chair is the Tatamia ($350)—this chair is billed as a "multi-purpose baby seat" since it also functions as a swing and bouncer. For 2011, Peg has improved the swing function and the one-hand tray release. Given the high price, reader feedback on this model has been thin, but in general, the few who have it, like it. In contrast to the Prima Pappa, the Tatamia is easy to clean. And fans like the multi-function swing/bouncer plus the compact fold.

New for 2012: Peg will introduce a brand new high chair, the Siesta. Peg bills this as a "multi-function, ultra-compact" model that has nine height positions and a full recline. We liked the hi-tech "eco-leather" covering, which should be easy to clean. As you'd expect, you also get a dishwasher safe tray, wheels that have a unique "stop and go" break system and a storage net on the back. When folded it measures just 11.8." That is a bit wider than the 9" depth of the Graco Contempo when folded, but overall, impressive. The Siesta will run $300 and will be out in early 2012.

Bottom line: skip the Prima Pappa. And if you have a rich uncle, consider the Tatamia for the gift registry. The Siesta isn't out as of this writing, but bears watching. **Rating: C+**

Phil & Teds philandteds.com Stroller maker Phil & Teds debuted their first high chair offering in the past year—the Highpod features a modern look and five height adjustments as well as an infant recline.

At $300, we'd expect this high chair to actually make a full breakfast for your baby. But sadly, the Highpod is just a high chair. Fans like the seamless chair/pad (no crevices for food to hide) and deep seat recline for infants.

But the negatives include a very small tray (a larger snack tray is a $30 accessory) that takes two hands to remove. Plus, it is too easy for babies to remove the dishwasher safe insert, in our opinion. Add in the fact that the safety bar is attached to the tray and not the seat (for safety reasons, we like it the other way around) and the lack of wheels, and you've got a mixed review for the Highpod. This high chair feels like a version 1.0 product . . . and for $300, we expect it to be perfect. Reader feedback on the Highpod has been sparse, probably due to the high price tag. **Rating: B-**

Safety 1st safety1st.com While parent Cosco sells bare-bones high chairs to the discount chains, Safety 1st focuses on a slightly more upscale market. Example: Safety 1st's Adjustable High Chair ($70 to $80, pictured) has all the standard features you expect in a high chair (machine-washable cushion, three position recline, one-hand tray

release) plus has an ultra-compact, standing fold. FYI: The Adjustable used to be called the AdapTable, which sold for the same price and had much the same features.

Safety 1st has two other high chair models: the Comfy Seat ($110) and the Serve 'n Store ($80), which comes in both regular and Disney versions.

The Comfy Seat has six height positions, one-hand tray release and a machine washable cloth seat with infant insert. Safety 1st will debut a deluxe version of this seat as a Babies R Us exclusive in 2011.

New this year, the Posh Pod is a sleek, IKEA-like high chair with a seat made from EVA foam. It runs $70 at Amazon. While it features a five-point harness and dishwasher safe tray, the Posh Pod doesn't fold up (but its legs remove). We suppose if you must have a modern high chair but want to spend less than $100, the Posh Pod is the most affordable option.

Overall, the quality of Safety 1st's high chairs is only average. They are neither innovative nor affordable. If you want a bare bones chair for Grandma, you're better off with one of Cosco's offerings for $30 less. If you want a full feature high chair, you're better off with Fisher Price or Graco, which are priced about the same as Safety 1st, yet offer enhanced features and better quality. *Rating:* **C+**

Stokke *stokkeUSA.com.* The Stokke Tripp Trapp is the revised version of the Kinderzeat, which we recommended in a previous edition. This $250 chair has a seat and footrest that adjusts to multiple positions— the result is you can use it from six months (once baby can sit up) to age eight or beyond.

The downsides? Well, the baby rail ($70) and seat cushion ($30 to $45) are extras—making this a very pricey investment. And the Tripp Trapp doesn't come with a tray . . . so baby will be making a mess on your table, not his high chair tray. Our view: the Tripp Trapp is probably best for older toddlers who have outgrown a regular high chair (as an alternative to a booster seat). The quality of the Stokke Tripp Trapp is excellent. *Rating:* **A-**

Summer *summerinfant.com.* Better known for their baby monitors, Summer has two high chairs under the Carter's license. The Carters Bumble Newborn to Toddler Folding High Chair ($100, pictured) has a five-position height adjustment and three-position seat recline. While this high chair is plastic and metal, Summer also offers a wood model: the Classic Comfort Reclining Wood High Chair ($140).

Like the Eddie Bauer wood high chairs, the Classic Comfort is a hybrid with wood base and plastic tray. One unique feature: the seat has a three position recline; most wood high chairs don't have this. FYI: The Classic Comfort seems to have much more distribution than the Carter's Bumble high chair, which we only see sold online.

Reader feedback on these chairs has been mixed. More than one reader complained about the difficulty in assembling the Classic Comfort. Overall quality on these chairs is only average—adjusting the tray, for example, can be difficult. On the Carter's

Bumble model, readers complained about straps that broke and fabric that fell apart after just a few months of use.

Bottom line: these chairs look pretty but don't have long-term quality. **Rating: D+**

Svan of Sweden scichild.com. Svan is a multi-function high chair imported from Europe, much like the Tripp Trapp (discussed earlier). The all-wood Svan (a plastic dishwasher-safe tray cover is included) morphs from a high chair to a

chair for toddlers and then older kids. Available in five finishes (including espresso), the Svan retails for $280 for the chair plus another $40 for cushions.

So is the Svan worth the $300 price tag? Fans tell us they love how sturdy the chair is, yet it's still light enough to move around the kitchen. The aesthetics and small footprint are the key selling points. On the other hand, this is a wood high chair, so there is no seat recline or other perks you find in plastic chairs. Adjusting the chair's height requires an Allen wrench, which is a pain—and several parents complained about the Svan's numerous nooks/crannies to clean. Overall, however, most of the reviews for the Swan are positive—this is a good chair if you can get past the drawbacks and price.

FYI: Svan also makes a simple wood high chair (the Anka) for $180. Reader feedback on this model is mixed and not as positive compared to the $300 Svan.

For 2012, Svan is tweaking their high chair with some improvements: the chair will now be dubbed the Signet and it will be easier to assemble. There is also a new five-point harness for infants. The Signet Essential will be the basic Svan chair for $220; the Signet Complete with include the tray and baby rail for $280. look for the rebranded chairs in January 2012. **Rating: B+**

Valco valcobaby.com. Stroller maker Valco debuted its first high chair in the past year. The simple $150 Astro is a basic high chair that folds flat (and comes with a travel bag). Recently, the Astro added a reclining seat. Reader feedback on the Astro has been quite positive—the real star here is its compact fold and light weight (about 15 lbs.), which makes it a good bet for travel.

On the downside, the tray is not dishwasher safe and requires two hands to remove. We also don't like how far it sits away from the child, although the deep lip is nice. Bottom line: this is proba-

FEEDING

bly a better bet for older babies and for parents with a small kitchen that need a high chair with a compact fold. FYI: As of this writing (August 2011), we noticed Toys R Us and Walmart has the Astro on sale for $130. ***Rating: B***

Zooper *zooperstrollers.com.* This high chair is reviewed on our web page BabyBargains.com, click on Bonus Material.

◆ **Other Brands.** Kettler is a brand better known in this country for their tricycles, but their Tipp Topp high chair has won fans for its simple design. We found it for $100 on BabiesRUs.com. Similar wood chairs are also made by Geuther, a European import sold on HighChairs.com.

high chairs

   If you like those wood high chairs at restaurants, you can buy a similar model online: the Lipper wood high chair is only $35 on Amazon.com.

Our Picks: Brand Recommendations

Here is our round up of the best high chair bets.

Good. Is space tight in your kitchen? *The Fisher-Price Space Saver* ($44-$60) lives up to its name—it straps to a regular chair and provides most of the features of a full-feature high chair, yet costs half as much. Another good option: the ***Graco Contempo*** ($92 to $130), which has the most compact fold of any high chair on the market and positive feedback. Also good in the compact fold, simple high chair category: ***Joovy's Nook*** ($110-$140), which has a swing-out tray and a sleek, modern look.

Better. *Graco's Blossom* takes second place with its more modern design and a slew of features. Among its best tricks: it converts to a toddler booster chair that straps to a regular kitchen chair for older babies. Yes, the Blossom is pricey at $145-$180, but worth it. One bummer: the Blossom doesn't fold away for storage.

Best. The *Fisher-Price Healthy Care* has got it all—great safety features, ease of use, cleanability and more. We like the snap-off dishwasher-safe tray, good design and easy-to-clean vinyl pad. At $70 to $125, it is about 30% to 50% cheaper than the Graco Blossom depending on the version. FYI: This high chair goes under several names, including Ocean Wonders, Adorable Animals and Precious Planet Blue Sky. The more expensive versions include an upgraded pad and toys.

Continued on page 308

HIGH CHAIRS

High chairs, compared

NAME	RATING	PRICE	TRAY HEIGHT	TRAY DEPTH
BABY BJORN	N/A	$300	5.5″	5.5
BABY TREND	C+	$60-$100	8.5	8
BOON FLAIR	A	$230-$280	5.5	7
BLOOM FRESCO	C	$400-$500	10	8
CHICCO POLLY	C+	$120-$180	7.5	7
COSCO FLAT FOLD	C+	$29	*	*
EDDIE BAUER CLASSIC	D	$12-$145	8	5
EVENFLO RIGHT HEIGHT	C-	$80	*	*
FISHER PRICE HEALTHY CARE	A	$70-$125	7.5	6
FISHER PRICE SPACE SAVER	A	$44-$60	7.5	5
GRACO BLOSSOM	B+	$145-$180	6	6
GRACO CONTEMPO	B+	$92-$130	7.5	6
IKEA ANTILOP	C+	$20	*	*
IKEA BLAMES	C+	$60	*	*
INGLESINA CUB	C	$120	5.5	8
INGLESINA ZUMA	C	$200-$250	7.5	7.25
JOVVY NOOK	A-	$110-$140	*	*
MAMAS & PAPAS GO EAT	N/A	$180	6	8
MAMAS & PAPAS JUICE	N/A	$150	7	9.5
OXO TOT	B+	$250	7	7
PEG PEREGO PRIMA PAPPA	C+	$180-$230	8.5	7
PEG PEREGO SIESTA	C+	$300	7.5	9
PHIL & TEDS HIGHPOD	B-	$300	*	*
SAFETY 1ST POSH POD	C+	$70	7	9
STOKKE TRIPP TRAPP	A-	$250	*	*
SUMMER CLASSIC WOOD	D+	$140	*	*
VALCO ASTRO	B	$150	8	9

KEY

TRAY HEIGHT: Distance from the seat to the top of the tray. Any measurement under 8″ is acceptable. Above 8″ is too tall.

DEPTH (tray to seat): Distance from the back of the seat to the tray. 5″ to 7″ is acceptable.

SUB?: Most high chairs have a special guard to prevent a child from submarining under the tray. Some models attach this to the chair; others to the tray. A better bet: those that attach to the seat. See discussion earlier in this chapter.

SUB?	PAD	COMMENT
SEAT	NONE	NO 5-PT. HARNESS, EASY CLEAN, SMALL SEAT
SEAT	CLOTH	PAD SHOULD BE HAND-WASHED, LINE DRIED.
SEAT	VINYL	SEAMLESS SEAT; AUTOMATIC HEIGHT ADJUST.
SEAT	CLOTH	SEAMLESS SEAT, AUTO HEIGHT, SEAT RECLINES
TRAY	VINYL	HARD TO CLEAN, DIFFICULT TO ADJUST HARNESS
SEAT	VINYL	LOWEST PRICE, GOOD FOR GRANDMA'S HOUSE.
TRAY	BOTH	WOOD WITH PLASTIC TRAY; HARD TO CLEAN.
SEAT	CLOTH	COMPACT FOLD, MACHINE WASHABLE PAD.
SEAT	VINYL	TOP RATED PICK; COMES IN 3 VERSIONS.
SEAT	VINYL	ATTACHES TO CHAIR; GREAT FOR SMALL SPACES.
TRAY	VINYL	CONVERTS TO TODDLER BOOSTER.
SEAT	VINYL	AMONG NARROWEST FOLD ON MARKET.
SEAT	NONE	TRAY IS $5 EXTRA; BETTER FOR OLDER TODDLERS.
NONE	NONE	NO HARNESS; BETTER FOR OLDER TODDLERS.
SEAT	VINYL	BEST FOR TODDLERS NOT READY FOR BOOSTER.
SEAT	CLOTH	SEAMLESS SEAT, MOD LOOK, VERY PRICEY.
SEAT	VINYL	EASY FOLD, LIKE A BEACH CHAIR.
SEAT	VINYL	COMPACT FOLD, BUT FEW OTHER ADJUSTMENTS.
SEAT	VINYL	LEGS POP OFF TO CONVERT TO A CHAIR.
TRAY	VINYL	DOESN'T FOLD; WOOD HYBRID.
SEAT	VINYL	STYLE LEADER; MANY COLORS, HARD TO CLEAN.
SEAT	VINYL	9 HEIGHT POSITIONS, COMPACT FOLD.
TRAY	VINYL	SEAMLESS PAD, BUT SMALL TRAY.
TRAY	FOAM	MODERN, LEGS REMOVE BUT NO FOLD.
SEAT	CLOTH	BABY RAIL IS $70 EXTRA; NO TRAY.
SEAT	CLOTH	3 POSITION SEAT RECLINE, WOOD BASE.
SEAT	VINYL	FOLDS FLAT, COMES WITH CARRY BAG.

high chairs

PAD: Is the seat made of cloth or vinyl? We prefer vinyl for easier clean up. Cloth seats must be laundered and some can't be thrown in the drier (requiring a long wait for it to line dry). Of course, this feature isn't black and white—some vinyl seats have cloth edging/piping.
* Not applicable or not available. Some of these models were new as of press time, so we didn't have these specs yet.

Grandma's house. For grandma's house, a simple *Cosco Flat Fold* ($29) should do the trick. No, it doesn't have casters or other fancy features, but Grandma doesn't need all that.

Hook-on Chairs and Boosters

Your toddler has outgrown his high chair, but doesn't quite fit into the adult chairs at the kitchen table. What to do? Consider a booster. There are three types of kitchen booster seats on the market today:

1 **HOOK-ON CHAIRS.** As the name implies, these seats hook on to a table, instead of attaching to a chair. Pros: Lightweight; yet most can hold toddlers up to 35 to 40 lbs. Very portable—many parents use these chairs as a sanitary alternative when they dine out since many restaurants seemed to have last cleaned their high chairs during the Carter administration. Cons: May not work with certain tables, like those with pedestal bases. Fear of tipping an unstable table leads some restaurants to prohibit these chairs. Hook-on chairs do not recline, a feature you see on regular boosters.

2 **BOOSTER SEATS WITH TRAYS.** These boosters strap to a chair and usually have a tray. Pros: Most fold flat for travel. Some have multiple seat levels. Can use with or without a tray. Cons: Child may not be sitting up at table height. Some brands have too-small trays and difficult to adjust straps make for a loose fit.

3 **PLAIN BOOSTERS (NO TRAY).** These chairs are just boosters— nothing fancy, no trays. Pros: Better bet for older toddlers (age four or five) who want to eat at the table. Cons: No restraint system or belt, so this isn't a choice for younger toddlers.

Our Picks: Brand Recommendations

◆ *Hook-on chair. Top pick:* Chicco's two entrants in this category are excellent. The *Caddy* ($40) has a compact fold, three point harness and "quick grip" table clamps. The seat pad is removable and machine  washable. FYI: Chicco makes a version of this hook-on chair with a seat that rotates, dubbed the 360 Hook On ($70). It's more expensive and doesn't earn quite the kudos from readers as the Caddy— stick with the lower price version.

◆ **Kitchen booster seat with tray. Top pick:** Fisher Price Healthy Care Booster Seat (fisher-price.com). Fisher Price has a winner here: we liked the snap-off feeding tray that can go into the dishwasher, easy fold and shoulder strap for road trips plus three different height settings. When your child gets older, the tray removes so the seat becomes a basic booster. The only caveat: the back does not recline, so your baby must be able to sit up on his own to use it safely. (No biggie for most toddlers, but we know some folks consider these boosters as high-chair replacements—not a good idea unless your child can sit upright). Price: $25 to $39, making this a good value.

Runner Up: Summer Infant Deluxe Comfort Booster (summerinfant.com). This affordable ($20-$25) booster is similar to our top pick, but adds one nice bonus: it features a compact fold for easy transport. No snack tray, but the full-size tray is dishwasher-safe. Be aware: this seat has a 33-pound limit—as a result this one won't work for larger toddlers. (FYI: The Fisher Price Healthy Care booster is good up to 45 pounds).

◆ **Kitchen booster seat without tray.** The BabySmart Cooshie Booster. This is our recommendation for older toddlers—the Cooshie Booster's super comfortable foam design is a winner. It's lightweight and non-skid. No, there isn't a safety harness, but older kids don't really need it. How old? The manufacturer says this seat would work for babies as young as 12 months, but we think that is a stretch. The optimum time to use this booster would be between ages three and five, in our opinion. Yes, we think some toddlers as young as two would be mature enough but any younger would be pushing it. Price: $40.

A brief warning: The Bumbo Baby Sitter ($35) is a popular seat designed for younger infants to sit upright. The problem? The Bumbo should ONLY be used on the floor (NOT on a raised surface like a chair or table). A report by a San Francisco TV station chronicled several cases of babies tipping out of their Bumbos . . . and toppling to the floor when the Bumbo was on a table. A 2007 recall focused on beefing up the warnings for how to use the Bumbo.

FEEDING

The Bottom Line:
A Wrap-Up of Our Best Buy Picks

What's the most affordable way to feed baby? Breastfeeding, by a mile. We estimate you can save $500 in just the first six months alone by choosing to breast-feed instead of bottle-feed.

Of course, that's easy for us to say—breastfeeding takes some practice, for both you and baby. One product that can help: a breast pump, to relieve engorgement or provide a long-term solution to baby's feeding if you go back to work. Which pumps are best? For manual pumps, we like Avent Isis ($40) and the Medela's Harmony ($35) for that occasional bottle. If you plan to pump so you can go back to work, a professional-grade pump works best. Tip: rent one first before you buy. If you like it and decide you are serious about pumping, we liked the Medela Pump In Style ($265-$370) or Ameda Purely Yours (about $160 to $300).

If you decide to bottle feed or need to wean your baby off breast milk, the most affordable formulas are the generic brands sold in discount stores under various private-label names. You'll save up to 40% by choosing generic over name brands, but your baby gets the exact same nutrition.

Who makes the best bottles? Our readers say Avent and Dr. Brown's are tops, but others find cheaper options like Playtex work just was well at half the price.

Let's talk baby food—besides the ubiquitous Gerber, there are several other brands that are good alternatives. One of the best is Earth's Best, although it is more pricey than affordable brands like Nature's Goodness and Beechnut. How can you save? Make your own baby food for pennies or buy jarred baby food in bulk at discount stores. And skip the toddler meals, which are a waste of money.

Finally, consider that quintessential piece of baby gear—the high chair. We felt the best bets were those that were easiest to clean (go for a vinyl, not cloth pad) and had snap-off dishwasher-safe trays. Our top pick is the Fisher Price Healthy Care ($70 to $125), although the Graco Blossom ($145-$180) is a stylish alternative, albeit at a higher price.

Now that you've got the food and kitchen covered, what about the rest of your house? We'll explore all the other baby gear you might need for your home next.

CHAPTER 7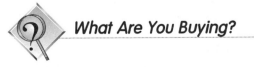

Around the House: Monitors, Diaper Pails, Safety

Inside this chapter

What's the best bathtub for baby? Which baby monitor can save you $40 a year in batteries? What's the best—and least stinky—diaper pail? In this chapter, we explore everything for baby that's around the house. From bouncer seats to safety gates, we'll give you tricks and tips to saving money. You'll learn about play yards and swings. Finally, let's talk safety— we'll give you advice on affordable baby proofing.

Getting Started: When Do You Need This Stuff?

The good news is you don't need all this stuff right away. While you'll probably purchase a monitor before the baby is born, other items like bouncer seats and even bath-time products aren't necessary immediately (you'll give the baby sponge baths for the first few weeks, until the belly button area heals). Of course, you still might want to register for these items before baby is born. In each section of this chapter, we'll be more specific about when you need certain items.

What Are You Buying?

Let's take a tour around the house to see what items you might consider for baby. Of course, these ideas are merely suggestions— none of these items are "mandatory." We've divided them into two categories: bath-time and the baby's room.

Bath

1 **TOYS/BOOKS.** What fun is taking a bath without toys? Many stores sell inexpensive plastic tub toys, but you can use other items like stacking cups in the tub as well. And don't forget about tub safety items, which can also double as toys. For example, Safety 1st (800) 739-7233 (safety1st.com) makes a ***TempGuard Rubber Ducky or Froggy***, a yellow duck or frog with attached thermometer (to make sure the water isn't too hot) for $2.50. ***Tubbly Bubbly*** by Kel-Gar (972) 250-3838 (kelgar.com) is a $12 elephant or hippo spout cover that protects against scalding, bumps and bruises. But it doesn't fit on some spouts that have a shower diverter.

2 **TOILETRIES.** Basic baby shampoo like the famous brand made by Johnson & Johnson works just fine, and you'll probably need some lotion as well. The best tip: first try lotion that is unscented in case your baby has any allergies. Also, never use talcum powder on your baby—it's a health hazard. If you need to use an absorbent powder, good old cornstarch will do the trick.

What about those natural baby products that are all the rage, like Mustela or Calidou? We got a gift basket of an expensive boutique's natural baby potions and didn't see what the big deal was. Worse yet, the $20-a-bottle shampoo dried out our baby's scalp so much he had scratching fits. We suppose the biggest advantage of these products is that they don't contain extraneous chemicals or petroleum by-products. Also, most don't have perfumes, but then, many low-price products now come in unscented versions as well. The bottom line: it's your comfort level. If you want to try them out without making a big investment, register for them as a shower gift.

If you have a history of allergies or skin problems in your family, consider washing baby's skin and hair with Dove or Cetaphil bar

---

Moms clubs great way to share, save

Mom's clubs today are a great way to meet other moms, learn about new products and save money. In Dallas, Metro Moms (metroplexbaby.com) holds monthly events that include dinner and numerous product giveaways. Some events feature a guest speaker (usually a parenting expert), guided museum tours, book signings and other seasonal events. In Chicago, the BumpClubChicago.com is aimed at both moms and moms-to-be with girl's night out, lunch and dinner seminars, shopping events and more. Many of these new moms' clubs spread the word via social media (Facebook, Twitter, Foursquare).

soap. These do not contain detergents that you find in even the most basic baby shampoo. And remember, just because a product is "organic" or "all-natural" doesn't mean it's non-allergenic. In fact, ingredients like shea butter (made from a tree nut), calendula and chamomile all have potential for reactions including rashes, breathing problems (anaphlaxis) and eye irritation. See our other book, *Baby 411* for more on alternative ingredients and their potential side effects.

3 **BABY BATHTUB.** While not a necessity, a baby bathtub is a nice convenience (especially if you are bathing baby solo). See page 314 for more info on bathtubs.

Safe & Sound

◆ **BATH SEATS SHOULD NOT BE USED.** It looks innocuous—the baby bath seat—but it can be a disaster waiting to happen. These seats suction to the bottom of a tub, holding baby in place while she takes a bath. The problem? Parents get a false sense of security from such items and often leave the bathroom to answer the phone, etc. We've seen several tragic reports of babies who've drowned when they fell out of the seats (or the seats became un-suctioned from the tub). The best advice: AVOID these seats and NEVER leave baby alone in the tub, even for just a few seconds.

◆ **TURN DOWN YOUR WATER HEATER.** Ideally, your water heater should be set at no more than 120° F. At 140° F it poses a safety hazard. You can also consider installing anti-scalding devices on your showers and faucets. One such device is called *ScaldShield* and sells at hardware stores for about $50.

◆ **NO SKID RUGS IN THE BATHROOM.** Invest in rugs that have rub-berized, no skid bottoms. You don't want to slip carrying your baby, and you don't want your new walking toddler to bang his head on the toilet or tub.

◆ **LOCK IT UP.** Install cabinet and toilet locks. This is just as impor-tant as safeguarding baby from dangers in the kitchen. And now is a great time to retrain your husband to put the lid down on the toilet seat. Locks don't work unless you actually use them.

Baby Bathtubs

Sometimes, it is the simplest products that are the best. Take baby bathtubs—if you look at the offerings in this category, you'll note some baby bathtubs convert to step stools and then, small compact cars. Okay, just kidding on the car, but these products are a good example of brand manager overkill—companies think the way to success with baby bath tubs is to make them work from birth to college.

So, it shouldn't be a surprise that our top picks for baby bathtub are, well, just bathtubs. Here's an overview

Best (full size tub). The *EuroBath by Primo* ($30; web: primobaby.com; pictured right) is a sturdy tub for babies, age birth to two. It weighs less than two pounds and is easy to use—just add baby, water and poof! Clean baby. The EuroBath is well designed, although it is big—almost three feet from end to end. It may be a tight fit if you have a small bathroom.

Another good choice is the **First Year's Infant to Toddler Tub with Sling** ($18). This simple tub includes a sling and foam pads to better fit a newborn.

Best (folding tub). The *Puj Tub* ($30) is a soft, foldable tub designed to fit in a sink. Made of foam, it unfolds when not in use and can hang on the back of a door—perfect if you live in a tiny urban apartment. The only caveat: it doesn't work with all sinks or faucets  (an oval sink with a 6.5" depth is best). And it is designed for infants to six month-olds, so this won't work for older babies and toddlers.

What about tubs with bells and whistles like built-in thermometers? A waste of money, say our readers, who complain the thermometers often don't work.

A baby bathtub is a great item to pick up second-hand or at a garage sale. Or borrow from a friend. Readers say they've snagged baby bath tubs for $2 or so at garage sales—with a little cleaning, they are just fine. What if you want to give baby a bath in a regular tub or kitchen sink? A bath sling like **Summer's Fold N Store Tub Time Bath Sling** ($10) will do the trick.

Now let's talk about that huge, scary and wonderful milestone, potty training.

Potty Seats

Potty seats come in two flavors: floor models and inserts. Inserts are molded (and sometimes padded) seats made for smaller bottoms. They are installed on top of the regular toilet seat. Floor models are traditional self-contained units with a base and seat.

Some potty seats start out as floor models and then the seat can be removed and used as an insert on the regular toilet. Our advice: go for the insert. Yes, you'll need a step stool for your little one to climb up, but it's much easier to transition to a regular toilet if your child is already using one. And think about how excited your child will be to use the same toilet as his parents (trust us, it is a big deal).

Our Picks: Brand Recommendations

Best (Seat Insert). The *Baby Bjorn Toilet Trainer* ($21) has an adjustment dial to fit most toilet seats and an angled splashguard. The contoured seat works well, says readers.

Best (Potty Chair). The *Fisher Price Precious Planet Potty* ($13) is shaped like a frog and is very simple. Does the trick at an affordable price. A closer runner-up is *Baby Bjorn's Potty Chair* at $30. Very good as well.

Ceiling Fans & White Noise

Many parents swear they'd never survive without the ceiling fan in their baby's room—the "white noise" made by a whirling fan soothed their fussy baby (and quieted sounds from the rest of the house).

Interestingly, a study in the *Archives of Pediatrics and Adolescent Medicine* published in 2008, showed that babies who sleep in a room with a ceiling fan have a much lower risk of dying of Sudden Infant Death Syndrome (SIDS). Why would a ceiling fan make a difference, you ask? Turns out that by circulating the air in your baby's room, you lower the chances that he or she will "re-breathe" exhaled carbon dioxide. This re-breathing has been suggested as one cause of SIDS. So we definitely recommend a ceiling fan, both for that low hum in the background and the recirculation of the room's air.

What about other white noise generators that play rain forest or ocean sounds? Our advice is to skip them. In a 2003 study published in the journal *Science*, researchers say using white noise can be dangerous to your child's developing hearing. Our advice now is to avoid those white noise generators, although a ceiling fan is fine.

Diaper Pails

Pop quiz! Remember our discussion of how many diapers you will change in your baby's first year? What was the amount?

Pencils down—yes, it is 2300 diapers! A staggering figure . . . only made more staggering by figuring out what do with the dirty ones once you've changed baby. Yes, we can hear first-time parents raising their hands right now and saying "Duh! They go in the trash!"

Oh, not so fast, new parental one. Stick a dirty diaper in a regular trashcan and you may quickly perfume your entire home—not to mention draw a curious pet and we won't even go there.

So, most parents use a diaper pail, that specialized trashcan designed by trained scientists to limit stink and keep out babies, pets and stray relatives. But which diaper pail? Here's our Diaper Pail 411:

Diaper pails fall into two camps: those that use refill cartridges to wrap diapers in deodorized plastic and pails that use regular kitchen trash bags.

As you'd guess, pails that use special refills are more expensive (the refills cost about $6 each) and wrap about 140 or so diapers. The pail can hold 20-25 diapers at a time, which is about three days worth of diapers. Bottom line: you'll about need to buy 16 refill cartridges per year—which means $100. And that's on top of the $30 to $40 that the pails cost.

So, should you just get a diaper pail that uses regular kitchen trash bags? Yes, they are less expensive to use—but there is sometimes a major trade-off. Stink. These pails tend to stink more and hence, have to be emptied more frequently (perhaps daily or every other day) than the diaper pails that use special deodorized plastic.

Obviously, the decision on which diaper pail is right for you and your baby's nursery depends on several factors. What is the distance to the trash? If you live in a house with easy access to an outside trashcan, it might be easier to go with the lower-cost alternatives and just take out the diapers more frequently. If you live in an apartment where the nearest dumpster is down three flights of stairs

---

Wipe Warmers: Not Recommended

These $20 gizmos warm wipes to a comfy 90 degrees, so baby isn't surprised by a cold wipe at 2am. While this sounds like a good idea, there have been a series of safety recalls for these devices, which have caused fires, electric shock and other problems. Besides, you can just warm the wipes up in your hands for a few seconds—voila! Warm wipe without spending $20.

and a long walk across a parking lot, well, it might make sense to go with an option that requires less work.

Another factor: how sensitive are you to the smell? Some folks don't have a major problem with this, while moms who are pregnant again with a second child may need an industrial strength diaper pail to keep from losing it when walking into baby's nursery. A great tip from our readers: dump the poop. Before tossing the diaper, dump the poop into the toilet.

Whatever your decision, remember you'll live with this diaper pail for three or more YEARS (that's how long before most children potty train).

And it's a fact of life: diapers get stinkier as your baby gets older . . . so the diaper removal strategy that works for a newborn may have to be chucked for a toddler. Yes, you may be able to use a plain trashcan with liner when your newborn is breastfeeding . . . but after you start solid foods, it will be time to buy a more stink-free diaper pail.

Given those caveats, here is an overview of what's out there:

CLEAN AIR ODOR FREE DIAPER DISPOSAL BY FIRST YEARS
Type: Kitchen trash bag.
Price: $40. Extra carbon filters $8 for two.
Web: learningcurve.com
Pros: Uses a fan and carbon filter to trap odors. Holds 40 diapers. Uses standard kitchen trash bags.
Cons: LOUD! Requires four D batteries. Smell escapes.
Comments: Like the Graco diaper pail reviewed below, First Years must have figured it needed some catchy gizmo to break into the diaper pail market. Voila! The first diaper pail with a fan and carbon filter! Readers have one universal complaint: it is too LOUD! When you put a diaper in, the pail cranks up the decibels like a 747 (okay, an exaggeration, but you get the idea). Other readers report diapers that jam and a general lack of stink control.
Bottom line: A loser. *Rating: F*

DIAPER CHAMP BY BABY TREND
Type: Kitchen trash bag.
Price: $30-$35.
Pros: Did we mention no expensive refills? The Diaper Champ uses regular ol' kitchen bags, yet the contraption works to seal out odor by using a flip handle design. Easy to use. Taller design means it holds more diapers than the Genie.
Cons: Not as stink-free as the Genie or Dekor, especially when

baby starts solid foods. Bigger footprint than other pails.

Comments: When you redesign a best-selling product, you're supposed to improve it, right? Yes, unless you are Baby Trend, a brand that seems to botch even the simplest task. Fans loved the original Diaper Champ, which started the concept of using regular kitchen trash bags (and hence, saved hundreds of dollars in refill cartridges). The most recent version of Diaper Champ, unfortunately, is a step backwards: yes it has a wider opening, but parents tell us it doesn't work as well (diapers get stuck, the smell can be atrocious, etc). And the diaper removal process may require an EPA HazMat Rapid Response team, given the stink level. Fans of this diaper pail seem to like it . . . until their baby starts solid foods. Then the smell can be overwhelming, forcing folks to buy a Dekor or Genie. One tip: if you go with the Champ, put a fabric softener sheet in the pail with each load (this cuts down on the smell). And be prepared to scrub it every month or two with bleach, leaving it outside to air out. And the Champ probably isn't the best bet if you have an older toddler, who can put toys into the slot (trust us, not a pretty sight). New this year, Baby Trend is offering Odor Grabber refills that can be used in any diaper pail on the market: Diaper Genie, Diaper Dekor and more.

Bottom Line: A mixed review: good for the first few months, not so good after baby starts solid food. A bargain—but beware the stink trade-offs. ***Rating: C+***

DIAPER DEKOR

Type: Refill canister.

Price: $42 to $75. Refill packs are $5-$7.50 each and wrap 1160 newborn diapers.

Pros: Hands free operation—you hit the foot pedal and drop in a diaper. Comes in three sizes, largest can holds 5+ days of diapers. Converts to a regular trashcan after baby is done with diapers. Parents say it is much easier to use than the Diaper Genie, reviewed below.

Cons: New "biodegradable" refills are terrible at containing stink, readers report. Hinges on the "trap door" seem prone to breakage, as does the foot pedal.

Comments: The only serious competition for the Diaper Genie, the Diaper Dekor comes in three sizes: regular ($30, holds 30 diapers), Plus ($40, 40 diapers) and XL ($90, 50+ diapers). The classic Diaper Dekor is best for newborns; the Plus is pitched for larger families (where more than one child is in diapers) and the XL is best for multiple births or a daycare center . . . or the Octomom. As of this writing, we saw more Plus versions for sale than the XL or Classic.

The Dekor was one of our top picks for diaper pails in our last edition—but then the company re-designed the refills . . . the result is a disaster. The worst part is a change in the plastic: the new refills are now "biodegradable." And in case you missed the eco-friendly message, the plastic is now green. The problem? The new refills are horrible at blocking odor, the main reason why you'd part with the big bucks to buy one of these pails.

While we are all for saving the environment, ruining the effectiveness of a product in order to make it more green is a colossal mistake.

Some good news: the stink about the new refills was so great, Regal Lager has brought back the original refills, which work great. So we will recommend this diaper pail, as long as you use the original refills.

Bottom Line: Re-designed refills are a disaster; stick with the original ones (which are white). ***Rating: A (original refills only)***

DIAPER GENIE II / ELITE BY PLAYTEX

Type: Refill canister.
Price: II: $25; Elite: $40. Refill cartridges ($6) hold 180 diapers.
Pros: Wraps each diaper in deodorized plastic. One-hand operation. Easy to remove diapers.
Some say better at stink control than Diaper Champ.
Cons: Expensive, since you have to keep buying those refills.
Comments: The revised Diaper Genie II addresses some of the key gripes with the original version (the Twistaway, now discontinued): there's no more twisting when diapers go in, enabling one-hand operation. A clamp keeps the diapers (and the smell) inside the container. The Genie II also holds more diapers, since there are no more chains of sausages as with the original. The removal process has also been improved: Playtex actually designed a cutter that, well, cuts.

The Diaper Genie comes in two versions: the II and the II Elite. The latter features a foot pedal, is taller and has anti-microbial coated plastic (to control odor). Both versions use the same refills (in case you find an old Twistaway Genie at a garage sale, it uses different refills that are still sold in some stores).

There used to be a three-way competition in diaper pails between the Genie, the Dekor and Baby Trend's Diaper Champ. But after Baby Trend muffed the re-design of the Champ, the Dekor changed the plastic on it's refills and Munchkin released its Arm & Hammer diaper pail, it looks to be a two way race for odor control between the Arm & Hammer and the Genie.

That doesn't mean the Genie doesn't have its detractors, many of whom cite the cost of refill cartridges as a major negative. Those parents think a steel trashcan with tight fitting lid (with frequent emptying) is just as effective as the Genie. That is debatable, but others object to the process of putting a diaper in the Genie, which requires pushing it below a clamp (ew, we know).

FYI: Between the two pails, the Genie II gets slightly better marks than the Elite—but the feedback on both is similar.

Bottom Line: The Genie is among the best in its field—but that doesn't mean its perfect. There is probably no such thing as a stink-free diaper pail, especially when baby starts solid foods. ***Rating: A***

MUNCHKIN ARM & HAMMER DIAPER PAIL

Type: Refill canister.

Price: $25; refills $18 for a three pack.

Pros: Baking soda+diapers = less stink.

Cons: Requires two hands to open the lid.

Comments: This diaper pail's secret weapon is baking soda—once you put a diaper in, a built-in dispenser sprinkles the diaper with baking soda to control odor. Yes, you still have to push in the diaper (like the Diaper Genie), but the self-sealing system is a bit easier to use and does what it supposed to do: control the stink.

Reader feedback on this has been trending more positive on this pail than in the past. Parents praise the lack of odor saying it seals better than other brands. And the little shot of baking soda from the refillable cartridge can't hurt. It's also easy to replace the bag and remove the dirty diapers.

Perhaps the biggest complaint we hear from readers is what's called the "squish factor." You have to really push the diaper down to get it into the pail—not fun when it's a really full diaper. And some enterprising toddlers have easily figured out how to get the door open in the base. Finally, it does take two hands to open the lid making for tough going if you have your baby in one hand.

Bottom Line: Despite its faults, Munchkin's Arm & Hammer diaper pail is a great option for odor control. ***Rating: A***

VIPP DIAPER PAIL

Type: Refill canister.

Price: $320. Plastic liners: $5.

Pros: Uh . . . it's from Denmark?

Cons: Yes, the world's first $300+ diaper pail!

Comments: We'll let one of our readers describe her experience with the Vipp: "So I gave in and bought the VIPP diaper pail. I thought that despite the obscene price this would be a worthwhile investment that would fight smell, not take up too much space, and look attractive in my Manhattan apartment. I saw that it is made in Denmark, used in doctor's offices and has a steel liner. Basically no plastic to absorb smell. And despite the many debates about Dekor/Genie, it seemed that neither one is quite ideal.

"Well this story does not end well. For $320, I also wanted ease of use (special bags are needed)—but even their special VIPP bag is rather difficult to get in and out. Sadly, I took my 39-week pregnant self to return the trashcan and the woman at Giggle confirmed that although it is great at keeping the smell at bay, it is difficult to change the bag. I really was shocked to find that this 80-year-old Danish company did not have this down to more of a science. While this is not an official 'diaper pail' I think this is aggravating even if using this for regular trash."

Bottom Line: You don't need to spend $320 on a trashcan.

Rating: F

◆ **More pails:** There are several other basic diaper pails on the market today, such as the $20 Safety 1st Simple Step Diaper Pail. Most are simple plastic trashcans with lids. Our suggestion: if you go this route, just get a stainless steel step-on trashcan ($40 to $80 at stores like Bed Bath & Beyond). Why steel? They are easier to clean—and less likely to stink like plastic. And you are getting a real trashcan you can repurpose to another part of the house after baby is done with diapers.

Humidifiers

We always know when its wintertime here at the ranch in Colorado—the furnace kicks in and everyone's skin dries out quicker than you can say Palm Desert. Hence, humidifiers are a way of life here. But even if you live in a moist climate, running a humidifier in your baby's room in the winter can keep throats, nasal passages and skin from drying out—and make everyone happier.

Here's the 411 on buying a humidifier. First, there are two basic types of humidifiers:

1 EVAPORATIVE HUMIDIFIERS. Water is soaked into a wick and then a fan blows the moisture out. While these are affordable, they can be rather noisy (the fan) and you have to replace the filters regularly.

2 ULTRASONIC HUMIDIFIERS. Sound waves disperse the moisture, so there's no fan—hence these humidifiers are quieter. The downside: sometime these humidifiers leave a coating of white dust on furniture.

There's also one more choice to make when it comes to humidifiers: warm or cool mist. Like the name implies, warm mist humidifiers use a heating element to warm the water. While that might sound appealing if you live in a cold climate, we do NOT recommend these humidifiers for baby's room. That's because warm mist humidifiers can overheat the room—and that is a risk factor for Sudden Infant Death Syndrome. Also: the warm mist coming out of the humidifier can cause a scalding injury if touched by a wayward toddler.

Some quick additional points:

◆ **CONSIDER ROOM SIZE.** Humidifiers are rated by gallon output and most will tell you the size room they cover—match this to the size room your baby is in. You don't need a giant humidifier for most bedrooms.

◆ **CLEAN IT REGULARLY.** Humidifiers have detailed cleaning instructions—follow these! If not, you risk mold or mildew build-up in the unit or shortening the life of the humidifier.

◆ **ADJUSTABLE HUMIDISTAT.** A humidistat works like a thermostat, setting the humidity at a certain level and turning on or off the humidifier until it reaches that level. This is a nice feature, but not completely necessary.

◆ **REMODELING? CONSIDER A WHOLE-HOUSE HUMIDIFIER.** If you are planning to do any HVAC work on your home, consider installing a whole-house humidifier. These automatically kick in when your furnace runs (or can be controlled by a thermostat). Since they are permanently installed and plumbed to a water line, you never have to refill the humidifier. You do have to change the filter and clean out the drip pan, but that's just once a year.

◆ **SKIP THE VAPORIZER.** A vaporizer is a humidifier that lets you disperse medication in your child's room. Generally, this is NOT recommended—that's because pediatricians rarely prescribe medication that needs to be vaporized these days.

Tracking Online Coupon Codes

If you've earned your black belt in online shopping, you know discount codes are a common way for web sites to lure customers or reward customer loyalty. And while there are sites that list coupon deals across the web (FatWallet.com, eDealFinder.com), how do you find the best coupon codes just for baby stuff? Check out our message boards (BabyBargains.com, click on Message Boards). On the Bargain Alert board, we keep a pinned thread with all the latest coupon deals, all submitted by our readers (spam isn't allowed). Updated regularly, this thread has all the best deals. (And there's even a separate pinned thread for freebies.)

Brand Recommendations: Our Picks

Good. The *Crane EE-5301* is a $40-$50 cool mist humidifier with a 2.3 gallon output and automatic shut-off feature. But it lacks a humidistat—you adjust the amount of output with a knob on the front. This is a very good model that is quiet. FYI: Crane also makes the same humidifier in a series of animal shapes—basically the same model, but these units are smaller and only hold one gallon of water.

Best. The *Air-O-Swiss 7135 Ultrasonic Humidifier* is pricey ($170) but features a built-in humidistat and a replaceable demineralization cartridge to cut down on white dust. Offers either warm or cool mist (when used in a baby's room, always use cool mist). A sleep mode turns the unit off after eight hours. Very quiet, 3.5 gallon tank. But the anti-microbial features of this unit come at a price: regular maintenance is a must—and that requires about $100 per year in supplies (demineralization cartridges and other parts).

Bouncer Seat/Activity Gyms

◆ **ACTIVITY GYM.** Among our favorites is the *Gymini by Tiny Love* (tinylove.com). The Gymini is a three-foot square blanket that has two criss-cross arches. You clip rattles, mirrors and other toys onto the arches, providing endless fun for baby as she lies on her back and reaches for the toys. The Gymini comes in several versions that range from $35 to $60. The *Gymini Super Deluxe Lights & Music* is a good bet at $60. A runner-up: the *Fisher Price Rainforest Melodies and Lights Deluxe Gym* is $49. Both of these activity gyms fold up for travel.

◆ **ACTIVITY SEAT/BOUNCER WITH TOY BAR.** An activity seat (also called a bouncer) provides a comfy place for baby to hang out while you eat dinner, and the toy bar adds some mild amusement. The latest twist to these products is a "Magic Fingers" vibration feature—the bouncer basically vibrates, simulating a car ride. Parents who have these bouncers tell us they'd rather have a kidney removed than give up their vibrating bouncer, as it appears the last line of defense in soothing a fussy baby, short of checking into a mental institution.

What features should you look for in a bouncer? Readers say a carrying handle is a big plus. Also: get a neutral fabric pattern, says another parent, since you'll probably be taking lots of photos of baby and a garish pattern may grate on your nerves.

What is the best brand for bouncers? Fisher Price (fisher-price.com) makes the most popular one in the category; most are about $30 to $75, depending on the version. A good choice: the **Fisher Price RainForest bouncer** ($45). Although some of the sounds were a little loud, the toys and waterfall got high marks. Yes, other compa-

nies make similar products (KIDS II is a good runner-up), but the feedback we get from parents is that Fisher-Price is the best.

Readers also give kudos to the **Fisher Price Newborn Rock 'n Play Sleeper** ($45) which doubles as both a place to sleep and a rocker.

One caveat: most bouncer seats have a 25-pound weight limit. If you want something that will last longer, consider the **Baby Bjorn Balance**. Yes, it is more pricey than the Fisher-Price (about $150, depending on the store) and lacks a vibrating feature . . . but you can use it up to 29 lbs. Fisher-Price does have a bouncer that can even be used up to 40 lbs.—the **Infant-to-Toddler** rocker ($36). Parent feedback on that model is very positive.

Graco has added a new sub-category to bouncers: a "soothing center." The **Graco Sweet Peace** ($140-$160; pictured) provides four cradling motions, six speeds and the removable carrier doubles as a floor rocker (or you can use it with a Graco infant car seat). Feedback on the Sweet Peace has been mostly positive with only a few complaints

that the motor is a bit loud. Parents really like that it plugs into the wall (battery-operation is optional) and is easy to put together.

What about those $100+ bouncers from Oeuf or Svan? Pretty to look at but not practical, say our readers. The lack of vibration or just about any other feature you find on a $50 bouncer makes these bouncers not worth the extra investment.

◆ **Toy Bars for your car seat.** Here's another money-saving tip: turn your infant car seat into an activity center with an attachable toy bar. Manhattan Toy makes a **Whoozit Activity Spiral** with dangling toys that wraps around carrier handles for $20. Another plus: your baby is safer in an infant car seat carrier than in other activity seats, thanks to that industrial-strength harness safety system. Safety warning: only use these toy bars when the car seat is NOT inside a vehicle (that is, at home, etc.). Toy bars are not safe in a vehicle as they can be a hazard/projectile in an accident.

One caveat: some parents and pediatricians believe that leaving an infant in a car seat for extended periods of time can contribute to breathing problems in very young infants. For older babies, excessive time in an infant seat could lead to flat head syndrome (plagiocephaly). Unfortunately, doctors don't agree on how much time in an infant seat is too much. Use your common sense and move your child out of the seat frequently.

Monitors

For her first nine months, your baby is tethered to you via the umbilical cord. After that, it's the baby monitor that becomes your surrogate umbilical cord—enabling you to work in the garden, wander about the house, and do many things that other, childless human beings do, while still keeping tabs on a sleeping baby. Hence, this is a pretty important piece of equipment you'll use every day—a good one will make your life easier . . . and a bad one will be a never-ending source of irritation.

Smart Shopper Tips for Monitors

Smart Shopper Tip #1
Bugging your house
"I saw a TV report where a reporter was able to drive around a neighborhood and peer in on folks' video baby monitors. Are these monitors secure?"

Let's consider what a baby monitor really is: the base unit is the transmitter and the receiver is, well, a receiver. So anyone with another baby monitor on the same frequency can often pick up your monitor—not just the sound of your baby crying, but also *any* conversations you have with your mate in the nursery.

Ditto for video monitors—most work at the same frequency. If you get another receiver and drive around the neighborhood, you'll probably be able to pick up other video signals.

The take home message: most audio and video monitors are not encrypted. Therefore the best advice is to remember that your house (or at least, your baby's room) is bugged. If you want to protect your privacy, don't have any sensitive conversations within earshot of the baby monitor. You never know who might be listening. It is wise to turn OFF the baby monitor when baby isn't in the room.

So are there any monitors that are private? Until just recently, the answer was no. But there is good news: several models feature "digital" (DECT) technology—their signals can't be intercepted, unlike older analog monitors. We'll discuss DECT later in this section and point out which models feature this technology in our product reviews.

As for baby video monitors, most are analog, not digital (and hence, not secure). However, there are a few digital models such as the Summer Infant Best View Handheld Color video monitor that do provide secure transmission. We'll note such monitors in the reviews later in this chapter.

Side note: you can use a network webcam as a baby monitor—and several of these cameras can be password protected (so not just anyone can look in on the signal). But setting up a network webcam to view online is rather geeky and beyond the scope of this book!

Smart Shopper Tip #2
Battery woes

"Boy, we should have bought stock in Duracell when our baby was born! We go through dozens of batteries each month to feed our very hungry baby monitor."

Most baby monitors have the option of running on batteries or regular current (by plugging it into a wall outlet). Our advice: use the wall outlet as often as possible. Batteries don't last long—as little as eight to ten hours with continual use. Another idea: you can buy another AC adapter from a source like Radio Shack for $10 or less—you can leave one AC adapter in your bedroom and have another one available in a different part of the house. (Warning: make sure you get the correct AC adapter for your monitor, in terms of voltage and polarity. Take your existing AC adapter to Radio Shack and ask for help to make sure you are getting the correct unit. If not, you can fry your monitor).

Another solution: several baby monitors (reviewed later in this chapter) feature rechargeable receivers! You'll never buy a set of batteries for these units—you just plug them into an outlet to recharge.

Smart Shopper Tip #3
Interference issues

"We have a cordless phone and a baby monitor. Boy, it took us two weeks to figure out how to use both without having a nervous breakdown."

If we could take a rocket launcher and zap one person in this world, it would have to be the idiot who decided that baby monitors and cordless phones should share the same radio frequency. What were they thinking? Gee, let's take two people who are already dangerously short of sleep and mess with their phone and baby monitor.

So, here are our tips to avoid frustration:

First, the higher the frequency, the longer the range of the monitor. Basic baby monitors work on the 49 MHz frequency—these will work for a few hundred feet. Step up to a 900 MHz monitor and you can double the distance the monitor will work (some makers claim up to 1000 feet). Finally, there are baby monitors that work on the 2.4 GHz frequency, where you can pick up your baby in Brazil. Okay, not that far, but you get the idea. Of course, "range" estimates are just that—your real-life range will probably be much less than what's touted on the box.

Now here's the rub: cordless phones and WiFi networks can often interfere with your baby monitor. Old cordless phones worked on the 49 MHz frequency, but modern models are more likely to be found in the 900 MHz or the 2.4 GHz (or even 5.8 GHz) bands. If you've got a baby monitor at 900 MHz and a cordless phone on the same frequency, expect trouble. Ironically, as more and more devices use the higher frequency, the old 49 MHz for baby monitors now seems to be the most trouble free when it comes to interference.

WiFi networks work on the 2.4 GHz band—yep, the same frequency used by some baby monitors. The same advice as above: don't get a baby monitor on the same frequency as your WiFi network. FYI: Baby VIDEO monitors work on either the 900 MHz or 2.4 GHz frequencies and can have the same interference issues as audio monitors.

New to the market are digital or DECT monitors, which work in the 1.9 GHz range. Since very few other electronics operate on this band, DECT monitors are virtually interference-free and work at even longer range than 2.4 GHz monitors. Another plus: DECT monitors can't be monitored by noisy neighbors. Bottom line: if your house is buzzing with electronics, consider a DECT monitor (we'll suggest specific models later in the reviews section).

So, to sum up, here is our advice: first, try to buy a baby monitor on a different frequency than your cordless phone or WiFi network. Second, always keep the receipt. Baby monitors have one of the biggest complaint rates of all products we review. We suspect all the electronic equipment in people's homes today (cell phones, WiFi routers, fax machines, large-screen TVs the size of a Sony Jumbotron), not to mention all the interference sources near your home (cell phone towers, etc.) must account for some of the problems folks have with baby monitors. Common complaints include static, lack of range, buzzing and worse—and those problems can happen with a baby monitor in any price range.

So, read our monitor recommendations later with a grain of salt. ANY monitor (even those we rate the highest) can still run into static and interference problems, based on your home's electronics.

Again, the best advice: always keep the receipt for any baby monitor you buy—you may have to take it back and exchange it for another brand if problems develop.

Smart Shopper Tip #4
The one-way dilemma

"Our baby monitor is nice, but it would be great to be able to buzz my husband so he could bring me something to drink while I'm feeding the baby. Are there any monitors out there that let you communicate two ways?"

Yep, Philips has models that do just that (see review on page 336). Of course, there is another alternative: you can always go to Radio Shack and buy a basic intercom for about $50. Most also have a "lock" feature that you can leave on to listen to the baby when he's sleeping. Another advantage to intercoms: you can always deploy the unit to another part of your house after you're done monitoring the baby. Of course, the only disadvantage to intercoms is that they aren't portable—most must be plugged into a wall outlet.

Here are other features to consider when shopping for monitors:

◆ *Out of range indicators.* If you plan to wander from the house and visit your garden, you may want to go for a monitor that warns you when you've strayed too far from its transmitter. Some models have a visual out of range indicator, while others beep at you. Of course, even if your monitor doesn't offer this feature, you'll probably realize when you're out of range—the background noise you hear in your home will disappear from the receiver.

◆ *Low battery indicator.* Considering how quickly monitors can eat batteries, you'd think this would be a standard feature for monitors. Nope—very few current models actually warn you when you're running out of juice. Most units will just die. If you plan to heavily use your monitor on battery power (out in the garden, for example), look for this feature.

◆ *What's the frequency?* As we discussed above, the right or wrong frequency can make a world of difference. Before selecting a monitor, think about the wireless gadgets you have in your home (particularly cordless phones). Then look carefully at packages . . . not all monitors put that info up front.

◆ *Extra receivers.* It is convenient to leave one receiver in your bedroom and then tote around another receiver in your home.

◆ *Digital technology.* New models use digital technology to prevent eavesdropping by your neighbors. Digital monitors also avoid static and interference from other electronics in your home.

◆ *Great, but not necessary.* Some monitors have a temperature display, which might help you spot a nursery that's too warm. Others have a base with nightlight or play lullabies to sooth baby. Nice, but most folks don't need this.

Smart Shopper Tip #5
The cordless phone trick
    "A techie friend of mind mentioned that some of the new cordless phones can double as baby monitors. Which phone does that?"

Here's a clever way to avoid spending $50 on a baby monitor. Simply use your cordless phone to monitor the baby's room. Uniden (uniden.com), for example, sells not one but 55 cordless phone models with a room monitor feature. A typical package includes two handsets for about $40—then you can buy extra handsets for about $20. FYI: Panasonic also has several models with this feature as well.

Basically, you put one handset in the baby's room, turn on the room monitor feature and you can listen in on a second handset. One caveat: with some models you can't both monitor a room and receive a phone call at the same time. Make sure your model can receive a call when in monitor mode.

The bottom line: if you need a new cordless phone for your house, consider buying one with a room-monitoring feature.

More Money Buys You

Basic baby monitors are just that—an audio monitor and transmitter. No-frills monitors start at $20 or $25. More money buys you a sound/light display (helpful in noisy environments, since the lights indicate if your baby is crying) and rechargeable batteries (you can go through $50 a year in 9-volts with regular monitors). More expensive monitors even have transmitters that also work on batteries (so you could take it outside if you wish) or dual receivers (helpful if you want to leave the main unit inside the house and take the second one outside if you need to work in the garage, etc.). Finally, the top-end monitors either have digital technology or intercom features, where you can use the receiver to talk to your baby as you walk back to the room. The most expensive monitor on the market, Philips' $200 Digital Monitor, adds a room temperature thermometer, adjustable sound sensitivity, music and a night light.

For video monitors, more money buys you a color viewing screen (the cheaper ones are just black and white). Some more expensive models have point-tilt-zoom capability (PTZ) as well as extra monitors (Summer's "complete" coverage video monitor comes with a 7" LCD screen and 1.8" handheld unit).

Audio Baby Monitors

The Name Game:
Audio Baby Monitors

Here's a look at the best audio baby monitors (video monitor reviews start on page 338).

Major caveat to these reviews: ANY baby monitor, even those that earn our highest ratings, can have problems with static, poor reception or interference (see earlier discussion). The best advice: keep your receipt and buy a monitor from a store with a good return policy. It might be trail and error to find one that works for you.

A quick safety tip for monitors: always keep the cord away from your baby's crib. Cords from cameras/monitors are a strangulation hazard.

The Ratings

    A **EXCELLENT**—*our top pick!*
    B **GOOD**— *above average quality, prices, and creativity.*
    C **FAIR**—*could stand some improvement.*
    D **POOR**—*yuck! could stand some major improvement.*

Angelcare angelcare-monitor.com. The Angelcare monitor launched in 1997 after engineer Maurice Pinsonnault bought the patent rights to a breathing monitor sold in the UK. In a nutshell, Angelcare has two functions: first, it is a regular audio baby monitor. Second, it measures baby's "breathing movements" through a sensor placed under the crib mattress. If baby stops moving for 20 seconds, an alarm sounds on the parent unit.

Here's our problem with this concept: Angelcare clearly preys on parents' fears of Sudden Infant Death Syndrome. However, experts such as the American Academy of Pediatrics say monitors like Angelcare don't work in preventing SIDS. And Angelcare is very careful to steer clear of such promises (its website doesn't refer to SIDS, only the "anxiety which all new parents face").

Bottom line: if your baby has a medical condition that requires a breathing monitor, you need to get a medical grade monitor from your pediatrician.

In Angelcare's defense, folks who have this monitor generally praise it for the "piece of mind." But you can get the same piece of mind from any audio monitor that costs half as much as the Angelcare ($90 for a single, $140 for a double receiver).

As a side note, we should mention that Angelcare does make an audio-only model (the AC430, $58). This model omits the breathing sensor and generally gets very good marks from parents. But it is rather pricey (by comparison, the Sony monitor we recommend is about 25% cheaper). And there is no dual receiver version of the Angelcare audio only monitor, limiting its appeal. They have expanded the line with other options as well: a color video monitor with movement sensor ($300), a movement only monitor ($70) and a couple analog models.

FYI: Angelcare is now owned by Graco, which oddly distances itself from the product. Angelcare has its own web site; Angelcare monitors don't appear on Graco's web site section on monitors.

So we will give Angelcare a failing grade: if experts say it doesn't prevent SIDS, what is the point? ***Rating: F***

BabySense *babysense.net.* The BabySense V Movement Monitor ($130) is similar to the Angelcare—using sensor pads, it detects baby's movements to prevent SIDS. If she stops breathing, the parent unit sounds an alarm. But it isn't an audio monitor so you won't hear your baby crying. Regardless, we don't recommend monitors like the BabySense; see the Angelcare review for our reasoning. ***Rating: F***

BebeSounds. *See Angelcare.*

Evoz *myevoz.com* And now for something really scary . . . want to monitor your baby's nursery from your smartphone? No matter where you are in the world?

Unlike normal baby monitors that have a limited range, Evoz is the first baby monitor that connects to the Internet and streams your baby's every coo over the web. Thanks to Evoz's free iphone app, you'll be able to hear this wherever you are . . . in the kitchen, across town or even overseas.

While that sounds cutting edge, there is one downside: unlike other monitors, this one requires a service contract. The Evoz baby monitor has three data plans: basic (30 minutes per day limit), standard (unlimited listening plus multiple guardians can access the monitor) and premium (get call, text or email alerts when baby is crying plus access to a parenting dashboard, with data on your baby's sleep and crying).

Basic is $120 (including the monitor), standard is $160 (six months of service) and premium is $180 (12 months of service). Each additional year of standard service runs $40; premium is $70 a year. FYI:

you can also use a iPhone or iPod touch as a monitor with a $5 accessory microphone.

This will take some getting used to, we suppose—since you use a baby monitor for three to four years, Evoz could turn into a $400 purchase. Whether that is worth the chunk of change is an open question.

As for the quality of the Evoz monitor, we hope to field test the unit shortly. There has been little parent feedback on the unit yet, as it is so new. Early user feedback on iTunes is encouraging, although a few folks complained about dropped connections between the app and the monitor. **Rating: Not Yet.**

First Years thefirstyears.com. The First Years' monitor line-up features four digital models. The A100 ($40) has an out of range and low battery indicator, sound-lights and a child unit that can be wall mounted. The A200 ($50) is the same model with two receivers.

The P300 ($55) has the same features but adds rechargeable batteries and an intercom features. Finally, the P400 ($65-$75) adds three-way communication (you can talk with the other parent or to baby).

Reader comments are mixed on First Years monitors. The A100 is generally panned for its poor quality and lack of clarity. Similar complaints dog the P300—poor range and audio that is too quiet are among the common refrains from parents.

The P400 gets somewhat better marks than the cheaper monitors, but still draws complaints of static and crackling noises. Again, quality issues dog the monitor: many users said the receiver will stop receiving a signal, forcing you to turn the unit on and off. This feedback dovetails with similar comments we received on First Years' previous generation of monitors, which were hampered by quality concerns.

In the past year, The First Years added a low-cost analog monitor to their line-up: the Y3040 ($35), which has two parent units, low battery indicator, sound/light display and works on the 49 Mhz frequency. Again, poor quality mars the user reviews of this monitor, which we would not recommend.

New for 2012, First Years will debut the Talk & Soothe Digital Audio monitor in both single ($65) and double receiver versions ($85). This monitor's key feature is a digital screen with some bells and whistles (nursery temperature, timer, backlight). You can remotely activate a nightlight and the Talk & Soothe features a two-way intercom. This monitor should be on the market in summer 2012.

Bottom line: we can't recommend this brand. First Years monitors aren't ready for prime time. **Rating: D**

Fisher Price fisher-price.com. Fisher Price has announced it will now longer make its own baby monitors; instead it will license out the Fisher Price name to Mobicam, which will make both audio and video monitors under the Fisher Price brand.

This confirms what we long suspected about Fisher Price: its aging analog monitor line was losing sales to newer digital and video models. It's sad that a brand that was once a leader in this category is now reduced to farming out production of monitors to a competitor. We're sure this probably makes sense on paper, but we wonder about Fisher Price's choice of partner, Mobicam. That company has at best a mixed track record in the video monitor segment and no experience in audio monitors.

So below we'll review the 2012 Fisher Price audio monitors (made by Mobicam). Meanwhile, an archive review of the old Fisher Price models is on our web site.

For 2012, Mobicam will be selling two audio monitors under the Fisher Price brand: the Clear & Secure and Talk to Baby. Clear & Secure ($50-$60) will feature DECT 6.0 digital transmission, rechargeable batteries, sound/light display and low battery/out of range alerts. The Talk to Baby Digital monitor ($60 to $70) has the same features, but adds a two-way intercom and room temperature display with high/low alerts. The parent unit can also remotely turn on a night light and lullabyes

Among Mobicam's biggest innovations with these monitors is their zero-transmission mode—when there is no sound detected by the monitor, it doesn't transmit a signal. This should help with battery life and overall longevity.

Of course, these are the very first Mobicam audio monitors, so there is no track record yet. And given Mobicam's mixed record with video monitors, we'd be cautious about being the very first to buy one of these. We also were puzzled by the lack of a dual receiver model, as that is a very popular feature. The prices are on the high side. **Rating: C**

Graco *gracobaby.com*. Graco has aggressively expanded in the monitor market in recent years, with offerings in the analog, digital and video segments. In 2008, Graco also bought BebeSounds, maker of the Angelcare movement monitors (reviewed earlier).

At the opening price point for audio monitors, the Simple Sounds analog monitor is aptly named—this 49 MHz monitor just has audio (no lights or other features) for $18.

The Ultra Clear Monitor ($23 single, $35 dual) adds vibration, nightlight and sound/lights display and works on the analog 49 MHz frequency with a low battery alarm.

For digital monitors, Graco has three offerings: the Secure Coverage, Direct Connect and imonitor.

Secure Coverage ($45) is a 900 MHz monitor with vibration,

sound/lights and a low battery alarm. Direct Connect ($60) is similar, but adds an intercom feature as well as a display of the baby's room temperature on the parent unit.

The imonitor Vibe ($60 single) is a simple digital monitor with 900 MHz frequency and vibration. This model will be discontinued shortly, although we notice it is still for sale on quite a few sites.

So how's the quality? Readers generally liked the simplest monitors best: the Ultra Clear won the best reviews, although a significant number of folks complained of static and interference (probably due to the monitor's simple 49 MHz frequency). Unfortunately, like many monitors, it will eat batteries (the parent unit only lasts a few hours on battery power); it is best to leave it plugged in.

Graco's digital monitors fared worse in reader feedback. The imonitor, for example, is often criticized for its lack of range and short battery life. Sound clarity is good, but more than one complained about lack of long-term durability (the monitor won't hold a charge after a year, etc.). No surprise that the imonitor is headed for the discontinued bin.

Similar complaints about quality and lack of range dog the Secure Coverage and Direct Connect monitors—Graco clearly over-promises (a 2000 foot range?) and under-performs (readers say it is more like 30 feet line of sight).

Overall, Graco falls short in this category. The simplest monitors (particularly the Ultra Clear) are probably the best bet. *Rating: C+*

Motorola *binatonetelecom.com* Electronics maker Binatone has licensed the Motorola name for a line of baby monitors that are mostly sold online.

The audio-only Digital Baby Monitor ($50; model MBP10L) is pretty basic: sound/lights, out of range warning and battery indicator. As the name implies, it has digital transmission. The MBP15L ($65) adds rechargeable batteries and a temperature monitor, with a display on the parent's unit.

In recent months, Binatone has rolled out two more digital audio monitors: the simple MBP11($40) has a basic sound/light display, out of range indicator, rechargeable batteries and . . . that's about it. The main difference between this model and the 10: the 10 has a transmitter that will also work on a battery (for five hours of wireless monitoring). The 11 lacks that feature (of course, it is also $10 cheaper).

Also new in recent months: the MBP16 ($60) adds a night light, two-way intercom, lullaby player and room temperature display.

So how's the quality? Binatone/Motorola audio baby monitors have just been on the market for about a year and are mostly sold online (Amazon is a good bet). So far, reviews are mostly positive. Perhaps the biggest drawback is the lack of continuous transmission—the monitor only makes a sound when baby cries (instead of constantly transmitting even background noise from your nursery). Adding to this negative: there is no way to adjust the sensitively of when the monitor trips on . . . and that frustrated quite a few folks.

Despite that negative, most parents who've used these monitors give it good marks—the simpler 10 or 11 model are the best bets, quality-wise. The digital DECT transmission (which translates into little static or interference issues) and the relatively low prices make these models decent choices. ***Rating: B+***

Philips Avent *consumer.philips.com.* Consumer products giant Philips is known for its innovative products . . . and, at the same time, monumentally inept marketing and poor customer service.

Case in point: Philips baby monitors. The European consumer products giant made a big push into the monitor market ten years ago with cutting-edge offerings that were way overpriced. No surprise, the monitors bombed, thanks in part to high prices and thin distribution (chain stores didn't want to stock $200 monitors). And when consumers had problems, their complaints fell on deaf ears at Philips' anemic customer service department.

So, Philips has hit the reset the button with three new monitors that are (dare we say it?) more affordable. At least, affordable for Philips.

Philips ace-in-the-hole is DECT technology; as we discussed earlier, this special frequency virtually guarantees interference-free reception. No static, no problem with cordless phones or WiFi networks, etc.

All Philips monitors offer DECT: the basic SCD510 features rechargeable batteries, adjustable microphone sensitivity, sound/light display, intercom feature and out-of-range indicator. Price: $90 $120.

New in the past year, Philips has come out with slightly revised models that have a new eco mode, which is basically a lower power consumption feature. The SCD525 ($120 to $150) includes music and a nightlight, intercom, rechargeable batteries and out of range and low battery indicators. The SCD535 ($150 to $190) has similar features but a cube style baby unit for a unique look.

Very few stores seem to be carrying the Philips monitors—Amazon is probably your best bet.

Reader feedback has been positive on these new models—parents like the ability to adjust the microphone sensitivity to screen out background noise in baby's room. Fans also laud the interference-free reception and long battery life (about 24 hours on a charge). But some readers report the volume on the parent unit is way too low, even at the highest setting. Other gripes: the temperature sensor is off by five degrees and the screen on the parent unit is hard to read in dim light, even with the backlight on.

monitors

Bottom line: while these audio monitors are pricey, the quality is excellent. If you live in an area with lots of interference, a simple DECT monitor like the $100 SCD510 is a good buy. Skip the more pricey models with the temperature display and just get a $10 digital thermometer at the hardware store. ***Rating: A***

Safety 1st *safety1st.com.* Like Graco, Safety 1st offers both audio and video monitors.

In the audio category, the company starts with a bare bones 49 MHz model with no sound and light display (Crystal Clear, $14). The Sound View Monitor ($24) is similar, but adds a sound/light display.

The Glow & Go also has a sound/light but adds a temperature display (on base) and comes in both single ($25) and dual ($35) versions. The baby's unit has a glow light with a 15 minute auto-shut off.

The Comfort Zone digital baby monitor ($40) adds a temperature monitor function—if the temperature in baby's room falls outside a preset level, an alert is sent to the parent unit.

New for 2012, Safety 1st will bring back their digital monitor, the High Def Monitor. This simple monitor will feature DECT technology, sound/light display, rechargeable battery, out of range and low battery indicators. At $40, this is one of the lowest price digital monitors on the market today.

So, how's the quality? The simple Crystal Clear monitor gets the best reviews here—perhaps after spending $16, folks don't have high expectations. While it worked for most parents, the Crystal Clear occasionally suffers from being less than crystal clear (static is the biggest issue for some parents).

Safety 1st's other analog monitors (especially the Glow & Go) generally received good marks, but readers were downright hostile on Safety 1st's digital offering (Comfort Zone). Complaints include quality issues (some units died after a month) and complicated programming and design. The redesigned High Def wasn't on the market yet as of this writing. ***Rating: C+***

Sony *sonystyle.com.* Sony keeps it simple with one audio baby monitor model: the Sony BabyCall NTM-910 is a 27 channel model with rechargeable batteries for $40 single, $70 dual. Yes, you read that right—the BabyCall has 27 channels (most monitors have at most one or two). The result is less chance for interference and that's what parents seem to love about Sony's BabyCall—it works without static, buzzing, clicking and all the other complaints you read about monitors.

The downside? Well, the receiver is rather bulky. And since this monitor isn't digital, it is possible to eavesdrop on the signal. And the 900 MHz frequency has less range than 2.4 GHz or DECT. But this model does have an out-of-range indicator and an optional sound-activated mode that silences the receiver until sufficient noise activates it.

Readers generally give the Sony BabyCall high marks for quality, audio clarity and range. Critics don't like the fact that the unit will beep at you when it is out of range (this occasionally goes off in the middle of the night for some users). And some folks have a problem with static, especially if there is something else in their house on the 900 MHz frequency. However, the positive reviews generally far outnumber the negative ones—and for a baby monitor, that is an achievement. *Rating: A*

Summer *summerinfant.com.* Summer is the market leader in video monitors—at last count, they offered ten models. Summer's offerings in the audio-only segment are simpler: two analog and one digital model.

For analog, Summer has the 49 MHz Close2You Cordless ($30, which features a transmitter that can operate on battery power) and the 900 MHz SecureSleep monitor ($60), which features a temperature read-out on both the receiver and transmitter, and doubles as a nightlight. Cool feature: the nightlight changes color based on the temperature (red is too hot, blue too cold, yellow just right).

The Slim & Clear Digital Audio Monitor ($50 single, $80 dual) is a 2.4 GHz monitor with sound/lights and rechargeable batteries. Reader feedback on this new model has been mixed: folks like the audio clarity, but the bright blue LED on the parent unit makes this one a pain to use a night (one reviewer said it was like a blue strobe light).

Bottom line: while Summer's video monitors get good marks (see review in next section), the audio monitors are disappointing. *Ratings: C-*

Our Picks: Brand Recommendations

Here are our picks for baby monitors, with one BIG caveat: how well a monitor will work in your house depends on interference sources (like cordless phones, wireless internet routers), the presence of other monitors in the neighborhood, etc. Since we get so many complaints about this category, it is imperative you buy a monitor from a place with a good return policy. Keep the receipts in case you have to make an exchange.

Good. The *Graco Ultra Clear* ($23 single, pictured, $35 dual) and *Safety 1st Crystal Clear* ($14) are very simple 49 MHz monitors. Nope, you don't get any fancy features with these models (no rechargeable batteries or two-way intercom), but they do their job just fine.

Better. If your house is buzzing with electronic equipment and you fear Baby Monitor Interference Hell, then it's time to check out our top-rated baby monitor, the *Sony BabyCall*

NTM-910. For $40 single (or $70 dual), you get a monitor with 27 selectable channels . . . odds are, one will work. Add in rechargeable batteries, an out-of-range indicator and very positive parent reviews and we've got a winner.

Best. Are the neighbors a bit too nosy? If so, you may want to consider a new digital monitor. The *Philips Avent SCD510* ($90-$120; pictured) features DECT digital technology to stop interference and eavesdropping. The SCD510 also has rechargeable batteries, out-of-range indicator and intercom feature.

Video Baby Monitors

The Name Game: Video Baby Monitors

Axis *axis.com*. See review on our web site, BabyBargains.com.

First Years *thefirstyears.com* The First Years launched its first video monitor in the past year: the Home & Away Portable ($140) features 3.5" monitor, 650 foot range, night vision, rechargeable batteries and the ability to expand up to four cameras. The camera is Skype-compatible, letting you view the camera from Windows-based PC's. You can even take pictures and it has an intercom feature. Reviews of the monitor were mixed. Parents complained that the range wasn't anywhere near 650 feet. Other complaints: the Skype feature was cumbersome and is not Mac compatible. (FYI: a version of this model, the Y7400, Home & Away Computer Connect, omits the receiver and instead turns your PC into a monitor for $120).

Undeterred, The First Years plans to launch a slew of additional digital video monitors in 2012. The Crisp & Clear Digital Video Monitor (Y7500) will debut in April 2012 and aims for the entry-price point market ($100). The monitor will have a small 1.8" color screen and features rechargeable batteries. A dual receiver model (Y520, $190) will debut in June 2012.

Also new: the Complete View Digital Video Monitor ($170) features a 2.4″ color screen, nursery temperature, 800 foot range and rechargeable batteries. This model should be out in January 2012.

Finally, The First Years will debut the Safety Shield Video Monitor ($250, Y7527) in July 2012. This top-of-the-line model will be the first baby monitor to feature what the company calls "safe zone technology." This monitor lets you draw a virtual border around part of the viewing area; you get an alert if anything enters or leves the boundary. Hence, you could be alerted if your cat jumps in the crib or your toddler throws a toy, for example. This model will also have nursery temperature, 3.5″ color touch screen, two-way intercom, rechargeable batteries and an 800 foot range.

Bottom line: the First Years is making a big bet on digital video monitors with their expansion in this category. Unfortunately, given the feedback on their first model, we can't recommend them. There are simply better choices in this category. **Rating: C+**

Fisher Price *fisher-price.com.* As we mentioned earlier, Fisher Price has partnered with Mobicam to launch three new video baby monitors under the Fisher Price brand in 2012. These models are similar to Mobicam's monitors in terms of features, albeit with smaller or lower resolutions screens.

The entry-level Instant View Secure Sleep digital monitor will have a small 2″ screen, 2.4 GHz digital frequency, night vision and rechargeable batteries. Price: $129.

The Instant View Deluxe Two-Way Talk Video Monitor offers a slighter larger display (2.4″) and two-way intercom feature, plus the ability to expand the system with up to four cameras. A USB connection allows remote viewing via Skype, Google Talk and a few other messaging programs. Price: $169.

The top of the line Instant View Premium Complete Care Video Monitor has all the above features, but adds a 3.5″ LCD display. Price: $199 to $229.

Interestingly, Mobicam's video monitors for 2012 will be similarly price (the Digital DXR is $200) but appear to offer higher resolution screens and other goodies (recording to a SD card, a quad split-screen for viewing four cameras at once, etc). We review Mobicam's namesake offerings separately.

We also gave Mobicam's video monitors a D, so we'll have to wait and see if the Fisher Price versions do a better job in terms of quality. The jury is still out. **Rating: Not Yet.**

Foscam Like our review of Axis cameras in this category, Foscom offers an easy-to-set-up network camera (the FI8918W, $87) with an impressive list of features: remote pan/tilt, night vision (you can turn this remotely on or off), two-way audio monitoring and a sharp picture. Built-in wi-fi means you don't have to run an ethernet cord to the camera. The one downside: there is no monitor to view the camera—you do that from your computer or smart phone.

Readers on our message boards have been quite happy with this monitor. Fair warning: like many network cams, it does take a fair amount of tech skill to set it up.

Bottom line: considering the affordable price and good quality, Foscam is a decent alternative to "baby" monitors, if you have the tech chops to set it up! ***Rating: A-***

Graco *gracobaby.com* Graco has struggled to get traction in this category. Their last effort (the ill-fated imonitor video) suffered from range, battery life and overall complaints. It is now discontinued.

Taking another swing at the category, Graco has launched the True Focus video monitor with 1000-foot range and pan and tilt feature. It also has night vision and rechargeable batteries. Price: $150. FYI: Even though Graco told us it is shipping the True Focus, we've yet to see it show up in stores or online as of this writing. So with no real world feedback, we'll take a wait and see approach on its rating.

Overall, Graco has had little success in video monitors. Our rating below reflects their past few monitors, not the True Focus as it is not quite available as of this writing. ***Rating: C+***

Levana *mylevana.com* Canada-based Levana is the baby monitor division of Svat, which makes security cameras. Levana has an affordable line of video monitors (mostly sold online), as well as an audio monitor. Levana's first effort in this category is the BabyView20 (aka the Interference-Free Digital Wireless Video Baby Monitor), a $130 monitor featuring rechargeable batteries, a magnetic base and hardware to mount the camera and a 2.3" color LCD screen. This digital video monitor works on the 2.4 GHz frequency and provides a secure connection. Range is about a 100 feet. Like many monitors, the Levana BabyView20 has a standby mode that mutes the audio and turns off the screen until baby cries. The base also doubles as a nightlight and has a lullaby feature. This model is being discontinued as of August 2011 although it's still for sale on several web sites.

Replacing the BabyView20 is the The LV-TW301 ClearVu Digital monitor ($140), which features longer range (350 feet) and an audio-only feature when the LCD screen is turned off. You can also add additional cameras.

If you'd prefer to view your baby over a smartphone, the LV-TW500 might be the trick. It is a $90 digital wireless camera that lets you monitor your baby online (note: it doesn't come with a receiver). Like the BabyView20, it has a night light feature, night vision and a digital signal. But . . . the software is difficult to set up without detailed tech knowledge. And several readers said the camera/software set up is buggy and prone to crashes.

Levana added two new models to its lineup in the past year. The LV-TW501 Safe N'See monitor ($127) features a 2.4" screen, 450-foot range, temperature monitor, intercom feature and sound-activated vibration. In case you want a bigger screen, Levana also offers this model with a 3.5" screen for $164 (the LV-TW501).

New for 2012, Levana plans to introduce the Era, a 500 foot range monitor that can take pictures and record video. The Era will have an intercom feature, temperature monitoring, digital zoom and is expandable up to four cameras. The Era will come in three versions that will range from $129 to $199 (the less expensive versions will omit the photo/video recording feature).

So how's the quality? Mixed is the best way to describe Levana's track record. Folks like the affordable prices and extensive feature list of these monitors. But more than one parent told us the range was nowhere close to the promises Levana makes in its marketing. Battery life is another gripe. And perhaps the biggest problem is long-term reliability—we saw more than one report of Levana monitors that just stopped working after a few months (in some cases, a few weeks).

Bottom line: Levana's video baby monitors are in the middle of the pack. On the plus side, we like the affordable prices and extensive features (intercom, temperature monitoring). Quality-wise, Levana ranks above competitors like Graco and First Years . . . but that isn't saying much. The company needs to improve long-term reliability of its monitors to be a player. **Rating: C+**

Lorex *lorextechnology.com* Like Levana, Lorex is a security camera maker that has branched out into baby monitors. The Lorex Live Snap baby monitor (LW2003; $135) features a 2.4" LCD display, secure digital transmission and the ability to add additional cameras. One unique feature: you can "snap and store" pictures on a microSD card.

While most of the reviews have been positive (picture quality is good, set up is easy), more than one reader complained that the cheap plastic camera broke after a few months of use. The hyped "picture store" feature produces blurry snapshots. There is no pan/tilt/zoom feature, but then again, that's something you'd see on more expensive units.

All in all, the Lorex is a good but not great baby video monitor. It is a decent runner-up choice, but still pales behind the market leading Summer video monitors. **Rating: B**

Mobicam *getmobi.com* Mobicam was among the first affordable video baby monitors ($87) with an LCD screen to score widespread distribution. You'd think after being on the market for five years, this company would have the video monitor thing down to a science. You'd think . . . but you'd be wrong.

Numerous quality woes have dogged Mobicam for years, including broken on/off switches, broken power cords, etc. Interference and static were other major issues for users—some of this is caused by the 2.4 GHz frequency that Mobicam uses . . . the same as WiFi internet routers.

Mobicam attempted to address these problems with an updated version dubbed Mobicam Ultra. The updated camera sports a larger display, voice activation and "new technology for clear sound and picture" (it now works on the 900 MHz frequency). And the verdict from consumers? Numerous gripes about constant static, poor night vision and poor customer service.

To their credit, Mobicam has steadily released new models with updated technology. Their latest: the Mobicam DL Digital Monitoring system for $150 retail ($111 on Amazon). This model features a high-resolution 2.4 inch TFT LCD monitor and camera as well as voice-activated audio and video alerts. The DL has a digital transmission that prevents eavesdropping—the company claims a 300 foot range. You can expand the system with up to three additional cameras. The Digital DL can work on regular batteries and AC power (but no rechargeable battery).

At the high end, Mobicam now offers the Digital DXR ($229 retail, $165 Amazon). This model features a larger LCD screen (3.5" versus the 2.4 for the DL), longer transmission range and a built-in rechargeable battery. Similar to the DL, the DXR features voice activation and an audio-only mode. But the DXR adds two-way audio communication and a SD card slot for recording.

FYI: Mobicam stills sells an internet monitoring version of their camera (the Mobicam AV, $150) that lets you view your camera online from any PC or Windows Media-enabled cell phone. Also: Mobicam now sells video monitors under the Fisher Price brand, reviewed separately.

Feedback on Mobicam's new models (such as the DXR) has been mixed. Glitches with volume control and multi-camera set-up are two common complaints. Others who are using the camera in single mode seem happier. Again, Mobicam just can't quite seem to get quality control right, even for its more pricey monitors.

Given Mobicam's mixed track record for quality in this category, we will take a pass on recommending these monitors. ***Rating: D***

Motorola *natonetelecom.com* Electronic gadget maker Binatone licensed the Motorola name for a line of baby monitors that debuted in 2011.

Binatone has been expanding their video offerings in recent months and now have four models (and a fifth coming in 2012). All video monitors include infrared night vision, lullabies, sound/light display, room temperature monitor and a two-way intercom feature. The main difference is the size of the screen.

The basic MBP20 ($130) has a 1.5″ color LCD screen, while the MBP33 ($160) has a 2.8″ screen. The MBP35 adds a 3.5″ screen, plus a sleep mode for power saving, The camera also has a battery for 3.5 hours of wireless monitoring.

The BMP36 ($200) also has a 3.5 screen, but adds a camera that can pan, tilt and zoom.

For 2012, Binatone will add a new model: the MBP2000 ($400) which works on a WiFi network and can be expanded with up to four cameras. You can record up to 30 hours of video on a Micro SD card. The receiver also doubles as a telephone and answering machine. At $400, it looks like Binatone is throwing in everything including the kitchen sink for this model.

Parent feedback on these video monitors has been quite positive, with few reports of static or interference. Much of that credit probably goes to the monitor's 2.4 GHz FHSS technology—FHSS stands for frequency-hopping spread spectrum—which enables strong, secure reception. Both the MBP33 and MBP36 have FHSS, while the simpler MBP20 works on DECT.

Perhaps the biggest complaint about these cameras is their weak night vision—compared to other brands, the Motorola night vision pictures are not very clear. ***Rating: A-***

Philips *usa.philips.com* New in the past year, Philips debuted its first digital video monitor, appropriately named the Digital Video Monitor ($150-$180). The unit features a private/secure connection, night vision and 2.4″ viewing screen. The screen automatically activates when noise is detected in the baby's room—that sounds good in theory, but is lousy in practice. That's because the monitor doesn't transmit any audio while in this rest mode. Unfortunately, it takes a very loud noise for the monitor to trigger on and that bugged more than one reader—it would make more sense for the audio to be on 24/7 and the video screen to activate when sound reaches a certain level you could set.

Otherwise, readers liked Philips video monitor—picture quality and range are good. However, more than one reader reported interference with their WiFi network; and the lack of a point/tilt/zoom feature is disappointing at this price point. ***Rating: B***

Safety 1st *safety1st.com* Safety 1st has two offerings: the Prism Color Video Monitor ($220) and the True View Color Video Monitor ($180). The Prism is a 2.4 GHz monitor with 2.5″ color screen, night vision and a zoom feature. A power save mode turns on the screen when audio is detected. Safety 1st says this unit has a 350 foot range and can accept additional cameras ($120).

The less expensive True View Color Video Monitor has a smaller screen (2″) and works on the same 2.4 GHz frequency, but lacks the zoom feature of the Prism.

Safety 1st plans an expansion of video monitors in 2012, with the debut of several new digital models. The most affordable will be the $139 ComfortView, with a 2.7″ screen. The PrivateView will be similar in specs, but has a 3.5″ table top receiver for $139.

Also new for 2012, Safety 1st will sell a three-piece monitor system that will include an additional audio-only receiver: the Secure Comfort handheld Digital Color Video Monitor with Audio for $169.

So, how's the quality? Overall, feedback has been negative. Readers knocked the Prism for its poor battery life and generally panned the unit, although a few fans liked the overall video quality, zoom function and the sound activation feature. The True View has somewhat better feedback than the Prism, although battery life is also a problem here. Video quality also came in for criticism and the audio is prone to static.

The new digital models mentioned above aren't on the market yet; it will be interesting to see if Safety 1st's new video monitors with their digital transmission will be able to improve the company's somewhat lackluster reputation in this category. **Rating: C+**

Samsung Samsung has four video monitors, the EzVIEW, RemoteVIEW, SmartVIEW and SecureVIEW. And just to confuse you, Amazon also sells a Samsung video monitor (model SEW3030, $160), which is among the site's top sellers but doesn't appear on Samsung's web site.

The Samsung video monitor on Amazon is an example of our advice that to save money, sometimes you shop at places that don't have "baby" in its name. Hence, this system is really pitched as a security system, not a baby monitor—and costs less than most baby video monitors. This monitor features a 3.5″ LCD, 2.4 GHZ camera with night vision and the ability to monitor the camera remotely via Skype. The Samsung Wireless Video Security Monitoring System also monitors the temperature in baby's room. And it has digital zoom and two-way intercom.

Parent reviews on this monitor are quite positive, with most saying the picture quality is better than other video monitors they've tried. Detractors say the "sound sensitivity sensor" (which beeps at you if it

detects baby moving) is a hassle, constantly beep
turn this down via a sensitivity setting. And th
about five to ten degrees above the actual roo

As for Samsung's other monitors, the EzVIEW and SmartVIEW are sold at Target for $179 and $199 respectively. The EzVIEW is the entry-level model with a 2.4" monitor, 2x digital zoom, built-in temperature sensor and remotely activated night light. The SmartVIEW is basically the same, but adds a 3.5" monitor and two-way talk feature.

Samsung's other two models offer slight variations on the theme. The RemoteVIEW has the smaller 2.4" screen but adds four remote-activated lullabies. The SecureVIEW is similar to the SmartVIEW.

All Samsung video monitors feature a digital signal with 350 feet of promised range. You can also add up to three additional cameras. Two models (the RemoteVIEW and SecureVIEW) allow you to view the baby video via Skype or MSN. All the monitors offer a SD card slot so you can record videos and share them with others via Facebook (this isn't automatic—you'd have to manually move the videos from the SD card to a computer and then upload to Facebook, of course).

Bottom line: in a field crowded with mediocre options, Samsung's video monitors are an affordable option that offer decent quality. The model on Amazon is probably the best deal, price-wise. *Rating: A*

Summer *summerinfant.com* Summer's video monitors are this brand's key mojo—you'll find monitors with black and white TV displays, color flat panel monitors, handheld models and more. Prices start at $100 for a black and white TV model and go up to $200 for a handheld or color flat screen.

The best-selling model is the Summer Infant Day and Night Handheld Color Video Monitor ($160-$180). Yep, it has a tiny 1.8" screen and works on the 900 MHz frequency, but the recharge-able batteries in the parent unit work up to ten hours (that's much longer than the competition). The LED sound/lights let you monitor audio even when the video isn't on.

Another good bet is the Summer Best View Handheld Color Video Monitor ($175), which features pan/tilt/zoom, digital transmission and a 2.5" color display. Since it works on the 2.4 GHz frequency, it has a longer range than the Day and Night monitor. Perhaps the biggest criticism of this monitor is the volume adjustment—you can't just flip a dial. Instead, you have to use the joystick to go into a menu option. That seems like a strange design decision. Also: the night vision LED's on the camera flash on and off every five seconds—again, a bad design feature.

Next, Summer offers the Sleek & Secure Handheld Color Video

onitor. The Sleek & Secure is a smaller, more streamlined design with 2.5″ color video display, intercom, rechargeable batteries, AV output jack and automatic channel switching for $230. Most parents like the Sleek & Secure but some complained about short battery life and poor quality. We'd stick with other Summer video monitors reviewed earlier.

The newest video monitor in the Summer line is the BabyTouch Digital Video Monitor ($240). It features a large 3.5 inch color LCD and pan/tilt/zoom, as well as rechargeable batteries. You can add additional cameras as well. Reader feedback has been positive so far.

BABY MONITORS — A quick look at various features and brands

NAME	MODEL	PRICE
THE FIRST YEARS	P300	$55
FISHER PRICE	CLEAR & SECURE	$50-$60
	TALK TO BABY DIGITAL	$60-$70
GRACO	SIMPLE SOUNDS	$18
	ULTRA CLEAR	$23/$35
	SECURE COVERAGE	$45
	DIRECT CONNECT	$60
	TRUE FOCUS VIDEO	$150
LEVANA	BABYVIEW20	$130
MOBICAM	DL DIGITAL MONITORING SYSTEM	$150
MOTOROLA	DIGITAL	$50
	MBP20	$130
PHILIPS	SCD 510	$90-$120
	SCD 525	$120-$150
	SCD 535	$150-$190
	DIGITAL VIDEO MONITOR	$150-$180
SAFETY 1ST	CRYSTAL CLEAR	$14
	GLOW & GO	$25/$35
	COMFORT ZONE DIGITAL	$40
	HI DEF MONITOR	$40
	TRUE VIEW COLOR VIDEO	$180
SAMSUNG	EzVIEW	$180
SONY	BABY CALL NTM-910	$40/$70
SUMMER	CLOSE2YOU	$30
	SECURESLEEP	$60
	SLIM & CLEAR	$50/$80
	DAY & NIGHT VIDEO HANDHELD	$160-$180

For 2012, Summer plans to launch their first app-based baby monitor, the Connect Internet Camera Set. This model includes a network
camera (which requires an ethernet connection) that can be viewed
on your iPhone or iPad with a free app. The app can take snapshots
of your baby. Price: $230. This model will be out in early 2012—it will
be interesting to see how this works in the real world.

Bottom line: Summer is the reigning king of video monitors, with
a mind numbing total of 21 offerings in the category. Quality is
good, but competitors like Motorola and Samsung are nipping at
their heals. ***Ratings: A-***

✔= Yes

900 MHz: A higher frequency that eliminates interference
with cordless phones and extends a monitor's range.

DIGITAL: Does the monitor have digital technology?

RECHARG. BATTERIES	DUAL RECEIVERS	900MHz	DIGITAL	VIDEO
✔			✔	
✔			✔	
✔			✔	
	✔ $35 VERSION			
		✔	✔	
			✔	
✔				✔
✔			✔	✔
				✔
✔				✔
✔			✔	
✔			✔	
✔			✔	
✔			✔	✔
	✔ $35 VERSION			
			✔	
✔			✔	
✔			✔	✔
✔				✔
✔	✔ $70 VERSION	✔		
		✔		
✔			✔	
✔		✔	✔	✔

...s.com. This brand is reviewed on our web site,

Our Picks: Brand Recommendations

Summer's Day & Night Handheld Color Video Monitor ($120-$160) features night vision, rechargeable batteries, LED sound lights and 900 MHz technology. A video on/off button turns the monitor into an audio-only monitor at night. In a field crowded by inferior video monitors, this one is the best of the field.

A runner-up would be *Summer's Best View Handheld Color Video* monitor ($175), which has a bigger LCD screen and pan/tilt/zoom feature. Those are nice features, but not completely necessary—it's your call whether they are worth the extra bucks.

Other runners-up in the video monitor sweepstakes: Motorola (Binatone) has a series of video monitors that run $130 to $200 and receive good reviews from parents. The downside: Motorola's night vision is weak. Another alternative is to consider a network cam from Axis or Foscam. It takes some tech skills to set these up, but a network cam give you the ability to view your nursery from a smartphone or computer. In many ways, this is more flexible than traditional video monitors—and you can repurpose the network cam to another part of your house once the nursery monitoring days are over.

Play Yards

The portable play yard has been so popular in recent years that many parents consider it a necessity. Compared to rickety playpens of old, today's play yards fold compactly for portability and offer such handy features as bassinets, wheels and more. Some shopping tips:

◆ *Don't buy a second-hand play yard or use a hand-me-down.* Many models have been the subject of recalls in recent years. Why? Those same features that make them convenient (the collapsibility to make the play yards "portable") worked too well in the past—some play yards collapsed with babies inside. Others had protruding rivets that caught some babies who wore pacifiers on a string (a BIG no-no, never have your baby wear a pacifier on a string). A slew of injuries and deaths have prompted the recall of ten million playpens over the years. Yes, you can search government recall lists (cpsc.gov) to see if that hand-me-down is recalled, but we'd skip the hassle and just buy new.

◆ *Go for the bassinet feature.* Some play yards feature bassinet inserts, which can be used for babies under three months of age (always check the weight guidelines). This is a handy feature that we recommend. Other worthwhile features: wheels for mobility, side-rail storage compartments and a canopy (if you plan to take the play yard outside or to the beach). If you want a play yard with canopy, look for those models that have "aluminized fabric" canopies—they reflect the sun's heat and UV rays to keep baby cooler.

◆ *Skip the "newborn napper."* Graco has recently added a "new-born napper" feature to some of its playpens. This is a separate sleep area designed to "cuddle your baby." You are supposed to use this napper before you use the bassinet feature. Our concern: the napper includes plush fabrics and a head pillow—we consider these an unsafe sleep environment. As we discussed in Chapter 2, Nursery, your baby should always be put down to sleep on his back on a flat surface with no soft bedding. Graco also makes a model (the Chadwick) that has non-removeable bumpers on the

safety

Playpen Bassinets: Naps vs. Sleeping?

As you may remember from Chapter 2, we recommend the bassinet feature of playpens as an alternative to a stand-alone bassinet for newborns.

However, some readers note that manufacturers like Graco advise the product is "intended for naps and play" and question whether a newborn should sleep full time in the bassinet.

We understand the confusion, but here's our advice: when it comes to newborns, there isn't much of a distinction between "naps" and nighttime sleep—day or night, most newborns are sleeping only four hours at a stretch (they need to feed at roughly that interval). Hence, we interpret Graco's advice to only use the Pack N Play for "naps or play" applies more to older babies—the product shouldn't take the place of a full-size crib (but is fine for occasional use at Grandma's house or a hotel room). The bottom line: we believe the bassinet feature is fine for full-time use for newborns who are under the weight limits (typically 15 pounds).

FYI: Be sure to check out some of our recommendations for play yard sheets in Chapter 3. While most parents love their play yards, the cheap-o sheets that come with most are a pain (they slip off the mattress too easily, etc). We discuss alternatives in Chapter 3 that solve this problem.

bassinet. We do not recommend this model play yard for the same reason we don't recommend you use bumpers in a crib.

◆ **Check the weight limits.** Play yards have two weight limits: one for the bassinet and one for the entire play yard (without the bassinet). Graco and most other play yard versions have an overall weight limit of 30 lbs. and height limit of 35" The exception is the Arms Reach Co-Sleeper which tops out at 50 lbs. However, there is more variation in the weight limits for the bassinet attachments. Here are the weight limits for the *bassinet attachments* on various play yards:

Arms Reach Co-Sleeper	30 lbs.
Graco Pack N Play	15 lbs.
Chicco Lullaby	15 lbs.
Compass Aluminum	18 lbs.
Combi Play Yard	15 lbs.

Our Picks: Brand Recommendations

Good. *Joovy's Room2 Portable Play Yard* ($150) has ten square feet of area—twice the size of most standard playpens, giving baby more room to play. No, it doesn't include many other features you see in other playpens (there is no bassinet, diaper changing area, etc). However, it does  what it does well—provide a large, safe area for baby to play. Readers love the easy set-up and heavy weight canvas fabric.

Better. *Chicco's Lullaby LX Play Yard* ($190) is loaded with all the bells and whistles: bassinet, changing station, toys, storage areas, remote control electronics and more. Readers love the quality and ease of set-up for the Chicco playpen, but a few critics  knocked the hefty 30-pound weight (which we admit stretches the definition of a *portable* play yard). And the two gimmicky features (a vibrating mattress that doesn't really vibrate) and a somewhat useless mobile had more than one reader scratching their heads. Overall, however, folks are generally happy with this unit.

Best (for home). Graco is the market leader in this category—and given the value and features they offer, that's no surprise. The company offers a dozen models of playpens and each is well designed. A

good example is the **Graco Pack N Play with Bassinet** ($90), which lacks all the whiz-bang electronics and toys of the Chicco playpen, but then again, is that really needed? It features a bassinet, changing table and wheels. Of course, if you want all the toys and gizmos, Graco has models with those features too—but you'll pay $150 to $200 for those versions. One final caveat: skip the Graco models with "newborn nappers." As we explained earlier, we don't recommend these for safety reasons.

Best (for travel). Baby Bjorn's **Travel Crib Light** ($200 to $250). Not cheap, but this ultra-light play yard folds up like an umbrella and fits in a smaller size carry case. Parent feedback has been universally positive. At 11 pounds, it is half the weight of a standard Graco Pack N Play.

Swings

You can't talk to new parents without hearing the heated debate on swings, those battery-operated surrogate parents. Some think they're a godsend, soothing a fussy baby when nothing else seems to work. Cynics refer to them as "neglect-o-matics," sinister devices that can become far too addictive for a society that thinks parenting is like a microwave meal—the quicker, the better.

Whatever side you come down on, we do have a few shopping tips. First, ALWAYS try a swing before you buy. Give it a whirl in the store or borrow one from a friend. Why? Some babies love swings. Others hate 'em. Don't spend $120 on a fancy swing only to discover your little one is a swing-hater.

When we last wrote on the topic of swings, you still had a choice between wind-up swings and battery-operated models. While you may still find some wind-up models at garage sales or on eBay, most swings sold in stores are battery-operated. On Craigslist, we've seen wind-up swings for as little as $20. Of course, check with the CPSC (cpsc.gov) to make sure a used swing hasn't been recalled. Good news: many swings now also include an AC adapter so you can plug the swing into a wall outlet. This saves tremendously on batteries. Fisher-Price has several options with adapters.

If you are in the market for a new swing, remember this rule: swings eat batteries faster than toddlers can scarf M&M's. Look for swings that use fewer batteries—some use as little as two or three (others up to four).

Swings range in price from $50 to $140. The more money you spend the more bells and whistles you get—toys, musics, etc.

Remember to observe safety warnings about swings, which are close to the top ten most dangerous products, as far as injuries go. You must always stay with your baby, use the safety belt, and stop using the swing once your baby reaches the weight limit (about 25 lbs. in most cases). Always remember that a swing is not a baby-sitter.

Our picks: Brand recommendations

Swings today come in three flavors: full-size, compact or travel. As you might guess, the latter category folds up for easy transport. Each work fine—if you have the space, go for a full-size model. If not, try a compact or travel version.

Who makes the best swings? Here are our picks:

Good. *Kids II's Bright Starts Comfort & Harmony Portable Swing* is a very affordable swing ($40-$60) with six speeds, timer and songs with auto shut-off.

Better. Graco's top-selling swing is the *Sweet Peace Newborn Soothing Center,* ($148-$170) which we discussed earlier in the bouncer section of this chapter. This one is a hybrid between a swing and bouncer and gets very good review from readers.

Best. Fisher-Price has the cradle swing down to a science. The *Fisher Price My Little Lamb Cradle Swing* ($100-$120) allows for both side-to-side and front-back motion, three seat positions and a plush seat. There are six speeds, eight musical tunes and two-position seat recline. FYI: Fisher Price makes many different versions of its cradle swing in prices that range from $100 to $160—the difference is typically fashion and toys. For example, the *Papasan Cradle Swing* ($130) is a reader favorite.

Portable. How about a swing for Grandma's house? We like the *Fisher Price Open Top Take-Along Swing*. This cool swing folds up for portability, making it a good bet for $60 to $70.

Baby Proofing

All parents want to create a safe environment for their baby. And safety begins at the place where baby spends the most time—your home.

Getting Started: When Do You Need This Stuff?

Whatever you do, start early. It's never too soon to think about baby proofing your house. Many parents we interviewed admitted

The Most Dangerous Baby Products

The Consumer Product Safety Commission releases yearly figures for injuries and deaths for children under five years old related to juvenile products. The latest figures from the CPSC are for 2010 and show a 5.6% increase in the number of injuries. The following chart details the statistics:

Product Category	Injuries	Deaths
Infant carries/car seats*	16,900	10
Cribs, mattresses	14,000	41
Strollers/carriages	12,800	1
High chairs	11,500	1
Changing tables	4,300	1
Walkers/jumpers	4,000	1
Baby gates/barriers	3,500	1
Bouncer seats	3,200	1
Portable Baby Swings	2,300	1
Play yards/ Playpens	2,300	12
Bottles/Warmers/Sterlizers	1,900	0
Bath Seats	**	10
Bassinets/Cradles	**	19
Other	3,100	2
Total	**81,700**	**101**

Key:
Deaths: This figure is an annual average from 2006-08, the latest figures available.
* Excludes motor vehicle incidents
** In the CPSC's latest report bath seat and bassinets/cradle injuries were not tabulated due to a low sample size.

they waited until their baby "almost did something" (like playing with extension cords or dipping into the dog's dish) before they panicked and began childproofing.

Remember Murphy's Law of Baby Proofing: your baby will be instantly attracted to any object that can cause harm. The more harm it will cause, the more attractive it will be to him or her. A word to the wise: start baby proofing as soon as your child begins to roll over.

Safe & Sound: Smart Baby Proofing Tips

The statistics are alarming—each year, over 100 children die and millions more are injured in avoidable household accidents. Obviously, no parent wants their child to be injured by a preventable accident, yet many folks are not aware of common dangers. Others think if they load up their house with safety gadgets, their baby will be safe. Yet, there is one basic truth about child safety: *safety devices are no substitute for adult supervision.* While this

---

E-MAIL FROM THE REAL WORLD
A solution for those coffee tables

Reader Jennifer K. came up with this affordable solution to expensive coffee table bumpers.

"When our son started to walk we were very worried about his head crashing into the glass top tables in our living room. We checked into the safety catalogs and found those fitted bumpers for about $60 just for the coffee table. Well, I guess being the selfish person that I am, and already removing everything else dangerous from my living room, I just didn't want to give up my tables! Where do we put the lamps, and where do I fold the laundry?

"My mother-in-law had the perfect solution. FOAM PIPE WRAPPING!!! We bought it at a home improvement store for $3. You can cut it to fit any table. It is already sliced down the middle and has adhesive, (the gummy kind that rolls right off the glass if you need to replace it). The only disadvantage that we've come across is that our son has learned to pull it off. But at $3 a bag we keep extras in the closet for 'touch-ups.'

"Now the novelty has worn off, so I have NOT had to replace it as often. And I'm happy to report that we've had plenty of collisions, but not one stitch!"

section is packed with safety must-haves like gates, you still have to watch your baby at all times.

Where do you start? Get down on your hands and knees and look at the house from your baby's point of view. Be sure to go room by room throughout the entire house. On our web site, BabyBargains.com (click on bonus material), we have room-by-room advice on how to baby proof on a shoestring.

Top 10 Baby Products That Should Be Banned

We asked Dr. Ari Brown, a pediatrician in Austin, TX and co-author of our book *Baby411* for a list of baby products that should be banned. Some are dangerous, others simply foolish and unnecessary. Here is her take:

1 **BABY WALKERS: NO!** There are so many cases of serious injury associated with these death traps on wheels that some countries (including Canada) completely ban baby walkers.

2 **DON'T GET YOUR KIDS HOOKED ON BABY EINSTEIN.** TV and electronic media of any type, even "educational videos" designed for babies, are bad for developing brains. Babies need active, not passive learning, and getting them used to watching TV is a bad habit.

3 **THROW AWAY THE PACIFIER AT SIX MONTHS.** As we discussed in the feeding chapter, pacifiers are now recommended after breastfeeding is well established (about one month). But . . . remember to STOP the pacifier at six months! Your baby needs to learn to fall asleep and/or comfort herself without a crutch.

4 **AVOID EAR THERMOMETERS.** They are notoriously unreliable, and since fever in infants (over 100.3 degrees) could be serious, an inaccurate reading might give parents a false sense of security. Rectal thermometers are the most accurate.

5 **DON'T FALL FOR THE BABY TOOTHPASTE HYPE.** The best way to clean your baby's teeth is to wipe them with a wet washcloth, twice daily. The sweet taste of baby toothpaste encourages your baby to suck on the toothbrush once in his mouth and you can't maneuver it around well.

6 **BEWARE OF NATURAL BABY SKIN-CARE PRODUCTS.** Over 25% of "natural" infant skin-care items contain common allergens including peanuts.

7 **YOU DON'T NEED TEETHING TABLETS** from the health food store. Some of these contain *caffeine* as an ingredient! Save the espresso for kindergarten! In 2010, the Food & Drug Administration recalled Hyland's Teething tablets because they contained belladonna, a potentially toxic substance that can cause serious harm at high doses. Specifically, the FDA found Hyland's Teething tablets contained "inconsistent amounts of belladonna"

Tummy Time Toys: A Waste of Money?

"Friends keep telling me that Tummy Time for my baby is a must. I've heard that my daughter might suffer developmental delays if I don't include tummy time in her day. What is it and why is it so important?"

Do babies spend too much time on their backs? That's one concern parents and child development specialists have brought up in recent years. Before the advent of the Back to Sleep campaign, the SIDS awareness program that encourages parents to put their babies to bed on their backs, babies were more likely to be placed in a variety of positions. Nowadays, however, babies spend an inordinate amount of time on their backs. And some folks wonder if that is causing a delay in creeping, crawling and walking.

The solution is a simple one: just put your baby on her tummy for a few minutes a day when she is awake. Yes, there is research that shows that extra tummy time can help your child reach developmental milestones sooner. But keep in mind that normal babies who don't participate in increased periods of tummy time typically still meet developmental milestones within the normal time period. So there is no need to panic if your baby isn't getting "15 minutes of tummy time daily."

In fact, many parents have noted that their babies hate being on their stomachs. For those babies who object to being on their tummies, you simply don't have to force them. Of course, baby products manufacturers have jumped on this new craze to come up with more stuff you can buy to make Tummy Time more fun. For example, Camp Kazoo, the makers of Boppy pillows (boppy.com) make a **Boppy Tummy Play Pad** for $30. This smaller version of the famous Boppy has a few toys attached to entertain your baby.

You don't need to buy extra stuff to make tummy time successful in your house, however. Save your money and just get down on the floor with your baby face to face. After all, you're the thing in her life she finds most fun, so get down there and spend some quality tummy time with her.

and has received reports of "serious adverse events in children taking this product."

8 **FORGET SIPPY CUPS.** They promote tooth decay because the flow of liquid heads straight to the back of the top front teeth. If your baby hasn't quite mastered drinking from a cup yet, offer her a straw instead.

9 **HANGING MOBILES ARE ONLY FOR NEWBORNS.** Remove all toys and decorations hanging over your baby's crib by the time he or she is five months old. They become hazardous when babies start to pull themselves up and grab for them.

10 **ENJOY THOSE BEAUTIFUL QUILTS AS WALL HANGINGS,** not in the crib.

Safety Gates: Our Picks

Safety gates are needed in four key areas:

◆ **STAIRS**. Gates should be permanently mounted at the top and bottom of stairs.

◆ **NO BABY ZONES.** You may want to gate off the dining room or other areas baby isn't allowed.

◆ **PLAY AREAS.** Some gates can be linked together to form playyards—a space where baby can play, but not escape.

◆ **WINDOWS/FIREPLACES**. Unless you plan to leave your windows closed and locked, safety gates are needed when a window is opened. Fireplaces hearths are another area that need gating.

Gates come in two flavors: hardware or pressure mounted. Hardware-mounted gates are permanently affixed to walls or door openings. Pressure-mounted gates use a spring to create pressure, holding the gate in place. In general, we recommend hardware-mounted gates at the top and bottom of stairs. Pressure-mounted gates are fine for no baby zones.

When it comes to hardware-mounted gates, it is always best to mount the gate's brackets into solid wood (not drywall). Use a "stud finder" (sold in hardware stores) to find wood studs in walls.

Here are specific recommendations by use:

Best stair gate. *KidCo's Safeway Gate* ($60) comes in differ-
ent versions: a steel gate (G20) for straight stair openings and a
model that can be mounted on angled stairways. The latter is available in both steel (G22) or wood (G32). The basic gate fits openings 24.75" to 43.5" and can be used for either stairs or windows.
Reader feedback on this gate is very positive, with fans loving the
ease of installation and small footprint (when open, it doesn't restrict
the stairway). Got a wider opening? Kidco sells an 24" extension of
the Safeway for $34.

Best soft gate. *Evenflo's Crosstown Pressure Mounted Soft
Gate* ($33-$40) is 20" tall and expands from 38" to 60" wide—perfect for funky openings you need to gate. Mesh lets baby see
through the gate. However, this gate isn't designed to be set-up
and removed frequently—it is better to set it up and have the adults
walk over it to access the non-baby zone.

Best play yard gate. Want to create a safe place for an infant to play in
the living room? *The North States
Superyard XT Gate Play Yard* ($50 to
$70) is an expandable panel system that
is 26" high and provides a play area of
18.5 square feet. A two-panel extension

kit ($18) nearly doubles the area. Some readers use this to protect
a Christmas tree from toddlers. Yes, it is all-plastic, but it is durable
enough to corral toddlers. A few parents say it is hard to open and
close the gate (the hinges are tight), but overall, readers give this
play yard solution the thumbs up.

Best fireplace hearth gate.
A fireplace is an obvious place
baby doesn't need to visit—but
how do you protect it? *KidCo's
HearthGate* ($185; model G70) is
pricey but does the trick. It is
29.95" tall and works on hearths

six feet wide by two feet deep; extensions are available for bigger
openings. The HearthGate also includes a walk-through gate.

Best window guard. *Guardian Angel* (angleguards.com) sells
affordable metal window guards that fit just about any type of window. A gate that works on windows 23" to 35" runs about $60 and
is hardware mounted. A must for low-windows your toddler can
access or if you live in a high-rise condo building. Remember

babies can climb furniture and access windows you think are safe—keep them locked or install a window guard. Runner-up: Kidco sells a *Mesh Window Guard* ($40) in case you don't want metal bars over your windows. Another idea: the *Super Stopper* from Parent Units ($9; parentunits.com) is a simple device that suctions on a window, preventing it from opening too far to let a toddler out.

Top 11 Safety Must Haves

To sum up, here's our list of top safety items to have for your home (in no particular order).

◆ *Fire extinguishers* rated "ABC," which means they are appropriate for any type of fire.

◆ *Outlet covers.*

◆ *Baby monitor*—unless your house or apartment is very small, and you don't think it will be useful.

◆ *Smoke alarms.* The best smoke alarms have two systems for detecting fires—a photoelectric sensor for early detection of smoldering fires and a dual chamber ionization sensor for early detection of flaming fires. An example of this is the First Alert "Dual Sensor" ($25 to $35). We'd recommend one smoke alarm for every bedroom, plus main hallways, basement and living rooms. And don't forget to replace the batteries twice a year. Both smoke alarms and carbon monoxide detectors can be found in warehouse clubs like Sam's and Costco at low prices.

◆ *Carbon monoxide detectors.* These special detectors sniff out dangerous carbon monoxide (CO) gas, which can result from a malfunctioning furnace. Put one CO detector in your baby's room and another in the main hallway of your home.

◆ *Cabinet and drawer locks.* For cabinets and drawers containing harmful cleaning supplies or utensils like knives, these are an essential investment. For playtime, designate at least one unsecured cabinet or drawer as "safe" and stock it with pots and pans for baby.

◆ *Spout cover for tub.*

◆ *Bath thermometer or anti-scald device.*

◆ *Toilet locks*—so your baby doesn't visit the Tidy Bowl Man. One of the best we've seen in years is KidCo's toilet lock ($15), an award-winning gizmo that does the trick. Check their web site at kidco-inc.com for a store that carries it.

◆ **Baby gates.** See the section earlier for recommendations.

◆ **Furniture wall straps.** Since 2000, over 100 deaths have been caused by TV's and furniture tipping over onto kids. We recommend you anchor all your large furniture to the wall, especially shelves and dressers in baby's room. Once your child becomes a climber, she'll climb anything so be prepared.

The Bottom Line: A Wrap-Up of Our Best Buy Picks

For baby bathtubs, we like the simple EuroBath by Primo ($30) or the First Years Infant to Toddler Tub with Sling for $18.

When it comes to potty seats, a seat insert like the Baby Bjorn Toilet Trainer ($21) when paired with a step stool is the best bet for most toddlers. For potty chairs, the **Fisher Price Precious Planet Potty** ($15) should do the trick.

What's the best diaper pail? We like the Diaper Dekor and the Diaper Genie best, although they require costly refill packages.

Many find a simple can with regular kitchen trash bags will do the trick.

Stay away from wipe warmers, which have safety concerns.

An activity/bouncer seat with a toy bar is a good idea, with prices ranging from $20 to $60—we like the Fisher Price bouncers best. An affordable alternative: adding a $10 toy bar to an infant seat.

For baby monitors, a simple Graco UltraClear ($23 single, $35 dual) will work for most folks. If you are concerned about interference, consider the Phillips Avent SCD510 ($90-$120), which has rechargeable batteries and DECT technology. Another great monitor with rechargeable batteries is the Sony BabyCall NTM-910 ($40).

Play yards are a great way to keep baby safe, but also provide a place to sleep (bassinet) for newborns. The Graco Pack N Play with bassinet is $90 and does the trick.

Our top pick for swings is the Fisher Price My Little Lamb Cradle Swing ($100-$120), although the Graco Sweet Peace Newborn Soothing Center combines both a swing and bouncer/soother for $148 to $170.

CHAPTER 8

CAR

SEATS

Car Seats: Picking the right child safety seat

Inside this chapter

What's the best car seat for your baby? What is the difference between an infant, convertible or booster seat? We'll discuss these issues and more in this chapter. You'll find complete reviews and ratings of the major car seat brands as well as informative charts that compare the best choices.

Here's a sobering figure: in the most recent year's statistics, motor vehicle crashes killed 1,670 children under age 14 and injured another 200,000. And 100 infants under age one were killed in traffic accidents in 2007.

While the majority of those injuries and deaths occurred to children who were not in safety seats, the toll from vehicle accidents in this country is still a statistic that can keep you awake all night. Just to make you feel a tiny bit better, the lives of 367 children under age five were saved last year because they were in a child restraint.

By law, every state in the U.S. (and every province in Canada) requires infants and children to ride in child safety seats, so this is one of the few products that every parent must buy. In fact you may find yourself buying multiple car seats as your baby grows older—and for secondary cars, grandma's car, a caregiver's vehicle and more.

So, which seat is the safest? Easiest to use? One thing you'll learn in this chapter is that there is not one "safest" or "best" seat. Yes, we will review and rate the various car seat brands and examine their recall/safety history. BUT, remember the best seat for your child is the one that correctly fits your child's weight and size—and can be correctly installed in your vehicle.

And that's the rub: roadside safety checks reveal 80% to 90% of child safety seats are NOT installed or used properly. Although the exact figure isn't known, a large number of child fatalities and injuries from crashes are caused by improper use or installation of seats.

Realizing that many of today's child safety seats are a failure due to complex installation and other hurdles, the federal government has rolled out a safety standard (called LATCH) for child seats and vows to fix loopholes in current crash testing. The results so far are mixed—we'll discuss these issues later in this chapter.

Getting Started: When Do You Need This Stuff?

You can't leave the hospital without a car seat. By law, all states require children to be restrained in a child safety seat. You'll want to get this item early (in your sixth to eighth month of pregnancy) so you can install it in your car before baby arrives.

Sources to Find Car Seats

1 **DISCOUNTERS.** Car seats have become a loss leader for many discount stores. Chains like Target and Walmart sell these items at small mark-ups in hopes you'll spend money elsewhere in the store. The only caveat: most discounters only carry a limited selection of seats, typically of the no-frills models.

E-MAIL FROM THE REAL WORLD
Car seats save lives

"When I was expecting my first child, I used your book extensively. I followed your recommendation for a car seat for my baby. I'm so glad I did because we recently were involved in a potentially deadly accident. My car's left back-side (where my ten-month-old baby was sitting), hit a lamp post. To give you an idea how serious it was, the car door was pushed in nearly a foot and a half.

"My son was riding in his Graco SnugRide infant seat, installed rear facing and attached to its base. He was actually injured by the collision when the door was damaged and the air bag deployed. We rushed him to the hospital where he was found to have superficial skull fractures and minor bruises. Good news: he recovered quickly without any permanent damage. Later, when we showed the hospital staff the photos of the vehicle, they were amazed that our son survived the accident."

2 **BABY SPECIALTY STORES.** Independent juvenile retailers carry car seats, but the selection is often limited by the size of the store (small boutiques may just have one or two brands).

3 **THE SUPERSTORES.** Chains like Babies R Us, Buy Buy Baby and Burlington Coat Factory's Baby Depot dominate the car seat business, thanks to a wider selection of models than discounters. Prices can be a few dollars higher than the discounters, but sales often bring better deals.

4 **ONLINE.** We'll discuss our favorite sites to buy a car seat online shortly, but remember this caveat: Prices are usually discounted, but watch out for shipping—the cost of shipping bulky items like car seats can outweigh the discount in some cases. Use an online coupon (see page 322 for coupon sites) to save and look for free shipping specials.

Best Online Sources

car seats

The web is teeming with both information and bargains on car seats. Here's the best of what's out there.

◆ **NHTSA.** The National Highway Traffic Safety Administration site (nhtsa.gov) is a treasure trove of car seat info—you can read about recalls, the latest news on changing standards and installation tips. Confused about how to use your LATCH car seat? The web site offers instructional videos for both rear and forward facing seats. You can also contact the government's Auto Safety Hotline at 800-424-9393 to ask car seat related questions. Even better: NHTSA now ranks car seats on their *ease of use* (assembly, instructions, securing a child, etc). The most recent report covers over 90 seats, from infant to booster. Note: these ratings do NOT cover how well a seat does in crash tests or compatibility with different vehicles.

◆ **The American Academy of Pediatrics** (aap.org, go to "Parenting Corner") is an excellent resource for buying tips.

◆ **The National Safe Kids Campaign** (safekids.org; click on United States) has a helpful interactive "safety seat guide" that helps you determine which seat is right for the age and weight of the child.

◆ **Safety Belt Safe USA** (carseat.org) has a good site with tips on picking the best seat for your child, as well as the latest recalls and info on child safety seats.

◆ *Our web site* has a message board dedicated to car seats. Plus: we have a brochure called "Buying a Better Car Seat Restraint" produced by a Canadian auto insurance company. This publication (downloadable as a PDF) has excellent advice on buying a seat. For a link to the brochure and the ratings web page, go to BabyBargains.com and click on the "Bonus Material" section.

◆ *Insurance Institute for Highway Safety* booster seat report is linked from our site at BabyBargains.com/boosters.

◆ *Where to buy online.* Our readers' favorite sites to buy car seats at a discount include BabyCatalog.com, Amazon, and Bed Bath & Beyond (owners of Buy Buy Baby). As always, look for a coupon code for additional savings, free shipping and the like. Check out the Bargain Alert message board on our site (BabyBargains.com/coupons) for a regularly updated list of coupon deals and discounts.

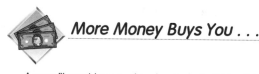

More Money Buys You . . .

As you'll read later in this chapter, all child safety seats are regulated by the federal government to meet minimum safety standards. So whether you buy a $50 seat from Walmart or a $400 brand from a specialty store, your baby is safe. When you pay extra money, however, there are some perks. First, on the safety front, the more expensive seats often have shock-absorbing foam that better protects a child from side-impact collisions. The more expensive seats are also easier to use and adjust . . . and clearly that is a major safety benefit. For infant seats, when you spend more money, you get an adjustable base (which enables a better fit in vehicles), a canopy to block the sun and plush padding.

Speaking of padding, the more money you spend, the cushier the seat—some makers throw in infant head pillows, body cushions and more . . . all of which raises the price. These are not marketed as a safety benefit, but more for the baby's "comfort." The problem? Newborns and infants don't really care. They are just fine in a seat with basic padding (versus the deluxe version). Of course, if you have a super long commute or an older child (say over two years), padding and comfort becomes more of a relevant issue. But for most babies, basic padding is just fine.

 *Smart Shopper Tips*

Smart Shopper Tip #1
So many seats, so much confusion

"I'm so confused by all the car seat options out there. For example, are infant car seats a waste of money? Should I go with a convertible seat? Or one of those models that is good from birth to college?"

Children's car seats come in four flavors: "infant," "convertible," "booster" and "hybrid." Let's break it down:

◆ **Infant** car seats are just that—these rear facing seats are designed for infants up to 35 lbs. or so and 33" in height (weight/height limits will vary; some models only works up to 22 lbs. and 29"). On average, parents get about six months of use out of an infant seat (of course, that varies with the size/height of the child). Infant car seats have an internal harness (usually five-point) that holds the infant to the carrier, which is then snapped into a base. The base is secured to the car. Why the snap-in base? That way you can release the seat and use the carrier to tote your baby around.

◆ **Convertible** car seats (see left) can be used for both infants *and* older children (most seats go up to 40 lbs., but newer models top out at 65, 70 and even 80 lbs.)—infants ride rear facing; older kids over one year of age ride facing forward. Convertible seats have different harness options (more on this later); unlike infant seats, however, they do not have snap-in bases.

◆ **Booster** seats come in three types: hybrid/combo seats, high back and backless boosters. We'll discuss each in-depth in a special section on boosters later in this chapter. In a nutshell, here's how they work: after your child outgrows his convertible seat, the booster correctly positions the safety belt. Most states have laws that require booster seat use until 60 or 80 lbs. (or up to age eight).

◆ **Hybrid** seats. Of course, real life doesn't always fit neatly into these categories—some seats pitch their use from birth to 100 lbs. The most well known is the Safety 1st Alpha Omega (also called the Eddie Bauer Three in One)—the pitch here is one seat that can be used for an infant, toddler and then older child. The Alpha Omega is used rear facing from 5 to 35 lbs., then forward facing 22 lbs. to 40 lbs. From 40 lbs. to 100 lbs. the Alpha Omega converts to a booster seat that uses the auto safety belt to restrain an older child. We'll review this seat later in this chapter. (There will be a quiz on this later as well).

So, does it make more sense to buy one car seat (that is a convertible model) and just skip the infant car seat? There is considerable debate on this subject. Some safety advocates think convertible car seats are safer, pointing to recalls of infant car seats. Others deride infant car seats for their overuse *outside* of a car (as a place for baby to nap), speculating that such babies are at risk for SIDS (Sudden Infant Death Syndrome, discussed in Chapter 2). Fuel was added to this fire in 2006, when a *British Medical Journal* study generated headlines, saying that babies in infant car seats are at risk for breathing problems.

But . . . we analyzed that study and found the researchers examined only nine babies in New Zealand to come up with that conclusion (see our *Baby 411* blog for a detailed discussion). And while babies born prematurely (less than 37 weeks in gestation) are at an increased risk for breathing problems while in a car seat, full term infants ARE NOT. Sure, you should always supervise a newborn in an infant seat (have someone ride in the back seat if possible). And limit your baby's time in an infant seat. But that doesn't mean infant seats are UNSAFE or dangerous for sleeping infants.

On the other side of the debate are advocates who say infant car seats fit newborns better—most are designed to accommodate a smaller body and baby travels in a semi-reclined position, which supports an infant's head and neck. Yes, some convertible seats recline—but the degree of recline can be affected by the angle of your vehicle's seat back.

Furthermore, most babies don't outgrow their infant car seats until six months (and some as late as 12 months, depending the baby's weight and seat's limits)—and that can be a very long period of time if you don't have an infant car seat.

Why? First, it's helpful to understand that an infant car seat is more than just a car seat—it's also an infant carrier when detached from its base. Big deal, you might say? Well, since infants spend much of their time sleeping (and often fall asleep in the car), this *is* a big deal. By detaching the carrier from the auto base, you don't have to wake the baby when you leave the car. Buy a convertible car seat, and you'll have to unbuckle the baby and move her into another type of carrier or stroller (and most likely wake her in the process). Take it from us: let sleeping babies lie and spend the additional $100 for an infant car seat, even if you use it for just six months.

Remember: babies should be REAR FACING until they reach one year of age, regardless of weight. If your child outgrows his infant car seat before one year of age, be sure to use a convertible seat in rear facing mode for as long as possible. Most convertible seats can be used rear facing until baby is 30 to 35 lbs. (depending on the model).

Smart Shopper Tip #2
New standards, new problems?
"I hear there are problems with LATCH. What is LATCH anyway?"

Stop any ten cars on the road with child safety seats and we'll bet eight or nine are not installed or used correctly. That's what road-side checks by local law enforcement in many states have uncovered: a recent study by the National Highway Traffic Safety Administration stopped 4000 drivers in four states and found a whopping 80% made mistakes in installing or securing a child safety seat.

What's causing all the problems?

Many child safety seats have failed parents, in our opinion. Installation of a car seat is an exercise in frustration—even parents who spend hours with the instructions still made mistakes. The number one culprit: the auto seat belt—it is great at restraining adults, but not so good at child safety seats. And those seats simply won't work well if they aren't attached to a car correctly . . . that's the crux of the problem. Simply put, thanks to the quirkiness of auto safety belts (different auto makers have different systems), putting a child safety seat in a car is still like trying to fit a square peg into a round hole. Some seats wobble too much; others can't be secured tightly to the back seat.

The bottom line: some child safety seats simply DON'T FIT in some vehicles. Which cars? Which seats? There is no easy answer. Often, parents find it's trial and error to see what works.

So, that's where LATCH comes in. The federal government rolled out a mandated "uniform" attachment (called LATCH or ISOFIX), required for all vehicles and safety seats made after 2002. LATCH stands for "Lower Anchors and Tethers for Children." ISOFIX stands for International Standards Organization FIX, which is the international version of LATCH.

CAR
SEATS

What is LATCH? Instead of using the auto's seat belt, car seats attach to two anchor bars in the lower seatback. The result: fewer confusing installations, no more locking clips or other apparatus needed to make sure the seat is correctly attached.

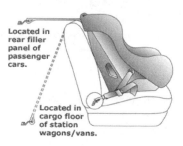

Located in rear filler panel of passenger cars.

Located in cargo floor of station wagons/vans.

(Another part of the new standard: tether straps, which are discussed later in this section.) See picture of a LATCH-installed car seat above.

Here is a sum up of frequent questions we get on LATCH seats:

◆ *Which manufacturers sell LATCH seats?* Answer: all. Every infant and convertible car seat sold now includes LATCH. However, booster car seats aren't required to us LATCH (although a few do).

◆ *Will I have to junk my old car seat?* Yes, car seat safety advocates do NOT recommend using a seat that is over five years old. Why? Belts, clips and interior parts in car seats wear out over time . . . hence, seats over five years old may no longer be safe to use.

◆ *My car does not have LATCH. What is the safest seat I can buy?* All LATCH seats are backward compatible—that is, they can be safely installed and used in older vehicles that do NOT have LATCH anchors. Remember the safest seat is the one that best fits your car *and* your child. There is no one "safest" seat. Get the best seat you can afford (we'll have recommendations later in this chapter) and use it with a tether strap. And get your car seat safety checked to make sure you have the best installation and fit.

◆ *I need to move my LATCH seat to a second car that doesn't have the new attachments. Will it work?* Yes, see above.

◆ *I know the safest place for a baby is in the middle of the back seat. But my car doesn't have LATCH anchors there, just in the outboard positions! Where should I put the seat?* Our advice: use the LATCH positions, even if they are only on the side. Some car seat and vehicle makers say it is okay to use a LATCH seat in the middle of the back seat if you use the LATCH anchors in the outboard positions—check with your car seat and vehicle owner's manual to see if this is permissible.

◆ *I got a LATCH seat that doesn't fit in my vehicle! I thought this was supposed to be universal.* LATCH has been sold to the public as some kind of magic pill that will instantly make all seats fit all vehicles. Hardly. Because of the wide variety of vehicles and seats (a SUV versus a compact, minivan versus pickup), it is unreasonable to expect any system would make this happen. While LATCH helps, it is not the cure-all.

◆ **I find LATCH hard to use.** You're not alone: a recent survey showed that 40% of parents aren't using LATCH. Problems with LATCH include hard-to-reach anchors that are buried in the seat back, making installation a challenge. Some LATCH clips are also easier to use than others. Car seat makers are trying to respond to these issues. Example: Evenflo's new Symphony car seat has an improved LATCH clip that is easier to install.

Smart Shopper Tip #3
Strap Me In

"What is a tether strap? Do I want one?"

Way back in 1999, the federal government mandated that all convertible child safety seats be sold with a tether strap—these prevent a car seat from moving forward in the event of a crash. How? One end of the tether strap attaches to the top of the car seat; the other is hooked to an "anchor bolt" that is permanently installed on the back of the rear seat or on the floor in your vehicle.

Most newer vehicles already have anchor bolts, making the use of a tether strap a snap. (Hint: check your vehicle's owner's manual to find instructions on using tether straps). Older vehicles may have pre-drilled anchorage points—just ask your car dealer for the "anchor bolt installation kit" (a part number that's listed in your owner's manual in the section on installing child safety seats). You can install the bolt or have the dealer do it.

Of course, really old cars are trickier since they lack anchor bolts or even pre-drilled holes—to install the anchor bolt, you may need to drill through your car's sub floor (a job for the car dealer, as you can guess). And just finding out the part number for the anchor bolt can be a challenge; some car dealers are clueless about this issue.

A side note: most seats can only use tether straps when FORWARD FACING. Only four models (the Britax Roundabout, Marathon and Boulevard and the Diono Radian have a tether that can be used in either rear or forward facing positions. Note: tether straps are typically not used with infant seats or booster seats (but always consult your seat's directions for specific advice on this).

So, is the tether strap worth all the hassle? Yes—crash tests show car seats are SAFER when used with a tether strap. The strap keeps the car seat (and hence, your baby's head) from moving forward in a crash, lowering the chance of injury. Unfortunately, parents don't seem to be getting this message: a 2006 survey from the NHTSA revealed that only 55% of parents are using a top tether.

Are seats used *without* tethers unsafe? No, the federal government requires seats to be safe even when a tether is not in use. Of course, the tether adds that extra measure of safety and is always preferable to a tether-less installation.

Smart Shopper Tip #4
One Size Does Not Fit All

"My friend has a car seat that just doesn't fit very well into her car. Does anyone put out a rating system that says which seats are most compatible? Easiest to use? Safest?"

There are two resources to check out: first, CarSeatData.org has a compatibility database—pick a vehicle or seat and read feedback from parents.

Also: the National Highway Traffic Safety Administration rates car seats on their ease of use and posts the results on the web at nhtsa.gov or call 888-327-4236. Note these are not crash test results. NHTSA rates seats on how a seat assembles, installs and secures a child. In the latest report, over 90 seats were rated. The government updates the report every year.

Smart Shopper Tip #5
Recalls

"I saw online that a particular car seat is being recalled. Should I be skeptical of other seats by that manufacturer?"

Here's a sobering fact of car seat shopping: most major brands of car seats have had a recall over the past five years. We've seen recalls on cheap seats sold in Walmart and $300 car seats sold in specialty stores, making recalls a reality no matter what brand you consider. So if all major brands have had recalls, how do you shop for the best seat?

First, understand that some recalls are more serious than others. Some car seats are recalled for minor problems, like incorrect warning labels. Other companies do voluntary recalls when their own testing reveals a problem. The key issue: look to see if there are any injuries associated with the defective product. Obviously, car seats that are so defective as to cause injury to babies are much more serious than minor labeling recalls.

Another issue: how does a company handle a recall? Do they fight the government, forcing regulators to order a recall? Or do they voluntarily recall the item and set up an efficient process to get replacements or retrofit kits to consumers? In the past, we have lowered our ratings for car seat manufacturers who bungled a recall effort.

When a company announces a recall, the product is typically removed from store shelves (if the recall is for the current production run). If the recall is for a product's previous production, you may still see it on store shelves (since the defect may have been corrected months before). That's why it is key to see WHEN the recalled product was manufactured. Of course, different car seats in the same manufacturer's line may be totally unaffected by a recall.

Another tip: make sure to fill out the registration card that comes with any car seat you buy . . . and send it in! In theory, this will get you expedited recall information and repair kits. Also: sign up for a recall email list on Recalls.gov.

Unfortunately, with some car seat makers, even if you fill out a registration card you may not get a recall notice. For more on this problem, see the box on pages 374-75.

Smart Shopper Tip #6
Watch the height limit

"My son isn't anywhere near the 26 lb. limit for his infant seat, but he's so tall I don't think it is safe anymore—he has to bend his legs when we put him in!"

Here's a little known fact about most infant seats: in addition to WEIGHT limits, all infant car seats also have HEIGHT limits. And like everything in the car seat world, each seat has different limits (check the sticker on the side of the carrier—by law, the manufacturer must list both height and weight limits). Once your baby exceeds EITHER the height or weight limit, you should move him to a convertible seat.

One note on this: while the weight limit is important, do one other test if your child is approaching the height limit—is there less than an inch of seat left above baby's head? If so, then move your baby to a convertible seat (facing the rear of the vehicle until they pass one year of age).

With the bigger babies everyone seems to be having these days, this isn't a moot point. A large infant might exceed the height limit BEFORE he or she passes the weight limit. And of course, different seats have different limits (see the seat reviews for specs).

Later in this section, we'll have a chart that lists the height and weight limits of all major infant car seats. See the box "How Big is Normal?" on page 383 for more on this topic.

Smart Shopper Tip #7
Do I have to buy THREE seats?

"My baby has outgrown his infant seat. Can I buy a combo seat that converts to a booster?"

The short answer: yes. Do we recommend it? No. Why? We think the safest place for an infant who has outgrown an infant seat is in a CONVERTIBLE seat in rear facing mode. Leave them there until they are AT LEAST a year of age—longer if they still are under the weight limit. Note: nearly all "combo" seats with five-point harnesses that convert to a belt-positioning booster are FORWARD FACING only seats.

So, what is best? When your child outgrows her convertible seat, THEN we recommend a booster seat (combo or belt-positioning). Now, we realize what you are thinking: have we lost our minds? We are recommending you buy THREE seats for your child: infant, convertible, and then a booster. Wouldn't it be cheaper to get one of those all-in-one seats or at least one that combines the convertible/booster function? No, not in our opinion. The all-in-one-seats (like the Safety 1st Alpha Omega) are generally a poor choice; see review on page 424.

And while those combo boosters are a good choice for a three or four year old child who has outgrown his convertible seat but is not mature enough to sit in a belt-positioning booster, combo seats are NOT good for infants—they often don't recline and have less sleeping support than convertibles.

Smart Shopper Tip #8
European seats

"I saw a cool European car seat online—is that safe or legal to use in the U.S.?

Short answer: no.

Thanks to the web, you can order a car seat from Switzerland . . . or South Africa. Making this more tempting: the belief among some safety advocates that Europe has better car seats than the U.S. or Canada.

But let's do a reality check: European standards are DIFFERENT than the U.S. or Canada. Different does not necessarily mean better, however. European seats are designed to work in European cars, which have different safety features compared to vehicles sold in North America.

Bottom line: it is ILLEGAL (and foolish) to use a seat from overseas here in the U.S. (Ditto for you Canadians—seats must be certified to meet Canadian standards before they can be sold or used in Canada. So if you are a Canadian reading this book, you can't buy a seat in the U.S. and use it legally in Canada.)

Smart Shopper Tip #9
Holding Your Baby Back: Safety Harness Advice
 "Which seats are easiest to adjust?"

You will adjust your baby's car seat's harness two ways: first, you will tighten or loosen it as they grow. And then you will adjust the HEIGHT of the harness as she gets taller.

The best car seats have upfront adjusters to tighten or loosen a harness. Unfortunately, some seats require you to do this from the back of the seat—that is a major pain. We'll note which seats have this feature in the review section of the book.

As for adjusting the height, the best seats have a harness that can be raised without having to re-thread the harness (which requires disassembling the seat to a certain degree). Again, we'll note this feature later in this chapter.

FYI: do not put your child in a bulky coat or snowsuit when sitting in a safety seat. In the case of an accident, the bulky coat might compress, compromising the safety of the seat. At most, only put a child in a thin coat (like a fleece) when they are riding in a child safety seat. (To keep an infant warm, consider a seat cover-up, which goes on the outside of the seat. We'll discuss examples of these products on page 389).

Here are nine more shopping tips for car seats:

◆ *How easily does it recline?* Many convertible seats have a recline feature to make sure baby is at a proper angle. Of course, how easily the seat reclines varies from model to model—and reaching that lever in a rear facing seat may be a challenge. Check it out in the store before you buy.

◆ *No-twist straps.* Better car seats have thicker straps that don't twist. The result: it is easier to get a child in and out of a seat. Cheaper seats have cheaper webbing that can be a nightmare—"twisty straps" are a key reason why parents hate their car seats. Later when we review specific car seat models, we'll note which ones have twisty straps.

◆ *Look at the chest clip.* The chest clip or harness tie holds the two belts in place. Lower-quality seats have a simple "slide-in" clip—you slip the belt under a tab. That's OK, but some older toddlers can slip out from this type of chest clip. A better bet: a chest clip that SNAPS the two belts together like a seat belt. This is more kid-proof.

car seats

CAR SEATS

◆ *Are the instructions in Greek?* Before you buy the car seat, take a minute to look at the set-up and use instructions. Make sure you can make sense of the seat's documentation. Another tip: if possible, ask the store for any installation tips and advice.

◆ *Is the pad cover machine-washable?* You'd think this would be a no-brainer, but a surprising number of seats (both convertible and infant) have covers that aren't removable or machine washable. Considering how grimy these covers can get, it's smart to look for this feature. Also check to see if you can wash the harness.

◆ *Will the seat be a sauna in the summer?* Speaking of the seat pad, check the material. Plush, velvet-like covers might seem nice in the store, but think about next August. Will your baby be sitting in a mini-sauna? Light weight, light colored fabric pads are better than heavier weight, dark fabrics.

◆ *Does the seat need to be installed with each use?* The best

It's Not In the Mail or Email: Finding Out About Car Seat Recalls The Hard Way

As a new parent, you try to do everything you can to make sure your baby is safe. Besides researching which products are safe, many parents also diligently fill out warranty and registration cards with the expectation they will be contacted in case of a future safety recall.

Yet many parents are surprised to learn that baby product companies fail to mail out notices of defective products to registered users. Why? Companies complain that mailing costs are too high—instead they issue a press release to the media, hoping web sites, local newspapers, radio and TV will spread the word about a defective product. No wonder experts estimate the response rate for recalls is an abysmal 50%.

Hello? Is this insane or what? Parents take the time to fill out and mail those registration cards that manufacturers include in product boxes, but for what? Instead of receiving a courtesy email, call or postcard that the car seat you are using might be dangerous, you are supposed to be watching the local news at exactly the right moment to hear your car seat is recalled? Or see page 16A of the local paper?

Last year, the Consumer Products Safety Commission (CPSC) issued 100+ recalls of baby products, including toys. That's more than two recalls per week! So, what can a parent do to keep up with what's safe and what's recalled? Here are our tips:

car seats are "permanently" installed in your car. When you put baby in, all you do is buckle them into the seat's harness system. Yet a few models need to be installed with each use—that means you have to belt the thing into your car every time you use it. Suffice it to say, that's a major drawback.

◆ *Watch out for hot buckles.* Some inexpensive car seats have exposed metal buckles and hardware. In the hot sun, these buckles can get toasty and possibly burn a child. Yes, you can cover these buckles with a blanket when you leave the car, but that's a hassle. A better bet is to buy a seat with a buckle cover or no exposed metal.

◆ *How heavy is it?* This is a critical factor for infant car seats, but also important for convertibles. Why? First, remember you are lugging that infant seat WITH a baby that will weigh seven to ten lbs. *to start.* When your baby outgrows the infant seat, she will weigh 22 to 35 lbs. *in addition to the seat weight!* To help you shop, we

◆ *Track your purchases.* In order to know whether you have a recalled product, you first have to know what you've got to begin with. One parent told us she kept a spreadsheet with the following info for all her baby products: manufacturer, model, serial number, date manufactured, company phone number/web site, where purchased and price paid. Okay, perhaps that's a bit overboard for most parents. But at least put all your receipts and product manuals into a file or shoebox. The goal: create ONE place you go to when a recall is announced.

◆ *Stay informed.* Register for free email alerts about recalls. Our blog (BabyBargains.com/blog) tracks the latest recalls. We can send you a text message or email when a product is recalled—enter your email and click subscribe when you are on the blog page. Of course, the Consumer Products Safety Commission also emails out recall notices—sign up at Recalls.gov or CPSC.gov.

◆ *Consider buying products from web sites that will inform you of recalls.* Case in point: Amazon does a good job of letting customers know of recalled products. One reader was amazed when Amazon sent her a recall notice (with detailed instructions on what to do) for a bassinet she bought over a year ago.

◆ *Be careful with second-hand purchases.* We don't recommend buying a used car seat off Craigslist. But if you insist, do a search of the NHTSA's web site (nhtsa.dot.gov) to make sure the seat isn't recalled.

car seats

list the weights for major infant car seat brands later in this chapter. What about convertible seats? If you buy one seat and plan to move it from car to car, weight may be a factor here as well.

◆ *Buying a new car?* Consider getting a built-in (also called integrated) child safety seat, which is a $200 to $400 option on vehicles like minivans. This is an option for parents who have a child who is older than one year of age and heavier than 20 lbs. The only caveat: most integrated seats lack side-impact protection and may not fit small children well. Of course, offerings vary by maker. For example, Volvo offers an integrated booster seat ($500 for two seats) that has won kudos for its innovative design.

Safe & Sound

1 **NEVER BUY A USED CAR SEAT.** If the seat has been in an accident, it may be damaged and no longer safe to use. Bottom line: used seats are a big risk unless you know their history. And the technology of car seats improves every year; a seat that is just five years old may lack important safety features compared to today's models. (And, as we discussed earlier, seats older than five years also have parts that may wear out and fail . . . a big reason not to use an old seat). Another tip: make sure the seat has not been recalled (see the contact info on page 379 for the National Highway Traffic Safety Administration). Safety seats made before 2000 may not meet current safety standards (unfortunately, most seats aren't stamped with their year of manufacture, so this may be difficult to determine). The bottom line: risky hand-me-downs aren't worth it. Brand new car seats (which start at $50) aren't that huge of an investment to ensure your child's safety.

2 **GET YOUR SEAT SAFETY CHECKED.** No matter how hard you try to buy and install the best seat for your child, mistakes with installation can still occur. There's nothing like the added peace of mind of having your car seat safety checked by an expert. Such checks are free and widely available. The National Highway Traffic Safety Administration's web site (nhtsa.dot.gov) has a national listing of fitting/inspection stations.

3 **DON'T TRUST THE LEVEL INDICATOR.** Yes, many infant car seats come with "level indicators" and instructions to make sure the seat is installed so the indicator is in the "green" area. When in the green, the seat is supposedly at the correct angle to protect your baby in case of a crash. Nice idea, but thanks to the myriad of back seat designs in dozens of cars, the seat may be incorrectly installed even if the indicator says it is fine. At car seat safety checks, many techs ignore the level indicator and instead use this test: They

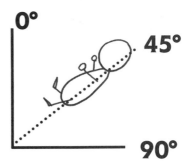

take a piece of paper and fold one corner to form a 45-degree angle. Then they place the side of the paper against the back of the infant car seat where the baby's back would lie. When the folded corner is level with the horizon, the seat is at the correct angle—even if the indicator says it ain't so. If you aren't sure your seat is installed to the correct angle, take it to a car seat safety check.

4 **FORGET CAR SEAT ADD-ONS.** We've seen all manner of travel "accessories" for kids in car seats, including bottle holders, activity trays and so on. The problem: all these objects are potential hazards in an accident, flying around the car and possibly striking you (the adult) or your child.

5 **HOW TALL IS TOO TALL?** You'll notice that most child safety seats utilize two types of limits: weight and height. It's the latter limit that creates some confusion among parents. Convertible seats have both a rear and forward facing height limit—this is required by federal law (for those inquiring minds, the standards are FMVSS 208, 213, 225). Most safety techs say the maximum height for a child is when their head is one inch below the top of the shell (the 1″ rule) or if your child's shoulders exceed the height of the top harness slot. The problem: some car seat makers have more strict height limits than the 1″ rule. Here's the frustrating part: kids often outgrow the seat's stated height limit *before* they reach that 1″ rule or their shoulders are taller than the top harness slot, leaving some parents to wonder if they should continue using the seat. The problem is one of interpretation: while the federal law requires every seat to have height limits, car seat makers are free to interpret this rule (and usage of the seat). Some seat makers just interpret the rules more strictly than others. Bottom line: while we understand seat makers might have their own take on federal safety standards, it is generally safe to use a seat until your child's head is 1″ below the top of the seat or their shoulders exceed the top harness slot—even if their height is slightly above the stated limit for the seat.

6 **READ THE DIRECTIONS VERY CAREFULLY.** Many car accidents end in tragedy because a car seat was installed improperly. If you have any questions about the directions, call the company or return the car seat for a model that is easier to use. Another tip: read your vehicle's owner's manual for any special installation instructions. Consult with your auto dealer if you have any additional questions.

What's the number-one problem with car seat installation? Getting a tight fit, say safety techs. Make sure the safety seat is held firmly against the back of the car seat and doesn't wobble from side to side (or front to back). One tip: put your knee in the seat and push down with your full weight while you tighten the seat belt or LATCH strap. This eliminates belt slack and ensures a snug installation.

7 **KEEP YOUR CHILD REAR FACING AS LONG AS POSSIBLE.** Safety experts agree that the longer a child is rear facing, the safer the child is in an accident. Why? Newborns and even young toddlers have undeveloped neck muscles—this can lead to an injury, especially if a child is forward facing in an accident. Good news: more and more seats have higher rear facing limits. Several infant car seats now work to 30 or 32 lbs. rear facing. And many convertibles also work up to 33 lbs. or even 40 lbs. rear facing. The take home message: keep your child rear facing as long as possible (to age two or three if you can).

8 **PUT THE CAR SEAT IN THE BACK SEAT.** Air bags and car seats don't mix—several reports of injuries and deaths have been attributed to passenger side air bags that deployed when a car seat was in the front seat. As a result, the safest place for kids is the back seat. In fact, whether the car has an air bag or not, the back is always safer—federal government statistics say putting a child in the back seat instead of the front reduces the risk of death by 27%.

And where is the safest part of the back seat? Safety experts say it's the middle—it is the furthest away from side-impact risks. The only problem with that advice is that some cars have a raised hump in the middle of the back seat that makes it difficult/impossible to safely install a car seat. Another problem: safety seats are best held against the car's back seat by a three-point belt—and some middle seats just have a two-point belt. Finally, consider the LATCH problem we noted above (where many vehicles have no LATCH anchors in the middle of the back seat, only the sides). Bottom line: while the middle of the back seat is the safest spot, sometimes you just can't install a seat there. The next best place is in an outboard position of the back seat with a lap/shoulder belt.

What about side curtain air bags you see in the back seats of

some cars? Many new cars come equipped with̶ ̶ ̶ ̶ ̶
bags or curtains. These air bags are NOT as dangerous as front air
bags, as they deploy with much less force in the event of a side
impact crash. Therefore, putting a car seat next to a door that has
a side curtain air bag is not a danger.

9 **REGISTER YOUR SEAT.** Don't forget to send the registration
card back to the manufacturer. Yes, earlier we discussed how
some manufacturers fail to send notices to registered users when a
car seat is recalled (instead, relying on a media announcement) . . .
but register your seat anyway just in case.

10 **PICKUP TRUCKS ARE OFTEN NOT SAFE FOR CAR SEATS.** "A
pickup truck should not be considered a family vehicle,"
concluded an article by the Children's Hospital of Philadelphia on
car seat safety—and we agree. Why? "Children in the rear seat of
compact extended-cab pickups are nearly five times as likely to be
injured as children seated in the back seat of other vehicles,"
according to a study by Partners for Child Passenger Safety, sponsored by the same hospital.

Of course, not all pickup trucks are alike. Some larger pickup
trucks with full-size rear seats do allow car seats (check your vehicle
manual for advice). Depending on the vehicle maker, pickup trucks
with these seats are called SuperCrew, Double Cab, Crew Cab or
Quad Cab. However, pickup trucks with jump seats should NEVER
be used with car seats—these are often referred to as Extended Cab
or SuperCab trucks. If your pickup truck does not have a rear seat
and you must use the front seat (again, not recommended), you
must disable the passenger-side air bag.

Even if your pickup truck has a full-size rear seat that allows for
car seat installations, think twice about using this vehicle with car
seats. Again, studies show that all passenger cars are generally safer
in an accident (for kids in a car seat) compared to pickup trucks.

11 **CONSIDER SEATS WITH SIDE IMPACT PROTECTION.** About 25%
of all vehicle accidents are side-impact collisions. Over the last
few years, more and more seats have been adding side-impact
protection. This would be especially important if your vehicle does
not have rear-curtain airbags to protect rear occupants. Yes, these
seats tend to cost a bit more than those without side-impact protection, but we think it is a wise investment.

Recalls

The National Highway Traffic Safety Administration (NHTSA) posts recalls online (nhtsa.dot.gov) and has a toll-free hot line to check for recalls or to report a safety problem. Call (800) 424-9393 or (202) 366-0123. You can have a list of recalled car seats automatically faxed to you at no charge (in case you don't have online access). Note that this is a different governmental agency than the Consumer Product Safety Commission, which regulates and recalls other juvenile products.

Money-Saving Secrets

1 TRACK AMAZON PRICES. Baby gear prices on Amazon often rise or fall with little notice. Tracking web sites like CamelCamelCamel.com will send you free email alerts when prices drop. You can also look up historical price charts (a Firefox plug-in lets you see this even while looking at the Amazon pages). We tracked the Britax Marathon and noticed the prices ranged between $210 and $280 in the past six months. And we saw Amazon drop the price on a Combi infant car seat by 21% in the past week.

2 GET A FREE SEAT! A reader emailed in this great tip—her health insurance carrier provides free infant car seats to parents who complete a parenting class. No specific class is required . . . you just provide proof of completion. And health insurance providers aren't the only ones with car seat deals—check with your auto insurance provider or employer as well. Some companies sell discounted car seats as a family-friendly perk, so check that too.

3 IF YOU HAVE TWO CARS, YOU DON'T NEED TO BUY TWO INFANT SEATS. Instead, just buy one seat and then get an extra stay-in-the-car base. Major infant seat makers sell their auto bases separately for $40 to $70. Retail stores rarely carry these bases; you'll probably have to buy an extra base online.

4 COUPONS! Find the latest coupons and discounts by popping over to our Bargain Alert message boards (BabyBargains.com/coupons). Right at the top, we keep a pinned thread with a list of the best online coupon codes, discounts and deals. The thread is updated regularly, so come back to visit when you need a code.

5 EXPENSIVE MODELS AREN'T NECESSARILY BETTER. If you spend $200 on a car seat, are you getting one that's twice as safe as a seat that's $100? Not necessarily. All car seats must meet federal minimum safety standards. In fact, we will recommend a simple

Cosco Scenera, which costs $40 to $60 as a good bet for your second car or Grandma's vehicle.

So what do you get when you spend more? First, plusher fabric and padding. That doesn't have anything to do with safety—it's more comfort. Based on our research, extra padding isn't worth the extra money for infant car seats; however, for convertible seats or boosters, we can see the point (especially for longer trips). That's because older infants and toddlers are more likely to notice skimpy padding than newborns.

Also when you spend more you get a car seat that is easier to adjust (and that is a major plus and safety advantage). And some of the most expensive seats have added side-impact crash protection, again worthy of the extra investment.

6 **LAST YEAR'S FASHION.** Car seat makers frequently discontinue fashions (not the seat, just the fabric). Look for closeouts and save. Example: we saw a closeout pattern for a Britax seat for 40% off on Amazon.

The Name Game: Reviews of Selected Manufacturers

Here are our reviews of the major car seat brands. FYI: many of the infant seats reviewed here are sold as travel systems that combine a car seat and stroller; the strollers are reviewed separately in the next chapter. Of course, you don't have to buy a travel system—nearly all infant seats are sold separately.

Special note: this section gives you an overview of each brand; we review each model seat separately later in this chapter!

The Ratings

 A **EXCELLENT**—*our top pick!*
 B **GOOD**— *above average quality, prices, and creativity.*
 C **FAIR**—*could stand some improvement.*
 D **POOR**—*yuck! could stand some major improvement.*

Baby Trend *babytrend.com.* Baby Trend sells both infant car seats and booster seats, the latter of which is new in the past year. Unfortunately Baby Trend, the company, has been dogged by poor customer service and other glitches. Example: the availability of Baby Trend's car seats has been inconsistent in recent years. And

Baby Trend recently had to declare bankruptcy after losing a multi-million dollar jury verdict in a patent dispute.

Safety Track Record. There have been no recalls on these seats as of this writing.

Baby Trend's infant seat is on page 391, boosters are on page 441.

Britax *britax.com.* European-car seat maker Britax came to the U.S. car seat market in 1996 and changed the rules of the game: the company introduced several premium car seats that were packed with extra safety features . . . and sold at premium prices. Britax was the first seat maker to cross the $200 price level (and some of its seats now top $300).

Britax's success is due to both its innovation (side impact crash protection, a tether can that can be used in rear or forward facing position) and ease of use. On that latter score, Britax's seats are easy to install (they are a favorite of safety techs) and simple for parents to use (the harness adjustments, etc).

Britax recently rolled out a new generation of its best-selling convertible seats, which now work to higher weight limits. The new seats feature deeper sidewalls for side-impact protection and a redesigned shell that features technology to absorb more energy in a crash.

While Britax has seen success in the convertible seat category, its efforts in other areas have fallen somewhat short. Britax's infant car seat (the Chaperone) has struggled against competitors like Graco and Chicco, although the company came out with a lower-price infant seat (B-Safe) in the last year. The weakness in infant seats has hampered Britax's efforts in the stroller market.

Meanwhile, Britax has had more success in booster seats, with a revised Frontier gaining ground against rivals in the past year.

Safety track record: Despite its emphasis on safety, Britax hasn't been immune to recalls for production defects and other snafus—the company has had several major recalls in the past ten years (including a recall in 2010 for the Chaperone infant car seat). But the company has handled these responsibly, offering repair kits and fessing up to its mistakes in a timely manner.

Britax infant seats begin on page 392. Britax's convertible seat reviews begin on page 408; booster seat reviews begin on page 441.

Chicco *chiccousa.com* Chicco makes an infant car seat (KeyFit) and a booster (Strada). While well known in Europe, Chicco took a while to get traction in North America. But their KeyFit infant car seat has been a smashing success in recent years.

Safety track record: In 2008, Chicco recalled 18,000 infant car seats for defective bases.

Chicco's infant car seat is reviewed on page 394; booster seat is on page 445.

How big is normal?

A quick glance at the "average" growth charts for infants makes you realize why kids outgrow their infant seats so quickly. Some infant seats are only rated for babies up to 22 lbs. and 29" in height. The average male infant hits 22 lbs. at about nine months (at the 50th percentile). But for boys at the top of the growth chart, that could happen at a mere six months! Girls are of course a bit behind that curve, hitting 22 lbs. on average at 12 months of age (at the 50th percentile). Girls at the top of the chart might hit 22 lbs. as soon as eight months.

When a child outgrows his infant seat, he must go into a convertible seat—and there is the rub. Safety advocates say babies should be rear facing to one year of age and AT LEAST 20 lbs. Our advice: make sure the convertible seat you buy is rear facing to at least 30 lbs. Or purchase an infant seat with a weight limit of at least 30 lbs.

What about height? Boys hit 29" at around ten months (again the 50th percentile). But some really tall baby boys can hit 29" as soon as eight months. For girls, the average age when most infants hit 29" is 12 months, but it can happen as soon as eight months.

Bottom line: some kids may outgrow their seats by HEIGHT long before they hit the weight limit.

And here's the take home message: keep your child REAR FACING as long as possible, given your seat's limits. It is the safest way for them to ride. *Source: National Center for Health Statistics, www.cdc.gov/ growthcharts.*

Combi *combi-intl.com.* While better known for its strollers, Combi is also a small player in the car seat market. The main emphasis here is on infant seats that pair with Combi strollers to form travel systems, although Combi does sell a couple of convertible and booster seats as well.

Combi's infant car seat is the Shuttle, which works with most of Combi's strollers.

In the convertible seat category, Combi has a couple of niche offerings. The Zeus, which rotates from rear to forward facing without having to reinstall it, has an anti-rebound bar and side impact protection. The Coccoro is a compact convertible that can fit three seats across in most vehicles.

In the booster category for older kids, Combi has the Kobuk Air-Thru.

Safety track record. Combi has had several major recalls in recent years, including a recall of all its infant car seats in 2008.

Combi's infant seats are reviewed on page 395. Combi's convertible seats are reviewed on page 413; boosters are on page 446.

Cosco djgusa.com. Owned by Canadian conglomerate Dorel Industries, Cosco is a big player in the car seat market with over six million seats sold each year. As one blogger once put it, Dorel/Cosco puts the industrial in the Baby Industrial Complex.

Dorel/Cosco sells its seats under a variety of brand names: Eddie Bauer, Alpha Elite, Alpha Sport, Safety 1st and Maxi Cosi, which is a European division.

In previous years, Cosco would take the same basic seat, change the fabric pad and sell it under various brand names, depending on the outlet. Hence, you'd see the same seat sold in Walmart under the Cosco brand, an upgraded version in Target sold under the Safety 1st nameplate and then a top-of-the-line model sold under the Eddie Bauer moniker at chains like Babies R Us.

Realizing parents aren't likely to be fooled by such small distinctions, Cosco told us they plan to make each brand more unique. So, you'll see basic seats under the Cosco name in discount stores . . . but Safety 1st car seats will now have brand-specific technology like "Air Protect" (side-impact technology).

Perhaps Cosco's most unique brand is the Maxi Cosi line of car seats—since these are imported (and designed) by Cosco's European division, these seats aren't simply rehashes of Cosco's domestic seats. The Maxi Cosi car seats pair with a line of strollers under the Quinny brand (another Dorel Euro import).

Safety track record: Cosco's safety track record has been marred by recalls—20+ at last count since 1990. Now, you could point out that since Cosco is the largest seller of car seats in North America, it follows the company would have more recalls than a smaller competitor. True, but it is the *type* of safety lapses that bother us.

Example: Cosco allegedly sold hundreds of thousands of Touriva convertible seats AFTER the company knew a plastic notch in the seat caused skull fractures in low-speed crashes. That allegation came to light in a 2007 investigation by the *Chicago Tribune* (July 14, 2007, "When car-seat safety, commerce collide"). Despite Dorel's own engineers labeling the notch a "child safety concern," Dorel continued to make Tourivas with the notch for three years. Why? The *Tribune* alleges that Cosco didn't want to shut down its production lines (losing roughly $4 million in Touriva sales) to switch molds to a notch-less seat.

For the record, Dorel maintains it did investigate the notch allegation and its own testing confirmed "these recesses will not injure a child." When asked point blank if it delayed fixing the Touriva to rack up extra sales, the company replied: "The suggestion that Dorel would sacrifice the safety of children for a few extra dollars of profit is insulting and not worthy of further comment."

Yet, this isn't the first time Cosco allegedly put profits ahead of safety—in 1996, the American Academy of Pediatrics told parents NOT to use shield boosters (a type of booster seat that uses a shield to hold a child in place) because of numerous injuries. Yet Dorel/Cosco continued to sell shield boosters until 2004, selling ten million of the $20 boosters in a 20-year period. Cosco has settled dozens of shield-booster lawsuits (without admitting fault), according to the *Chicago Tribune.*

Cosco's infant seat is reviewed on page 396, while Cosco's convertible seat reviews start on page 414. Cosco's booster seats are reviewed starting on page 447.

Diono *diono.com.* Formerly Sunshine Kids. Diono's key entry in this category is a combination convertible seat plus booster called the Radian. Available in versions that work up to 100 or 120 pounds, the Radian the only folding car seat on the market. Diono accomplishes this by omitting the typical base you see on a convertible seat—this clever design trick makes the Radian perfect for car pools.

In the past year, Diono rolled out upgraded versions of the Radian, with a version that now adds side impact protection (the Radian RXT).

In addition to their convertible seats, Diono also has two entries in the booster category: the Monterey, which features a deep seat with width adjustment and a backless booster called the Santa Fe.

Safety track record: No recalls as of this writing.

Diono's convertible seat is reviewed on page 415; the booster on page 448.

Eddie Bauer. *See Cosco.*

EPP vs. EPS foam

When you take the fancy fabric cover off a car seat, you'll notice that many car seats are lined with foam for crash protection. Car seat makers use two types of foam: EPS and EPP. EPS (expanded polystyrene foam) is the hard yet lightweight foam used in bicycle helmets. EPP (expanded polypropylene foam) is similar to EPS but softer (and hence more comfortable) for older toddlers. The take-home message: either foam is fine, but more makers are using EPP foam as an upgrade.

Evenflo *evenflo.com.* Evenflo has struggled in this category, thanks to a string of disastrous recalls and other snafus. Yes, Evenflo has tried to add innovative features (mostly to their convertible seats), but the company has had a tough time overcoming its poor reputation in the marketplace. All in all, Evenflo often seems outflanked in the car seat market; Britax trumps them on safety features and Graco outguns them in infant seats and travel systems. Even downscale Cosco has a hotter license (Eddie Bauer).

Judging from parent reviews posted to our web site, Evenflo has a ways to go to win the hearts of car seat buyers. Ease of use (or lack thereof) is a common gripe, with seats that have difficult-to-adjust belts and other frustrations.

In recent years, Evenflo has been rolling out seats with side-impact technology, dubbed e3. As the name implies, e3 has three layers of foam and is seen on Evenflo's high-price seats.

Safety track record: Evenflo's safety track record is mixed, with many recalls of their infant car seats during the past 15 years. Example: the 2008 recall of one million Discovery infant seats that separated from their bases in a crash. This followed a 2006 recall of the Embrace infant seat for defective handles that unexpectedly released, causing some infants to tumble out of the seat. If that sounds familiar, you may remember the huge recalls of Evenflo infant car seats from the 1990's for a similar issue.

In 2010, Evenflo recalled Maestro combination toddler booster seats after *Consumer Reports* said the seat failed their crash tests.

That new car seat smell?

Given all the toy recalls for lead paint and the general anxiety among parents regarding environmental hazards, it's no surprise that environmental groups have turned an eye toward that one safety item everyone must buy: the car seat.

HealthyCar.org tested dozens of car seats for toxic chemicals, measuring the amount of bromine, chlorine and lead and assigning ratings from low to high concern.

The results showed some car seat makers do a better job at keeping toxic chemicals to a minimum. Example: Diono scored at the top of the ratings for the "healthiest" car seats—that's probably thanks to the company's intentional efforts to use a unique flame-retardant treatment that nearly eliminates out-gassing.

Other companies had a mix of good and bad news: Britax generally scored well, but a couple of Britax fabrics (specifically Onyx) had high levels of bromine.

You can see the entire results at HealthyStuff.org.

Reviews of Evenflo's infant seats start on page 398, while Evenflo's convertible seat reviews start on page 417. Evenflo's booster seats are reviewed on page 449.

First Years thefirstyears.com. These seats debuted in 2004 under the name Compass, but the company lacked the marketing clout to compete with the big boys like Britax and Graco. Hence it wasn't much of a surprise when baby gear and toy maker Learning Curve acquired Compass in 2007. The Compass name is now limited to booster seats; the company uses The First Years brand for infant and convertible seats.

The line includes an infant seat (the Via), a convertible (True Fit) and a booster (the Folding Booster car seat). The company's niche seems to be car seats that are a step up in features, safety and design from the mass market brands like Dorel/Cosco . . . but priced below the premium that Britax charges.

Despite the new corporate parent, these seats are still hard to find in retail stores (but are sold online).

Safety track record. First Years/Compass recalled the I420 infant car seat in 2006 because of a defective harness strap.

First Years' infant seat is reviewed on page 400; convertible seats are on page 420; booster seats on page 452.

Graco gracobaby.com. Graco's success in the car seat market boils down to one model: its best-selling infant seat, the SnugRide. That gave Graco a major leg-up in the travel system market (travel systems combine both an infant car seat and stroller). As a result, when you walk into chain stores, you'll see many Graco car seats.

Graco has had less success with its convertible seat line, which has struggled to compete against Britax. To amp up the competition, Graco has focused on higher-weight limit seats in recent years. In 2012, Graco releases several new seats with enhanced side impact protection called Safety Surround.

In the booster seat category, Graco has had a home run with its TurboBooster and Nautilus seats.

Safety track record: Compared to brands like Dorel/Cosco and Evenflo, Graco's safety record is good. That doesn't mean Graco is perfect, of course—there have been nine recalls in the past decade. In 2008, Graco recalled 277,000 convertible seats for a mis-assembled anchor belt. Four years prior to that recall, Graco recalled 650,000 SnugRide infant seats for missing hardware used to attach the carrier to the base. Most of Graco's recalls have been for minor issues (incorrect labels, etc).

Graco's infant seat is reviewed on page 401. Graco's convertible seat is reviewed on page 421. Graco's booster seats are reviewed starting on page 453.

Harmony *harmonyjuvenile.com* Montreal, Canada-based Harmony is a small manufacturer of booster car seats. Its two models (Baby Armor and Dreamtime) are belt-positioning boosters reviewed later in this chapter. Despite winning an industry innovation award in 2009, the company has little distribution in the U.S.

Kiddy *kiddy.de* German juvenile product company Kiddy plans to launch a couple of booster seats in the U.S. in the coming year. Their unique feature: an energy absorbing shield that the company claims offers the best impact protection in a head-on collision. Check our web site for updates on this brand.

Orbit *orbitbaby.com* "High style" aren't two words you'd normally associate with a travel system, that combination of infant car seat and stroller often sold in discount stores. Orbit's aim is to take the travel system to the next level. The brainchild of two Palo Alto-based designers, Orbit started out with an infant car seat and stroller and has been slowing expanding, adding a toddler car seat and, in 2012, a booster.

Described on a parenting blog as looking like a crock-pot (bummer that we didn't think of that first), the Orbit infant seat has two soft carrying straps and is only sold as part of a system (base and stroller) for a whopping $900.

Orbit has updated the infant seat and stroller with a series of small improvements, dubbed G2. There is also a toddler car seat ($360) that "docks" with its car base and fits on the stroller frame.

While we give Orbit bonus points for creativity, the high price of this seat sharply limits its appeal.

Safety track record: Orbit got into a spat with *Consumer Reports* in 2009, after the magazine deemed its infant seat unsafe. Orbit disputed the findings and the government (that is, the NHTSA) declared the seat safe. CR then pulled this report off its web site, but still says the seat is a safety risk. A detailed report about this is archived on our blog.

The Orbit infant seat is reviewed on page 404; toddler seat is on page 425; the booster is on page 456.

Peg Perego *perego.com.* Peg's key entry in this category is an infant car seat, the Primo Viaggio. Launched to stop the loss of stroller sales to cheaper "travel systems," the Viaggio has gone on to be quite a hit, despite its relatively high price tag (about $100 more than Graco's popular seat). Chalk that up to Peg's sense of style (the Viaggio features luxury Italian fabrics) and pairing with

Peg's popular strollers. In recent years, Perego has only made a few small modifications to the seat, most notably adding side impact protection.

Peg is expanding their car seat offerings in 2012 with their first convertible car seat and even a high-back booster. Confusingly, Peg calls all its car seats the Primo Viaggio. So there will be a Primo Viaggio infant seat and a Primo Viaggio convertible seat, for those scoring along at home. And the booster seat is called, wait for it, the Viaggio High Back Booster.

Safety track record: Peg had a 2009 recall on its infant seat for sharp plastic edges that cut some babies. Other than that, the company has had a good safety track record.

Peg Perego's infant seat is reviewed on page 405; convertible seat is on page 425.

Radian *See Diono.*

Recaro *recaro.com.* Recaro is a 100-year old German-based company well known in Europe for their racing seats and other safety gear. After watching Britax's success on this side of the Atlantic, Recaro decided to give the U.S. market a try. So far, Recaro has had

---

Seat cover-ups provide warmth

Okay, you aren't supposed to put baby in a car seat with a bulky coat. But what if you live in, say, Maine and it's currently ten degrees outside as you read this? Try a cover-up that fits OVER the car seat and hence doesn't compromise the seat's safety. One of our favorites: **Kiddopotamus's**  *"Poppit"* ($28), a multi-purpose cover-up that can be used as a front carrier warmer. . . or on top of a car seat. The same company also offers several other innovative travel products, including the RayShade (a cover for strollers).

What about other infant body pillows or warmers that fit between baby and the car seat? If it does not come in the box with your infant or convertible car seat, we wouldn't use it. Add-on or after-market products that are not manufacturer-tested may compromise the seat's safety. The same thing goes for car seat toy bars or special mirrors so you can see baby from the front seat. Don't use them in a vehicle—they could come loose in an accident, becoming a dangerous projectile.

---

limited success in cracking the market (their prices are on the high end), but we give them credit for persistence as well as rolling out innovative models. "These seats scream quality," said one of our readers—you can tell when you take a Recaro seat out of the box that the company does NOT skimp on construction details. So if you can afford it, we suggest giving these seats a look-see.

Recaro recently moved most of its car seat production to Michigan; at the same time, it changed its model names. Now the convertible seats are called ProRIDE, the combo seats are ProSPORT and boosters are ProBOOSTER. FYI: The Vivo and Euro are made in China.

Recaro's distribution is a bit thin in retail stores; seeing it in person can be a challenge.

Safety track record: Recaro had a recall on its convertible seats (Signo and Como) in 2007 for defective harnesses. This recall was extended in 2009 to cover more seats.

Recaro's convertible seats are reviewed on page 426 and booster seats start on page 457.

Safety 1st *See Cosco.*

Summer *summerinfant.com.* Summer Infant is probably best known for its video monitors, but it has been slowly expanding into

---

What is the lightest infant car seat carrier?

Here at *Baby* Bargains, we have Ivy League-trained scientists who help us determine important stuff like which infant car seat weighs the least (and hence, is easiest to lug around).

Oh, we're just kidding. Actually, we the authors just went to our local baby store and stood there in the aisles lifting each infant seat and saying things like "Yep, this one is lighter!" For this edition, we actually employed a scale to get accurate readings (and you thought only the folks in lab coats at *Consumer Reports* got to play with such toys). Our official results: the lightest seat is the Evenflo Discovery (5.5 lbs.) followed by the Safety 1st Envoy Air (9.4 lbs.). The heaviest seats? That crown goes to the Orbit at 12 lbs and Britax Chaperone (11.2 lbs). The Combi Shuttle and Peg Perego Primo Viaggio were close behind at 11.1 lbs.

We list the weights for infant car seat carriers in a chart on page 430. Of course, the weight of an infant seat isn't the only factor we used to decide which was best, but it certainly is important.

other gear categories. The latest: infant car seats. The Summer Prodigy features a slew of new technologies, including a harness than automatically adjusts for the height of your child. Also new: SmartScreen tells you whether you have installed the seat correctly. Since Summer is brand new to this category, there is no safety track record here yet.

Summer's infant car seat is reviewed on page 406.

Teutonia teutoniausa.com. Owned by Graco, this German brand of strollers has a matching infant car seat (the t-tario 32), which is the same as the Graco SnugRide.

Infant Car Seats (model by model reviews)

APRICA A30

Comments: The Aprica A30 is the infant seat sold as part of the Aprica Moto travel system. The seat is the same as the Graco SnugRide 30, but adds upgraded fabrics.

BABY TREND FLEX-LOC

Price: $80 to $130. Extra bases $40.
Limits: 30 lbs. and 30″
NHTSA ease of use rating: ★★★★☆
Pros: Top rated seat in recent crash test.
Cons: Carrier is quite heavy; hard to find in some stores—mostly sold as part of a travel system with an inferior stroller.
Comments: Baby Trend's Flex-Loc features a four-position height adjustable base and EPS foam for head protection. Some models come with a boot for extra warmth.

The downsides? Well, the carrier is quite heavy (9.4 lbs.). And, confusingly, Baby Trend markets two versions of this seat, one that works to 22 lbs. and one to 30 . . . except they go by the same name (Flex-Loc). More criticism: the handle release button can be hard to reach and stiff to release. And the strange triangle handle takes a bit of getting used to.

Baby Trend advertises this as the #1 rated infant car seat—we assume they are referring to a 2007 report from *Consumer Reports* that named the seat a "Best Buy." But that was 2007 . . . in CR's most recent report, the Flex Loc dropped to seventh out of ten infant car seats. We would probably attribute this to the seat starting to show its age—the Flex-Loc hasn't been updated in years.

CHAPTER 8: CAR SEATS   391

CAR
SEATS

While we will recommend this seat with an above-average grade, we should note that Baby Trend is a company with a checkered history. As of press time, the company is still languishing in bankruptcy after it lost a multi-million dollar verdict in a patent dispute. Baby Trend's customer service, or lack thereof, is also disappointing. Unanswered emails, un-returned phone calls and a general "we don't care" attitude mar Baby Trend's brand.

Just to confuse you, Baby Trend sells a 22 lb. limit version of this seat as the EZ Flex-Loc (some sites just call it the Flex-Loc so check the weight limit to make sure which seat you're getting). This seat has the same latch straps, but some versions don't have a height adjustable base. *Rating: B-*

BRITAX B-SAFE
Price: $140-$180 **Limits:** 4-30 lbs., 32"
NHTSA ease of use rating: ★★★★☆
Pros: Under $200, lighter carrier. Side-impact protection, tangle-free harness.
Cons: Omits rebound bar and no-rethread harness found on Britax Chaperone, not compatible with most strollers.

Comments: Britax has always finished back in the pack for infant car seats, thanks to its slow-selling models. One big reason: price. The brand's flagship model (the Chaperone) is $230 at retail (though often discounted below $200 online).

We gave the Chaperone a B in our ratings—we liked the innovative features (anti-rebound bar, no-rethread harness), but the heavy carrier weight (11.2 pounds), lack of compatible strollers and high retail price are major drawbacks.

Given the state of the economy, Britax decided to scale back the Chaperone and lower the price. The result: the B-SAFE, a less-expensive version of the Chaperone that clocks in $180 (which matches the price of the Chicco KeyFit 30), or $50 less than the Chaperone.

So what are the trade-offs? The B-SAFE omits the anti-rebound bar and no-thread harness of the Chaperone—those were key features that impressed us. The anti-rebound bar is an excellent safety feature, but most seats with this feature haven't really caught on in the U.S. On the plus side, the B-SAFE is lighter than the Chaperone (9.6 lbs) and the base is shorter, so those of you with small cars should find it easier to fit compared with the bulky Chaperone.

Another negative: while the B-SAFE has basic side-impact protection, the Chaperone features adjustable, "True" side impact protection wings.

Real world feedback on the B-SAFE has been positive overall. Compared to the Chicco KeyFit, Chicco gets higher marks for ease of install, but the Britax has better fabric (albeit only two choices) and a superior canopy. As for fit, it is probably a tie.

One major consideration for this seat: stroller compatibility. If you are getting a Britax stroller, then this infant seat or the Chaperone would be a no-brainer. As for compatibility with other strollers, well, that's going to be hit and miss (mostly miss). Fewer strollers are compatible with Britax's infant seat, compared with Graco and Chicco.

The bottom line on the B-SAFE: overall this seat is a winner. We like the lower price and weight. But if you are getting a Britax stroller, it might be worth the extra $50 to splurge on the Chaperone for the anti-rebound bar and no-rethread harness. *Rating: A-*

BRITAX CHAPERONE
Price: $180-$195 Type:
Limits: 4-30 lbs., 32"
NHTSA ease of use rating: ★★★★☆
Pros: Anti-rebound bar, side-impact protection, EPS foam.
Cons: Price, not compatible with most strollers.

Comments: Britax's previous infant car seat, the Companion, was a critical success but commercial flop. The seat drew kudos from safety techs for its design, which included an anti-rebound bar, side impact protection and ease of installation. We gave it an A- in our last book. But at $200, it's high price and low weight limit (22 lbs.) doomed the seat. And the lack of compatibility with strollers made it a no go. So does the new Chaperone fair better? The Chaperone works up to 30 lbs. and is compatible with a Britax stroller to make a travel system. So has Britax hit a home run?

Yes and no. While we like the anti-rebound bar and no re-thread harness, this seat has a major problem: it is too darn big to fit in many vehicles. Its long base may make it a difficult install, even in a midsize car. And with the carrier clocking in at 11.2 lbs. empty, it is significantly heavier than most infant seats. Mix in the nearly $200 price tag, the fact most strollers don't have an adapter for this seat and you can see why the Chaperone has not been a top-seller.

That said, Britax has released a new series of strollers (reviewed in the next chapter) that are finally breathing life into the Chaperone's sales.

Bottom line: for parents who have a big enough vehicle, this seat is a winner, earning praise for its ease of use. So it is a mixed review for the Chaperone. *Rating: B*

Chicco KeyFit 30

Price: $155-$180, extra base $70-$80.

Limits: 4-30 lbs., 30"

NHTSA ease of use rating: ★★★★☆

Pros: EPS foam, newborn insert, adapters available to work with other strollers.

Cons: Skimpy canopy. Large base may be tight fit for smaller vehicles.

Comments: The Chicco KeyFit scored at the top of *Consumer Reports* latest car seat report and that has helped propel the sales of this already popular seat into best-seller status. It is well deserved.

The Chicco KeyFit boasts a nice list of features: a seat lined with EPS foam for improved side impact protection, thick seat padding, multi-position canopy and comfort grip handle. Chicco hired a former Graco engineer who worked on the SnugRide to design the KeyFit and it shows in the details . . . the base has a "single-pull" LATCH adjustment, a leveling foot to account for uneven back seats

Leaving On a Jet Plane

Which car seats can be taken on an airplane? Most of the infant and convertible seats reviewed in this section are certified for use in an airplane. But will they fit? That's a tougher question—each airline has different size seats. Hence, wide car seats like the Evenflo Triumph may not fit (especially if you're required to keep the armrests down for take-off). Check with the airline before you get to the airport if you have questions about car seat compatibility. A better bet: simple seats like the Graco ComfortSport (which is narrow and light in weight) usually do the trick.

Here's a listing of convertible car seats with the narrowest bases: Cosco Scenera (16.5"), Evenflo Tribute (16") and Combi Coccoro (16"). By comparison, a seat like the Britax Advocate is 21.5" wide.

FYI: There is a way to avoid lugging your own car seat on a plane: the FAA has approved the first child safety harness for airlines, the *AmSafe Aviation Cares* (KidsFlySafe.com). This $75 seat can be purchased online and provides additional belt and shoulder harnesses for a child weighing 22 to 44 lbs.—perfect for infants that have outgrown their infant seat (and for parents who don't want to lug a heavy convertible seat in the airport).

and even a smooth underside to keep from damaging your back seat upholstery. As you'd expect from Chicco, the fashion of this seat boasts Italian flair and there is even a newborn insert for a better fit.

Our readers have been very positive about the KeyFit's ease of use, lauding the no-twist, easy-to-adjust straps, the ability to leave the handle in the up position when driving (most seats require it to be lowered), and overall ease of installation. Quibbles? The KeyFit carrier weighs 9.4 lbs., a tad heavier than other similar seats. It takes two hands to release the handle on the seat. And the sunshade is too small. A few readers also report the fabric doesn't breathe, so the seat can get hot.

Perhaps the biggest drawback to the Chicco KeyFit 30 is the large base, which may not fit in smaller vehicles. And more than one reader complained that the KeyFit doesn't fit into shopping carts you see in grocery stores.

FYI: Chicco makes two versions of the KeyFit—one that works to 22 lbs. (called the Key-Fit) and one to 30 lbs. (KeyFit 30). Between the two, we'd suggest the 30 lb. version. And also note: the same base works with either the 22 lb. or the 30 lb. carriers.

In recent years, more stroller companies have rolled out adapters for the KeyFit and that's great news. Of course, you can also use it in Chicco's strollers, which are generally well regarded.

Overall, this is an excellent seat that is highly recommended.
Rating: A

COMBI SHUTTLE 33
Price: $160-$180. Extra base: $70.
Limits: 33 lbs., 33"
NHTSA ease of use rating: ★★★★☆
Pros: EPS foam, one-pull harness adjustment, nice padding. Works to 33 lbs.
Cons: Complex belt path and puzzle buckle. Large seat.

Comments: The Combi Shuttle works to 33 lbs. and features EPS foam for crash protection, comfort pads on the harness and one-pull harness adjustment. The seat has an anti-rebound bar, which keeps the seat more stable in the case of a crash.

In the past year, Combi has improved the Shuttle's base, making it smaller and easier to use, thanks to a new locking clip design. But the belt path on the new Shuttle base had us scratching our heads: it is way too complex compared to other seats. FYI: The latest Shuttle works to 33 lbs. and 33"—earlier versions worked to just 22 lbs.

All of Combi's strollers work with the Shuttle infant seat, with the odd exception of Combi's own stroller frame (the Flash), now discontinued.

Reader and expert feedback on the Shuttle 33 has been mixed. *Consumer Reports* ranked it second in a recent survey of seats, giving it above average remarks for ease of use and crash protection. Readers weren't so generous, with numerous complaints about the anti-rebound bar (baby's feet can caught on the bar when being put in the seat) and the complex puzzle buckle, which more than one reader said requires three hands to buckle (ok, that's an exaggeration, but we can see the point). The carrier is also heavy at 10.1 lbs. Fans of the seat like that the handle can be left in the upright position when in a vehicle. But be forewarned: the Shuttle is a large seat that won't fit into some smaller vehicles (and even mid-size sedans).

Overall, readers gave the Shuttle merely average marks—for the same money, folks felt the Chicco KeyFit was better made and easier to use.

Regarding safety, Combi's track record has been mixed, with several major recalls in recent years. Example: a 2008 recall for 67,000 Shuttle and Centre seats after testing revealed the seats could separate from the base in a crash. ***Rating: C+***

COSCO COMFY CARRY
Price: $60; extra base $35.
Limits: 22 lbs., 29"
NHTSA ease of use rating: Not rated.
Pros: Low price.
Cons: Base isn't adjustable; no level indicator. Very basic seat.

Comments: This is Cosco's newest, low-price infant seat. Like the Cosco Starter, it features a 22 lb. weight and 29" height limit. And that's about it: the base isn't adjustable, nor is there a level indicator. The only difference we see between this and the Cosco Starter are lower side walls on the base, which Cosco says enables it to be lifted out of the base easier. This seat was brand new as of this writing, so parent feedback yet.

As usual, Dorel makes different versions of this seat, marketed under their Cosco and Safety 1st brands. Here's an overview:

The Cosco Comfy Carry: $60. As we mentioned above, it is rather bare bones: no head support insert, the harness adjusts from the rear and the base is non adjustable. Sold at Walmart and online retailers.

The Safety 1st Comfy Carry Elite: $70. This version adds a head support insert and front harness adjuster. Available in chain stores like Sears, Toys R Us, etc.

The Safety 1st Comfy Carry Elite Plus: $80-$90. All the features of the Elite plus an adjustable base and upgraded fabrics. This model is available from Amazon and BabiesRUs.com. Of all the versions of the seat, this is probably the best bet as we prefer the adjustable base and front harness adjuster. ***Rating: Not Yet***

CYBEX ATON

Price: $200-$230
Limits: 4 to 32 lbs., 30".
NHTSA ease of use rating: ★★★☆☆
Pros: Light carrier weight, very easy to install. Short shell might fit compact cars better than others.

Cons: Funky canopy has skimpy coverage. Steep price tag.

Comments: German baby gear maker Cybex launched in the U.S. in 2009 with a brightly colored stroller line that largely flopped in stores (see review in our stroller section). But the company is still trying to crack the U.S. market. And since the key to stroller success in the U.S. requires a popular infant car seat, Cybex rolled out the Aton in May 2011.

The Aton has a striking, Euro-minimal look (complete with the

The NYC Taxi Dilemma

Here's a common email we get from parents in New York and other urban areas: are there any portable car seats that can be used in taxis? Something that is lightweight, easy to install and collapses to fit inside a small purse when not in use? Well, the answer is no—there's no perfect solution. But we have a few ideas. Let's break out our advice for New Yorkers by age:

◆ *Infant (birth to six months).* The safest way for an infant to ride in a taxi is in an infant car seat. Most (but not all) can be strapped in without the stay-in-the-car base. However, always check the manual BEFORE buying any seat to confirm this feature.

◆ *Babies/toddlers (six months to four years).* Many infant car seats can be used up to 30 or 32 pounds—use the seat as long as you can. For older babies, there aren't many good options. If you use a car service to go to or from an airport, you can usually request a car seat in advance. Otherwise, using public transport is probably the safest option.

◆ *Older kids.* A booster seat is the safest way to go—and a simple backless booster such as the Graco TurboBooster (backless version) is lightweight and portable.

infant seats

bright colors so adored for baby gear over there), but its key features are a secure belt-tightening system and sleek hidden canopy. Safety-wise, the Aton's steel base-to-car seat connectors provide a rock solid installation. You also get infant inserts (a newborn inlay for babies up to 11 lbs. and an infant insert for babies up to 22 lbs.) and a padded harness. Of course, the Aton snaps into most Cybex strollers to form a travel system (there are also adapters for Maxi Cosi strollers). In fact, you can use Maxi Cosi adapters made for other strollers with the Aton.

What's not to like? Well, the seat shell is rather short—about 17" for the seatback. That compares to 20" for most other seats (like the Britax Chaperone, Graco SnugRide, etc.). So some larger babies might outgrow the seat before they reach 32 lbs. On the plus side, the shorter shell might work better for small, compact vehicles.

So is it worth the steep $200+ price tag? Well, we like the carrier's light weight (8.8 lbs). And early reports from parents say the seat is very easy to install.

But the Aton's canopy gets mixed reviews. Folks like how it hides away and its fabric quality. But the coverage is rather skimpy compared to other brands. And we worry the giant piece of plastic that borders the canopy might break after extended use.

Since this seat has only been on the market for such a short time and with little real world feedback, we'll wait on assigning a rating. **Rating: Not Yet.**

Evenflo Discovery 5

Price: $55 to $60; extra base $25.
Limits: 22 lbs., 26"
NHTSA ease of use rating: ★★☆☆☆
Pros: Lightweight carrier, low price. Z-shaped handle is easy to carry.
Cons: Not easy to use.

Comments: This bare-bones seat is sold in discount stores like Walmart. The carrier (at 5.5 lbs.) is one of the lightest on the market. And yes, Evenflo has added EPS foam to the seat (a few years after the competition). But . . . you don't get many features with this seat—the base doesn't adjust, there is just one crotch strap position and so on. Want to adjust the straps? You'll have to do that from the back of the seat, a major pain.

And the list of negatives goes on: the handle must be in the down position when travelling in a car, an extra step that takes up extra space. Amazingly, a version of this seat first debuted in 1998, yet it is still on the market (albeit, in an updated form). Using a car seat with 90's technology is hard to imagine, considering all the advances in child passenger safety since then.

That probably explains why the Evenflo Discovery scored at the very bottom of *Consumer Reports* most recent report on infant car seats—that report weighed ease of use heavily in their rankings. And our feedback from parents is similar: yes, this seat is cheap, but in this case, you get what you pay for. ***Rating: F***

EVENFLO EMBRACE
Price: $65 to $70; extra base $35.
Limits: 22 lbs., 29″
NHTSA ease of use rating: ★★★☆☆
Pros: Three-position adjustable base, easier to release base and handle.
Cons: Recalled in 2007 for faulty handle.

Comments: Here, in a nutshell, is why Evenflo is in last place in the car seat biz: the Embrace infant seat was supposed to be a fresh start for Evenflo, after their last major car seat (the PortAbout) was recalled for failing a crash test back in 2005. The Embrace features a new, easier release mechanism for the carrier (this was a gripe for past models). The seat also has a three-position adjustable base and Z-handle with the "Press 'n' Go" system that releases the handle with one hand.

Yet, Evenflo had to recall 450,000 Embrace infant seats in 2007 after 679 reports of the handle of the carrier unexpectedly releasing, causing 160 injuries to children. (As a side note, 679 reports? 160 injuries? At what point did Evenflo think it was time to pull the plug?).

As for ease of use, the Embrace scored second to last in *Consumer Reports* most recent infant car seat rankings; Evenflo's Discovery 5 was in last place. The Embrace was judged better for crash protections than the Discovery 5, but otherwise ranked far behind the competition. Another example: the Embrace only works

Fabric vs. Model Names

When shopping for a car seat online, you'll note that some sites refer to seats by their fabric AND model name. For example, Amazon sells the Britax Roundabout Davenport. Britax is the manufacturer; Roundabout is the model name; Davenport is the fabric.

In this section, we refer to brands and models of car seats—since color or fabric patterns change frequently, we don't reference this. Just beware that a seat like the Graco Metropolitan SnugRide and Graco Family Tree SnugRide (as examples) are basically the same seat. Yes, the fabric might be fancier on one version, but you are talking the same basic seat! When we recommend a seat like the Graco SnugRide, our recommendation applies to all the fabrics/versions of that seat.

infant seats

to 22 lbs., while many competitor's seats go to 30 or 35 lbs.

About the best we can say for this seat is it is a bit easier to install and use than the Evenflo Discovery . . . but that's not saying much. Given the past safety issues with this seat and Evenflo's track record, we say pass. **Rating: D+**

EVENFLO SERENADE
Also known as the Secure Ride 35
Price: $128 to $145.
Limits: 35 lbs.; 29"
NHTSA ease of use rating: ⭐⭐⭐⭐⭐
Pros: Upgrades include infinite slide harness for easier adjustments.

Cons: $140 for an Evenflo seat?

Comments: This is Evenflo's top of the line model—the Serenade works to 35 lbs. and features Evenflo's "SureLATCH" technology for quicker installation. An infinite slide harness adjust and upgraded canopy round out the features. Evenflo claims this seat is side impact tested; Evenflo has tests for a side-impact crash similar to the ones used by the government for vehicles. But since there is no federal side impact standard, it's hard to know how this seat compares to other models that also claim side impact protection.

Consumer Reports testing of the Serenade puts it in the middle of the pack, with very good crash protection but only fair "fit to vehicle" when secured with a safety belt. Reader feedback on the Serenade has been mixed. On the one hand, the Serenade is much better than the Evenflo Discovery or Embrace—but that's a low bar to cross. And the $140 price tag has some folks wondering if Evenflo has hidden a stroller (or lottery tickets) in the box somewhere, as one wag put it. It's hard to imagine spending this much money on an infant car seat from a brand that is such an also-ran in the infant car seat business.

FYI: This seat is also marketed as the SecureRide 35 e3—basically the same seat, but with added side impact protection.

Bottom line: this seat is much better than Evenflo's other offerings, but the company still has a way to go to compete with the top sellers in this category. **Rating: Not Yet.**

FIRST YEARS VIA
Price: $150-$170
Limits: 5-35 lbs.
NHTSA ease of use rating: ⭐⭐⭐⭐⭐
Pros: Carrier is completely lined with foam. Widest, deepest carrier. Light weight.
Cons: Must use carrier with base. Doesn't fit

into shopping carts or stroller frames.

Comments: The First Years Via is a very good infant seat . . . which is impossible to find in most retail stores. That, in a nutshell, is what is wrong with The First Years and their efforts in this category. When the company bought out Compass in 2007, we had high hopes they'd expand distribution of Compass' innovative (yet under-marketed) seats. But two years later, the seats languish in no man's land.

Take the Via, which features a carrier entirely lined in EPS foam (yet still weighing only 8.4 lbs.), a padded handle, side impact protection, washable pad, height adjustable base and more. We like the built-in belt lock-off for non-LATCH installations and steel-on-steel construction for latching the carrier to the base (some cheaper seats use plastic hooks, which can break and have led to past recalls).

Consumer Reports ranked this seat third out of eight seats that work to 22 lbs. in a recent ranking, with "very good" marks on crash protection and ease of use. Feedback from our readers has been similar—most folks love this seat.

The downside? The First Years Via doesn't work without its base (hence this isn't the best choice for urban dwellers who want to use it on the go in a taxi), nor is it compatible with most stroller frames. On the plus side, the newest versions of the Via now work up to 35 lbs. (older models were just 22 lbs).

Amazon is one of the few places you can find this seat for sale.
Rating: A-

GRACO SNUGRIDE 30, 32, 35

Also known as the Teutonia t-tario, Aprica A30
Price: $77-$160; extra base $50.
Limits: SnugRide: 22 lbs., 29"; SnugRide 30: 30 lbs., 30"; SnugRide 32: 32 lbs., 32"; Snug Ride 35: 35 lbs., 32"
NHTSA ease of use rating: ★★★☆☆

Pros: Lightweight carrier (for the base model), level indicator, canopy, easy to use. Front belt adjuster on some models. Works with many strollers.

Cons: Only one crotch position.

Comments: Here is the country's top-selling infant car seat—and it deserves the crown. The Graco SnugRide is an affordable infant seat with excellent features: EPS foam lining, adjustable base and good fit in most vehicles.

Heads up: Graco sells four versions of the SnugRide. See above for the weight and height limits for each version. With so many versions, check the box or online description carefully if you want the higher weight model.

The overall reader verdict on the SnugRide: thumbs up. For ease of use, the SnugRide earns good marks. The few complaints centered on the "annoying" handle, which takes two hands to lower. And be aware of the harness adjuster: the cheapest SnugRides require you to adjust the harness from the back. Our advice: buy a model with a FRONT adjuster, which is much easier to use.

As always, Graco makes a zillion versions of the SnugRide with the main difference being the fabric. A simple SnugRide in discount stores runs $85, while plusher versions with boot can top out at $160. One tip: newborns don't really care how much padding there is in the seat—that's really an issue for older kids in convertible seats. Hence, the less-expensive SnugRides are just fine.

So which SnugRide should you get? We'd suggest the 30, 32 or 35. If the ultrasound says your going to have a big baby, consider the 32 or 35. We'd skip the SnugRide that works to 22 pounds, as that is typically too small for today's babies.

FYI: be aware the SnugRide 32/35 is a heavier carrier (9.5 lbs. versus 8 lbs. for the basic version).

New for 2012: the SnugRide 35 will come with an infant insert cushion for babies as little as four pounds (up from the previous 5 lb. starting limit). Parents of preemies, take note.

Are there trade-offs between the SnugRide and more expensive seats? Well, the SnugRide does lack extra side-impact protection like you see on the Peg Perego and Britax seats. And the seat lacks an anti-rebound bar, seen on the Britax and Combi seats. More than one reader complained about the crotch position on the SnugRide— with only one position it is harder for larger, older babies to fit.

On the other hand, one big advantage to getting the ever-popular SnugRide: it is compatible with a wide range of strollers and stroller frames, many more than other brands.

One negative note: *Consumer Reports* recent ranking of infant car seats only ranked the basic SnugRide in the middle of the pack, while the SnugRide 32 and 35 ranked dead last. "Fair" fit to vehicle using a safety belt and average crash protection held down the SnugRide 32 and 35 seats.

That probably brings up a good point: Graco could beef up the side impact protection of these seats. That doesn't mean the current models are unsafe; but when the competition is racing ahead in terms of side impact protection, you could see how other seats would edge out the Graco SnugRide in such crash tests. Hence, we would recommend this seat if your car already has side-curtain airbags in the rear seats; if not, consider a seat like the Britax, Chicco or Perego with added side-impact protection.

Despite those points, overall, this seat is a winner—good crash test ratings, excellent ease of use and features. Add in the affordable price and we have a winner. ***Rating: A***

MAXI COSI MICO

Price: $150-$180.

Limits: 22 lbs., 29″

NHTSA ease of use rating: ★★★★☆

Pros: Works with Quinny strollers, EPP foam, four harness heights, deep side wings.

Cons: Canopy doesn't stay up, pricey for what is essentially a Cosco seat.

Comments: Cosco imports this seat from their European subsidiary, adapted for the U.S. market and designed to work with its Quinny strollers. This seat is sold in both specialty stores and chains, but not discounters.

Reader feedback has been mixed: fans say it is easy to use and install, plus the EPP foam is softer than the EPS foam you see on most other seats.

Detractors hate the canopy (which does not stay in place) and the large handle that is awkward to carry. Dorel suffered a black eye for the Mico when 28,350 seats were recalled in 2009 for a defective base attachment system.

In the past year, the feedback on this seat has trended in a more positive direction. Fans point out that even though the weight limit is 22 lbs., it is one of the biggest seats (the shell is longer) compared to other 22 lb. seats. And at eight pounds, the carrier is among the

Chocolate donuts with sprinkles?

Here's a confusing thing about car seat shopping: most car seat makers offer their models in a plethora of versions. At one point a couple of years ago, one infant seat maker had FIVE different versions of the same seat: the Classic, Plus, Elite, Supreme and the Extra Crispy. Okay, there wasn't an Extra Crispy, but you get the point. The key thing to remember: the seat was basically the very same seat in each configuration, just with minor cosmetic variations (an extra bit of padding here, a pillow there, etc). Yes, sometimes there are more significant variations like a five-point harness (versus three-point) or an adjustable base. But often there isn't much difference. Think of it this way: car seat makers produce a chocolate donut and top it with different color sprinkles—the rainbow sprinkle version goes to Walmart, the green sprinkle donut goes to Target, etc. That way the companies can offer "exclusives" on certain models to large retailers, so the chains don't have the same exact offerings. But remember this: basically, it's the same donut. Bottom line: don't get caught up in all the version stuff. If the basic seat has the features you want, it doesn't really matter whether you buy the Plus or the Elite. Or the Extra Crispy.

infant seats

lighter weight options out there. The Maxi Cosi scored second in *Consumer Reports* latest infant seat crash tests; and the government gives this seat a four star rating for ease of use.

So we'll tick up the rating a bit this year—but we still think spending $170 on what is essentially a Cosco car seat seems a bit overdone. ***Rating: B***

MAXI COSI PREZI INFANT SEAT

Comments: This seat will be released in May 2012 and come in two versions: regular ($229) and premium ($249), the latter of which features an "easy-out" harness. This is a harness that is lined with a foam pad that enables you to quickly get baby in and out of the seat. With a weight limit to 30 lbs., the Prezi will have an antirebound bar and five-position adjustable base, as well as a no-rethread harness. FYI: The Prezi isn't replacing Maxi Cosi's previous infant seat (the Mico), but is an addition to the line.

MIA MODA CERTO

This seat is reviewed on our web site, BabyBargains.com.

ORBIT

Price: $900, as part of a travel system with stroller frame. $400 sold as a stand-alone seat.
Limits: 4-30 lbs., 32"
NHTSA ease of use rating: ★★★★☆

Pros: Well, it is stylish.
Cons: Did we mention it is sold as part of a travel system that's $900?
Comments: Orbit is a start-up company that aims to inject a bit of cache into the travel system market. Their first offering, the Orbit Baby Infant System, includes an infant car seat, in-car base and stroller frame that attempts a Bugaboo-like vibe. The infant car seat is a bit strange looking (one parenting blog compared it to a crock pot), with an innovative soft-strap handle and rotating base. We liked Orbit's "SmartHub" base technology, that lets you "dock" the seat at any angle. The base also has a front knob that ensures a tight fit to the vehicle.

The feedback on the Orbit has been mixed. Fans love the Orbit's technology and ergonomic design. Tall parents particularly love the tall handles; others love how it is a conversation starter with other parents.

But . . . detractors point out the bulky 12 lb. carrier is beyond HEAVY, providing a serious upper body workout as baby gets bigger. The limited 22 lb. weight limit means larger babies are going to outgrow the Orbit seat quickly (the company does sell a toddler car seat, more on that later). The bulk of the Orbit seat makes for a tight fit in smaller cars.

And let's get real for a second: does anyone really need to spend $900 on an infant car seat and stroller frame? Most babies will outgrow the Orbit infant car seat at six months or earlier. Then you have to pony up another $200 for a toddler stroller seat. So that means you are now spending a total of $1100. (A new bassinet cradle that docks to the stroller frame is another $280).

In the past year, Orbit began offering the infant car seat separately, for an eye-popping $400.

So, it's a mixed review for the Orbit. Kudos to the company for their innovative features and design. But let's do the math. You could buy an Orbit system for $900. . . or buy a Graco Snugride for $150 plus a stroller frame for $50 and take the $700 savings and start a college fund for your infant.

FYI: Orbit got into a spat with *Consumer Reports* magazine in 2009 after CR reported the Orbit infant seat failed its safety tests. Orbit disputed the results and the government (NHTSA) weighed in, declaring the seat safe. *Consumer Reports* removed the report from its site, but still brands the seat as not recommended. See our blog for an archived review of the controversy. ***Rating: B***

PEG PEREGO PRIMO VIAGGIO SIP 30/30
Price: $225-$300. extra base: $60.
Limits: 5-30 lbs., 30"
NHTSA ease of use rating: ★★★★☆
Pros: Matches Perego's hot-selling strollers. Side impact protection, auto harness adjustment, improved canopy, luxe fabrics.
Cons: Price.

Comments: Peg Perego has had much success in this category, despite the seat's high price tag. Some of that success can be chalked up to Peg's slow but steady improvements to the Primo Viaggio. In recent years, the company has added side impact protection, an automatic adjustable harness and a better canopy to the seat, which now works up to 30 lbs. and can be used with or without the base.

Of course, a big part of Peg's mojo here is their Italian fabrics and style—plus the fact this seat mates with many of Peg's fashionable strollers. The luxe Italian fabrics are sharp, but most of Peg's competitors have caught up in the looks department in recent years.

As for ease of use, most of our readers give the Viaggio good marks, although not quite as high as the Graco SnugRide. Negatives include a bulky, heavy carrier that clocks in at 11.1 lbs.

Obviously, the price of the Viaggio is its biggest drawback—Peg has let the price of this seat creep dangerously close to $300. Seriously, $300 for an infant car seat? While it is a well made, safe infant car seat, it's hard to justify the $100 to $150 price premium over similar seats from Chicco and Graco. Heck, Peg makes Britax look affordable at this price.

On the plus side, there are many bargain Primo Viaggio seats sold online—most are previous years' models that are in the $170 to $200 range. Be aware, however, that many earlier models only work to 22 lbs. and omit the side impact protection.

As for the latest crash tests, the Primo Viaggio scores in the middle of the pack in *Consumer Reports* latest tests—good crash protection but only fair fit to vehicle using a safety belt. The government gave this seat a four-star rating for ease of use. ***Rating: A-***

SAFETY 1ST ONBOARD 35/35 AIR

Price: OnBoard 35 is $100 to $130. Extra base: $85. OnBoard 35 Air is $160 to $180.

Limits: 35 lbs., 32″

NHTSA ease of use rating: ★★★☆☆

Pros: One of the few seats designed to work with preemies.

Cons: Have to pay an extra $60 to get the version with additional side impact protection.

Comments: This seat features a special insert for preemies (you can use the OnBoard for babies from four lbs. and up). You also get EPP foam, four harness height positions and an adjustable base. Otherwise, the OnBoard is a plain Jane infant seat without any special bells or whistles.

The Safety 1st OnBoard is only sold in a handful of stores, which probably explains why we've had very little feedback on it.

FYI: Safety 1st sells an upgraded version of this seat, the OnBoard 35 Air. It is the infant car seat version of the brand's successful Complete Air convertible seat (reviewed on page 427). It features the same Air Protect side impact protection and works to 35 lbs.

Reader feedback on this seat has been positive. As for crash tests, the OnBoard Air scored better than the regular OnBoard in *Consumer Reports* latest tests (excellent versus very good), although the basic version was judged easier to use. The magazine gave the OnBoard a best buy rating, since its affordable price ($100) is on the low-end for seats that work to 35 lbs. The government gives both OnBoard versions a three star rating for ease of use— not the worst, and better than most of Dorel's offerings. ***Rating: B***

SUMMER PRODIGY

Price: $161; extra base $80.

Limits: 32 lbs., 32″

NHTSA ease of use rating: Not rated yet.

Pros: Auto height harness adjustment, high-tech screen to advise on correction installation.
Cons: Version 1.0 of any car seat is usually best to skip.

Comments: Summer's first effort at an infant car seat will be on the market by the time you read this. We got a preview of the Prodigy and thought the features were impressive: auto height and harness adjustment, side-impact tested and a gizmo called a SmartScreen. This LCD readout tells you when you've correctly installed the belt, testing the install to ensure safety.

At 9.9 lbs, the carrier (which has two crotch positions) is on the heavy side, but oddly lacks any EPS foam. By pricing the seat at $160+, Summer is swinging for the fences here, hoping to compete with the Chicco and Graco in the 32 lb. weight capacity. That seems like a stretch for a company better known for its baby video monitors—and car seats isn't like the other categories Summer has recently entered, so the jury is out on whether this will succeed.

Summer plans to pair the Prodigy with a stroller to create a $300 travel system. We'll review the stroller in our stroller section, but its 29.2 lb. weight is going to make it a tough sell.

While the infant car seat definitely has nice features, we wonder how the SmartScreen will work in the real world. Any gizmo like this has to be weatherized to withstand the extreme heat and cold a car endures—so we'll have to wait and see how this performs in the cold of a Maine winter . . . or Texas summer.

After writing this book for nearly 20 years, we generally advise folks to NOT buy the first generation of any baby product—and the learning curve on car seats is as steep as they come. We'll wait to see how these seats perform out in the wild before assigning a rating. ***Rating: Not Yet.***

◆ ***Car beds.*** How do you transport a preemie home from the hospital? The smallest infants may not be able to sit in a regular infant seat—in that case, a "car bed" enables an infant to travel lying down. Check with your hospital—some rent out car beds for preemies for free (one mom said she had to pay a $50 deposit, refundable when she returned the car bed). If you have to purchase a car bed, we'd recommend the ***Cosco Dream Ride*** ($80, rating: A). FYI: ALL premature infants should be given a car seat test at the hospital to check for breathing problems—ask your pediatrician for details.

Convertible and Forward Facing-Only Car Seats (model by model reviews)

ALPHA OMEGA THREE IN ONE *See Eddie Bauer Three In One convertible seat.*

BRITAX ADVOCATE 70 CS
Price: $370 retail, about $275-$325 online.
Type: Convertible seat.
Limits: 5 to 40 lbs. rear facing, 20 to 70 lbs. forward facing, 49″ tall.
NHTSA ease of use rating:
★★★★☆ Rear-facing.
★★★★☆ Foward-facing.

Pros: Same as Boulevard but with added side impact protection.

Cons: Price. Big seat—may not fit into smaller vehicles.

Comments: This seat is the same as the Britax Boulevard CS, with one major difference: the Advocate has added side-impact protection cushions that compress to protect the child during a crash. Yep, think of these as side-impact air bags for your car seat. The CS in the seat's model name stands for Click and Safe—when the harness is correctly adjusted, you hear a click . . . a nice feature.

Two major caveats to this seat: it is much heavier and bigger than other Britax seats (21.2 lbs), which will make it less convenient to switch between vehicles. The Advocate's huge footprint will make it a tough fit in smaller vehicles. Also, the height of this seat is short—and since you have to stop using it when your child's ears reach the top of the shell (in forward facing mode), you're child will probably outgrow it by height long before he hits the 70 lb. limit.

One nice feature can also be a negative: the cover is easy to remove for washing. But we noted more than a few readers said it came off way too easily when in the car.

This second generation of the Advocate features a series of upgrades (common to all Britax seats now): SafeCell technology to minimize seat movement in a crash, integrated steel bars for strength and an energy-absorbing Versa-Tether that can be used forward or rear facing.

Reader feedback on this seat has been very positive. It scored well in *Consumer Reports'* most recent report on convertible seats. The NHTSA gives this a seat a four-star rating for ease of use, which is improved over the last version. One criticism: we heard from more than one reader who was stumped by the instruction manual, which is heavy on illustrations and light on text.

Overall, this is an excellent seat—the rating only falls short of an A because of the high price and seat shell's shortness. ***Rating: B+***

Britax Boulevard/Boulevard 70 CS

Price: $340 retail, $240 online.

Type: Convertible seat.

Limits: 5 to 40 lbs. rear facing, 20 to 70 lbs. forward facing, 49" tall.

NHTSA ease of use rating:

★★★★☆ Rear-facing.

★★★★☆ Foward-facing.

Pros: Same as the Marathon, but seat adds height-adjuster knob. Additional side impact protection with headrest.

Cons: Price. Big seat—may not fit into smaller vehicles. EPS foam only in headrest.

Comments: This seat is virtually the same as the Marathon (see later review), with two significant differences.

First, you get a height adjuster knob that lets you make numerous adjustments to the harness heights (instead of being stuck with the four positions you see in the Marathon). Hence, you don't have to re-thread the belts every time your child grows.

The second difference is what Britax calls "true impact protection." Basically, this is a reinforced headrest lined with EPS foam that protects your child in a side-impact collision. The first version of this seat (called the Wizard) had a headrest that many felt was too restrictive, so Britax revised the headrest to make it wider. Britax also added an infant pillow, like the Decathlon.

Like all of Britax's second-generation seats, the Boulevard comes with SafeCell, integrated steel bars and the Versa-Tether (see review of Advocate above for details).

The Boulevard comes in two flavors: regular (pictured) and CS, that latter stands for Click and Safe—you hear a click when you adjust the harness to make sure it is as snug as possible. The Boulevard CS is $330 retail ($250 online).

The Boulevard gets good crash test marks from *Consumer Reports*; the government's ease of use rating has improved, thanks to easier rear-facing installation. Reader feedback on this seat has been very positive—perhaps the only complaint we heard is about the crotch strap, which isn't adjustable. ***Rating: A-***

Britax Marathon 70

Price: $290 retail, $215-$260 online.

Type: Convertible seat.

Limits: 5 to 40 lbs. rear facing, 20 to 70 lbs. forward facing, 49" tall.

NHTSA ease of use rating:

★★★★☆ Rear-facing.

★★★★☆ Foward-facing.

CAR
SEATS

Pros: Up to 70 lbs. with a five-point harness. Plush pad, EPS foam, same pros as Roundabout.

Cons: HUGS harness system gets mixed reviews.

Comments: The Marathon is Britax's best-selling seat and it's no wonder: this model was one of the first to work to 65 lbs. with a harness (the newest version now works to 70 lbs.). Since its release, Britax has done a series of Marathon spin-offs that add side impact protection (Boulevard, Advocate). Despite being more old school, the Marathon is still worthy of consideration.

The Marathon has four harness heights (the top is 18"), Britax's "Versa-Tether" (which means the seat can be tethered rear or forward facing) and EPS foam.

Thanks to its wide distribution, you can find the Marathon sold in many stores and online. That means you can often snag one on sale: as of this writing—Amazon was selling it for $225 as we went to press. One tip: watch for discontinued patterns, which can sell for 20% to 30% less. Same seat, just last's year fashion.

So, what's not to like about the Marathon? Well, first, this is a big seat. At 26" tall (the seat back), the Britax is a few inches taller than other brand convertible seats. But that means it may not fit into smaller cars, especially when in rear facing mode.

And let's talk about the HUGS system, which appears on the Marathon. Britax says this harness system is designed to "better distribute webbing loads to reduce head movement and minimize the chance for webbing edge loading on the child's neck in the case of an impact. In addition, it is designed to reduce the chance of improper positioning of the chest clip."

The first version of HUGS generated many complaints from parents, who said it didn't fit larger children and was confusing to use. Britax tweaked the system by coming out with larger HUGS straps and clarifying its use in the seat's instructions. But some folks still dislike HUGS and find it difficult to use.

New this year: the Marathon has added a no re-thread harness making it easier to adjust harness height.

The Marathon does have side impact protection (deep side walls), but Britax's other models (Boulevard, Advocate) go a step further with additional head cushions. Those cushions have both fans and detractors—the safety benefit is obvious, but some kids don't like the wings/cushions around their heads, limiting vision and movement.

Reader feedback on this seat has been very positive, with fans citing its ease of use and installation. All in all, we recommend the Marathon—IF you have a vehicle in which it can fit!

FYI: A few web sites are still selling the old Marathon (now called the Marathon Classic); given all the new technology in the Marathon 70, we'd recommend the 70 over the Classic. ***Rating: A***

BRITAX ROUNDABOUT (55, 50 CLASSIC)

Price: $200 retail, $160-$170 online.

Type: Convertible seat.

Limits: 5 to 40 lbs. rear facing, 20 to 55 lbs. forward facing (Roundabout 50 works to 50 lbs). 40" tall.

NHTSA ease of use rating:

★★★☆☆ Rear-facing.

★★★☆☆ Foward-facing.

Pros: Excellent features—EPS foam, no-twist straps, can be tethered rear or forward facing, easy to adjust harness, double-strap LATCH, nice colors.

Cons: Pricey; harness not as easy to adjust as Marathon.

Comments: The Roundabout was Britax's first convertible to be sold in the U.S. and has been a best-seller thanks to its rock-solid installation—the lock-off clips provide snug belt install and Britax's double-strap LATCH connectors are among the best in the business. We also found Britax's harness to be easy to use and the straps don't twist. Finally, we should mention that you can tether the Roundabout either rear or forward facing, a key safety advantage.

Britax revised the Roundabout last year with the same technological improvements it rolled out across its entire line, including the SafeCell feature that keeps the seat from rebounding in a crash. Also new: a Roundabout 55 with a higher weight (pictured; the 50 lbs. Classic is still available), deeper sidewalls for side impact protection and a new, lower first harness height (8"). That addresses a complaint we had about previous Roundabouts, whose lowest harness height was too tall for the smallest infants.

What's not to like? Well, the Roundabout is the same height as the Marathon (26"), which as we pointed out in that review, makes it a snug fit when rear facing in smaller vehicles. And, again like the Marathon, the Roundabout is old school: you have to manually rethread the harness to change the harness height. As we were going to press, we had a reader email us with a concern that the Roundabout 55 harness was much harder to adjust than on her previous Roundabout. And that seemed to be confirmed by another car seat tech we consulted on this issue—for some reason, the new Roundabout has a harness that requires much more effort to adjust.

In the past, we recommended the Roundabout, giving it a slight edge over the Marathon since it had a smaller shell (both in back height and width)—that made it a better fit in smaller vehicles. However, now that the Marathon and Roundabout share the same dimensions, we'd suggest the Marathon. That's because you can use it longer with bigger toddlers (thanks to the higher top harness slot)—for kids up to 49" in height, versus 46" for the Roundabout. The

Marathon also has a cover that much more easily removes for cleaning, a feature the Roundabout lacks. Hence, it might be worth it to spend the extra $25 for a Marathon, since the street price of the Marathon (on Amazon, for example) is $225 compared to the Roundabout's $200 retail. That said, the Roundabout is still an excellent seat—and if that is all your budget will allow, this is a good compromise. FYI: Britax still sells the old version of the Roundabout (now called the Roundabout 50 Classic)—given all the improvements in the new model, we'd suggest skipping the older one. ***Rating: A***

CLEK FOONF
Price: $450-$500.
Type: Convertible seat.
Limits: 15 to 40 lbs. rear facing, up to 65 or 70 lbs. forward facing, 49" tall.
NHTSA ease of use rating: Not yet.

Pros: Premium seat that can fit three across in a backseat. Rigid LATCH for front-facing mode. Unique crumple zone for crash protection.

Cons: $500? And it doesn't work with infants.

Comments: Perhaps the most anticipated new car seat for 2012 is Clek's Foonf, from the Canadian company known for its popular booster seats with rigid LATCH connectors. Yes, this is Clek's first foray into the convertible seat market and they will bring all the goodwill they've earned in the booster seat category to the Foonf (which continues Clek's tradition of funky names).

We got a sneak peak at the Foonf (which should be out in spring 2012) and liked it. It will feature a narrow base that will allow three-across seating, an aluminum "crumple zone" in the seat for energy absorption, anti-rebound bar and more. There are also little interesting touches like magnets that hold open the harness when putting baby in or out of the seat.

So will it be worth the nearly $500 price tag? Well, you do get quite a few premium features, such as the IMMI flexible LATCH attachments for rear facing and rigid LATCH for forward-facing mode. Like the Oobr, there is also an integrated headrest. And there will be a recline feature (two for front facing, one for rear). The Foonf will work to either 65 or 70 lbs. (it hasn't been tested yet).

The negatives: the seat will not be rated for infant use (a child will have to be 15 lbs. or more to use the Foonf), which is odd for a convertible seat.

But is it really worth half a grand? That's tough to answer before we see real-world reviews from parents. There is probably a market for a premium seat that can fit three-across in the backseat of a car. But . . . this probably isn't the best time to launch what could be the market's most expensive car seat. So we'll wait and see if the Foonf lives up to its billing and price tag. ***Rating: Not Yet.***

COMBI COCCORO

Price: $200 to $240

Type: Convertible seat.

Limits: 5 to 30 lbs. rear facing, 20 to 40 lbs. forward facing, 40″ tall.

NHTSA ease of use rating:

★★★☆☆ Rear-facing.

★★★☆☆ Foward-facing.

Pros: Small size = good fit for compact vehicles.

Cons: Can be hard to install rear facing.

Comments: The Coccoro is a compact car seat (it weighs just 11 lbs.) pitched for parents with small cars. Thanks to its small base size, Combi pitches this seat as a solution for parents who need to fit three car seats across the backseat. The top harness slot is 15,″ which is impressive for a compact seat. Another plus: the Coccoro has built-in lock off clips, a nice safety feature. And the Coccoro comes in a series of bright colors.

Parent feedback on this seat has been positive, although a few have complained that it is hard to install rear facing. *Consumer Reports* echoed that view, with a "poor" rating for the Coccoro's fit to vehicle, rear facing. That dragged down CR's overall opinion of the seat, which scored second to bottom overall even though crash protection was judged very good. The NHTSA gives the Coccoro an overall three-star rating for ease of use, although again installation in rear facing mode comes in for criticism. So it is a mixed review for the Coccoro—this is a good seat if you have a smaller child (and only need a seat with a 40 lb. limit) and/or you have a smaller car. But be aware of the poor fit and installation when in rear facing mode. ***Rating: B***

COMBI ZEUS 360°

Price: $400 retail, $360-$380 online.

Type: Convertible

Limits: 5 to 33 lbs. rear facing, 20 to 40 lbs. forward facing,

NHTSA ease of use rating:

★★★☆☆ Rear-facing.

★★★☆☆ Foward-facing.

Pros: Base rotates from rear to forward facing without reinstallation.

Cons: Pricey, hard to find in stores.

Comments: Combi's Zeus 360° has a unique feature: a turnable base—you can flip the seat from rear to forward-facing without reinstallation. In our first review of the Zeus we flunked it because its rear-facing limit was only 22 lbs. Good news: Combi has re-certified the seat to 33 lbs.

Reader feedback on the Zeus is mixed—parents who love the Zeus

convertible seats

like the ability to rotate the seat to remove a rear-facing infant from the car. Others laud the overall quality and sturdiness of the Zeus.

On the other hand, critics point out this seat is HUGE, making it at tight fit even in mid-size cars. At $330, this seat is very expensive, yet can only be used to 40 lbs. (most $300+ seats work to 65 lbs.). And Combi's distribution on the Zeus is rather thin, making it hard to see the seat in person. ***Rating: B***

COSCO ALPHA OMEGA *See Eddie Bauer 3-in-1.*

COSCO APT

Price: $55
Type: Convertible seat.
NHTSA ease of use rating: Not yet.
Limits: 5-40 lbs. rear facing, 22-40 front-facing.
Comments: This new seat debuted January 2012 and is basically an updated Scenera, Cosco's popular and affordable convertible seat. The differences? The Apt has deep side walls for side impact protection and two intergrated cup holders. Those cup holders will make the Apt a bit wider than the Scenera, which might make three across seating more difficult.

The Apt will be sold in Cosco's usual retailers (Target, etc) and there may also be a deluxe model. No rating yet, as it wasn't out on the market as of this writing.

COSCO SCENERA / SCENERA 40RF

Price: $40-$60
Type: Convertible seat.
Limits: 5-35 lbs. rear facing, 22-40 lbs. front-facing. The 40RF works to 40 lbs. rear-facing.
NHTSA ease of use rating (Scenera):

⭐⭐☆☆☆ Rear-facing.
⭐⭐☆☆☆ Foward-facing.

Pros: Affordable car seat for a second car.
Cons: No side impact protection or EPS foam.
Comments: This simple seat is our top pick for that occasionally-used second car or Grandma's vehicle. The Scenera isn't fancy: you get a five-point harness with four height positions and three crotch slots. The padding is very simple and there isn't any EPS foam, side-impact protection or other goodies. But then again, this seat is just $40—perfect when you need an affordable seat that is easy to install and use.

Consumer Reports picked this seat as a best buy in their most recent rankings, giving it an "excellent" in crash protection. As for ease of use, the Scenera earned just two stars from the NHTSA, with rear facing installation holding the seat's rating down. Nonetheless, we think this is a good, basic seat for secondary use.

FYI: Cosco has come out with a new version of the Scenera, dubbed the Scenera 40RF ($55). The main feature: this version works to 40 lbs. rear-facing. Otherwise, the seat is very similar to the regular Scenera. The 40RF scored three stars on the government's ease of use ratings. ***Rating: B+***

DIONO RADIAN RXT / R120 / R100

Price: RXT $340, R120 $310, R100 $260
Type: Convertible (RXT converts to belt-positioning booster)
Limits: to 80, 100 or 120 lbs. Height up to 57".
NHTSA ease of use rating: Not yet.
Pros: Folds up! Works to 80/100/120 lbs, depending on the model. EPS foam. RXT has added side impact protection. Narrow base lets you fit three across.
Cons: Heavy weight. Biggest kids may find crotch strap too tight. Not as ideal for kids under one year of age riding rear facing.
Comments: Diono, formally known as Sunshine Kids, is a small company that focuses on car seats and travel accessories. Their claim to fame is their Radian car seat line, which was among the first to have extended use harnesses (most convertible seats used to stop at 40 lbs). And the seats are car pool friendly—yes, they fold up!

The Radian accomplishes its folding trick by omitting the base you see on so many convertible seats—the seat actually sits along the back of the vehicle's seat. One plus to this: the Radian's narrow base allows for a three-across install in the back of a vehicle.

The Radian has recently been refreshed and now comes in three versions: RXT, R120 and R100. All the seats feature a steel alloy frames. And you can use LATCH up to 80 lbs., much higher than other seats on the market.

The RXT is the flagship and features a new trick: the harness removes so the seat can become a belt positioning booster (up to 120 lbs). The pitch: you can use this from birth (starting at 5 pounds), rear-facing for infants, forward-facing for toddlers with a harness that works to 80 lbs. . . . and then in belt-positioning mode to 120 lbs. The RXT also features memory foam and side impact protection (wings that are near the top of the seat).

The R120 omits the side impact protection wings, but otherwise is much like the RXT (example: you still get the memory foam, etc) and has the same weight limits.

The entry level R100 is more bare bones: no memory foam and the booster mode is only rated to 100 lbs.

Diono is rumored to be coming out with a recline angle adjuster for their seats, but no news as of this writing. And that's perhaps one of the few negatives to these seats: in rear-facing mode, their isn't much recline to these seats (and hence they may not be the best bet for the smallest newborns). Another negative: these seats are heavy (20+ lbs.), which means that even though they fold up and are pitched for car poolers, actually lugging around these seats isn't easy.

We gave the last generation of Radian seats an A- and expect to recommend these seats as well. However, since the RXT/R120/R100 just shipped as of press time, we haven't seen any real world feedback on the new models—we're especially watching how well the seats preform in booster mode, which is new. So we'll wait a bit before a final rating is issued. ***Rating: Not Yet.***

EDDIE BAUER DELUXE 3-IN-1 (a.k.a. Alpha Omega Elite, Safety 1st Alpha Omega Elite, Alpha Echelon)
Price: $190 to $200.
Type: Convertible, five-point harness.
Limits: 5 to 35 lbs. rear-facing, 22 to 40 lbs. front-facing, 30 to 100 lbs. as a booster.
NHTSA ease of use rating:

★★★☆☆ Rear facing.
★★★★☆ Forward facing.
★★★★☆ Booster.

IIHS rating for booster mode: Not recommended.
Pros: It's an infant seat! It's a convertible! It's a booster!
Cons: Twisty straps. Poor recline. And much more!
Comments: This best-selling seat is sold under a zillion aliases, as you'd expect from Cosco. It is marketed under the Eddie Bauer, Safety 1st, Cosco and Alpha brands in a variety of price points and spin-offs. We've seen it in a stripped-down version for $100 at Costco . . . and deluxe version for $200 online. A typical offering is the tricked-out Eddie Bauer version sold for $180.

The pitch for this seat is simple: you can use it from birth to college. Ok, perhaps not college, but this seat aims for a triple play: rear-facing for infants up to 33 lbs., as a convertible with five-point harness up to 40 lbs. . . . and then as a belt-positioning booster up to a whopping 100 lbs. for toddlers and older kids.

The problem: it just doesn't live up to the hype. It is poorly designed, hard to use and expensive. Our reader feedback hasn't been kind to this seat: readers knock the instructions as "vague and confusing," the belts are hard to adjust in the rear-facing mode and the straps are so thin they constantly get twisted and snagged. Yet another problem: the highest harness slot in this seat (14.5") is a full inch lower than other seats like the Britax Roundabout. Why is this a problem? That low slot means some parents will be forced to convert this seat to booster mode too soon for larger children.

As for safety, this seat scored better in crash tests with LATCH than just with a safety belt. *Consumer Reports* latest tests pegged this seat as only "good" (most other seats in this price range scored "very good" or "excellent") for crash protection with a safety belt. And we're disappointed that this seat doesn't have EPS foam or side impact protection.

FYI: Cosco makes two versions of this seat under the Cosco label: the Alpha Omega and the Alpha Omega Elite. While similar (both add EPP foam), the Elite goes to 50 lbs. with a five-point harness and 100 lbs. as a belt-positioning booster (the regular Omega is 80) and adds armrests and an adjustable headrest. Safety 1st sells a version of this seat called the Alpha Luxe for $100.

Bottom line: despite its pitch, this seat is too expensive and hard to use. *Rating: D*

EDDIE BAUER DELUXE CAR SEAT

This seat is reviewed on our web site, BabyBargains.com.

EVENFLO MOMENTUM 65
Price: $200 retail, $150-$185 online.
Type: Convertible seat.
Limits: 5-40 lbs. rear facing, 20-65 forward facing.
NHTSA ease of use rating:
★★★★☆ Rear facing.
★★★★☆ Forward facing.

Pros: Enhanced side-impact protection, lower price than Britax.
Cons: Massive, bulky seat.
Comments: This new seat is Evenflo's attempt to upscale their offerings and compete with Britax's premium seats. The headline here is side-impact technology, which Evenflo dubs e3 for an expanded zone of protection. You also get the same SureLatch technology that is on the Triumph, plus an infinite slide harness for easier belt adjustments and an easy-off washable pad. Early feedback on the seat has been positive, with parents saying it is easy to use and install. But more than one reader said the seat's sheer bulk (it is a massive 31" tall and 21" wide—nearly three inches wider than the already-big Britax Marathon), makes this a tough fit in even mid-size vehicles, especially rear facing. Perhaps Evenflo didn't get the memo that GM has discontinued its Hummer brand, but we are hard pressed to see how this seat fits into anything other than a big SUV. And if you put it in the outboard position rear facing, we'd guess there would be little or no room for a passenger in the front seat, since that seat will be jammed into the dash. New this year, Evenflo now has three trim levels: plain 65, 65 LX and 65 DLX. The difference is basically padding and fabric. Prices are similar. *Rating: B*

EVENFLO SYMPHONY 65

Price: $165-$250.

Type: Convertible seat.

Limits: 5-35 lbs. rear-facing, 20-65 lbs. for-ward-facing with five-point harness, 30-100 lbs. as a belt-positioning booster.

NHTSA ease of use rating:

★★★☆☆ Rear facing.

★★★☆☆ Forward facing.

★★★☆☆ Booster.

IIHS rating for booster mode: Base model: Good bet. e3 version: Best bet.

Comments: The Symphony is Evenflo's answer to the Safety 1st Alpha Omega seat . . . it aims to work with newborns to older kids up to 100 lbs.

SureLATCH is the headline here: Evenflo's new LATCH connectors that tout a "super-fast, tight and safe installation." SureLATCH features built-in retractors that eliminate belt slack—this makes the Symphony one of the easier seats to install with LATCH.

Parent feedback on the seat has been positive. Fans like the removable padding for infants and excellent harness adjuster.

New for 2011, Evenflo is increasing the size of the Symphony's head wings. Also new: an aluminum bar inside the shell for stability, Evenflo's new E3 side impact protection and a new feature called TruTether, which indicates whether the tether strap has been correctly tightened. This model is dubbed the Symphony 65 e3.

As for ease of use, Evenflo seats generally score at the bottom of the government's ratings, although the Symphony itself has yet to be evaluated. *Consumer Reports* puts the Symphony in the middle of the pack, with poor rear fit-to-vehicle holding down its overall score.

We found the Symphony's booster mode better designed than Eddie Bauer's—it's easy to adjust and will provide a good fit for older kids. BUT, the Symphony is not a very tall booster . . . that means kids will probably outgrow it by height long before the stated 100 lb. limit.

Bottom line: this seat is probably one of the better attempts at an "all in one" seat. If you have your heart set on buying just one seat that works from birth to 100 pounds, skip the Safety 1st option and go with this one. ***Rating: B+***

EVENFLO TITAN ELITE/SPORT

Price: $100 retail, $80 online.

Type: Convertible; comes in five-point and bar-shield versions.

Limits: 5 to 30 lbs. rear facing, 20 to 50 lbs. forward facing.

NHTSA ease of use rating:

★★★☆☆ Rear facing.

★★☆☆☆ Forward facing.

Pros: Value, excellent crash tests.

Cons: Hard to clean cover and adjust straps. Twisty straps.

Comments: Here's another seat to consider for grandma's car—the Evenflo Titan is a bare-bones seat where the price (under $100) is right. Nothing fancy here: you get a five-point harness, four shoulder positions and simple padding. Yet the Titan shows how simpler is sometimes better.

FYI: Evenflo makes several versions of the Titan, including a Titan Sport sold online for $80. We're not sure what makes this seat sporty, except for the different fabric.

Like the Cosco Scenera, the Evenflo Titan has no side-impact protection, fancy padding or EPS foam, but, hey, it's affordable. The big gripe we heard from parents on the Titan were the straps—some found the harness hard to adjust, especially when the seat is rear facing. *Consumer Reports* echoed this complaint with a "fair" rating for the Titan Elite's fit-to-vehicle in rear facing mode—overall, the seat ranked dead last among convertible seats with greater than 40 lb. forward facing harness capacity.

So we will caveat our review: the Titan is probably best as a seat for kids over a year (and not riding rear facing). ***Rating: B+***

EVENFLO TRIUMPH 65 ADVANCE LX/DLX

Price: $140-$180.

Type: Convertible seat.

Limits: 5 to 35 lbs. rear facing, 20 to 65 lbs. forward facing.

NHTSA ease of use rating:

★★☆☆☆ Rear facing.

★★☆☆☆ Forward facing.

Pros: Special harness "remembers" last setting, EPP foam, up-front five-position recline and harness adjustment (no re-threading). Half the price of Britax.

Cons: Tension knob is hard to adjust when seat is in rear facing mode. Wide base may not fit in smaller cars. Can only use the top harness slot when forward facing, making the seat difficult to use for larger (but young) infants.

Comments: Evenflo has made steady improvements to this seat over the years and that's a good thing. Older versions of the Triumph garnered a large number of reader complaints about ease of use.

The latest Triumph is dubbed the Advance. Available in two trim levels (LX, DLX) the Advance works to 65 lbs. (older Triumphs only work to 40 or 50 lbs.). The difference in the trim levels is just fabric

convertible seats

and a bit more padding with the DLX version. Also new: EPP foam and improvements to harness adjustment system.

The Triumph's key features are the TensionRight knob that tightens the harness from the side of the seat and the infinite slide harness adjustment system (no rethreading). All the knobs on the Evenflo seat have both fans and detractors—give it a try in the store to see if you find it easy to adjust.

Parent feedback on the Triumph has been positive and the seat scored at the top of *Consumer Reports* recent rankings of convertible car seats—that's a coup for Evenflo, since most of its other models dwell at the bottom of CR's rankings. The NHTSA's ease of use rating, however, isn't as effusive, with the Triumph earning just two out of five stars. That's probably due to the difficulty in adjusting the TensionRight knob when the seat is rear facing. Another negative: the wide base (19.5″) may make it a tight fit in smaller vehicles.

Bottom line: The Triumph Advance is much improved over its previous versions. And the price (50% less than a Britax Marathon) make this one worthy to consider if money is tight but you still want a seat that works to 65 lbs. with a five-point harness. ***Rating: A-***

FIRST YEARS TRUE FIT
Price: $145-$250.
Type: Convertible seat.
Limits: 5 to 35 lbs. rear facing, 20 to 65 lbs. forward facing
NHTSA ease of use rating:
⭐⭐⭐⭐⭐Rear facing.
⭐⭐⭐⭐⭐Forward facing.
(Rating is for True Fit Premier, C670)

Pros: Headrest pops off for easier rear facing installation. EPP foam, easy-off pad for hand-washing, affordable price.
Cons: Harness can be hard to adjust when rear facing.
Comments: Here's a great alternative to the Britax Marathon that costs $100 less: the First Years True Fit is an excellent seat that works up to 65 lbs. This seat's most amazing feature is a headrest that pops off. That makes the True Fit easier to install rear facing in smaller vehicles (you won't need the headrest for newborns riding rear facing). We also like the automatic harness adjustments (no rethreading), side-impact wings, a seat entirely lined with EPP foam and three crotch positions to adjust for growing babies. Add in the 65 lb. top weight and an affordable under $200 and we have a winner!

We should point there are three True Fit models: the regular version (C630, $145), the Premier (C670, $200-$250, pictured), and the Recline (C650, $150-$200). The Premier adds an anti-rebound bar, making it the only convertible seat on the market with that feature.

The bar helps stop the seat from moving in an accident. Meanwhile, the True Fit Recline adds a reclining seat, but lacks the anti-rebound bar. (Just to confuse you, the Premier also reclines).

Like the Diono Radian seats, the True Fit does not have a base—this enables the seat to be deeper on the inside without increasing its overall dimensions.

Feedback on the True Fit has been very positive: fans love the roomy seat, the "easy off" pad that enables quick cleaning and the overall ease of installation (belt lock-offs are a plus). The downsides? The True Fit doesn't have wide distribution, which can make seeing it in person a challenge. And the harness can be hard to adjust when the seat is in the rear facing position.

The True Fit Premier earned a unique distinction in 2009: it was the first seat to earn a five-star ease of use rating from government, which is impressive. (The regular version of the True Fit earned four stars; the Recline version was too new to be evaluated as of press time). *Consumer Reports* only evaluated the regular True Fit, putting it in the middle of the pack (rear facing fit-to-vehicle was a concern).

One caveat to the True Fit: in rear facing mode with the head-rest removed, the weight limit is just 22 lbs. With the headrest on, it is 35 lbs. ***Rating: A***

GRACO COMFORTSPORT
Price: $80-$100
Type: Convertible seat.
Limits: up to 30 lbs. rear facing, 20 to 40 lbs. forward facing.
NHTSA ease of use rating:
★★★☆☆ Rear facing.
★★★☆☆ Forward facing.

Pros: Front belt-adjuster, level adjuster, EPS foam.

Cons: Very low harness slots for forward facing. Cheaper versions have skimpy padding; next to impossible to adjust straps in rear facing mode.

Comments: Despite Graco's success with infant seats, the company hasn't been able to translate this to convertible models. Exhibit A: The ComfortSport.

This seat first debuted in 1999 as the Century Accel. Yes, the technology on this seat is that old—why Graco keeps this seat around is puzzling. Yes, it has EPS and a front harness adjuster. And since it sells for less than $100, we can see why folks may be tempted.

But . . . the seat is seriously flawed. The top slots of the ComfortSport are a measly 14" tall—the lowest slots on the market. That means your child will quickly outgrow this seat long before the stated limits. And you can only use the bottom two slots for rear facing (and the top two slots for forward facing only). That's a strange configuration that truly limits the usage of the seat.

The low weight limits are another major drawback: most seats on the market today work to 35 lbs. rear facing (the ComfortSport stops at 30) and even Evenflo's similarly priced Titan work up to 50 lbs. forward facing (the ComfortSport is only 40).

Hence while this seat LOOKS like a bargain, it isn't—your child will outgrow it way too soon. And the ComfortSport is very difficult to install in most vehicles (it lacks belt lock-offs, etc). It's not a big surprise that most reader feedback on this seat has been negative. Bottom line: this seat is a loser. *Rating: D*

GRACO MYRIDE 65
Price: $130-$180
Type: Convertible seat.
Limits: 4-40 lbs., rear facing, up to 65 lbs. forward facing
NHTSA ease of use rating:
★★★★☆ Rear facing.
★★★★☆ Forward facing.

Pros: Yes, it works to 40 lbs. rear facing! Affordable.

Cons: Difficult LATCH installation, strap adjustments.

Comments: This is Graco's effort at an affordable convertible seat that works to 65 lbs. Reaction from readers, however, is mixed and mostly negative. Yes, folks love the 40 lb. rear-facing limit, but the complicated LATCH installation (Graco uses a single strap that runs under the seat in rear facing mode) makes a tight fit difficult in some vehicles. The recessed cup holders are now built into the seat (in earlier versions of the MyRide, they weren't—and that generated quite a few complaints). Adjusting the straps is quite difficult, especially when compared to Britax's seats.

Despite the mixed reader feedback, this seat earned four out of five stars in the government's ease of use ratings. And *Consumer Reports* picked this seat as a best buy, even though it ended up scoring in the middle of the pack in their most recent report on convertible car seats. We can see their point on affordability: $120 (Walmart's price) for a seat that works to 65 pounds is a value.

Given the split opinion, we'll side with our readers on this seat and only give it an average rating. Bottom line: while we salute Graco's effort to make an affordable 65 lb. limit seat, the trade-offs in ease of use and design drag down the MyRide's rating.

New for 2012, Graco is adding enhanced side impact protection to the MyRide. Dubbed "Safety Surround," this feature adds an optional/removeable head cushion for infants and built-in side impact protection for older kids. The head cushion for infants adjusts up or down to accommodate a growing child. The MyRide 65 with Safety Surround will be out in December for $180 at Babies R Us. See pictures at right and below for more details.

Also new for 2012: the MyRide 65 features a special newborn insert cushion that will enable the seat to accommodate infants as small as four pounds (parents of preemies, take note). The previous seat started at five lbs. *Rating: C*

GRACO MY SIZE 65
Price: $180.
Limits: 4-40 lbs. rear-facing, 20-65 lbs. forward.
Comments: This brand new seat is set to debut in the 2nd quarter of 2012. It will feature a height position adjustable headrest and no rethread harness. The My Size 65 will aso have a three-position recline and upgraded LATCH connectors (called In Right LATCH).

GRACO SMART SEAT
Price: $300-$330.
Type: Convertible seat.
Limits: 5 to 40 lbs., rear facing, 20 to 65 forward facing, up to 100 lbs. as a belt-positioning booster.
NHTSA ease of use rating:
★★★★★ Rear facing.
★★★★★ Forward facing.
★★★★★ Booster.

IIHS rating for booster mode: Check fit.
Pros: First seat with stay in car base, side impact protection, no rethread harness. Converts to booster.
Cons: $300 for a Graco car seat?
Comments: And now for something totally different: Graco's Smart Seat aims to be one of the first convertible seat with a stay-in-the-car base (like infant car seats). Yes, you install this base once and then snap in the seat, either front or rear facing. Add in a no rethread harness, six position headrest, seat recline, integrated cup holder and the ability to work as a booster (the base and five-point harness are removed) to 100 lbs. and you have one impressive seat. We also liked how the Smart Seat features side impact protection, a first for Graco. So what's not to love? Well, at $300+, customer expectations will be very high—this seat better be as easy to use as Britax's most expensive models. And on that score, Graco has a less than stellar track record. As you can read in the reviews for Graco's other convertible seats, this brand struggles to earn over a C in our book. So we'll have to wait to see

convertible seats

how this seat works in the real world. For those brave pioneers who get it first, email us with your thoughts! ***Rating: Not Yet***

LILLY GOLD PLAY SIT ´ N´ STROLL
This seat is reviewed on our web site, BabyBargains.com.

MAXI COSI PRIA 70
Price: $250
Type: Convertible seat.
Limits: 4-40 lbs. rear facing, 22-70 lbs. forward.
NHTSA ease of use rating: Not yet.
Pros: TinyFit infant insert good for preemies (starting at 4 lbs). Side impact protection. Small footprint means seat will fit into smaller vehicles. Nice fabric, padding.
Cons: Can only use tether in forward-facing position. TinyFit makes install rear-facing somewhat challenging. Must rethread harness when changing height.
Comments: Maxi Cosi is Dorel's European subsidiary that has been imported to the U.S. to help shore up Dorel's car seat offerings.

The Pria 70 replaces the Priori and aims to solve two problems: car seats that don't fit small infants well—and seats that don't fit small cars.

On the first score, the Pria 70 features a "TinyFit" seat—basically a car seat within a car seat for newborns as small as four lbs. It even has a smaller chest clip for newborns.

Unlike the Priori, the Pria 70 has higher rear-facing limit (40 lbs.) and a 70 lbs. forward facing limit. And the Pria 70 has the Air Protect feature for side impact protection (seen on Safety 1st seats). The seat also has three recline positions.

So is it worth $250? At this price, Dorel/Maxi Cosi is competing against Britax and Diono. . . and as such, our expectations are high. On some scores (padding, crash protection) the Pria 70 is equal to Britax. And the TinyFit seat does Britax one better (the Pria 70 starts at four pounds; Britax at five) . . . so if you know you're going to have a small newborn (parents of twins, take note), then the Pria is an excellent choice.

More than one parent we spoke with said they preferred the fabric on the Pria over Britax—the Pria's smooth fabric might be a better choice in hot/humid climates than the current crop of Britax seats, which features a less impressive fabric. Another plus for the Pria 70: its relatively small footprint means it will fit nicely in a compact vehicle.

The downsides? The Pria can only be tethered only in a forward-facing position (Britax can be tether either in forward or rear facing, which gives an extra measure of protection). Another negative: the cover for the headrest isn't removable.

And while the TinyFit seat is innovative, it makes the installation of this seat more complex than others (especially rear-facing). Finally, the Pria 70 lacks the no rethread harness feature you get on a Britax Boulevard, which is selling for the same price as the Pria 70 online.

Overall, we'll give this seat a B+. While not perfect, the Pria 70 is a good option, especially if you know you will be having a newborn on the small side. ***Rating: B+***

ORBIT TODDLER CAR SEAT

Price: $360.
Type: Convertible seat.
NHTSA ease of use rating:

★★★☆☆ Rear facing.
★★★☆☆ Forward facing.

Pros: Docks with Orbit travel system, sunshade, pad removes for easy cleaning.

Cons: Orbit travel system is $900—this $280 "accessory" is extra.

Comments: This unique convertible seat snaps into the Orbit base (see review of the infant car seat earlier in this chapter), but only in the rear facing mode (so you'll have to rotate it to get it forward facing). The seat also docks with Orbit's stroller frame, which is unique (it includes a detachable UV sunshade just for that purpose). The Orbit features side-impact braces, which are supposed to be used when the seat is in forward facing mode. We liked the fully removable seat cushion, which doesn't require the harness to be removed.

Feedback on this seat has been limited, given the Orbit system's high price (you first buy the Orbit's $900 infant seat and stroller frame combo before you graduate to this car seat). What we have heard is mixed: while folks like the Orbit system in general, the toddler seat is criticized for its weight and bulk. That seems to defeat the purpose of being able to take it from car to stroller frame. More than one reader said the Orbit was hard to adjust. And since $360 will buy you a top of the line Britax seat with change left over, we say pass on this one even if you decide you like the Orbit infant car seat. ***Rating: C***

PEG PEREGO
PRIMO VIAGGIO SIP CONVERTIBLE

Price: $329-$379
Limits: 5-45 lbs. rear-facing, 22-70 lbs. forward.
NHTSA ease of use rating: Not rated yet.
Comments: Stroller maker Peg Perego has long been a player in the infant car seat market, but this is their first shot at a convertible seat. We saw a prototype of their first effort at a trade show and thought it had promise: the Primo Viaggio SIP Convertible will work to 70 lbs. with a five-point harness and features an adjustable headrest, three recline positions

convertible seats

and a newborn insert. The winged headrest will provide a measure of side impact protection and shock absorbing foam in the base will add to crash protection.

Perego plans to offer two options for the cover: fabric for $329 and a leatherette for $380.

As always, Perego prices its products on the premium end of the market, hoping its fashion sense justifies the markup. But it's not like the competition is so lacking in the fashion/style department that there is much of an opening here. Given the fierce competition at the $300+ price level from Britax, Perego needs to offer more than just a me-too seat here—they should bring some innovation to the table. And from what we saw from the Viaggio prototype, we're not sure this is it. **Rating: Not Yet**

RECARO EURO
Price: $230.
Type: Convertible seat.
Limits: 5-35 lbs. rear-facing, 20-70 lbs. forward.
NHTSA ease of use rating: Not rated yet.
Comments: This new, lower-priced seat will debut in early 2012—it is basically the same as the Recaro ProRide, but omits the no rethread (infinite adjustable) harness. In a way, it is similar to the old Recaro Como. FYI: The Euro is made in China; the ProRide is made in the U.S. Also new in this seat: Safety Stripe stitching, a visual reminder to help parents avoid twisted straps. Since this seat wasn't out as of this writing, we don't have a rating yet.

RECARO PRORIDE
Price: $280 retail, $224 online.
Type: Convertible seat.
Limits: 5-35 lbs. rear-facing, 20-70 lbs. forward.
NHTSA ease of use rating:
★★★★☆ Rear facing.
★★★★☆ Forward facing.
Pros: Works to 70 lbs., adjustable headrest, EPP foam, side-impact protection wings. Higher harness slots than the Marathon.
Cons: May not fit rear facing in smaller vehicles. Hard to find in stores.
Comments: German car seat maker Recaro hopes to give Britax a run for its money with its new convertible, the ProRIDE. And yes, Recaro did come out with the first convertible seat to work to 70 lbs. (Britax caught up a year later).

Among the ProRIDE's unique features: side-impact protection wings made of cushy EPP foam. Similar to the Britax Boulevard, these wings provide both crash protection and head support for napping toddlers. The seat has many seat adjustments and the plush, microfiber fabric is impressive.

The negatives? Well, like the Britax Marathon, this is a big seat—it may not fit rear facing into smaller vehicles. A few parents told us they found the ProRIDE's head pillows to be too restrictive for their older toddlers. And Recaro's thinner distribution (as of this writing, Recaro isn't in as many stores as Britax) means you may have to search for a local store that carries it to see this seat in person.

Recaro has seen quite a few changes in the past year—first, the company moved all its production to Michigan. Then the company combined its previous convertible seat models into the new ProRIDE. Hence, some of our feedback for Recaro is based on the older Signo and Como models, which are now discontinued.

In general, parent feedback on the ProRIDE is quite positive—most folks say it is easy to use, although more than one noted the seat's large size makes it a tight fit in smaller vehicles. Compared to the similar Britax seats, readers like the head cushions (side-impact protection) somewhat better. Overall, this is an excellent seat that may be hard to find in stores. **Rating: A-**

Safety 1st Chart 65 Air

Comments: This newest addition to the "Air" family from Safety 1st will feature a 65 lb. weight limit and a headrest that adjusts separately from the back of the seat. The Chart Air 65 will be $145 at Target in early 2012. We just caught a glimpse of a prototype of this seat, so we'll do a more in-depth review when it is released into the wild. As you'd expect, the seat will feature the "Air Protect" side impact protection seen on other Air seats.

Safety 1st Complete Air 65
Price: $155 $240.
Type: Convertible seat.
Limits: 5 to 40 lbs. (19" to 40") rear facing, 22 to 65 lbs. (and 34" to 45") forward facing.
NHTSA ease of use rating:
★★★☆☆ Rear facing.
★★★☆☆ Forward facing.

Pros: 40 lbs. rear facing! Side impact protection.
Cons: Huge seat makes for a tough fit in small or mid-size cars.
Comments: "Revolutionary side impact technology" is how Safety 1st describes the new Complete Air, a convertible seat that works to an impressive 40 lbs. rear facing. The side impact shields inflate during a crash, providing more protection for baby in case of a crash.

The Complete Air also features a "QuickFit" harness system that adjusts the harness height without rethreading.

FYI: Safety 1st sells three versions of the Complete Air: the base

0, a LX and SE. The LX adds a three-position recline for $2~ d the SE or special edition, has upgraded fabric for $240 (although we've seen it online for closer to $200). And new for 2012, the Safety 1st Comfort Zone Complete Air SE features a built-in, battery-powered fan to cool sweaty toddlers. Price: $300.

Parent feedback on this seat has been mixed: more than one reader mentioned the seat's large size makes it a tough fit even in mid-size sedans, especially in rear facing mode. We were struck by the large number of reports of this seat not fitting in vehicles as large as the Honda Pilot, among others.

That said, folks who do like this seat cite its overall quality—the no-rethread harness particularly wins praise for ease of use.

Bottom line: kudos to Dorel for making a seat that works to 40 lbs. rear facing. But you better have a large vehicle to make it work.
Rating: B

SAFETY 1ST EASY FIT 65
Price: $90.
Type: Convertible seat.
Limits: 5-40 lbs. rear facing, 22-65 lbs. forward.
NHTSA ease of use rating: Not yet.
Pros: 40 lb. rear facing; compact seat. EPP foam. Easy to install.
Cons: No recline. Must rethread harness to adjust height.
Comments: This seat is a Babies R Us exclusive—the Easy Fit 65 features a 40 lb. rear-facing limit, four harness slots, three crotch positions and a relatively compact size. We liked the multi-position headrest, although the clunky cup holder might make installation near a door problematic (the cup holder is removeable). The key downside to the Easy Fit 65: you have to rethread the harness to adjust the harness height, which of course is common on lower price convertibles. And there are no recline positions for the Easy Fit 65.

Feedback on this seat has been sparse, but mostly positive. Folks like the overall fit and easy install plus the EPP foam is a nice feature at this price point.

FYI: This seat is also sold as the Eddie Bauer XRS 65 at Target for $130. Same seat, just upgraded fabric. And if you used to own a Safety 1st Uptown or Avenue and think this seat looks familiar, it is—the Easy Fit 65 has the same shell as those seats (but adds the headrest).

Finally, we should note that Safety 1st will release a version of this seat that will be available everywhere (not just Babies R Us) called the Guide 65. Look for it in January 2012; it will be similar to the Easy Fit 65. Price: $100.

And if the rethread harness on the Easy 65 is a deal killer for you, Safety 1st will release a version of this seat in 2012 with a no-rethread harness, dubbed the Able 65. Price: $150. ***Rating: A-***

SAFETY 1ST GUIDE 65
This seat is the same as the Safety 1st East Fit (and Eddie Bauer XRS 65). See review above.

SAFETY 1ST onSIDE AIR
Price: $80.
Type: Convertible seat.
Limits: 5-40 lbs. rear facing, 22-40 lbs. forward.
NHTSA ease of use rating:
★★★☆☆ Rear facing.
★★★★☆ Forward facing.
Pros: 40 lbs. rear facing! Side impact protection.
Cons: Only works to 40 lbs. front facing.
Comments: Safety 1st debuted this seat in 2010 as a more affordable alternative in its new Air Protect line. While it works to the same amazing 40 lbs. rear facing as the $180 Complete Air, the onSide Air tops out at the same 40 lbs. forward facing. That's odd, but we suppose the attraction here is a seat that can be used rear facing to 40 lbs. AND costs under $100. Plus you get the Air Protect side impact technology, which deploys in a crash to better protect a baby's head. Parent reviews on this seat have been positive. And given the value here with a price under $100, we'll recommend it. ***Rating: B+***

As you can imagine, the child safety seat world changes quickly—read our blog (BabyBargains.com) for the latest news, recalls and more with car seats.

Our Picks: Brand Recommendations

Here are our top picks for infant and convertible seats. Are these seats safer than others? No—all child safety seats sold in the U.S. and Canada must meet minimum safety standards. These seats are our top picks because they combine the best features, usability (including ease of installation) and value. Remember the safest and best seat for your baby is the one that best fits your child and vehicle. Finding the right car seat can be a bit of trial and error; you may find a seat CANNOT be installed safely in your vehicle because of the quirks of the seat or your vehicle's safety belt system. All seats do NOT fit all cars. Hence it is always wise to buy a seat from a store or web site with a good return policy.

FYI: See the chart on pages 432-433 for a comparison of features for both infant and convertible/front-facing car seats.

Best Bets: Infant Car Seats

Good. Let's be honest: if you're on a super-tight budget, consider not buying an infant car seat at all. A good five-point, convertible car seat (see below for recommendations) will work for both infants and children.

Better. The *Chicco KeyFit 30* is an excellent seat that works to 30 lbs. The KeyFit gets high scores from our readers on ease of use—installation is a snap and adjusting the harness is easy. The seat also features EPS foam and a newborn insert. The downsides? The seat is pricey at $180 and doesn't work with as many strollers as our top choice below.

Best. *Graco SnugRide 35* is easy to use and install, and features EPS foam. FYI: Graco makes this seat in four versions, the main difference is weight limits—22, 30, 32 or 35 lbs. While we are recommending the 35-pound version as our top pick, the 30 or 32 lb. version would work as well for most folks. At $150, the SnugRide is a good value.

Dark Horses. The *Britax Chaperone* features rock solid protection and an anti-rebound bar—but it is pricey at $180-$195 and heavy (11.2 lbs.). However, if you are getting a Britax stroller, this would be a good add-on. On the more affordable end of the dark horse spectrum, the *First Years Via* ($150-$170) has side impact protection, EPS foam lining the entire seat and a washable pad.

Best Bets: Convertible Car Seats

Good. For a decent, no-frills car seat, we recommend the *Cosco Scenera*. Yes, we realize Cosco's safety track record has been rocky, but this seat is still worth considering for that little-used second car or Grandma's vehicle. The Scenera is a basic, bare-bones convertible that works to 40 lbs., is easy to install and costs $40—no, that's not a typo. With the prices of some car seats pushing $300, it's nice to know you can find a decent seat for well under $100. Another good bet for Grandma: the *Evenflo Titan Elite* ($100), which has a bit more padding than the Scenera.

Better. The *Diono Radian RXT* is pricey ($340 retail, $277 online) but has some amazing stats: it can work rear-facing to 5-45 pounds, forward-facing to 80 lbs. in a five-point harness . . . and then to 120 pounds as a belt-positioning booster. Add in memory foam, side-impact protection and the ability to fold flat for storage and you've got a winner!

If you have a compact car, the *First Years True Fit* ($145-$250) is an excellent seat that works to 65 lbs. but adds this nifty trick: its head-rest pops off to make it easier to install rear facing in compact cars.

Best. So, what is our top recommendation for convertible car seats? The **Britax Marathon** takes the crown this year. The Marathon ($290) enables you to keep your child rear facing to 40 lbs. and forward facing to 70 with the five-point harness. The seat features EPS foam, side-impact protection, steel bar construction and can be tethered forward or rear facing. Britax has improved the seat in the last year with new technology that absorbs energy in a crash (SafeCell) and a harness that can be height adjusted without re-threading. All in all, an excellent seat worth the extra price.

If Grandma is buying. What if money isn't an issue when buying a seat? One obvious seat that we'd suggest is the top-of-the-line **Britax Boulevard 70 CS** ($340), which is much like the Marathon, but adds a height-adjuster knob (to better fit the harness to a growing child) and additional side-impact protection.

Another excellent seat if Grandma is buying would be the **Recaro ProRIDE** at $280. Recaro has many of the same features as Britax seats, but is priced about 20% lower.

Booster Seats

So what is a booster? Simply put, this seat boosts a child to correctly sit in an auto safety belt. Yes, some boosters have five-point harnesses (more on this later), but most boosters work with your vehicle's safety belt.

Most parents know they have to put an infant or toddler into a car seat. What some folks don't realize, however, is that child passenger safety doesn't end when baby outgrows that convertible car seat—any child from 40 to 80 lbs. and less than 4'9" (generally, kids age four to eight) should be restrained in a booster seat (or one of the new harnessed seats that work up to 80 lbs.). And in most states, booster seat use is mandated by law. Numerous states have passed laws requiring the use of booster seats. And more states are following their lead.

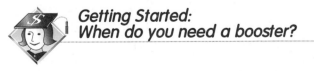

Getting Started: When do you need a booster?

Your child needs a booster seat when he outgrows his convert-

Continued on page 434

The following is a selection of better known infant car seats and how they compare on features:

Maker	Model	Price	Weight/Height Limits
Baby Trend	Flex-Loc	$80-$130	30 lbs./30" *
Britax	B-Safe	$140-$180	30 lbs./32"
Britax	Chaperone	$180-$195	30 lbs./32"
Chicco	KeyFit 30	$155-$180	30 lbs./30"
Combi	Shuttle 33	$160-$180	33 lbs./33"
Cosco	Comfy Carry	$60	22 lbs./29"
Cybex	Aton	$200-$230	32 lbs./30"
Evenflo	Discovery 5	$55-$60	22 lbs./26"
	Embrace	$65-$70	22 lbs./29"
First Years	Via/I140	$150-$170	35 lbs./30"
Graco	SnugRide 35	$160	35 lbs./32"
Maxi Cosi	Mico	$150-$180	22 lbs./29"
Orbit	Orbit	$400	30 lbs./32"
Peg Perego	Primo Viaggio SIP	$225-$300	30 lbs./30"
Safety 1st	OnBoard 35 Air	$160-$180	35 lbs./32"

Convertible Seats

The following is a selection of popular convertible car seats and how they compare on features:

Maker	Model	Price	Weight Limits (in pounds)	
			Rear	Forward
Britax	Boulevard 70	$240-$340	40 lbs.	70 lbs.
	Marathon 70	$215-$290	40	70
	Roundabout 55	$160-$200	40	55
Combi	Coccoro	$200-$240	30	40
Cosco	Scenera 40RF	$40-$60	40	40
Diono	Radian	$260-$340	44/45	80/100/120
Evenflo	Symphony 65	$165-$250	35	65/100
	Triumph Advance	$140-$180	35	65
First Years	True Fit	$145-$250	35	65
Maxi Cosi	Pria 70	$250	40	70
Recaro	ProRIDE	$224-$280	35	70
Safety 1st	Complete Air 65	$155-$240	40	65

KEY **SIDE IMPACT:** Does the seat have side-impact protection?

FOAM TYPE: Does the seat have a EPS or EPP foam (or none at all)? See box on page 385 for a discussion.

LEVEL IND.: Does the seat have a level indicator for easier installation?

CARRIER WEIGHT: This is the weight of the carrier only (not the base).

SIDE IMPACT	LEVEL IND.	FOAM TYPE	BASE WIDTH	CARRIER WEIGHT	OUR RATING
◆	◆	EPS	16.5"	9.7 LBS.	B–
◆	◆	EPS	17.5	11.2	A–
◆		EPS	18.3	11.2	B
◆	◆	EPS	17	9.4	A
	◆	EPS	17	11.1	C+
		NONE	17	6.6	N/A
◆	◆	EPS	15	8.8	N/A
		EPS	17.5	5.5	F
	◆	EPS	18	7.0	D+
◆		EPS	18.5	8.4	A–
	◆	EPS	19	9.5	A
◆		EPP	17	8	B
	◆	EPP	15.25	12	B
◆	◆	EPS	15.5	11.1	A–
◆	◆	EPP	15	9	B

boosters

RATING	COMMENT
A–	"CS" VERSION MAKES HARNESS EASIER TO USE.
A	MUST RETHREAD BELTS TO ADJUST HARNESS HEIGHT.
A	EPS FOAM, NO-TWIST STRAPS, TETHER REAR OR FORWARD.
B	COMPACT CAR SEAT WEIGHTS JUST 11 LBS.
B+	SIMPLE SEAT, GREAT FOR AIR TRAVEL OR GRANDPARENTS.
N/A	ONLY SEAT THAT FOLDS UP; CAN USE TETHER REAR-FACING.
B+	NEW LATCH SYSTEM MAKES IT EASIER TO INSTALL.
A–	MEMORY HARNESS; CAN ADJUST BELTS WITHOUT RETHREAD.
A	EPP FOAM; HEADREST POPS OFF FOR EASIER INSTALL.
B+	INFANT INSERT LETS SEAT START AT 4 LBS.
A–	ADJUSTABLE HEADREST, EPP FOAM, SIDE IMPACT WINGS.
B	SIDE IMPACT WINGS, QUICK FIT HARNESS BUT LARGE SEAT.

ible seat. This happens when he exceeds the weight limit or when he is too tall for the harness (his shoulders are taller than the top slots in the seat). For most children, this happens around ages three to five.

Booster seats use the vehicle's safety belt and hence require your child to be mature enough to stay in the seat. The seat belt is all that is holding your child in the seat—unlike the escape-proof five-point harness of a convertible seat.

What if your child has outgrown a convertible seat but isn't mature enough to stay in a booster? Then consider a hybrid seat that uses a five-point harness up to 65 or 85 pounds.

Best Online Sources

◆ *SafetyBeltSafeUSA* (carseat.org) has three good reports on booster seats (click on the button, Booster Seats) that explain proper installation and offer other tips. Another great site is CarSeatData.org.

◆ *The National Highway Traffic Safety Administration* (nhtsa. gov) has excellent videos showing proper booster seat installation and use. Click on Child Safety Seats, then on Booster Seats. Also cool: the NHTSA now rates and reviews booster seats for ease of use and other factors.

Smart Shopping Tips

Smart Shopper Tip #1
Booster Laws
"My daughter just turned four, and my state doesn't require her to use a car seat anymore. Does she really need a booster?"

A number of states have recently enacted stiffer car seat laws, usually requiring children to use "appropriate restraints" until age six or 60 lbs. (some state laws are now up to age eight or nine and 80 lbs). But other states still only require a car seat until a child turns four (some even just two) years old. So why should you continue to hassle with a car seat or booster after this time?

We like to remind parents that there is the law . . . and then there is the law of physics. Car seat belts are made for adults, and children (as well as some short adults) just don't fit well, and don't get good protection from those belts. Lap belts used with four- to eight-year old children routinely cause such severe injuries and paralysis that the injuries even have their own name: "lap belt syndrome." Children using lap/shoulder belts often put the shoulder belt behind their back (since it is so darn uncomfortable), giving them no more protection than a lap belt alone. Ejections are another common problem with young children in adult belts, even if they are using both the lap and shoulder belt.

Booster seats (and of course regular car seats) work very simply to eliminate this problem. Boosters properly position the lap part of the belt on a child's hip bone, not their soft internal organs. They elevate the child and include a special adjuster so that the lap shoulder belt fits right on the strong shoulder bones. Booster seats should be used until a child fits the adult belts like an adult. Try out the Five Step Test (later in this section) to see if your child is ready.

See our web page for pictures of good and bad fit for a booster (BabyBargains.com, click on Bonus Material).

Smart Shopper Tip #2
Different seats, lots of confusion?

"When I was shopping for a booster seat, I was confused with all the types of seats out there. Why isn't there just one type of booster?"

Good question. We've noticed that buying a booster seat can be a bit more complex than buying another car seat. For example, an infant car seat is, well, an infant car seat. But a booster can come in several versions: high back boosters, backless boosters, combination seat/boosters, and more.

In this chapter, we'll try to simplify things a bit. Any time we refer to a *belt-positioning booster*, we mean a seat that uses the lap/shoulder belt to secure the child. Most other car seats (like convertible seats) use an internal harness to hold the child, while the seat itself is attached to the car with the seat belt or the LATCH system.

What's made this so confusing is that car seat makers have blurred the lines between convertible seats and boosters in recent years by coming out with hybrid models that use a five-point harness up to 65 (or 80) pounds and then convert to a belt-positioning booster. The Britax Frontier and Graco Nautilus are two examples.

Confusing, yes we know. But we want this section to cover all the options for older children who've outgrown their traditional convertible seat . . . so you'll see a variety of options in this section. Let's break down what's out there:

◆ **High back boosters (HBB):** Belt-positioning boosters come in two flavors: high back boosters and backless boosters. High back boosters have often been called "kid's captain's chairs," which they kind of resemble. They are designed to be simple, but provide vital safety features for children who've out-grown a harnessed seats. These boosters properly position the lap belt on a child's strong hip bones, rather than letting it ride up on the soft internal organs. And they provide correct positioning of the shoulder belt, so the child can comfortably wear it and get critical upper body support. The high back also protects the child's head from whiplash if there are no head restraints in the vehicle, and the high back may also give some side sleeping support. ALL of these boosters require a lap and shoulder belt. FYI: Some high back boost-ers convert into backless boosters for older kids.

◆ **Backless boosters:** These belt-posi-tioning boosters work the same way as high back boosters—they just don't have a back. Safety-wise, these can be a bit better than a high back booster, since the child sits against the vehicle seat. They do the same job positioning the lap belt, and usually include some sort of strap to adjust the shoulder belt. But they don't provide head sup-port if you have low seat backs, and they don't give any side or sleep-ing support. On the other hand, they are often popular with older kids, since they can be quite inconspicuous.

Harnessed seats that work to 70+ lbs.

Safety experts say it is best to keep a child in a five-point har-ness as long as possible. Here are some examples:

NAME	TOP WEIGHT LIMIT (HARNESS)	PRICE
Britax		
Advocate	70 lbs.	$370
Boulevard 70	70	$310-$330
Frontier 85	85	$280
Marathon	70	$280
Diono		
Radian RXT/R120/R100	80	$230-$300
Maxi Cosi		
Pria 70	70	$250
Peg Perego		
Primo Viaggio SIP	70	$329-$379
Recaro		
Euro	70	$230
ProRIDE	70	$280

◆ *Hybrid/Combo seats:* These are probably the most confusing "booster" seats because
sometimes they are a booster, and sometimes
they aren't. They come with a five-point harness,
which can generally be used up to 40 lbs. (some
seats now to 65 and even 80 lbs.). Then the harness comes off, and the seat can be used as a
belt-positioning booster, usually to 80 or 100 lbs. They get the name
"combination," or "combo" for short, from the two jobs they do.

A recent report by the Insurance Institute for Highway Safety criticized many older combo seats, saying they poorly fit kids when in
booster mode. We factored this report into our ratings.

Newer combo seats (namely the Britax Frontier, Graco Nautilus,
among others) now work to 65 or 80 pounds. These combo seats do
a better job at fitting older kids, whether in harness or booster mode.

The take-home message: hybrid/combo boosters are great for
children that have outgrown their convertible seats but aren't mature
enough to sit in a belt-positioning booster (the types described earlier). The five-point harness provides that extra measure of safety and
security while they are still young (typically, a child has to be three or
older to be mature enough to handle the belt-positioners).

◆ *Special Needs Seats:* There are a few seats on the market
now that don't really fit into any category. One is the Britax Traveler
Plus, which is designed for special needs kids up to 105 lbs.

Smart Shopper Tip #3
Avoid Seat Belt Adjusters

*"The shoulder belt was bugging my son's neck, so I bought a lit-
tle adjuster thing. Is that as good as a booster?"*

Several companies make inexpensive belt adjusters ($10 or so),
which help to properly position the shoulder belt on your child.
Sounds good, right? Wrong. Look closely at the pictures on the box.
In order to pull the shoulder belt down, and make it more comfortable for a short passenger, virtually all of these devices also pull the lap
part of the belt UP, right back onto the tummy. Marketed to kids 50
lbs. and up, these devices are also packed with statements that confuse even the most safety conscious parents, like "designed to meet
FMVSS 213," a reference to a federal safety standard in crash testing.
What's wrong with that picture? That federal standard doesn't even
apply to items marketed for children 50 lbs. and up! Worse yet, government crash tests show that a three-year-old dummy is less protected when using one of these adjusters compared to using the regular
vehicle safety belt. When tested with a six-year-old dummy, same
result. Bottom line: forget these adjusters and use a booster seat.

boosters

CAR
SEATS

Smart Shopper Tip #4
Cars with only lap belts
"What if my car has only lap belts in the back seat?"

While lap belts are just fine with infant and convertible seats, they are a no-no when it comes to boosters. If your vehicle doesn't have shoulder belts, check with your vehicle's manufacturer to see if they offer a retrofit kit. If that doesn't work, consider buying a newer vehicle with lap/shoulder belts in the back seat. In the meantime, there are a few seats that can be used with a lap belt for kids over 40 lbs. See the convertible seat reviews earlier in this chapter for details.

Smart Shopper Tip #5
LATCH system and boosters
"My car has LATCH attachments. Do booster seats work with this?"

We discussed LATCH earlier in this chapter; in short, most booster seats do NOT work with LATCH. There are a couple of exceptions: see reviews of Clek and Diono's boosters.

Smart Shopper Tip #6
Back Harness Adjuster
"I loved our combo seat—until the day I discovered its fatal flaw. When it was cold, my daughter's thick coat required me to loosen the belts on her five-point harness. I discovered this could only be done from the BACK of the seat! What a pain!"

More booster seats are adding five-point harnesses so they can be used at younger ages/weights (some seats start as little as 20 lbs.). The problem? The cheapest combo boosters do NOT have up-front belt adjustments. You must adjust the belts from the back of the seat, which is a pain especially in cold weather. A word to the wise: if you get a combo seat, make sure the belt adjustments are UP FRONT and easy to access. The question of coats/snowsuits and car seats comes up frequently—we should stress that most safety advocates suggest that a child in a safety seat wear a coat that is no thicker than a polar fleece. Big bulky coats are a hazard. Why? In the event of a crash, the coat will compress, creating a gap between the child and the restraint (and possibly ejecting the child from the seat).

Smart Shopper Tip #7
Too Tall for a Convertible
"My daughter is too tall for her convertible car seat but is only 32 lbs. Now what?"

Many children outgrow their convertibles by height before weight. Most convertibles say that they are good from 40" to 49" tall, but a better measure is to make sure the child's shoulders are no higher than the top harness slot. Another guideline: when a child's ears reach the top of the car seat shell, he's outgrown the seat.

Remember that while weight limits are set in stone, height rules are more like guidelines. Example: two children could both be 48" tall, but one still fits in her convertible car seat while the other clearly needs to be a booster. Why? Because a child could be 48" tall, but have a long torso—and if a child's ears are at the top of the car seat shell, it's time to move to a booster. Yet the other child who is 48" tall may be shorter in the torso (but have longer legs) and may still fit in the convertible.

Smart Shopper Tip #8

Who crash tests booster seats?

"Are there independent sources to find boost seat crash test ratings?"

There are three sources for booster seat ratings: *Consumer Reports*; The National Highway Traffic and Safety Administration (NHTSA) and the Insurance Institute for Highway Safety (IIHS).

Consumer Reports magazine independently crash tests and evaluates boosters for ease of use. The NHTSA assigns ease of use ratings (on a one to five star scale) for booster seats—these are based on "vehicle installation features" and how well the seat secures a child. In the review section later in this chapter, we list this as the NHTSA ease of use rating.

The Insurance Institute for Highway Safety (IIHS) evaluates how well a booster seat fits the lap and shoulder belt on a four to eight year old child. The IIHS doesn't crash test seats, just evaluates belt fit. Seats are judged best bets, good bets or not recommended. In the review section, we list the IIHS rating for each booster. FYI: In some cases, the IIHS says a booster is rated "check fit." That means these seats may work in *some* vehicles; you need to check the fit.

At *Baby Bargains*, we look at tests and information from these three sources and combine that with parent feedback to come up with our booster seat ratings.

Safe & Sound

1 **CHECK YOUR VEHICLE'S OWNERS MANUAL.** We're amazed at the detailed info on installing child safety seats you can find in your vehicle's owners manual, especially for newer vehicles. Car seats also include detailed installation instructions.

2 **ALWAYS USE THE LAP/SHOULDER BELT WITH THE BOOSTER**—this provides crucial upper body protection in the case of an accident. NEVER use just the lap belt.

3 **DON'T EXPECT TO USE THAT BOOSTER ON AN AIRPLANE.** FAA rules prohibit the use of booster seats on airlines. Why? Booster seats must be used with a shoulder belt to be effective—and airplanes only have lap belts. Our advice: if you travel a lot, consider a harnessed seat that works to 65+ pounds that is certified to work on airplanes—the Diono Radian is an example.

4 **BE CAREFUL OF HAND-ME-DOWN AND SECOND-HAND BARGAINS.** Most old booster seats don't meet current safety standards. If you do find a newer used booster, make sure you ask the original owner if it has been in a crash, and then check the seat for recalls (Safety Belt Safe has a great recall list at carseat.org). And if your seat has been in a crash, is over six years old or missing its proper labels, stick it in a black garbage bag and throw it away.

5 **ONLY USE CARDBOARD CUPS IN BOOSTER SEAT CUP HOLDERS.** You'll note that some seats now come with cup or juice box holders. These are a great convenience, but most manufacturers only recommend cardboard cups (like to-go cups) or juice boxes be used. Anything harder could become a dangerous projectile in a crash.

6 **WHEN IS A CHILD BIG ENOUGH TO USE JUST THE AUTO'S SAFETY BELT?** When a child is over 4'9" and can sit with his or her back straight against the back seat cushion (with knees bent over the seat's edge), then he or she can go with just the auto's safety belt. Still have doubts? Try this Five-Step Test from Safety Belt Safe, USA:

◆ Does the child sit all the way back against the auto seat?
◆ Does the belt cross the shoulder between neck and arm?
◆ Is the lap belt as low as possible, touching the thighs?
◆ Can the child stay seated like this for the whole trip?
◆ Do the child's knees bend comfortably at the edge of the seat?

If you answered no to any of these questions, your child needs a booster seat, and will probably be more comfortable in one too.

7 **DON'T USE A BOOSTER TOO SOON.** Most safety techs say a child should stay in a harnessed seat as long as possible—many seats can now keep a kid harnessed until 65, 70 or even 80 pounds. Some parents try to switch a too-young toddler to a booster . . . but kids that are under four are often not mature enough to correctly sit in a belt-positioning booster.

Booster Car Seats (model by model reviews)

BABY TREND FAST BACK
Booster type: Combo
Limits: up to 120 lbs.; 22 to 70 lbs. with harness, belt-positioning booster for 30 to 100 lbs. Backless 40-120 lbs.
Price: $200
IIHS rating: Not yet.
NHTSA ease of use rating: Not yet.
Pros: Harnessed works to 70 lbs. Rigid LATCH.
Cons: New, so no parent feedback yet.
Comments: This new seat is a Babies R Us exclusive for the first half of 2012. The Baby Trend Fast Back is a harnessed booster that works up to 70 lbs. with a harness and then as a belt-positioning booster to 100 lbs. Finally, pop off the back and you'll have a backless booster to 120 lbs. The Fast Back features rigid LATCH built into the steel frame and EPS foam lining on the side and head wings of the seat. The "snug sides" are what Baby Trend refers to the seat's head wings. The Fast back will also have eight harness positions and two crotch buckle positions, plus cup holders (naturally).

This seat just debuted as of press time, so our only first impressions were the prototype we saw at a trade show. In short, we thought the seat hit all the right design notes, but as we've commented on in other Baby Trend reviews, the company itself is a bit wonky. And the initial reviews for Baby Trend's other new booster seat (Euro Sport) were quite negative, so we'll have to wait and see if the Fast Back gets any traction. ***Rating: Not Yet.***

BABY TREND TRENDZ EUROSPORT 3-IN-1
Booster type: Combo
Limits: 22-100 lbs.; 22 to 50 lbs. with harness, belt-positioning booster for 30 to 100 lbs.
Price: $100-$130.
IIHS rating: Not yet.
NHTSA ease of use rating: Not yet.
Pros: Tension indicators show when harness is tightened correctly.
Cons: Low harness weight, low top harness slot means kids will outgrow this seat too quickly. Baby Trend's overall funkiness.
Comments: Baby Trend has been a long-time player in the infant car seat market, but this is their first foray into booster seats. The Baby Trend trendZ Euro Sport 3-in-1 booster has a harness that works up to 50 lbs, after which it becomes a high back booster (and then backless) up to 100 lbs. Tension indictors on the harness on LATCH straps indicate a correct fit. Another cool feature: the

smart safety buckle beeps if the harness is unbuckled, in case you have a child who is a little Houdini.

So what's not to like? Well, the seat only has a small piece of EPS foam behind the headrest—the sidewings are not foam lined. The 50 lb. harness limit seems skimpy compared to other combo seats that go to 65 lbs and beyond. The low top harness slot (15″) is another concern—most children will outgrow this seat's harness far too quickly. The narrow seat and one crotch position will also be a negative for bigger toddlers. And we are not impressed with the Baby Trend brand overall. Their customer service and overall quality lags other seat makers, in our opinion.

Bottom line: we say pass on this one. There are better combo/harnessed seats out there. ***Rating: D+***

BRITAX FRONTIER 85 / SICT

Limits: 20-85 lbs. with harness, up to 120 lbs. as a belt-positioning booster. For kids at least two years old, 25 lbs. and 30-57″ for the harness, 42″ to 65″ in height for belt-positioning booster.
Booster type: Combo
Price: $215-$340.
IIHS rating: Best Bet (both models).
NHTSA ease of use rating:

★★★☆☆ Booster mode
★★★★☆ Harness mode

Pros: Works to 85 lbs. with five-point harness. A bit wider, deeper than the Graco Nautilus. New SICT version adds side-impact cushions.
Cons: Large seat, expensive.
Comments: The Frontier aims for a market similar to the Graco Nautilus (see review later)—it is a harnessed seat that works to a whopping 85 lbs. and then a belt-positioning booster to 120 lbs. after that. The Frontier is targeted at kids at least two years old who have outgrown their convertible seats but aren't mature enough to sit in a belt-positioning booster.

In a past edition of this book, we only gave the Frontier a C because it was challenging to install and the top harness slots were below that of the Graco Nautilus. That meant kids could outgrow the seat long before the stated top weight limit.

Well, there is good news: the Frontier 85 is much improved over the past Frontier—the top harness slot is now nearly 20″ (from the old 18.25″) and installation is easier. The overall weight and height limits are higher and there are a series of small improvements (example: the cup holders inset in the seat, rather than stick out from the side, etc.).

So kudos to Britax for listening to its customers and improving the Frontier. Are there any negatives to this seat? Well, just as before, this is a big, bulky seat. Although the Frontier 85 weighs a couple of pounds less than the last version, it's still nearly 20 lbs. Carrying it through an airport isn't going to be fun (the Frontier is certified for use in an airplane, but only with its five-point harness—not as a booster).

The Frontier is 19.5" wide—that means fitting it three across in a carpool won't be easy for most vehicles. Also: the Frontier has limited recline settings and that might be a negative for some. Finally, we should note more than a few readers complained about the long-term durability of the mesh fabric on the seat, which is prone to snags. On the plus side, the mesh fabric doesn't extend as far on the new Frontier 85, so this probably will help. Overall, reader feedback on the Frontier 85 has been very positive.

Of course, the price of the Frontier 85 is perhaps its biggest draw-back—the similar Graco Nautilus is HALF the price. That said, the Britax Frontier 85 is an excellent seat and is highly recommended. FYI: The Frontier 85's list price is $300, but it is sold for as little as $215 on Amazon and $240 on Diapers.com.

In mid 2011, Britax launched an additional version of the Frontier, called the Frontier 85 SICT. SICT stands for side impact cushion technology. The Frontier SICT adds these side-impact cushions, plus a new "Easy Remove" two-piece cover so you can clean the fabric without disassembling the seat. Also new: the Frontier 85 SICT can be used without a top tether (we still strongly recommend using the tether, but we realize some vehicles make this a challenge).

The list price for the Britax 85 SICT is $400, but Babies R Us has it for $340, Diapers.com for $271 and Amazon for $255. **Rating: A**

BRITAX PARKWAY SG/SGL

Booster type: High back

Limits: 40 to 100 lbs., 38-63" in height, as a belt-positioning booster.

Price: $95 to $125

IIHS rating: Parkway SG backless: Check fit. Parkway SG high back: Good bet. Parkway SGL backless: Check fit. Parkway SGL high back: Best bet.

NHTSA ease of use rating: ★★★☆☆

Pros: Side-impact protection, plush cover.

Cons: Pricey, narrow seat, skimpy armrests.

Comments: Britax brought this seat back from the discontinued graveyard in 2009 in order to have a more affordable seat to compete against the Graco TurboBooster (apparently, having just the $250 Frontier to sell in a down economy wasn't a smart move). The main difference between the new Parkway and the old model is the Slide Guard (SG) feature—this keeps a child from submarining out of the seat in a crash. Also new: the back of the Parkway removes so it can be a backless booster.

In the past year, Britax introduced a version of the Parkway that has LATCH connectors (SGL model). It runs $125. Otherwise, the SGL is the same as the SG. The LATCH feature is helpful for keeping the seat in place when unoccupied.

Comparing the Parkway to the Graco TurboBooster, we'd give Britax the advantage when it comes to seat covers—the fabric Britax uses is much nicer than Graco's. That said, the Graco TurboBooster's armrests are bigger than the Parkway's, which are not adjustable. And the Parkway has a somewhat narrower seat than the TurboBooster, which might mean a tight fit for larger toddlers.

Bottom line: this is a good seat, but at a price that is double the Graco TurboBooster, we'd give the Graco seat the edge in overall value. ***Rating: A-***

BUBBLEBUM

Booster type: Backless
Limits: 40 lbs. to 80 lbs. (kids over age 4)
Price: $40
IIHS rating: Best Bet
NHTSA ease of use rating: Not yet.
Pros: Small and lightweight. Deflates and rolls up into carry bag for travel. Good for three-across situation.
Cons: Unstable, wobbly to sit on. Not comfortable for a long car ride.
Comments: BubbleBum is an inflatable, backless booster seat invented by a certified car seat tech from Northern Ireland (it's been available in the UK for quite a while). The idea was to have an easy-to-carry booster seat option when you travel and have to rent a car. But it's also a great option if you live in a place like New York and need a portable option for taxis.

Another plus: it's affordable ($40). But does it work well? Car seat techs report that the BubbleBum does provide good lap and shoulder belt fit (the IIHS gave it a "Best Bet" rating). The seat belt is threaded through a lap belt positioner, which keeps the belt in the proper position.

A couple complaints, however: it can be confusing to use the positioner at first. Techs recommend threading the seat belt through the positioner after you have buckled your child into the seat to get a tighter fit. Also, it's a small seat and doesn't provide much thigh support. So the BumbleBum isn't going to be comfortable for long-term use. On the plus side, however, the small size of the seat makes it possible to use for three kids in the same row.

We like the BumbleBum for it's portability, price and safety. When used for short-term situations and travel, it's a great option. So we'll give it a top rating. ***Rating: A***

CHICCO KEYFIT STRADA

Booster type: High back
Limits: 33 to 100 lbs.
Price: $140-$180
IIHS rating: High back: Best Bet. Backless: Check fit.
NHTSA ease of use rating: ☆☆☆☆☆

Comments: The KeyFit Strada is the first belt-positioning booster from Chicco, a brand better known for its strollers and high chairs. The KeyFit Strada's unique features include a headrest and side wings that adjust up and out and more EPS foam than other seats. The seat converts to a backless booster for kids up to 100 lbs. and features an adjustable, clip-on cup holder.

The price seems high: $140 to $180 is a bit much, when you consider the similar Graco TurboBooster starts at $50. It's hard to image how an adjustable headrest and side wings would justify such a price premium.

Reader feedback on this seat has been limited, since it hadn't been on the market for long as of press time. However, most folks like it and the Strada earned a Best Bet from the IIHS in high back mode. A few critics note some kids found the little hump on the seat base uncomfortable, especially for longer trips. And Chicco notes the seat cover can only be sponged off for cleaning, instead of hand washing— that's a problem if there's a serious stain that needs to be cleaned.

Other than that, we will recommend the Strada—it is a well designed, if pricey booster. ***Rating: B***

CLEK OLLI/OZZI

Booster type: Backless booster
Limits: 40 to 120 lbs., 57" tall.
Price: $95 to $105 Olli, $70 to $80 Ozzi
IIHS rating: Check fit.
NHTSA ease of use rating: ☆☆☆☆☆

Pros: Only LATCH backless booster. Removable, washable seat cover.

Cons: No cup holders. High price.

Comments: Canadian car seat maker Magna's (magnaclek.com) backless booster is unique: it is one of only a few backless boosters that use LATCH for a secure fit to the car. Your child then buckles in with the auto safety belt. The main advantage of the Clek is that the LATCH connectors hold the seat in place when it is unoccupied. Nice, but is it worth $100 when most other (LATCH-less) backless boosters run $20?

Reader feedback on the Clek Olli (pictured) has been positive— readers love how easy it is to install and use. The downsides: it is

CAR SEATS

CAR
SEATS

pricey and lacks a cup holder, seen on most other boosters. FYI: Clek makes a scaled down version of the Olli called the Ozzi: it omits the quick release strap, mesh side storage pocket, carry bag and armrest padding. The Olli comes in several colors and is made of a micro fiber; the Ozzi comes in one color (black) and has less expensive fabric. The Ozzi is $30 cheaper. **Rating: A-**

CLEK OOBR
Limits: 33 to 100 lbs., 57" tall.
Booster type: High back and backless.
Price: $200-$300
IIHS rating: Backless: Check fit. High back: Best Bet.

NHTSA ease of use rating: ★★★★★
Comments: The Clek Oobr is a high back booster that has a removable back. As with the Clek Olli/Ozzi, the Oobr features LATCH for a secure fit to the car. The Oobr's other main point is that the seat reclines up to 12 degrees and has an adjustable head restraint. At prices approaching $300, however, this is a tough sell for most parents. With the top-selling high back booster (the Graco TurboBooster) selling for $200 less, it is unclear whether these features make it worth the investment.

Despite the price, reader feedback on this seat has been very positive, with folks saying the overall quality and LATCH feature outweigh the cost issue. Quality and safety-wise, this seat would earn an A if it wasn't priced so high. **Rating: B**

COMBI KOBUCK
Limits: 33 to 125 lbs.; 33" to 57" in height.
Booster type: High back and backless booster.
Price: $90 to $120
IIHS rating: Good Bet.
NHTSA ease of use rating: ★★★★☆
Pros: Side impact protection; can be used as a backless booster. Picked as a "good bet" by IIHS.
Backless booster scored as a "best bet" in same survey.
Cons: Funky cup holder; not sold in many stores so it may be hard to see in person.
Comments: Want side impact protection but turned off by the restrictive wings of other booster seats? Combi's Kobuk aims to fill this niche with a protective headrest, minus the tight-fitting wings. We liked the padding of this seat (even the armrests are padded), but the cheesy cup holder that sticks straight out of the seat and relatively high price (twice the price of a Graco TurboBooster) are negatives.

On the plus side, the entire seat is lined with EPS and "egg shock" (comfort) foam. Combi's pitch for the Kobuk includes a claim that its front air vents allow for "healthy ventilation." Well, given parent feedback, we don't think this seat is any cooler than other boosters, but it's hard to measure that claim. In the past year, Combi hasn't made many changes to this seat but it is now rated to 125 lbs. (up from 100 lbs.).

Parent feedback on this seat has been positive. The Kobuk scored as a good bet on the latest IIHS rating and four out of five stars in the government's ease of use tests. Unfortunately, like many Combi products, this seat may be hard to find at retail. That is more of a problem for a booster seat, as it is best to sit your child in the seat before purchasing. ***Rating: B+***

Cosco Ambassador
This seat is reviewed on our web site, BabyBargains.com.

Cosco High Back Booster
(a.k.a. Cosco Complete Voyager)
Booster type: Combo
Limits: 22-40 lbs. with harness, 40-80 as belt positioning booster.
IIHS rating: Check fit.
NHTSA ease of use rating:

⭐⭐☆☆☆ Booster mode:
⭐⭐☆☆☆ Harness mode:

Price: Two different versions, $55 to $70.
Pros: Inexpensive, fits great in cars, five-point harness option from 22 to 40 lbs., headrest, armrests, storage bag.
Cons: Straps twist, Cosco's abysmal safety record. Poor ease of use.
Comments: The Cosco High Back Booster is a combo booster with a five-point harness from 22 to 40 lbs., then works as a booster from 40 to 80 lbs. But this seat has cut corners at every turn. First and foremost, the top harness slots on this seat are the same as an earlier Cosco convertible seat that worked to 40 lbs.—that means lots of kids get too tall for this seat before they reach 40 lbs. Second, the tether strap is a total pain to adjust and get tight.

While this seat does fit well in cars, we don't give it high marks. The too-low harness heights are a deal killer. We also note that parent reviews of Cosco's boosters have been mixed. For every parent we interviewed who liked their Cosco booster, another gave it a thumbs down—some gripes were minor (Cosco's light tan fabric on some of the boosters stains too easily), while other frustrations were more serious (quality complaints, straps that twist and are hard to adjust, etc.). Finally, we should note the government only gives this model two out of five stars for ease of use, among the lowest rated seats in this category. ***Rating: D***

CAR SEATS

COSCO PRONTO
Booster type: High back and backless booster
Limits: 30-100 lbs. as belt positioning booster, 40-100 lbs. as backless booster.
Price: $35-45.
IIHS rating: Backless mode: Check fit. High back mode: Best Bet.
NHTSA ease of use rating: ★★★★☆

Pros: Low price, machine washable pad, cup holder.
Cons: None.
Comments: This booster has a roomy seat and adjusts for taller kids. We also like the machine washable pad. And you can't beat the price. This might be a good booster for Grandma's car. Unlike Cosco's High Back Booster, this seat earns a better rating from the government for ease of use (four out of five stars) and a Best Bet from the IIHS. Reader feedback has also been positive. **Rating: B**

CYBEX SOLUTION X-FIX
Limits: 33-80 lbs.
Booster type: High back
Price: $200 (retail); $140 on Amazon
IIHS rating: Best Bet
NHTSA ease of use rating: ★★★★☆
Pros: Rigid LATCH, side impact protection.
Cons: Pricey, doesn't convert into a backless booster.

Comments: This LATCH-compatible booster debuted in 2010 and features a rigid LATCH connector, much like the Clek Oober. We liked the Solution X-Fix's adjustable back and side impact protection. One unique feature: the headrest reclines in three positions.

Reader feedback on this seat has been sparse, probably due to Cybex's thin distribution in stores and its relatively recent debut. However, the IIHS picked it as a Best Bet and the government scored it as four out of five stars in ease of use. So we'll recommend this one, even though it is pricey. FYI: As we went to press, we noticed Target was selling this seat for just $100. **Rating: B+**

DIONO MONTEREY BOOSTER
Limits: 30 to 120 lbs., 63" in height.
Booster type: High back
Price: $105-$150.
IIHS rating: Backless mode: Check fit. High back mode: Best bet.
NHTSA ease of use rating: ★★★☆☆
Pros: Works with LATCH, height adjustable,

EPS foam, retractable cup holder, seat recline.

Cons: Short LATCH connectors hard to install, difficult to remove.

Comments: The Monterey features a dial-adjustable seat width, EPS foam, a deep seat, retractable cup holders, two recline positions and a cushy foam seat. The Monterey also works with LATCH, among the few boosters on the market with this feature. But . . . the LATCH connectors are very short and hard to attach. Hence moving this seat from car to car would be a chore. Despite that drawback, most parent feedback on this seat has been very positive. Folks like the roomy seat and easy adjustments. Critics note it is a nightmare to clean—small black pins must be removed to take off the cover and the mesh fabric is a hassle to hand wash.

The Monterey is marketed as a backless booster, called the Sante Fe ($55-70). *Rating: A-*

EDDIE BAUER DELUXE HIGHBACK BOOSTER

Limits: 22 to 100 lbs.

Booster type: High back belt-positioning booster

Price: $90-$140.

IIHS rating: (for the earlier Auto Booster version): Backless mode: Check fit. High back mode: Best bet.

NHTSA ease of use rating: ★★★☆☆

Pros: Affordable.

Cons: Easy to use.

Comments: The Eddie Bauer Deluxe Highback Booster features extra padding, double cup holders and converts to a backless booster (40 to 100 lbs.). It is similar to the Cosco Pronto, but has armrests that pivot and an adjustable headrest plus an extra cup holder.

FYI: An earlier version of this seat called simply the Eddie Bauer Auto Booster is still for sale for $70 to $75 online; it works from 30 to 100 lbs. and then converts to a backless booster. Compared to the Deluxe above, the Auto Booster has a lower base and different headrest design. We assume it is being discontinued, as it has disappeared from the Eddie Bauer/Cosco site. *Rating: B*

EVENFLO BIG KID AMP

Booster type: Backless booster

Limits: 40-100 lbs. Kids must be 57" or less.

Price: $15-$25.

IIHS rating: Best bet.

NHTSA ease of use rating: ★★★★★

Pros: Neon colors; affordable.

Cons: None.

Comments: Basic backless booster that aims to appeal to kids with bright neon colors. Parent feedback very positive. ***Rating: A***

EVENFLO BIG KID
Limits: 30 to 100 lbs.
Booster type: High back booster
Price: $30-$50.
IIHS ratings:
Big Kid LX: Check fit.
Big Kid No Back: Check fit.
Big Kid Sport backless: Best bet.
Big Kid Sport high back: Check fit.

NHTSA ease of use rating: ★★★★☆
Pros: Low price, extras like reading lights, EPS foam.
Cons: Skimpy padding in low-end version.
Comments: Evenflo's answer to Graco's TurboBooster, the Big Kid adds a few bells and whistles that Graco doesn't have. Example: two reading lights for "evening activities." Also unique: The Big Kid is adjustable in both height and lap depth (most boosters are just height adjustable). The back removes as kids grow bigger, adding a discreet boost to older kids without having them look "uncool."

On the plus side, the Big Kid is less expensive than the Graco Turbo Booster (a $40 version called the Big Kid Amp at Babies R Us is especially affordable). On the downside, the padding is a bit skimpier than the Graco, making this seat less comfy for longer trips. And the Big Kid has less side impact protection than other seats. As usual, it is the little things about Evenflo that drive you crazy: the reading lights are nice, but lack an auto shut-off feature (and hence, will consume batteries fast if left on).

Like most Evenflo products, the Big Kid comes in several different versions, including a LX and DLX (Deluxe; pictured). The more expensive Deluxe includes upgraded fabric and padding. A Walmart exclusive version of the Big Kid (called the Big Kid Sport) is $30. The Sport omits the activity lights, the one-hand adjustment, energy-absorbing foam liner and pivoting armrests.

Reader feedback on this seat has been positive, with parents lauding the many features and adjustments. And the government awarded this seat its four-out-of-five star rating for ease of use. On the downside, the IIHS didn't pick the high back version of this seat as a best or good bet. ***Rating: B***

EVENFLO CHASE (LX & DLX)
This seat is reviewed on our web site, BabyBargains.com.

EVENFLO GENERATIONS
This seat is reviewed on our web site, BabyBargains.com.

EVENFLO MAESTRO

Limits: 20-100 lbs.; 20 to 50 lbs. with harness, belt-positioning booster for 40 to 100 lbs. and up to 57".
Price: $75-$85
IIHS rating: Best Bet.
NHTSA ease of use rating:

★★★★☆ Booster mode
★★★★☆ Harness mode

Pros: LATCH connectors, Best Bet from IIHS.
Cons: Must disassemble the seat to clean the pad; harness must be re-threaded to change height.
Comments: The Evenflo Maestro is a new model that is exclusive to Babies R Us, as of this writing. Like other combo seats, you can use the five-point harness up to 50 pounds (note the Evenflo Generations is 65). After a child outgrows the harness, the Maestro becomes a belt-positioning booster up to 100 lbs.

The Maestro has performed better than Evenflo's other boosters, which are showing their age. The Insurance Institute for Highway Safety gives the seat a Best Bet rating and it earned four out of five stars for ease of use. Reader feedback has been limited, but folks generally like the Maestro. Fans cite the LATCH attachments, upfront harness adjustment and two crotch positions. Critics note the harness must be re-threaded when you need to change the height and you have to dissemble the seat to clean the pad.

Bottom line: this is a better effort than Evenflo's other boosters and it is affordable . . . but the relatively skimpy 50 pound harness limit (compared to others that are 65 or 85 pounds) makes the Maestro less appealing. ***Rating: B+***

EVENFLO SECURE KID 300/400

Booster type: Combo booster
Limits: 20-65 lbs. with harness; 30 to 100 lbs. as a booster
Price: $129/ $159
IIHS rating: Not rated
NHTSA ease of use rating: Not yet.
Pros: Side impact protection plus 65 lb. harness.
Cons: Not available yet.
Comments: Set to debut in early 2012, The Secure Kid is Evenflo's latest booster seat—and the first to have enhanced side impact protection and a 65 lb. weight limit harness. Built on the Maestro platform, the Secure Kid comes in two versions: the 300 has basic LATCH connectors and sells for $129. The 400 adds SureLATCH self-ratcheting connectors and e3 side impact protection, which is

added foam. Both models have integrated cup holders and an adjustable headrest. ***Rating: Not Yet.***

FERRARI DREAMWAY SP
This seat is reviewed on our web site, BabyBargains.com.

FIRST YEARS PATHWAY B570
Also sold under Learning Curve, Compass brands
Booster type: High back booster
Limits: 30-100 lbs.
Price: $90-100
IIHS rating: Best Bet (B570 only). Other models are rated "check fit."

NHTSA ease of use rating: ⭐⭐⭐⭐⭐

Pros: Folds up, nicely padded, flip-up armrests, extra wide seat.
Cons: Earlier models not recommended in previous IIHS report.
Comments: This seat started life as the Compass Folding booster and is still sold that way, even though Compass was acquired by Learning Curve's The First Years brand a couple of years ago. As you might have guessed from the name, this seat's key selling feature is the ability to fold, unique in the market. That's a boon for carpoolers or anyone who has to shuttle a booster between vehicles. The Folding Booster features excellent padding, side impact protection (EPS foam) and extras like two cup holders, flip-up armrests and six-position height adjustment.

Over the years, The First Years has come out with several different versions of this seat—the Deluxe, Ultra, Premiere, etc. Each is very similar, with the plushness of the fabric being the main difference. The basic model is $60, while some versions are closer to $100. The most current model numbers for this seat are the B505, B510, B530, B540, B570—the higher the number, the newer the model (and generally the more plush the fabric).

The latest version of this seat is the B570 Pathway. It adds color-coded belt paths and LATCH attachments. The seat also features three position adjustable shoulder belt and side impact protection. That last feature is unique for First Years and is similar to the Clek Oober booster, which also features LATCH. Of course, the Pathway folds up like all the other Compass boosters.

There's been a split opinion on this seat. On one hand, reader feedback has been very positive (parents find it very easy to use, excellent adjustments and overall quality). Plus the government gave this booster its top rating for ease of use.

However, in a 2009 report, the Insurance Institute for Highway Safety declared earlier models not recommended (the IIHS looks at belt fit). Then, in 2010, the IIHS picked the B570 Pathway as a Best Bet, but said the older models (B505, 510, 530, 540) were in the middle range (not as bad as the not recommended seats, but not as good as the best bets).

So we'll raise our recommendation of this seat this time out; if you think this is the one for you, we'd recommend the Pathway B570 version (skip the earlier models). *Rating: B*

FIRST YEARS UNITE B830
A preview of this new seat is on our web site, BabyBargains.com.

GRACO ARGOS 70
Type: Combo
Limits: 20 to 70 lbs. with harness, up to 100 lbs has a belt-positioning booster, up to 120 lbs. as a backless booster.
NHTSA ease of use rating: Not rated yet.
IIHS rating: High back mode: Best bet. Backless mode: Check fit.

Comments: This brand new seat debuted in August 2011 and is exclusive to Target and Babies R Us. The big headline here is a no-rethread harness. Graco is also promoting this seat's side-impact testing and EPS foam. The Argos also has a three-position recline.

Basically, the Argos is like the Nautilus, but works to 70 lbs. with a five-point harness (the Nautilus works to 65 lbs.) and then to 120 lbs., as a backless booster (the Nautilus stops as 100 lbs.). And the no-rethread harness is a big pro over the Nautilus.

So what's not to like? Well, the harness slots are the same height as the Nautilus. You'd think if they are promoting the higher weight, Graco would throw you a harness height an inch or so above the Nautilus. And the price premium is another issue: the Argos is about $200, while the Nautilus can be found online for as little as $137 on Walmart.com. Of course, we expect the usual suspects will discount the Argos, but the price gap will need to close for this seat to be worth the extra cash.

FYI: an "Elite" version of the Argos 70 features belt lock-offs and an adjustable headrest.

Early feedback on the Argos is positive, but we haven't received enough reports yet to give it a rating. *Rating: Not Yet*

GRACO NAUTILUS 3-IN-1
Booster type: Combo
Limits: 20-65 lbs. with harness, 30 to 100 lbs. as high back booster. Backless booster from 40 to 100 lbs.
Price: $140-200
IIHS rating: Check fit.

NHTSA ease of use rating:

★★★★☆ Booster mode

★★★☆☆ Harness mode

Pros: Works to 65 lbs. with a five-point harness.

Cons: Harness must be re-threaded to adjust height.

Comments: Graco's Nautilus is a combo booster that works with a five-point harness to 65 lbs. and then converts to a high back booster (100 lbs.) and even a backless booster for older kids. The harness is a big plus if you have a toddler who has outgrown his convertible seat, but wish to keep him in the harness for a while longer (the 65 lb. limit should fit most five year olds).

The Nautilus' other features include over molded armrests (with side storage), three-position recline and decent padding. The seat is lined with EPS foam. Like most Graco seats, Graco makes a few different versions of the Nautilus, which boils down to fabric plushness. The basic one is $140; Babies R Us sells a slightly upgraded version that is $180. There is even a "Nautilus Elite" for $200 with a memory foam seat and adjustable head wings.

The Nautilus's biggest competitor is the Britax Frontier, so let's look how they compare. The Britax Frontier is bigger and wider than the Nautilus—and the Britax seat works up to 85 lbs. with the five-point harness. It is much easier to adjust the harness height with the Frontier. Folks generally give the Frontier better marks for padding, although the more expensive Nautilus models offer similar padding.

In the past, we gave the Nautilus the edge over the Frontier for its ease of install; however, Britax redesigned the Frontier in 2010 and caught up to the Nautilus.

There are a couple of key differences: to adjust the harness height with the Graco Nautilus, you have to rethread the harness. The Frontier doesn't require rethreading, which makes it much easier to use. The Frontier has three crotch strap adjustments; the Graco only two. On the other hand, the mesh fabric on the Britax Frontier is much more prone to wear and show stains compared to the Nautilus, which doesn't have this problem.

So it now basically comes down to price: the basic Nautilus is HALF the cost of the Britax Frontier . . . and we know that's nothing to sneeze at. However, if you are tempted to get an the upgraded Nautilus Elite, then you might as well spring for the Britax Frontier, as the price difference isn't as great here.

As for reader feedback, the Graco Nautilus earns positive marks from readers for its overall ease of use. The IIHS rates the Graco Nautilus as a "Check Fit"—that means it isn't a good bet or best bet. By contrast, the Britax Frontier 85 earned a Best Bet. Bottom line: we like the Nautilus—it is among our top picks in this category. ***Rating: A***

GRACO TURBOBOOSTER

Limits: 30 to 100 lbs. as high back boost-er (backless, it is 40 to 100 lbs).
Booster type: High back and backless booster
Price: $45 to $80. Backless version is $22-30.
IIHS rating: High back mode: Best Bet. Backless mode: Check fit.
NHTSA ease of use rating: ★★★☆☆

Pros: Top choice in booster market—both affordable and well designed.

Cons: No five-point harness; little side impact protection.

Comments: This is our top pick as a great, affordable booster seat. The TurboBooster features padded armrests that are height adjustable, EPS foam, hide-away cup holders and a one-hand adjustment for the headrest. The seat pad removes for cleaning; the TurboBooster converts into a backless booster for older kids.

As usual, Graco makes this in sixteen colors and styles. Hence, you'll find a basic version for $45 at Walmart and upgraded models (the Elite) for $90 in specialty stores. What's the difference? Just the fabric pad. More money, fancier pad.

So what are the drawbacks to the Graco TurboBooster? Well, unlike the Graco Nautilus or Britax Frontier, this seat lacks a five-point harness. Hence you must have an older toddler who is mature enough to sit in a regular seat belt. Finally, the TurboBooster requires quite a bit of assembly with various screws (that's the reason this seat only earned three out of five stars in the government's ease of use rating).

One flaw for the TurboBooster (the lack of side impact protection) is being addressed for 2012: Graco is adding their "Safety Surround" side impact protection to the seat. See our review of the Graco My Ride 65 for details on Safety Surround. The version of the Graco TurboBooster with this feature will debut in the 1st quarter of 2012 for $70.

Bottom line: this is a good option for older toddlers who no longer need a seat with a five-point harness. ***Rating: A***

HARMONY BABY ARMOR, CRUZ, DREAMTIME, LITERIDER

These seats are reviewed on our web site, BabyBargains.com.

KIDSEMBRACE DALE EARNHARDT JR. BOOSTER

This seat is reviewed on our web site, BabyBargains.com.

boosters

Maxi Cosi Rodi XR

Limits: 30 to 100 lbs.
Booster type: High back booster
Price: $160-$180
IIHS rating: High back mode: Best Bet. Backless mode: Check fit.
NHTSA ease of use rating: ★★★★☆

Pros: Extra large side wings provide sleep support, adjustable headrest. Seat recline.

Cons: Requires vehicles with rear headrests.

Comments: Maxi Cosi is a European subsidiary of Dorel, the juvenile products giant home to the Cosco, Eddie Bauer and Safety 1st brands.

The Rodi first debuted as a $100 booster with deep side wings for side impact protection and sleeping support. The Rodi also had a recline feature, yet lacked an adjustable headrest. And at $100, it was hard to justify the extra 50% price premium over seats like the Graco TurboBooster, which basically do the same thing.

The new Rodi XR adds an adjustable headrest but is similar to the old Rodi (seat recline, etc.). At $160-$180, it's overpriced when compared to similar booster seats. Another major negative: like most Dorel boosters, the Rodi requires the rear seat in your vehicle have headrest support—something lacking in many cars.

That said, reader feedback on this seat has been positive. And it earned a Best Bet (in high back mode) from the Insurance Institute for Highway Safety. So we'll tick up the Rodi's rating this year. However, the lack of value keeps this seat from earning a top grade. FYI: MaxiCosi's web site shows this seat with the name XP but we continue to see only the XR for sale. *Rating: B-*

Orbit Booster

Comments: Orbit plans to debut its first high-back, belt-positioning booster in spring 2012. The Orbit Booster will feature a 40 to 100 lb. weight limit (38-60″ in height), extendable headrest (see picture at bottom right), two cup holders and a backless booster mode. It will have a rigid LATCH connector. Price: $200. Our first impression of this seat was that it will probably appeal to die-hard Orbit fans. And they probably won't blink an eye at the $200 price tag, especially after shelling out $900 for the Orbit travel system to start with. As for everyone else, we think this one will have very limited appeal. For the same price, you can pick up a Britax Frontier with a five-point harness that works to 85 lbs., has side-impact protection and more.

Peg Perego Viaggio HBB 120 Booster

A preview of this new seat is on our web site, BabyBargains.com.

RECARO ProBOOSTER

Booster type: High back booster
Limits: 30 to 120 lbs., 37" to 61" tall.
Price: $130
IIHS rating: Best Bet.
NHTSA ease of use rating: ★★★☆☆
Pros: Side impact protection, works to 120 lbs.
Cons: Hard to find in retail stores, no LATCH.

Comments: Side impact protection is the headline here—the ProBOOSTER is similar to the Vivo (see below), but works to 120 lbs. and has a wider seat. This model has "cool mesh" air ventilation and a recline feature to better fit the slope of a vehicle's back seat. This seat is still relatively new and we haven't had much reader feedback on it yet. That said, early reports are positive and the seat won a Best Bet rating from the IIHS. Price and feature-wise, this seat's closest competitor is probably the Britax Parkway. Comparing the two, the ProBOOSTER lacks the LATCH feature on the Parkway SGL, which keeps the seat in place when unoccupied.

That said, the ProBOOSTER gets better marks on comfort and fabric quality, compared to the Parkway, which is similarly priced.

Even though this seat is still new, we'll give it a recommendation based on Recaro's overall track record and quality. **Rating: A**

RECARO ProSPORT

Booster type: Combo
Limits: 20 to 120 lbs.; five-point harness to 90 lbs. Up to 59"
Price: $225 to $280
IIHS rating: Best Bet.
NHTSA ease of use rating:
★☆☆☆☆ Booster mode
★★★☆☆ Harness mode
Pros: Very comfortable, EPS foam, side impact protection.
Cons: Price. Hard to find in retail stores.
Comments: The ProSPORT is an updated version of Recaro's best-selling Young Sport combo seat. It has a five-point harness that works up to 90 lbs.—yep, you read that right. That is the highest harness weight on the market as of this writing. After your child outgrows the harness, the ProSPORT works as a booster up to 120 lbs.

Like the Recaro ProBOOSTER, side impact protection is the star here. You also get a harness height adjustment that works without re-threading, EPS foam for crash protection, and extra seat padding. The ProSport also features LATCH connectors, which is handy to keep the seat in position when not occupied.

Reader feedback on this seat has been very positive and it

boosters

earned a Best Bet from the Insurance Institute for Highway Safety. One negative: the government only gave this seat an abysmal one-star rating for ease of use when in the booster mode. The harness mode eeked out three stars, however. ***Rating: A***

RECARO VIVO

Booster type: High back booster
Limits: 30 to 100 lbs.
Price: $90-$100
IIHS rating: Best Bet.
NHTSA ease of use rating: ★★★☆☆

Pros: Side wings provide impact protection and sleep support. Nice fabrics.

Cons: Hard to find in retail stores.

Comments: Recaro's Vivo high-back booster is an excellent choice. The side wings provide side-impact protection and the seat is lined with EPS foam. The Vivo has a microfiber pad that earns good marks for comfort.

Reader feedback on the Vivo has been very positive—parents like the side impact protection and the overall quality of Recaro's seats . . . you can tell the company doesn't cut any corners. Unfortunately, seeing one of these seats in person can take a bit of persistence, as Recaro's retail distribution is thin.

This seat earned a Best Bet rating from the Insurance Institute of Highway Safety. Given how similar it is to the new Recaro ProBOOSTER, we'd suggest that seat over the Vivo since it can be used to 120 pounds and is a newer model with a wider seat. That said, the Vivo is still an excellent pick. ***Rating: A***

SAFETY 1ST APEX 65

(a.k.a. Safety 1st Apex 65, Alpha Elite Apex)
Type: Combo
Limits: 22 to 65 lbs. with internal harness; 40 to 100 lbs. as a belt-positioning booster. Kids must be 57" or less.
Price: $190 to $230

IIHS rating: Not rated.
NHTSA ease of use rating:
★★★☆☆ Booster mode.
★★☆☆☆ Harness mode.

Pros: 65 lb. limit with a five-point harness.

Cons: Limiting top harness slot and crotch strap means larger toddlers will outgrow the harness before 65 lbs. Difficult to install. Requires vehicle headrest.

Comments: The Apex was one of the first harnessed booster seats to work to 65 lbs. with a five-point harness. This seat features an adjustable headrest, padded armrests, cup holder and padded insert to fit smaller toddlers.

As a hybrid seat, the Apex morphs into a belt-positioning booster after a toddler has outgrown the harness. And that's the rub with this seat: the top harness slot is only 17.5". Given that height, we'd guess that many toddlers will be too tall for the harness before they reach 65 lbs. And the lack of an adjustable crotch strap (it only has two positions) also limits the Apex's harness use. Another downside to this seat: the arm pads come off too easily, according to reader feedback. As with all Cosco's boosters, your vehicle must have rear headrests, which may be another negative.

Reader feedback on this seat has been mixed—fans like the affordable price and 65 lb. harness limit. But while the Apex was once a trend setter, the competition has caught up. Seats like the Graco Nautilus get better reviews, but cost the same. Example: while Apex has a slightly wider seat than the Graco Nautilus, it doesn't convert to a backless booster. And with Britax and Recaro turning up the top weight limit to 85 and 90 lbs. respectively (albeit at twice the price), the Apex 65 is looking a bit dated.

Rating: B-

SAFETY 1ST BOOST AIR PROTECT
Booster type: High back
Limits: 30 to 100 lbs.
Price: $65 to $85.
IIHS rating: High back mode: Best Bet. Backless mode: Check fit.
NHTSA ease of use rating: ★★★☆☆

Pros: Affordable. Side impact protection.
Cons: EPS foam only lines headrest.
Comments: Safety 1st's "Air Protect" feature is the headline here—air cushions that release air if the seat is in a crash. This same technology is used on Safety 1st's infant and convertible seats.

The Boost Air Protect converts to a backless booster and has an adjustable headrest and slide-out cup holders.

Reader feedback on this seat has been sparse; we saw a sample at a local chain store and weren't that impressed. EPS foam only lines the headrest, not the rest of the seat.

While we like the Air Protect feature, this seat looks like Safety 1st rushed it out without much thought. If you want side impact protection but only have $100 or so to spend on a booster, the Compass Pathway is a better bet. Even though it earns a Best Bet from the Insurance Institute for Highway Safety, we will take a pass on it. *Rating: C*

SAFETY 1ST ESSENTIAL AIR

Booster type: Combo
Limits: 22-65 pounds with harness; converts to belt-positioning booster from 40-100 lbs.
Price: $180 to $215.
IIHS rating: Best Bet.
NHTSA ease of use rating:

★★★★☆ Booster mode.
★★★★☆ Harness mode.

Pros: "Quick Fit" harness does not need to be re-threaded.

Cons: Five-point harness only works to 65 lbs. Seats like Britax Frontier work to 85 lbs. with harness.

Comments: Featuring a five-point harness that works up to 65 lbs., the Essential Air converts to a booster that will work to 100 lbs. Available in a standard and premium version, the Essential Air has Safety 1st's Air Protect side-impact protection feature—which releases air to protect a child if the vehicle is in an accident. It is priced about $162 to $180 online, although the premium version may top $200 in some stores. FYI: This seat was originally called the S1 Rumi Air (get it? Roomy! Rumi!) and some sites still refer to it by that name.

As for parent reviews, this seat came out recently, so there's been little reader feedback yet. We'll wait to assign a rating until we get more real-world feedback. ***Rating: Not Yet.***

SAFETY 1ST GO HYBRID

Limits: 30 to 100 lbs. To 60 lbs. with five-point harness. 34"-52" height for the five-point harness; 43"-57" for the backless booster.
Booster type: Combo seat and backless booster.
Price: $185-$200.
IIHS rating (backless mode only): Check fit.
NHTSA ease of use rating:

★★★★☆ Booster mode.
★★★★☆ Harness mode.

Pros: Innovative hybrid seat that works up to 60 lbs. with five-point harness; great for taxis.

Cons: Requires a top tether when used with five-point harness. No cup holder. LATCH limit in your vehicle may limit usefulness.

Comments: Safety 1st acquired this seat when maker Safeguard exited the business. The Safety 1st Go Hybrid features a five-point harness that can be used to 60 lbs. . . . and then the seat converts to a backless booster to 100 lbs. And, weighing just 11 lbs., it all folds into a travel bag, a boon for carpools or taxis (take note, New Yorkers).

One caveat to the Go—it can only be used with its five-point harness in vehicles with LATCH and a top tether. That's not a problem if your car was made after 2003 . . . but if you are driving an older vehicle, it may not be compatible (some car makers added LATCH before 2003, but others did not).

And remember that your vehicle may have low LATCH limits—Honda's limit is just 40 lbs., for example. Most are 48 lbs.; Subaru is 60. If your vehicle has a low limit, you won't be able to use the five-point harness—and hence you just bought yourself a $200 backless booster.

And just to add another layer of confusion: some vehicles have different (lower) limit for tethers. If you own such a vehicle, this would be a poor choice.

Safety 1st hasn't changed this seat, other than raising the price by $50. Bottom line: this is a good seat IF your vehicle has high enough LATCH and tether limits to take advantage of its unique design. Reader feedback on this seat has been very positive.

The Go earned a top rating (Best Bet) in an earlier report from the Insurance Institute for Highway Safety. In their most recent report, however, the IIHS says this seat is in the middle range: neither a Best Bet nor a Not Recommended. Considering the seat hasn't changed, we'll go with the earlier assessment as a guide.

Overall reader feedback on the Go Hybrid has been quite positive. The seat has quite a few fans among urban dwellers that don't own a car, but rely on taxis—the light weight and travel bag make this one a winner. *Rating: B+*

SAFETY 1ST SUMMIT, VANTAGE

These seats are reviewed on our web site, BabyBargains.com.

Best Bets: Booster Seats

◆ *Best Bets: Harness Seats.* Our top pick is the *Graco Nautilus*—this combo seat has a five-point harness that can be used up to 65 lbs. The Nautilus also converts to a belt-positioning booster and even a backless booster to 100 lbs. Starting at $140, the Nautilus is half the price of our other best bet in this category: the Britax Frontier 85.

Despite costing twice as much as a Nautilus, we think the *Britax Frontier 85* is also worth a look. Yes, it works up to 85 pounds with a five-point harness—and that is impressive. Reader feedback on this seat has been very positive.

◆ *Best Bets: Belt-Positioning Booster.* We have one clear winner here and several other strong runners-ups.

The *Graco TurboBooster* ($45 to $80) is the best belt-positioning booster on the market today. It packs a good number of features into an affordable package: height-adjustable headrest, open belt loop design, armrests, back recline, cup holders and more. Note it comes in two versions: a high-back version and backless (the latter is about $25).

Runner up: **Recaro ProBooster** features side impact protection and sleep support, plus EPS foam and Recaro's overall strong reputation for quality. At $130, it is worth a look compared to the TurboBooster. One advantage: the Recaro seat works to 120 pounds, versus 100 for the TurboBooster.

◆ **Best Bets: Booster for Carpools.** First Years/Compass Pathway B570 ($90) is an excellent booster seat that has a killer feature for carpools: it folds up. Add in side impact protection and six-position height adjustment and you have the perfect pick for parents who need to shuffle a seat between daycare and home.

◆ **Best Bets: Booster for Taxis.** If you live in a big city and don't own a car, you'll be relying on taxi cabs to get to the airport, the zoo and other special trips. In that case, we recommend the **Safety 1st Go Hybrid**. This excellent seat ($185 to $200) works with a five-point harness up to 60 pounds, yet installs in just one minute. Weighing only 11 pounds, the Go Hybrid also folds down to a compact size and fits in a travel bag—perfect for taxis! One caveat: this seat can only be used with its five-point harness if the vehicle has LATCH and a top tether. Most modern vehicles have these vehicles, but it is one important caveat!

◆ **Best Bets: Backless Booster.** The best backless boosters on the market are the **Graco TurboBooster** backless ($25) and the **Evenflo Big Kid Amp** ($15-$25). Both are affordable and easy to use boosters for older kids who don't need a high back booster.

Whew! You made it through the car seat chapter. Yes, we know—it was slightly shorter than the last Harry Potter book. Next up: strollers: which brands are best? How can you pick the best stroller for what you need? We've got it covered, starting on the next page.

CHAPTER 9

Strollers, Diaper Bags, Carriers & Other Gear To Go

Inside this chapter

What are the best strollers? Which brands are the most durable AND affordable? We'll discuss this plus other tips on how to make your baby portable— from front carriers to diaper bags and more. And what do you put in that diaper bag anyway? We've got nine suggestions, plus advice on the best baby carriers.

Getting Started: When Do You Need This Stuff?

While you don't need a stroller, diaper bag or carrier immediately after baby is born, most parents purchase them before baby arrives anyway. And some of the best deals for strollers and other to-go gear are found online, which necessitates leaving time for shipping.

Sources to Find Strollers, Carriers

As with other baby products, discounters like Target and Walmart tend to specialize in just a handful of models from mass-market companies like Cosco, Kolcraft, Graco and so on (lately, they've been adding premium brands to their web sites although they aren't available in their stores). The baby superstores like Babies R Us and Buy Buy Baby have a wider selection and (sometimes) better brands. Meanwhile, juvenile specialty stores almost always carry the more exclusive brands.

Yet perhaps the best deals for strollers, carriers and diaper bags are found online—for some reason, this seems to be one area the web covers very well. This is because strollers are relatively easy to ship (compared to other more bulky juvenile items). Of course, more competition often means lower prices, so you'll see many deals online. Another plus: the web may be the only way to find certain premium-brand strollers if you live in less-populous parts of the U.S. and Canada.

Beware of shipping costs when ordering online or from a catalog—many strollers may run 20 or 30 lbs., which can translate into hefty shipping fees. Use an online coupon (see Chapter 7 for coupon sites) to save and look for free shipping specials.

Parents in Cyberspace: What's on the Web?

Baby Catalog of America

babycatalog.com. Baby Catalog sells strollers from Graco, Phil & Teds, UPPAbaby and more. We liked the wide variety of double stroller models. The site divides its offerings by stroller type and accessories; unfortunately, you can't search by brand. On the plus side, Baby Catalog offers free ground shipping on orders over $99. There's also a handy maple leaf icon to note which strollers can't be shipped to Canada. If you join their membership program ($25 for one year; $50 for three years), you can get an additional 10% discount. If you're active duty military, you qualify for free membership for one year. *Rating: A*

◆ **Discount codes.** Stroller deals come and go by the day—track the latest deals on our message boards. Our stroller message board (BabyBargains.com/strollers) hosts a lively discussion on all things stroller-wise, while the bargain board (BabyBargains.com/coupons) tracks the latest discount codes for major stroller retailers.

◆ **Craigslist.** Stroller deals abound on Craigslist—on the New York City board, we found a Bugaboo Cameleon with extras for $450 (regularly $900), a free Graco stroller in San Francisco and a Chicco Cortina for half price in Dallas. Sure, some deals are dogs . . . but there are also steals. Spend a few moments on Craigslist and you'll quickly see the going rate for used name-brand strollers.

Strollers

Baby stores offer a bewildering array of strollers for parents. Do you want the model that converts from a car seat to a stroller? What about a stroller that would work for a quick trip to the mall? Or do you want a stroller for jogging? Hiking trails? The urban jungle of New York City or beaches near LA?

And what about all the different brand names? Will a basic brand found at a discount store work? Or do you pine after one of the stylish Euro-designed imports? What about strollers with anti-lock brakes and air bags? (Just kidding on that last one).

The $274 million dollar stroller industry is not dominated by one or two players, like you might see in car seats or high chairs. Instead, you'll find a couple *dozen* stroller makers offering just about anything on wheels, ranging from $30 for a bare-bones model to $900 for a Dutch-designed über stroller. A recent hot trend: all-terrain strollers with three wheels, where the front wheel swivels.

We hope this section takes some of the mystery out of the stroller buying process. First, we'll look at the six different types of strollers on the market today. Next, we'll zero in on features and help you decided what's important and what's not. Then, it's brand ratings and our picks as the best recommendations for different lifestyles. Finally, we'll go over several safety tips, money saving hints, and wastes of money.

Whew! Take a deep breath and let's go.

What Are You Buying?

There are six types of strollers you can buy:

◆ **Umbrella Strollers.** The name comes from the appearance of the stroller when it's folded, similar to an umbrella.

WHAT'S COOL: They're lightweight and generally cheap—that is, low in price (about $20 to $40). We should note that a handful of premium stroller makers (Maclaren and Peg Perego) also offer pricey umbrella strollers that sell for $150 to $300—we discuss them in the next category. Pictured is a no-frills Kolcraft umbrella stroller.

WHAT'S NOT: They're cheap—that is, low in quality. You typically don't get any fancy features like canopies, storage baskets, reclining seats, and so on. Another problem: most umbrella strollers have hammock-style seats with little head support, so they won't work well for babies under six months of age.

◆ **Lightweight Strollers.** These strollers are our
top recommendation: they're basically souped-up
umbrella strollers with many convenience features.

WHAT'S COOL: Most offer easy set-up and fold-
down; some even fold up similar to umbrella
strollers. Many models have great features
(canopies, storage baskets, high-quality wheels) at
amazingly light weights (as little as eight lbs.). Graco and Maclaren
probably make the most popular lightweight strollers.

WHAT'S NOT: Can be expensive—most high-quality brands run
$150 to $300. The smaller wheels on lightweight strollers make
maneuvering in the mall or stores easy . . . but those same wheels
don't perform well on uneven surfaces or on gravel trails. Skimpy
baskets are another trade-off.

◆ **Full-size Strollers.** Full-size strollers used
to be called carriages or prams. Sort of like a
bed on wheels—the seat lies flat and the leg
rest pulls up to form a bassinet-like feature.
Clearly, this feature focuses on newborns . . .
but these strollers can then be configured for
older babies with a seat that sits upright.

WHAT'S COOL: Full recline is great for newborns—they spend most
of their time sleeping. Most combo carriage/strollers have lots of
high-end features like plush seats, quilted canopies and other accessories to keep the weather out. The best carriage strollers and prams
have a dreamy ride, with amazing suspensions and big wheels.

WHAT'S NOT: Hefty weight (not easy to transport or set up) and
hefty price tags. Another negative: most Euro-style "prams" have
fixed front wheels, which make maneuvering difficult on quick trips.
Some carriage/stroller models can top $500, although entry-level
carriage strollers start at $200. These strollers once dominated the
market but have lost favor as more parents opt for "travel systems"
that combine an infant seat and stroller (see below).

◆ **Multi-function Strollers.** These
strollers morph from infant carriages to
toddler strollers, with either an infant car
seat adapter or bassinet accessory. With
fully reclining seats, these strollers can be
used from birth. Some multi-functions even
have second seat options, morphing from
a single to a double stroller. Examples

include the UPPAbaby Vista and the Britax B-Ready (pictured).

WHAT'S COOL: In a word, flexibility—parents who buy these

strollers love the ability to morph them into several different uses.

◆ *Jogging (or Sport) Strollers.* These strollers feature three big bicycle-tire wheels and lightweight frames—perfect for jogging or walking on rough roads. The front wheel is fixed to maximize glide.

WHAT'S COOL: How many other strollers can do 15 mph on a jogging trail? Some have plush features like padded seats and canopies—and the best fold up quickly for easy storage in the trunk. This category was hip a few years ago, but is now in decline: more popular are the all-terrain strollers (see below).

WHAT'S NOT: They can be darn expensive, topping $300. Jogging strollers are a single-purpose item—thanks to their sheer bulk and a lack of steering (joggers usually have fixed front wheels), you can't use one in a mall or other location. On the plus side, the flood of new models is helping lower prices. New, low-end jogging strollers run $100 to $150. The trade-offs to the new bargain price models: heavier steel frames and a lack of features.

◆ *All-terrain Strollers.* The baby equivalent of sport-utility vehicles, these strollers are pitched to parents who want to go on hikes or other outdoor adventures. All-terrain strollers are similar to joggers with one big difference—the front wheel swivels.

WHAT'S COOL: Big air-filled tires and high clearances work better on gravel trails/roads than standard strollers. These strollers are great for neighborhoods with broken or rough sidewalks. All-terrain strollers have many convenience features (baskets, canopies, etc.) as well as one key advantage over jogging strollers: most all-terrains have swivel front wheels. That makes them easy to maneuver, whether on a trail or at the mall. Pictured above is the Phil & Ted's Explorer stroller.

WHAT'S NOT: All-terrain strollers are wider and heavier than other strollers, which make them less useful in a mall or store with tight aisles. And air-filled tires are great for trails . . . but a pain in the neck if you get a flat. If you really want to run with a stroller, all-terrains with a swivel front wheel are not the best choice (a jogger with a fixed front wheel is better). And let's not forget the cost—most all terrains are pricey, some topping $400.

◆ *Travel Systems.* It's the current rage among stroller makers—models that combine infant car seats and strollers. Century (now part of Graco) kicked off this craze way back in 1994 with its "4-in-1"

model that featured four uses (infant carrier, infant car seat, carriage and toddler stroller). Since then, just about every major stroller maker has jumped into the travel system market. Pictured here is the Graco Quattro travel system.

WHAT'S COOL: Great convenience—you can take the infant car seat out of the car and then snap it into the stroller frame. Voila! Instant baby carriage, complete with canopy and basket. Later, you can use the stroller as, well, just a stroller.

WHAT'S NOT: The strollers are often junk—especially those by mass market makers Cosco and Evenflo. Quality problems plague this category, as does something we call "feature bloat." Popular travel systems from Graco, for example, are so loaded with features that they tip the scales at nearly 30 lbs.! The result: many parents abandon their travel system strollers for lighter weight models after baby outgrows his infant seat. And considering these puppies can cost $150 to $250 (some even more), that's a big investment for such limited use. On the up side, better strollers brands such as Maclaren, Perego and Chicco have also jumped into the travel system market, offering alternatives to the heavyweight mass market strollers.

Safe & Sound

Next to defective car seats, the most dangerous juvenile product on the market today is the stroller. That's according to the U.S. Consumer Product Safety Commission, which estimates that over 11,000 injuries a year occur from improper use or defects. The problems? Babies can slide out of the stroller (falling to the ground) and small parts can be a choking hazard. Seat belts have broken in some models, while other babies are injured when a stroller's brakes fail on a slope. Serious mishaps with strollers have involved entanglements and entrapments (where an unrestrained baby slides down and gets caught in a leg opening) and lacerations when parents fold up the stroller and kids get their hands caught. Here are some safety tips:

1 NEVER HANG BAGS FROM THE STROLLER HANDLE—it's a tipping hazard.

2 DON'T LEAVE YOUR BABY ASLEEP UNATTENDED IN A STROLLER. Many injuries happen when infants who are lying down in a stroller roll or creep and then manage to get their head stuck in the stroller's leg openings. Be safe: take a sleeping baby out of a stroller and move them to a crib or bassinet.

3 **THE BRAKES SHOULDN'T BE TRUSTED.** The best stroller models have brakes on two wheels; cheaper ones just have one wheel that brakes. Even with the best brakes, don't leave the stroller unattended on an incline.

4 **FOLLOW THE WEIGHT LIMITS.** Most strollers shouldn't be used by children over 35 lbs..

5 **JOGGING STROLLERS ARE BEST FOR BABIES OVER ONE YEAR OF AGE.** Yes, some stroller makers tout their joggers for babies as young as six weeks (or six months) of age. But after consulting with pediatric experts, we suggest waiting until one year of age to run with baby in a stroller. Why? The neck muscles of infants under a year of age can't take the shocks of jogging or walking on rough paths (or going over curbs). Ask your pediatrician if you need more advice on when it is safe to use a jogger.

6 **FOLD AND UNFOLD YOUR STROLLER WHEN BABY IS NOT NEAR.** Simply because they are foldable, strollers have various pinch points where baby's fingers may get caught. While some stroller makers have included protective shields over those points, it's best to open and close strollers when your baby is not around—leave them buckled in their car seat or keep them a distance away while you set up or put away your stroller.

Smart Shopper Tips

Smart Shopper Tip #1
Give it a Test Drive

"My friend was thinking of buying a stroller online, sight unseen. Should you really buy a stroller without trying it first?"

It's best to try before you buy. Most stores have at least one stroller set up as a floor model. Give it a whirl, practice folding it up, and check the steering. One smart tip: put some weight in the stroller seat (borrow a friend's toddler or use a backpack full of books that weighs about 15 lbs.). The steering and maneuverability will feel different if the stroller is weighted—obviously, that's a more real world test-drive.

Once you've tried it out, shop for price through 'net or mail order sources. Ask retailers if they will meet or beat prices quoted to you online (many quietly do so). What if you live in Kansas and the nearest dealer for a stroller you want is in, say, Texas? Then you may have no choice but to buy sight unseen—but just make sure the web site has a good return policy. Another tip: use message boards like those on our web site (BabyBargains.com) to quiz other parents about stroller models.

If you buy a stroller from a store, we strongly recommend opening the box and making sure everything is in there BEFORE you leave the store!

Guaranteed Frustration: Baby gear warranties can leave you fuming

It's a fact of life: sometimes you buy a product that breaks only days after purchase. So, you pick up the phone and call the manufacturer and ask about their warranty. "Sure, we'll help," says the customer service rep. In no time, you have a replacement product and a happy parent.

Fast forward to real life. Most parents find warranties only guarantee frustration—especially with baby products like strollers and other travel gear. Numerous hassles confront parents who find they have a defective product, from unreturned emails to endless waits on hold waiting for a customer service rep (on a non-toll free line, naturally).

Consider the process of actually registering an item. Filling out a warranty card often requires information that you can only find on the product box or carton. Some parents find this out the hard way . . . after they've hauled all the boxes off to the trash. Even worse: some baby product makers like Peg Perego actually request a copy of the sales receipt for their warranty form. Hello? What about gifts?

Then, let's say something goes wrong. Your new stroller breaks a wheel. That brand new baby monitor goes on the fritz after one week. If it is a gift or you lost the receipt, the store you bought it from may say "tough luck"—call the manufacturer. With many warranties, you have to return the defective item to the manufacturer *at your expense*. And then you wait a few more weeks while they decide to fix or replace the item. Typically you have to pay for return shipping—and that can be expensive for a bulky item like a stroller. And then you must do without the product for weeks while they fix it.

Dealing with the customer service departments at some baby product makers can add insult to injury. It seems like some companies can count their customer service staff on one hand—or one finger, in some cases. The result: long waits on hold. Or it takes days to get responses to emails. The U.S. offices of foreign baby product companies seem to be the worst at customer service staffing, while mass-market companies

Smart Shopper Tip #2
What Features Really Matter?

"Let's cut through the clutter here. Do I really need a stroller that has electronic stability assist and anti-lock brakes? What features are really important?"

Walk into any baby store and you'll encounter a blizzard of strollers. Do you want a stroller with a full recline? Boot and retractable canopy? What the heck is a boot, anyway? Here's a look at the features in the stroller market today:

such as Graco and Evenflo have better customer service.

And customer service can go from good to bad in the blink of an eye. Recalls can cause a huge surge in customer service requests—and many companies fail to adequately staff their customer service departments during such events. Hence, even good companies can fall flat on their face during such episodes.

The bottom line: it's no wonder that when something goes wrong, consumers just consider trashing the product and buying a new one. And let's be realistic: paying $30 in shipping to send back a broken $50 stroller doesn't make much sense. Here's our advice:

◆ *Keep your receipts.* You don't have to get fancy—a shoebox will do. That way you can prove you bought that defective product. If the item was a gift, keep the product manual and serial number. Ask for gift receipts when possible.

◆ *If something goes wrong, call the manufacturer.* We're always surprised by how many consumers don't call the manufacturer FIRST when a problem arises. You might be surprised at how responsive some companies are at fixing an issue.

◆ *If the problem is a safety defect, immediately stop using the product* and file a complaint with the Consumer Product Safety Commission (cpsc.gov). Also contact the company.

◆ *Attack the problem multiple ways.* Don't just call; also send an email and perhaps a written letter. Be reasonable: allow the company one to two business days to reply to a phone call or email.

◆ *Let other parents know about your experiences.* The best way to fix lousy customer service? Shame companies into doing it better. Post your experiences to the message boards on our site (BabyBargains.com) and other parenting sites. Trust us, companies are sensitive to such criticism.

Features for baby:

◆ *Reclining seat.* Since babies less than six months of age sleep most of the time and can't hold their heads up, strollers that have reclining seats are a plus. Yet, the *extent* of a stroller's seat recline varies by model. Some have full reclines, a few recline part of the way (120 degrees) and some don't recline at all. FYI: just because a stroller has a "full recline" does NOT mean it reclines to 180 degrees. It may recline slightly less than that for safety reasons.

◆ *Front (or napper) bar.* As a safety precaution, many strollers have a front bar (also called a napper bar) that keeps baby secure (though you should always use the stroller's safety harness). Better strollers have a bar that's padded and removable. Why removable? Later, when your baby gets to toddler hood, you may need to remove the bar to make it easier for the older child to access the stroller. Some strollers have a kid snack tray, which serves much the same function as a napper bar.

◆ *Footrest.* Footrests can range from a simple strap extending between the two side bars of the stroller or as complex as a ratcheting adjustable footrest with leg support. FYI: If a stroller has a fully reclining seat, voluntary safety regulations require the stroller to have an adjustable footrest that can fold out to fully enclose the entire stroller seat—this keeps baby from sliding out.

◆ *Seat padding.* You'll find every possible padding option out there, from bare bones models with a single piece of fabric to strollers with deluxe-quilted padding made from fine fabrics hand woven by monks in Luxembourg. (Okay, just kidding—the monks actually live in Switzerland). For seating, some strollers have cardboard platforms (these can be uncomfortable for long rides) and other models have fabric that isn't removable or machine washable (see below for more on this).

◆ *Shock absorbers or suspension systems.* Yes, a few strollers do have wheels equipped with shock absorbers or suspension springs for a smoother ride. This is a nice feature if you live in a neighborhood with uneven or rough sidewalks.

◆ *Wheels.* In reality, how smooth a stroller rides is more related to the type of wheels. The general rule: the more the better. Strollers with double wheels on each leg ride smoother than single wheels. Most strollers have plastic wheels. In recent years, some stroller makers have rolled out models with "pneumatic" or inflated wheels. These offer a smoother ride—but they are heavier and can go flat.

◆ *Weather protection.* Yes, you can buy a stroller that's outfitted for battle with a winter in New England, for example. The options include retractable hoods/canopies and "boots" (which protect a child's feet) to block out wind, rain or cold. Fabrics play a role here too—some strollers feature quilted hoods to keep baby warm and others claim they are water repellent. While a boot is an option some may not need, hoods/canopies are rather important, even if just to keep the sun out of baby's eyes. Some strollers only have a canopy (or "sunshade") that partially covers baby, while other models have a full hood that can completely cover the stroller. Look for canopies that have lots of adjustments (to block a setting sun) and have "peek-a-boo" windows that let you see baby even when closed.

What if the stroller you've fallen in love with only has a skimpy canopy? Or lacks a rain cover? Good news: after-market accessories can fill the gap (see box below).

Features for parents:
◆ **Storage baskets.** Many strollers have deep, under-seat baskets for storage of coats, purses, bags, etc. Yet, the amount of storage can vary sharply from model to model. Inexpensive umbrella strollers may have no basket at all, while other models have tiny baskets. Mass-market strollers (Graco, etc.) typically have the most storage; other stroller makers have been playing catch-up in the basket game. One tip: it's not just the *size* of the storage basket but the *access* to it that counts. Some strollers have big baskets but are practically inaccessible when the seat is reclined. A support bar blocks access to some baskets. Tip: when stroller shopping, recline the seat and see if you can access the basket.

strollers

Handy stroller accessories

What if your stroller doesn't have a rain cover? One option is the **Protect a Bub Wind & Rain Cover**, which comes in both single ($23) and double versions ($45; protect-a-bubusa.com).

You're in love with a fancy stroller. . . except for that skimpy canopy. What's the solution? Try the **RayShade** ($15, single; $30 double) by Summer. This shade extends your stroller canopy and is excellent for blocking low-angle sun (take note, Californians). It also blocks ultraviolet rays and has a hidden bottle pocket.

◆ **Removable seat cushion for washing.** Let's be honest: strollers can get icky in a jiffy. Crushed-in cookies, spilt juice and the usual grime can make a stroller a mobile dirt-fest. Some strollers have removable seat cushions that are machine washable—other models let you remove *all* of the fabric for a washing. Watch out for those models with non-removable fabric/seat cushions—while you can clean these strollers in one of those manual car washes (with a high-pressure nozzle), it's definitely a hassle, especially in the winter.

◆ **Lockable wheels.** Some strollers have front wheels that can be locked in a forward position—this enables you to more quickly push the stroller in a straight line (nice for exercising).

◆ **Wheel size.** You'll see just about every conceivable size wheel out there on strollers today. As you might guess, the smaller wheels are good for maneuverability in the mall, but larger wheels handle rough sidewalks (or gravel paths) much better.

◆ **Handle/Steering.** This is an important area to consider—most strollers have a single bar handle, which enables one-handed steering. Other strollers have two handles (example: Maclaren as well as Perego's Pliko line). Two handles require two hands to push, but enable a stroller to fold up compactly, like an umbrella. It's sort of a trade-off: steer-ability versus easier fold. There are other handle issues to consider as well. A handful of strollers feature a "reversible" handle. Why would you want that? Initially, you can push the stroller while the baby faces you (better for small infants). Later, you can reverse the handle so an older child can look out while being pushed from behind. (Note: models with reversible handles seem increasingly rare in recent years; instead some strollers now have reversible *seats*. We'll note which have this feature later).

Another important factor: consider the handle *height*. Some handles have adjustable heights to better accommodate taller parents. However, just because a stroller touts this feature doesn't mean it adjusts to accommodate a seven-foot tall parent (at most, you get an extra inch or two of height). Later in this chapter, we'll mention which have height adjustable handles as we review stroller brands. Finally, a few stroller makers offer "one-touch fold" handles. Hit a button on the stroller and it can be folded up with one motion.

◆ **Compact fold.** We call it the trunk factor—when a stroller is folded, will it fit in your trunk? Some strollers fold compactly and can fit in a narrow trunk. Other strollers are still quite bulky when folded—think about your trunk space before buying. Unfortunately, we are not aware of any web site that lists the size/footprint of strollers when folded. You are on your own to size up models when folded in a store, compared to your trunk (hint: take trunk measurements before you go stroller shopping). Not only should you consider how compactly a stroller folds, but also how it folds in general. The best strollers fold with just one or two quick motions; others require you to hit 17 levers and latches. The latest stroller fold fad: strollers that fold standing UP instead of down. Why is this better? Because strollers that fold down to the ground can get dirty/scratched in a parking lot.

◆ *Durability.* Should you go for a lower-price stroller or a premium brand? Let's be honest: the lower-priced strollers (say, under $100) have nowhere near the durability of the models that cost $200 to $400. Levers that break, reclining seats that stop reclining and other glitches can make you despise a cheap stroller mighty quick. Yet, some parents don't need a stroller that will make it through the next world war. If all you do is a couple of quick trips to the mall every week or so, then a less expensive stroller will probably be fine. However, if you plan to use the stroller for more than one child, live in an urban environment with rough sidewalks, or plan extensive outdoor adventures with baby, then invest in a better stroller. Later in this chapter, we'll go over specific models and give you brand recommendations for certain lifestyles.

◆ *Overall weight.* Yes, it's a dilemma: the more feature-laden the stroller, the more it weighs. And strollers are often priced via the Bikini Principle: the less it weighs, the more it costs. Yet it doesn't take lugging a 30-pound stroller in and out of a car trunk more than a few times to justify the expense of a lighter-weight design. Carefully consider a stroller's weight before purchase. Some parents end up with two strollers—a lightweight/umbrella-type stroller for quick trips (or air travel) and then a more feature intensive model for extensive outdoor outings.

One factor to consider with weight: steel vs. aluminum frames. Steel is heavier than aluminum, but some parents prefer steel because it gives the stroller a stiffer feel. Along the same lines, sometimes we get complaints from parents who own aluminum strollers because they feel the stroller is too "wobbly"—while it's lightweight, one of aluminum's disadvantages is its flexibility. One tip for dealing with a wobbly stroller: lock the front wheels so you can push the stroller in a straight line. That helps to smooth the ride.

Smart Shopper Tip #3
The Cadillac Escalade or Ford Focus Dilemma
"This is nuts! I see cheap umbrella strollers that sell for $30 on one hand and then fancy designer brands for $900 on the other. Do I really need to spend a fortune on a stroller?"

Whether you drive a Cadillac Escalade or a Ford Focus, you'll still get to your destination. And that fact pretty much applies to strollers too—most function well enough to get you and baby from point A to point B, no matter what the price.

So, should you buy the cheapest stroller you can find? Well, no. There *is* a significant difference in quality between a cheap $30 umbrella stroller and a name brand that costs $150, $250 or more. Unless you want the endless headaches of a cheap stroller (wheels that break, parts that fall off), it's important to invest in a stroller that's durable.

The real question is: do you need a fancy stroller loaded with features or will a simple model do? To answer that, you need to consider *how* you will use the stroller. Do you live in the suburbs and just need the stroller once a week for a quick spin at the mall? Or do you live in an big city where a stroller is your primary vehicle, taking all the abuse that a big city can dish out? Climate plays another factor—in the Northeast, strollers have to be winterized to handle the cold and snow. Meanwhile, in Southern California, full canopies are helpful for shading baby's eyes from late afternoon sunshine.

Figuring out how different stroller options fit your lifestyle/climate is the key to stroller happiness. Starting on page 533, we'll recommend several specific strollers for certain lifestyles and climates.

One final note: name-brand strollers with cachet actually have resale value. You can sell that pricey stroller on eBay, at a second-hand store, or via Craigslist and recoup some of your investment. The better the brand name (say, Bugaboo), the more the resale value. Unfortunately, the cheap brands like Graco, Evenflo and Kolcraft are worth little or nothing on the second-hand market—there is a reason for that (beyond snob appeal). Take a quick look at eBay or your local Craigslist stroller section to see what we mean.

Smart Shopper Tip #4
Too tall for their own good

"I love our stroller, but my husband hates it. He's six feet tall and has to stoop over to push it. Even worse, when he walks, he hits the back of the stroller with his feet."

Strollers are made for *women* of average height. What's that? About 5'6". If you (or your spouse) are taller than that, you'll find certain stroller models will be a pain to use.

This is probably one of the biggest complaints we get from parents about strollers. Unfortunately, just a few stroller models have height-adjustable handles that let a six-foot tall person comfortably push a stroller without stooping over or hitting the back of the stroller with his or her feet. One smart shopping tip: if you have a tall spouse, make sure you take him or her stroller shopping with you. Checking out handle heights in person is the only way to avoid this problem.

The best stroller brands for taller parents: Maclaren and Peg Perego (particularly, the Pliko, which has height adjustable handles). The worst? Combi, a Japanese brand that has low-handle heights.

Smart Shopper Tip #5
The Myth of the Magic Bullet Stroller

"I'd like to buy just one stroller—a model that works with an infant car seat and then converts to full-featured pram and then finally a jogger for kids up to age four. And I want it to weigh less than ten lbs.. And sell for just under $50. What model do you suggest?"

Boy, that sounds like our email some days! We hear from parents all the time looking for that one model that will do it all. We call it the Myth of the Magic Bullet Stroller—an affordable product that morphs into seven different uses for children from birth to college. Sorry, we haven't found one yet.

The reality: most parents own more than one stroller. A typical set-up: one stroller (or a stroller frame) that holds an infant car seat and then a lightweight stroller that folds compactly for the mall/travel. Of course, we hear from parents who own four, five or six strollers, including specialty models like joggers, tandem units for two kids and more. First-time parents wonder if these folks have lost their minds, investing the equivalent of the gross national product of Aruba on baby transportation. Alas, most parents realize that as their baby grows and their needs change, so must their stroller.

Far be it for us to suggest you buy multiple strollers, but at the same time, it is hard to recommend just one model that works for everyone. That's why the recommendations later in this chapter are organized by lifestyle and use.

Wastes of Money

1 **SILLY ACCESSORIES.** Entrepreneurs have worked overtime to invent all kinds of silly accessories that you "must have" for your stroller. We've seen stroller "snack trays" ($15) for babies who like to eat on the run. Another company made a clip-on bug repellent, which allegedly used sound waves to scare away insects. Yet another money-waster: extra seat cushions or head supports for infants made in your stroller's matching fabric. You can find these same items in solid colors at discount stores for 40% less.

So which stroller accessories are worth the money? One accessory we do recommend is a toy bar (about $10 to $20), which attaches to the stroller. Why is this a good buy? If toys are not attached, your baby will probably punt them out the stroller.

Does your stroller lack a cup holder? Hard to believe, but some pricey strollers actually omit this feature, which you would think would be a no-brainer. As a fix, we like Kelgar's Stroll'r Hold'r cup holder ($8, call 972-250-3838 or kelgar.com).

Valco also makes a Universal Cup Holder for $16 (twice the Kelgar option above) as does Baby Jogger (Liquid Holster, $20). Parents seem to like the Valco, but the Baby Jogger Holster is a disappointment. Apparently it only stays upright (not spilling) some of the time. One parent recommended it only for water bottles, not for cups.

What about stroller handle extensions? If you find yourself kicking the back of the stroller as you walk, you might want to invest in one of these $20 devices. An example: the Stroller Handle Extender from MBS (mbsolutionsinc.com) for $23. It attaches to the stroller handle with Velcro and adds about eight inches.

2 **"NEW" OLD STOCK.** A reader alerted us to this online scam— the problem of "new" old stock. A stroller she ordered from a small web site was described as a "new Chicco stroller." Turns out, the stroller she got was seven years old. Yes, technically it was "new," as in "not previously used" and still in its original box. Unfortunately, since it was sitting in a warehouse for seven years, it had a cracked canopy, torn fabric and other problems. Apparently, there must be warehouses full of "new" old baby products out there for whatever reason. Our advice: request MODEL YEAR info on strollers or other products when that isn't clearly listed online. While previous year models can be a great deal, we wouldn't buy anything over three years old. . . even if a web site says it is "new."

3 **GIVE THE "BOOT" THE BOOT.** Some expensive strollers offer a "boot" or apron that fits over the baby's feet. This padded cover is supposed to keep the baby's feet dry and warm when it rains or snows. Sometimes you have to spend an extra $50 to $100 to get a stroller with this accessory. But do you really need this? We say save the extra cost and use a blanket instead. Or try a product like the Cozy Rosie or Bundle Me (mentioned later in this chapter), which are made of fleece and provide more warmth than a typical stroller boot. Or, if you decide you need a boot, buy a stroller model that includes this feature—several models now include a boot as standard equipment.

Money-Saving Tips

1 **STOP! DON'T BUY A FULL FEATURE STROLLER BEFORE THE BABY ARRIVES.** Here's a classic first-time parent mistake: buying an expensive, giant travel system stroller (a.k.a, the Baby Bus), thinking you need all those whiz-bang features. But the huge bulk and weight of those strollers will have you cursing the thing before your baby hits six months. A better bet: get a basic stroller frame for $60 (more details on these later), strap in an infant seat and voila! You have transport for an infant for at least six months. Trust us, after you've hung out with your baby for a few months, you'll have a much better idea what your stroller needs are. As your baby nears the limits on an infant car seat, THEN you buy a regular stroller.

2 **WHY NOT A BASIC UMBRELLA STROLLER?** If you only plan to use a stroller on infrequent trips to the mall, then a plain umbrella stroller for $40 to $50 will suffice. One caveat: most plain umbrella strollers do NOT recline—you will not be able to use it until your baby is able to hold up his head (around six months). And they may not have any storage.

3 **CONSIDER A CARRIER FOR NEWBORNS.** Yes, a simple baby carrier (sling, wrap, front carrier, etc.) can be a much more affordable alternative to expensive strollers. The best carriers have padded straps and lumbar support to keep the strain off your back. Sure you will need a stroller at some point as your baby grows . . . but a carrier can be a cost-effective option to take your newborn or young infant to the store or mall.

4 **CHECK FOR SALES.** We're always amazed by the number of sales on strollers. We've seen frequent sales at the Burlington Coat Factory's Baby Depot, with good markdowns on even premium brand strollers. Coupons are also common. Babies R Us offers occasional coupons in newspaper circulars as well as to parents on their mailing list. Another reason strollers go on sale: the manufacturers are constantly coming out with new models and have to clear out the old. Which leads us to the next tip.

5 **LOOK FOR LAST YEAR'S MODELS.** Every year, manufacturers roll out new models. In some cases, they add features; other times, they just change the fabric. What do they do with last year's stock? They discontinue it—and then it's sale time. You'll see these models on sale for as much as 50% off in stores and on the web. And it's not like stroller fabric fashion varies much from year to year—

strollers

E-Mail from The Real World
Last year's fashion, 50% off

A reader emailed her tip on how she saved over $100 on a stroller:

"When looking for strollers you can often get last year's version for a big discount. I purchased a previous year Maclaren model online for $190. That compares to the $300 price tag for the current year model from Babies R Us. As far as my research could tell, the models are identical except for the color pattern. A quick web search can turn up a number of sources that are selling last year's strollers; colors are limited (dmartstores.com had the widest selection) but it is a great way to save over $100 for a very nice stroller."

---

is there really much difference between "navy pin dot" and "navy with a raspberry diamond"? We say go for last year's fabric and save a bundle. See the Email from the Real World above for a mom's story on her last year model deal.

6 SCOPE OUT FACTORY SECONDS. Believe it or not, some stroller manufacturers sell "factory seconds" at good discounts—these "cosmetically imperfect" models might have a few blemishes, but are otherwise fine. An example: one reader told us Peg Perego occasionally has factory sales from their Indiana headquarters. See Peg's contact info on page 521 to find the latest schedule.

7 DON'T FALL VICTIM TO STROLLER OVERKILL. Seriously evaluate how you'll use the stroller and don't over buy. If a Toyota Camry will do, why buy a Lexus? You don't really need an all-terrain stroller or full-feature pram for mall trips. Flashy strollers can be status symbols for some parents—try to avoid "stroller envy!"

8 SELL YOUR STROLLER TO RECOUP YOUR INVESTMENT. When you're done with the stroller, consign it at a second-hand store or sell it on Craigslist. You'd be surprised how much it can fetch. The best brands for resale are, not surprisingly, the better names we recommend in this chapter.

Of course, the strollers with the best resale value are those that are in excellent condition. If you keep an expensive jogging stroller in your garage or on your deck, consider a cover. BuggyBonnets.com sells a $85 cover for single strollers, $110 for a double, made from heavy duty, water-resistant fabric.

9 **WAREHOUSE CLUB DEALS.** Yes, Sam's and Costco periodically sell strollers, including joggers. At one point before going to press, Costco was selling Schwinn jogging strollers from their web site (Costco.com) at 45% under retail. Of course, these deals come and go—and like anything you see at the warehouse clubs, you have to snap it up quickly or it will be gone.

10 **eBAY/CRAIGSLIST**. It's highly addictive and for good reason—these sites are more than just folks trying to unload a junky stroller they bought at K-Mart. Increasingly, baby gear retailers are using eBay to discreetly clear out overstock. Better to unload online the stuff that isn't moving than risk the wrath of local customers who bought the model for full price last week. An example: a reader scored a brand new Peg Perego for HALF the stroller's retail price through an eBay auction. Other readers regularly report saving $100 to $200 through eBay. Hint: many strollers sold online are last year's model or fashion. Be sure to confirm what you are buying (is it in the original box? No damage? Which model year?) before bidding.

And don't forget Craigslist either. Yes, this site has both junk and jewels. Be patient and search carefully to find worthwhile stroller buys.

The Name Game: Reviews of Selected Manufacturers

So, how do we rate and review strollers? First, we do hands-on inspections in stores and trade shows. That involves giving the stroller a test spin, checking the fold and more. Next, we listen to you, the reader. The stroller message board on our web site is one of the most popular forums, brimming with over 1000 posts a month. As always, parent feedback is our secret sauce.

One key point to remember: the ratings in this section apply to the ENTIRE line of a company's strollers. No, we don't assign ratings to individual strollers, but we will comment on what we think are a company's best models. Following this section, we will give you several "lifestyle recommendations"—specific models of strollers to fit different parent lifestyles.

The Ratings

A **EXCELLENT**—*our top pick!*
B **GOOD**— *above average quality, prices, and creativity.*
C **FAIR**—*could stand some improvement.*
D **POOR**—*yuck! could stand some major improvement.*

Abiie *abiie.com.* This brand is reviewed online at BabyBargains.com

Aprica *apricausa.com.* The iconic Japanese stroller brand Aprica was bought by Graco in 2008 and relaunched in the U.S. as a premium lightweight stroller line. Graco's first effort is the Presto ($200, 13.9 lbs. although we've seen it online for as little as $115), a lightweight stroller that sits a bit higher than other models—this enables more legroom for older children. The Presto's self-standing fold, four-wheel suspension and extended canopy are the other draws here.

In the past year, Graco released an upgraded version of the Presto, dubbed the Presto Flat ($230, 15 lbs; online as little as $180). It features a fully reclining seat and a footrest that folds up when the seat reclines to form a bassinet. The Presto Flat can hold a Graco infant car seat. FYI: The Presto is scheduled to be discontinued in 2012, but the Presto Flat will live on.

New for 2012, Aprica is launching its first travel system: the Moto ($230) at Babies R Us. The Moto combines the Aprica A30 car seat (which is the same as a Graco SnugRide 30) with a stroller that features a bigger basket, a smartphone cradle in a kids tray and a one-

Stroller Shopping Secret: Rear Wheel Width

Weight may be the most important factor to urban parents looking for a new stroller, but we suggest looking at one additional criteria: rear wheel width. Many new strollers have a wide spread between the rear wheels. The problem? Many urban parents have to negotiate tight spaces (grocery store aisles, subways, etc). A stroller with a wide wheelbase may not squeeze through small doorways and into tight elevators. Here is a look at the rear wheel widths for some popular urban strollers.

STROLLER	REAR WHEEL WIDTH
Maclaren Techno XT	19.5″
Bugaboo Bee	20.0
Stokke Xplory	22.0
Bugaboo Cameleon	23.0
Peg Perego Skate	23.75
Microlite Toro	24.0
Orbit	24.0
UPPAbaby Vista	25.0
Quinny Buzz	25.5

Our advice: go for the narrowest wheelbase you can find—23″ and under is probably best (some doors are a narrow 24″ wide).

hand, standing fold. The Moto stroller weighs 20 lbs.

One of Aprica's key selling features is a 70 lb. weight limit on all its strollers—yes, that is quite unusual for umbrella strollers (few are rated beyond 50 lbs.). So if your child has already been signed up as a future linebacker for the New York Jets, this might be the stroller for you.

What's the verdict on the new Aprica? Well, we like the elevated seat design and the high-tech mesh fabric. The handles are not adjustable, but will work for most tall parents.

Reader feedback on the new Apricas has been quite positive—and readers report they are finding them on sales for as little as $80 on clearance at Babies R Us (Amazon currently has the Presto for $145). At those price levels, folks seem to be happy with this brand. Highlights include a recline feature, which is lacking on the similarly price Maclaren Volo. Critics find the five-point harness complicated and the rear brakes are too easily engaged when going down stairs. Another bummer: the Presto has a maximum height of 45"—which makes that 70 lb., weight limit moot if you have a tall toddler.

The new Moto travel system was brand new as of this writing, so we've had little feedback on it yet. We saw a prototype of the Moto and weren't that impressed. Unlike the Aprica Presto, the Moto feels like a Graco stroller that's been slapped with a fancier label. And we've seen early reports from consumers who complain the Moto's car seat doesn't latch properly in the stroller.

So it is a mixed review for this brand: if you can find it at a discount and can live with the shortcomings (no cup holder, etc.), then go for it. But at full retail, Aprica just doesn't measure up to category leaders like Maclaren. *Rating: B*

Babyhome. Spanish stroller maker Baby Home will debut in the U.S. in 2012 with their Emotion stroller. This lightweight ($300, 16.9 lbs.) stroller features a curved frame, rain cover, mosquito net, fully reclining seat and is car seat adaptable (Chicco, Graco, Maxi Cosi). The stroller's unique feature: polyurethane wheels (with ball bearing suspension) give a smooth ride. Made in China, the Emotion comes in six solid color fashions. This stroller wasn't out as of this writing, so no rating yet. *Rating: Not Yet*

Baby Jogger *babyjogger.com*. Baby Jogger literally invented the jogging stroller category 30 years ago with the first stroller with bicycle tires designed for runners. Since then, the company has been through numerous ups and downs . . . including a bankruptcy back in 2003 that led to new ownership. The company has since refocused on all-terrain strollers with swivel front wheels. Their new models have met with much success, despite the fact the company has drifted away from its "jogger" name.

The models. Baby Jogger has three main stroller models: the City Series, Summit and Performance. The City Series has the easiest fold we've seen for such models: one-hand and zip! It's done. That probably explains the strong sales for this series, which boasts four models: the Micro, Mini, Elite and Select.

The City Micro (single $160, 17.2 lbs.; double $230, 26.4 lbs.) appears to have been discontinued. It features small (6") wheels in front and is designed for the mall. It also has a partial seat recline. You may see a few still available online at discounted prices.

The City Mini (single $200, 17.1 lbs.; double $400, 26.6 lbs.) is similar to the Micro, but adds a full recline, fancier canopy and slightly larger wheels. For 2012, the City Mini gets a few tweaks: a slightly larger seat, an easier to access storage basket and an auto lock feature when the stroller is folded. Also new for 2012, Baby Jogger will debut a new version of the City Mini, the City Mini GT ($350, 21.5 lbs.). The GT adds an adjustable handle bar with brake, a redesigned seat/canopy that provides more headroom, an easier to access storage basket and bigger, no-flat tires. It is scheduled to be released in Spring 2012.

At the top end, the City Elite (single $400, 31.3 lbs.; double $650, 42 lbs.) features 12" air-filled wide tread tires and a parent console. While those air-filled tires make the Elite more of an all-terrain stroller, the trade-off is added weight.

FYI: One major difference between the City models is weight capacity. The City Elite works to 75 lbs. single, 100 double. The City Mini and Micro's limits are 50/100 lbs.

The biggest stroller launch for Baby Jogger in recent years was the 2010 debut of the City Select, which is sort of like the Swiss Army Knife of strollers. It can be configured 16 ways, with an optional second seat. With a telescoping handle and foam tires, the Select (28.1 lbs.) costs $500 (plus $160 for the second seat). A bassinet accessory is $90. For 2011, Baby Jogger has made only small changes to the Select, upping the amount of seat padding yet keeping the price the same.

If you can't decide between the City Mini and the Select, there is a new option for spring 2012: the City Versa (23.7 lbs). This hybrid is a cross between those two models: the seat on the Versa reverses (like the Select), but the stroller doesn't expand to a double. You do get a full canopy and recline, an adjustable leg rest, all wheel suspension, hand brake and a flat fold. Price: $450.

If you want to actually jog with a Baby Jogger, the company offers the Performance (single $430, 24 lbs.; double $500, 30 lbs.). This stroller has a one-step, quick-release seat recline, floating canopy for extra sun coverage, and a direct-pull brake. Baby Jogger recently added the FIT ($300, 25.4 lbs.) to the line, with a

Different Versions Spark Confusion

Here's a common question we get at the home office: readers go into a chain store like Babies R Us and see a major brand stroller they like. Then, they visit a specialty store and see a similar model, but with some cosmetic differences . . . and a higher price tag. What's up with that? Big stroller makers like Graco have to serve two masters—chain stores and specialty retailers. Here's a little trick of the baby biz: stroller makers often take the same basic model of stroller and make various versions for different retailers. Hence, you'll see a Graco stroller with basic fabric in Babies R Us—and then the same model sold with fancier fabric in specialty stores. So is there any real difference besides the fabric color to justify the increase in price? Yes, sometimes the fabrics are upgraded (or there is more padding). But overall, you are basically seeing the same stroller. Our advice: if you can live with the basic version, go for it.

fixed front wheel, deep seat recline and aluminum frame. FYI: The Performance will be discontinued in 2012, but the FIT will live on.

For more serious all-terrain use, the Summit 360 comes in single ($400, 25.4 lbs.), double ($650, 38.8 lbs.) and even triple versions ($900, 48.5 lbs.). The Summit is Baby Jogger's top-of-the-line model, with 16" rear and 12" front air-filled tires, swivel front wheel that locks, suspension, and the same quick-fold technology you see on the City Series.

Finally, Baby Jogger has a hybrid jogging stroller/bike trailer model, the Switchback ($650). It morphs back and forth between being a jogger and bike trailer without any special kit or tools. FYI: The Switchback will be discontinued in 2011 and replaced by the Pod. This new model will be sold as a chassis for $500—you can add a stroller kit for $80, jogger for $59 and bike trailer adapter for $40. The Pod will be 30" wide so it can fit through most standard doorways, yet still accommodate up to two kids.

Our view. Baby Jogger's biggest problem would probably the envy of most other stroller companies: its products are so popular, they have often run out of stock. Example: the City Mini spent most of 2010 in a backorder twilight zone. Much of that popularity is probably due to the company's overall quality, which is excellent.

Our readers love the quick-fold feature and wide selection of accessories . . . at least when they are in stock! More than one reader grumbled about the lack of availability of the second seat for the Select. A word to the wise: if you want a Select, get all the accessories at once if they are in stock. One final note: Baby Jogger sells a car seat adapter that works with most infant car seats, including Graco and Peg Perego. ***Rating: A***

Baby Planet baby-planet.com. This brand is reviewed on our web site, BabyBargains.com (click on Bonus Material).

Baby Trend babytrend.com. Baby Trend's biggest selling stroller isn't really a stroller at all—it's a stroller frame. Here's an overview of the line:

The models. The Snap N Go is such a simple concept it's amazing someone else didn't think of it years ago—basically it's a stroller frame that lets you snap in most major-brand infant car seats. Presto! Instant travel system at a fraction of the price. The basic Snap & Go is $70 (less online); a double version that holds two car seats is $100. Be aware that while most infant car seats snap into the Snap & Go, others merely rest on the top bar. In either case, Baby Trend recommends using the supplied safety belt to make sure the seat is secure.

The Snap N Go has been so successful it has spawned knock-offs from several competitors, namely Kolcraft, Cosco and Graco. We will review those options later.

Besides the stroller frame, Baby Trend also offers travel systems, double strollers and joggers. Baby Trend's travel systems combine their Flex-Loc infant seat with basic low-end strollers. Example: the Envy travel system is $150 (car seat and stroller). That's a low price, but the stroller (21 lbs.) is nothing fancy—steel frame, five-point harness and multi-position recline. You do get a decent canopy, one-hand fold and big basket.

FYI: The company refers to its travel systems by the fabric name (the Spunky Plaid travel system, for example)—it's the same stroller, just a different fabric.

Besides its basic stroller, the company sells a smattering of other stroller models, including a Bugaboo knock off (Euro Buggy, $140) and the Stride Sport Stroller ($90-100).

Baby Trend is a big player in the jogging stroller market—their flagship model is the Expedition. This steel frame jogger is loaded with features (reclining seat, five-point harness, parent tray with cup holders and ratcheting canopy) and is sold as a travel system ($200-$345) or separately ($120-$185).

We should also note that Baby Trend markets their products under the name "Swan" for specialty stores. Basically, these are the same products/models as Baby Trend makes, albeit with a few cosmetic differences (fabric color, etc.).

FYI: Baby Trend still sells the Sit N Stand stroller, a "pushcart" that combines a stroller with a jump seat for an older child, despite being sued by rival Joovy over a patent dispute. See Joovey's review for more info on this.

Baby Trend recently rolled out a redesigned Sit N Stand double that holds two car seats and has a napper bar that rotates away when not in use. It comes in both steel (36 lbs.) and aluminum (30 lbs.) versions that run $160 to $200. The redesigned single Sit N Stand will let you attach a car seat in front or back.

Our view. After writing about baby gear for 18 years, there are still some companies that are mysteries. Baby Trend is Exhibit One.

The company rarely releases new stroller models, content to sell basically the same products year after year in chain stores like Babies R Us and Walmart. Despite quality and customer service that our readers peg as merely average, the company seems to merrily chug along. Basically, these are strollers that are sold on price—if it breaks, that's your problem.

Baby Trend hit a speed bump in 2009 when it lost an $8.4 million verdict in a wrongful termination lawsuit. A jury found the company "acted with malice, oppression and fraud" in firing an employee who was a marketing executive. As a result of the verdict, Baby Trend filed for bankruptcy in 2010. That case is still winding its way through the courts as of press time.

If that weren't enough, Baby Trend has also become embroiled in multiple patent lawsuits. Joovy has sued Baby Trend over the patent rights to the Sit N Stand stroller. And in 2010, Graco sued Baby Trend for allegedly violating the patents for its playpens. This was followed by a lawsuit in 2011 by Kids II that alleged Baby Trend infringed on its patents for a bouncer. For good measure, Baby Trend has also sued Dorel for alleged infringement on its patent for

E-MAIL FROM THE REAL WORLD
The Weight Game

"I saw the same stroller listed with two different weights online. How can the same model weigh five lbs. less on one site?"

Good question—call it the weight shell game. We've noticed some web sites play fast and loose with the weights of strollers listed on their sites. Why? What parents' value most in a stroller is LIGHT overall weight—and online sellers know this. So, why not cheat and list a stroller's weight . . . minus a few items like a canopy, basket or other amenities? Another explanation: stroller manufacturers often tweak their models from year to year, adding new features. This can add additional ounces, but some web sites "forget" to update the weight. Yes, it is deceptive—but there are ways around the problem. First, this book lists the true weight for most models. Also check the manufacturer's web site, which usually lists the correct weight.

a car seat harness.

Even if you set aside Baby Trend's legal and financial woes, its products are becoming passé. The unique niche once occupied by the Snap & Go has now been matched by competing stroller frames. And now many strollers are sold with car seat adapters, making the Snap & Go an unnecessary expense. As for Baby Trend's other strollers, there's not much to write home about. Bottom line: we'd avoid this brand until it resolves its problems. ***Rating: C-***

Bloom *bloombaby.com* The mini-boomlet of modern baby gear companies turned into a bust when the recession hit, taking with it a raft of companies that thought the market for $2000 cribs was ever expanding.

Yet a few companies somehow made it through these trying times. Among the survivors is Bloom, which is probably most famous for their Bloom high chair and Alma mini crib. And now Bloom adds strollers to its stable of products.

Count us among the skeptical when we toured Bloom's booth at a trade show and got the full court press for the new stroller. Does the world need another $800+ stroller?

But we have to admit: Bloom's new stroller, the babyZEN, is darn impressive. The stroller's flat fold system is something you have to see to believe (there is an online demo video, naturally).

Invented by the French designer who thought up the BAEBA brand, the babyZEN features an adjustable frame, a reclining seat that can be swapped out for a lay-flat bassinet and a footprint when folded that can fit into the smallest compact car.

The babyZEN stroller is $800. The Yoga newborn nest (the bassinet) is $250.

Ok, there are some gimmicky features here, most notably a remote-activated headlight that is rather superfluous. But it's the little design touches that impressed us most: the babyZEN stands when folded and then can be wheeled about, thanks to small casters in the handle.

The negatives? Well, the seat recline is a series of zippers and catches, which seems overly complicated. And the weight (25.5 lbs) in the toddler mode is on the cusp of hefty.

Another bummer: the stroller will launch with just two color schemes: monochrome (silver, grey) and something Bloom calls CMYK. For those not in print production, that stands for cyan, magenta, yellow and black—hence this model looks like something a Cirque du Soleil costume designer might dream up.

This model wasn't yet out in the wild as we went to press, so we'll have to wait to see how it works in the real world. But we think Bloom may have a winner on its hands. ***Rating: Not Yet***

BOB Strollers *bobgear.com*. BOB has won accolades for their innovative joggers—you can tell these were designed by runners for runners. (Trivia note: BOB stands for Beast of Burden trailers—they decided BOB was easier to spell . . . and would avoid a lawsuit from Mick Jagger). BOB's strollers are billed as "sport utility" strollers and that's an apt moniker, as their rugged design (polymer wheels to

Shopping Cart Covers: Advice & Picks

Grocery store carts aren't exactly the cleanest form of transportation—yet once your baby outgrows her infant car seat, you will put likely baby in the little seat up front . . . and quickly realize that keeping the carts clean doesn't seem to be a high priority for most stores. Some stores have added in a wipes dispenser near the carts, but you can't get the gook off the fabric belts—that's just gross.

To the rescue comes the shopping cart cover, basically a fabric seat that provides a clean and safe space for baby while you shop. Here are our top picks for shopping cart covers:

◆ *OhSewCuteBoutique.net* Looking for a shopping cart cover that will even work on those oversized warehouse store carts? Oh Sew Cute's $85 cover 100% washable and comes in a plethora of fabrics and colors.

◆ *Itzy Ritzy.* These shopping cart covers are more fashionable than the ones you see in stores and run $68. Readers say Itzy Ritzy covers (itzyritzy.com) are easy to use and work on both regular grocery store carts and those large carts at Costco. Price includes a carrying case.

◆ *Bellingham Baby's* (bellinghambabycompany.com) shopping cart covers were recommended by readers for their reversible covers in cool fabrics. Covers include two toy loops plus pockets and are available in 17 fabric choices. Prices are about $68.

Our readers also recommended the BuggyBagg ($50-$90), and the Original Clean Shopper ($25). The latter just has quilted cotton fabric, no batting— it is no frills, but does the job. Readers gave much lower marks to covers from Infantino and Nojo, which we would avoid.

strollers

prevent rust, for example) and plush ride make these strollers best sellers despite their $300+ price tags. The BOB Sport Utility stroller sells for $379 (duallie: $450 to $500) and comes with polymer wheels

If you are a serious runner, the BOB Ironman Stroller (single: $350 to $410, 21 lbs.; double: $480 to $560, 31.4 lbs.) is probably the pick of the litter, with smooth tires, stiffer shocks, suspension wheels and more. Plus the bright yellow color gives it great visibility. For more casual walkers, the BOB Stroller Stride model ($400 to $440) is basically a BOB Revolution with an added handlebar console and tension tubing for resistance exercise. In the past year, BOB debuted a new universal accessory adapter that can be removed without tools. The adapter can fit a snack tray or BOB's infant car seat adapter ($60) and works with the Graco SnugRide, SafeSeat, and Peg Primo Viaggio.

Also new, the Revolution and other models now feature a heat-pressed seat for more support, adjustable crotch strap, new multi-position canopy and a storage basket with easier access. Strollers with polymer wheels are now referred to as the Sport Experience (SE; single $450, dualie $660) while those with aluminum wheels are called the City Experience (CE; single $470). The CE models will feature smaller wheels than the current offerings. We weighed the new Revolution SE at 24.9 lbs., so the redesigned models are about a pound or two heavier.

Parents give BOB excellent marks on quality and durability. Yes, these strollers are expensive, but worth it. Minor quibbles: the handlebars are not height adjustable, frustrating some parents. And BOB needs to keep an eye on its weight, as that new Revolution is now approaching 25 lbs. (which can be a bit much to haul in and out of a trunk). That said, BOB is a great brand and earns our highest rating.

FYI: In October 2011, BOB was acquired by Britax. No news yet on whether Britax will run BOB as a stand-alone brand or fold it into its stroller offerings. **Rating: A**

Britax britaxusa.com. Best-known for its well-made car seats, Britax launched a stroller line in 2005 so it could compete in the travel system market.

The models. Britax offers four stand alone strollers: B-Agile, B-Ready, B-Nimble and B-Scene. The B-Ready ($500–we've seen it online for as little as $376, 28.1 lbs.) is Britax's flagship stroller and their first stab at a modular stroller that works with an optional bassinet and second seat. Designed to integrate with Britax's infant car seat (the Chaperone), the B-Ready has 14 different configurations, much like the Baby Jogger Select and Uppa Baby Vista.

Out of the box, the stroller will work with Britax's infant car seats (a separate $50 adapter is needed for Graco and Chicco seats). The B-Ready features a seat that reverses to face forward or rear, full tire suspension, large storage basket and full seat recline. Got two kids? A second seat ($150; $120 online) transforms the B-Ready into a double stroller.

The B-Nimble ($200, online as little as $163; 15.5 lbs.) is the B-Ready's much lighter cousin— it is infant car seat compatible and features a removable/reversible seat liner, cup holder and rain cover. It works with the Britax infant seat out of the box.

Finally, B-Scene ($400, as little as $350 online; 29 lbs.) is a tri-wheel version of the B-Ready. It lacks the B-Ready's second seat, but does come with a rain cover. And a quick fyi: in the closeout bin, you might see two old Britax models, the Chaperone and the Blink. Both were nothing special, but if you can get them at 70% off, go for it.

New in the past year, Britax has rolled out their version of the Baby Jogger City Mini: the B-Agile weighs in at 16.5 lbs. and runs $250 ($195 online). It features a one-hand quick-fold, large canopy and no-rethread harness.

For 2012, Britax has rolled out a new travel accessory: a $70 car seat travel cart that let's you use a car seat's LATCH connectors. The travel cart folds for storage in an aircraft overhead bin.

Our view. Britax has struggled in this category, racking up five years of failure before finally getting it right with its current offerings. Why the struggle? Ironically, Britax's strength in car seats has been a weakness when it comes to strollers. That's because what works with car seats (strong engineering focus and innovation) doesn't necessary translate to the world of strollers, where success is often a meld of function, style and value.

As for the function part, the new Britax strollers are much closer to the mark. We liked the B-Ready's ability to morph into different configurations—many more than the comparable Uppa Baby Vista (which notably, runs $180 more than the B-Ready). And you can fold the B-Ready with the second (toddler) seat attached—that's something the competition can't do.

Critics, however, knock the B-Ready's overall bulk and weight (about two lbs. heavier than the comparable Vista).

So we have the function and value, but what about style? That's probably Britax's weakness. . . and we aren't just talking about the B-Ready's plain Jane fashion and the line's goofy model names (B-Ready? B-Scene? B-serious). Britax strollers lack a certain je ne sais quoi when compared with Baby Jogger (see: Quick Fold, definition of) and Uppa Baby. And when you are trying to sell a $500 stroller like the B-Ready, you need some zing.

On a more positive note, the Britax B-Agile gets good marks on quality. The price (under $200 online) makes it a good deal. Parents like the smooth glide, large canopy and easy to adjust harness. We recommend the B-Agile as a credible alternative to the Baby

Jogger City Mini.

As for Britax's other strollers (the B-Scene and B-Nimble), we have much less parent feedback on these models. They aren't as popular as the B-Ready or B-Agile.

Despite its shortcomings, we will recommend the new Britax stroller line. The B-Ready in particular is a credible and affordable alternative to the Uppa Baby Vista; and the B-Agile is a good bet compared to the Baby Jogger City Mini. ***Rating: A-***

Bugaboo *bugaboo.com.* Bugaboo. It's Dutch for "priced as if from a hotel mini-bar."

The models. Here's an unlikely recipe for success in the stroller biz. Take a Dutch-designed stroller, attach a $700 price tag and voila! Instant hit, right? Well, chalk this one up to some creative marketing (or at least, lucky timing).

Bugaboo's breakthrough success was the Frog, named as such for its small wheels in front that give it a frog-like look. The Frog ($760) is a clever hybrid of an all-terrain and carriage stroller, pitched to parents for its multiple uses. The Frog comprises three parts: an aluminum frame and bassinet that can later be replaced by a stroller seat (included with canopy and basket). It weighs about 20 lbs., which is rather amazing. (Bugaboo is closing out the Frog although it was still available at press time.)

Oh, and we forgot the fourth ingredient of the Bugaboo—hype.

The Bugaboo folks were in the right place at the right time. How did the Bugaboo become so hot? Sure, it was fashionable, but that doesn't quite explain it. Nope, the answer is Bugaboo had one of the great product placements of all time . . . it was the featured stroller on HBO's "Sex in the City." The rest is stroller history. In no time, celebs like Gwyneth Paltrow were swishing their Bugaboos across the pages of *People* magazine. The Bugaboo was the first baby stroller to cross paths with the white-hot supernova that is celebrity culture these days.

It didn't hurt that Bugaboo debuted during the boom in baby luxury products during the early 2000's (remember those days?).

Cleverly, Bugaboo played on its Dutch design roots . . . even though (shhh! don't tell anyone!) the Bugaboo is made in Taiwan, not Amsterdam.

Bugaboo's sequel to the Frog—the aptly named Cameleon (20 lbs.) runs $880. The Cameleon adds a more springy suspension on the front wheels, plus a slightly larger seat frame and higher chassis. Unlike the Frog, the Cameleon is available in a wide range of color combinations—you can choose from six base colors and nine top colors, mix and match. Also new: a height adjustable handle.

Bugaboo has added to its line at a slow pace. In 2007, the company launched its first compact stroller, the Bee ($600, 22 lbs.). Pitched to urban dwellers with its narrow width (20"; about four inches narrower than other Bugaboo's), the Bee has an oversized canopy, reversible seat, and four-position seat recline.

Yet the Bee was never the runaway hit that the Frog or Cameleon were, so Bugaboo went back to the drawing board and launched a refreshed Bee in 2010. Dubbed the Bee Plus, it features a wider, height adjustable seat, adjustable canopy height and upgraded wheels. The company seemed to listen to its critics when it dropped the original Bee's much-hated seat "wings."

The big news in the past year was Bugaboo's first double stroller, the unfortunately named Donkey. The unique feature here is a frame that can expand to accommodate a bassinet, storage basket or second baby seat. In its single or mono configuration, the stroller is 23" wide; for a duo, it expands to 29." Unfortunately, all this presto-chango goodness comes at a price, both literally and figuratively. The weight of the Donkey is a hefty 32 lbs. as a single and a whopping 40.3 lbs. as a duo (with the added second seat). And the cost? $1200 for a "mono" version, $1500-$1650 for a double. No kidding.

FYI: Bugaboo also sells a raft of accessories for its strollers such as cup holders (what? You thought that would be included?). Example: a $45 car seat adapter lets you attach most major brand infant car seats to the frame. That cup holder is $25, parasol $40, foot muff $130.

Our view. The rise and fall of Bugaboo at first blush looks like a tale that mirrors the economy: at first, parents (and grand parents) couldn't wait to spend nearly $1000 on a Bugaboo stroller, wanting the very best for their baby. Now frugal is in and luxe is out—so naturally, Bugaboo has suffered.

But some of Bugaboo's woes go beyond macroeconomics . . . and are more self-inflicted. The company's notoriously slow and arrogant customer service is Exhibit One. When you spend this much on a stroller and something breaks, you expect white glove treat-ment from the company. Yet reader reports and online reviews again and again slam Bugaboo for indifferent customer service, long waits for parts and other hassles.

Quality issues have also dogged Bugaboo (plastic parts that break, inflated tires that go flat and so on) and that's on top of some of the built-in design hassles of the strollers, particularly on the Cameleon. In 2011, Bugaboo recalled Bee strollers for defective wheels.

Readers gripe that the assembly and folding on the stroller takes too darn long. To fold a Bugaboo Frog or Cameleon, you must first remove the seat—that's a major pain, especially for folks who live in the suburbs and plan to fold it up frequently to fit in a trunk (and you'll need a big trunk). Hence, setting up the Bugaboo requires re-

strollers

attaching the seat to the frame. Sure, this takes 30 seconds or so, which isn't forever—but about 25 seconds longer than most strollers.

Bottom line: a Bugaboo is probably best for urban dwellers or folks who don't plan to frequently disassemble and throw it in a trunk. (The Bee is an exception—it is easy to fold and set-up).

Fans of Bugaboo love the strollers' smooth steering, ride and suspension. The multi-function aspect of the Cameleon also earns kudos, although this has been matched in recent years by the Uppa Baby Vista and even Britax. And while we think the Donkey's amazing expandable frame is a key innovation, it's hard for us to suggest anyone spend $1500 on a stroller.

Given its quality and customer service issues, we will drop our rating for Bugaboo this time out. Except for a few well-heeled urban parents, the hassle and expense of Bugaboo's flagship Cameleon or Frog makes this a questionable purchase. ***Rating: B***

Bumbleride bumbleride.com. In a stroller market marked by look-a-like models in varying shades of navy, Bumbleride's niche is all-terrain and umbrella strollers with more than a touch of style. Started by a husband and wife team in San Diego, Bumbleride is a small stroller company with four basic models: Flyer, Indie, Queen B and Flite.

The models. The Flyer is a $370 carriage stroller (19 lbs.) that features a five-point harness, reversible handle (which is nice), four-position recline, adjustable footrest and mesh basket. Best of all, it is compatible with several major infant car seats. The only negative: it is quite bulky when folded, so you'll need a large trunk to haul it around. In a recent update, Bumbleride made the rear wheels of the Flyer unlock and swivel, which makes pushing easier when the handle is reversed. A detachable cup holder rounds out the features.

The Indie ($500, 20 lbs.) is a tri-wheel, all-terrain stroller with quick release 12" inflated tires, boot, adjustable handle, full recline and deep storage basket. Basically, the Indie is a more stylish version of the Mountain Buggy Urban Single or BOB Revolution. FYI: A twin version of the Indie runs $680 and now can hold two infant car seats.

Bumbleride's most expensive model is the Queen B ($650, 31 lbs.), a pram-style stroller with wire basket. Yes, it comes with plush padding, reclining seat, boot and front swivel wheels.

New in the past year, the Flite ($250, 13 lbs.) is a lightweight stroller with two handles (a la the Peg Pliko or Maclaren Techno), a big canopy, two recline positions and car seat adapter bar. We liked all the included accessories such as a rain cover and travel bag.

Also new: special editions of their strollers that feature waterproof fabric (the Movement Edition) and recycled fabrics (Natural Edition). And the company has a new car seat adapter for the Maxi Cosi.

Our view. Reviews for Bumbleride are mixed at best—folks tell us they "like but don't love" their Flyers. Fans like the handle that reverses, letting you look at a newborn as you push the stroller and then switch the position for older babies. Other readers laud the Flyer's overall design (decent storage basket, sturdy frame, easy fold, etc). But detractors point out Bumbleride's inconsistent quality (reports of strollers with squeaky wheels, steering that pulls to one side), which mars the brand's overall rating. The Flyer's lack of a smooth glide and large size when folded are other negatives.

The Indie gets somewhat better marks from readers, who often compare it to the BOB Revolution. The Indie is three lbs. lighter than the Revolution and fans like its easy fold, adjustable height handle, car seat adapter and more. But critics point out the Indie doesn't have as smooth of a glide as the Revolution and the Indie only has a partial seat recline. The canopy on the Indie also gets low marks for its skimpy coverage and gaps near the frame. Considering both strollers cost about the same, the advantage goes to the BOB Revolution.

The Flite also is a mixed bag. Readers like the compact fold and car seat adapter—plus the overall style of the stroller is a winner. Critics say similar strollers like the Maclaren Techno have a smoother ride and easier access to the storage basket (the Flite's puny basket is a loser). One big difference between this stroller and the Techno: the Flite doesn't have a height adjustable handle, so if you are short and your partner isn't, this could be a major problem.

So it is a mixed review for this brand. Customer service, design and fashion are good; but inconsistent quality (especially for the Flyer) drags down Bumbleride's rating a bit. *Rating: B-*

Carter's *See Kolcraft.*

Chariot *chariotcarriers.com.* Canadian outdoor brand Chariot takes a different approach to the jogger market—Chariot makes bicycle trailers that covert into jogging strollers. If you are an avid bicyclist who also wants to occasionally jog with baby, Chariot offers six models of bike trailers with optional kits that turn the trailers into jogging strollers. Example: the Cougar ($535), which features plush harness straps, padded seats and adjustable suspension. Add a $90 jogging kit and you've got a stroller. In the past year, Chariot has redesigned the Cougar with expanded legroom.

New to the line is the Corsair bike trailer that features Chariot's largest child cockpit, side air vents, padded seat and 20" remove-able wheels. Price: $775.

While this brand is pricey (some Chariot models run close to $800), we've been impressed with Chariot's quality—no, they aren't cheap . . . but you'll be amazed by the ease of use and adjustments. (Yes, there is even a cross-country ski kit). The downside: these trailers/joggers are too wide to take into most stores, so this isn't a good solution for shopping. Obviously, unless you are a serious biker or runner, a Chariot is probably overkill. But if you want a quality bike trailer that can morph into a stroller, this brand should be on the top of your shopping list. ***Rating: A***

Chicco *chiccousa.com.* Chicco (pronounced Kee-ko) has a 50-year history as one of Europe's leading juvenile products makers. Along with Peg Perego, Chicco is one of Europe's biggest producer of baby gear and toys.

When we first started writing these books, Chicco always played second fiddle to Peg, whose strollers outsold Chicco by a large margin. In recent years, their fortunes have switched: Chicco has seen a string of successes in America, with a popular infant car seat and several lightweight stroller models. Peg, meanwhile, has languished with too-high prices and a lack of new models.

The models. Chicco's emphasis is on lightweight strollers designed for the mall—the company offers two compact models (Liteway, C6/Capri) and three full-size options (Cortina, Trevi, and S3).

In the compact category, the Liteway ($140, 17 lbs.) features two handles, rear wheel suspension, padded five-point harness, cup holder and a full recline. We like the boot that tucks away.

The entry-level C6 (also known as the Capri; $65, 11 lbs.) features a two-position seat recline, five-point harness and basic canopy . . . a bit like the Maclaren Volo, but almost half the price. The C6 and the Capri are basically the same, but the Capri has an upgraded canopy.

The Cortina, Chicco's marquee stroller, is sold separately ($170, 23 lbs.) or as part of a travel system ($300, paired with Chicco's excellent KeyFit infant seat). The Cortina features a more traditional design with height-adjustable handles and decent size basket. We thought it was well designed—we liked the one-hand fold and fully reclining seat.

The Trevi ($140, 19 lbs.) is also designed to work with Chicco's infant car seat and features a full recline, umbrella-style fold, two handles, cup holder and removable child tray.

Rounding out the line is Chicco's first tri-wheeled stroller, the S3 ($430, 23 lbs.). This swivel wheel stroller features suspension, foot muff and quick release wheels.

Chicco offers two double strollers: the Trevi Twin and the Cortina Together. The Trevi Twin ($170, 23 lbs.) is a side-by-side stroller that has fully reclining seats and upgraded canopies. By contrast, the Cortina Together ($300, 30 lbs.) is a front/back tandem stroller that holds two car seats and features an aluminum frame, a storage basket with trap door access, three-position handle and flat fold.

New in the past year, Chicco debuted their first stroller frame, dubbed the KeyFit Caddy ($100, 11 lbs.). As you might guess, it fits a Chicco KeyFit infant car seat (which pops in with a click) and has a big storage basket plus a height adjustable handle.

FYI: The prices we quoted above are full retail; we often seen Chicco discounted online below those prices. Also: the Trevi Twin was in short supply as we went to press.

Our view. "Cute and cheap" is how our readers sum up Chicco. Take the 11 lb. Chicco C6 (Capri)—it's half the price of a Maclaren and 40% lighter than the Peg Pliko. That makes it ideal for quick trips to the mall or airplane travel.

Detractors point out that Chicco strollers don't work well for tall folks, who often find the handle heights uncomfortable. And the canopies on many of their low price strollers don't offer much shade.

But that's the minority view: most readers say they are happy with their Chicco, especially those who mainly use the strollers for quick shopping trips.

So which Chicco strollers get the best marks? Readers give the full-featured Cortina and Trevi very good reviews—fans cheer the easy steering, one-hand fold and padding (critics point out both are a bit bulky).

How about the lightweight strollers? Readers seem to like the C6 and Liteway equally. Detractors point out the Liteway isn't that light—at nearly 20 lbs., it stretches the definition of lightweight. The skimpy baskets also come in for criticism on the Liteway and C6. On the other hand, most parents are happy with the overall quality of Chicco—and the customer service is good.

Chicco's new stroller frame was too new for us to give a verdict, but the prototype we had a chance to play with seemed well designed. It seems a bit pricey at $100 (since other stroller frames are about $70), but the height adjustable handle and snap-in capability for the Chicco KeyFit may make it worth it for some.

Overall, we think Chicco is a good brand and the prices are a decent value. If you like the look of Maclaren but don't have a Maclaren bank account, Chicco is a good alternative. *Rating: B+*

Combi combi-intl.com. Japanese-owned Combi had its heyday in the '90's with a string of best-selling lightweight strollers, but the company has struggled in recent years. Combi has gone through several management changes and shifts in strategy, which has hurt its brand.

The models. Combi's focus is on lightweight, compact strollers. The company's flagship model, the Cosmo, is a good starting point. The Cosmo ($105 to $130, 13 lbs.) features a compact fold, full seat recline for infants, and removable napper bar plus it holds Combi's Shuttle infant car seat.

Next is Combi's Cabria, which is basically a pimped out Cosmo. It features an extended canopy, larger basket, larger wheels, parent storage console and cup holder. This adds about a pound to the stroller (14.8 lbs.). Price: $180 (seen online for as little as $160). For 2012, The Cabria gets a few tweaks: bigger wheels, a bigger basket and cup holder.

Combi's sole entry in the twin market is the Twin Sport ($200 to $250, 22 lbs.), a side-by-side model that can fit one Combi infant car seat. The Twin Sport features a removable napper bar, machine washable cushions, 165-degree reclining seats and a separate canopy for each seat. Babies R Us sells an exclusive version of the Twin Sport (the EX) for $210 to $260—same stroller, different fashion.

Reeling from the tough economy, Combi has decided to discontinue a slew of slow-selling models. These include the Savvy, Flare and their stroller frames (Flash, Coccoro Flash) as well as travel systems. Also gone: the Strollee versions of Combi strollers.

New for 2012, Combi will debut the Catalyst, a very un-Combi like stroller that will weigh in at 28.1 lbs. This $450 stroller features a reversible seat, extendable handles, and a bassinet that morphs into a seat. It will be car seat compatible with Combi's Shuttle infant seat and adapters for other brands (Graco, Chicco). While this stroller is innovative, we were scratching our heads at why Combi would attempt to compete in the full-size stroller market with a nearly 30 lb. model.

Our view. Combi's woes in the stroller market can be traced to one major problem: its infant car seat. Unlike competitors Perego and Chicco, Combi has yet to figure out this market (its weak Shuttle car seat has suffered from slow sales amid recalls and other issues). As a result, Combi has missed out on the entire travel system market.

Design snafus have also dogged the brand. Parents have complained for years about Combi's handles (too short) and storage baskets (too small, hard to access). You'd think Combi's designers would have better adapted these models to America after being here for 20 years. And while parents universally like Combi for their lightweight and easy folds, there always seems to be some fatal flaw that pops up . . . front wheels that are easily damaged when the stroller is folded up, an overall lack of durability, etc.

When you spend $40 on a bare-bones umbrella stroller, you might put up with some of these issues. But at the $100+ price level, that's a tough sell, especially when competitors like Chicco and Maclaren offer similar strollers without the hassles mentioned above.

As for parent feedback, the most positive reviews for this line come for the Combi double Twin Sport stroller. The reviews for the Cosmo and Cabria are more mixed. ***Rating: B-***

Compass *See the First Years*

Cosco *djgusa.com.* Baby products conglomerate Dorel takes a divide and conquer approach to its stroller offerings. In mass-market discounters like Walmart, Dorel sells travel systems under the brands Cosco and Safety 1st. For chains like Babies R Us, it sells more upscale versions of its strollers under the Eddie Bauer brand. Finally, at the top end, Dorel uses its European sister brands (Quinny, Maxi Cosi) to sell strollers in specialty stores and chains.

Since Quinny and Maxi Cosi are marketed as their own separate brands, we review them separately. Below is a review of Cosco, Safety 1st and Eddie Bauer.

The models. Cosco's niche is entry-price point strollers such as the Sprinter Travel System. This $130 travel system combines the Cosco Designer 22 car seat and a no-frills stroller with one-hand fold and three-point harness. Cosco also sells a handful of low-price umbrella strollers ($18 to $35) and what it calls "convenience strollers" (the Altura, Avila and Umbria) in stores like Sears and K-Mart for $35 to $90.

Eddie Bauer and Safety 1st offer more options and upscale fabrics—these strollers are sold at Babies R Us and Diapers.com. A typical offering: the Eddie Bauer Adventure Sport Travel System, combining the Designer 22 infant car seat with a stroller with one-hand fold, large basket and fully reclining seat. Price: $229. Eddie Bauer offers five travel systems, while Safety 1st has 12 models.

In the past year, Dorel debuted its first stroller frame, the Safety 1st Clic ($70, 13 lbs.). It features a large storage basket, two cup holders, a click-in feature for Dorel seats and a strap-in system for other infant car seats.

Safety 1st's marquee stroller is the AeroLite LX ($150 to $215), which is combined with the OnBoard Air infant car seat to make a travel system. This model features a curved frame, ultra compact fold, multi-position canopy and seat recline. There are multiple versions of this travel system ranging in price from $180 to $240.

New for 2012, Safety 1st will debut its first stand-on stroller for transporting three kids: the Stand Onboard has a stroller seat and then can hold an infant car seat. A stand-on platform at the back can transport an older toddler. Price: $150, 23.7 lbs. Also new for 2012: the 3-Ease (17.7 lbs.), a tri-wheel stroller with one-hand fold, seat recline, parent organizer and large storage basket (but only a three point harness). It can hold a Comfy Carry or onBoard car seat with no additional hardware. Price: $140 as a stroller, $230 as a travel system.

Cosco is a big player in the double stroller market—their Safety 1st Two Ways tandem ($160) has a reversible front seat so kids can face each other.

Our view. The Achilles heal of Cosco's stroller line is their travel systems—many are paired with Cosco's poor Designer 22 infant car seat, which only works to 22 lbs. and receives low marks from readers. This drags down folks' overall impression of the strollers, which themselves are of only average quality.

Eddie Bauer strollers are basically pimped out versions of Cosco's offerings—we say pass. Better marks are earned by Safety 1st, whose models offer more innovative features compared to Cosco. That said, no one would say Safety 1st is the Mercedes of strollers.

Take the Safety 1st Aerolite, for example. Parents tell us the strollers' vaunted one-hand fold/step-up is a pain to use in real life (the stiff release mechanism frustrates users) and design goofs like the wider rear wheelbase causes the stroller to get caught in tight spaces at the mall. Also: the travel system's paired infant car seat (OnBoard 35) has such a huge base, it only fits in the largest of vehicles.

Bottom line: we aren't impressed with these strollers. Unless you are picking up one as a steal on Craigslist, we suggest skipping it. **Rating: C+**

Cybex *cybex-online.com* German stroller brand Cybex had the misfortune of launching in the U.S. during the economic meltdown of 2009. As a result, Cybex hasn't made much of a mark yet.

The models. These brightly colored models combined features similar to Maclaren at $200+ price points. But the white frames and white solid wheels turned off parents, who perhaps thought they'd quickly lose that pristine look after a spin in the mall parking lot.

So it's back to the drawing board for Cybex, which recently showed us revised models that featured silver frames and improved features. Example: the Ruby ($150, 13.2 lbs.) has a foam handle, two-step fold and full canopy that is even height adjustable. An infant car seat adapter will be an extra accessory.

The Onyx ($230, 16 lbs.) features more padding and full seat recline. (For 2012, Cybex plans to roll out a double version of the Onyx). The Callisto is Cybex's most expensive current offering ($350, 22 lbs.) with plush fabric and wheel suspension.

Reader feedback on the Cybex has been thin, probably due to their poor sales. One mom who bought an Onyx posted to our stroller message board that she loved the stroller's canopy, high handles and decent steering. But the ride was rickety, especially on cracked sidewalks. Overall, she was impressed—but she only paid $65 for the stroller on Overstock.com. "It would absolutely not be worth it at the full $200 retail price point."

Other readers agreed, saying they liked but didn't love their Cybex. While most folks love the bright colors and overall features, critics knock the use of flimsy plastic (such as the canopy attachment) and too high prices. If you can find one of these strollers at a steep discount, go for it. Otherwise, we'd take a wait and see on whether the line refresh addresses Cybex's shortcomings. **Rating: B**

Easy Walker *This brand is reviewed on our web site, BabyBargains. com (click on Bonus Material).*

Eddie Bauer *See Cosco.*

Evenflo *evenflo.com.* Evenflo's claim to fame, stroller-wise, is their one-hand steering. All of Evenflo's strollers and travel systems have this feature. Here is a breakdown:

The models. Evenflo's flagship stroller is the Aura, which is paired with Evenflo's Embrace infant seat in a travel system. The Aura ($140) has probably one of the most amazing parent trays on the market, complete with two cup holders with "automotive cup grippers" and a storage area with "privacy lid." If only Evenflo had put as much effort into the rest of the stroller as they did the parent tray.

While the Aura has a one-hand fold feature, folding it is not easy or intuitive—and once folded, this thing is big and bulky, clocking in at nearly 30 lbs. and filling up most of just about any vehicle's trunk space. The Aura travel system sells for $180.

Evenflo's other major stroller offering is the Journey. Similar in size and weight to the Aura, it lacks the one-hand fold, cool parent tray (the Journey's parent tray is much simpler) or retracting child tray (to keep it from getting scuffed when folded). The Journey is sold as a stand-alone stroller ($50) and travel system paired with the Evenflo Embrace ($135). For $10 more, Evenflo sells an upgraded version (Elite) with better fabric.

Evenflo's "premium" travel system is the EuroTrek ($160, 20 lbs.). We're not sure what makes this stroller "Euro," but it does offer a few upgrades not seen on Evenflo's lower-end models such as a height adjustable handle and full coverage canopy. The EuroTrek's aluminum frame makes it significantly lighter than the Aura. The EuroTrek stroller is paired with the Evenflo Embrace 30 and Secure Ride 35 for a travel system at $200.

In the past year, Evenflo debuted a new compact stroller called the Zing (20 lbs.). It is paired with the Embrace 30 infant seat for a $170 travel system. Evenflo used to be a small player in the double stroller market, but its main offering (Take Me Too tandem) was discontinued as of this writing.

For 2012, Evenflo plans to debut a new stroller: the Feather Lite 400. As the name implies, this travel system will be 20% lighter than Evenflo's other offerings with the stroller clocking in at 14.2 lbs. It will feature a full recline and five point harness. Retail: $200 to $300. We saw a prototype of the Feather Lite and were impressed: you don't see too many affordable travel system strollers in the 14 lb. range.

Evenflo plans to discontinue the Aura and Zing in 2012, although the Journey will live on.

Our view. Evenflo has slowly improved its quality and durability in recent years. Its travel systems generally win kudos from readers, who say easy assembly and good quality are what they like most about models like the Evenflo Aura.

Detractors point out the bulk and weight of most Evenflo strollers (the Aura clocks in at 27 lbs. empty) make it hard to haul in and out of a trunk. And we're not enamored with Evenflo's infant car seats, which of course are part of any Evenflo travel system. That said, we'd put these travel systems ahead of competitors like Cosco/Eddie Bauer in quality. But . . . competitors like Chicco and Graco have better infant car seats, which make their travel systems a better bet than Evenflo.

It looks like Evenflo is getting the message on their stroller's weight—the new Feather Lite 400 is a step in the right direction.

So, it's a mixed bag for Evenflo. Thumbs up for the overall value of this line—it is hard to find a travel system in the sub-$150 price range these days. And we also give a shout out to Evenflo's customer service department, which earns good marks from our readers for promptly taking care of problems.

But the bulk and weight of Evenflo's travel system strollers—plus the sub-par performance of Evenflo's infant car seats—drags down their overall rating. We'll have to see if the new Feather Lite 400 stroller will mark a turnaround for the brand. ***Rating: B***

First Years *learningcurve.com* Better known for their feeding accessories and toys, First Years (part of the Learning Curve family) launched an affordable line of strollers in 2010. Here's an overview.

The models. The super affordable Jet ($33 to $40, 11.4 lbs.) is a good place to start: this no frills umbrella stroller features a simple design and basic basket. The compact umbrella fold and $40 price are the stars here—a basic, safe stroller for under $50. Who would've thought?

For another $20, the Ignite ($50, 15.8 lbs.) adds upgraded fabric, a bigger seat and partial seat recline. The Ignite features both a storage basket AND a "parent bag," an additional storage compartment near the handles.

The First Years also offers two more expensive models: the Indigo ($130 to $180, 22 lbs.) and the Wave ($255 to $330, 24 lbs.). The Indigo features a reversible seat, adjustable handle height and universal car seat adapter. The Wave's unique selling point is a seat that can swivel 360 degrees. It also has larger rear wheels and a seat that makes into a bassinet, plus an universal car seat adapter.

In the past year, The First Years has released its first travel system: the Wisp ($180-$250) combines First Years' Via infant seat with a 16.6 lb. stroller that has a removable child tray and rather tall handles.

Our view. Given the current state of the economy, why didn't anyone think of this before First Years: an affordable line of strollers with good quality, smart design and many included extras?

Take the basic Jet and Ignite strollers—readers tell us these strollers are great for travel and quick outings to the mall. And yes, they cost just $40 and $60, respectively. That's not a typo!

What's the downside? Well, the canopy on the Ignite is basic and the basket is a bit hard to access. Both strollers are fine for smaller babies, but larger toddlers may quickly outgrow the smallish seats.

The more expensive Indigo stroller also earns kudos for its value and ease of use. Yes, that included car seat adapter is a big plus— you can buy this stroller as a stand-alone model or part of a travel system with the First Years Via infant car seat for $230.

We've had less feedback on the Wave, but the reports we hear from readers are generally positive—that swivel seat enables you to switch the seat from front to rear facing without removing it. The huge, full coverage canopy is also a winner. The only negative: the seat has to be removed to fold the stroller.

So what's not to love about the First Years strollers? Well, many of the models lack cup holders, which is an odd oversight. Yes, you can add an aftermarket cup holder—and considering the value of these models, that seems like a fair trade-off. First Years strollers also lack other common accessories like a boot. And the storage baskets are a bit hard to access and rather skimpy (especially on the Wave). But those are minor quibbles, considering the prices. The Wave is the dark horse here— $300 for such an amazing stroller seems like a steal compared to strollers like the Uppa Baby Vista.

All in all, First Years strollers are winners. ***Rating: A***

Go-Go Babyz *gogobabyz.com. This brand is reviewed by on our web page, BabyBargains.com (click on Bonus Material).*

Graco *gracobaby.com.* Graco's main stroller niche is the travel system combining an infant car seat and stroller and aimed at first-time parents who want all the bells and whistles. The secret to their success is their excellent infant car seat, the SnugRide. Like Dorel, Graco uses its own name to sell strollers in discount stores (Walmart) and in baby specialty chains like Babies R Us and Buy Buy Baby. In recent years, Graco has experimented with new upper-end brands (Teutonia and Aprica), with models sold at specialty stores and high-end chains. Those brands are reviewed separately.

Graco is like the Honda of strollers—a mid-priced brand with decent quality, but not a lot of pizzazz. The company leaves the low-end market to Dorel/Cosco.

Graco's line is huge, so let's get to the highlights:

The models. Graco divides their stroller line into three areas: lightweight, full-size travel systems (seven different models) and multi-child strollers.

The lightweight models include the Ipo, Mosaic, MetroLite, UrbanLite and LiteRider.

The full-size strollers are the Quattro Tour Deluxe and Sport, Vie4, Alano and Alano Flipit, plus the new Trekko and Signature. In the double or multi-child category, Graco offers the DuoGlider, Quattro Tour Duo, and Twin Ipo. Whew. Deep breath. In the lightweight category, Graco's key offerings are the Ipo, Mosaic and MetroLite. The Ipo ($80 to $100, 17 lbs.) is Graco's riff on the Peg Perego Pliko—two handles, large basket, one hand fold and tinted sun visor.

The Mosaic ($100 to $120, 18 lb.) is an umbrella stroller with two handles, deep basket and partial recline. This stroller has a "three-dimensional" fold—that basically means it folds down to the ground but doesn't scrape or dirty the stroller in the process.

The MetroLite ($100 to $160 stand alone; $250 to 300 travel system) is an 18 lb. stroller that features rubber tires for a smooth ride, three-position reclining seat and plush padding. The MetroLite also has a full recline and height adjustable handle.

In the past year, Graco added to its lightweight offerings with the Urban Lite, a 20 lb. stroller with three positions, full recline, height adjustable handle, large basket and one-hand fold. The canopy on the Urban Lite fully covers the seat. Price: $270 as part of a travel system, $150 as a stand-alone model.

Graco's best-known full-size stroller is the Quattro Tour, a Hummer-like stroller that weighs 26+ lbs. empty. The Quattro comes in two versions: Deluxe and Sport. Both feature a one-hand gravity fold, fully reclining seat, and large parent storage tray that holds two drinks. The difference: the Sport features a more modern, elliptical frame. The Quattro is available as a stand-alone stroller ($150) or part of a travel system ($235 to $250). FYI: The Quattro comes in two trim levels, basic and "sport" (the latter has a contoured frame and upgraded fabric).

Graco's other full-size strollers are basically scaled down versions of the Quattro. The Vie4 ($100 to $135) features a height adjustable handle and one-hand, standing fold. The Alano Flipit's ($120 to $140) main selling point is its reversible handle. We're not sure if Graco has thought this one out, however—the Alano Flipit has fixed rear wheels. So when you reverse the handle, the front of the stroller won't be able to maneuver easily.

Coming in 2012, Graco will debut a new full-size model dubbed the Dynamo Lite (17.5 lbs.) It will feature a full recline, large basket and be sold as a travel system ($180 to $200) or stand-alone model ($120).

New in the past year, Graco debuted its first modular stroller, the Signature 3-in-1 ($300, 26.4 lbs.). It features a reversible, fully reclin-

STROLLERS AND MORE

ing seat, one-touch brake, suspension and the ability to hold a Graco infant car seat. But you can't fold the stroller with the seat (it must be removed first), which is a pain.

But why buy a 3-in-1 stroller when you can get a 12-in-1? Graco will debut a new model in 2012 called the Ready to Grow that features 12 seating positions, the ability to hold two infant seats, and a removable rear jump seat with harness that can hold an older toddler. The Room to Grow will run $180 to $200 and weigh in at a hefty 32.4 lbs. This stroller seems squarely aimed at the Joovy Big Caboose market.

Also new: the Quattro Tour Reverse (30.6 lbs.) features a seat that rotates to face forward or rear, plus a three position recline, one-hand fold and large basket. It will be sold as a travel system with the SnugRide 30 or 35 ($280 to $400).

Buy Buy Baby had a Graco exclusive in the past year: the Stylus Edge ($260). This stroller features a three position, fully reclining seat, height adjustable handle, elliptical tube frame and one-hand gravity fold. That exclusive ended in January 2012, as Amazon gets a Stylus model as well. For 2012, the Stylus gets a new bassinet feature, thanks to a leg rest that folds up to enclose the seat.

New for 2012, Graco is hoping to conjure up some of that Baby Jogger Quick Fold magic with its new FastAction Fold LX stroller ($130, 20.9 lbs). As the name implies, this stroller folds in a single-step and stands when folded. It features a multi-position reclining seat, three or five-point harness and all the standard Graco stroller features you'd expect (large storage basket, parent tray with cup holders, etc). It holds all Graco infant seats. Sold as a stand-alone model or as a travel system ($200-$240).

Also new: Graco is giving the three-wheel, all-terrain stroller market another try with the Trekko ($160 stand-alone, $280 travel system). This full-size stroller has a front wheel that can be locked and features a 180 degree rotating canopy, full seat recline, one-hand fold, rubber tires, and a height adjustable handle. And it works with any Graco infant car seat. Our only concern with this stroller: the rear-wheel width at 25.5" may make negotiating tight spaces difficult (most strollers have a 20-24" rear wheel width). Also this stroller clocks in at 26.9 lbs., about 10% heavier than the similar Valco Tri-Mode.

Finally, double strollers are Graco's last major forte—the brand offers two tandem and one side-by-side model. The DuoGlider ($130 to $150, 29 lbs.). is a front/back tandem. Graco's claim to fame in this niche is "stadium seating," where the rear seat is elevated. Of course, you get all the standard features: huge storage baskets, removable canopies, etc. Cool feature: The DuoGlider holds two Graco infant car seats.

Graco's other tandem is the Quattro Tour Duo (32 lbs., $200-$250), which features a curvy frame, fancy cup holders, stadium seating,

strollers

one-hand "gravity" fold, large basket and a back seat with full recline. The Quattro Tour Duo is about 20% smaller than the DuoGlider.

The side-by-side double Twin Ipo ($164-$190, 32 lbs.) features a one-hand fold—this model will eventually replace the DuoGlider as Graco's main side-by-side stroller.

New for 2012, Graco will release a new model that is like the Baby Trend's Sit N Stand: the Room for 2. This stroller will hold a 50 lb. child in both front or rear jump seat and feature a large basket, one-hand fold, parent tray and the ability to hold a car seat in front. The child in the rear can sit or stand. Price: $139, 24.7 lbs.

Graco's entry in the stroller frame category, the Snug Rider, is a winner—this $70 frame holds the (what else?) Graco Snug Ride infant car seat with a secure lock-in feature and has a one-hand fold and basket.

Our view. Graco has come a long way and now sits atop the mountain as the top-selling mass market brand for strollers.

We don't fault Graco for focusing on the lucrative first-time parent niche, but we can't help but point out to folks that NO, you do not need a 30 lb. stroller to push around baby. In fact, many parents end up cursing their Graco Hummers as impossible to wrestle in and out of a trunk, among other sins. Stick with the lighter-weight models (Ipo, Mosaic, MetroLite) and you'll be happier here.

And even though Graco's lightweight strollers generally get good marks, we should point out that these strollers stretch the definition of "lightweight"—the Ipo is 17 lbs. . . . that's significantly heavier than the similarly in price UPPAbaby G-lite, which weighs a mere 10 lbs. The "lightweight" Mosaic and MetroLite are even heavier (18 lbs.). Heck, a top-of-the-line Maclaren (such as the Techno) still weighs less than that.

If your heart is set on getting a full-size stroller, our pick in this line would be the Quattro Tour Sport—yep, it is way too heavy at 26 lbs. but at least it is loaded with just about every feature you can think of in a stroller. At $180, this model is a decent value.

Much of Graco's good reader feedback stems from their travel systems, which get a halo effect from the strong sales of Graco's infant car seats. While we aren't big fans of travel systems, the best Graco option here would probably be the MetroLite travel system, which combines a relatively lightweight (for Graco) stroller at a reasonable price ($260 to $310).

We liked Graco's first attempt at modular strollers (the Signature) and the $300 price point is way under similar models from Britax and Baby Jogger. But . . . you can't fold the stroller with the seat attached and there is no second seat option, which is the main point to modular strollers. Hence, you are paying less here for the Signature, but it might be worth it to spend more on a Britax B-

Ready or Baby Jogger Select if you plan to use it with two kids.

Of course, despite the generally positive reviews, Graco strollers aren't without their faults. Look at how some Graco strollers fold up . . . when folded, the front tray hits the ground, inevitably damaging or scratching it in a parking lot. Parents also complain about canopies that offer less than full coverage (note that several of Graco's new models include fully enclosing canopies). And the steering on most Graco strollers is only so-so. These strollers were designed for the mall or smooth sidewalks.

Graco strollers are bulky when folded—even the lightweight ones like the MetroLite will eat up the entire trunk of an average sized car. Factor this into your decision if your ride is a small compact.

Bottom line: Graco's strollers are designed for the mall or other light duty shopping trips. Don't expect these strollers to do well in urban environs with cracked sidewalks. Stick with Graco's lightest weight models and set your expectations accordingly. ***Rating:*** B

Grand Touring Baby (aka, i'coo, Hauck) gtbaby.com. This brand is reviewed online at BabyBargains.com

iCandy icandyworld.com British stroller maker iCandy launched in the U.S. in 2010 with their fruit-themed stroller line.

The models. The Cherry ($400, 17.5 lbs.) is iCandy's entry-level model with three-position reclining seat, adjustable footrest, reversible seat and machine-washable fabric. Car seat adapters are available for the Maxi Cosi Mico and Graco infant seats. An optional bassinet is $130.

The Apple ($450; $525 for "flavour edition", 28 lbs.) strikes a pose with larger, air-filled tires, height adjustable handle, and rear wheel suspension. Like the Cherry, there are a multitude of accessories for the Apple including a bassinet and foot muff. There is also an "apple to pear" upgrade kit ($250) that turns the Apple into a double stroller with two seats, two rain covers and larger wheels.

Next is the Pear ($780), a modular stroller that can hold two infant car seats (adapters sold separately), one or two seats for use with twins or an infant/toddler configuration.

The latest model to join the iCandy line is the Peach. This $900 stroller (30.7 lbs.) features a reversible seat and the ability to morph into a double stroller with the "peach blossom converter" ($1050). In 2012, iCandy plans to release a jogger version of this stroller (dubbed, wait for it . . . the Peach Jogger). It's hard to imagine anyone who would be up for running with this 30+ lb. stroller, but iCandy will give it a try.

New for 2012, iCandy will continue its fruit expansion theme with an entirely new model: the Strawberry. This model's key feature: you can fold it with the seat in any position. The Strawberry will feature a one-hand fold, fully reclining seat, rain cover, and foam handle. No pricing info yet, as this model probably won't debut until late 2012.

Our view. Despite being on the market here for almost two years, feedback on the iCandy line is rather thin—that's probably due to the line's sky-high prices. Take the Peach stroller. This model is comparable to the Uppa Baby Vista, but costs $200 more.

Parents on our message boards who've compared the two say the Peach has much better fabrics than the Vista; and we'd say the overall quality of the iCandy line is good. But there are some big negatives: the first is seat size. The smallish seat on the Peach means a child will probably outgrow it before age 2—that's a deal killer for a $900 stroller.

We liked the multi-function design, but the weight on many models (the Apple and Peach are about 30 lbs.) seems excessive, especially for folks who plan to lug these strollers in and out of a trunk.

We noticed the reviews of iCandy from parents on British parenting boards like reviewcentre.com have voiced similar concerns about the weight and bulk of the models. Fans love the steering and multi-function design of iCandy, especially the Apple. However, critics say you better hope nothing ever breaks on your iCandy stroller. The company's unresponsive customer service and refusal to honor its two-year warranty were troubling. Let's hope the company doesn't plan to bring that customer service attitude to the U.S.

Bottom line: we'll give iCandy only an average rating—too expensive and heavy to be serious contenders for the U.S. multi-function stroller market. *Rating: C*

Inglesina *Inglesina.com.* Given the success of fellow Italian stroller makers Peg Perego and Chicco, you'd think Inglesina would be another slam-dunk here in the U.S. Yet the company has struggled for several reasons. First, it lacks an infant car seat—that means Inglesina is frozen out of the big travel system market. Second, prices: Inglesina has raised its prices in recent years, pricing their strollers out of the reach of average buyers. Let's look at the line.

The models. The Zippy is Inglesina's flagship model. Its claim to fame is its amazing one-hand fold—you lift up on a lever on the back of the stroller and poof! Instant folded stroller. This 23 lb. model is aimed at urban parents—it has a full recline, adjustable backrest, removable front bumper and storage basket. Best of all: the Zippy has a universal car seat adapter that lets you secure an infant car seat to the stroller (yes, the Graco SnugRide works well with it). The Zippy's handles are height adjustable and the back wheels sport suspension for a smoother ride.

So what's not to love? Well, the Zippy is darn expensive: $390. Yes, you can find previous year models or certain colors online for

$300, but it just seems too pricey for what you get. Sure, it is made in Italy, but so are Peg Perego strollers . . . and the similar Pliko P3 is $80 less than the Zippy.

On the plus side, the Zippy does include a car seat adapter and rain cover for that price.

Inglesina has two other models: the Trip and Swift. The Trip ($180 to $200, 14.9 lbs.) is a lightweight umbrella model with a four-position seat recline, adjustable footrest, cup holder and included rain cover. The Swift (13 lbs., $130) is a scaled down version of the Trip, but still has the same seat recline. It omits the cup holder and rain cover and has a less fancy canopy. FYI: the Trip and Swift are made in China.

In the past year, Inglesina made some small improvements to the Trip: bigger wheels, improved suspension and a larger extended canopy. For 2012, the Trip gets a bumper bar and rain cover with no increase in price.

New in the past year, Inglesina has debuted an entirely new model: the Avio ($450 to $530, 22.3 lbs.) is billed as Inglesina's re-interpretation of the Zippy. It features an ultra-smooth glide (thanks to ball bearings), optional bassinet plus a one-hand, self-standing fold. Car seat adapters for Graco and Peg Perego are available ($60 extra). For 2012, the Avio gets all-wheel suspension and an easy to remove canopy.

Our view. We've always liked this brand, despite its struggles in recent years. The new Avio has helped inject a bit of life here—reviews from parents on our message boards have been quite positive. Folks like the sturdy frame, plush fabrics and smooth steering.

Reader feedback on the Zippy, Trip and Swift is also positive—parents tell us the brand gets good marks for quality, durability and function. And while the Zippy and Avio are quite pricey, at least the company includes extras like a cup holder and rain cover— many other upper-end stroller makers force you to shell out additional bucks for such accessories. *Rating: A*

InStep See Schwinn.

i'coo/Traxx See Grand Touring Baby.

Jeep See Kolcraft.

Joovy joovy.com. Joovy was launched in 2002 by a former Baby Trend executive who secured the rights to the English pushcart better known as the Baby Trend Sit N Stand. Joovy re-christened this model as the Caboose Stand-on Tandem ($150, 26 lbs.). Compared to the old Sit N Stand, Joovy's Caboose features a higher handle height, foam handle, improved car seat attachment and nicer canopy. The company also brightened up the fashion.

Over the last few years, Joovy has refined the Caboose—now the seat recline doesn't interfere with the space for the toddler. And the infant car seat attachment sits higher than the previous model. FYI: the Joovy works with 13 infant seats, including the Graco SnugRide and Chicco KeyFit.

In recent years, Joovy has rolled out several spin-offs of the Caboose: the Caboose Ultralight, Big Caboose, Ergo Caboose and Big Caboose Stand On Triple.

The Caboose Ultralight ($200 to $270, 24.3 lbs.) is 20% lighter than the original Caboose and features a larger canopy and neoprene parent organizer. In the past year, this stroller got a fancier canopy and taller seat.

Got three kids? The Big Caboose ($380, 37 lbs.) has two seats plus a toddler jump seat/standing area. This model can also handle two infant car seats—so if you have twins and an older toddler, this would be one of the few models out there to hold all three tykes.

The Ergo Caboose ($400, 28.5 lbs.) looks like a pregnant Bugaboo—it features air-filed rear tires, ergonomic mesh seat with two-position recline, a longer frame with better access to the storage basket and a slew of accessories (rain cover, fleece canopy, etc).

While the Caboose is Joovy's flagship model, the company has several other strollers. The Scooter ($100 to $150, 18.5 lbs.) is a new lightweight stroller with a funky elevated handle and elliptical frame. It also features a deep (but not full) seat recline. Like all Joovy strollers, the Scooter features an oversized canopy and large storage basket. Yes, there is a cup holder, perched between the two handles. The ScooterX2 ($230) is a side-by-side twin stroller.

Similar but a bit smaller in size is the Kooper ($180, 15.5 lbs.). It features a compact fold and quick release wheels. The compact Groove ($200) has been updated in the past year with a new frame design.

Joovy's Zoom ATS ($200 to $270) is a jogger with fixed front wheel, no rear axle (so you can run without kicking the back), full canopy and parent tray. Yep, it is pricey—but it does include a rain cover. A version of this stroller (Zoom 360, $270) is available with a front swivel wheel.

New to the Joovy line is the Roo stroller frame, formally called the Dock. A double version (Twin Roo) is also available. These will ship in February 2012 (no pricing yet).

Also new for 2012: Joovy will distribute Silver Cross strollers, the UK brand that had an unsuccessful run in the U.S. a few years ago. First up will be the Silver Cross Surf stroller, coming in May 2012.

Our view. Of all the Caboose variations, we recommend the Joovy Caboose Ultralight as tops. Reader feedback on this model is mostly positive—the lighter weight makes it a worthy upgrade over the regular Caboose.

Feedback on Joovy's other strollers has been generally positive. The Kooper earns kudos for its huge canopy and basket, although more than a few parents bemoaned the lack of height adjustable handles. If you are 5'6" or taller, this isn't the stroller for you. Quality control also seemed inconsistent on the Kooper, as we had more than a few reports of unbalanced wheels and difficult steering. Readers were more uniformly positive about the Zoom, especially the 360 model. The Zoom is a great value, but a few parents criticized the weight (27 lbs.) and smallish seat, which means larger toddlers will quickly out grow it.

As for Joovy's other offerings, the Scooter also gets good marks for its easy fold, although it takes two hands. This stroller is a good bet if you find the price of a Baby Jogger City Mini too spendy.

Overall, we would recommend Joovy for its value and key features like those oversized canopies. If the company can keep its quality consistent, it could be among the industry's top players. ***Rating: B+***

Kelty See our web page BabyBargains.com for a review.

Kolcraft kolcraft.com. Kolcraft has always been an also-ran in the stroller market—that is, until their recent hot selling Jeep-branded strollers took off. Since Kolcraft exited the car seat business in 2001, the company has no travel systems to offer. That's a blessing in disguise: many Kolcraft models hold other major brands of car seats, giving parents more flexibility.

The models. Kolcraft sells strollers under three brands: Kolcraft, Jeep and Contours. Kolcraft is sold as entry-level models at chains stores like Walmart. The real standout, however, is the Jeep line—Kolcraft has an entire line of Jeep strollers, complete with SUV-like knobby wheels, beefed up suspension, and sporty fabrics at affordable prices (most are under $150). Clever touches like simulated lug nuts on the wheels and a toy steering wheel for baby have made these models quite popular.

The best selling Jeep is the Liberty Limited—a three-wheel stroller with turnable front wheel that can be locked in a forward position. This hybrid between jogging and sport strollers fits many major brand infant car seats and features a reclining seat, height-adjustable five-point harness and more. At about $150 at Walmart and Amazon, it's no surprise this one has been a hot seller.

Parent reviews have been generally positive on this model, albeit with a stray complaint about inflated tires that go flat and a too-short handle for tall parents.

Kolcraft sells several versions of the Liberty—the more expensive models add extra storage (a bag on the side of the basket), fancier padding and an electronic toy steering wheel.

Kolcraft also makes a raft of other Jeep models, including an umbrella style (Wrangler All Weather, 18.5 lbs., $40) and a more traditional lightweight model, the Cherokee Sport ($70). The Wrangler Twin Sport is a side-by-side model for $100.

There's also a couple joggers, the Jeep Overland Limited ($220) and the Jeep Overland Sport ($160).

Besides the Jeep line, Kolcraft also offers strollers under its own brand. Kolcraft's stroller frame (the Universal 2 Car Seat Carrier, $50, 13 lbs.) competes against the Baby Trend Snap & Go, fitting most major brands of car seats. It has a large basket and one-hand fold. This stroller frame is also sold under the Jeep name.

Kolcraft's other major stroller label is Contours, which features a bit more style than one would expect from a mass market brand like Kolcraft (bright red fabrics, curved tubular frames, etc.).

The Contours Option 3 Wheel Stroller ($130 to $170, 26 lbs.) has an infant car seat adapter and reversible seat, so you can see baby while pushing, while the Contours Options II Tandem ($200 to $240, 32 lbs.) is a double stroller with Bugaboo-like front wheels. It has seats that can face each other—and the stroller comes with a car seat adapter (a second one is available as an accessory).

Speaking of the Bugaboo, Kolcraft also offers the Contours Lite stroller ($55-$70, 15.5 lbs.), a credible knock-off of the Dutch best seller. In the double stroller (tandem) category, the Jeep Traveler ($190, 28 lbs.) features a compact fold and height adjustable handle. The Traveler's rear seat fits a variety of infant car seat brands.

In the past year, Kolcraft has rolled out an all-aluminum version of the Contours Optima Tandem ($260 to $290), which weighs 10 lbs. lighter than the current model. It features height adjustable canopies.

New for 2012, Kolcraft launch an extensive expansion of the Contours line with three new strollers. The goal is to address the weight issue—the new models will be significantly lighter than the original Contours models.

First up is the Contours Cruiser, which will take an infant car seat and features an oversized canopy, one-hand steering and one-hand fold. Price: $130, due in spring of 2012.

The Contours Bliss Toddler and Baby Pram stroller has a stroller seat that converts into a pram or carry cot—with no extra parts! The carry cot is detachable and the seat is reversible. The Contours Bliss also has a telescoping handle. Price: $350, also due in spring of 2012.

Finally, the new Contours Options LT Tandem has the same features of the Options Tandem but is about eight lbs. lighter, thanks to a new aluminum frame. The fold is also compact and you don't have to remove the seats. Price: $230.

Our view. Dollar for dollar, these are the best affordable strollers on the market. Compared to other low-end brands (Graco, Cosco),

Kolcraft shines.

The Contours Lite is a winner—we liked the affordable price tag and overall lightweight design. Critics, however note the seat doesn't quite sit upright, which bothers some older toddlers. The canopy's coverage is also a bit skimpy, the toddler tray and cup holder are in an awkwardly high position and the stroller doesn't offer a compact fold. But then again, it is just $55 on Amazon.

Readers also like the Contours Options 3 Wheeler (but be forewarned: the stroller can't be folded when the seat is in the rear-facing position) as well as Kolcraft's double strollers. The Jeep Liberty three-wheeler isn't a bad option for an affordable all-terrain stroller, but it is showing its age. It needs to be updated.

Perhaps the biggest complaint about this line is weight: that 30 lb. tandem stroller Kolcraft sells is a beast. But there is good news: the new Contours stroller we discuss above that will debut in 2012 will address this issue.

Bottom line: for suburbanites who need a sturdy stroller with lots of storage for the mall, Kolcraft/Jeep fits the bill. **Rating: B+**

Kool Stop *See our web page (BabyBargains.com, click on Bonus Material) for a review.*

Maclaren *maclarenbaby. com.* Maclaren is the brand with British roots that specializes in premium-priced, high-quality umbrella strollers made from lightweight aluminum.

Founded in 1965 by a British test pilot, Maclaren's strollers were a sharp departure from the bulky prams that were the norm back then. By inventing a lightweight stroller that folded up to the size of an umbrella, Maclaren appealed to a generation of mobile parents who wanted to take their strollers on planes, subways, etc.

Maclaren's first efforts to crack the U.S. market were centered on the East Coast, appealing to New Yorkers and Bostonians who needed sturdy yet lightweight strollers that could be hauled up and down subway station stairs. In the last decade, Maclaren has expanded its market by rolling out the brand nationwide to chain stores like Target and Babies R Us.

Most Maclaren strollers run $200 to $300. So, you might be wondering, why buy a Maclaren when you can find a cheap umbrella stroller for under $100 in discounters? Maclaren fans point out these strollers are much more durable, lighter in weight and packed with more urban-friendly features (one-hand folds) than the competition. As a result, Maclaren strollers can last for more than one child and have resale value. Pop onto Craigslist and search for Maclaren versus Evenflo or Graco strollers . . . you'll see what we mean.

The models. Okay, let's take a deep breath. Maclaren offers

EIGHT models, so there is much to cover. There will be a quiz at the end of this review.

FYI: Maclaren quotes weights for its strollers without adding in the canopy or mesh shopping basket. Hence, you'll need to add a couple lbs. to each of weights you see online to compare apples to apples with other brands.

Maclaren's entry-level model, the Volo ($130 although there are discounts on some fabrics online, 9.4 lbs.) is a super light, stripped down stroller. You get a canopy, five-point harness and mesh seat and basket—but that's about it. You also get a removable seat cushion.

A more full-featured model from Maclaren is their Triumph, ($180) which weighs 12 lbs. and features a fully enclosed protective hood and one-hand fold. This seat does have a two-position recline (it is designed for babies three months and up).

Next up is the Quest ($200-$250, 12.9 lbs.), which adds more padding, a four-position partial seat recline and an extendable footrest. New for 2012, the Quest will feature a fully reclining seat, so it can be used from birth.

The Techno XT ($250 to $320, 15 lbs.) is the top of the line Maclaren—it features the most padding, a flip-down sun visor and three-position adjusting handles that can be extended to a height of 42 inches. And yes, Maclaren throws in a cup holder for the Techno, which also has upgraded wheels and reflective trim. The Techno XLR ($360, 16.5 lbs.) is an inch and a half wider than the Techno XT. You can also use this stroller for a child who weights up to 65 lbs.—10 lbs. more than most other Maclarens.

Maclaren sells two side-by-side strollers, the Twin Triumph ($300, 23.4 lbs.) and the Twin Techno ($330 to $380, 26.9 lbs.). The basic difference between these models: the Twin Techno is more plush and comes with a boot, head support and upgraded canopy. Parents of twins rave about these strollers, which are among the best side-by-side models on the market. Maclaren's doubles are good for older child/infant needs as well.

New for 2012, Maclaren will debut a brand new model: the Globetrotter. This 10.6 lb. stroller will include a rain cover and par-tial, mutli-position seat recline for $140. Since the seat doesn't fully recline, this stroller is recommended for babies six months and older.

In the coming year, Maclaren will pare its line and discontinue a series of strollers that didn't quite cut it. That includes the Grand Tour LX, which was Maclaren's first full-sized stroller that cost $900+. Also gone: the Easy Traveller stroller frame, the customizable Volos and the Four Seasons strollers.

In the past year or two, Maclaren has been concentrating on beefing up its accessories rather than rolling out new models (the Globetrotter notwithstanding). One key accessory: a $20 universal stroller organizer that fits on the back handles—it includes two bottle pockets that can hold drinks, a cell phone pocket and a mesh storage bag. This helps address parent complaints that Maclarens lack adequate storage. They also offer new eco-liners made of corn, bamboo, organic cotton or recycled polyester. Cost: $40 to $75.

One important caveat to this line: all Maclaren strollers lack napper or bumper bars on the front of the seat. Yes, these models all have five-point harnesses to keep baby securely inside the strollers, but the absence of a napper bar will turn off some parents.

Our view. Maclaren suffered a major black eye in 2009 when they recalled over a million strollers after the company received a dozen reports of finger amputations—kids who got their fingers caught in a hinge when the stroller was folded or unfolded. The company shipped out a hinge cover that solved the hazard.

Yes, it is a problem when you recall your entire production from the last ten years . . . and Maclaren struggled to contain the PR damage during the early days of the recall, when their web site crashed and phone lines were jammed. But in the end, Maclaren 'fessed up to the problem and fixed it.

Despite the recall apocalypse, we still think Maclaren is one of the best quality stroller brands on the market, but there are a couple of caveats. First, while this brand still trumpets its British heritage, Maclaren switched all its production to China back in 2001. Maclaren is no more British than Bugaboo is Dutch or Graco is American—all these strollers are made in China (ok, Bugaboo is made in Taiwan, but you get the idea). The point is, don't buy this stroller thinking you are avoiding a made-in-China product.

Another issue: Maclaren's finicky fold. Retailers who sell many Macs tell us you must be careful to correctly fold up the stroller (you have to make sure the backrest is completely upright and the canopy is back before folding). You never want to force or jam the stroller, which can bend the frame.

The other perennial Maclaren complaint: skimpy canopies. To address this issue, Maclaren is coming out with a new sunshade in the summer of 2012 for $45. That's nice, but when you pay $200+ for a stroller, you'd think that would be standard.

Now that we've got the complaints out of the way, we should point out that the majority of reader feedback on Maclaren is very positive. The company has enhanced its customer service reputation by rolling out 35 service centers nationwide in case you need to get your stroller repaired.

However, the massive safety recall was troubling to say the least. Among the most disturbing aspect: Maclaren knew about the finger amputation risk for several years before the 2009 recall. As a result, we are knocking Mac's grade down this year. ***Rating: B***

Mamas and Papas *mamasandpapas.com* No, not the 1960's folk rock group. Mamas and Papas is the UK-based baby product manufacturer and retailer that landed in the U.S. in 2010. In Britain, the brand is like Graco, selling products across several categories. Unlike U.S. competitors, Mamas and Papas not only makes baby gear but also runs their own chain of stores in Britain.

The models. Mamas and Papas launched in the U.S. with eight models, sold in Babies R Us (some are in stores, all are online). Their flagship is the Urbo ($530), a 22.3 lb. shiny aluminum model with reversible seat, large canopy and fully reclining seat. Infant car seat adapters are available for the Graco and Maxi Cosi infant seats ($60). An "elite" version of this stroller with all black frame runs $630—it includes a foot muff and upgraded fabric.

The spider-like Mylo stroller is heavy (29 lbs.) and pricey ($1000), but includes a carrycot, foot muff, fully reclining seat that reverses, telescoping handle and adjustable footrest.

The Sola ($420) is Mamas and Papas' riff on the Bugaboo, with smaller front wheels and reversible seat. Like the Urbo, it has an optional infant car seat adapter and features adjustable handle height.

Mamas and Papas' Luna Mix ($310) is similar to the Baby Jogger City Mini, although it lacks that model's quick fold. Instead, the Luna Mix features an adjustable handle, infant seat capability (Graco and Maxi Cosi) and fully reclining seat.

New for 2012, Mamas and Papas is debuting a new tri-wheel model, the o3 Sport. This model features air-filled, quick-release wheels, height adjustable handle, adjustable leg rest and rain cover. With a fully reclining seat, the o3 Sport will sell for $350. A car seat adapter accessory that fits the Perego infant seat will also be available.

If that weren't enough, Mamas and Papas has a slate of five light-weight strollers that mimic Chicco's and Maclaren's strollers. These include the Trip ($130, 11.5 lbs.), Trek ($160 to $180, 13 lbs.), Tour ($200, 14 lbs.), Cruise ($200 to $270, 16 lbs.) and Voyage ($310 to $330, 20 lbs.). As you might expect, the more you pay, the better the features. The Trip is a simple umbrella stroller, the Trek adds an adjustable leg rest and multi-position recline, the Cruise offers wheel suspension, and the top-of-the-line Voyage has more padding, sun visor and adjustable handles.

Our view. Mamas and Papas may be the largest stroller brand in the UK, but like warm beer and the BBC, some things just don't translate well to America. Take the Urbo stroller, for example. The Brits want us to shell out $500 for a shiny stroller that has a dinky, useless basket and no cup holder. How did this company so blow their market research?

Ditto for the odd Mylo stroller: the market here for a heavy $1000 stroller that includes a carrycot is probably in the low double digits.

More promising are the Sola and Luna strollers, which are clear-ly riffs on Bugaboo and the Baby Jogger City Mini. But again price here makes these strollers tough sells: when you can get a City Mini for $230, why spend $300 for a Luna . . . and not get the quick fold feature of the Mini?

Since this brand is so new to the U.S., feedback from our read-ers has been limited. A quick search of UK-based product review sites like ReviewCentre.com shows Mamas and Papas has a mixed track record. British parents panned the Luna for its poor quality and design (example: when folded, the foam handle and mesh hood can be easily damaged).

While the company's lightweight strollers fare better in reviews by UK parents, we will take a wait and see approach to Mamas and Papas. The company needs to better adapt its models to American tastes and address quality issues before we can recom-mend it. *Rating: C-*

Maxi Cosi *maxi-cosi.com* Dorel brought its European subsidiaries Maxi Cosi and Quinny to the U.S. a couple of years ago to bolster the brand's efforts in the upper end of the stroller market.

The models. Maxi Cosi sells both car seats and strollers here in the U.S. The brand's marquee stroller is the Foray LX ($400, 23.4 lbs.), which clearly riffs off that Bugaboo vibe. The Foray LX is a modular system that starts with a stroller frame that fits a Maxi Cosi infant car seat and continues with a stroller seat that can face forward or rear. Yes, there's even a cup holder, telescoping handle and weather shield.

Reader feedback on the Foray LX is mostly positive: fans love the smooth glide, thanks to the wheel design (larger air-filled tires in back, smaller wheels up front). The one-touch push brake is a wel come design improvement over other stroller brakes that can scuff shoes. Of course, the Foray's affordability (less than half the price of a Bugaboo) is a big plus.

But the Foray is about 30% heavier than a Bugaboo, so there's one trade-off. The fold is improved on the LX version from the orig-inal Foray. It's much more compact now. The Foray LX only works with the Maxi Cosi Mico infant car seat, which we only give a C rating. And the long-term durability of the Foray LX has been a thorn in the side of some owners, who complain the canopy can tear (among other quality woes) after just a few months of use. If Dorel wants to compete in the luxury stroller segment, it can't cheap out on the quality or fail to answer emails sent to customer service, as some readers allege.

Maxi Cosi's other key model, the Perle ($180 to $230, 17 lbs.) also works with the Mico infant car seat as a travel system. The Perle has a two-handle design like the Peg Pliko and features an umbrella fold, partial seat recline, adjustable leg rest and rain cover. Unlike the cumbersome fold for the Foray, the Perle is much simpler and requires just one hand. On the other hand, the Perle's fashion choices are as limited as the Foray: there's just one beige/grey color scheme.

Reader feedback on the Perle isn't as positive as the Foray—quality woes (like fabric that tears after just a few months of use) also dog this stroller. While fans love the easy fold and plush seat, detractors say the kid cup holder is a joke and the weight is several lbs. more than a similarly priced Maclaren. The canopy's lack of coverage is another major negative.

A bit heavier than the Perle but similar in size is the Mila ($250, 18.1 lbs.). It features a compact fold, adjustable footrest and basic storage basket. We've receive little reader feedback on this model. On the plus side, the Mila stands when folded and offers a deep seat recline—two features similar Maclaren models like the Triumph don't offer. And the Mila comes in a variety of colors, unlike the rather limited pallette for other Maxi Cosi strollers. One negative: the basket under the Mila is a bit hard to access.

The Loola ($400) with its reversible seat will be discontinued.

Our view. Maxi Cosi gets a mixed review: the Foray gets better marks than the Perle. But lack of long-term durability holds down this brand's overall rating. ***Rating: B-***

Mia Moda *This brand is reviewed on our web site, BabyBargains.com*

Micralite *This brand is reviewed on our web site, BabyBagains.com*

Mountain Buggy mountainbuggy.com. Mountain Buggy got a second chance at the U.S. market when rival Phil & Teds scooped them out of bankruptcy in 2009. After moving the production of the New Zealand brand to China, Phil & Teds also updated Mountain Buggy's aging designs and lowered prices.

Mountain Buggy's forte is the all-terrain, tri-wheel stroller, with lightweight aluminum frames (21 to 24 lbs., depending on the model), 12" air-filled tires with polymer rims, fully reclining seats, height adjustable handles and one-step folds.

The brand's flagship model is the Urban Jungle ($450 to $500 single, 24 lbs.; $680 duo, 36 lbs.). It has a front wheel that can swivel or lock into place, plus a raft of available accessories, including a car seat adapter, carry cot, rain cover and more. Unfortunately, the cup holder is an extra expense.

If you don't need the swivel wheel, the brand offers a fixed-wheel model: the Terrain ($450 to $500). It is designed more as a jogger with 16" wheels and a hand brake.

Mountain Buggy's last model is a compact version of the Urban

Jungle—the Swift ($450, 21 lbs.) has smaller, 10" tires. In the last year, Mountain Buggy has added a higher canopy with extendable visor and bumper bar to the stroller.

Not much change is happening here for 2012: the company has launched a new designer collection of updated fashions. These new two-tone fabrics give a shot of style to a stroller brand that hasn't exactly been known as fashion forward.

Our view. Phil & Ted's has done a nice job with the revisions to this line—we liked the small changes, such as the streamlined designs that now hide the wheel hubs. The Duo now has separate canopies (replacing the oft-criticized single canopy) and other improvements, including a better harness.

Of course, we also like the lower prices—at one point, the Urban was closing in on $600. The new price points make more sense.

The feedback on the new Chinese-made Mountain Buggies has been positive—folks love the revised designs and overall durability of the brand. The Duo, despite its $680 price, is a fave among readers, who like the steering. If you live somewhere where the weather is a beast (think Chicago), Mountain Buggy is a good bet. ***Rating: A***

Mutsy mutsy.com. Dutch-bred Mutsy hoped to follow in the footstep of that other Holland stroller company that made a splash in the U.S. Like Bugaboo, Mutsy offers a series of stroller frames that can fit an infant car seat, stroller frame or bassinet. And like Bugaboo, Mutsy imports its strollers from Asia. So is Mutsy a hit or a flop? Read on.

The models. Mutsy's flagship model is the 4Rider ($480 to $569, 33.5 lbs.), which has 10" single-spoke wheels, a car seat adapter and optional bassinet. The 4Rider Light ($455 to $570, 29 lbs.) swaps the 4Rider's air-filled tires for rubber versions.

The Slider ($630, 29.1 lbs.) features foam wheels (they provide the lighter overall weight), reversible/telescoping handle, bassinet and stroller seat, micro fiber fabric and more. This model is probably Mutsy's closest competitor to the Bugaboo since it also has a reversible seat, infant car seat adapter and bassinet option. However, the model is being discontinued.

New to the Mutsy line is the Transporter ($320 to $400, 24 lbs.), which features a partially reclining seat, height adjustable handle and 10" rear wheels. Car seat adapters and a bassinet ($150) are available.

Also new: the Easy Rider, a basic umbrella-style folding stroller with a reclining seat. Price: $145 to $170, 14 lbs.

Our view. On paper, Mutsy looked like a slam-dunk—multifunction strollers that just oozed cool Euro chic. Unlike other models that tout a faux "European-inspired" label, Mutsy is the real deal. These strollers are head turners.

Yet, so far, Mutsy has barely been a blip on the sales radar at baby

strollers

stores. Why the washout? In a word: weight. These strollers are too darn heavy. Even the "light" version of the 4Rider is 29 lbs. (don't believe the weights listed on their web site—we weighed the stroller ourselves). Bulk when folded is another major negative: the 4Rider when folded takes up most of the trunk in an average vehicle.

Fans of Mutsy cite the super-adjustable handles, plush fabrics and ease of use. We also liked the more affordable Transporter, although the seat recline requires two hands and the canopy is somewhat skimpy. Quality, overall, is excellent.

So we'll tick up our rating for Mutsy this time out. If you can get past the Sumo wrestler heftiness, these are good strollers. ***Rating: B+***

Orbit *orbitbaby.com.* Fans of *The Office* may remember the Orbit stroller, after Dwight Schrute spent an entire episode trying to destroy the pricey travel system to no avail. While that episode may qualify as the best baby product placement in a TV series ever, it showcased the Orbit's quality to withstand the show's extreme road test (you can see the episode on Orbit's web site).

The model. What set off Dwight? It was Orbit's über expensive price tag (" $1200 is more than I spent on my entire bomb shelter!"). Actually, the Orbit runs $900, including the infant car seat reviewed in the past chapter. And no, the Orbit doesn't come with a toddler stroller seat—that's an extra $250.

New for 2012, Orbit is debuting their first double stroller: the Double Helix. This $1200 twin stroller offers numerous combinations—you can have an infant seat in back, toddler in front, etc. The frame weighs 17 lbs. (that's before any seats) and features telescoping handles, parent's tray and more. The Double Helix will be available two ways: as a complete double stroller or as a $300 upgrade kit that can transform an Orbit into a Helix.

What's cool about the Double Helix: the ability of the stroller seats to swivel will let older toddler get in and out of the stroller easier than other doubles.

Our view. If Apple designed a stroller, it would probably look like the Orbit.

But how does it work in the real world? Folks who have the Orbit love it—the unique car seat base makes for simple, rock solid installation, as we noted in the last chapter. The engineering on the Orbit is top notch: parents like the stroller frame's simple one-hand fold and ergonomic handles. And the frame lets you shift the car seat in a 360-degree range of motion. The Orbit's ride is excellent.

Downsides? The Orbit car seat only works up to 30 lbs. When your baby outgrows the car seat, you have to pony up another $220 for a toddler stroller seat—but that means a total investment of $1120. Compare that to the Uppa Baby Vista, which can easily fit a toddler for a total price of $680 retail (as little as $500 or so online). Granted, the Vista isn't as cool looking as the Orbit—but is this worth $500+?

As we noted in the Orbit car seat review, the carrier is heavy (nearly 10 lbs.) and bulky, making it a tight fit in smaller vehicles. Once your baby is near the weight limits of the seat, carrying the Orbit's 30 lb. weight (baby plus car seat) will be a hardy upper-body workout.

The lack of storage is a major Orbit negative—the dinky basket doesn't hold much. Another bummer: the Orbit only comes in three colors—brown, black and red.

In the past year, Orbit launched the second generation of its travel systems (these are dubbed G2). The revisions included a bigger sunshade, new foam tires and other refinements.

The take-home message: if you are looking for a travel system that is a conversation starter, then Orbit is your brand. Parents love the Jetsons-like look . . . and having a stroller/car seat that no one on the block has is appealing. While we understand this, we would be much more excited about the Orbit if it were half the price. That's something we (and Dwight) can agree on.

FYI: In November 2011, Orbit was acquired by the parent of the Ergo baby carrier company (Compass Diversified Holdings). No word yet on what changes the new owners may make with Orbit, but Orbit's founders will continue to work for the new company for the near future. ***Rating: B***

Peg Perego *perego.com*. Peg Perego is the Italian stroller maker that was among the first European brands to land in North America, way back in the 1980's. The company traces its roots back to 1949 when its founder Giuseppe Perego created a carriage for his infant son.

Unlike most other European brands who long ago moved production to China, Peg Perego still makes all its strollers in Italy. (Okay, there was a brief time when Perego flirted with Chinese imports with one model—the Aria—but that didn't go well and the company returned back to an all-Italian line).

That all-Italian mantra for Peg has been both a blessing and curse. On the upside, the company's fabrics are considered among the most fashionable (although, admittedly, other companies have since closed the fashion gap). Peg's reputation for quality is also excellent. In an era where parents are concerned about Chinese imports and their safety, recalls on Perego strollers are rare.

But . . . the made-in-Europe label has its price—in the last few years, Peg's strollers have jumped in price to compensate for a strong Euro. Most Peg strollers run $300, $400 and more . . . that's a tough sell in this economy.

Adding to Peg's woes is a failure to innovate. The company seems content to rest on its laurels. Example: Peg missed out on the all-terrain three-wheel stroller craze and waited five years after the Bugaboo to launch a competitor, which promptly bombed. Peg also lost a bit of its cache after letting its overstock strollers be sold in discounters like Marshall's.

So can Peg get its mojo back? Let's look at their current line up.

The models. Perego has a lengthy list of strollers that includes single models, doubles and what they dub "systems," modular models that include an infant car seat.

Making matters more confusing: Peg often uses overlapping model names, mixing these from year to year. Example: in 2011, Peg had a stroller called the Pliko Switch. For 2012, there will be two models: the Switch Four and the Pliko Four. Fun, no?

So below is the 2012 model line-up. We'll break this down into single, double and systems.

Single strollers: Peg's 2012 line-up includes seven single strollers: the Uno, Switch Four, Pliko Four, Si, Vela Easy Drive, Pliko Mini and Book.

The Uno ($370 to $400, 23 lbs.), which features a Bugaboo-ish wheel design with smaller wheels up front and larger ones in the back. It includes a reversible handle so you can face baby, as well as a boot and height adjustable handle. The only bummer: when you reverse the handle on the Uno, you have the turnable wheels in back (rear-wheel drive), which is awkward.

The new Switch Four ($500, 23.8 lbs.) has a 150 degree reclining seat, reversible seat, foot muff and rain shield.

The new Pliko Four ($400, 18.7 lbs.) features four wheels that have suspension and ball bearings for a smooth ride. (FYI: The Switch Four has the same wheel system). This latest generation Pliko features a two-handle design, 150 degree reclining seat, adjustable leg rest, adjustable height handle and removable/washable seat cushions. There is also a one-hand fold. Compared to past versions of the Pliko, this model has a more compact fold.

The Si ($180 to $300, 16.5 lbs.) features height adjustable handles, standing one-hand fold and a seat recline with three positions. The Si holds a Peg car seat, as well as other brands. (In fact, all Peg's strollers work with Peg's infant car seat).

The Vela ($200, 16.4 lbs.) is Peg's belated entry into the tri-wheel, all-terrain market. It features a large storage basket, one hand, standing fold and can accommodate a car seat. The double front wheels can lock in place or swivel. In the past year, the Vela (now dubbed the Vela Easy Drive) morphed into a four-wheel stroller with the same wheels that are found on the Skate. We see both the old Vela and the new Vela Easy Drive sold as of this writing.

Also in the past year: a Pliko spin-off called the Pliko Mini ($200, 14 lbs.) Peg's lightest weight stroller. The Mini features a three-position reclining seat, cup holder, adjustable footrest and height adjustable handle.

New for 2012, the Perego Book stroller ($400, 19 lbs.) gets its name form its fold: yes, it folds up like a book (and stands when folded). The Book features wider front wheels with suspension and a wider seat (it can also hold a car seat). The Book will also be sold as a travel system, paired with Peg's infant car seat.

Double strollers. Peg makes two double strollers: the Aria Twin ($300, 17 lbs.), a side-by-side model and the Duette SW ($800, 32 lbs.), a tandem model. The Aria has a 60/40 configuration that holds a car seat in the larger space.

Got triplets? Peg even makes triple stroller, dubbed the Triplette SW for $1000. It weighs a whopping 61 lbs!

Modular systems. Peg sells two modular models: the Switch Four Modular System and the Skate.

The Switch Four Modular System is like the single version described above, but adds a bassinet and infant car seat plus a raft of accessories (bassinet stand, child tray, rain cover, foot muff, etc). Price: $1000.

The Skate was introduced in 2008 with much fanfare—it featured a Bugaboo-like multifunction frame, a height-adjustable handle, four-wheel suspension, ball-bearing wheels for a smooth glide, three seat heights and (drum roll) a cup holder. But it also cost an outrageous $900 and weighed 33.7 lbs. . . . 68% more than the Bugaboo. The Skate was like a Ford Expedition to the Bugaboo's BMW Z3. As you might guess, the Skate bombed big time.

Peg has tweaked the Skate to fix its shortcomings. The current version now weighs 28.8 lbs. and features a $700 price tag, which includes a bassinet, an improved fold and other refinements. Yes, there's even a storage basket now.

Our view. Despite Peg's extensive history as a top stroller brand, the company has made some bone-headed moves that have damaged its reputation in recent years. Exhibit one: the Aria. For a while, Peg decided to move production on this model from Italy to China . . . and the results were disastrous, with numerous reader complaints about quality and other woes. It's no surprise the Aria was recently sent to the discontinued graveyard.

Another major problem for Peg: price. While we were happy Peg lowered its prices somewhat in the past year, the strollers are still priced at the outer realm of reality in this economy. Then to further muddle its brand, Peg has dumped unsold strollers at deep discounts, both online and offline.

Finally, the failure of the Skate is another black mark on Peg's history. Even some of the company's fixes to this stroller have been questionable. For example, the new jumper seat should make the seat more comparable to similar offerings from Phil & Teds and

Baby Jogger. But . . . the jumper only has a three-point harness and lacks a canopy. Note most competitors offer a five-point harness and some have canopies.

Of course, it isn't all doom and gloom here. We like the newer lightweight models like the Si and Pliko Mini. Fans like the Si's overall design and canopy, but more than one parent complained that the front wheels wobble and shake.

The Pliko line is another good bet here—the Pliko Mini and new Pliko Four are winners.

We're less enthusiastic about the rest of the Peg line. The Aria Twin gets lower marks from readers . . . there are better double strollers out there than this. The Vela Easy Drive only gets mixed reviews. ***Rating: B***

Phil & Teds *philandteds.com.* When the sales of its in-line, all terrain strollers took off a few years ago, Phil & Teds committed one of the seven deadly sins of business—it over-expanded. The company quickly rolled out spin-offs to its tri-wheel stroller . . . and then suffered when quality control snafus led to a series of embarrassing safety recalls.

If that weren't enough, the company parted ways with its longtime distributor in 2009, setting up its own operation instead. And then to top it off, it acquired competitor Mountain Buggy's business out of bankruptcy. Digesting that acquisition and the hangover from the past years' expansion efforts has dogged the brand.

The models. Phil & Ted's key model is a tri-wheel stroller with inflated tires that can morph from a single stroller to a double with a toddler seat accessory. Car seat-compatible or with an optional bassinet, a Phil & Ted in-line stroller can go from birth to the toddler years with ease.

The best-selling Phil & Teds is probably the Explorer (which used to be called the Sport). The Explorer ($500, 30.1 lbs.) features a large canopy and one-hand fold. You can also use the doubles kit (the extra toddler seat) and an infant car seat at the same time.

What sets Phil & Ted apart is their second-child seat ($90 to $100 extra; for kids six months and up), which can attach to the FRONT or BACK of the stroller (for comparison, Valco's toddler seat only attaches to the front). The rear seat configuration turns off some parents (safety hint: the child in the backseat has to be removed first to prevent tipping). And if you put a larger toddler in the back seat, the access to the stroller's storage basket is limited. But that caveat aside, folks seem to love the Explorer. Parents tell us the all-terrain 12″ air-filled wheels are perfect for both the mall and hiking trails, plus the wide seat accommodates children for many years.

If the Explorer is too expensive for your budget, the company sells a stripped down version of the Explorer, dubbed the Classic

($370, 24 lbs.). The Classic omits the Explorer's height adjustable handle and has less fancy padding. But it still has a large canopy and one-hand fold.

Phil & Teds also makes three more expensive variations of the Explorer: the Dash, Hammerhead and Vibe. The Dash ($550, 23 lbs.) features upgraded padding and canopy. The unfortunately named Hammerhead ($500, 26 lbs.) is much like the Sport, but with two wheels at front that are lockable to push in a straight line. Finally, the Vibe ($700, 22 lbs.) has an exposed aluminum frame, plus extras like a kid snack tray and a canopy with additional adjustments.

If all these presto-chango features are too much for your tastes, Phil & Teds does make a simple lightweight stroller. The Smart ($250, 12 lbs.) has smaller wheels up front and bigger tires in back, and features a compact fold and one-touch brake, but no cup holder. The Smart also has a reversible seat and a car seat adapter accessory ($29).

In the past year, Phil & Teds debuted its first true jogging stroller, the Sub 4 ($800). It features wishbone suspension, disc brakes and quick-release wheels.

New for 2012, Phil & Teds is jumping into the modular system market with a brand-new offering: the Promenade ($850, 27.9 lbs.). This will be Phil & Ted's first stroller with a reversible seat that morphs into a lay-flat bassinet. The Promenade also features a telescoping handle and EVA (never flat) tires. Like all Phil & Ted's, you can add a second seat that can also lay flat as a bassinet (perfect for twins). The Promenade is infant car seat compatible (adapters are accessories).

Also new for 2012: the Dot, a new, smaller version of the Explorer. About 10% smaller than the Explorer, the Dot will have much the same features as the Explorer. The weight of the prototype we tried out was 29.5 lbs. Price: $529. A doubles kit will be $100.

Our view. These strollers are perfect for the outdoors—the air-filled tires are great for hikes, gravel paths or rough sidewalks.

Readers give the Explorer an enthusiastic thumbs up for its smooth ride and second-seat functionality. The height adjustable handle also wins raves. We like the little touches such as the flip-flop friendly brake pedal and new, bigger canopy. Cons to this stroller: a few parents complain of tire blowouts (requiring the purchase of extra tubes). And why no included cup holder? For 500 bucks, the least Phil & Teds could do is include a place to hold a water bottle.

What about Phil & Ted's more expensive versions of the Explorer? We say skip them—reports of quality issues with the Dash and Vibe make these models not ready for prime time. If Phil & Teds really wants to compete in the $600 or $700 stroller market, it needs to do a better job on quality control and customer service.

strollers

These models don't cut it.

The new Promenade is interesting and clearly aiming at the Baby Jogger Select market; we though it was very innovative, but bulky—the frame alone weighs 20.4 lbs. Add in a 7.5 lb. seat and you've got a stroller that's near 28 lbs. without the second seat. If Phil & Ted's could slim that down a bit, the Promenade could be a winner. While the Baby Jogger Select is about the same weight, it is $350 cheaper.

Bottom line: if you need to transport two kids and like the idea of an in-line, all-terrain stroller, then Phil & Teds is a good bet. Stick with the Classic or the Explorer. Our rating is for those models only.
Rating: A-

Quinny *quinny.com.* Quinny launched in 2007 amid much fanfare as parent Dorel/Cosco tried to steal a bit of the Bugaboo mojo and tap the premium part of the stroller market. Quinny is Dorel's Dutch subsidiary known for its stylish multi-function strollers.

The models. The Buzz (26.4 lbs.) is Quinny's flagship model—this clever tri-wheel stroller has an innovative "automatic unfolding" feature plus a sleek look with a fully reclining seat that can face forward or back toward the parent. Like the Bugaboo, the Buzz is a modular system, albeit sold separately: $580 for a stroller, $100 to $190 for a carrycot (Dreami) and $135-190 for a Maxi Cosi Mico infant car seat. There is even a two-tone fashion option, like the Bugaboo Cameleon.

In the past year, the Buzz got a larger storage basket, replacing the dinky previous offering.

The Zapp ($270 to $300, 13 lbs.) is Quinny's lightweight stroller with compact fold. This model also accommodates a Maxi Cosi car seat. Unlike the Zapp's European counterpart, the U.S. Zapp has a storage basket. A cup holder, however, is an extra $20. The major flaw: the Zapp doesn't recline.

To address that shortcoming, Quinny rolled out a new version of Zapp in the past year: the Zapp Xtra ($300, 19.1 lbs). This stroller DOES recline (and a full recline at that) and the seat is reversible. The only bummer: the seat has to be removed from the frame for folding. And the Zapp Xtra weighs six lbs. (almost 50%) heavier than the regular Zapp. FYI: The Zapp Xtra is replacing the original Zapp in 2012.

In the past year, Quinny rolled out the Senzz ($260 to $400, 19.8 lbs.) with a curvy frame, compact, one-hand fold and a partial seat recline. It works with the Mico car seat and the Mico bassinet.

New for 2012: Quinny is debuting a new model, dubbed the Moodd ($700, 30 lbs.). The Moodd features an easy fold and unfold feature, plus a one-hand seat recline, reversible handle and air tires in back. Also included is a rain cover and a funky t-bar bumper bar in front. The Moodd comes in a variety of colors in black or white frames.

If that weren't enough, Quinny has a new ultra-lightweight stroller on tap for 2012: the Yezz is a 11 lb. tri-wheel stroller features a compact fold and carry strap. Pricing wasn't available as of press time.

Our view. Dorel largely mis-fired when it launched Quinny state-side a few years ago. Amid all the buzz for Bugaboo and the luxury market, you'd think Quinny would be a slam dunk.

And there was stroller lust when Quinny launched—folks loved its sleek design and gee-whiz features like the Buzz's automatic unfolding trick. But then folks actually used their Quinnys. And lust became buyer's remorse.

Take the Buzz. It lacks all the features most parents take for granted in a good stroller—easy, one-hand fold, generous canopy, a place to put a cup of coffee, kid's snack tray and so on. The Buzz has none of that. Instead, you get a stroller with a 25.5" wide rear wheels. This makes negotiating tight spaces difficult. The Buzz's fold can be a challenge, with levers that are hard to push. Add in that 26 lb. weight and you can see why the buzz on the Buzz has evaporated.

The Zapp has similar faults. Yes, it is much lighter in weight than the Buzz, but it lacks a seat recline, which is hard to believe for a $200 stroller. One-touch fold? Forget about it—the Zapp requires multiple steps, buttons you have to push, a bottom latch that must be wrestled with. The skimpy canopy and lack of cup holder is the final capper.

Yes, the Zapp Xtra addresses the original Zapp's faults by adding a seat that not only reclines but also reverses. That is a neat trick—but this pushes the price close to $300 and nearly doubles the weight. That said, the reviews on the new Zapp Xtra are more positive on than the original Zapp.

We've heard little feedback on the Senzz, as it has very little distribution as of this writing. At $400, it seems grossly overpriced for its meager features. And the new Moodd and Yezz strollers weren't released yet as of this writing.

Bottom line: Quinny needs a reboot. Dorel must better adapt these European models to American tastes. Yes, the company has made a few small improvements here and there, but key design problems remain. For now, we say skip this line. ***Rating: C***

Safety 1st *See Cosco.*

Schwinn/InStep *This brand is reviewed online at BabyBagains.com*

Stokke *stokkeusa.com.* And now for something totally different: the Stokke Xplory looks like something George Jetson might have pushed Elroy around in, but it's more than a vision of what strollers might look like in the year 2050. We will give Stokke bonus points for creativity (they've tried to push it as the next Bugaboo), but the

strollers

$1050 Xplory is a bit too funky for its own good.

The model. Like the Bugaboo, you get a modular system that includes a frame with rubber tires and a seat that can attach to the frame either forward or rear facing. The Stokke's key feature is its high-altitude seating. The pitch, according to Stokke, is to keep baby higher off the ground so they are away from exhaust fumes, slobbering Labradors, etc. (the target market is urban parents).

Our view. So why haven't you seen the über rich pushing the Stokke Xplory around Greenwich Village? That's because for the most part, the Xplory has been a bust. First, the handle and most of the Xplory's frame is injection-molded plastic, not something you'd expect from a $1000+ stroller. The "plastic-y" feel turns off many, while the lack of a basket is another major negative. Instead the Xplory has a "shopping bag" that attaches to the frame . . . close, but no cigar.

In the past year, Stokke has rolled out a Complete Xplory for $1250 that includes a bassinet (a la the Bugaboo). Also new: a car seat adapter accessory ($55 to $80) for the Perego Primo Viaggio, Maxi Cosi or Graco SnugRide, which addresses a key complaint about past versions. So while we still wouldn't recommend the Xplory (its high price alone is a deal killer), we will raise the rating a touch this year to reflect the new car seat adapter. **Rating: C-**

Stroll Air *This brand is reviewed online at BabyBagains.com*

Summer *summerinfant.com* Best known for its video baby monitors, Summer has been rapidly expanding recently, entering new categories like cribs, high chairs and, now, strollers and car seats.

The models. The big news at Summer is their first travel system, Prodigy, which debuted in mid 2011 at Babies R Us for $265 to $280. Summer's infant car seat is probably the headliner here, with its new technology (see review in the car seat chapter). However, the Prodigy stroller deserves mention: it offers a one-hand, self-standing fold, multi-position seat recline and height-adjustable handle.

Summer sells the Prodigy stroller as a stand-alone model under the name Upstart for $136, again exclusive to Babies R Us.

Our view. This is Summer's first foray into travel systems and even though the stroller has been out since mid 2011, we've had little parent feedback on it. The few initial reviews we saw are positive, however. The full-size stroller hits all the right notes feature-wise, but the weight (29.2 lbs.) gives us pause.

Summer clearly is aiming this offering at the first-time parent travel system market so dominated by Graco, Evenflo and Dorel. But when the weight of an empty Prodigy stroller clocks in three lbs. heavier than an already hefty Graco Quattro, it makes us wonder if Summer has done their homework here. **Rating: Not Yet.**

Teutonia *teutoniausa.com* Teutonia is a 60-year-old German brand of strollers that, like many European stroller makers, churns out large prams and bulky carriage strollers. Owned for several years by Britax, Teutonia tried and failed to crack the U.S. market, thanks to designs that were way to heavy for domestic tastes.

Enter Graco, which bought Teutonia from Britax in 2007 and remade the brand into a stylish stroller system that lets you customize various frames, seating options and colors. But unlike Graco's strollers, you won't see Teutonia in chain stores—the brand is only sold in specialty store boutiques. Let's take a look at the offerings.

The models. Teutonia offers two basic options: design your own stroller or a pre-made system, the T-Linx. The latter is offered as a stroller ($400 to $500) or as part of a "system" which includes the T-Tario 35 infant car seat for $600. The T-Tario is the same as the Graco SnugRide 35. The T-Linx (25.7 lbs.) features a reversible handle and seat and front wheel suspension with no-flat tires.

If you go the custom route, you can pick from two stroller chassis, the t-160 ($425) or the t-460 for $500. The t-460 frame folds with the seat attached and features a bigger canopy, one-touch footrest and two-stage front suspension. Then you can pick a stroller seat ($150 to $175, 10.7 lbs.) or a carrycot/bassinet ($150, 9 lbs.).

Of course, there are a slew of accessories (diaper bag, $50 to $75; foot muff, $65 to $80; mosquito net, $15 to $25; etc.) but oddly, no cup holder. At least Graco/Teutonia offers you a wide choice of fashion options: nine solid colors, three floral prints and another 15 accent colors available on an optional reversible seat insert.

Our view. Reader feedback on this line is limited, but what we've heard so far is quite positive. Quality is good. Made in Germany and Poland, the Teutonia strollers are easy to steer one-handed, report readers. Folks like the foam-filled tires (no flats), suspension to smooth out bumps and height adjustable handle.

But . . . these strollers are HEAVY. The new 460 series clocks in at 31 lbs. for both the frame and seat. Add baby plus a few items in the basket and you've got 40+ lbs. to push. We're amazed that Graco put all this time and effort into this line and came out with such a heavy stroller . . . what are they thinking? Can an average parent who isn't on steroids actually lift this thing in and out of a trunk?

While we are happy that the newer T-LInx is "only" 25.7 lbs., if Graco wants to give the competition a run for its money, it should aim for something closer to 20 lbs.

Bottom line: if you have your heart set on custom-designing a stroller and live in a big city where you won't be lugging this stroller in and out of a car trunk, Teutonia should be on your list of brands to consider. But the heavy weight bulk makes this brand a tough sell if you live in the suburbs. ***Rating: B***

Tike Tech *This brand is reviewed online at BabyBagains.com*

Trends For Kids *This brand is reviewed online at BabyBagains.com*

UPPAbaby *uppababy.com.* Newcomer UPPAbaby was started by Bostonians Bob and Lauren Monahan. Bob worked for First Years and Safety 1st in product development before striking out on his own; Lauren provides the PR and design mojo. Obviously, Bob and Lauren have kids, as you can tell from the well thought-out designs of their first strollers.

The models. UPPAbaby has a hit with their flagship model, the multi-function Vista ($700, 26.3 lbs.). Made of an aircraft alloy frame, the VISTA stroller system includes a bassinet and stroller seat, telescoping handle and easy fold. We liked all the included extras, such as a rain shield, mesh sunshade and bug cover. Plus the Vista uses rubber-like foam wheels that give a smooth ride, but don't go flat. Unlike the Bugaboo, you can fold the Vista with the seat attached.

Yes, it is pricey at a $700 retail, but we often see the Vista discounted as low as $500 online.

In the past year, the Vista got a few minor tweaks and upgrades, including an improved canopy with pop-down sunshade and easier-to-adjust harness. Also new: a $100 to $130 rumble seat for a second child that can be used when the Vista is either in infant car seat or stroller seat mode. The latest model includes a slightly taller seat and lower basket, plus a new push-button brake. Besides a new wheel lock mechanism, there isn't much changing here in 2012.

UPPAbaby offers car seat adapters for Graco, Chicco and Peg infant seats. While the Vista does include a weather shield, mesh sunshade and bug cover there are few additional accessories available (travel bag, cup holder, all terrain wheels).

UPPAbaby's second offering is the G-Lite ($120, 8.3 lbs.), a super lightweight umbrella stroller with a standing fold and mesh seat (like the Mac Volo) and seat pad. The G-lite doesn't recline, so it is best for babies six months and up.

If a partial seat recline is important, consider the upgraded version of the G-Lite, dubbed the G-Luxe ($190, 11.9 lbs.). It features a standing fold, bigger wheels, and partial seat recline. For 2011, the G-Luxe gets a removable, washable seat pad and an improved canopy.

In the past year, UPPAbaby launched a new model, the Cruz ($460, 22.2 lbs.), positioned price-wise between the G-Lite and the Vista. It features a reversible seat (but no bassinet) and adjustable height handle. The Cruz is car seat compatible with Graco, Peg, Chicco and Maxi Cosi. FYI: The Cruz has the same seat dimensions as the Vista; there is a full recline and an adjustable foot rest and handle. We liked the smart design touches such as a sunshade that pulls up for taller toddlers.

Our view. Parent feedback on UPPAbaby has been positive. Readers who like the Vista praise its quality, huge basket and high-riding seat and bassinet. The no-flat foam tires also win raves.

The negatives include a basket that is a bit hard to reach with the bassinet attached—and the rear wheelbase (25″) on the Vista is rather wide, making the stroller harder to maneuver in tight aisles or doorways. Another bummer: the seat doesn't have a full recline, which irks some users. But . . . the footrest is adjustable (something the Bugaboo lacks) and the fold is much easier and compact compared to the Bugaboo or i'coo Targo.

Another parent told us she loved the stroller as a single, less so as a double (the attached toddler seat made the steering difficult). We blogged about that issue in November 2011. We would agree: if you need a double, look elsewhere than the Vista.

Those criticisms aside, folks who have the Vista give it high marks for quality and durability. The company's customer service is also excellent. If you live in the city and need a durable, multi-function stroller (and can live with the weight/bulk), the Vista is a good choice.

The G-lite wins similar kudos, with fans citing its super lightweight and included cushions. Readers debate whether the G-lite is really better than a Maclaren—the lack of seat recline in the G-lite is one major negative, but folks with older toddlers say it is fine for them. All in all, we'd give Maclaren a slight edge in overall quality and construction . . . but a typical Mac costs much more than a G-lite.

The Cruz was too new as of press time for any reader feedback. We liked the prototype we played with a trade show and think it will be a winner.

So, we will recommend UPPAbaby—no, the Vista isn't cheap. But at least for the money, you get decent value (example: the sun canopy is included for the Vista; a $40 add-on for Bugaboo Cameleon, which is already $200 more than the Vista!). ***Rating: A***

Valco *valcobaby.com.* Australia-based Valco has made a splash in the all-terrain stroller market with their Tri-Mode EX, a tri-wheel stroller whose key selling point is its expandability.

The models. The Tri-Mode EX comes in both a single ($500, 23 lbs.) and double ($630 to $700, 33 lbs.) version and features a five-position, fully reclining seat, large storage basket, aluminum frame, newborn insert and swivel front wheel that can be locked in a fixed position. The Tri-Mode has 12″ air-filled tires.

That's nice, but what really has parents jazzed are Valco's add-ons: a bassinet ($180) and toddler seat ($80) that extend the use of this stroller. The bassinet is fine, but the toddler seat is really cool, turning the Valco into a double stroller. Valco's other accessories

strollers

include a car seat adapter ($40, which holds a Graco or Peg seat) and foot muff ($80).

How does the Valco stack up versus its main competitors in the swivel wheel, all terrain category? Well the Valco is a touch heavier than the Mountain Buggy Urban, although Valco has reduced its weight in the past year to be more comparable. And folks seem to like the Valco's toddler seat configuration better than Phil & Ted, although there is a split opinion here.

For 2012, The Tri-Mode will get a new easier fold—and Valco continues to try to shave a few ounces off the weight with mesh fabrics.

While the Tri-Mode is Valco's flagship stroller, the brand also has two other models: the Latitude EX and Ion EX.

The Latitude EX is a tri-wheel model with smaller (non-air filled) tires and standing, umbrella-like fold. The Latitude comes in both single ($220 to $350, 19 lbs.) and double versions ($340 to $500, 30 lbs.) and features a telescoping handle, fully reclining seat and a rather amazing fold. Like most Valcos, you get all the accessories included: rain cover, boot, front napper bar, etc. Both Latitudes are car seat compatible (they include straps for a Graco car seat), but the double only fits one car seat.

The Ion EX ($240 to $400, 17 lbs.) features a full recline and flat fold. A double, side-byside version (Ion 4 Two) is $585 (26 lbs.). The Ion is similar to the Latitude, but the former has a funky circular handle. The Latitude's handle is more traditional.

In the past year, Valco debuted a less-expensive version of the Tri-Mode called the Matrix ($280 to $375) as well as a four-wheel spin-off dubbed the Quad ($500, 22 lbs.).

FYI: The Latitude, Ion and Quad will be phased out sometime in 2012. They will be replaced by three new models: the Zee, Spark and Snap.

The Zee ($330, 18.3 lbs.) a lightweight model with full recline, wheel suspension and full extension canopy. Accessories for Tri-Mode will work on the Zee.

The Spark ($440) is similar to the Zee but adds an adjustable handle and a seat that can be forward or rear-facing. The Spark folds with the seat, which can even morph into a bassinet.

The Snap ($230) is a lightweight model that will come in a three-wheel (13.9 lbs.) and four-wheel (15.8 lbs.) version. It will feature an auto-lock standing fold, fully reclining seat and will be car seat adaptable.

Our view. Parent feedback on the Tri-Mode EX has been positive, with folks lauding the stroller's quality, maneuverability and sturdy ride. We've been impressed with how Valco has trimmed the weight on the Tri-Mode EX, as that was previously a major drawback.

Readers love all the storage and air-filled tires, which make the Tri-Mode EX a better bet for folks who want to use it on trails or rough sidewalks. We have much less reader input on Valco's other models, which are clearly designed more for the mall than off-road adventure. These strollers have sold in much lower quantity than the Tri-Mode.

All in all, Valco is a winner. **Rating: A**

Zooper *This brand is reviewed online at BabyBagains.com*

Our Picks: The Best Strollers

Lifestyle #1: Mall Crawl

You live in the suburbs and drive just about everywhere you go. Besides the mall, you take quick strolls around the block, which has paved sidewalks in good condition.

The ideal mall crawler stroller has small wheels that enable tight cornering in narrow aisles—it can't be too wide or bulky. As for weight, you'll be hauling this stroller in and out of a trunk several times a day . . . so anything over 20 lbs. is asking for trouble.

Trunk space is a concern when considering the fold of a mall stroller—some strollers are more bulky than others. If you have a compact car, take a second to compare the measurements of the folded stroller and your trunk. Other nice features for a mall stroller include a decent cup holder and good-sized basket. The canopy and accessories like a rain cover are a bit less important, since this stroller is used more indoors than out.

Common first-time parent mistake: buying a giant travel system, with matching infant car seat and stroller. These are common shower gifts and many folks fall for that coordinated look . . . and think their stroller should be built like a tank to protect a newborn from thermonuclear attack. But many travel system strollers are behemoths—and that huge weight and bulk make them impossible to use as baby gets older, not to mention wrestling it in and out of trunk.

Good. Ok, you have two choices here: get a stroller that is infant-car seat compatible or go for a stroller frame.

Good news: more stroller models now can fit other brand car seats (but check for compatibility), so you don't have to buy a giant Evenflo or Graco travel system. We note which strollers have car seat adapters in the reviews earlier in this chapter. A good example is the Baby Jogger City Mini (see below)—its car seat adapter accessory ($60) works with most major brand car seats.

Another option: buy a simple stroller frame, like the **Graco Snug Rider** ($70) or **Baby Trend Snap & Go** ($60). If you can't decide what main stroller you want just yet, this could be a placeholder. When your baby outgrows the infant car seat, you'll end up buying a good

STROLLERS
AND MORE

lightweight stroller like the ones recommended below.

FYI: When trying out different stroller frames, take a second and snap your favorite infant car seat into the various stroller frames in the store before purchasing. Some car seats will lock into place; others must be held with straps. Locking is best for safety, of course.

Finally, a caveat about over-use of the infant car seat for newborns in strollers. Pediatricians generally recommend limiting the amount of time newborns spend in an infant car seat—this is especially true for preemies or infants with certain medical conditions (ask your doctor for advice if there is a concern). While there is no hard and fast rule, it makes sense to take your baby out of the seat frequently so there is a change in position.

Better. Your baby has now outgrown the infant car seat and you are looking for a lightweight stroller. Among the better bets would be the *Chicco C6* (aka the Capri; $65, 11 lbs.; pictured) which features a two-position seat recline, five-point harness and basic canopy . . . it is a best bet for the mall. Yes, you read right— it is just $65.

A bit more money but still excellent would be the *Uppababy G-Lite* ($100 8.3 lbs.) or *Maclaren Volo* ($100-130, 8.8 lbs.). FYI: Both of these strollers are best for babies over six months of age since they don't have fully reclining seats.

STROLLER ROUND-UP

Here's our round-up of popular lightweight models by the major stroller manufacturers.

MAKER	MODEL	WEIGHT	PRICE	RECLINE
APRICA	PRESTO FLAT	15 LBS.	$180-$300	FULL
BABY JOGGER	CITY MINI	17.1	$200	FULL
CHICCO	C6 / CAPRI	11.0	$65	PARTIAL
COMBI	COSMO	13.0	$105-$130	FULL
CYBEX	RUBY	13.2	$150	PARTIAL
FIRST YEARS	JET	11.4	$33-$40	PARTIAL
GRACO	IPO	17.0	$80-100	PARTIAL
INGLESINA	SWIFT	13.0	$130	PARTIAL
KOLCRAFT	CONTOURS LITE	15.5	$55-$70	PARTIAL
MACLAREN	VOLO	9.4	$130	NONE
PEG PEREGO	SI	16.5	$180-$300	PARTIAL
UPPA BABY	G-LITE	8.3	$120	NONE
VALCO	ION EX	17.0	$240-$400	FULL

Best. We have two top picks for the best stroller for the mall crawl: the *Baby Jogger City Mini* ($230, 17.1 lbs.) and the *Maclaren Quest* ($200-$250, 12.1 lbs.).

The Baby Jogger City Mini is an excellent tri-wheel stroller with oversized canopy and fully reclining seat. Baby Jogger's quick fold technology is amazing—you lift a strap in the middle of the stroller and zip! It's folded.

The Maclaren Quest includes a four position seat recline and linked brakes (one button locks both wheels), plus foam grip handles. It is lightweight and easy to fold and use. FYI: The 2011 Quest model will feature a new, fully reclining seat so it can be used from birth.

One difference between these two models: The Baby Jogger has a car seat adapter; the Quest does not. Both these strollers have small wheels, which makes them great for the mall, airports and city sidewalks. However, the smaller wheels don't work on grass, gravel paths or other more rugged terrain.

Airline travel. Experienced parent rule #429: never gate-check your expensive Maclaren or Baby Jogger stroller. Instead, if you plan to do much airline travel, go for a super cheap, lightweight model. Our suggestion: the *First Years Jet* ($40, 11.4 lbs.) It's no frills, but is lightweight and has a compact fold and basic basket. And at $40, it is easily replaced if the airline mangles it in the cargo hold.

strollers

COMMENTS

Higher seat, self-standing fold, four wheel suspension.

Quick-fold technology, extended sun canopy, tri-wheel.

Compact umbrella fold, decent-size basket. aka the Capri.

Affordable, compact fold, can be paired with Combi infant seat.

Two-step fold, one-touch brake; height adjustable canopy.

No frills, compact umbrella fold. Basic basket.

One-hand fold, no napper bar; doesn't work with infant seat.

Skimpy canopy, no cup holder, two handle design.

Affordable, but seat doesn't sit upright. Skimpy canopy.

Mesh seat but no seat recline (new '11 version adds this feature).

Height adjustable handle, standing one-hand fold.

Lightest weight. Standing fold, mesh seat, machine-washable pad.

Flat fold; double version also available. Funky handle.

Lifestyle #2: Urban Jungle

When you live in a city like New York, Boston or Washington D.C., your stroller is more than just baby transportation—it's your primary vehicle. You stroll to the market, on outings to a park or longer trips on weekend getaways.

Weight is crucial for these parents as well. While you are not lugging a stroller in or out of a trunk like a suburbanite, you may find yourself climbing up subway stairs or trudging up to a fourth-floor walk-up apartment. It's a major trade-off here: full-featured strollers that are outfitted for the weather (full boot, rain cover) can weigh more than lightweight models designed for the mall. Basically, you want a rugged stroller that can take all the abuse a big city can dish

BUGABOO SMACKDOWN!	*The Bugaboo Cameleon ($880, 20 lbs.) is the reining champ of ultra expensive, three component strollers (combining a bassinet, stroller frame and seat). Whether you think it is a cleverly designed*

CONTENDER		PRICE	WEIGHT	BUGABOO-ISH?
BABY JOGGER CITY SELECT		$500	28.1 LBS.	🥿🥿
BLOOM babyZEN		$800	25.5 LBS.	🥿🥿🥿
BRITAX B-READY		$376-$500	28.1 LBS.	🥿🥿🥿
MAXI COSI FORAY LX		$400	23.4 LBS.	🥿
MUTSY 4RIDER LIGHT		$455-$570	29 LBS.	🥿🥿🥿🥿
PEG PEREGO SKATE ELITE		$700	28.8 LBS.	🥿🥿
STROLL AIR ZOOM		$500	24 LBS.	🥿🥿
TUETONIA T-LINX		$400-$500	25.7 LBS.	🥿🥿
UPPA BABY VISTA		$700	26.3 LBS.	🥿🥿🥿

out—giant potholes, uneven sidewalks, the winter from Hell . . . without the weight of a bulldozer.

In the past, carriage strollers or prams were the primary "urban jungle" stroller, but these have fallen out of favor for their bulk, weight and other disadvantages (prams typically have front wheels that don't turn).

Multi-function strollers are now the rage for urbanites—these combine a chassis with stroller seat for older babies and a bassinet for newborns. Some models include the bassinet, others offer it as an optional accessory.

While multi-function strollers are nice, they do have one disadvantage. They're heavy (many are 20+ lbs.) and most don't fold compactly. When you are trying to ascend subway stairs with baby

---

stroller that embodies urban chic . . . or a sign of wretched yuppie excess, Bugaboo sure has been one thing: a hit. Now competitors are nipping at Bugaboo's wooden shoes. We rate the contenders on a scale of one to three klompen! (Google it.)

COMMENTS/VERDICT

Swiss Army knife of strollers with 16 configurations. 2nd seat runs $160, bassinet is $90. **But it weighs 40% more than Bugaboo.**

Coolest alternative. Flat fold, adjustable frame, reclining seat can be swapped out for a lay-flat bassinet. New in 2012.

Reversible seat, 14 different seat configurations. 2nd seat is $150. wheel suspension, large storage basket. Fashion is a bit dull.

Reversible seat, weather shield, cup holder. But can't fold with seat on and fold is complex. **Only works with mediocre Maxi Cosi car seat.**

Solid rubber tires. Includes car seat adapter, but bassinet is extra. Quality is good, but heavy weight makes this a tough sell.

Folds with seat, **includes accessories like car seat adapter,** rain cover and boot. But it is 45% heavier than Bugaboo. Expensive.

Includes bassinet, reversible seat, adj. handle, plush padding, rain cover, diaper bag, umbrella. **Can fold with seat on.**

Works with Graco car seat. Foam (no flat) tires, front suspension, height adjustable, reversible handle. **Storage basket is skimpy.**

Pricey, but includes bassinet, height adj. handle, rain shield, mesh sun shade, rubber-like foam wheels. Bonus: extra rumble seat for toddlers.

strollers

in one arm and a stroller in another, the last thing you need is a bulky stroller.

So we recommend a lightweight second stroller—but unlike a stroller for the mall, this one needs more weatherproofing for the city. Of course, if you live in a studio apartment, all you may have room for is the lightweight stroller.

Hence, we will break down our picks for the urban jungle into two categories: multi-function and lightweight, but weather proof:

Best (multi-function). The winner here is the **UPPAbaby Vista** ($670, 26.3 lbs., pictured), which includes a bassinet and stroller seat, plus many extras (rain shield, mesh sun shade, bug cover, etc). Readers love how functional this stroller is (you can fold it with the stroller seat attached, for example), plus  its smooth ride on no-flat foam tires is a must for urban dwellers.

If you plan to have two kids close in age, we'd suggest the **Baby Jogger City Select** ($500, 28.1 lbs.). It can be configured 16 ways with an optional second seat ($160). An excellent stroller with a quick fold.

Finally, a dark horse in the multi-function stroller race is the **Britax B-Ready** ($500, 28.1 lbs.). It also has the second seat option, but lacks the cool quick-fold of the Baby Jogger. The B-Ready works out of the box with the Britax infant car seat, which is a nice plus.

You'll note we didn't mention Bugaboo in the above picks—sorry, their $880 Cameleon just doesn't offer the same value and features as the others we mentioned. See the "Bugaboo Smackdown" box on the previous page for a look at how the Bugaboo stacks up to the competition.

Best (light weight). In years past, this crown would probably have gone to a Maclaren stroller. And Mac still makes several good bets for urban city dwellers. But this year, our top pick is the **Baby Jogger City Mini** ($230, 17.1 lbs.; pictured)

There are two key reasons to go with the City Mini over a Maclaren: fold and canopy. Baby Jogger's "quick fold" is amazing—grab it by a strap on the seat and zip! It's folded in one simple step. That's a key advantage over Maclaren, which involves hitting two levers before you fold the stroller onto itself, requiring you to lean over to the ground. It's not that it takes forever, but when you live in New York or Boston, seconds count.

Ditto for the canopy. The City Mini has an awesome, giant canopy that completely shields baby from sun, wind and all the urban weather you can think of. Maclaren's canopy? Not so much.

That said, a Maclaren would be our runner-up choice here: either the Maclaren Triumph or Quest would be a good bet. However, once you get into Mac's more expensive models (the Techno XT or XLR), you've likely topped 20 lbs. when you include the canopy, basket and other accessories. That's probably a line you don't want to cross when climbing subway stairs.

A dark horse choice in this category would be *Joovy's Kooper* ($200, 15.5 lbs.) with a generous canopy and compact fold. Even though the list price is $200, we've seen it discounted to $150 online. Joovy's new *Scooter* ($150, 18.5 lbs.) is also one to watch. Joovy doesn't have the name recognition of Maclaren or Peg Perego, but quality and durability are good.

Lifestyle #3: Green Acres

If you live on a dirt or gravel road or in a neighborhood with no sidewalks, you need a stroller to do double duty. First, it must handle rough surfaces without bouncing baby all over the place. Second, it must be able to "go to town," folding easily to fit into a trunk for a trip to a mall or other store. And what about snow? Most mall strollers simply don't work in snow.

The answer: an all-terrain stroller with air-filled tires.

Good. *Phil & Ted's Explorer* ($480, 30.1 lbs.) is a tri-wheel stroller with swivel front wheel and air-filled tires. What's unique about the Sport: a toddler seat accessory ($110) that attaches to the BACK of the seat, giving you added flexibility if you have multiple kids. That's what makes Phil & Ted special: the flex-  ibility to use the same stroller for newborn, toddler, BOTH toddler and newborn at the same time and two toddlers. Hence, this is a good bet if you are planning on having more than one kid. If not, consider one of the next two picks.

Better. Similar to the Phil & Ted's Explorer (in fact, they are owned by the same company), the *Mountain Buggy Urban Jungle* ($500, 24 lbs.) is our better pick in this category. The polymer spoke wheels won't earn fashion points, but at least they don't rust (helpful for folks who live near an ocean). Fans of  Mountain Buggy love the way these strollers push and handle the most extreme weather (Snow? Sleet? Bring it on). We also like the stroller's overall weight (24 lbs.). Although it does have a infant car seat adapter accessory, there is no second seat option.

Best. The crown for best all-terrain stroller goes to the *BOB Revolution* stroller ($390, 24.9 lbs.). It comes in two versions: polymer wheels (SE or Sport Experience) or aluminum alloy rims (CE or City Experience). The polymer wheels are a pound heavier (24.9 lbs.) than the aluminum option (23.9 lbs.); the aluminum version is about $10 more expensive. We love the new infant car seat adapter accessory ($60) that can be removed from the stroller without tools. Fans of BOB love the stroller's quality and durability. The only slight negative: the handle bar isn't height adjustable. So if one parent is much taller than the other, this might be an issue.

See the chart below for a comparison of all-terrain models.

Lifestyle #4: Exercise (Jogging & Sport Strollers)

If you want to exercise with a stroller, you have two choices: tri-wheel strollers with fixed front wheels, or a model with a front wheel that swivels.

Fixed-wheel jogging strollers with air-filled tires are best for folks who want to actually jog or run with a stroller—you can push them in a straight line. The disadvantage to these strollers: to turn them, you have to pick up the front wheel and move it. Hence, fixed wheel joggers aren't good for walking or shopping trips.

Strollers with turnable front wheels are NOT recommended for folks who want to run—even if the stroller has the option to lock the

ALL-TERRAIN STROLLERS	*How top all-terrain strollers compare—each of these*		
MODEL	**WEIGHT**	**PRICE**	**BRAND RATING**
BABY JOGGER CITY ELITE	31.3 LBS.	$400	A
BOB REVOLUTION SE	24.9	$450	A
BRITAX B-SCENE	29.0	$350-$400	A-
BUMBLERIDE INDIE	20.0	$500	B-
JEEP LIBERTY LIMITED	29.2	$150	B+
MOUNTAIN BUGGY URBAN	24.0	$450-$500	A
PHIL & TED EXPLORER	30.1	$500	A-
VALCO TRI-MODE	23.0	$500	A

front wheel.

That said, strollers with a swivel front wheel are great for folks who just want to walk the neighborhood or trails. So you need to ask yourself, exactly how do you plan to exercise with the stroller?

Another issue to consider: how young can your baby be and ride in a jogger? First, determine whether the seat reclines (not all models do). If it doesn't, wait until baby is at least six months old and can hold his or her head up. If you want to jog or run with the stroller, it might be best to wait until baby is at least a year old since all the jostling can be dangerous for a younger infant (their neck muscles can't handle the bumps). Ask your pediatrician for advice if you are unsure.

Another decision area: the frame. The cheapest strollers (under $200) have steel frames—they're strong but also heavy (and that could be a drawback for serious runners). The most expensive models ($300 to $400) have aluminum frames, which are the lightest in weight. Once again, if you plan casual walks, a steel frame is fine. Runners should go for aluminum.

Finally, remember the Trunk Rule. Any jogger is a lousy choice if you can't get it easily in your trunk. Check the DEPTH of the jogger when it is folded—compared this to your vehicle's trunk. Many joggers are rather bulky even when folded. Yes, quick release wheels help reduce the bulk, so check for that option.

So, which jogging stroller do we recommend? Let's break that down into two categories: power walking and serious runners. Note that all these strollers have fixed front wheels; if you want a stroller with a turnable front wheel (more suited to the mall or light duty outdoor activities), see the Green Acres section above.

Best (power walking). *Jeep Overland Limited* ($220, 28 lbs.)

---

models are tri-wheels with air-filled tires and front wheels that swivel.

COMMENT

12″ AIR-FILLED TIRES, PARENT CONSOLE, QUICKEST FOLD ON MARKET.
POLYMER RIMS (OR ALUMINUM $20 EXTRA). CAR SEAT ADAPTER $60 EXTRA.
TRI-WHEEL VERSION OF B-READY, BUT LACKS 2ND SEAT OPTION.
ADJUSTABLE HANDLE, FULL RECLINE, BOOT AND BIG STORAGE BASKET.
ONE-HAND FOLD, PARENT AND CHILD TRAY, ADJUSTABLE FOOT REST. HEAVY.
MANY ACCESSORIES, SMOOTH GLIDE, FULL RECLINE.
WIDE SEAT, HEIGHT ADJUSTABLE HANDLE. OPTIONAL SECOND CHILD SEAT.
FULLY RECLINING SEAT, LARGE BASKET, TODDLER SEAT ACCESSORY.

has a fixed front wheel and a boatload of convenience features: parent tray that can hold two water bottles, compartment to store an mp3 player, height adjustable handle and an easy fold. Since it is heavy, we think this would be a better bet for power walkers than serious runners, but the price is right: we've seen it discounted under $200 on Amazon.

Three mistakes to avoid when buying a jogging stroller

With jogging strollers available everywhere from Target to high-end bike stores, it is easy to get confused by all the options. Keep in mind these traps when shopping for a jogger:

◆ *Rust.* Warning: cheaper jogging strollers are made of steel—rust can turn your jogging stroller into junk in short order. This is especially a problem on the coasts, but can happen anywhere. Hint: the best joggers have ALUMINUM frames. And make sure the wheel rims are alloy, not steel. All-terrain strollers like Mountain Buggy use polymer wheels (in most models) to get around the rust problem.

◆ *Suspended animation.* The latest rage with joggers is cushiony suspensions, which smooth out bumps but can add to the price. But do you really need it? Most jogging strollers give a smooth ride by design, so no added suspension is necessary. And some kids actually LIKE small bumps or jostling—it helps them fall asleep in the stroller.

◆ *Too narrow seats.* Unlike other baby products, a good jogging stroller could last you until your child is five years old—that is, if you pick one with a wide enough seat to accommodate an older child. The problem: some joggers (specifically, Baby Jogger and Kelty) have rather narrow seats. Great for infants, not good for older kids. We noticed this issue after our neighbors stopped using their Baby Jogger when their child hit age three, but our son kept riding in his until five and beyond. Brands with bigger seats include Dreamer Design and BOB. (As always, confirm seat dimensions before committing to a specific stroller; seats can vary from model to model).

Best (serious running). BOB Ironman ($350, 21 lbs.) has all the quality features of a regular BOB, but adds adjustable tracking, stainless steel wheel spokes, new smooth 16″ tires and bright yellow fabric. Thanks to an aluminum frame, this jogger weighs just 21 lbs. A runner up to the BOB: the **Baby Jogger Performance** ($430, 24 lbs.) with 20″ wheels.

Need a double jogger? Our advice would be the same: BOB would come first, followed by Baby Jogger.

Plan to take your jogger out in the cold weather? Instead of bundling up baby, consider a stroller blanket. One of our favorites is the **JJ Cole Bundle Me** (bundleme.com), which comes in several versions for $50. And what can you use to keep a blanket on your stroller? Try the **BlankyClip**, a $12.50 tension clip (blanky-clip.com) cleverly disguised as a stuffed bear or duck.

Of course, you could have the opposite problem: you live somewhere where the summer weather is brutal. If your stroller seat fabric doesn't breathe, consider a **Cool Mee Seat Liner** from Meeno Babies (MeenoBabies.com). Their machine washable seat liner ($35) is made of three-ply mesh material that promotes airflow to cool baby.

Double The Fun: Strollers for two

There are two types of strollers that can transport two tikes: tandem models and side-by-side styles. A tandem stroller has a "front-back" configuration, where the younger child rides in back while the older child gets the view. These strollers are best for parents with a toddler and a new baby.

Side-by-side strollers, on the other hand, are best for parents of twins or babies close in age. In this case, there's never any competition for the view seat. The only downside: some of these strollers are so wide, they can't fit through narrow doorways or store aisles. (Hint: make sure the stroller is not wider than 30″ to insure door compatibility). Another bummer: few have napper bars or fully reclining seats, making them impractical for infants.

So, what to buy—a tandem or side by side? Our reader feedback shows parents are much happier with their side-by-side models than tandems. Why? The tandems can get darn near impossible to push when weighted down with two kids, due to their length-wise design. Yes, side by sides may not be able to fit through some narrow shopping aisles, but they seem to work better overall.

Double strollers can be frustrating—your basic choices are low-price duos from Graco or Kolcraft or high-price doubles like those from Maclaren and Baby Jogger. There doesn't seem to be much in between the low-price ($200 range) and the high-end ($400 and up).

Best tandem (front/back double strollers). *Kolcraft Contours Options II Tandem* ($240, 32 lbs.). Cool feature: the seats reverse to face the parents or each other. This model features a few upgrades over other tandems, including adjustable leg rests and each seat can fully recline. Minor quibble: while there are cup holders for each child, there is no child snack tray. And, yes, this stroller is heavy and quite bulky when folded—but so are most tandem strollers.

Runner's up: Chicco has a winner with the **Chicco Cortina Together** ($300, 30 lbs.). This front/back tandem stroller holds two car seats and features an aluminum frame, a storage basket with trap door access, three-position handle and flat fold. Readers love the steering and overall quality of this stroller.

Another runner up in this category: the **Joovy Caboose Stand-on Tandem** ($150, 26 lbs.). It really isn't a tandem, but a pushcart—the younger child sits in front while the older child *stands* in back (there is also a jump seat for the older child to sit on). This is a better solution when you have an older toddler who doesn't want to ride all the time in a stroller . . . but still gets tired and needs a place to sit on long outings.

E-MAIL FROM THE REAL WORLD
Biting the bullet on a pricey twin stroller

Cheapo twin strollers sound like a good deal for parents of twins, but listen to this mother of multiples:

"Twins tend to ride in their strollers more often and longer, and having an unreliable, bulky or inconvenient stroller is a big mistake. As you suggest, it's a false economy to buy an inexpensive Graco or other model, as these most likely will break down before you're done with the stroller. My husband and I couldn't believe that we'd have to spend $400 on a stroller, but after talking to parents of multiples, we understand why it's best to just bite the bullet on this one. We've heard universally positive feedback about the Maclaren side-by-side for its maneuverability, durability and practicality. It fits through most doorways and the higher end model (Twin Techno) also has seats that fully recline for infants. We've heard much less positive things about front-back tandems for twins. These often are less versatile, as only one seat reclines, so you can't use them when both babies are small (or tired). And when the babies get bigger, they're more likely to get into mischief by pulling each others' hair and stuff."

Best side by side strollers. For parents of two little ones on a tight budget, we suggest the *Jeep Twin Sport All Weather Umbrella Stroller* (27 lbs., pictured) for $100 on Amazon. It's bare bones (no basket) but will get the job done with reclining seats and a compact fold.

If you can afford to spend another $90, we'd suggest the *Graco Twin Ipo* ($190, 32 lbs.). Yes, it is five lbs. heavier than the Jeep, but you get a storage basket, better canopies with sun shield as well as adjustable leg rests. Readers say the Graco Twin Ipo is an excellent stroller.

Is Grandma offering to buy your twin stroller? If so and the budget allows, we recommend the *Maclaren Twin Techno* ($380, 26.9 lbs.) with its fully reclining seats, plush seats, and excellent overall quality. Ditto for the *Baby Jogger City Mini Duo* ($400, 26.6 lbs., pictured), with its excellent extended canopies and quick fold.

Finally, for outdoor treks with two kids, we'd suggest looking at our top-rated all-terrain stroller brands (Phil & Ted, Mountain Buggy and BOB). They each make swivel wheel doubles that, while pricey, feature great quality and comfort.

Bike Trailers, Seats & Helmets

Bike Trailers. Yes, lots of companies make bike trailers, but the gold standard is *Burley* (866-248-5634; burley.com). Their trailers (sold in bicycle stores) are considered the best in the industry. A good example is the *Burley D'Lite.* It features a multi-point safety harness, built-in rear storage, 100 lb. carrying capacity and compact fold (to store in a trunk). Okay, it's expensive at $580 but check around for second-hand bargains. And there is a $160 jogger conversion kit that turns a Burley into a jogging stroller (we've heard mixed reviews on this for its wobbly steering).

A close runner-up to Burley in the bike trailer race is Canada's *Chariot* (chariotcarriers.com). "These are the best engineered bike trailers I've ever seen," opined a reader and we agree. Sold at REI, the basic Cheetah runs $400, although they sell pricier versions that can run up to $1000.

Baby Jogger, the jogging stroller company reviewed earlier, has an entry in the bike trailer race as well. The Pod is a modular system that lets you add accessories to your trailer. A chassis is $500—

bike trailers/seats

you can add a stroller kit for $80, jogger for $65 and bike trailer adapter for $45. The Pod will be 30″ wide so it can fit through most standard doorways, yet still accommodate up to two kids.

What about the "discount" bike trailers you see for $150 to $200? **InStep** makes a few of these models:, including the Quick N Easy ($120). InStep also makes four Schwinn bike trailers, which are upgraded versions of their regular line. Cost: $115 to $350.

What do you give up for the price? In general, lower priced bike trailers have steel frames and are heavier than the Burleys (which are made of aluminum). And the cheaper bike trailers don't fold as easily or compactly as the Burleys, nor do they attach as easily to a bike.

The key feature to look for with any bike trailer is the ease (or lack thereof) of attaching the trailer to a bike. Quick, compact fold is important as well. Look for the total carrying capacity and the quality of the nylon fabric.

So, should you spring for an expensive bike trailer or one of the $150 ones? Like jogging strollers, consider how much you'll use it. For an occasional (once a week?) bike trip, we'd recommend the cheaper models. Plan to do more serious cycling, say two or three times a week? Then go for a Burley or Chariot. Yes, they are expensive but worth it if you really plan to use the trailer extensively. Hint: this might be a great item to buy second-hand on eBay or Craigslist.

Safety information: you should wait on using a bike trailer until your child is OVER one year of age. Why? Infants under age one don't have neck muscles to withstand the jolts and bumps they'll encounter with bike trailers, which don't have shock absorbers. Remember you might hit a pothole at 15+ mph—that's not something that is safe for an infant to ride out. Be sure your child is able to hold his head up while wearing a helmet as well. Your child should always wear a helmet while riding in a bike trailer—no exceptions. And, no, there is no bike trailer on the market that safely holds an infant car seat, which might cushion the bumps. Most trailers will accommodate children up to about age six.

Bike seats & helmets. When considering whether to buy a bike seat or a bike trailer, the low price of many bike seats (which start at $100) may be tempting. However, for safety reasons, we recommend a bike trailer.

Why? Bike seats are inherently less safe for baby than a trailer. That's because if you crash on a bike with a bike seat, both you and baby hit the ground. Even if your baby is wearing a helmet, that can still be ugly. Meanwhile, a trailer doesn't hit the ground the same way in a crash—and it is closer to the ground to begin with.

Also: bike seats can make even the best of bikes unstable. That's because the additional weight of a child plus the bike seat can make a bike hard to handle even for experienced riders.

Of course, bike trailers have their own issues—since they sit lower to the ground, they can be hard for motorists to see (always use an orange flag on the trailer). And they can be tippy, especially on tight turns. Since a trailer is wider than a bike, you have to be careful when negotiating tight spaces.

That said, we still think bike trailers are a better (and safer bet) than a bike seat. As a result, we will no longer recommend bike seats in this edition.

One final tip: don't forget the helmet. If your child is strapped in securely to a bike trailer, she still needs a helmet that is properly fitted and adjusted. *Consumer Reports* does a good job rating and reviewing kid bike helmets: we agree that their most recent top pick (the **Gyro Me2** helmet) is a good option. It comes in both infant or toddler versions for about $30.

A few tips on helmets: sometimes it is hard to fit a helmet on a toddler. The best advice is to go to a bike store for help. One tip: add in thick pads (sold with some bike helmets) to give a better fit. Don't glue pads on top of pads, however—and adding a thick hat isn't a safety solution either. If your child cannot wear a bike helmet safely, put off those bike adventures until they are older. Be sure your child wears the helmet well forward on his head. If a helmet is pushed back and your child hits the ground face first, there is no protection for the forehead.

Diaper Bags

We consider ourselves experts at diaper bags—we got five of them as gifts. While you don't need five, this important piece of luggage may feel like an extra appendage after your baby's first year. And diaper bags are for more than just holding diapers—many include compartments for baby bottles, clothes, and changing pads. With that in mind, let's take a look at what separates great diaper bags from the rest of the pack. In addition, we'll give you our list of nine items for a well-stocked diaper bag.

Best Online Sources

Just because you have a new baby doesn't mean you have to lose all sense of style. And there is good news: an entire cottage industry of custom diaper-bag makers has sprung up to help fill the style gap. One good place to start: our message boards. Go to BabyBargains.com, click on the message boards and then to Places to Go (All Other Gear, Diaper Bags, etc). There you'll find dozens of moms swapping tips on the best and most fashionable diaper bags. Here's a round up of our readers' favorite custom diaper bag makers (most sell direct off their sites, but a few also sell on other sites):

Amy Michelle	amymichellebags.com
California Innovations	californiainnovations.com
Fleurville	fleurville.com
Haiku Diaper Bags	haikubags.com
Holly Aiken	hollyaiken.com
I'm Still Me	imstillme.com
Ju Ju Be	ju-ju-be.com
Kate Spade	katespade.com.
Kipling	kipling.com
Lexie Barnes	lexiebarnes.com
Oi Oi	oioi.com.au
One Cool Chick	onecoolchick.com
Reese Li	reeseli.com
Skip Hop	skiphop.com
Timbuk2	timbuk2.com
Tumi	tumi.com
Vera Bradley	verabradley.com

No doubt there are dozens more, but that's a great starting point. You can expect prices to be commensurate with style. Kate Spade can cost over $300 a diaper bag. But there are some great looking options for under a $100 too. One caveat: many of these manufacturers are small boutique companies. Often it may be the owner who's taking the order. . . and also sewing the bag! While we admire the entrepreneurship of these companies, many are so small that a minor event can put them off kilter. All it takes is one hurricane or a deluge of orders to turn a reputable company into a customer service nightmare. Check the feedback on these companies on our message boards before ordering.

Smart Shopper Tips

Smart Shopper Tip #1
Diaper Bag Science
"I was in a store the other day, and they had about one zillion

different diaper bags. Some had cute prints and others were plain. Should I buy the cheapest one or invest a little more money?"

The best diaper bags are made of tear-resistant fabric and have all sorts of useful pockets, features and gizmos. Contrast that with low-quality brands that lack many pockets and are made of cheap, thin vinyl—after a couple of uses, they start to split and crack. Yes, high-quality diaper bags will cost more ($50 to $150 versus $30 to $45), but you'll be much happier in the long run. High-end diaper bags (like those made by Kate Spade and other designers) can reach the $300 mark or more. Of course, many of our readers have found deals on these bags, so check out our message boards for shopping tips.

Here's our best piece of advice: buy a diaper bag that doesn't *look* like a diaper bag. Sure those bags with dinosaurs and pastel animal prints look cute now, but what are you going to do with it when your baby gets older? A well-made diaper bag that doesn't look like a diaper bag will make a great piece of carry-on luggage later in life.

Smart Shopper Tip #2
Make your own

"Who needs a fancy diaper bag? I just put all the necessary changing items into my favorite backpack."

That's a good point. Most folks have a favorite bag or backpack that can double as a diaper bag. Besides the obvious (wipes and diapers), put in a large zip-lock bag as a holder for dirty/wet items. Add a couple of receiving blankets (as changing pads) plus the key items listed below, and you have a complete diaper bag.

You can buy many items found in a diaper bag (such as a changing pad) a la carte at most baby stores.

Top 9 Items for a Well-Stocked Diaper Bag

After much scientific experimentation, we believe we have perfected the exact mix of ingredients for the best-equipped diaper bag. Here's our recipe:

1 **GET TWO DIAPER BAGS**—one that is a full-size, all-option big hummer for longer trips (or overnight stays) and the other that is a mini-bag for a short hop to dinner or the shopping mall. Here's what each should have:

The full-size bag: This needs a waterproof changing pad that folds up, waterproof pouch or pocket for wet clothes, a couple

diaper bags

compartments for diapers, blankets/clothes, etc. Super-deluxe brands have bottle compartments with Thinsulate to keep bottles warm or cold. Another plus: outside pockets for books and small toys. A zippered outside pocket is good for change or your wallet. A cell phone pocket is also a plus.

The small bag: This has enough room for a couple diapers, travel wipe package, keys, wallet and/or cell phone. Some models have a bottle pocket and room for one change of clothes. If money is tight, just go for the small bag. To be honest, the full-size bag is often just a security blanket for first-time parents—some think they need to lug around every possible item in case of a diaper catastrophe. But, in the real world, you'll quickly discover schlepping that big full-size bag everywhere isn't practical. While a big bag is nice for overnight or long trips, we'll bet you will be using the small bag much more often.

2 **EXTRA DIAPERS.** Put a dozen in the big bag, two or three in the small one. Why so many? Babies can go through quite a few in a very short time. Of course, when baby gets older (say over a year), you can cut back on the number of diapers you need for a trip. Another wise tip: put whole packages of diapers and wipes in your car(s). We did this after we forgot our diaper bag one too many times and needed an emergency diaper. (The only bummer: here in Colorado, the wipes we keep in the car sometimes freeze in the winter! As they say, you don't know cold . . .)

3 **A TRAVEL-SIZE WIPE PACKAGE.** A good idea: a plastic Tupperware container that holds a small stack of wipes. Some wipe makers sell travel packs that are allegedly "re-sealable" to retain moisture; we found that they aren't. And they are expensive. For example, a Huggies travel pack of 16 wipes is $6. That works out to 38¢ per wipe compared to 2¢ per wipe if you buy a Huggies refill box of 384 from Kmart.

4 **BLANKET AND CHANGE OF CLOTHES.** Despite the reams of scientists who work on diapers, they still aren't leak-proof—plan for it. A change of clothes is most useful for babies under six months of age, when leaks are more common. After that point, this becomes less necessary.

5 **A HAT OR CAP.** We like the foreign legion-type hats that have flaps to cover your baby's neck and ears (about $10 to $20). Warmer caps are helpful to chase away a chill, since the head is where babies lose the most heat.

6 **BABY TOILETRIES.** Babies can't take much direct exposure to sunlight—sunscreen is a good bet for all infants. Besides sunscreen, other optional accessories include bottles of lotion and diaper rash cream. The best bet: buy these in small travel or trial sizes. Don't forget insect repellent as well. This can be applied to infants two months of age and older.

7 **DON'T FORGET THE TOYS.** We like compact rattles, board books, teethers, etc.

8 **SNACKS.** When baby starts to eat solid foods, having a few snacks in the diaper bag (a bottle of water or milk, crackers, a small box of cereal) is a smart move. But don't bring them in plastic bags. Instead bring reusable plastic containers. Plastic bags are a suffocation hazard and should be kept far away from babies and toddlers.

9 **YOUR OWN PERSONAL STUFF.** Be careful putting your wallet or checkbook into the diaper bag—we advise against it. We left our diaper bag behind one too many times before we learned this lesson. Put your name and phone number in the bag in case it is lost.

Our Picks: Brand Recommendations

Here we go with our top picks for best diaper bag. We realize a diaper bag is a fashion choice and our tastes may not always agree with yours, but if one style by the following manufacturers doesn't appeal to you, check out the other options by that brand. You may find something else you like and you'll be getting commensurate quality.

Good. Surprisingly, one of our top picks is a diaper bag made by Gerber. Yeah, we usually knock these guys' products as cheap, cheesy and low quality. But their diaper bags (made by AD Sutton) are affordable and fashionable. At only $20 to $30 (it's often on sale), the ***Gerber Tote Diaper Bag*** is one of the most affordable out there. It features a large shoulder strap, a large zip front pocket with elastic bottle holders, two more front pockets and one in back as well as a changing pad with spacious interior. The polyester fabric wipes clean and the style is rather cool in chocolate brown with green trim.

Better. Lands End has long been one of our favorites for diapers bags. They aren't super stylish (like our earlier list), but they do a workman like job of caching all your diaper and baby food needs. The Do-

It-All diaper bag ($40) is the biggest option and this year the company has shaped it like a doctor's bag. The main compartment is large and is ringed with mesh pockets. A front zippered pocket is useful for parent stuff like keys and there is a zip-lock plastic pocket for any wet stuff. A little more manly choice might be the **Convertible Backpack** diaper bag ($40) which can be used as either a tote or a backpack. Similar features to the Do-It-All, the Convertible just repackages the storage. Finally, if you just need a small one or two diaper bag with changing pad, the Little Tripper ($24.50) fits the bill. This item is for those short trips, not any all day or over night outings. All three Lands End bags are made of heavy-duty polyester fabric in six solid colors.

Best. Okay, you want to be the coolest mama on the block when you go out with your baby. No basic bag for you. But you don't want to spend the equivalent of a used car on your diaper bag. What's the solution? Our readers love the Skip Hop line of bags. Skip Hop offers eight different designs, but our favorite is the **Duo** ($55). The Duo is their largest bag with eleven pockets including a cell phone pocket, magnetic closures instead of zippers and their cool Shuttle Clips, which allow you to clip it to a stroller. Yes, it has a shoulder strap too and changing pad as you'd expect. Some parents say the bag holds less than they expected and the magnetic closures don't work as well if you stuff the bag really full. But with 15 different fabric options, you will be the style leader in your neighborhood and still be prepared for diaper duty.

Carriers

Advocates of baby wearing from pediatricians to your next-door neighbor tout the benefits of closeness with your child. But even if you don't subscribe to attachment parenting, you have to admit carriers are darn convenient. When you have a baby who just won't take a nap and you've got dinner to get on the table, a carrier that gives you two hands free is a godsend.

Just to make it more confusing, though, it seems like there are 437 different carrier makes and models on the market, from simple slings to fancy backpacks. And we've noticed over the years that every single one of those models has a fan. Of course, the key is to find the right carrier for you. One idea: we like an instructional DVD on baby wearing called Tummy 2 Tummy (tummy2tummy.com). It covers different types of carriers and how to wear them—a good introduction to the world of carriers. Another tip: we recommend buying a carrier that either has a DVD with instructions or provides an instructional video on their web site.

Best Online Resource

The Baby Wearer

thebabywearer.com. The Baby Wearer is just the right resource for parents interested in "baby wearing." Yes you've seen Guatemalan natives wearing their babies in PBS specials and you love the idea of that kind of closeness. And take it from us, there's nothing quite like it. But there are so many different options available today. So this is the site to visit when you're not sure if you want a sling, a wrap, a hip carrier and so on.

Here you'll find articles, reviews, product listings, ads, you name it. The main emphasis seems to be on sling-type carriers, not so much front carriers. There are a couple of great charts that offer detailed comparisons for carriers. In fact, there is so much here, you could spend days on the site. If you're a newbie to baby wearing, be sure to start with the basic articles as well as the glossary of terms. Then you can join chats and message boards or click on product links. Our biggest criticism of the site: there's a lot of advertising here. And the site is very jumbled. You're probably smart to take their recommendations with a grain of salt and verify reviews with other sites before you buy. ***Rating: B***

What Are You Buying?

Carriers come in several flavors: slings, hip carriers, front carriers, mei tais, wrap arounds and frame carriers. Here's a look at each:

◆ ***Slings and Pouches.*** Slings allow you to hold your baby horizontally or upright. Made of soft fabric with an adjustable strap, slings drape your baby across your body and uses rings to connect the strap (see picture). The best-known sling is made by NoJo, but many other manufac-turers have jumped into the sling market.  Whichever brand you choose, devoted sling user Darien Wilson from Austin, Texas has a great tip for new moms: "The trick for avoiding backache when using a sling is to have the bulk of the baby's weight at the parent's waist or above."

Some parents complain that there isn't much between your baby's head and a collision with a wall, furniture, etc. It's true you have to watch where you're going and what you're doing, but sling aficionados say once you get the hang of it, slings are simple to use.

Slings come in padded and unpadded versions in a variety of fabrics. They may also be called Rebozos (they tie together instead of using rings).

Pouches work in a similar way to slings across mom's body, but they are really just one continuous piece of fabric with an area of fabric that forms a pouch.

◆ *Mei Tai or Asian Carriers.* This type of carrier is made up of fabric with straps at each corner. The bottom straps tie around your waste while the top straps go over your shoulders and attach to the carrier or are tied together.

◆ *Wrap Around Carrier.* These are like those Guatemalan carriers we mentioned earlier. They are basically made by wrapping a long piece of fabric around and around your body forming a pouch around baby. This type needs some practice to learn to use.

◆ *Hip Carriers.* Hip carriers are a minimalist version of the sling. With less fabric to cradle baby, they generally work better for older babies (over six months). Baby is in a more upright position all the time, rather than lying horizontally. And like a sling, the hip carrier fits across your body with baby resting on your hip.

◆ *Front (Soft) Carriers.* Front carriers are basically a fabric bag worn on your chest. Your baby sort of dangles there in an upright position either looking in at you (when they're very young) or out at the world (when they gain more head control). Some front carriers will convert to a back carrier.

◆ *Frame (or backpack) Carriers.* Need to get some fresh air? Just because you have a baby doesn't mean you can never go hiking again. Backpack manufacturers have responded to parents' wish to find a way to take their small children with them on hikes and long walks. The good news is that most of these frame carriers are made with lightweight aluminum, high quality fabrics and well-positioned straps. Accessories abound with some models including sunshades, diaper packs that Velcro on, and adjustable seating so Junior gets a good view.

Safe & Sound

In 2010, the Consumer Product Safety Commission issued a warning to parents about sling use for infants under four months of age.

At least 14 deaths have been associated with the use of slings in the last 20 years. Here are the CPSC's tips for using a sling:

◆ *Premature infants and those with low birth weight (including twins or infants with breathing issues such as a cold) should not be placed in a sling.*

◆ *Make sure the infant's face is not covered* and can be seen at all times.

◆ *Frequently check on your baby to make sure he is breathing.*

◆ *Check the graphic below.* This shows both the correct way (chin up, face visible, nose and mouth free) and the improper way to wear your baby.

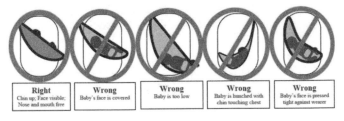

| Right | Wrong | Wrong | Wrong | Wrong |
| Chin up; Face visible; Nose and mouth free | Baby's face is covered | Baby is too low | Baby is hunched with chin touching chest | Baby's face is pressed tight against wearer |

The Name Game: Carrier Reviews

carriers

Slings and Pouches

BABY K'TAN
babyktan.com
Price: $55 to $70.
Maximum weight: 42 lbs.
Comments: The best thing about a Baby K'Tan carrier: it rests on both shoulders. That's right, unlike the usual slings, which lay across your body and puts the weight on one shoulder the K'Tan distributes your weight evenly. Another plus: it works like a mei tai, but you don't have to do any wrapping or knotting and you don't have all that excess fabric. The disadvantage readers tell us is it works best for young or small babies. Once you get beyond 20 lbs., it's too small.
Rating: A-

BALBOA BABY ADJUSTABLE SLING BY DR. SEARS

BalboaBaby.com

Price: $45 to $60.

Maximum weight: 25 lbs.

Comments: Dr. Sears was the original advocate for "baby wearing." He worked for years with NoJo (owned by Crown Crafts) who manufactured his version of a sling. Now he's moved on to a new manufacturer, Balboa Baby, which also has it's own line of slings. The sling is basically a pouch with a contoured and padded strap that slips through an adjustable ring system. There is elastic around the edges that help create a pouch. Parent feedback is mixed on this sling: fans liked the comfortable padded strap while others complain that if they don't position baby just right, the sling becomes quite uncomfortable.

Rating: B

MAMMA'S MILK BABY SLING

MammasMilk.com.

Price: $30 to $75 depending on fabric.

Maximum weight: no limit given; birth to three years.

Comments: Made of stretch cotton, the Mamma's Milk slings are probably the simplest style of sling available. They come in two options: adjustable and non-adjustable. Aplix (a stronger version of Velcro) is used in the adjustable versions, while the non-adjustable rely on stretchy fabric to keep baby in position. Comfortable foam padding is included in the area where baby's legs rest. Videos are available online as well as photos to help you use and adjust your sling. Feedback is positive.

Rating: A

MAYA WRAP

MayaWrap.com

Price: $75 to $95 depending on fabric and padding.

Maximum weight: 35 lbs.

Comments: Maya Wrap has consistently been recommended to us by readers who love its flexibility and comfort. A helpful instructional DVD comes with the wrap. Fabrics are 100% cotton hand-loomed and are only made of one layer of fabric. As a result, the May Wrap is quite lightweight. It comes in four sizes. Reader feedback on the Maya Wrap is positive, although some parents complain about the long piece of fabric that hangs from the rings when the sling is being used.

Rating: A

NEW NATIVE BABY SLING

NewNativeBaby.com

Price: $31 to $55.

Maximum weight: 35 lbs.

Comments: New Native's focus is eco-friendly slings made from organic cotton. This sling is styled as a one-piece pouch with no adjustments. Check the size chart carefully since you can make the sling smaller, but not larger. That lack of adjustment is a negative here, as are the high prices (up to $90). On the plus side, there are also a couple non-organic options for a more affordable $42 to $66. Included in the price for all their slings is an instructional DVD.

Rating: B-

THE PEANUT SHELL

thePeanutShell.com

Price: $40 to $100.

Maximum weight: Varies by model.

Comments: The Peanut Shell should win an award for best-named baby sling—this cute design is available in two versions: original and heirloom. The original sling is basically a pouch style with no straps, clips, belts or adjustments—be sure to pick the right size (it comes in six sizes). Their web site has sizing charts as well as video clips to make this decision easier. A fancier Heirloom version comes in ruffled or embroidered fabrics for $99. Reader feedback on the Peanut Shell has been decidedly mixed. Some readers complained that the strap hurt their shoulder or that it was difficult to put baby in or take her out. Others gave the Peanut Shell a rave review, once they got the hang of it.

Rating: B-

SLING BABY SLING

WalkingRockFarm.com

Price: $68.

Maximum weight:

Comments: Readers love the Sling Baby Sling because it's so easy to use—no rings, no knots or ties, no tails of fabric hanging down. The strap works like a duffle bag strap—just slide it one way or the other to lengthen or shorten. It's so easy to adjust, maker Walking Rock claims you can hand baby off from one parent to the other without waking your baby. The Sling Baby is available in three fabrics: "climate-control" micro fleece for cold climates, Air Max fabric for warm climates and "all-climate" cotton. Unfortunately, this sling appears to only be available directly from the Walking Rock Farm web site.

Rating: A-

carriers

ZoloWear Sling

ZoloWear.com

Price: $50 to $125 depending on fabric.

Maximum weight: 40 lbs.

Comments: Zolo Wear's mojo are cool fabrics: cotton (including organic), silk brocade and breathable mesh. Yep, it's the gorgeous silk material (machine washable) that catches your eye. Designed with a front ring, these slings include a front pouch and come in four sizes. The Zolo Wear sling can be used with baby in six different positions. Check their web site for sales, plus there is a factory outlet. Reader feedback on Zolo Wear is positive, although a few moms told us it takes a bit of practice to use the sling. An instructional video is helpful.

Rating: A

ZoloWear Baby Pouches

See review online at BabyBargains.com

Front Carriers

Baby Bjorn

BabyBjorn.com

Price: $60 to $200.

Maximum weight: Original : 22 lbs.; Air: 25 lbs.; Comfort: 31 lbs.; Synergy: 26 lbs.; Active: 26 lbs.

Comments: Baby Bjorn is the 800-pound gorilla in the carrier category. This Swedish import comes in five flavors: Original (and Original Spirit in brighter colors or Original Organic; pictured), Comfort, Air, Synergy and Active (also available in organic fabric). The Original ($60) is easy to use and adjust (baby can ride facing forward or rear). Best of all, you can snap off the front of the Bjorn to put a sleeping baby down in a crib.

The Active ($130) adds lumbar support and wider straps for longer walks and the Air version features a mesh fabric to keep baby cooler in warmer climates. The Synergy ($180) combines the mesh of the Air and the lumbar support of the Active.

The Comfort ($200) has an ergonomic waste belt and is for children from three months to two years of age—not for newborns.

Bjorn has added yet another carrier to their line-up: the Miracle. Released in October 2011, the Miracle builds on some of the features of its other carriers including the Comfort. Like the Comfort, the Miracle has an adjustable weight belt. But that's just for starters. The carrier also includes a measuring tape adjustment inside the carrier so you can make sure the seat is a best fit for your child. For parents, the adjustable weight belt combines with infinite adjust shoulder belts allowing parents to evenly distribute the weight on shoulders and waist, or take weight off either the waist or the shoulders. This makes the fit even more customized. Also, the waist belt flexes as it pivots meaning it stays flat on the stomach and doesn't dig in. The new Miracle is available in three price points: the basic at $185, the organic at $199 and the mesh at $209. Not cheap certainly and considerably more than the Mamas and Papas Morph with similar features.

Baby Bjorn consistently gets high ratings from parents who purchase front carriers—they like the ease of use and the fact that baby can face outward eventually. But detractors point to the high price and limited use (babies outgrow it fast). Back/neck strain is a common complaint of Bjorn users (the Bjorn Active generates fewer complaints on this, thanks to the lumbar support and we expect the Miracle with also have fewer complaints). Some babies also don't like the Bjorn for whatever reason. We recommend keeping the receipt just in case you have a picky baby. **Rating: B**

BABY TREKKER
babytrekker.com
Price: $150.
Maximum weight: 40 lbs.
Comments: Baby Trekker was first recommended to us by our Canadian readers who raved about this made-in-Canada, multi-use carrier. Yes, it works as your typical front carrier with baby facing in when young and out when older. But the carrier also has a cool nursing option; a backpack position allows baby to either face your back or out to see the world (though not until your baby is at least three months old or 15 lbs.). The Trekker stores in its own attached pocket making it easy to pack in your diaper bag. We liked the extra padding under every buckle for baby's comfort. Canadians also like the fact that it is easy to use when baby is dressed in a snowsuit—not a problem for Florida readers, but you get the idea. An instructional video is available on YouTube. **Rating: A**

BECO BUTTERFLY 2
BecoBabyCarrier.com
Price: $125-$150.
Maximum weight: 35 lbs.
Comments: The Butterfly 2 baby carrier was designed by a mom who is also a rock climber. Yep, it is pricey—but seems to fit shorter parents a bit better than the Ergo. Included in the price is an infant insert for babies as small as 7 lbs., a separate hood, a removable headrest and an instruction book with DVD. FYI: Babies can only face in (toward you) in this carrier. **Rating: A-**

carriers

BECO GEMINI

BecoBabyCarrier.com

Price: $115-$130.

Maximum weight: 35 lbs.

Comments: Unlike Beco's Butterfly 2 carrier, the Gemini allows baby to face forward. It comes with head support, waist belt, adjustable chest strap and adjustable base. This base alternates to allow for small infants facing mom, then, when baby gets bigger, facing out. Unlike the Butterfly 2, you don't need an infant insert. And you can also adjust the carrier so baby rides on your back or hip. Reader feedback on the Gemini is positive. Yes it is pricey, but a bit less than the Butterfly 2.

Rating: A

BELLE BABY CARRIER

BelleBabyCarriers.com

Price: $90-$110.

Maximum weight: 30 lbs.

Comments: Looking for a lightweight, easy to pack carrier? Belle Baby carriers forgo all the extra padding to make a lighter, cooler carrier that allows baby to face both in and out. Made in Colorado, they are available in five organic cotton/hemp designs as well as seven polyester options. We liked the ergonomic design and how densely padded straps cross in the back like the Baby Trekker. An independent waist belt puts the weight on your hips, not your back. Unlike other carriers, Belle's removable head support is extra: $10.

Rating: A-

ERGO BABY CARRIER

ErgoBabyCarrier.com

Price: $115 to $160.

Maximum weight: 40 lbs.

Comments: Made by Hawaii-based ERGOBaby, the Ergo carrier has won kudos on our boards for its ease of use (you can wear it in front or back) and less strain on the back. While most front carriers put the strain on your shoulders and back, the Ergo comes with a padded hip belt that takes the strain off your upper back. Best of all, you can use it from birth (with a newborn insert, $25-$38) up to an amazing 40 lbs. (toddlers)—most front carriers can only be used for a short time (the Bjorn limit is 22 lbs.). And the Ergo can be used as a hip carrier. One important caveat: you *cannot* face your baby out when wearing it in the front position; baby always rides facing you. On the plus side, Ergo offers five versions: Original, Performance (spe-

cial light-weight fabric), Sport (extra long waist belt and shoulder straps), Organic and Options (black carrier with optional fabric covers for an addition $30). Reader feedback on this carrier is positive.
Rating: A-

MACLAREN BABY CARRIER
MaclarenBaby.com
Price: $70.
Maximum weight: 25 lbs.
Comments: Better known for its strollers, Maclaren also has a line of simple baby carriers.
These front carriers ($80 to $100) work from eight to 12 lbs. with a "pod insert" and up to 25 lbs. otherwise. We liked the one-hand, quick-release buckles and enclosed harness system. Baby faces in first and later can face out. Readers mentioned this carrier seems to work better on parents with bigger frames—very petite moms complained that they couldn't get a good fit.
Rating: B

MORPH
Mamasandpapas.com
Price: $139.
Maximum weight: 7.7-26.4 lbs.
Comments: The Morph is meant to be intuitive out of the box. The straps go on just like a jacket (not over your head) and snaps/zips together. Another plus: the Morph allows parents to adjust the shoulder straps and waist strap easily for a great fit. The carrier comes in two sizes (sm/med and med/lg) and additional harnesses are available ($65 each). Baby can be positioned facing in or out. Compared to the Baby Bjorn Miracle, the Morph is certainly more affordable. Parent feedback is positive, although a few noted the Morph is more complicated to use than the company claims. Favorite feature: how easy it is to transfer baby from one person to another (if you buy a second harness). **Rating: A**

PIKKOLO
CatBirdBaby.com
Price: $130.
Maximum weight: 40 lbs.
Comments: Maker Catbird Baby started off with a mei tai carrier, but recently expanded into a soft carrier with buckles instead of ties. The straps are shorter than a mei tai, addressing a common complaint with those carriers. The Pikkolo can be used front and rear facing, on the back and on the hip like a mei tai. They offer it in only one size and recommend their original mei tai if you

are very petite or large. The Pikkolo comes with an optional hood, memory foam straps, optional chest strap to use in the piggyback position and instruction booklet. Fabric options are limited (one solid, two patterns), made of brushed cotton canvas. Reader feedback on the Pikkolo has been very positive—the hybrid style of a soft carrier with mei tai like options makes it a favorite. FYI: the Pikkolo is sold on Amazon and in specialty stores.

Rating: A

Mei Tai or Asian Carriers

BABYHAWK

BabyHawk.com

Price: $95 to $150.

Maximum weight: 40 lbs.

Comments: BabyHawk offers quite a few options if you want to custom design your own mei tai. Start with a strap color (17 options) and main body color (over 500), and then decide whether you want extra long straps ($5), a pocket ($10), toy rings ($5 each) or reversible fabric ($10). Without all the extras, a basic BabyHawk is $80. Toddler sized mei tais start at $85. If you just want to buy an in stock mei tai, the options are equally numerous. We like all the unique fabrics including Amy Butler designs as well as florals, Asian prints, and geometrics. Like other mei tais, BabyHawk can be used in front, back or on the hip. Readers most like the customization options (but be forewarned: customized BabyHawks are non-returnable) and the comfortable fabrics. On the other hand, some readers complained that the straps were too long . . . and it takes a while to figure out how to use these carriers.

Rating: A

ELLA ROO MEI TAI

EllaRoo.com

Price: $75 to $125.

Maximum weight: 35 lbs.

Comments: Ella Roo's version of the mei tai gets rave reviews from readers. Fans like the short learning curve and the fact that either mom or dad can wear it—it easily adjusts to different sizes and body types. Baby can face in or out in the Ella Roo or on the back as with most mei tais. Shoulder straps are lightly padded and there is a padded headrest as well. All carriers are made of 100% organic cotton and must be hand washed/hung dry. The only complaint: The Ella Roo takes some time to put on or take off.

Rating: A

Kozy Carrier

KozyCarrier.com

Price: $80 to $105.

Maximum weight: 40 lbs.

Comments: Kozy Carrier's web site touts that this mei tai-inspired carrier has no buckles or rings—just tie it on. You'll notice it has wide shoulder straps with light padding, a lightly padded curved head support and is reversible. Extra long straps are available as an option. Customization is the headline here: pick a base fabric and a solid or print accent fabric. Like other mei tai carriers, baby can be worn in front (facing in or out), on the side or on your back and used for infants up to toddlers. You'll need to check the web site for instructions on how to use the carrier. Reader feedback has been quite positive on the Kozy Carrier.

Rating: A

Wrap Around Carriers

Moby Wrap

MobyWrap.com

Price: $40 to $140.

Maximum weight: 35 lbs.

Comments: Moby Wraps are one-size-fits-all carriers designed to allow moms to adjust the fit by how tight they wrap the baby. The wrap uses three sections of fabric for extra security but has no additional padding. Moby Wraps are machine washable, although the company does caution that there will be some shrinkage when first washed. Another downside: it takes a bit of time to learn to use it, and even once you have it figured out, the Moby Wrap takes some time to put on. The Moby Wrap can be used for both front and back wearing. Parent reviews are mostly positive, with the exception of the learning curve. **Rating: A-**

Wrapsody

GypsyMama.com

Price: $64 to $84.

Maximum weight: 35 lbs.

Comments: Gypsy Mama makes three Wrapsody wraps in different fabrics: the Water Wrap (to use in the water, of course), Baby Breeze Wraps (cotton gauze), and Bali Baby Stretch Wraps (like t-shirt material). The Baby Breeze wraps are the lightest weight but not stretchy. The maker recommends the stretch wraps for beginners as they are "more forgiving of sloppy wrap jobs." Online instructions (both videos and printed) were

carriers

clear and easy to follow. We recommend the Baby Breeze for parents in hot climates or summer wearing. **Rating: A**

VATANAI
PieceofCloth.com
Price: $99 to $118.
Maximum weight: 35 lbs.
Comments: Manufactured in the Czech Republic, Vatanai wraps have a world-wide following. In the US, they are sold on PieceofCloth.com and in Canada through RaspberryRouge.com. Vatanai is made of lightweight cotton and, like the Wrapsody carriers above, are recommended for warm climates. They claim to have a unique "cross-wise stretch" that makes them easier to tie. These wraps are available in three sizes from 3.5 to 5 meters of fabric. **Rating: A**

Hip Carriers

CUDDLE KARRIER
CuddleKarrier.com
Price: $47 to $74.
Maximum weight: up to six years of age; we recommend three years

Comments: Cuddle Karrier won't win any design awards for their web site, but their hip carrier is the Swiss Army knife of carriers. It converts from carrier to shopping cart restraint, high chair cover . . . and four more uses. The Cuddle Karrier adjusts and repositions with just one hand (the online video is helpful to see this). One caveat: you may need a waist belt to make the Cuddle Karrier work most comfortably. Oddly, the company doesn't sell this accessory, but instructions are available to show you how to make your own.
Rating: B-

HIP BABY
WalkingRockFarm.com
Price: $88 to $108.
Maximum weight: 44 lbs.

Comments: We mentioned Walking Rock Farm's sling earlier in the chapter, but their hip carrier is the company's biggest seller. The Hip Baby comes in three types of fabric: Inprints, which is a lycra knit with heat reducing lining; Cooler II, a waterproof fabric with breathable lining; and Air Flow, a special water proof athletic fabric. Walking Rock touts their strap for its length and no-slip padding. A few readers complain the strap digs into their necks, despite the padding. The Hip Baby adjusts pretty much the same way all-hip carriers work with a backslide adjustment. All in all, this is a good choice among hip carriers.

Rating: B+

MEI HIP
Ellaroo.com
Price: $90.
Maximum weight: 35 lbs.
Comments: Ella Roo's Mei Hip carrier wins rave reviews from our readers. It has a waist strap that you buckle on first, then a strap that wraps around the back and clips to the carrier in front. The straps are wide and very long—an advantage if you're tall but annoying to some parents. Both straps can be tightened by pulling on the loose ends (that sounds like a flight attendant talking!). One frustrating aspect: we heard from parents that directions weren't included in their order. Instead, you have to download them from Ella Roo's web site, which lacks any instructional videos.

Rating: A-

ORIGINAL HIP HAMMOCK
swankeltd.com
Price: $48.
Maximum weight: up to three years of age
Comments: The Original Hip Hammock was designed to make the usual baby-on-the-hip carry easier on moms' backs. Attach the waist belt, slide your baby into the seat, then wrap the shoulder strap around your back and snap to the front of the carrier. In a nutshell, it is similar to a messenger bag. The Hip Hammock only works with children who are at least 14 lbs., so it's not for newborns. FYI: avoid the Playtex version of the Hip Hammock—readers didn't like it much, although it's a bit cheaper.

Rating: B

Frame (Backpack) Carriers

DEUTER KID COMFORT III
DeuterUSA.com
Price: $290.
Maximum weight: 48.5 lbs.
Comments: Deuter is a German company with a long history in this category—Deuter rucksacks debuted in 1934 and were used on expeditions to the Himalayas in 1953. The company branched out into child carriers in 1991 and

now offer four models. The most popular version is the Kid Comfort III, which features sun roof, contoured hip belt, chin pad, 3D air mesh, large storage pockets, and child dimensioned safety belt with height adjustment. Parents love the multiple adjustments for parent and child, as well as the storage. Others rave about how comfortable it is. The only complaint: more than one reader told us they hate the Kid Comfort's numerous zippers.

Rating: A-

Kelty TC 3.0 Transit Child Carrier
kelty.com
Price: $180.
Maximum weight: 40 lbs.

Comments: While the Kelty TC 3.0 requires a lot of adjustment at first to get baby strapped in, readers tell us this backpack carrier is one of the best options on the market. The adjustable lumbar support gets kudos, parents find it easy to get on and off, and it is comfortable for long hikes. Kelty offers four other frame carrier options—readers like the TC 3.0 best.

Rating: A

Sherpani Rumba Superlight
SherpaniPacks.com
Price: $250.
Maximum weight: 55 lbs.

Comments: Sherpani offers two different carriers: the Rumba and the Rumba Superlight. Readers prefer the lighter weight Superlight—every pound counts when you're on a hike. The pack is a bit stripped down from the regular Rumba with less storage, but still includes their great five point harness system, stirrups that improve leg circulation for baby, large mesh pocket and storage compartment, and sunshade and storm cover. Parents complain that the sunshade doesn't cover their baby but they praise the pack's ease of use and comfort. Price is definitely a factor in our rating here: you pay nearly as much as the Deuter, but don't get nearly the amenities. On the other hand, the Deuter is 50% heavier (6 lbs, 13 oz versus the Rumba Superlight at 4 lbs. 8 oz.) So the decision here comes down to the trade-off between weight and features. If you don't need all the bells and whistles, then the Rumba Superlight is an excellent choice.

Rating: B+

TOUGH TRAVELER KID CARRIER

ToughTraveler.com

Price: $184.

Maximum weight: three years of age

Comments: Tough Traveler makes a wide array of frame carriers for kids, from ultra lightweight stripped down versions up to full-featured options with extra padding and straps. The most popular version is somewhere in the middle: the Kid Carrier. It has a five-point safety harness, high padded sides, full seat, footrest for small children and an optional set of stirrups for toddlers. It doesn't include a rain/sun hood ($45 extra) and only offers a mesh pocket for storage. Tabs are attached to the bottom, ostensibly to carry additional items. The lack of storage or included rain cover are negatives. On the other hand, we like the 4 lb. weight, making it one of the lighter frame carriers on the market.

Rating: B

Our picks: Brand recommendations

Baby wearing has become the norm today for most of our readers and the options available have multiplied exponentially since we began writing *Baby Bargains*. Gone are the days when you basically had a choice between a Baby Bjorn and a Snugli.

With all these new options, which do we recommend as our top picks? In the sling category, we have a tie: the **Mama's Milk** baby sling and the **Maya Wrap**. Parents love the simplicity of the Mama's Milk and the flexibility and comfort of the Maya Wrap.

In the front carrier category, our top pick this year is the **Pikkolo** from Cat Bird Baby. It's really a mash-up of a front carrier and a mei tai with buckles instead of long ties. It's also more flexible than other front carriers—it can be used in front facing both in and out, on the back and as a hip carrier. Our runner up favorite is the **Ergo** with it's padded ergonomic hip belt. But baby can only face toward the parent in an Ergo.

Speaking of hip carriers, some parents only need a carrier that offers a hands-free option with baby riding on the hip. Our top choice here: the **Mei Hip** from Ella Roo. Great fabrics and padding make this a stylish and comfortable hip carrier.

Mei tais or Asian carriers have really made inroads in the carrier market. Our top pick for this category is the **BabyHawk**. The customization options, great fabrics and ease of use made this mei tai a favorite. The **Ella Roo** mei tai is our runner-up in this category.

Wrap carriers also have front and back carrying flexibility and our favorite is the **Wrapsody Baby Breeze** gauze carrier. If you get hot when wearing your baby, this is the coolest, lightest fabric on the market.

Finally, frame carriers. For those committed to long hikes with baby, a frame carrier is a great option. Our favorite is the **Kelty TC 3.0**. It's comfortable for parents and baby, easy to use and reasonably priced. If you've just inherited a bit of money from a long lost uncle, the **Deuter Kid Comfort III** would be an excellent choice here. It's got everything you could ever need: adjustability, storage and great safety features. It's just ridiculously expensive.

The Bottom Line: A Wrap-Up of Our Best Buy Picks

Wow . . . and you thought car seats were complex!

Here's the take-home message on strollers: match a stroller to your lifestyle. That means thinking about HOW you'll use the stroller. Mall? Park? Hikes? Read our lifestyle recommendations to match the right stroller to your needs.

Overall, the best strollers brands are UPPAbaby, Phil & Ted's and BOB. But even brands that get a lukewarm rating can have an occasional winner—witness Graco's twin strollers or Kolcraft/Jeep's affordable all-terrain models.

No matter which stroller you get, it is always smart to go for the lightest weight model you can find. Another key factor: rear wheel width, especially for urban parents. Some new strollers have wide rear wheel widths . . . making negotiating a narrow doorway or tight elevator darn near impossible.

For diaper bags, we like Land's End and Skip Hop's offerings. Designer diaper bags are nice to get as gifts . . . but go for practical here and you'll be happier.

Carriers fall into five categories: slings, hip carriers, wraps, front carriers and backpack. Options from Pikkolo, Mother's Milk, Ella Roo, Kelty and BabyHawk are among our favorites. But every baby (and mom) is different so make sure you can return a carrier if it doesn't work for you.

Let's see: you've got the nursery picked out . . . and a car seat, stroller and carrier. Plus a high chair and breast pump. And your home is ready for baby with safety gates and more. Let's sum up all the savings next.

CHAPTER 10 CONCLUSION

What Does it All Mean?

How much money can you save if you follow all the tips and suggestions in this book? Let's take a look at the average cost of having a baby from the introduction and compare it with our Baby Bargains budget.

Your Baby's First Year

ITEM	AVERAGE	BABY BARGAINS BUDGET
Crib, mattress, dresser, rocker	$1375	$1320
Bedding / Decor	$345	$158
Baby Clothes	$630	$311
Disposable Diapers	$890	$300
Maternity/Nursing Clothes	$1210	$550
Nursery items, high chair, toys	$520	$225
Baby Food/Formula	$960	$350
Stroller, Car Seats, Carrier	$675	$490
Miscellaneous	$600	$500
TOTAL	$7205	$4204
TOTAL SAVINGS:		**$3001**

WOW! You just saved $3000. We hope the savings makes it worth the price of this book. We'd love to hear from you on how much you saved with our book—feel free to email, write or call us. See the "How to Reach Us" page at the back of this book.

What does it all mean?

At this point, we usually have something pithy to say as we end the book. But, as parents of two boys, we're just too tired. We're going to bed, so feel free to make up your own ending.

And thanks for reading *Baby Bargains*.

APPENDIX A
Sample registry

Here's the coolest thing about registering for baby products at Babies R Us—that neato bar code scanner gun. You're supposed to walk (waddle?) around the store and zap the bar codes of products you want to add to the registry. This is cool for about 15 seconds, until you realize you have to make DECISIONS about WHAT to zap.

What to do? Yes, you could page through this book as you do the registry, but that's a bit of a pain, no? To help speed the process, here's a list of what stuff you need and what to avoid. Consider it *Baby Bargains* in a nutshell:

The order of these recommendations follows the Babies R Us Registry form:

Car Seats/Strollers/Carriers/Accessories

◆ **Full Size Convertible Car Seat.** Basically, we urge waiting on this one—most babies don't need to go into a full-size convertible seat until they outgrow an infant seat (that could be in four to six months or as much as a year). In the meantime, new models are always coming out with better safety features. Hence, don't register for this and wait to buy it later.

If want to ignore this advice, go for the *Britax Marathon 70* ($290). For Grandma's car, we like the *Cosco Scenera* ($40). The *Diono Radian RXT* is another good pick (and converts to a booster) for $340.

◆ **Infant car seat.** Best bet: the *Graco SnugRide*—we recommend the 35 pound version ($150).

◆ **Strollers.** There is no "one size fits all" recommendation in this section. Read the lifestyle recommendations in Chapter 8 to find a stroller that best fits your needs. In general, stay away from the pre-packaged "travel systems"—remember that many of the better stroller brands now can be used with infant seats.

◆ **Baby Carriers.** *Pikkolo* ($130; sold on Amazon) from the Catbird Baby is our top carrier. You really don't need another carrier (like a backpack) unless you plan to do serious outdoor hikes. If that is the case, check Chapter 8 for suggestions.

◆ **Misc.** Yes, your infant car seat should come with an infant head support pillow, so if you buy one of these separately, use it in your stroller. There really isn't a specific brand preference in this category (all basically do the same thing). Any other stroller accessories are purely optional.

Travel Yards/High Chairs/Exercisers

◆ **Gates.** The best brand is *KidCo* (which makes the Gateway, Safeway and Elongate). Don't forget window guards (*Guardian Angel* is a good brand) and fireplace hearth gates.

◆ **Travel Yard/Playard.** *Graco's Pack 'N Play* is the best bet. Go for one with a bassinet feature for $90.

◆ **High Chair.** The best high chair is the *Fisher Price Healthy Care* ($80-$120).

◆ **Walker/Exerciser.** Skip the walker; an excerciser is optional. Good model: *Evenflo Splash Mega ExerSaucer.*

✓◆ **Swing.** The *Fisher Price My Little Lamb Cradle Swing* ($105) is a *(m)*op pick here.

◆ **Hook on high chair.** The *Chicco Caddy* ($40) is a good choice.

✓◆ **Infant jumper.** Too many injuries with this product; pass on it.
m

✗◆ **Bed rail.** Don't need this either.

✓◆ **Bouncer.** *Fisher Price* makes the most popular one in the category—their Rainforest bouncer is about $50.
Rink. N play

Cribs/Furniture

✓◆ **Crib.** For cribs, you've got two basic choices: a simple model that is, well, just a crib or a "convertible" model that eventually morphs into a twin or full size bed. In the simple category for best buys, *Graco's* Lauren crib is a basic hardwood crib for just $145 to $165. If you fancy a convertible crib, we like the **Baby Cache** cribs (made by Munire) $400 as well as the **Bedford Baby** (Westwood) Tribeca crib.

✗◆ **Bassinet.** Skip it. See Chapter 2 for details. If you buy a playpen with bassinet feature, you don't need a separate bassinet.

✗◆ **Dressing/changing table.** Skip it. Just use the top of your dresser as a changing area. (See dresser recommendation below.)

✓◆ **Glider/rocker and ottoman.** In a word: *Dutailier*. Whatever
mm

style/fabric you chose, you can't go wrong with that brand. Hint: this is a great product to buy online at a discount, so you might want to skip registering for one.

◆ **Dresser.** Dressers and other case pieces by **Munire** is our top pick—prices run about $600 for a dresser. Quality is excellent. FYI: Munire sells furniture under the **Baby Cache** label in Babies R Us. Other good brands for dressers include **Westwood**, **Ragazzi** and **Romina**.

◆ **Misc.** Babies R Us recommends registering for all sorts of miscellaneous items like cradles, toy boxes and the like. These are clearly optional.

Bedding/Room Décor/Crib Accessories

◆ **Crib set.** Don't—don't register for this waste of money. Instead, just get two or three good crib sheets and a nice cotton blanket or the Halo SleepSack. See Chapter 3 for brands.

✗◆ **Bumper pads, dust ruffle, diaper stacker.** Ditto—a waste.

◆ **Lamp, mobile.** These are optional, of course. We don't have any specific brand preferences.

◆ **Mattress.** The *Sealy Soybean Foam-Core* crib mattress is a good deal at $122. Unfortunately, Babies R Us doesn't sell many of our top matterss picks—you have may have to shop other stores or online.

◆ **Misc.** Babies R Us has lots of miscellaneous items in this area like rugs, wallpaper border, bassinet skirts and so on. We have ideas for décor on the cheap in Chapter 3.

Infant Toys, Care & Feeding

◆ **Toys.** All of this (crib toys, bath toys, blocks) is truly optional. We have ideas for this in Chapter 6.

◆ **Nursery monitor.** The simple *Graco Ultraclear* is a good buy at $23. Among the digital offerings, we liked *the Phillips Avent SCD510* for about $100—its DECT technology stops interference. A key tip: keep the receipt. Many baby monitors don't work well because of electronic interference in the home

◆ **Humidifier.** A good bet is the *Crane EE-5301*, a $40 cool mist humidifier.

◆ **Diaper pail.** The *Diaper Dekor* and *Diaper Genie* are best bets.

◆ **Bathtub.** While not a necessity, a baby bath tub is a nice convenience—try to borrow one or buy it second hand to save. As a best bet, we suggest the *EuroBath by Primo*—it's a $30 bath tub that works well.

◆ **Bottles.** *Avent* and *Dr. Brown's* are the best bet, according to our readers. But cheaper options like Playtex can work just as well.

◆ **Bottle Warmer.** Also optional—remember, baby doesn't need to have a warm bottle! But if you insist, go for the Avent's *iQ Electronic Bottle and Baby Food Warmer* ($60). It can heat a bottle in four minutes.

◆ **Sterilizer.** Also optional, *Avent's* "Digital Bottle and Baby Food Warmer" ($46) is a good choice.

◆ **Thermometer.** Don't register for a fancy thermometer—the cheap options at the drug store work just as well. *First Years* has a high-speed digital thermometer ($8) that gives a rectal temp in 20 seconds and an underarm in 30 seconds. Ear thermometers are not recommended, as they are not accurate.

◆ **Breast pump.** There isn't a "one size fits all" recommendation here. Read Chapter 5 Maternity/Nursing for details.

◆ **Misc.** In this category, Babies R Us throws in items like bibs, hooded towels, washcloths, pacifiers and so on. See Chapter 4 "Reality Layette" for ideas in this category.

Diapers/Wipes

◆ **Diapers.** For disposables, the best deals are in warehouse clubs like *Sam's* and *Costco*. Generic diapers at *Walmart* and *Target* are also good deals. We have a slew of deals on cloth diapers in Chapter 4.

◆ **Wipes.** Brands like *Pampers* and *Huggies* are the better bets, although some parents love the generic wipes that Costco stocks.

Clothing/Layette

◆ See the "Reality Layette" list (Ch. 4) for suggestions on quantities/brands.

APPENDIX B

Advice for multiples

Yes, this year, one in 32 births in the US will be twins. As a parent-to-be of twins, that can mean double the fun when it comes to buying for baby. Here's our round-up of what products are best for parents of multiples:

◆ **Cribs.** Since twins tend to be smaller than most infants, parents of multiples can use bassinets or cradles for an extended period of time. We discuss this category in depth in Chapter 2, but generally recommend looking at a portable playpen (Graco Pak N Play is one popular choice) with a bassinet feature as an alternative.

Cool idea: a mom of twins emailed us about the **Leachco Crib Divider** for $30 that lets you use one crib for twins. Available on BabiesRUs.com.

Baby's Dream offers a great crib for parents of twin: the Cube ($500) converts to two twin platform beds.

◆ **Nursing help.** Check out **EZ-2-NURSE's** pillow (800-584-TWIN; sold on Amazon). A mom told us this was the "absolute best" for her twins, adding "I could not successfully nurse my girls together without this pillow. It was wonderful." This pillow comes in both foam and inflatable versions (including a pump). Cost: $50.

Walmart has a breastfeeding collection with **Lansinoh** products (including their amazing nipple cream). Check the special displays in the store or on their web site at walmart.com.

Yes, nursing one baby can be a challenge, but two? You might need some help. To the rescue comes **Mothering Multiples: Breastfeeding & Caring for Twins and More** by Karen Kerkoff Gromada ($14.95). This book was recommend to us by more than one mother of twins for its clear and concise advice.

FYI: Skip buying a glider-rocker if you plan to nurse your twins. The large nursing pillows won't fit! Instead, go for a loveseat.

◆ **Car seats.** Most multiples are born before their due date. The smallest infants may have to ride in special "car beds" that enable them to lie flat (instead of car seats that require an infant to be at least five or six pounds and ride in a sitting position). The car beds then rotate to become regular infant car seats so older infants can ride in a sitting position.

Some hospitals sell or rent infant car beds—they can be used for premature infants up to nine pounds. The key feature: a wrap-around harness to protect a preemie in an accident. FYI: ALL premature infants should be given a car seat test at the hospital to check for breathing problems—ask your pediatrician for details.

Another idea: check with your hospital to see if you can RENT a car bed until your baby is large enough to fit in a regular infant car seat.

◆ *Strollers.* Our complete wrap-up of recommendations for double strollers is in Chapter 8 (see Double the Fun in the lifestyle recommendations). In brief, we should mention that the *Chicco Cortina Together* accepts two infant seats ($300).

Another top pick for tandem strollers: the *Kolcraft Contours Options II Tandem* ($240, 32 lbs.). Cool feature: the seats reverse to face the parents or each other. This model features a few upgrades over Graco, including adjustable leg rests and each seat can fully recline (only the back seat of the Quattro Tour Duo reclines fully).

For side-by-side strollers, we suggest the *Jeep Twin Sport All Weather Umbrella* (27 lbs.) for $100 at Walmart. If you've got a bit more budget, the *Maclaren Twin Techno* ($380, 26.9 lbs.) features fully reclining seats. We also liked the *Baby Jogger City Mini Duo* ($400, 26.6 lbs., pictured), with its excellent extended canopies and quick fold.

◆ *Deals/Freebies.* Chain stores like Babies R Us and Baby Depot offer a 10% discount if you buy multiples of identical items like cribs. Get a *$7 off coupon for the Diaper Genie from Playtex* when you send proof of multiple births to Playtex (800) 222-0453; playtex.com.

Kimberly Clark Twins Program: Get a gift of "high-value coupons" for Huggies diapers by submitting birth certificates or published birth announcements. (800) 544-1847). *The First Years* offers free rattles for parents of multiples when you send in copies of birth certificates. Web: thefirstyears.com.

The National Mothers of Twins Clubs (nomotc.org) has fantastic yard/garage sales. Check their web page for a club near you.

Don't forget to check out the freebie list on our message board, updated frequently: babybargains.com/freebies.

Another good source: Twins Magazine is a bi-monthly, full-color magazine published by The Business Word (twinsmagazine.com).

◆ *Miscellaneous.* For clothes, make sure you get "preemie" sizes instead of the suggestions in our layette chapter—twins are smaller at birth than singleton babies.

One of our readers with multiples sent us an extensive list of tips from her experience with twins. Go to BabyBargains.com/twins to download this free PDF.

multiples

index

index

INDEX

index

index

index

BabyBargains.com

What's on our web page?

◆ Updated blog with news and safety recalls.

◆ Download ebooks for your Kindle, iPad or Nook.

◆ Message boards with in-depth reader feedback.

◆ The latest coupon codes and freebies!

◆ Corrections and clarifications.

◆ Links to our Facebook page and Twitter feed.

◆ Subscribe to read the latest, up-to-date reviews!

BabyBargains.com
Email: authors@babybargains.com
Phone: (303) 442-8792